de Gruyter Textbook

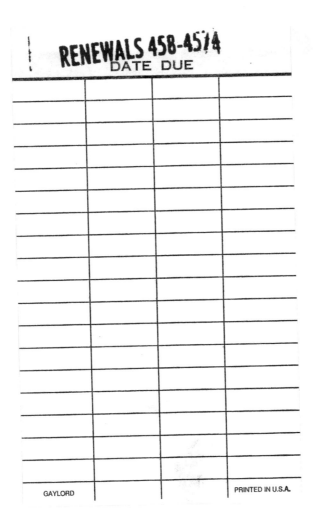

Michael Meier-Brügger

Indo-European Linguistics

In cooperation with Matthias Fritz and Manfred Mayrhofer

Translated by Charles Gertmenian

Walter de Gruyter · Berlin · New York
2003

Michael Meier-Brügger holds the Chair in Comparative and Indo-European Linguistics at the Free University of Berlin, Germany.

Matthias Fritz is Research Fellow in the Department of Comparative and Indo-European Linguistics at the Free University of Berlin, Germany.

Manfred Mayrhofer is Emeritus Professor of Comparative and Indo-European Linguistics at the University of Vienna, Austria.

♾ Printed on acid-free paper which falls within the guidelines of the ANSI to ensure permanence and durability.

ISBN 3-11-017433-2

Bibliographic information published by Die Deutsche Bibliothek

Die Deutsche Bibliothek lists this publication in the Deutsche Nationalbibliografie; detailed bibliographic data is available on the Internet at <http://dnb.ddb.de>.

Cover design: Hansbernd Lindemann, Berlin
Printing and Binding: WB-Druck, Rieden am Forggensee
Printed in Germany

Contents

Preface to the Seventh German Edition (2000)

The field of Indo-European linguistics has been represented in the Sammlung Göschen (SG)[1] for a long time. Rudolf Meringer, author of the first treatise, was a professor at the University of Vienna at the time of the first edition and at the University of Graz at the time of the third. The first edition[2] comprised the following parts: Section 1, "The Science of Language and its Developments"; Section 2, "The Indo-European Languages"; Section 3, "The Proto-Indo-European Language" (with accentuation, phonology and morphology); and Section 4, "Culture and Geographical Origin of the Indo-Europeans." Pages 1 through 66 were printed in Fraktur. The second edition,[3] was not altered. For the third revised edition,[4] in the second main section, a subsection *n* on rules of pronunciation was added and the fourth chapter evolved into one of the main sections. Further, a section on abbreviations was added to the end.

Soon after the Second World War, Hans Krahe was engaged as a new author at the publishing house. He had been a professor at the University of Würzburg at the time of the publication of his first edition; at the time of the publication of the second edition, he was a professor in Heidelberg. Since the publication of his third edition, he has been at the University of Tübingen. The first Krahe edition[5] includes: Part 1, "The Indo-European Language Group"; Part 2, "Phonetics"; and Part 3, "Morphology." The second edition[6] was unchanged. The third edition was revised in two volumes. The first of these, *Introduction and Phonology*,[7] includes: Part 1, "General Information" and Part 2, "Phonology." The second volume[8] treats *Morphology*. The fourth edition was a revision of these volumes:

---

[1] First located in Leipzig, then in Berlin.
[2] 1897 (SG 59) 136 pages.
[3] 1899 (SG 59) 136 pages.
[4] 1903 (SG 59) 151 pages.
[5] 1945 (SG 59) 134 pages.
[6] 1948 (SG 59) 134 pages.
[7] 1958 (SG 59) 106 pages.
[8] 1959 (SG 64) 100 pages.

Volume I. *Introduction and Phonology,*[9] Volume II. *Morphology.*[10] The two volumes of the fifth edition (1966 and 1969) were unchanged. In its sixth edition the work remained unchanged, though issued in a single volume[11].

Krahe's volume is now more than fifty years old. Although the sixth edition has the external appearance of a new volume of the Sammlung Göschen, the content remains a child of the third edition of the 1960s. Typical of the state of research at that time is Krahe's comment on laryngeals (vol. I p. 101): "A number of Indo-European scholars have recently represented the so-called laryngeal theory, according to which, in addition to the phonemes included here, the basic Indo-European language included certain laryngeals (glottals and schwas), which are not taken into account in this short work. The author is of the opinion that in a work that is primarily conceived for students and as an introduction to a field, only the most proven research should be presented. The laryngeal theory has been affirmed neither in its methodology nor in its technique." The last sentence is decidedly incorrect: The common expression 'laryngeal theory' is historically conditioned and can be misleading, but this should not lend credence to the idea that the laryngeals are only vague and theoretical. Today laryngeals are part of the attested body of phonemes of the Indo-European language.[12] One often finds in Krahe's book information and reconstructions, about which we either know more, or have acquired more adequate insights today.

In the middle of the 1980s, the publisher retained Heiner Eichner and Manfred Mayrhofer to write a new *Indo-European Linguistics* for the Göschen series. By 1985 Dr. Mayrhofer had written the section on phonology; Dr. Eichner was to provide the introduction and the section on morphology. A 1988 publication date was announced, but the volume was never published. A number of difficulties hindered publication, particularly on the side of Dr. Eichner. Dr. Eichner and his manuscript, which in the meantime had grown, were faced with space and time constraints, including that difficulty, known to every author, of putting one's own name on something less than completely perfect, which hindered him finally, from bringing the project to completion.

---

9 1962 (SG 59) 110 pages.
10 1963 (SG 64) 100 pages.
11 1985 (SG 2227).
12 see below L 314 ff.

In December 1993, the publisher offered to me the role of Dr. Eichner. After exchanges with all concerned parties, a contract was signed with February 1996 as the agreed upon date of completion. The offer of a position to me at the Freie University in Berlin rendered the bold timeframe impossible. The change from Hamburg to Berlin brought everything with it except the necessary leisure to produce a manuscript. I am grateful to Brigitte Schöning, who, while showing kind understanding of my time constraints, was able to make sure the actual deadline of the publisher was met. Although I would like very much to have expanded and embellished my manuscript, I must now give it up to those who will publish it.

By fall 1998 I had covered only half the intended material but was informed that I had considerably exceeded the page allowance for one Göschen volume. Thus, a currently expanding series, the "de Gruyter Studienbücher," was attractive. They offer greater spatial freedom. Further, they do not demand a particular format of proof. Hence, the manuscript, prepared with the help of Microsoft Word 7.0 for Windows 95, can be used directly for publication. No more galleys. On the part of the publisher, Ingeborg Klak took care that the typography does not come off too old-fashioned.

While Dr. Mayrhofer and Dr. Eichner, following the precedent set by Krahe, intended on only covering phonology and morphology, now syntax and vocabulary are receiving the recognition they deserve.

The explanations in the section on morphology are based on the text written by M. Mayrhofer in 1985, as Dr. Mayrhofer had given me complete freedom to determine the arrangement and the organization of the definitive version. I take sole responsibility for the present version of the section on phonology. Happily, I was able to have Matthias Fritz write the section on syntax. Further, he contributed to the part of the introduction on the history of Indo-European linguistics as well as the overview of Indo-European languages and their sources.

M. Fritz, M. Mayrhofer, Elisabeth Rieken, Bernfried Schlerath and Antje Schwinger read individual excerpts with a critical eye and shared their criticisms with me. Veronika Rittner and Thorsteinn Hjaltason reviewed individual texts electronically. Mr. Hjaltason and Ms. Schwinger helped me with certain data processing problems, Mr. Hjaltason especially with the creation of particular symbols, and Ms. Schwinger with the layout. A sincere thanks to you all!

As is appropriate for a volume in the Sammlung Göschen and a "de Gruyter Studienbuch," the book should offer an introduction to Indo-European linguistics. The textbook should provide an informative and comprehensive treatment of the issues and areas of focus from a contemporary perspective. I allow myself a special style in presenting both information on the field in general and on the course of study in the introduction. In the main text, on the other hand, I present inconclusive material in a usable way, to encourage possibilities of more in-depth study. The treatment proceeds according to good science and good conscience. Completeness is nowhere attempted. To keep this in the reader's mind, the chapter titles begin often with "on." Most of the examples in the sections morphology, syntax and vocabulary come from Latin, Ancient Greek and Indian (Indo-Aryan). In the section on phonology, the examples are intentionally more numerous and are taken from the entire realm of Indo-European languages, which include Hittite, Germanic and Slavic, in addition to the above-mentioned three. The index appended at the end should give support to the reader and facilitate his or her access to information. The state of research reflected in the text is that of September 1999. Last additions will be inserted after this deadline just before the definitive layout is made in December.

The current textbook is not without competition. Still good is Rix's *Historische Grammatik des Griechischen* (1976). Starting from Greek, Rix presents pertinent information on all aspects of Proto-Indo-European phonology and morphology. But the treatment is done without any reference to discussion in the field. Recent works worthy of mention are Szemerényi, *Einführung*, fourth edition (1990), Beekes, *Introduction*, (1995), Schmitt-Brandt, *Indogermanistik*, (1998) and in a certain sense also Meiser, *Historische Laut- und Formenlehre der lateinischen Sprache*, (1998) (compare pp. 27-46, the chapter "Grundzüge der urindogermanischen Grammatik"). All four titles have strengths and weaknesses, and so shall it be with mine. The comprehensive bibliographical information in Szemerényi is a treasure trove, but the skepticism regarding laryngeals is bothersome. Beekes' book is illustrative and very readable, but in phonology and morphology he leans too much on views shared only by himself and F. Kortlandt. Schmitt-Brandt's work is in a praiseworthy fashion aimed at beginners and concentrates especially in morphology on a broad argumentation that encourages creativity. However, his book cannot be recommended because he leads the reader into unsignaled idiosyncrasies that stray from the *communis opinio*. Meiser, like Rix, treats only phonology and morphology. He grounds himself competently, but of necessity briefly (too briefly), on the realities of the Proto-Indo-European language. I should not speak of typographical errors. He who sits in a glass house is well advised to throw no stones.

I am thankful for any feedback and request that it be sent to the *Seminar für Vergleichende und Indogermanische Sprachwissenschaft* at the Freie University in Berlin (FU), Fabeckstraße 7, D-14195 Berlin-Dahlem. Tel.: 030-838-55028; Fax: 030-838-54207; e-mail: drmeier@ zedat.fu-berlin.de; internet site: http//www.fu-berlin.de/indogermanistik.

I dare try to create a rubric on our web site: "De Gruyter Studienbuch Indogermanische Sprachwissenschaft: Addenda and Corrigenda." I've resolved, starting with the appearance of the book, on the first weekday of each month, to note addenda and corrigenda as I learn about them.

Berlin-Dahlem, September 15, 1999

Michael Meier-Brügger

Preface to the Eighth German Edition (2002)

The occasion to publish the present eighth edition presented itself unexpectedly soon after the publication of the seventh edition.

I know that I am joined by M. Fritz and M. Mayrhofer in my gratitude for the responses of goodwill and for the positive reception of the previous edition, which appeared in March 2000. We are pleased that the text has found its place as an introduction to the current status of Indo-European linguistic research. It is encouraging that this text and E. Tichy's depiction of fundamentals of Indo-European linguistics (Bremen 2001) complement each other wonderfully without any prior arrangement having taken place. E. Tichy sketches a concise treatment of the main characteristics, while the present text fills them out with details. I can easily imagine that the interested reader would first consult Tichy's treatment, and then, given the page references from that text, would reach for the present text.

Happily, the requested feedback was furnished with intensity. On the other hand, my planned internet rubric, "Addenda and Corrigenda" did not come to be. Among the reasons for this are juridical problems that prevent one from presenting special characters that were created at the Seminar on the Internet. Other reasons include the ever-growing burden of tasks in teaching and administration: Constant reductions and transformations due the scarcity of public funds claim most of our energies.

I am happy about the positive feedback and thankful for having been sent entire lists of comments, inquiries, and tips about typographical errors and unclear points. The lists complemented each other wonderfully: Each person sees something different; no one sees everything. Imperfections, and the corresponding need for correction, were found mostly where generally accepted opinion does not apply: Hence, in the assessment of the role of the laryngeal h_3 in the Hittite language (see below L 334), or in the evaluation of the stative diathesis and its connection to perfect and medium diatheses (see below F 211), or in the case of genders, where one must likely draw the conclusion that the formation of three-way masculine/feminine/neuter took place only after the splitting off of Anatolian, thus in a phase that followed the phase of the original Indo-European language (see below F303), or in the earlier common assessment of the IE *g^wou̯- 'steer' as an hysterodynamically declined noun. In contrast to this representation, *g^wóu̯- must be categorized as primarily acrostatic with a strong stem *g^wóu̯- and a weak stem *g^wéu̯-. The adjustment to amphidynamically declined root nouns such as IE *di̯eu̯- 'sky, god of the sky, day' with the strong stem *di̯éu̯- and the weak stem *diu̯-´ is secondary. The strong nominative singular *g^wóu̯-s remains, but the weak genitive singular *g^wéu̯-s is replaced by the new weak genitive singular *g^wou̯-és (see below F 318 § 6). The eighth edition introduces modified content in such cases. The numbering of paragraphs from the seventh edition was conserved whenever possible. What I could not yet accomplish in the eighth edition includes the addition of a complete index of vocabulary, and the expansion of the rather brief treatment of vocabulary.

Altogether, as many as possible of the typographical errors and oversights were corrected. Imperfections were either eliminated, or at least clearly marked as such. As a result of such work, an eighth edition appeared which I can stand by with a good conscience. The responsibility for all remaining mistakes lies with me. M. Fritz kindly agreed to correct the work, and thus took responsibility for the section on syntax.

My particular thanks for criticism goes to: Augustinus Bal (Amsterdam), Irene Balles (Jena), Wolfgang Beck (Würzburg), Joachim Becker (Göttingen), Martin Braun (Vienna), Emilio Crespo (Madrid), Roberto Gusmani (Udine), Heinrich Hettrich (Würzburg), Katharina Kupfer (Freiburg), Christoph Landolt (Zürich), Gyula Mayer (Budapest), H. Craig Melchert (Chapell Hill), Peter-Arnold Mumm (Munich), Sergio Neri (Salzburg), Oswald Panagl (Salzburg), Bernfried Schlerath (Berlin), Diether Schürr (Gründau) and Stefan Schumacher (Halle and Freiburg). Klaus-Jürgen Grundner help with the corrections on this edition as well as with the seventh. Ms. Susanne Rade supported me kindly on the part of the publisher and guided me, such that the eighth edition could appear in the winter semester of 2002.

The addresses are the same as on page XIII.

Berlin-Dahlem, September 15, 2001

Michael Meier-Brügger

Preface to the English Translation of the Eighth German Edition

In recent years, the English language has attained a position similar to that enjoyed by Latin in the Middle Ages. While Indo-European linguistics has traditionally had a strong basis in the German-speaking world, the field is happily becoming ever more internationally and intercontinentally oriented. It is thus not surprising that I have received several inquiries regarding the possibility of an English translation of the original German-language edition.

But where could one find a suitable translator? Good fortune played a role: Charles Gertmenian attended my introductory course in the winter semester of 2000-2001. In the course of conversation, the idea arose of translating the textbook, then in its seventh edition, into English, thus making it accessible to a larger public. The 1000 copies of the seventh edition were sold quickly and the eighth edition sold equally well. Such success encouraged the publisher to give his support: H. Hartmann gave the green light following a publishing industry gathering in late autumn 2001. Mr. Gertmenian wrestled with the work for two years. The work was time-consuming and thorny; the difficulties of rendering scientifically formulated subtleties while retaining both precision and readability are well-known. Mr. Gertmenian solved the problem wonderfully. Reading his propositions I took the opportunity to reformulate some facts being presented in the German version in a too dense manner. It only remains for my co-authors M. Fritz and M. Mayrhofer, as well as myself, to express gratitude for the successful translation. A particular thanks for addenda and corrigenda concerning the eighth edition goes once more to Augustinus Bal (Amsterdam).

Indo-European linguistics is a science that is wonderfully alive. The eighth edition reflects the status of research as of summer 2001. In the two years that have since gone by, important new books and essays have appeared, of which I wish to mention: *The Luwians*, ed. by H. Craig Melchert, Leiden 2003; H. Rix, *Sabellische Texte*, Heidelberg 2002; J. H. Jasanoff, *Hittite and the Indo-European Verb*, Oxford 2003; *Indogermanische Syntax, - Fragen und Perspektiven -*, ed. by H. Hettrich, Wiesbaden 2002.

For practical reasons, we have agreed to abide by the text of the eighth edition. By the same measure, I shall make good on the promise made in the seventh edition by offering addenda and corrigenda concerning the various sections and paragraphs on our web site (http://www.fu-berlin.de/indogermanistik) on a regular basis. The first installment will be posted February 1, 2004. Existing reviews of the seventh and eighth editions shall then receive their due, including that of Ch. de Lamberterie in BSL 97/2 2002, p. 103-114. Feedback is welcome. The adresses are still the same as on page XIII.

Berlin-Dahlem, September 15, 2003

Michael Meier-Brügger

Terminology, Symbols, Abbreviations

1. Terminology

The terminology used in this textbook is without extravagances. It is that customary of textbooks in Indo-European linguistics. In individual cases more will be added on the subject, for example in the case of terms ablaut and declension patterns of the nouns (see below F 315 §3-4).

The Index at the back of the book provides an additional orientation, referring to relevant paragraphs and helpful literature. If a question should remain unanswered, for example in the domain of general linguistics, which is not further handled here, competent, informative reference works offering advice are available: → Bussmann *Lexikon d. Sprachw.* 2d ed. 1990; Lewandowski *Linguist. Wörterbuch* 1-3 1994; *Metzler Lexikon Sprache* 2000. In special terminological particularities in Indo-European phonetics, consult the glossary of Mayrhofer *Lautlehre* 1986 p. 182-185. For terminological particularities in the system of Forms of the Proto-Indo-European verb, consult the foreword of LIV 1998 = *Lexikon der indogermanischen Verben* 1998 p. 1ff. For questions about the formation of nouns, vocabulary and its problems, see the introduction to terminology in Kluge / Seebold 1995 p. XIVff. Further, the index of the *Zeitschrift für Vergleichende Sprachforschung*, see below in the bibliography under the entry HS = *Historische Sprachforschung*. Last tip: → *Duden Grammatik* 1995 p. 828 ff. (Index of technical terms).

The terminology originates essentially from the Greeks. Theoretical-linguistic examination dates back to at least the 5th century B.C. The Grammar of Dionysius Thrax offers a good insight into the status of grammatical research in the hellenistic period: → Dionysios Thrax *Grammatik*. In the course of the 2nd century B.C. Roman intellectuals took up the Greek terminology and more or less latinised it: → Wackernagel *Vorlesungen* I 1926 p. 13ff.

The motives for naming terms are often for us Moderns at first glance no longer clear, for example the Greek term πτῶσις, which as Latin *cāsus* and German *Fall* remains in use even today. The starting point for this *terminus technicus* is probably the idea that each noun in its nominative form is like a pin in a vertical, straight position (hence *casus rectus*). The uses as accusative, genitive, etc. differ from the 'straight' position, and are thus not straight (= *casus obliquus*) and can be described in the comparison as variously slanted positions (πτῶσις) of the pin: → Wackernagel *Vorlesungen* I 1926 p. 15. In another tradition, the image of a die ("knuckle") serves as a basis instead of a pin: → F. Murru in MSS 39 1980 p. 73ff. As a further example, compare the various terms Greek οὐδέτερον, Latin *neutrum*, German: *sächliches Geschlecht*. Behind these terms, one does not primarily find the idea of 'neither, nor', (neither masculine, nor feminine gender), but rather the idea of a third independent natural gender, in addition to masculine and feminine; a "male-female" gender: → K. Strunk "*Neutrum: zum antiken Benennungsmotiv eines grammatischen Terminus*" in *FS Untermann* Innsbruck 1993 p. 455ff.

One must always keep in mind the history of individual specialized terms in linguistics. All newer assessments are based as a rule on the so-called traditional grammar, which received its first systems through analysis of the classical Latin. But the application of traditional grammar in languages other than Latin is not without problems: → Bussmann *Lexikon d. Sprachw.* 2nd ed. 1990 p. 798f. Further, one must not overlook that in modern linguistics one and the same term may be used variously according to different theories: → Lewandowski *Linguist. Wörterbuch* 3 1994 under the heading '*Terminus*'.

2. Symbols, Writing Conventions, Quotations

a. Symbols

As a rule, the symbols used here speak for themselves. The meanings of the cover-symbols are not, however evident:

H = any particular laryngeal (h_1, h_2 and h_3 stand for real laryngeals), see below, L 314

K = any particular consonant (*d*, d^h, *t* etc. stand, in contrast, for real consonants.)

R = any particular sonant (*l*, *r* etc. stand, in contrast, for real sonants)

V = any particular vowel (*e*, *o* etc. stand, in contrast, for real vowels)

$\breve{\bar{a}}$ = long or short vowel *a*, etc.

——

\# = Beginning or end of a word
\## = Beginning or end of a sentence

——

**mon-u̯o-*, *k^{w}*i*- etc. = - marks morphological segmenting
**mon.u̯o-*, **ra.í-* etc. = . marks syllabic segmenting

——

ø or *z* = zero-step, - suffix, -ending
° = weak vowel, see below L 203
W = root
S = suffix
E = ending
W(*e*) = -*e*- full grade of the root
W(*ē*) = -*ē*- lengthened grade of the root
W(*o*) = -*o*- full grade of the root
W(*ō*) = -*ō*- lengthened grade of the root
W(*ø*) = zero grade of the root
W(°) = reduced grade of the root with weak vowel, see L 203

accordingly:
S(*e*) = -*e*-full grade of the suffix, etc.
E(*e*) = -*e*-full grade of the ending, etc.

——

* = A purely reconstructed form, without an attestation (if known, the probable time of the reconstruction will be given with terms such as Proto-Germanic, Proto-Indo-European, and pre-Proto-Indo-European)

——

< = derived phonetically from
> = developed phonetically into
= = corresponds to, see below E 507 § 5
⇒ = is replaced by
\+ for example Hom. + = Homer and later
→ The arrow refers to helpful literature (the key to reference citations is given below in section VI).

——

/*a*/ Forward slashes refer to the corresponding phonological value
[*ŋ*] Brackets refer to the corresponding phonetical value.
<*z*> Pointed brackets indicate graphemes

——

b. Writing conventions

1) For notation of Indo-European, see below L 100f.

2) In the cases of individual Indo-European languages, the accepted modes of writing are respected. I would like to call attention to a couple of details:

Latin <*c*> is always to be taken as /*k*/, and <*qu*> in contrast, as /k^{w}/, without regard for whether it represents /*ku̯*/ or comes from /k^{w}/, see below E 506 § 3. Please note as well that a word, such as <*maius*> should be read as /*mai̯i̯us*/ and a <*conicio*> as /*kon-i̯iki̯ō*/: → Leumann LLFL 1977 p. 127f.

In the examples from Mycenaean Greek, the instance of a word is given as a rule first, just as it is represented in Mycenaean Greek Linear-B. The probable phonological interpretation is then given equally in Latin script, but not in Greek script. (Graphemically indicated phonetic transitional sounds are taken into account as well, and often a modern morphological segmenting follows.) Compare *i-je-ro-wo-ko* i.e. *hii̯ero-u̯orgos* 'priest'. For the sake of simplicity, the symbols < > and / / are not written here. — Where an aspiration is probable, it is marked with an *h*, such as in the preceding example. — In the interpretation of the *z*-series, either a k^{j}, a g^{j} , a t^{j} or a d^{j} will be inserted according to etymological origin, for example: *to-pe-za* i.e. *torped*^{j}*a* 'table' < *(k^{w})*tr̥-ped-i̯a* '(thing) having four-legs'. — The sources of quoted forms are not cited, but they can easily be found in Aura Jorro *DMic.* I 1985 II 1993. — Examples from Greek dialects are represented without accents.

The model for Ancient Indian (Vedic) is Mayrhofer EWAia. As is common practice in IE linguistics, Vedic and Old Indian nominal forms are cited as a rule as stems without an ending (thus, for example, the Vedic *ávi-* 'sheep'). Older manuals often cite the nominative singular in the sandhi form with *-ḥ* (so-called Visarga), cf. a reference such as Latin *ovis* 'sheep' = Vedic *áviḥ*. For more information see below L 309 § 3. — The cited form for Vedic and Old Indian is the third person singular (see *bhárati* 'carries'), also on the subject the full grade verbal root (e.g. Vedic *bhar-* 'carry'). Accents are used in finite verb forms only when they are textually attestable.

In the case of Avestan, I follow the example of → Hoffmann / Forssman *Avestische Laut- und Flexionslehre* 1996.

In Anatolian (Hittite) *ḫ* should be written in transliteration from cuneiform as well as in the transcription, but *š* should be written in the transliteration, and not in the case of the transcription, compare, for example, *pa-aḫ-ḫu-e-na-aš* i.e. *paḫḫu̯enas*. The *z* that was introduced in the transliteration is given as t^s. Further, apparently stressed syllable marks such as *ták* in *ták-na-a-aš* do not refer to the place of the accent. In accordance with the conventions of Ancient Oriental Studies, the mark *á* is merely suggests that in addition to the usual form *tak* (= *tak* number one) a second form of symbol (= *tak* number two) is in use.

On Gothic: → Binnig *Gotisch* 1999.

c. Citing Conventions

Note that methods of citing are not handled in the same way in all ancient Indo-European languages, compare for example the verbal forms of Latin and Greek, in which the first person singular is cited, whereas in Vedic the third person singular is the traditionally cited form.

In Mayrhofer KEWA, the verb forms are listed according to the third person singular form, whereas in Mayrhofer EWAia they are indexed by their full-grade verbal roots, compare KEWA p. III 562f. the entry *svárati* 'gives off a sound, sounds, sings', with EWAia II p. 792f., the corresponding entry under *SVAR* 'giving off a sound, sounding, singing'. The citing convention of nouns as well varies from the KEWA to the EWAia, compare in the KEWA *svargáḥ*, while the EWAia lists *svargá-*.

3. Abbreviations

Certain of the most common abbreviations have been omitted from the following list. As a rule, the abbreviations that are used are long established or clear in their context.

N.B.: Abbreviations of periodicals are found in the bibliography.

§	paragraph
abl.	ablative
acc.	accusative
act.	active voice
adj.	adjective
ad l.	*ad locum*
adv.	adverb
aor.	aorist
Arm.	Armenian
AV	Atharva Veda
Avest.	Avestan
col.	column
coll.	collective
dat.	dative
encl.	enclitic
etc.	*et cetera*

ex. gr.	*exempli gratia*
f.	(genus) feminine
FS	Festschrift
fut.	future
gen.	genitive
Gr.	Greek
GS	*Gedenkschrift*
H	laryngeal, see L 314
Hell.	Hellenistic
Hitt.	Hittite
Hom.	Homeric
ibid.	*ibidem*
i.e.	*id est*
ind.	indicative
inf.	infinitive
inj.	injunctive
instr.	instrumental
intr.	intransitive
K	consonant
KN	Knossos
KS	*Kleine Schriften*
Lat.	Latin
LAv.	Later (Younger) Avestan
Lith.	Lithuanian
loc.	locative
m.	(genus) masculine
MHG	Middle High German
mid.	middle voice
Myc.	Mycenean
n.	(genus) neutral
N.B.	*nota bene*
NHG	New High German
nom.	nominative
OAv.	Old Avestan
OCS	Old Church Slavic
OE	Old English
OHG	Old High German
OHitt.	Old Hittite
OL	Old Latin
ON	Old Norse
OPers.	Old Persian
opt.	optative
OSax.	Old Saxon
p.	page
pass.	passive
perf.	perfect
pers.	person
pl.	plural
plpf.	pluperfect
poss.	possessive
pres.	present
pron.	pronoun
PY	Pylos
R	sonant
refl.	reflexive
RV	Rgveda
ŚB	Śatapatha Brahmana
sc.	*scilicet*
sg.	singular
str.	strong
subj.	subjunctive
subst.	substantive
s.v.	*sub voce*
TB	Taittiriya Brahmana
TS	Taittiriya Samhita
TH	Thebes
them.	thematic
Toch.	Tocharian
tr.	transitive
V	vowel
vs.	*versus*
w.	weak

I. Introduction

A. The Field and its Study

E 100. The field of Indo-European linguistics is established at German-speaking universities under various names, for example *Indogermanistik* (Friedrich-Schiller-Universität, Jena), *Indogermanische Sprachwissenschaft* (Ludwig-Maximilians-Universität, Munich), *Indogermanische and Allgemeine Sprachwissenschaft* (Albert-Ludwigs-Universität, Freiburg im Breisgau), *Allgemeine and Indogermanische Sprachwissenschaft* (Georg-August-Universität, Göttingen), *Historisch-Vergleichende Sprachwissenschaft* (Universität zu Köln), *Historisch-vergleichende Sprachwissenschaft/Indogermanistik* (Humboldt-Universität zu Berlin), *Vergleichende Sprachwissenschaft* (Julius-Maximilians-Universität Würzburg), *Vergleichende Indogermanische Sprachwissenschaft* (Universität Zürich), and *Vergleichende and Indogermanische Sprachwissenschaft* (Freie Universität, Berlin).

Among the programs offered in the English-speaking world are: *Historical linguistics and Indo-European* (Harvard University), *Comparative Philology* (Oxford University). The French-speaking realm includes: *Linguistique comparative* (Lausanne), *Grammaire comparée* (Paris, École Pratique des Hautes Études IVe Section), *Étude comparative des langues indo-européennes* and *Méthode comparative en linguistique historique* (thus Antoine Meillet in his publications, see the bibliography).

The web site, → http://www.fu-berlin.de/indogermanistik, prepared by our institute at the Freie Universität in Berlin, offers a continually updated list of internet links to departments and institutes in Europe and North America. The site features information on all areas of the field.

One must be aware that the structure of curricula, establishment, and interrelationship of Indo-European linguistics with other fields in the Romance language-speaking countries Italy, France, and Spain differ greatly from corresponding aspects in Germany, Austria, and German-speaking

Switzerland. Within the German-speaking realm there are also fine differences that can have to do with local tradition or teachers. In its information on curricula in Indo-European linguistics, the following account concentrates on the situation in Germany. Additionally, the local circumstances in Berlin may occasionally shine through.

The field of Indo-European linguistics is represented at every major university. The "*Indogermanische Gesellschaft*" represents the interests of the field as a professional association, see below E 201 § 2. It organizes a conference every four years, see the bibliography under the heading '*Fachtagung.*' In addition, there are individual colloquia, see the bibliography under the heading '*Kolloquium.*'

E 101. There is a whole series of positions taken regarding the nature and aim of Indo-European linguistics: → Arbeitsausschuß der Indogermanischen Gesellschaft in *Kratylos* 13 1968 p. 222f. (= *Linguistische Berichte* 9 1970 p. 78-80); Szemerényi *Einführung* 1990 p. 32-36; R. Lühr *Indogermanistik am Wendepunkt*? "*Thesen zur zukunftsorientierten Ausrichtung einer Disziplin*" in the *Gießener Universitätsblätter* 25 1992 p. 77-90; G. Neumann "*Zur Interdisziplinarität der Geisteswissenschaften. Ein Beispiel: Die Vergleichende Sprachwissenschaft*" in the *Gießener Universitätsblätter* 29 1996 p. 61-67; G. E. Dunkel "*Zürcher Indogermanistik zwischen Vergangenheit and Zukunft*" in the *Informationsblatt der Universität Zürich* 6 1990 p. 10-12.

In this context it is further worth taking a look at the definitions of the field that appear in increasing numbers on the web sites of departments and institutes for Indo-European linguistics. Examples from Cologne, Munich and Würzburg are printed here as examples. As of March 1999 they were obtainable under their corresponding addresses and are still worth reading today. As is characteristic and typical of today's fast-moving world, the texts from 1999 are, as a rule, no longer the same as texts of 2001. I encourage the interested reader to visit these web sites and consult the most current information.

E 102. The *Institut für Sprachwissenschaft* at the Universität zu Kölln (→ Link on our web site [see above E 100] see the heading for Indo-European linguistics in Europe) offered the following definition in March 1999:

> "The focus of historical-comparitive linguistics are languages, which through systematic similarities in declension, word formation, syntax,

and vocabulary are recognizable as 'related.' The comparison of these languages yields information about the history, pre-history, and origins and development of individual traits of each of them that could otherwise never be obtained. Historical-comparitive linguistics concerns itself empirically and theoretically both with processes of linguistic history, such as the splitting of originally unified languages into different descendent languages, and with language-inherent and extra-lingual circumstances for linguistic development. In addition, it investigates what historical linguistic description is capable of saying about cultural transformation. — Historical-comparative linguistics has developed most fully in the area of the so-called Indo-European languages, which include great European and Asian languages of cultural importance (Indian, Iranian, Greek, Slavic, Latin, Germanic and Celtic languages), and since its founding at the beginning of the 19th century it devotes the greater part of its interest to these languages."

E 103. The web site of the *Institut für Allgemeine and Indogermanische Sprachwissenschaft* of the Ludwig-Maximilians Universität in Munich (→ Link on our web site [see above E 100] under the heading Indo-European linguistics in Europe) offered in March 1999 the following description of the field:

"Indo-European linguistics is an empirical-historical, theoretically oriented discipline. The goal of its research is manifold: On the one hand, through comparisons of individual Indo-European languages (particularly their earliest available stages, such as Old High German, Vedic, Hittite), it aims to gain knowledge about language and culture of the common predecessor of these languages, namely of Proto-Indo-European. Meanwhile, the grammatical system of this mother language and its various changes after the moment of splitting off of the individual languages is in the foreground. On the other hand, Indo-European linguistics contributes to the better understanding of historical phenomena in the language and culture of all Indo-European peoples through knowledge of established rules that is acquired in the above-mentioned processes. As a connector of philologies, Indo-European linguistics includes the cultural realms from northern Europe, the Mediterranean of classical antiquity and the ancient and modern Orient, reaching all the way to India and central Asia. The most important language groups, or rather individual languages are Old Indian, and Greek, as well as Old Iranian, Latin, Germanic, Celtic, Slavic, Baltic,

Hittite, Armenian, Tocharian, and Albanian. — In the context of its outlined research objective, the field is additionally concerned with general linguistic problems, such as those of linguistic change and the relationship between historical and typological linguistic comparison. — By its nature, Indo-European linguistics is interdisciplinary, with natural connections with neighboring linguistic, philological, and cultural-historical fields (for example, pre- and early history)."

E 104. On the web site of the *Lehrstuhl für Vergleichende Sprachwissenschaft* of Julius-Maximilians Universität in Würzburg (→ Link on our web site [see above E 100] under the heading Indo-European linguistics in Europe) the field was defined as of March 1999 as the following:

"Comparative Indo-European linguistics is an empirical-historical, theoretically based discipline. It has several research goals: It compares the individual Indo-European languages (particularly their earliest known stages of development, for example, Latin, Ancient Greek, Old Indian, Gothic, Hittite, among others, but also the more recent stages) and gains, through processes of reconstruction, knowledge about grammar and vocabulary of earlier, non-written stages of language, and of the common predecessor of all these languages, Proto-Indo-European. Through the background of comparison furnished by the large number of languages and their diachronic perspectives, comparative linguistics contributes to a deeper understanding of grammar and vocabulary of the individual Indo-European languages. — Thorough research on these languages leads both to knowledge about the cultural background of a given language community (including history, social structure, religion, philosophy, poetry, etc.), to the theoretical study of general linguistic objects (e.g. the structural organization of language systems, phenomena of language development, relationship between genetic and typological language comparison.) — Comparative linguistics is an interdisciplinarily oriented field and is seen as a connecting member between the cultural regions of northern Europe over the Mediterranean and the ancient Orient through India and central Asia."

E 105. There is nothing more exciting and creative than historical-comparative linguistics. I am not alone in making this assertion.

But first a warning: The way to academic employment in the realm of linguistics is rocky and full of thorns. Whoever sets out to do this can win, but can also lose. Those who would like a large amount of money in their account ought to choose another route.

The fundamental prerequisite of promising studies in the field is a lively personal interest in languages and speech. A preference for a historical perspective must also be present. In addition to the general maturity expected at the university level, knowledge of Latin and Greek (preferably learned in school) are also important. Where today's school curricula have not provided this option, the necessary knowledge of Latin (to the extent of the so-called *kleines Latinum*) and Greek can be acquired in the first years of university education. Knowledge of English, German, and French is imperative for the reading of literature in the field. Spanish, Italian, and Russian are also helpful.

Latin, Greek, and Vedic are the pillars of Indo-European linguistics, if only because discussion in the field since its beginnings has referred to problems in terms of these languages. Only appropriate language ability allows independent assessment.

Along with the study of the three languages mentioned above, it is reccommended that one acquire good knowledge of Anatolian Hittite, as well as an Old Germanic language (such as Gothic, Old High German, or Old Saxon) and Old Church Slavic or Lithuanian.

Nothing can replace the reading of primary texts. It is also a personal gain to read, not just partially and according to immediate need, but really from A to Z, works and essays in Indo-European linguistics that have become classics. I enjoy thinking back to when I read Wackernagel (*Kleine Schriften* I / II 1969 III 1979, and *Vorlesungen* I 1926 II 1928) and Schulze (*Kleine Schriften* and *Nachträge* 2nd ed. 1966) during my own years at university. The texts read like detective novels.

It is worthwhile setting high personal standards and looking around to see how other linguists have become what they are: → *Autobiographische Berichte* 1991 and *Portraits* I / II 1966.

Like every other field, Indo-European linguistics has its unwritten rules of the guild. Thus, it is the duty of each and every researcher to keep new developements "in dialogue" with past research and to pay homage to prior accomplishments through frequent citation. The constantly growing quantity of data that one must master for this purpose is problematic. But the dealings with, and the reverence for what has preceded ought not to block new insights into the future.

E 106. At the time of my own studies (1967-1973), the study of Indo-European linguistics was still very simply structured. One was educated by attending lectures, lower-level seminars, and upper-level seminars; one engaged in individual reading, wrote papers, and after five or six years, chose a dissertation topic and completed his studies directly after the dissertation with doctoral exams.

Studies of Indo-European linguistics have become ever more reglemented due to dramatic changes in European universities (in view here are particularly the German ones). Today, following as a rule four semesters each of *Grundstudium* and *Hauptstudium*, and a semester of exams, one attains the *Magister* (M.A.) degree. But only the completion of a dissertation allows one to think of a career in Indo-European linguistics. Whoever chooses Indo-European linguistics as an occupation learns for a lifetime.

And new changes continue to threaten courses of study: The latest form of this threat is the introduction of a *Bachelor's degree* (B.A.) after only six semesters. Indo-European linguistics cannot be conveyed with sufficient thoroughness in three years. While the Bachelor candidate can obtain a good Indo-European linguistic education, he still needs at least an M.A. and a dissertation as qualifications in the field.

B. Indo-European Linguistics in the Age of the PC and the Internet

E 200. Indo-European linguistics, like any other science, can no longer make do without computers and the internet. While PCs are indeed variously used, (the palette of uses ranges from those of a simple typewriter, to professional use in the word-processing of texts in a variety of languages), the potential uses of the internet lead to an ever-greater density of information: → *Studia Iranica, Mesopotamica et Anatolica* (i.e. SIMA) 2 / 1996, published by J. Gippert and P. Vavroušek. Prague 1997. Here, one finds the files of the fourth *Internationale Arbeitstagung für Computereinsatz in der Historischen Sprachwissenschaft* 1995 in Vienna, edited by H. Eichner and H. C. Luschützky.

Today, good, practically oriented introductions for PCs and the internet are available. Examples include those of the *Wissentschaftliche Buchgesellschaft*: → H. Schröder, I. Steinhaus *Mit dem PC durchs Studium.*

Darmstadt 2000; D. Kaufmann, P. Tiedemann *Internet für Althistoriker and Altphilologen*. Darmstadt 1999.

E 201. I would like to call attention to three institutions specializing in Indo-European linguistics and the information that they offer. Their web sites include further information and a large variety of links. It should be clear to each user that the information on web sites changes constantly (The information included here is current as of March 1999.) and that many departments and institutes (and I include our department at the Freie University among these) are in the course of creating better, more informative web page.

1) TITUS (*Thesaurus Indogermanischer Text- und Sprachmaterialien*) Begun by J. Gippert, the goal of this institution, based for the moment in Frankfurt, is to process all linguistic materials that are relevant in questions of Indo-European linguistics into digital form that may easily be analyzed: → http://titus.uni-frankfurt.de. A constantly growing quantity of data is available under the headings "Actualia," "Didactica," "Textus" and "TITUS." J. Gippert offers an overview in the above-mentioned (E 200) SIMA-volume p. 49-76. He also offers further descriptions of his project as of March 1999 under the heading "TITUS" as *Beschreibung A* (called "TITUS, *Das Projekt eines indogermanistischen Thesaurus in LDV-Forum*" [i.e. *Forum der Gesellschaft für Linguistische Datenverarbeitung*] Band 12 / 1 1995 p. 35-74) and *Beschreibung B* (which refers to "*TITUS: Von der Keilschrift zur Textdatenbank*" in *Frankfurter Forschung* 4 1995 p. 46-56). A more detailed text may be found under the title *Beschreibung C* : C.-M. Bunz "*Der Thesaurus indogermanischer Text- and Sprachmaterialen* (TITUS) *ein Pionierprojekt der EDV in der Historisch-Vergleichenden Sprachwissenschaft*." — J. Gippert describes his comprehensive vision of the future in the Frankfurt research as the following:

> "Beyond the archiving of field-specific data, the project, which since the third conference on 'The use of computers in historical-comparative linguistics' in Dresden (October 1994) has been led under the succinct name "TITUS" (*Thesaurus Indogermanischer Text- und Sprachmaterialien*), should be extended increasingly to other areas of linguistic research. A comprehensive bibliographical information system should play a central role, featuring new material in all areas that touch upon the field with a claim to the greatest possible timeliness. The internet will perform a decisive function here as well: The aspired-to timeliness may only be obtained

if the information is not printed, but rather only processed online; and the compilation of individual pieces of information, which an individual institute could scarcely accomplish, should be distributed as quickly as possible to many partners whose common contact is the internet. There already exist firm agreements among colleagues at the universities of Prague, Vienna, Copenhagen, Leyden, Maynooth, among others. (A 'test-run' of the bibliography is was being conducted from Frankfurt at the time of publication.) Under the same prerequisites (participation of as many partners as possible in order to assemble complementary information), a couple of other areas of application of the TITUS project are emerging that should allow it to mature into a comprehensive field-specific information system. Thus, current regular notifications about events in the field (congresses, and conferences, as well as university programs), open positions and offers, projects, research plans, etc. can all be viewed. The assembly of all such information requires, thanks to the internet, only a very small amount of space and time on site. In order to call attention to a conference that will take place at an American university, the address of the invitation text must merely be entered on the given internet page –provided, naturally, that event organizers place their text on the internet."

2) The *Indogermanische Gesellschaft*, which is momentarily located in Halle (see link on our web site [see above E 100] under the heading, Indo-European linguistics in Europe): Up to date news from the *Indogermanische Gesellschaft* (about, among other things, the nature and goal of Indo-European linguistics and work with media) is offered, as well as addresses and general information. The *Hallisches Institut für Indogermanistik, Allgemeine and Angewandte Sprachwissenschaft* is currently responsible for maintenance of the page.

3) The Institute for Linguistics at the University of Cologne. The rubrics "*Sprachen and Schriften der Welt*," "*Indogermanisch allgemein*," "*Antike allgemein*" among others, and the links to individual Indo-European languages are available through the thankfully provided thematically organized links. There is a link to the University of Cologne on our web site (see above E 100 under the heading Indo-European linguistics in Europe).

C. A Word on the History of Indo-European Linguistics

E 300. It is not at all uninteresting to look up the entries under the heading 'Indo-European linguistics' in a general encyclopedia.

1) The *große Knaur* (Munich / Zürich 1967) offers an astonishingly competent treatment, which is given below without changes (the citations in this paragraph [→] refer to the encyclopedia; information about particular researchers is provided in the index of this volume):

> "Indo-European linguistics, a science that explores the Indo-European languages. Following the recognition, already in the 18th century, by W. Jones (1786) of the relatedness of Sanskrit to European languages, R. Rask (1814), F. Bopp (1816), and J. Grimm (1819) founded Indo-European linguistics. Rask and particularly Grimm (*Deutsche Grammatik*, 1819 ff.) researched the historical stages of the Germanic languages (see Consonant shift) in an exemplary manner. Whereas Bopp (*Vergleichende Grammatik* 1833ff.) analyzed and compared forms, A.F. Pott provided underpinning →etymology (*Etymologische Forschungen,* 1833-36) through exact comparisons of phonetic equivalences. Working with fixed rules of phonetic development, the first to try to attain an original Indo-European language was A. Schleicher (*Compendium der vergleichenden Grammatik der indogermanischen Sprachen*, 1861/62); he was also the first to bring Slavic and particularly Lithuanian into consideration. Researchers next tried to define methods and phonetic rules more clearly: 1863 H. G. Grassmann's Law (dissimilation of aspirates), 1877 K. Verner's Law (→Grammatical change), 1876-78 *Ausnahmslosigkeit der Lautgesetze* (A. Leskien, H. Osthoff and F. K. Brugmann; →Neogrammarians). Amelung, Brugmann, H. Collitz, F. de Saussure, J. Schmidt resolved the problem of the Indo-European '*a*' (European *a*, *e*, *o*); G. I. Ascoli discovered the two Indo-European guttural series; Brugmann ('*Nasalis sonans in der indogermanischen Grundsprache*,' 1876), the syllabic *m* and *n*; de Saussure ('*Mémoire sur le système primitif des voyelles dans les langues indoeuropéennes*,' 1878/79) formed the vowel theory of Proto-Indo-European through systematic representation of ablaut degrees of short and long vowels, discovery of and of two-syllable →Roots. H. Paul ('*Prinzipien der Sprachgeschichte*,' 1880) contributed the theory of Analogy, the effect of which Brugmann and Osthoff

treated in their '*Morphologische Untersuchungen*' (1878 ff.). H. Hübschmann recognized the →Armenian language as a separate language group. B. G. G. Delbrück contributed his *Syntax* (1893-1900) to Brugmann's '*Grundriß der vergleichenden Grammatik der indogermanischen Sprachen*' (1886 ff.).

Significant investigations into the philology of individual languages were provided by: Ch. Bartholomae (Indo-Iranian), J. Wackernagel, W. Schulze, and later P. Kretschmer (Greek), Fr. Kluge, H. Paul, E. Sievers, and still later W. Streitberg (Germanic), R. Thurneysen (Celtic). H. Hirt contributed in the areas of →accent (1895) and →ablaut (1900) as well as to those of the original homeland and language of Indo-Europeans ('*Die Indogermanen*,' 1905-07; '*Indogermanische Grammatik,*' 1921-37). Tocharian and Hittite were discovered at the beginning of the 20th century and worked on by W. Schulze, E. Sieg, W. Siegling, W. Krause (Tocharian), and F. Hrozný, F. Sommer, J. Friedrich (Hittite), H. Pedersen (both). Along with Hittite, Luwian and Palaic were also revealed; Phrygian, Lycian, and Lydian were also researched. Krahe analyzed the remains of the →Illyrian language. Indo-European linguistics became increasingly focused on questions of detail and individual philologies. Since de Saussure's demand for a synchronized, systematic linguistics ('*Cours de la linguistique générale*,' 1916), Indo-European linguistics, which is historically ('diachronically') oriented, has been replaced by various movements in modern →linguistics, particularly abroad (Geneva, Prague, Copenhagen, USA)."

2) *Meyer's Enzyklopädisches Lexikon* (Mannheim/Wien/Zürich. 9th ed. 1974) offers a comparably competent overview under the heading. Dissappointing, on the other hand – yet for this day and age, perhaps typical – is a newly conceived reference such as Haremberg, *Kompaktlexikon in 3 Bänden*. Dortmund 1996. The field of Indo-European linguistics is no longer mentioned; one is rather summarily referred to the "Indo-European language group" and the "Indo-Europeans."

3) An exhaustive treatment of the history of Indo-European linguistics from its beginning is lacking to this day.

Helpful literature: — a) On the subject of the history of Indo-European linguistics, with a particular focus on its beginnings and on the subject of the history of linguistics in general: → Benfey *Geschichte der Sprachwissenschaft* 1869; Delbrück *Einleitung* 1904; Windisch *Sanskrit-philologie* I 1917 II 1920; *Portraits* I / II 1966; Neumann, *Indogermanistik* 1967; Koerner, *Practicing Linguistic Historiography*

1989; Einhauser *Junggrammatiker* 1989; Szemerényi *Einführung* 1990 p. 1ff.; Bartschat *Methoden der Sprachwissenschaft* 1996; Morpurgo Davies *Ottocento* 1996. — b) with focus on the 20th century (until 1960): → Szemerényi *Richtungen der modernen Sprachwissenschaft* II 1982.

4) A couple of important steps of development from § 1 are clarified in the following.

E 301. Similarities and relationships in vocabulary between European languages such as Latin and Greek and Sanskrit have been increasingly studied since the eighteenth century. → Thumb / Hauschild *Handbuch des Sanskrit* I / 1 1958 p. 168ff. (The work concerns Sanskrit studies in Europe). On Sir W. Jones: → p. 173f.; *Portraits* I 1966 p. 1-57; *Lexicon Grammaticorum* 1996 p. 489f.; Mayrhofer *Sanskrit and die Sprachen Alteuropas* 1983.

In his German-language work, J. Klaproth (*Asia polyglotta* Paris 1823 p. 42ff.) refers commonly to the language group that joins Europe and India as "*indo(-)germanisch.*" But this term is clearly not Klaproth's invention. He uses the word as an established term, that at the time competed with the term 'Indo-European' and was employed by Bopp. Before Klaproth, the Danish geographer K. Malte-Brun had evidently used the term "*langues indo-germaniques*": → Thumb / Hauschild *Handbuch des-Sanskrit I* / 1 1958 p. 42f.; F. R. Shapiro "*On the Origin of the term 'Indo-Germanic'*" in HL 8 1981 p. 165-170; K. Koerner "*Observations of the Sources, Transmission, and Meaning of 'Indo-European' and Related Terms in the Development of Linguistics*" in IF 86 1982 p.1-29; by the same author, *Practicing Linguistic Historiography* 1989 p. 149-177; Szemerényi *Einführung* 1990 p. 12f. note 1; G. Bolognesi "*Sul termine* 'indogermanisch'" in *FS Belardi* I 1994 p. 327-338; F. Bader in *langues indoeuropéennes* 1994 p. 23.

While the term 'Indo-European' established itself in English and in the Romance languages, the term '*indo-germanisch*' has become accepted in the German-speaking world: → Committee of the *Indogermanische Gesellschaft* in *Kratylos* 27 1982 [1983] p. 221f. (Position with regard to the juxtaposition of 'Indo-Germanic' and 'Indo-European': "*Eine Abkehr von dem eingebürgerten wissenschaftlichen Terminus 'indogermanisch' ist also nicht geboten*"). A consciously anti-West German development, the term '*indoeuropäisch*' was the term of choice in the German Democratic Republic: → E. Seidel in *Wissenschaftliche Zeitschrift der Humboldt-Universität zu Berlin, Gesellschafts- and Sprachwissenschaftliche Reihe* XVIII 1969 p.297 ("In dealing indirectly with West German servants of imperialism, I see no reason to avoid using the term '*indogermanische Sprachwissenschaft* ... Nonetheless, I shall respect the wishes of the editor and use '*indoeuropäisch.*'")

E 302. The actual history of Indo-European linguistics begins with Franz Bopp (1791-1867). In 1816 he proved the relationship of the Indo-European languages. The foreword of his fundamental work, "*Über das Conjugationssystem der Sanskritsprache in Vergleichung mit jenem der griechischen, lateinischen, persischen and germanischen Sprache*" is dated 16 May, the date on which Bopp celebrated the birth of Indo-European linguistics. Whereas earlier suppositions were only supported by comparisons of words, Bopp proved the existence of relationships through grammatical comparison. Bopp's study of Vedic was prompted by Friedrich Schlegel's "*Ueber die Sprache and Weisheit der Indier*" (Heidelberg, 1808). For more information on Bopp: → B. Schlerath *Berlinische Lebensbilder - Geisteswissenschaftler* 1989 p. 55-72; Szemerényi *Einführung* 1990 p. 6f.

Along with Bopp, Jacob Grimm (1785-1863) is of great significance in the history of Indo-European linguistics. With his *Deutsche Grammatik* (1819ff.), he introduced the historical dimension in linguistic research: linguistic comparison and history constitute the foundaton of Indo-European linguistics: → Szemerényi *Richtungen* I 1971 p. 13ff.

E 303. The institutionalization of the field began with the appointment of Bopp in 1821, on the recommendation of Wilhelm von Humboldt, to the then new Berlin University. Bopp received the newly created chair for "*Orientalische Literatur und Allgemeine Sprachkunde.*"

In its first decades, the field remained closely associated with Sanskrit studies, given that familiarity with Sanskrit rendered the discovery of the Indo-European language group possible. Because of this tight connection to Sanskrit studies, Indo-European linguistics in its beginnings was closest to oriental studies, such that professors at the time usually carried the words 'Sanskrit' and 'oriental' in their titles. Yet the descriptions 'Indian studies' and 'oriental studies' have just as little to do with their present meanings as Bopp's chair of '*allgemeine Sprachkunde*' had to do with today's understanding of general linguistics. August Wilhelm Schlegel received the first chair in Indian Studies in 1818 in Bonn.

Chairs in Indo-European linguistics without particular ties to Sanskrit were created starting only in the 1870's. Thus, for example, Karl Brugmann's chair in Leipzig was created by simply renaming the chair for Classical Philology occupied by his teacher, Georg Curtius, who had been a student of Bopp in Berlin.

E 304. Bopp's circle of students was very large. For example, Friedrich Rückert, who held a chair for oriental studies in Erlangen and taught in Berlin, is significant beyond the confines of Indo-European linguistics. The circle included Wilhelm von Humboldt, August Wilhelm Schlegel and many representatives of Indo-European linguistics and Indian studies, such as August Friedrich Pott, Theodor Aufrecht, Otto von Böhtlingk, Adalbert Kuhn, Adolf Friedrich Stenzler, and Albrecht Weber, who became Bopp's successor.

In 1872, Hermann Ebel received the first chair for comparative linguistics in Berlin. In 1876, Johannes Schmidt, a student of August Schleicher, became his successor. Hermann Ebel founded the "*Berliner Schule*" of philological Indo-European linguistics, which is to be distinguished from the "*Leipziger Schule*" of systematic "neogrammarians."

E 305. The introduction of various new methods is associated with the names Pott, Schleicher, and Schmidt: Thus, with A. F. Pott from Halle is associated a more rigorous observation of consonant shift in the study of etymology (→ *Etymologische Forschungen auf dem Gebiete der Indogermanischen Sprachen mit besonderem Bezug auf die Lautumwandlung im Sanskrit, Griechischen, Lateinischen, Litauischen and Gothischen.* Lemgo 1833-1836); with A. Schleicher from Jena, reconstruction and theories of linguistic lineage; (→ *Compendium der vergleichenden Grammatik der indogermanischen Sprachen.* Weimar 1861); with J. Schmidt from Berlin, the wave theory (→ *Verwandtschaftsverhältnisse* 1872). The name Adalbert Kuhn calls to mind both Indo-European mythology as well as the founding of a review in the field of Indo-European linguistics, a review which, with only minimal changes in the title, has appeared from 1852 to the present day, and is still referred to as "*Kuhns Zeitschrift*": HS (previously ZVS or KZ). See the bibliography.

E 306. Representatives of different philological disciplines belonged to the group of so-called neogrammarians, which included for example, the slavist August Leskien and the germanist Hermann Paul. Literature: → Einhauser *Junggrammatiker* 1989.

The principle that phonetic rules are without exceptions (which includes the consonant shift as a phonetic rule) can be traced to the neogrammarians. Numerous durable phonetic rules were discovered by researchers from this circle: Jacob Grimm's Law (*Germanische Lautverschiebung*, see below L 336 § 4); Karl Verner's Law (see below L 421); Karl Brugmann's Law (see below L 412; On his discovery of the *nasalis sonans*, see below. L 305); Hermann Osthoff's Law (a long diphthong before a consonant becomes a short diphthong); Hermann Grassmann's Law concerning dissimilation of aspirates (see below L 348); Christian Bartholomae's Law concerning aspirates (see below L 347 § 2).

E 307. A decisive place in the history of Indo-European linguistics belongs to Ferdinand de Saussure (1857-1913). Not only did he enrich Indo-European phonetics with his discovery of laryngeals, he also founded modern synchronic linguistics. (Common headings include: synchronic vs. diachronic, langue vs. parole, signifiant vs. signifié.) → Szemerényi *Richtungen I* 1971 p. 19-52; for further information, see the bibliography under Saussure *Cours* (1916) and Saussure *Mémoire* (1879); further, see below, L 315.

As a rule, synchronic linguistics and general linguistics are considered to be one and the same. Since de Saussure, the field has gained impetus and diversified widely: → Szemerényi *Richtungen der modernen Sprachwissenschaft* II 1982.

At some universities, general linguistics has outstripped Indo-European linguistics. This is equally true in the cases of the large philologies, such as Germanic studies, Latin language studies, and English studies, where historically interested linguists are in the minority and are threatening to become lone voices in the desert. With its higher numbers of students, general linguistics has a trump card that cannot easily be overcome. But even general linguistics needs the historical dimension. A juxtapositioning of general and historical-comparative linguistics is the only appropriate approach. When the general linguist, who for the most part has only English as a foreign language and finds all of his examples in that language, the one-sidedness becomes egregious.

E 308. The contribution of new ideas and addition of new linguistic material has changed the state of research in Indo-European linguistics repeatedly: → Szemerényi *Richtungen der modernen Sprachwissenschaft* II 1982 p. 107ff. Following is a list of the individual Indo-European languages in the order of their incorporation into the group of Indo-European languages: Albanian (→ Bopp *Albanesisch* 1855); Armenian (H. Hübschmann 1875, see below E 424); Tocharian (E. Sieg, W. Siegling, W. Schulze 1908, see below E 408); Hittite (F. Hrozný 1915, see below E

410); Mycenaean / Linear B (M. Ventris and J. Chadwick 1953, see below E 418); Celtiberian (first Botorrita inscription found 1970, see below E 431 § 1c); Carian (See below E 415: → *Historia de la investigación* in *Adiego Studia Carica* 1993 p. 101ff.).

E 309. How Indo-European linguistics will evolve in the next millenium remains to be seen.

Indo-European linguistics has never been so well-documented as it today. Precision of description and argumentation have never been so good. One must continue on this path and examine our linguistic past with ever greater precision and adequacy. Openness to new approaches is of great importance.

It is a social responsibility to call attention to the historical dimension in all discussions of language and languages, and not to allow it to be forgotten. And this is all the more true today, as knowledge of the ancient Indo-European cultural languages Latin and Greek is threatened by suppression and marginalization.

Indo-European linguistics devotes itself to the linguistic past and, in so doing, makes the future intelligible. The motto, 'Without a past, no future' comes to mind. But Indo-European linguistics and historical linguistics must never be misused for political goals. (See index, under the headings 'Celts' and 'National Socialism.')

E 310. Indispensible to any perspective of the future is financial support of chairs for Indo-European linguistics at universities. In the present age of empty coffers in the public sector, so-called minor fields like Indo-European linguistics are often confronted with the crucial question of social relevance and called into question. Responsible faculties and university administrations are sometimes even willing to refuse the appointment of an Indo-European specialist in favor of material needs in other fields with greater numbers of students, and keep the field of Indo-European linguistics more or less alive through temporary teaching contracts. Thus has been the case recently in Basel, Fribourg (Switzerland), Giessen, Heidelberg, and Tübingen.

R. Wachter of the University of Basel offered a flaming appeal in March 1999 in favor of our fine, but small, field on the internet (link to Basel from our web site [see above E 100] under the heading Indo-European linguistics in Europe) entitled: "*Orchidee Indogermanistik: zähe Wurzel, zugkräftige Stammbildung, zerbrechliche Endungen*." In the following excerpt, "*Wozu Indogermanistik heute?*" the reader will easily recognize the statements that regard issues specific to the situation at the University of Basel and Switzerland in general.):

> "Here I should, in conclusion, accommodate today's utilitarianism by naming several additional factors that in my opinion clarify a well-grounded historical-comparative, and particularly an Indo-European curriculum as something useful, even outside of the more narrow area of classical philology and Indology, factors that can relativize the orchid-status of Indo-European linguistics: — Firstly, Indo-European linguistics can like no other science mediate between most languages of Europe, and particularly between the four languages of our country: It guides the regard to the common linguistic fund and the differences that have grown over time. It helps us to be familiarized ourselves, likewise archeologically, with the confusion of different historical layers, to keep them distinct from one another, and to be mindful of the historical context of inherited linguistic material, influences of languages of classical antiquity and the renaissance, exchanged linguistic material from the Roman-Germanic symbiosis of the early middle ages, scientific terms of the high middle ages that originated in Arabic, borrowings from the courtly culture of France, Anglo-Saxon technological-commercial vocabulary of the last hundred years, and much else. The historical-comparative perspective could, and furthermore should be made once again increasingly fruitful in language studies in the sense of applied linguistics. This is particularly useful for the Romance languages, of which three are official languages in Switzerland, and a fourth is among the most widespread languages of the world, further in the area of European common cultural vocabulary, which in many cases is common to all four official languages of Switzerland, as well as to English and the other European languages, and finally more or less in the structure of sentences and the typological changes of the last 2000 years, which likewise in nearly all of Europe reveal more commonalities than differences. And not least, the historical-analytical perspective, as I see it, encourages individual linguistic competence, trains sensitivity to style and broadens available linguistic resources. — Secondly, historical-comparative linguistics can help general linguistics to regain dimensions that the latter has for some time neglected, namely the historical and comparative dimensions. Lately, a convergence has been discernible, and here in Basel the signs of fruitful collaboration seem to me particularly promising. — Thirdly, Indo-European linguistics contributes greatly to the color of a university, for it brings its own bases of research and is at the same time a helpful field for many others, is cen-

trally important for classical philology among other fields, and meaningfully complementary to most other philologies, and it broadens significantly the selection of available fields through the inclusion of languages that would otherwise never be taught or researched. Through its multilingual integrating effect, Indo-European linguistics creates, along with history and comparative literature, an additional, particularly linguistically-oriented network of the most diverse fields. As an etymological science *par excellence*, it is particularly capable of finding a broader audience. — Last but not least, Indo-European linguistics does not cost very much: This is true in absolute terms, because it requires, aside from a minimum to assure continuity, very little personnel; books, reviews and other resources as well are required, commensurately with the breadth of the field, in modest quantity. But also considered relatively, the cost-benefit relationship is not at all bad, because here not only are the numbers of students relevant, but also just as much the qualitative aspect of the contribution of Indo-European linguistics to the functioning of many other fields and of the broadening of the choice of fields ... — It is a particularly desirable and effective reinforcement of the successful functioning of this small field that is full of tradition that the many other fields actually take advantage of its capacity to help. To achieve this, the field, or rather its representative, must contribute his part in his teaching, in his relations to students and representatives of the other fields, among others, as well as – today more than ever – toward the general public."

D. Overview of the Indo-European Languages and their Sources

1. General Information

E 400. Attestation and extent of documentation of the Indo-European languages varies from language to language. This is dependent on when the individual groups of IE language speakers found their way from the spoken word, originally prevalent in all of them, to the written one.

As a rule, this development took place at the time of contact with an established culture that employed writing. Compare for example the

Anatolian Hittites, who may be integrated in the Mesopotamian cuneiform tradition (cf. E 410 below), or the Mycenaean Greeks, who borrowed Linear B from the Cretan family of scripts (cf. E 418 below), or the Celts, who, depending on the region, wrote their inscriptions with the Greek, Latin, Etruscan, and even Iberian alphabets (cf. E 431, §1 below), or the Tochari, who, through their participation in the life marked by the Buddhism of the Tarim Basin of the sixth century AD, created language monuments of their own (see below E 408).

The earliest attestations of some language branches are translations of Christian content. These include Gothic, Old Church Slavic, and Armenian. A table of entry dates of individual languages into the world of written language is offered in Benveniste *Institutions* II 1969 in the opening text to the "*note bibliographique*."

In the best of all cases, the age of the language is consistent with that of those who created its records, as is the case with contemporary inscriptions. In other cases, the documents originate at a much later date, such as is the case as a rule with manuscripts. Thus, there is a period of oral tradition, or also of written tradition between the attested linguistic phase and the point at which the physical document can be dated.

Some languages have only come to be known in the last century, whether it be because they had remained undiscovered, or because the written documents could only then be deciphered.

The capacity to decode the languages concerned here varies both according to whether or not the given language has a modern descendent, and according to the length of its philological tradition.

E 401. General overviews of the individual representatives of the Indo-European language families are available in: → Cowgill *Einleitung* 1986 p. 17ff.; Lockwood *Überblick* 1979; *Lingue indoeuropee* 1994 = *Indo-European languages* 1998; *langues indo-européennes* 1994; Beekes *Introduction* 1995 p. 17ff.; *Convegno Udine (Restsprachen)* 1981 [1983].

2. The Individual Indo-European Language Families and their Sources

E 402. A short initial enumeration follows here in the order of the earliest attestation of the individual language. In each case, I shall mention the earliest evidence, and in the case of datable records the actual evidence shall also be mentioned. Further, an indication is given of an indirectly transmitted text if it is significant for the particular language because of age or size.

The current order is as follows: — Anatolian (Old Hittite, original documents from the 16th century BC, copies of texts from the 17th century BC); — Greek (Mycenaean original documents of the 17th and 14th/13th centuries BC); — Indian (13th century BC: the handing-down of the Rigveda must have taken place purely orally until far into the last millenium, but the creation of individual verses and of some philosophical content dates probably from the 13th century BC; further, material transmitted through secondary sources, including some names of deities and terms dates back to the Hurrian Mitanni empire of the 16th to 14th centuries BC.); — Iranian (the core of the Old Avestan text corpus dates back to Zarathustra, founder of zarathustranism, and thereby to the 10th century BC, but after a long period of oral transfer, the conserved texts were only preserved in written form starting in the 13th century AD, in the Middle Persian period); — Italic (perhaps the so-called *fibula praenestina* [if it is even authentic, and not a forgery: → Wachter *Altlateinische Inschriften* 1987 pp. 55-65] with its inscription can be dated to the first half of the 7th century BC; whereas other Latin monuments, such as the so-called Duenos inscription, only date from the 6th century); — Celtic (continental celtic inscriptions date from the 2nd century BC); — Germanic (Wulfila's Bible translation in Gothic is dated c. 350 AD; Germanic names on coins and in indirect records are attested from the 1st century BC); — Armenian (5th century AD); — Tocharian (6th century AD); — Slavic (9th century AD); — Baltic (14th century AD); — Albanian (15th century AD).

E 403. The following somewhat more thorough enumeration proceeds generally from geographical east to west, and follows, within each region, the order of first attested occurrence. References to helpful literature are kept quite brief.

1) Indian subcontinent and Chinese Turkestan: Indo-Iranian with Indian and Iranian (which adjoins from the west) ; Tocharian.

2) Asia Minor, Greece, and the Balkan peninsula: — From the 2nd century BC Anatolian in the east, Greek in the west. — From the 1st millenium BC Phrygian in Asia Minor. — Armenian in the east and Albanian in the Balkans beginning after Christ.

3) Italian peninsula: Italic.

4) Europe north of the Alps: Celtic, Germanic, Balto-Slavic.

E 404. Indian, or Indo-Aryan:

Indian and Iranian are closely linked both linguistically and culturally in their early stages. Even the name for the people, *ar̯ia-*, shared by both language branches, is an expression of intertwined Indo-Iranian cultures, cf. W 304. For a good overview of Indo-Iranian: → M. Mayrhofer in *langues indo-européennes* 1994 p. 101-120; *Arbeitstagung Erlangen* 1997 [2000].

1) Indian or – with reference to the non-Indo-European languages of India – Indo-Aryan is first attested ($16^{th}/14^{th}$ centuries BC) indirectly in other traditions, and in fact in the form of borrowed words and proper nouns in the Hurrian of kingdom of Mitanni ("Mitanni-Indian"): → Mayrhofer *Indo-Arier* 1966; Kammenhuber *Arier* 1968; M. Mayrhofer *Welches Material aus dem Indo-Arischen von Mitanni verbleibt für eine selektive Darstellung?* in *Kleine Schriften* II 1996 (an essay from 1982) p. 304-322; O. Carruba *Zur Überlieferung einiger Namen and Appellativa der Arier von Mitanni: "A Luwian look?"* in *Arbeitstagung* Erlangen 1997 [2000] p. 51-67. On the subject of Hurrian itself: → Neu *Hurritisch* 1988; Wegner *Hurritisch* 2000.

2) The oldest layer of the Indian language, which has continually developed through the present day, is tangible in the Vedic of the Rigveda, which may be dated to the middle of the 13th century BC and represents the Indian language of the Punjab region in the north-west of India. The dating concerns however only the language, and not the documents, since written transmission of Vedic texts began only two thousand years later. Because the oldest Vedic texts are ceremonial literature in verse, a genre in which exact phonetic observation and preservation are of the highest priority, the greatest reliability on the part of the oral tradition is assumed. Within Vedic Indian, different phases of language may be differentiated, which are connected with the various texts: Rigveda, Samaveda, Yajurveda, Atharvaveda, Brahmanas, Upanishads, Aranyakas. Even within the Rigveda, the collected hymns are not all of the same age; the oldest being those of the books two through seven, the so-called 'family books'. Different dialects of Vedic may also be distinguished.

Literature: — a) general: → Thumb / Hauschild *Handbuch des Sanskrit* 1958 / 1959; Wackernagel / Debrunner *Altindische Grammatik* 1957 / 1954 / 1930. — b) Vedic: → MacDonell *Vedic Grammar* 1910; Aufrecht *Hymnen des Rigveda* I / II 1877; Geldner *RV Übersetzung* 1951-1957; Grassmann *Wörterbuch* 1873; Mayrhofer *EWAia*; Hoffmann *Injunktiv* 1967; Narten *Sig-*

matische Aoriste 1964; Gotō, I. *Präsensklasse* 1987 and by the same author, *Materialien* Nr. 1-29 1990-1997; Zehnder *AVP* 2 1999; M. Witzel, "Tracing the Vedic Dialects" in *Dialectes indo-aryennes* 1986 [1989] p. 97-265; by the same author, *Die sprachliche Situation Nordindiens in vedischer Zeit* in *Arbeitstagung Erlangen* 1997 [2000] p. 543-579.

3) The earliest directly handed-down Indian pieces of linguistic evidence are inscriptions from the Buddhist Emperor Aśoka of 250 BC. The development of Prākrit begins in around 500 BC. Part of Prākrit is Pāli, the canonical language of southern Buddhism: → Geiger *Pāli* 1916; Mayrhofer *Pāli* 1951; von Hinüber *Älteres Mittelindisch* 1986.

4) Classical Sanskrit, which as a literary and intellectual language is used to the present day, appeared only after Middle Indian in the second half of the first millenium BC under the influence of the grammarian Pāṇini (c. 400 BC) and others: → Mayrhofer *Sanskrit-Grammatik* 1978.

5) Among the New Indian languages, Hindī and Urdū are particularly worth mentioning. For information on the present linguistic situation: → P. Gaeffke and H. Bechert in *Indologie* 1979 p. 32ff.

E 405. Already in its oldest attestations, Old Iranian may be divided into an eastern and a western branch. East Iranian is represented by Avestan; West Iranian by Old Persian. Avestan and Old Persian developed separate scripts: Avestan is written from right to left in an alphabet that is based upon the cursive Pahlavi alphabet of the 4th century AD and which, thanks to its wealth of characters, can take into account fine phonetic differences. Old Persian, however, is written in a simple cuneiform that developed separately around 520 BC.

The fragmentary attestation of Old Iranian leads great importance to the successive Middle and New Iranian languages. See an example of Khotanese in L 211 § 5.

Literature: → *Compendium Linguarum Iranicarum* 1989 with articles on all aspects of Iranian (from Old Iranian and Middle Iranian to New Iranian); R. Schmitt *Die iranischen Sprachen, Eine Einführung in 5 Teilen* in *Spektrum Iran* 8,4 1995 p. 6-27; 9,2 1996 p. 6-32; 9,3-4 1996 p. 6-32; 10,1 1997 p. 10-38; 11,1 1998 p. 14-42 = Schmitt *Iranische Sprachen* 2000; M. Mayrhofer '*L'Indo-iranien*' in *langues indo-européennes* 1994 p. 101-120; Bartholomae *Altiranisches Wörterbuch* 1904 (1979); Hoffmann *Altiranisch* in *Aufsätze* I 1975 p. 58-76 (Article from 1958; otherwise compare the essays I-III, which contain Hoffmann's central studies on

Old Iranian); R. S. P. Beekes *"Historical Phonology of Iranian"* in JIES 25 1997 p. 1-26.

E 406. The oldest occurrences of Avestan are the so-called Gathas of Zarathustra ("Gatha-Avestan"), which are hymns to the deity Ahura Mazda. These excerpts, together with the Yasna Haptaŋhāiti, a ceremonial text in prose date from the 10th century BC. — Later Avestan is a later dialect of Old Avestan and dates from around the 6th and 5th centuries BC. The oldest known manuscript text dates from 1288 AD.

Literature: → Beekes *Gatha-Avestan* 1988; J. Kellens in *Compendium Linguarum Iranicarum* 1989 p. 32-55; Kellens / Pirart *Textes vieil-avestiques* I-III 1988-1991; Hoffmann / Forssman *Avestische Laut- and Flexionslehre* 1996 (p. 247ff. A compilation of writings on Avestan by B. Forssman).

E 407. Old Persian is first attested at the time of the Old Persian cuneiform script, thus c. 520 BC; but the inscriptions from the 3rd century BC already contain linguistic mistakes that indicate that Old Persian was already no longer a contemporary language. In some cases, Old Persian also contains "medisms." The entire fund of Old Persian texts is comprised of a small corpus of inscriptions: → Brandenstein / Mayrhofer *Altpersisch* 1964; Mayrhofer *Supplement* 1978; R. Schmitt in *Compendium Linguarum Iranicum* 1989 p. 56-85; Schmitt *Bisitun Inscriptions* 1991; by the same author *Altpersische Inschriften* 1999; M. Mayrhofer *Über die Verschriftung des Altpersischen* in *Kleine Schriften* II 1996 p. 387-399 (essay from 1989).

For information on the Parthian Empire under the Arsacids (247 BC - 224 AD): → *Partherreich* [1996] 1998 (which contains, among others, R. Schmitt *Parthische Sprach- and Namenüberlieferung aus arsakidischer Zeit* p. 163-204. The oldest Pahlavi-inscription comes from the founder of the Sassanid dynasty, Ardashir I (Papakan = Ardashir) (224-241 n. Chr.): → Overviews in *Compendium Linguarum Iranicarum* 1989 p. 95ff.

E 408. Two languages may be distinguished in the case of Tocharian: East Tocharian, or Tocharian A, and West Tocharian, or Tocharian B. Both were used in eastern Turkestan starting in the 2nd century BC. The earliest attestations date from the 6th century AD; the latest from the 8th century AD. — Tocharian A was a purely written language. Tocharian B, on the other hand, was a lingua franca in Turfan, Qarasahr, Sorcuq, and Kuca. Contents of literary texts include poetry, religious, and scientific material. Extant religious, Buddhist texts, of which several are for the most part translations from Sanskrit, including some that are bilingual, and others that are copies of a known original. In addition, in Tocharian B, there are reports from monasteries, caravan passes, a letter, and text from mural paintings. A modified Northern Indian Brahmi alphabet was used. — Around 1900, expeditions explored the Chinese province Xinjiang. In 1904, A. Le Coq and A. Grünwedel discovered a distinctly Tocharian language in manuscripts from eastern Turkestan. The language was further researched by E. Sieg and W. Siegling: → W. Siegling *Tocharisch, die Sprache der Indoskythen* in *Sitzungsberichte der Berliner Akademie* 1908 p. 915-932 (Sergej Th. Oldenburg first postulated the Indo-European character of Tocharian in 1892: → E. N. Tyomkin in TIES 7 1997 p. 205ff.).

Literature: → An excellent introduction may be found in Pinault *Tokharien* 1989; *Fachtagung Tocharisch* Berlin 1990 [1994] (which contains, among others, p. 310ff. G. Klingenschmitt *Das Tocharische in indogermanistischer Sicht*, see also, by the same author, *Tocharisch and Urindogermanisch* in *Fachtagung Regensburg* 1973 [1975] p. 148-163); TIES (see the information in the bibliography); Adams *Tocharian* 1988; Adams *Dictionary* (Tocharian B) 1999; Ringe *Sound Changes in Tocharian* I 1996; Hackstein *Sigmatische Präsensstammbildungen* 1995; Carling *Lokale Kasus im Tocharischen* 2000.

E 409. With its Old Hittite cuneiform texts from the 16th century BC, the Anatolian group of languages offers the oldest attested occurrence of an Indo-European language. Eight Anatolian languages are attested: Hittite, Luwian, Palaic, Lycian, Lydian, Carian, Pisidian, and Sidetic. — The Anatolian languages use three different systems of writing: A type of babylonian-Assyrian cuneiform (Hittite, Palaic, Luwian), hieroglyphics (Luwian), alphabet (Lycian, Lydian, Carian, Pisidian, Sidetic).

Literature: → Melchert "Anatolian" in *langues indo-européennes* 1994 p. 121ff.; N. Oettinger "*Die Gliederung des anatolischen Sprachgebietes*" in ZVS 92 1978 [1979] p. 74-92; by the same author, in DNP under the heading *Kleinasien* column 555-559.

E 410. An archive of clay tablets was discovered in 1906 in Hattuša/Bogažköy, 150 kilometers east of Ankara. The linguistic material found in the Arzawa letters from the Amarna correspondence, found in 1887/88 in Middle Egypt moved Knudtzon to express the supposition in

1902 that the language is Indo-European. The deciphering of the script was performed by Bedřich Hrozný in 1915.

Hittite, the administrative language of the Hittite empire, offers the most textual material of the Anatolian languages. Hittite texts can thus be ordered chronologically into various phases: Three phases may be distinguished: Old Hittite (1570-1450), Middle Hittite (1450-1380) and Late Hittite (1380-1220). Meanwhile, the absolute chronology varies in research. In the two and a half century older Assyrian tradition, two Hittite borrowed words are attested (*išpatalu* 'lodging,' *išḫiuli* 'wage contract'). The latest Hittite attestations come from the 13th century BC. Hittite texts are written in cuneiform and, with the exception of one bronze tablet, are found on fired clay tablets. Most have been found in central Anatolia.

Literature: — a) General: → Bittel *Hattusha* 1970 by the same author *Hethiter* 1976; Bryce *Kingdom* 1998; Neve *Ḫattuša* 1996; C. Melchert *"Anatolian"* in *langues indo-européennes* 1994 p. 121-136; Benveniste *Hittite et indo-européen* 1962; *Bibliographie der Hethitologie* 1996 (1998): 1 p. 275ff. (writing); 2 p. 11ff. (languages and philology); A. Kammenhuber *Kleine Schriften* 1993; F. Starke in *DNP* (see the headings Ḫattusha and *Hethitisch*). — b) Writings / Texts: → Rüster / Neu *Hethitisches Zeichenlexikon* 1989; Neu *Althethitische Ritualtexte* 1980 and Neu *Althethitisches Glossar* 1983. — c) Language, lexicon: → Friedrich *Elementarbuch* I 1960; Oettinger *Verbum* 1979; Rieken *Nominale Stammbildung* 1999; *Grammatica ittita* 1992; Friedrich / Kammenhuber *HW*; Tischler *HEG*; *CHD*.

E 411. Palaic is only very fragmentarily handed down; it disappeared in the 13th century BC. It was the spoken idiom of Pala, an area northwest of the Hittite center: → Carruba *Palaisch* 1970, by the same author *Beiträge zum Palaischen*. Istanbul 1972.

E 412. Luwian, a language from southern and southwestern Anatolia, is attested in two dialects: one was handed down in cuneiform (14th/13th centuries BC), the other in hieroglyphics (15th-8th centuries BC). Many Luwian texts in cuneiform differ from one another very little such that the vocabulary that has been handed down is very limited. Other Luwian words are found as borrowed or adapted words in Hittite texts. For the most part, the hieroglyphic Luwian texts originate after the fall of the Hittite empire. Most of these are stone inscriptions found in the region comprised by southern Anatolia and northern Syria. Descendents of the Luwian language group, which include Lycian (see below E 413) and Carian (see below E 415) persisted in southwestern Anatolia into the first millenium BC.

Literature: — a) general: F. Starke in *DNP* under the heading *Luwisch.* — b) Cuneiform Luwian: → Laroche *Louvite* 1959; Melchert *Cuneiform Luvian* 1993; Starke *Keilschrift-luwische Texte* 1985, by the same author *Keilschrift-luwische Nomen* 1990. — c) Hieroglyphic Luwian: Laroche *Hiéroglyphes hittites* I 1960; Marazzi *Geroglifico* 1990; Hawkins *Corpus* 1 2000 and 2 1999; M. Marazzi, *Il geroglifico anatolico: stato delle ricerche* in Graz 2000 p. 317-326. — d) Luwian in the first millenium BC → Neumann *Weiterleben* 1961; Houwink ten Cate *Luwian Population Groups* 1965.

E 413. Lycian is the language of the Lycian landscape. Aside from the more broadly attested 'normal Lycian' (or Lycian A), a second dialect (Lycian B, or 'Milyan') is attested in a few occurrences. Stone inscriptions, which represent the majority of Lycian attestations, come from the 5th and 4th centuries BC and include, aside from grave inscriptions, among others the famous "Stele of Xanthos" and the trilingual stele of the Letoon in Xanthos, which contains Lycian, Greek, and Aramaic and was discovered in 1973. The Lycian alphabet belongs to the group of so-called Anatolian alphabets.

Literature: → Neumann *Kleine Schriften* 1994 p. 109-223 (with selected writings on); Hajnal *Lyk. Vokalismus* 1995 (p. 3ff. Introduction with an inventory of Lycian inscriptions and an overview of the history of research).

E 414. Lydian, the language of the kingdom of Lydia in West Anatolia, is attested at the earliest by texts on coins from the 8th century. Stone inscriptions, among which are to be a found a couple of Lydian-Aramaic bilingual tablets, are dated from the 5th and 4th centuries BC. The Lydian alphabet belongs to the same alphabet group as that of Lycian, but is independent.

Literature: → Gusmani *Lydisches Wörterbuch* 1964 and *Lydisches Wörterbuch Ergänzungsband* 1986; H. Eichner *Die Akzentuation des Lydischen* in *Sprache* 32 1986 p. 7-21; F. Starke in *DNP* under the heading *Lydisch*.

E 415. Carian is linguistically adjacent to Lycian. Its language monuments come from both Egypt (6th century BC) and the original area of Carian in southwestern Anatolia ($5\text{-}4^{th}$ century BC). Graffiti like that found in Iasos dates from as early as the 7th century BC; the Carian-Greek bilingual stele from Athens dates from the end of the 6th century BC. The alphabet is of the Anatolian type, but an independent creation. The appropriate attribution of phonetic values, which was only recently achieved, was confirmed through the discovery of a Carian-Greek bilingual stele in Kaunos.

Literature: → Adiego *Studia Carica* 1993; Cario 1993 [1994]; *Colloquium Caricum* 1998 (on the bilingual stele from Kaunos); I. Hajnal in *Kadmos* 36 1997 p. 141-166 and 37 1998 p. 80-108.

E 416. In the southern Anatolian area of Pisidia and around the city Side, successor languages of Luwian are attested to have been spoken. We have a whole series of names as well as a few inscriptions from Side.

Literature: → Neumann *Kleine Schriften* 1994 p. 227ff. (Essays on Sidetic may be found under the numbers 33, 39, 43, 48, 49.)

E 417. Greek is a language that can be documented over a period of 4000 years. — The oldest documents are clay tablets in Linear-B, see below, E 418. Greek inscriptions in alphabet script date from as early as the 8th century BC. With the exception of Cypriot, which employed a syllabic script similar to that of Mycenaean which dates back to the second millenium BC, Greek texts are written with an alphabet. The Greek alphabet was probably adapted from a northwest Semitic alphabet around 800 BC. — In the following, the most important texts are given first. Paragraphs have been added for Mycenaean Greek (see below, E 418), Homer (see below, E 419) and the dialects (see below, E 420).

Literature: — a) General: → Schwyzer *Griechische Grammatik* I 1939; Schwyzer / Debrunner *Griechische Grammatik* II 1950; E. Risch in LAW 1965 under the heading *Griechisch*; Meier-Brügger *Griechische Sprachwissenschaft* I / II 1992; K. Strunk *Vom Mykenischen bis zum klassischen Griechisch* in *Griechische Philologie* 1997 p. 135ff.; B. Forssman in *DNP* under the heading *Altgriechisch*; Meillet *Aperçu* 1975; Hiersche *Grundzüge* 1970; Risch *Kleine Schriften* 1981 (compare *Indices*); Ruijgh *Scripta Minora* I 1991 II 1996 (compare *Indices*). — b) Phonetics and morphology: → Lejeune *Phonétique* 1972; Allen *Vox Graeca* 1987; Zinsmeister *Griechische Grammatik* I 1954; Rix *Historische Grammatik des Griechischen* 1976; Bornemann / Risch *Grieschische Grammatik* 1978. — c) Syntax: → Delaunois *Syntaxe* 1988; *Kolloquium Kühner* Amsterdam 1986 [1988]. — d) Vocabulary: → Frisk GEW; Chantraine DELG; DGE (compare Anejo III); CEG.

E 418. The earliest written evidence of Greek that has survived, is comprised of inscriptions in a syllabic script ("Linear B"). The oldest known document comes from the area around Olympia, contains the proper noun _$K^{h}arok^{w}s$_ (compare the Homeric Χάροψ), and dates from 1650 BC: → P. Arapogianni, J. Rambach, L. Godard in *Floreant Studia Mycenaea* I 1995 [1999] p. 39-43. Part of the clay tablets from Knossos originate in the 14th century BC, the rest are dated around 1200 BC. Aside from Knossos on Crete, mainland sites include palaces in Pylos, Mycenae, Tiryns, and (in Boetia) Thebes. The language of the inscriptions is referred to as Mycenaean Greek or simply as Mycenaean. This early phase of Greek came to be a focus of research only in 1952, after Michael Ventris, along with J. Chadwick, deciphered Linear-B script. It is notable that Greek linguistics has only been able to integrate Mycenaean material in its discussion since the 60s. A textbook such as Schwyzer's *Griechische Grammatik* I 1939 can certainly maintain particular assertions that were at the time thinkable, but which today may no longer be maintained, for example the formerly common analysis of ἕνεκα 'because' < _*en-u̯eka_ 'with regard to the will,' which because of Mycenaean *e-ne-ka,* i.e. *eneka* must be rejected (In the case of _*enu̯eka_, _*e-we-ka_ would be expected!). The questionable ἕνεκα must now be seen as the fossilized root word _*h$_1$nek̑-m̥_ in the accusative singular case, which means 'for the attainment of (with a genitive complement)': → Meier-Brügger *Griechische Sprachwissenschaft* I 1992 p. 88f.

Literature: → SMID; Chadwick *Documents* 1973; Hiller / Panagl *Frühgr. Texte aus myk. Zeit* 1976; Aura Jorro *Diccionario micénico.* I 1985 II 1993; Meier-Brügger *Griechische Sprachwissenschaft* I 1992 p. 43ff.; Hooker *Linear B* 1980; Lejeune *Mémoires* I-IV 1958-1997. — The last colloquia: → *Colloquium Mycenaeum* 1975 [1979]; *Res Mycenaeae* 1981 [1983]; *Tractata Mycenaea* 1985 [1987]; *Mykenaïka* 1990 [1992]; Floreant *Studia Mycenaea* 1995 [1999]. — Concerning new finds in Thebes: → V. Aravantinos in Floreant *Studia Mycenaea* I p. 45ff. Further, compare the CRAI-lectures by L. Godart and A. Sacconi: *Les dieux thébains dans les archives mycéniennes* in volume *1996* p. 99-113; *Les archives de Thèbes et le monde mycénien* in volume 1997 p. 889-906; *La géographie des états mycéniens* in volume XX 1999 p. 527-546

E 419. The first Ancient Greek literary texts are the two epics by Homer; the Iliad and the Odyssey, the writing of which is probably correctly dated to the 8th century BC. The oldest evidence of the written transmittal of these texts are papyri from the third century BC. Although there had probably been a couple of editions before this date, well into the Hellenistic period, the normal Greek probably only knew his Homer text from the oral tradition.

Literature: → Latacz *Homer* 1989; by the same author: *Troia and Homer* 2001; by the same author in *DNP* see under the headings: *Der epische Zyklus, Epos, Homer, Homerische Frage*; Ruipérez *Ilias and Odyssee* 1999; *Iliad* I-VI 1985-1993; *Homers Ilias Prolegomena* 2000; *Homers Ilias Gesamtkommentar* 2000ff.; *Odyssey* I-III 1988-1992; LfgrE; Chantraine *Grammaire homérique* I 1958 II 1953; Risch *Wortbildung* 1973; *Colloquium Rauricum* 2 1991; *Homeric Questions* 1995.

E 420. Ancient Greek dialects: Ionic-Attic, Doric-Northwest Greek, Aeolic (Boeotian, Thessalian, Lesbian), Arcadian-Cypriot-Pamphylian; there is still a debate going on about a possible separation in Ionic, Doric, and Achaean, the latter of which is divided further into North Achaean (Aeolic) and South Achaean (Arcadian-Cypriot-Pamphylian). Early attestations of dialectal splitting in inscriptions and genre-specific literary use of different dialects (e.g. scientific prose in Ionic, lyrical writings in Aeolic, Doric chorus text in Attic tragedy) are particularities of Greek dialectology. In the course of time, the various dialects were replaced by the so-called Koine.

Literature: a) Overviews: → Bechtel *Griechische Dialekte* 1921-1924; Buck *Greek Dialects* 1955; Schmitt *Griechische Dialekte* 1977; Meier-Brügger *Griechische Sprachwissenschaft* I 1992 p. 76ff.; García-Ramón in *DNP* see under the headings *Äolisch, Arkadisch, Attisch, Dorisch, Ionisch*; *Katà diálekton* 1996 [1999]. — b) individual monographs: → Masson ICS 1961 + Add. 1983 (on Cyprus, also *Greek Language in Cyprus* 1988); Brixhe *Pamphylie* 1976; Threatte *Attic* I 1980 II 1996; Blümel *Aiolische Dialekte* 1982; Dubois *Arcadien* 1986; Bile *Crétois* 1988; Hodot *Éolien* 1990; Vottéro *Béotien* I 1998; Dobias-Lalou *Cyrène* 2000. — c) For information on Koine: → *Koiné* I-III 1993-1998.

E 421. The Macedonian of the ancient kingdom of northern Greece is probably nothing other than a northern Greek dialect of Doric: → C. Brixhe / A. Panayotou *Le macédonien* in *langues indo-européennes* 1994 p. 205-220; SEG 43 1993 Nr. 434; C. Brixhe in *Katà diálekton* 1996 [1999] p. 41ff.

In contrast, in the present Macedonia, of which the capital is Skopje, a southern Slavic language, similar to Bulgarian, is spoken. See below, E 433.

E 422. Illyrian and Thracian are languages of the southern Balkans. Whether or not they are Indo-European, is still discussed. They have not preserved any written language, but are probably reflected in the corpus of proper nouns in the region, the interpretation of which is difficult: → Krahe *Illyrier* I 1955; H. Kronasser, *Illyrier and Illyricum* in *Sprache* 11 1965 p. 155-183 (criticism apropos of Krahe); Katičić *Languages of the Balkans* 1976; C. Brixhe / A. Panayotou *Le thrace* in *langues indo-européennes* 1994 p. 179-203.

According to inscriptions found in southern Italy, Messapian – an IE language of the Italic branch ? - was spoken in the area of Brindisi and Lecce. Whether Messapian is linguistically linked to the Balkans has been open to discussion since Krahe: → C. de Simone and J. Untermann in Krahe *Illyrier* II 1964; O. Parlangeli and C. Santoro in LDIA 1978 p. 913ff.; C. de Simone *Iscrizione messapiche della grotta della Poesia* in ASNP Serie III Vol. XVIII / 2 1988 p. 325-415.

E 423. Phrygian is a language that was spoken in what is now central Turkey. The capital of the Phrygians, Gordion, lay 120 miles southwest of Ankara. Phrygian is attested in about 200 inscriptions in the Greek alphabet in two different phases: Old Phrygian (8th-4th centuries BC) and Late Phrygian ($2^{nd}/3^{rd}$ centuries AD).

Literature: → C. Brixhe *Le phrygien* in *langues indo-européennes* 1994 p. 165-178; Brixhe / Lejeune *Paléo-phrygien* 1984; Neumann *Phrygisch und Griechisch* 1988; *Frigi e Frigio* 1995 [1997].

E 424. Evidence of Armenian begins with the 5th century AD, likely soon after the creation of the Armenian script in 407 by the missionary Mesrop († 441) in order to translate the Bible into Armenian in 410. Prior to this time, only a few Armenian names are given in Aramaic, Greek, and Syrian texts. The Old Armenian language until 460 AD is also called Classical Armenian; in the 7th and 8th centuries follows the post-classical period of Old Armenian, followed in turn by Early Middle Armenian, which lasted from the 8th to the 11th centuries. Middle Armenian (Cilician-Armenian, among others) follows in the 12th century. The earliest preserved inscriptions date from the end of the 5th century AD. The oldest preserved manuscript dates from 887, while a greater quantity of manuscripts was preserved starting at the end of the 12th century. Most of the oldest Armenian literature consists of translations of Syrian and Greek; most Old Armenian texts consist of Christian literature or historiography. — After Armenian had been thought to be a part of the Indo-Iranian language branch, Heinrich Hübschmann showed in 1875 that Armenian represents its own Indo-European language branch: → *Ueber die stellung des armenischen im kreise der indogermanischen Sprachen* in KZ 23,1 1875 p. 5-49 = *Kleine Schriften* 1976 p. 1-45. — A peculiarity of Armenian is that in the case of plosives, a consonant shift just like that in Germanic took place. The lexicon contains many words borrowed from Persian, Syrian, and Greek.

Literature: → Lamberterie *Arménien classique* 1992 (A very good introduction); R. Schmitt *Forschungsbericht: Die Erforschung des Klassisch-Armenischen seit Meillet* (1936) in *Kratylos* 17 1972 [1974] p. 1-68; Meillet *Arménien classique* 1936; Jensen *Altarmenische Grammatik* 1959; Godel *Classical Armenian* 1975; Schmitt *Klassisches Armenisch* 1981; Ritter *Armeno antiguo* 1996; Klingenschmitt *Altarmenisches Verbum* 1982; Solta *Stellung des Armenischen* 1960; Clackson *Armenisch and Greek* 1994; Olsen *Noun* 1999.

E 425. The earliest evidence of Albanian is from the 15th century AD, which includes the baptismal formula of the Archbishop of Durazzo, Paolo Angelo, from the year 1462. The oldest preserved Albanian book is Gjon Buzuku's *Missals*, which was created in 1555. Albanian seems, however, to have been written in the 14th century. Albanian is divided into two dialects: Geg in the North and Tosk in the South.

Literature: → Bopp *Albanesisch* 1855; B. Demiraj *Albanische Etymologien* 1997; S. Demiraj *Albanisch* 1993; G. Klingenschmitt *Albanisch and Urindogermanisch* in MSS 40 1981 p. 93-131; by the same author *Das Albanische als Glied der indogermanischen Sprachfamilie* (handout) in *Kolloquium Pedersen* Copenhagen 1993 [1994] p. 221-233; J. Matzinger in *Sprache* 40 1998 p. 102-132 (Review of V. Orel *A Concise Historical Grammar of the Albanian Language*. Leiden / Boston / Köln 2000).

E 426. The ancient Italian ethnic groups offer a great diversity in a small area: → *Italia alumna* 1990 (which contains: *La civiltà dei Veneti, Reti, Liguri, Celti, Piceni, Umbri, Latini, Campani e Iapigi*); *Italia parens* 1991 (which contains: *La civiltà degli Enotri, Choni, Ausoni, Sanniti, Lucani, Brettii, Sicani, Siculi, Elimi*). Overview of the languages of Italy: → G. Meiser in DNP under the headings: *Italien, Sprachen*, column 1167-1170.

1) Latino-Faliscan and Sabellic together form the Italic branch of the Indo-European languages. Venetian probably split off before the differentiation of Latino-Faliscan and Sabellic. — The concrete hypothesis of H. Rix (in *Incontri*

Linguistici 17 1994 p. 24f.) is as follows: The Italic people was first a part of the northwest Indo-Europeans (see below, E 435, §4) but then settled as the independent original Italic language group in the area of Pannonia (from the upper Sava basin to the mid-Drava river area). From there they migrated into Italy in several distinct thrusts. The order of migrations: "Proto-Venetians" (on Venetian, see below, E 430), "Proto-Sabellians" (on Sabellic, see below E 429), "Proto-Latins" (on Latino-Faliscan, see below, E 427, E 428). Sabellians and Latino-Faliscans met again after a period of separation, in the middle Italic Koine of the 7th-5th centuries BC, see below §3A. — On the problem of Proto-Italic: → H. Rix *Latein and Sabellisch, Stammbaum und/oder Sprachband?* in *Incontri Linguistici* 17 1994 p. 13-29; J. Untermann *'Urverwandtschaft' and historische Nachbarschaft im Wortschatz der italischen Sprachen* in *Incontri Linguistici* 16 1993 p. 93-101; P. de Bernardo Stempel, *Kernitalisch, Latein, Venetisch: ein Etappenmodell* in Graz 2000 p. 47-70.

2) Alongside the Indo-European languages of the Italic family, other Indo-European languages were spoken in ancient Italy: Greek in the south (Greek colonies in Sicily and in all of southern Italy), and in the north, Celtic Lepontic (see below, E 431 § 1c). For information on Messapian, see above, E 422.

3) The non-Indo-European languages of ancient Italy are Etruscan (A) and Punic (B).

A) Etruscan: The Etruscans, probably having come by sea from the east, settled in Etruria. The Latino-Faliscans and Sabellians must have already been established in the region. The Etruscans marked the ancient Italian linguistic landscape. But their influence on Latin was overestimated early on. From around 650-450 BC there existed a cultural Koine between Etruscans, Latino-Faliscan, and Sabellians that exercised influence on the alphabet, numeral systems, the system of familiy names, and religious customs and names of the peoples of the region across ethnic boundaries. Literature: — a) General on Etruscans: → H. Rix *Schrift and Sprache in Etrusker* 1985 p. 210-238; Rix *Etruskische Texte* I / II 1991. — b) On the interrelation of Rome and Etruria: → *Etrusci e Roma* 1979 [1981]. — c) On the interrelation of Etruscan - Rhaetic - Lemnian (Proto-Tyrrhenian): → H. Rix *Eine morpho-syntaktische Übereinstimmung zwischen Etruskisch and Lemnisch: die Datierungsformel* in *GS Brandenstein* 1968 p. 213-222; by the same author, *Rätisch and Etruskisch* 1998.

B) Punic: Punic is a form of Phoenician. It is the language of Carthage, the great opponent of Rome up until its destruction in 146 BC. The Punic-Etruscan bilingual tablet from Pyrgi / Cerveteri (north of Rome) dates from the 5th century BC: → W. Fischer and H. Rix in GGA 220 1968 p. 64-94.

— The comedy *Poenulus* is by Plautus. — Further literature on Punic: → M. G. Guzzo Amadasi in LDIA 1978 p. 1013ff.

E 427. Latin is by far the best attested of the Indo-European languages of ancient Italy.

1) The Latin language was originally the dialect of the city of Rome and was closely connected to the landscape of Latium: → Kolb *Rom* 1995.

2) The earliest occurrences are inscriptions found in the city of Rome from the 6th century BC. From the 5th to the 1st centuries BC, the language is known as Old Latin. The majority of preserved texts come from the period from the 1st century BC to the 1st century AD. Classical Latin, strictly speaking, includes only the prose writings of Cicero and Caesar, which date from the 1st century BC.

3) For information on Old Latin inscriptions: → Ernout *Recueil* 1947; Diehl *Altlateinische Inschriften* 1965; Warmington *Remains of Old Latin* IV 1940; Degrassi *Inscriptiones* I-II 1965-1972; by the same author *Imagines* 1965; *Römische Inschriften*, by L. Schumacher. Stuttgart 1988 (= Reclam, Universal-Bibliothek Nr. 8512) and *Die römische Literatur in Text and Darstellung.* volume 1: *Republikanische Zeit* I (*Poesie*) by H. and A. Petersmann. Stuttgart 1991 (= Reclam, Universal-Bibliothek Nr. 8066); Meyer *Lateinische Epigraphik* 1973; Blümel *Untersuchungen* 1972; Radke *Archaisches Latein* 1981; Wachter *Altlateinische Inschriften* 1987; Vine *Archaic Latin* 1993.

4) The first Latin literary texts are only attested from the 3rd century BC: → H. Rix "*Schrift and Schriftgebrauch im vorliterarischen Mittelitalien*" in Hoffmann *Gedenkfeier* 1996 [1997] p. 27-42.

5) Literature on Latin: — a) History of the Latin language: → Meillet *Esquisse* 1928; Devoto *Lingua di Roma* 1940; M. Leumann *Geschichte der lateinischen Sprache* in Leumann / Hofmann / Szantyr *Allgemeiner Teil* 1965 p. 10*ff.; Solta *Stellung der lateinischen Sprache* 1974; Giacomelli *Lingua latina* 1993; J. Kramer *Geschichte der lateinischen Sprache* in *Lateinische Philologie* 1996 p. 115-162; M. Meier-Brügger in RGA 18 2001 under the heading 'Latein'. — b) General Latin: → Leumann / Hofmann / Szantyr *Allgemeiner Teil* 1965; H. Rix in DNP 6 1999 column 1160-1163 under the heading 'Latein'; *Kolloquium Latein and Indogermanisch* Salzburg 1986 [1992]; Sommer *Handbuch* 1948; Sommer / Pfister *Lautlehre* 1977; Leumann LLFL 1977; Meiser *Laut- and Formenlehre* 1998; Schrijver *Laryngeals in Latin* 1991; Benedetti *Composti radicali* 1988. Further, compare the series IKLL (ICLL / CILL), see the bibliography, under IKLL.

6) Of particular importance is also Vulgar Latin, the spoken language out of which in the various Roman provinces the individual Romance languages (Romanian, Romansch, Sardic, French, Dalmatian, Italian, Provençal, Spanish, Catalan, and Portugese) developed. In a unique way, the relationship of the mother language to its offspring may be observed and documented. On Vulgar Latin: → Väänänen *Latin vulgaire* 1981.

E 428. The oldest occurrences of Faliscan, the language of Falerii and the surrounding area, are inscriptions from the 6th century BC; the latest Faliscan inscriptions are from the 2nd century BC. Aside from the sparse inscriptions, there are no attestations of Faliscan. Literature: → Vetter *Handbuch der italischen Dialekte* I 1953 p. 277ff.; Giacomelli *Lingua Falisca* 1963; G. Giacomelli in LDIA 1978 p. 505ff.

E 429. Among the languages of the Sabellian branch of languages are so-called South Picene, Oscan, Umbrian, and a couple of other, only slightly varied languages, such as Volscian. Of particular interest is South Picene, the oldest attestations of which date from the 6th century BC. South Picene is particularly interesting. Three different alphabets were employed in Oscan inscriptions: the Greek alphabet, the Latin alphabet, and the Oscan alphabet. The oldest inscriptions date from the 3rd century BC. The so-called Iguvine Tables are the main source for Umbrian and come from the 3rd-2nd centuries BC.

Literature: → Meiser *Umbrisch* 1986; G. Meiser, *Pälignisch, Latein und Südpikenisch* in *Glotta* 65 1987 p. 104-125; H. Rix *Umbro e Proto-Osco-Umbro* in *Convegno Udine* (minor languages) 1991 [1993]; Marinetti *Iscrizioni sudpicene* 1985; G. Meiser and H. Rix in *Tavole di Agnone* 1994 [1996] p. 187ff. and p. 243ff.; H. Rix, *Südpikenisch kduiú* in HS 107 1994 p. 105-122; Schirmer *Wortschatz* 1998; Untermann *Wörterbuch Oskisch-Umbrisch* 2000.

E 430. Venetian represents a separate Italic language of what is now the Veneto region (inscriptions from the 6th-2nd centuries BC): → Pellegrini / Prosdocimi *Lingua Venetica* I / II 1967; Lejeune *Vénète* 1974; A. L. Prosdocimi *Il venetico* in LDIA 1978 p. 257ff. by the same author in *Convegno Udine* (minor languages) 1981 [1983] p. 153ff.

E 431. Celtic can roughly be divided into Continental Celtic (from the European continent) and Insular Celtic (from the British Isles [and from there, through migrations, Brittany connects linguistically with Breton]).

While Continental Celtic offers the oldest occurrences of Celtic, Insular Celtic offers by far the greater quantity of documents.

General literature: → *Kolloquium Keltisch* Bonn 1976 [1977]; Birkhan *Kelten* 1997; *Deutschsprachige Keltologen* 1992 [1993] (which includes K. H. Schmidt *Stand and Aufgaben der deutschsprachigen Keltologie* p. 1-35); K. H. Schmidt *Celtic Movements in the First Millennium B.C.* in JIES 20 1992 p. 145-178; K. McCone *Relative Chronologie: Keltisch* in *Fachtagung Leiden* 1987 [1992] p. 11-39; *Keltologen-Symposium* II 1997 [1999]; DNP see under the headings *Kelten, Keltische Sprachen*; RGA see under the headings *Kelten, Keltische Ortsnamen, Hercynia Silva, Helvetier.*

1) Apart from occurrences of Celtic (in toponymy, for example) in documents in other languages, the oldest occurrences of Celtic come from the 3rd century BC, which includes Continental Celtic inscriptions above all from Gaul, but also from Spain (Botorrita) and Italy (southern extremity of the Alps). The latest date from as late as the 3rd century AD. Literature: — a) General → J. F. Eska / D. E. Evans *Continental Celtic in Celtic Languages* 1993 p. 26-63 (which includes a good bibliography, p. 52-64); K. H. Schmidt *Grundlagen einer festlandkeltischen Grammatik* in *Convegno Udine* (Restsprachen) 1981 [1983] p. 65ff.; W. Meid *Forschungsbericht Altkeltische Sprachen* in *Kratylos*: I in 43 1998 p. 1-31, II in 44 1999 p. 1-19; III in 45 2000 p. 1-28. — b) Gaulish: → RGA 10 1998 see under *Gallien* (various authors); Lambert *Langue gauloise* 1977; RIG I-III 1985-1988; Meid *Gaulish Inscriptions* 1992; *Größere altkeltische Sprachdenkmäler* 1993 [1996] p. 11ff. (Contributions by D. E. Evans, K. H. Schmidt, J. T. Koch, W. Meid, P.-Y. Lambert, K. McCone). — c) Lepontic: Lejeune *Lepontica* 1971; J. Uhlich, *Zur sprachlichen Einordnung des Lepontischen* in *Keltologen-Symposium* II 1997 [1999] p. 277-304. — d) Celtiberian: → Untermann *Monumenta* IV 1997 p. 349ff.; Meid *Botorrita* 1993; *Größere altkeltische Sprachdenkmäler* 1993 [1996] p. 124ff. (Contributions by J. de Hoz, W. Meid, R. Ködderitzsch); Villar *Celtiberian Grammar* 1995; by the same author, *The Celtiberian language* in ZCP 49-50 1997 p. 898-947; W. Meid in *Kratylos* 45 2000 p. 1-28; F. Villar and C. Jordan in *Kratylos* 46 2001 p. 166-181 (review of Untermann *Monumenta* IV).

2) Insular Celtic may in turn be divided into Goidelic and Brythonic. The earliest occurrences of Insular Celtic are the Ogam Inscriptions, which date from the 4th to the 7th century AD. The following period, from the 7th to the 10th centuries, is accepted as the period of Old Irish; glosses in large quantities are found in a manuscript of Paul's Epistles, dated from the middle of the 8th

century, and named "Würzburger Glosses" after their present location. The linguistic phase of Irish that precedes that of the Würzburger Glosses is called Archaic Irish, and is attested in a few further glosses and Middle and New Irish manuscripts of archaic legal texts. Brythonic, which is only very sparsely attested in the earliest period, is divided into three dialects: Old Welsh is attested starting in the late 8th century AD (Middle Welsh starts in the middle of the 12th century AD); evidence of Old Cornish in Cornwall exists starting in the late 9th century AD and ending in the first quarter of the 12th century AD; similarly, Old Breton is attested starting at the end of the 9th century and ending in the first quarter of the twelfth century. Alongside Goidelic and Brythonic, there remains Pictish, which is only attested in names.

Literature: → *Celtic Languages* 1992; Ziegler *Ogam-Inschriften* 1994; McCone / Simms *Progress in Medieval Irish Studies* 1996; McCone *Old Irish Nasal Presents* 1991; ZCP 49-50 1997; Schulze-Thulin *o-stufige Kausativa / Iterativa and Nasalpräsentien im Kymrischen* 2001.

E 432. Germanic is represented by three language branches: East, North, and West Germanic. The preliminary phase of the latter two is called Northwest Germanic. The earliest traces of Germanic, which date from the 1st century BC, are proper nouns found on coins and, latinized, in Caesar's writings. From the 3rd century on, there are North Germanic runic writings. The first more comprehensive textual evidence of a Germanic language is the 4th century AD Bible translation of Bishop Wulfila († 383) into Gothic, an East Germanic language. A peculiarity of Germanic, compared with other Indo-European language branches with the exception of Armenian, is that in the case of plosives a consonant shift took place, see below L 336 § 4. Apart from runic writings, the Latin alphabet is used in the Germanic languages.

Literature: — a) General (Proto-Germanic; general Germanic): → *Germanenprobleme in heutiger Sicht* 1986 (which includes, among others, the contribution of E. Seebold *Die Konstituierung des Germanischen in sprachlicher Sicht* p. 168ff.); RGA 11 1998 under the headings *Germanen, Germania, Germanische Altertumskunde*. (which includes *Sprache und Schrift* p. 275ff. by E. Seebold); *Der Kleine Pauly* 4 1998 under the heading *Germanische Sprachen* (by S. Ziegler); Kluge *Urgermanisch* 1913; Kluge *Stammbildungslehre* 1926; Krahe / Meid *Germanische Sprachwissenschaft* 1965-1969; Streitberg *Urgermanische Grammatik* 1896; Bammesberger *Germanische Verbalsystem* 1986; Bammesberger *Urgermanische Nomen* 1990. — b) Runes: → R. Nedoma *Neueres zu älteren Runeninschriften* in *Sprache* 37 1995 [1997] p. 105-115; H. Rix

Thesen zum Ursprung der Runenschrift in Etrusker nördlich von Etrurien, Akten des Symposions von Wien - Schloß Neuwaldegg 1989, edited by L. Aigner-Foresti. Vienna 1992 (= SbÖAW vol. 589) p. 411ff.; by the same author, *Germanische Runen und venetische Phonetik in Festschrift* O. Werner, *Vergleichende germanische Philologie und Skandinavistik*, edited by Th. Birkmann et al. Tübingen 1997 p. 231-248; E. Seebold Fuþark, Beith-Luis-Nion, He-Lamedh, *Abğad und Alphabet, Über die Systematik der Zeichenaufzählung bei Buchstaben-Schriften* in *FS Untermann* 1993 p. 411-444; *Old English Runes* 1991; *Frisian Runes* 1996 (which includes, among others, A. Bammesberger *Frisian and Anglo-Saxon Runes: From the Linguistic Angle* p. 14-23; bibliography p. 22f.); Bammesberger *Pforzen und Bergakker* 1999; A. Griffiths in IF 104 1999 p. 164-210.

1) The main representative of the East Germanic branch is Gothic. Extant attestations include, on the one hand the above-mentioned Bible translation, on the other, a few trade documents from the 6th century AD. Apparently, an emmissary of the Holy Roman Empire, Ogier Ghislain de Busbecq, was able, during a stay in Constantinople between 1554 and 1562, to assemble a list of 86 Gothic words (referred to as 'Crimean Gothic'). Unfortunately, only small fragments of Burgundian and Vandalic have survived.

Literature on Gothic: → RGA 12 1998 see under the headings, *Goten*, *Gotische Schrift*, and *gotische Sprache* (various authors); Krause *Handbuch des Gotischen* 1968; Braune / Ebbinghaus *Gotische Grammatik* 1981; Feist *Gothisches Wörterbuch* 1939; Binnig *Gotisch* 1998. On the phonetic system, see below, K. Dietz in L 222 § 5.

2) In the North Germanic, or Scandinavian branch (Old Norse), which is first attested in runic writings of the 3rd century AD (which one may call 'Early Norse'; the name Proto-Norse being misleading in the case of an attested language), are to be included Old Icelandic, Old Norwegian, Old Swedish, and Old Danish, which could all be distinguished from one another at the time of the first preserved manuscripts in the 12th century. Old Icelandic and Old Norwegian are classified as Old West Norse; Old Swedish and Old Danish, as Old East Norse. The most attested in terms of literature is Old West Norse (since the 9th century AD), particularly Old Icelandic; that is why Old Icelandic forms are traditionally cited.

Literature: → Noreen *Altisländisch and Altnorwegisch* 1923; Noreen *Altschwedisch* 1904; Vries *Altnordisches etymologisches Wörterbuch* 1962; Lühr Egill 2000. — Modern Scandinavian languages: → Braunmüller *Skandinavische Sprachen* 1992 (with a review by J. A. Harðarson).

3) West Germanic, of which only a few runic writings remain, is composed of Old English, Old Frisian, Old Saxon (i.e. Old Low German) and Old Low Frankish (i.e. Old Netherlandish) on the one hand, and Old High German, with a second consonant shift, on the other. Old English, Old Frisian, and Old Saxon are placed under the rubrics, North Sea Germanic or Ingvaeonic. Old English is attested from the early 8th century AD, Old High German from the late 8th century, Old Saxon from the 9th century AD, Old Low Frankish from the 10th century AD, and Old Frisian from the 13th century AD.

Literature: — a) Old English (Old Saxon): → Brunner *Altenglische Grammatik* 1965; Krogh *Stellung des Altsächsischen* 1996. — b) Old High German and German: → Sonderegger *Althochdeutsch* 1987; Lühr *Hildebrandlied* I / II 1982; Seebold *Etymologie* 1981 p. 73ff. (*Die deutsche Sprache*); Riecke jan-Verben 1996; *Sprachgeschichte* 1 1998 and 2 1985; *dtv-Atlas Deutsche Sprache* 1998; Schwerdt *2. LV* 2000.

E 433. The Slavic group of languages may be divided into three subgroups: South Slavic (Bulgarian, Macedonian, Serbian, Croat, Slovenian), East Slavic (Russian, Belarusian, Ukrainian [Ruthenian], and West Slavic (Polish, Upper Sorbian, Lower Sorbian, Czech, Slovakian, [{Dravano-}Polabian {Lüneburg Wendland}, Pomeranian {Pomeranian Baltic Coast}, Slovincian {which, as the last representative of Pomeranian, died out in the 20th century}, Kashubian {still spoken today as a dialect}]). The oldest extant Old Church Slavic document is not written in a linguistically unified form, but is rather marked by the individual languages Bulgarian, Serbian, and Russian. Additionally, it does not contain a perfectly representative excerpt in any one of the concerned Slavic languages.

South Slavic: The oldest attested Slavic language (second half of the 9th century AD) is the Old Church Slavic that was employed by the Slavic mission in Mähren to translate Christian texts from Greek, and which is founded on a Salonikian dialekt. Due to predominantly Bulgarian qualities of the Salonikian dialect, Old Church Slavic is also called Old Bulgarian. In order to establish a system of writing, the Slavic apostle Cyril (originally named Constantine) created, on the basis of the Greek lower-case alphabet, the separate Glagolitic alphabet, which was replaced around 900 AD by the Cyrillic alphabet which is based on the capital letters of the Greek alphabet. The earliest inscriptions date from the 10th and 11th centuries AD — Middle Bulgarian begins in the 12th century. — Serbo-Croatian has been transmitted since the 12th century in Church Slavic texts with Serbo-Croatian characteristics. Two different alphabets are used, namely Cyrillic in Serbian texts of the orthodox church, and Glagolitic in the Croatian texts of the Roman church. — Slovenian has been continually attested since the 15th century; the oldest Slovenian linguistic evidence is found in the Friesinger records of about 1000 AD.

East Slavic: Transmittal of Russian begins in the middle of the 11th century AD through documents in Church Slavic which bear characteristics of East Slavic. Russian uses its own system of writing, the Cyrillic alphabet. — Belorusian and Ukrainian have both been attested since the 12th century on Old Russian language monuments, which bear dialectal qualities.

West Slavic: Polish has been attested since the 12th century. Polabian was spoken in the area of the lower reaches of the Elbe; it died out in Hannover in the 18th century.

Literature: — a) General: → Bräuer *Slavische Sprachwissenschaft* 1961-1969; Panzer *Slavische Sprachen* 1991; Pohl *Le balte et le slave* in *langues indo-européennes* 1994 p. 233-*250;* Rheder *Slav. Sprachwissenschaft* 1998. — b) Old Church Slavic: → Leskien *Handbuch der Altbulgarische Sprache* 1962; Aitzetmüller *Altbulgarische Grammatik* 1978; Koch *Old Church Slavic Verbum* I / II 1990 (I p. 17f. A good sketch of the history of Old Church Slavic).

E 434. The Baltic group is composed of three languages: Lithuanian, Latvian (East Baltic) and Old Prussian (West Baltic). Other Baltic languages may only be researched through borrowed words in Lithuanian and Latvian: among others, Jatvingian and Curonian.

The oldest Baltic linguistic record is the Elbinger lexicon of the beginning of the 14th century AD. It contains 802 Old Prussian equivalents of Old Middle German words. The oldest Baltic text is Old Prussian as well; it comes from the middle of the 14th century AD and includes only eleven words. Old Prussian textual material is otherwise also very limited. The language died out in the 17th century AD.

The first Old Lithuanian and Old Latvian texts come from the 16th century and appear already in book form. The oldest Lithuanian book is a catechism from 1547 translated into Lithuanian. The earliest Latvian text is a translation of the Lord's Prayer from the first half of the 16th century AD.

In the case of Lithuanian, one can distinguish two dialects, Lower Lithuanian (Žemaitisch) in the Northwest of the Lithuanian language-area, and High Lithuanian (Aukštaitisch); both dialects may in turn be divided into subdialects.

Literature: — a) General Baltic: → Stang *Vergleichende Grammatik* 1966; *Baltische Sprachen* 1994; *Baltistik* 1998. — b) Lithuanian: → Senn *Handbuch der lithauischen Sprache* 1966; Fraenkel *Lithautisches etymologisches Wörterbuch* 1962-1965; Bammesberger *Abstraktbildungen* 1973; Petit *Lituanien* 1999.

E 435. Within the group of Indo-European languages, some individual languages are more closely associated with one another owing to morphological or lexical similarities. The cause for this, as a rule, is a prehistoric geographic proximity (perhaps even constituting single linguistic community) or a common preliminiary linguistic phase, a middle mother-language phase, which would however then be posterior to the period of the mother language.

In the case of Anatolian, the question is asked inversely. Did it separate first as a language branch from Proto-Indo-European, and to what extent was it thus spared developments common to the remaining Proto-Indo-European language group? See below §5.

On the general problematics: → Porzig *Gliederung* 1954; *Ancient IE Dialects* 1963 [1966] (which includes, among others, H. M. Hoenigswald, "Criteria for the Subgrouping of Languages" p. 1ff.); E. Seebold in RGA 11 1998 p. 289ff.; G. Klingenschmitt *Die Verwandtschaftsverhältnisse der indogermanischen Sprachen* in *Kolloquium Pedersen* Copenhagen 1993 [1994] p. 235ff. (On Anatolian, among others.); W. Hock, *Balto-Slavisch, Indo-Iranisch, Italo-Keltisch: Kriterien für die Annahme von Sprachgemeinschaften in der Indogermania* in *Aspekte baltistischer Forschung* 2000 p. 119-145.

1) For more information on similarities between Greek, Armenian, and Phrygian (which all likely come from the same geographical area): → Neumann *Phrygisch und Griechisch* 1988; Clackson *Armenian and Greek* 1994.

2) Notions of Italo-Celtic, which was emphasized in earlier research must be modified. In all probability, there was no Italo-Celtic preliminary phase. Rather, Celtic contacts with eastern Indo-Europe are ancient. Compare the case, among others, of relative pronouns, which in Celtic, contrarily to the Italic *k^wo- / *k^wi-, is represented by *$H\underset{^}{i}o$- (cf. F 404), a characteristic that it shares with Greek, Phrygian, Indo-Iranian and Slavic. Celtic contacts with Italic are of a later date: → C. Watkins *"Italo-Celtic Revisited"* in *Ancient Indo-European Dialects* 1963 [1966] p. 29-50 (also published as *Selected Writings* I 1994 p. 105-126); K. H. Schmidt *"Latein und Keltisch"* in *Kollo-*

quium Lateinisch und Indogermanisch. Salzburg 1986 [1992] p. 29-51; by the same author, *Celtic* 1996.

3) On Balto-Slavic: → *Forschungsbericht* in *Baltische Sprachen* 1994 p. 36ff.; Andersen *Prehistoric Dialects* 1996.

4) On Northwest Indo-European: → N. Oettinger *Grundsätzliche Überlegungen zum Nordwest-Indogermanischen* in *Incontri Linguistici* 20 1997 p. 93-111 (On the common preliminary phase of Celtic, Italic, Germanic, and Balto-Slavic); by the same author "*Zum nordwestindogermanischen Lexikon*" in *FS Meid* *70 1999 p. 261-267; M. E. Huld in *Indo-Europeanization of Northern Europe* 1996 p. 109-125.

5) On the place of Anatolian and Hittite within Indo-European (Heading, among others, 'Indo-Hittite'): → N. Oettinger *'Indo-Hittite'-Hypothesen und Wortbildung*. Innsbruck 1986 (= IBS, Lectures and shorter writings 37); A. Lehrman *Indo-Hittite Revisited* in IF 101 1996 p. 73-88; G. Klingenschmitt at the beginning of the paragraph before § 1. Further, see below, F 207 § 3 and F 304 § 1. The position taken by H. Craig Melchert is central for us: "The Dialectal Position of Anatolian within IE in IE Subgrouping" 1998 p. 24ff. Melchert pleads for the following model (in his treatment it carries the name I.D.: "I now conclude that there is a growing consensus among many in favor of model I.D."):

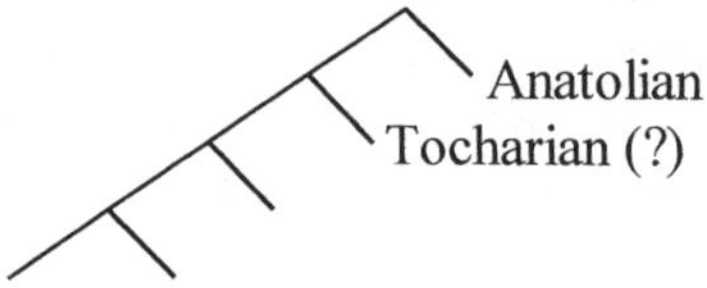

E 436. Ancient linguistic connections among Uralic languages (especially Finno-Hungarian) and Indo-European language groups (Germanic, Iranian, Baltic, Russian) have been confirmed. Foreign and borrowed words of Indo-European origin in Uralic offer an interesting secondary record. However, all recommendations must be critically examined: → Joki *Uralier und Indogermanen* 1973; Katz *Lehnwörter* 1985; Rédei *Indogermanische-Uralische Sprachkontakte* 1986; Koivulehtu *Uralische Evidenz für die Laryngaltheorie* 1991. (As R. P. Ritter [in PFU 1 1994 / 1995 p. 3-8 and in *GS Katz* 2001 p. 223-227] impressively demonstrates, the greatest care is required in the examination of apparent examples of words with laryngeal content.)

E 437. The hypothesis that the Indo-European language family bears evidence of a relationship to the Ural-Altaic, Afro-Asian, and Karvelian languages is found under the variously defined generic term 'Nostratic.' This theory can neither be confirmed nor denied.

Literature: → J. Reinhart *Holzwege der nostratischen Sprachwissenschaft* in *Akten 13. Österreich. Linguistentagung* 1988 p. 275-285; B. Vine *"Indo-European and Nostratic"* in IF 96 1991 p. 9-35; D. A. Ringe *"'Nostratic' and the Factor of Change"* in *Diachronica* 12 1995 p. 55-74; K. H. Schmidt in *Kratylos* 40 1995 p. 81 ff. and J.-P. Levet in BSL 93 / 2 1998 p. 111-116 (review of A. R. Bomhard and J. C. Kerns *The Nostratic Macrofamily* Berlin / New York 1994); G. Doerfer "*The Recent Development of Nostratism*" in IF 100 1995 p. 252-267; A. Manaster Ramer "*Nostratic from a Typological Point of View*" in JIES 25 1997 p. 79ff.; A. R. Bomhard in *Diachronica* 14 1997 p. 131-136 (Review of S. Levin, "*Semitic and Indo-European: The principal etymologies.*" Amsterdam / Philadelphia 1995); J. Gippert "*Die Glottaltheorie und die Frage urindogermanisch-kaukasischer Sprachkontakte*" in *Kolloquium Pedersen* Copenhagen 1993 [1994] p. 107-123.

Th. Vennemann develops a new dynamic. He includes Basque and Hamito-Semitic in his theories on the linguistic pre-history of Europe and allows for an ancient coexistence of Vasconian, Atlantic, and Indo-European languages. His hypotheses are universally rich with fantasy. An official response on the part of Indo-European linguistics is still pending, but it will have much to correct. Among his many publications, I shall name here: → *Linguistic Reconstruction in the Context of European Prehistory* in TPS 92 1994 p. 215-284; by the same author, "*Basken, Semiten, Indogermanen: Urheimatfragen in linguistischer and anthropologischer Sicht*" in *Fachtagung Innsbruck* 1996 [1998] p. 119ff.

E. The Reconstruction of Proto-Indo-European

1. Examples of Reconstruction

E 500. In order to clarify the various problems of reconstruction, I shall begin with three examples from the areas of phonology (E 501), verbal morphology (E 502-505), and lexicon (E 506).

E 501. The first example focuses on phonology and is often used in academic instruction: → M. Mayrhofer in AÖAW 117 1980 p. 364.

1) The phonetic deviation from the Latin nominative singular _nix_ (with <x>, i.e. _ks_) 'snow,' genitive singular _niv-is_ and verbal form _ni-n-gu-it_ 'it snows' allows the introduction of a method of investigation that had already been applied in Old Indian and Byzantine grammar: internal reconstruction (which means that assertions are based on the realities of a single language). Internal reconstruction assumes that the three forms, _nik-s, niv-is_ and _ni-n-gu-it_, must have come from a single root. In a first try, if one takes _nik-_ as the original root form, then it is not clear why morphologically appropriate Latin forms such as the genitive singular _*nik-is_ *<_nicis_> and the verb _*nin-k-it_ *<_ni-n-c-it_> do not correspond to it. Second try: If _niv-_ is primary, then we expect the nominative _*nips_ < _*nivs_ and the verb _*ninvit_. Third try: The calculation succeeds if the root _*nig_^{w}- <_ni-gu-_>, which is present in the verbal form _ni-n-gu-it_ is considered primary. One must then accept that in the case of the nominative singular _*nig_^{w}_-s_, the _-g_^{w}- which precedes _-s_ , in a phonetically plausible way, first lost its labial element ^{w}, and then its voiced quality (The assimilation from _-g-s_ to _-k-s_ is thus unsurprising). Likewise, the change from gen. sg. _*nig_^{w}_is_ to _nivis_ is credible. Thus, applying internal reconstruction, an original form _*nig_^{w}- of the root in question is deduced from Latin.

2) Comparative, also called external reconstruction, which incorporates evidence from all related languages, confirms the result achieved internally by completing it. From the Greek accusative singular νίφ-α, which occurs once in Hesiod and means 'falling snow,' it follows that the labiovelar was aspirated; thus, instead of _*nig_^{w}-, more precisely, _*nig_^{wh}- must be accepted. (On the phonetic shift of Greek _p_^{h} < _g_^{wh}, see below L 345; on Lat. _ni-n-gu-_ < _*ni-n-g_^{wh}- see L 345). — From Lithuanian _sniẽgas_, Old Church Slavic, _sněgъ_ 'snow,' German _Schnee_ etc., it becomes discernible that Latin and Greek _n-_ may be traced via _*zn-_ to _*sn-_. The Epic Greek ἀγά-ννιφος 'having much snow,' in which the double consonant _-nn-_ may be traced to _-sn-_, conveys the same message indirectly. Comparative reconstruction thus complements the initial investigation of the PIE _*snig_^{wh}- (_-e_-full grade PIE _*snei̯g_^{wh}-).

3) Finally, the Vedic _snih-_ 'to be sticky' could require a semantic clarification, i.e. the acceptance of a further meaning, 'to be sticky,' alongside 'snow' and 'to snow': → Hoffmann _Aufsätze_ II 1976 (in an essay of 1965) p. 453f. ("'snow' is that which 'sticks' to plants, living things, etc., or rather 'lays' on the earth"); Mayrhofer _EWAia_ II p. 772; LIV 1998 p. 521f.

E 502. A second example of reconstruction comes from the realm of verbal morphology and concerns the paradigm of PIE *h_1es- ‘to exist, to be.’ I shall begin in a first step with evidence from Vedic, and try, through internal comparison, to gain preliminary historico-linguistic insights.

1) A good overview of the relevant parts of the paradigm of the indicative present active of the Vedic present stem *as-* ‘to be’ may be gained through their arrangement in tabular form (for a collection of all Vedic forms of *as-*: → Gotō *Materialien Nr. 3* 1990):

	Forms	Analysis
1 sg.	*ásmi*	*ás-m-i*
2 sg.	*ási*	*á-s-i*
3 sg.	*ásti*	*ás-t-i*
1 pl.	*smás*	*s-más*
2 pl.	*sthá*	*s-thá*
3 pl.	*sánti*	*s-ánt-i*

2) The verb forms, like all verbs and nouns, consist of the lexically meaningful stem (the lexeme) and the syntactically meaningful ending (the morpheme). The verb stem *as-* (about the *a-* of the second person singular, see below § 3) cannot be further broken down into component parts, but rather consists of the verbal root alone, which shows, from singular to plural, a change from *as-* to *s-* (the so-called ablaut): In the singular, the root is full grade and accented (= *ás-*), in the plural, it is zero grade and not accented (= *s-*). The ablaut *as-* : *s-* may be understood as a direct consequence of the accent: In the singular, the verbal root is stressed and thus exhibits full grade, in the plural, the verbal root is unstressed and thus exhibits zero grade.

3) A word on the 2 sg. *ási*: it stands out relative to the other present forms. Without a doubt, one expects an **ás-si* as a point of departure and must then understand the simple *-s-* within the word as a simplification of the older *-s.s-* , which probably occurred very early, in the pre-Proto-Indo-European phase, see below, L 312.

4) The presently described construction of the paradigm *as-* is not singular, but rather a characteristic of the well-documented group of so-called athematic root presents (see below F 203 Type 1a): These show the characteristic construction with a finishing verbal root, to which the ending is added athematically (i.e. without the insertion of a so-called thematic vowel *–e/o-*, as is clearly

recognizeable in the PIE **bhér-e-ti* 'he carries', cf. F 203 § 1 with LIV type 1n).

5) A clear example, parallel to the Vedic *as*-, is the Vedic *ay*- 'to go.' (For detailed information concerning morphology: → Gotō *Materialien* Nr. 2 1990.) The singular *e* forms may be traced back to **ai̯*-. They are marked with * because they are not attested, see below § 6.

	Forms	Reconstruction
1 sg.	*émi*	**ái̯-m-i*
2 sg.	*éṣi*	**ái̯-s-i*
3 sg.	*éti*	**ái̯-t-i*
1 pl.	*imás*	*i-más*
2 pl.	*ithá*	*i-thá*
3 pl.	*yánti*	*i̯-ánt-i*

6) The singular contains full grade, accented *é*-. This monophthong *e*- (which is traditionally represented as the short vowel <*e*>) has been proven to originate from a diphthong *ai̯*-: Since the Vedic period, it occurs frequently that while the diphthongs *ai̯* and *au̯* before a vowel remain unchanged as <*ay*> and <*av*>, when they are followed by a consonant, they become monophthongs *ē* <*e*> and *ō* <*o*>. Cf. for the first case the Vedic subjunctive forms exhibiting full grade the 2nd person singular *áy-as* and the 3 sg. *áy-at*, and for the second case, the 3 sg. *é-ti*. See below L 220 § 3. In Vedic, an *s* which follows *r*, *r̥*, *u*, *k* or *i* becomes *ṣ* (a phenomenon called the *ruki*-rule), see below L 309 §3. The 2 sg. *eṣi* with a cerebral *ṣ* is only comprehensible if we accept that *eṣi* must have been an **ái̯si* that was subject to the *ruki*-rule.

7) In the plural, the verbal root *é*- < **ay*- contains zero grade *i*-. Before the ending of the 3rd person singular, which begins with a vowel, the consonant *i̯*- < *y*-> appears in place of *i*.

8) Observations regarding the endings of the *as*- and *ay*- paradigms: The 1 sg. *-m-i*, the 2 sg. *-s-i*, the 3 sg. *-t-i* and the 3 pl. *-ánt-i* end with *–i*, as opposed to the 1 pl. *-más* and the 2nd person plural *-thá*, where there is no *-i*. One must add, however, that the 1 pl. *-mas-i* exists in Vedic as a later variant. These endings are indicative of the present tense and are referred to as 'primary endings.' See below § 11.

9) The primary endings of the present tense (*-mi*, *-si*, *-ti*, *-más*, *-thá*, *-ánti*) stand in contrast to the non-present tense 'secondary endings,' -(*a*)*m*, *-s*, *-t*, *-ma*, *-ta*, *-an*.

10) The Vedic verb *bhara-* 'to carry' provides a good example of this contrast in the paradigms of the indicative present active versus indicative imperfect active:

	ind. pres. act.	ind. imp. act.
1 sg.	*bhár-ā-m-i*	*á-bhar-a-m*
2 sg.	*bhár-a-s-i*	*á-bhar-a-s*
3 sg.	*bhár-a-t-i*	*á-bhar-a-t*
1 pl.	*bhár-ā-mas(-i)*	*á-bhar-ā-ma*
2 pl.	*bhár-a-tha*	*á-bhar-a-ta(na)*
3 pl.	*bhár-a-nt-i*	*á-bhar-a-n*

Although not all of the twelve forms of *bhar-* are attested, they are safely deducible: → Macdonell *Vedic Grammar* 1910 p. 319 ff.; concerning the verb: → Gotō I. *Präsensklasse* 1987 p. 225 ff.; on the thematic vowel *-a-* / *-ā-* (< PIE **-e-* / **-o-*), see below, F 101 § 4.

11) The contrast between present and non-present is established through two different formal means: On the one hand through the augment, which is placed before the verb stem in the past tense (for more information, see below, F 213), on the other hand through the two series of endings: primary endings for the present, and the secondary endings for the non-present. In the 1st, 2nd, and 3rd singular and 3rd plural, the presence or absence of *-i* differentiates the two series, whereas in the 1st and 2nd person singular, the endings *-mas*(*-i*) vs. *-ma* and *-tha* vs. *-ta*(*na*), which differ from one another only slightly, perform this task. In place of *-nt-i* : **-nt*, in the 3rd person plural, the later *-nti*: *-n* is found (with simplification of *-nt* to *-n* in word-final position).

12) The Vedic imperfect forms of *as-* (for information on the status of research on attestations: → Gotō *Materialien* Nr. 3 1990 under appropriate heading; the Vedic verb forms are only given accents when they are attested in accented form; the verb in the main clause, as is generally known, normally carries no accent; for further information, see below F 211):

	attested	expected
1 sg.	*ā́sam*	**á-as-m̥*
2 sg.	*āsīs*	**á-as-s*
3 sg.	*ās, ā́sīt*	**á-as-t*
3 pl.	*ā́san*	**á-s-ant*

13) The investigation of the theoretically expected forms in § 12 is based on the analysis from § 1 in combination with the structure of *á-bhar-a-m* in § 10. Unproblematically comprehensible, the initial sound in the 1st person singular, in which the augment *a-*, with the full grade *a* in the root syllable *a*, through contraction directly produces *ā́s-*. Additional information regarding the ending *-am*: On the basis of the thematic 1st sg. *-a-m*, in the case of the athematic ending following a consonant-final verb stem, one expects to find *-m̥, or rather the *-a that phonetically results from it. The *-am* that is attested in its place, may thus be categorized as a form arrived at through analogical differentiation.

14) The 2 sg. **a-as-s* and the 3 sg. **a-as-t* both lead to **ās* with a contracted *ā* and final *-s*, because the final consonant groups **-ss* and **-st* are both simplified according to phonetic laws and result in simple *-s*. The rarely attested 3 sg. *ās* is thus old. The extent to which it belonged to the contemporary language is questionable. The formal similarity between the 2nd person singular and the 3rd person singular cannot have been practicable in the long term, and must have led to a new differentiation. — The new forms with the 2nd person singular *ās-ī-s* and the 3 sg. *ā́s-ī-t* appear already in the Rgveda. They evidently have their model in verbs such as *bravⁱ-* 'to speak, say, talk' (< PIE **-eu̯H-*: For further information on the so-called *seṭ*-roots, see below L 315 § 1). There, for example, the form of the subjunctive present active 3 sg. is *bráv-a-t* (< PIE **-éu̯H-e-t*; the *-e-* is the subjunctive suffix, see below F 207 § 1). In contrast, the form of the indicative present active 3 sg. is *brávī-ti* (< PIE **-eu̯H-ti*; the interconsonantal laryngeal is represented by *ĭ̄* in Indo-Iranian, see below L 325 - L 327) and the form of the indicative imperfect active 3 sg. is *á-bravī-t* (< PIE **-eu̯H-t*). Parallel to *bráv-a-t* and to *á-brav-ī-t* (which is result of new analysis, replacing *á-bravī-t*), an imperfect active 3 sg. *ā́s-ī-t* could be created on the base of the similar subjunctive present active 3 sg. *ás-a-t*. On the unexpected *ā-* of the 3 pl. *ā́san*, see below E 504 § 10.

E 503. In a second (this time language-external) step, the corresponding forms from the classical Latin paradigm are introduced for comparison in order to establish further clarity.

1) I have again chosen the tabular form for the relevant paradigm (For information on the details: → Leumann LLFL 1997 § 400 A):

	Forms	Reconstruction
1 sg.	*sum*	< **es-mi*
	inscr. *esom*	
2 sg.	*es*	< **esi* < **es-si*
3 sg.	*est*	< **es-ti*
1 pl.	*sumus*	< **s-mos*
2 pl.	*estis*	< **s-te-s*
3 pl.	*sunt*	< **s-onti*
	inscr. *sont*	

2) The reconstruction is based upon analysis of the Vedic paradigm. However, Latin *e*-vocalism predates Indo-Iranian *a*-vocalism. See below L 206. In the case of the endings (→ Leumann LLFL 1977 p. 512ff.), *-mus* results from **-mos*, *-ti-s* from **-te-s*, and *-unt* via *–ont* from *–onti* (perhaps preserved in the *tremonti,* quoted by Festus: → Leumann op. cit.p. 92). Next to *-énti*, *-onti* is secondary, see below, § 11.

3) The classical Latin paradigm is most easily understood if one uses the 3 sg. *est* and the 3 pl. *sunt* as a starting point. The verbal root reveals in both these forms the Ablaut change expected from Vedic, from full grade, singular *es-* to zero grade, plural *s-*.

4) In contrast to the Vedic endings (3 sg. *-t-i* and 3 pl. *-ánt-i*) the Latin endings (3 sg. *-t* and 3 pl. *-ont*) are missing the short final, unstressed *i*-vowels. While Vedic conserves these, they are eliminated in Latin: → Leumann LLFL 1977 p. 92 and see below, L 423 § 1. Note: The elimination of the *-i* is much older than what is called rhotacism, which, in the fourth century BC, would have to have changed a remaining **esi* into **eri*, see below L 309 § 1. — That which applies to the 3rd person singular and plural, also applies to the 2 sg. *es* as it relates to the postulated Proto-Italic **esi*.

5) In the singular paradigm, *sum* stands out in relation to the expected ablaut. Starting from the Vedic, first Proto-Italic **esmi*, or at least **esum* is to be expected. The newly discovered South Picene *esom* (→ Marinetti *Iscrizione sudpicene* 1985 p. 214) confirms this hypothesis. An inscribed Latin *esom* was also found recently: → M. Cristofani in *Quaderni di Archeologia Etrusco-Italica* 25 1996 p. 21. One may thus quite rightly accept that an existing Proto-Italic **és-mi* became *esom* after it eliminated the final *-i* from **es-m* and a weak vowel was inserted, via the form **es°m*: → H. Rix in *Kolloquium Latein und Indogermanisch* Salzburg 1986 [1992] p. 230. The later replacement of *esom* by *sum* came about through the analogy of the 1st person plural *sumus*. There, the cause is the regular, zero grade, **s-mos* (in which, the initial **sm-* > **s°m-* > *sum-*).

6) In the plural paradigm, the initial full grade *es-* of the 2nd person plural *estis* stands out. It should be regarded as analogous to the 3 sg. *est.*

7) The new analogous relationships between the first person singular and plural (§ 5) and between the 3rd person singular and the 2nd person plural (§ 6) show that the ablaut change between the singular *es-* and the plural *s-*, at the time of the replacement of the Latin *esom* by *sum* and of **ste-* by *estis* was no longer in use as a living tool for the formation of verbs.

8) Obscure areas of older ablaut structures may also be observed in the classical Latin paradigm *i-* 'to go' (On the material: → Leumann LLFL 1977 § 399):

	Forms	Reconstruction
1 sg.	*eō*	< **ei̯-ō*
2 sg.	*īs*	< **ei̯-si*
3 sg.	*it*	< **ei̯-ti*
1 pl.	*īmus*	< **i-mos*
2 pl.	*ītis*	< **i-te-s*
3 pl.	*eunt*	< **i̯-enti*

9) The forms on the right may be postulated starting from Vedic (see above, E 502 § 5). Taking into account the typical Latin monophthongization of *ei̯* > *ī* (see below, L 220 § 1) as well as the changes that we have already observed in the area of endings in the case of *sum* (see above, § 4), the 2 sg. *īs* <**ei̯s* <**ei̯si* is easily comprehensible. The same is true for the 3 sg. *it* <**īt* <**ei̯t* < **ei̯ti*, particularly if one bears in mind that long vowels preceding *t* in endings were shortened around 200 BC: → Leumann LLFL 1977 § 123.

10) In the plural, information about the zero grade root form *i-* is no longer attested. The long-vowel beginning of the 1st and 2nd person plural is comprehensible if we accept that there was strong analogous impact from the full grade singular. Singular *ei-* would probably already have entered in the plural as well before the 4th century BC (with later development of the newly introduced *ei̯-* > *ī-*). The 3 pl. *eunt* may also have provided the point of departure for the full grade plural. See below, §11.

11) The 1 sg. *eō* and the 3 pl. *eunt* are problematic in themselves. — Particularly concerning the 3rd person plural: Did the replacement of the expected **i̯-énti* by **éi̯-onti* occur via the model of the semi-thematic *-i̯e-/-i-* present conjugation? Cp. the type *facere* with thematic 1 sg. *faciō*, with athematic 3 sg. *facit* and thematic 3 pl. *faciunt* (on the *-i̯e-/-i-*present forms: → Meiser *Laut- und Formenlehre* 1998 p. 195f.; H. Rix in *GS Schindler* 1999 p. 524). Thus, from the 3 sg. **éi̯-ti* directly to **éi̯-onti*? — 1 sg.: In *eō* < **éi̯-ō* (on the disappearance of the inner *i̯*, see below, L 215) one notices that in place of the ending **-mi* (see above, § 5) suggested by *sum*, the otherwise widely current (originally thematic) *-ō* is introduced. The reason for this along with the analogy to semi-thematic conjugation can be the fact that regular **éi̯mi*, via **ei̯m* led to the morphologically unclear **īm*, or rather led, via an **ei̯°m*, which contains a weak vowel, to the morphologically unclear **eum*. See also G. E. Dunkel *"On the 'Thematisation' of Latin sum, volo, eo, and edo and the System of Endings in the IE Subjunctive Active"* in *FS Watkins* 1998 p. 83ff.

E 504. In a third step, the comparison with the classical Attic Greek paradigm is added.

1) As always, the tabular form is given first. On the status of attestations: → Kühner / Blass *Ausführliche Grammatik der Griechischen Sprache* I / 2 1892 p. 220 ff.; Schwyzer *Griechische Grammatik* I 1939 p. 676ff. Nr. 4; Chantraine *Morphologie* 1967 § 235 ff; Chantraine DELG *s.v.* In the accentuation of the *verbum substantivum*, one may note that with the exception of the 2nd person singular, it is used enclitically. It forms an accentual unity with the preceding word and is accentless, see below, F 214 § 2. The marking of the last syllable with an acute is purely a grammatical convention:

	forms	first preliminary reconstruction
1 sg.	εἰμί	< *és-mi*
2 sg.	εἶ	< **ési* < * *és-si*
3 sg.	ἐστί(ν)	< **és-ti*
1 pl.	ἐσμέν	< **(e)s-mén*
2 pl.	ἐστέ	< **(e)s-té*
3 pl.	εἰσί(ν)	< **(e)s-énti*

2) The ablaut difference between singular *es-* and plural *s-*, which is expected because of Vedic and Latin material, is not visible in Greek. The Greek forms all lead surprisingly to *es-*: 1 sg. εἰμί i.e. /*ēmi*/ < **ez-mi* < **és-mi*, 1 pl. ἐσμέν < **es-mé-*, see below § 9. I thus employ only *es-* in the following discussion. The *-sm-* series of sounds that occurs in both forms comes about in different ways. In the 1st person plural, it stays because of analogy to the 3rd person singular and 2nd person plural, according to the phonological rules of which *s* precedes *t*. Contrarily, the 1st person singular contains, according to phonological rules <*ei̯m-*> i.e. *ēm-* < **ezm-*: → Chantraine *Morphologie* 1961 p. 205, bottom of page; on <*ei̯*> i.e. *ẹ̄* Lejeune *Phonétique* 1972, p. 229.

3) The 2 sg. εἶ may be traced back via **éhi* to **ési*. The dialectal Epic/Ionic form εἶς is based on this εἶ, with an *-s*, which characterizes the 2nd person. In contrast to εἶ, it is enclitic. The Aeolic/Epic ἐσσι may best be seen as a new form, analogous to the 3 sg., *es-ti*. For information on **ési* < **és-si*, see above, E 502 § 3. See now O. Hackstein *Die Sprachform der hom. Epen* Wiesbaden 2002 p. 103f.

4) The 3 pl. εἰσί(ν) i.e. /*ẹ̄si*/ may be traced via **ẹ̄nsi* < **e.ensi*[1] < *ehensi* (thus Mycenaean in *e-e-si*) back to **es-énsi*[2]. (with Southern Greek/Ionic-Attic *-si* instead of Northern Greek/Doric *-ti*). The Doric form which corresponds to the Attic εἰσί is ἐντι: *enti* < **ẹ̄nti* < **e.enti* < **ehenti* < **es-énti*: → E. Risch in *FS Neumann* 1982 p. 324 with note 10. — According to the primary **es-énti*, an originally secondary **é es-ent* may be postulated as a 3rd person imperfect. The resulting form, according to phonological rules, is ἦεν. Surprisingly, the form was already in use in Early Greek as a 3rd person singular. The transformation from plural to singular must have taken place in the

1 *Nota bene*: The period marks the separation of syllables.

2 The hyphen marks morphological segmenting.

context of *collectiva*, see below, F 304 § 2. The form ἦσαν is in use as a new 3rd person plural imperfect, see § 5.

5) In the 3rd person plural, in addition to the Ionic/Attic εἰσί and the Doric ἐντι, there is also the Homeric/Ionic ἔασι: This is traced via **éh-ansi* back to **éh-anti* < **és-anti* < **és-ati* (*-anti* is found in place of *-ati* in order to clearly mark the 3rd person plural) < **és-n̥ti*. This **és-n̥ti* is found with the secondary ending *-n̥t* as well in the 3 pl. imperfect ἦσαν < **é-es-ant* < **é-es-n̥t*: → E. Risch in *FS Neumann* 1982 p. 331. — Incidentally: The endings **-énti* and **-n̥ti* of the 3rd person plural originate lastly from two different paradigms: **-énti* from a proterdynamic one of the type **éi̯-mi* / **i-més i̯-énti*, or of the type **stistéh$_2$-mi* / **stisth$_2$-énti*, **-n̥ti* from an acrodynamic one of the type **stḗu̯-mi* / **stéu̯-n̥ti*, or of the type **d^héd^hoh$_1$-mi* / **d^héd^hh$_1$-n̥ti*. See below, F 203 § 1 (LIV-types 1a, 1b and 1g).

6) The already observed presence of *es-* instead of zero grade *s-* in the plural is found in the case of εἰμί elsewhere as well. In the participle and the optative, one should expect the zero grade of the verbal root, cf. the Vedic participle *sant-*, Latin *(ab)sent-*, in the optative Vedic 2 sg. *syā́s*, and in Old Latin *siēs*. In fact, Greek contains in this case everywhere *es-* as well (indeed already in Mycenaean): On the participle, cf. the Mycenaean singular *e-o* i.e. *ehōn*, plural *-e-o-te* i.e. *-ehontes* etc., Ionic ἐών, Doric ἐών as well, or rather, then ἰών (Attic ὤν ὄντος is secondary: → M. Meier-Brügger in *Katà diálekton* 1996 [1999] p. 518), all forms < **es-ont-*; On the optative, compare the 2 sg. εἴης < **ei̯i̯ē-s* < **es-i̯eh$_1$-s* and εἶμεν < **ehīmen* < **es-ī-men* < **es-ih$_1$-men*.

7) Constructed in a parallel fashion to εἰμί, the verb εἶμι 'to go' (used often to indicate the future), with its regular ablaut *ei̯-* : *i-*, makes clear that there is something peculiar in the the consistent *es-* in εἰμί:

	Forms	Reconstruction
1 sg.	εἶμι	= **ei̯mi*
2 sg.	εἶ	< **ei̯si*
3 sg.	εἶσι(ν)	< **ei̯ti*
1 pl.	ἴμεν	= **i-men*
2 pl.	ἴτε	= **i-te*
3 pl.	ἴασι	= **i̯i̯-n̥ti*

8) In the singular, the 2 sg. ει can be traced back to **ei̯hi* < **ei̯-si*. The 3rd person singular contains Southern Greek/Ionic/Attic *–si* instead of Northern

Greek/Doric *–ti*. The ending of the 3rd person plural in -ασι may be compared with ἔασι from § 5.

9) The questionable Greek peculiarity of the constant *es-* for full grade and zero grade, may most easily be explained by accepting that the Proto-Indo-European verbal root **es-* originally contained a word-initial laryngeal, and thus read **$h_1$es-*, but otherwise was conjugated in a normal proterodynamic fashion. Full grade **$h_1$es-* and zero grade **h_1s-* both produce in fact, according to phonological rules, *es-* in Greek, see below, L 322 § 1 and L 328 § 1. Full (*e*-) grade Greek **$h_1$es-* lives on after the disappearance of laryngeals before a vowel as *es-*, whereas the word-initial consonance of the zero grade Greek **h_1s-* developed with the help of a weak vowel via **h_1°s-* > **$h_1$es-* > also to *es-*. — This is not the case in Vedic and Italic, in which the full grade *es-* stands in clearly visible contrast to the zero grade *s-*: While the full grade **$h_1$es-* does result, parallel to Greek, in Vedic *as-* (on the intermediary grade **es-*, see below, L 206) and the Latin *es-*, the zero grade **h_1s-* leads, in contrast, through simplification of the double consonance, from **h_1s-* to *s-*. The singular of the Vedic participial negation *ā́sat-* (with a long initial vowel Rgveda IV 5, 14 and VII 104,8; also attested several times with a short initial vowel *ásat-*) 'not being' proves indirectly that at the time of this construction the initial double-consonance must still have been present, for this alone explains the stretched initial secondary form: PIE **n̥-h_1s-n̥t-* > Proto-Indo-Iranian **a-Hsat-* > Vedic *ā́sat-*. The short vowel is to be understood in contrast as a later analogous form of the participial *sat-*, with the usual prefix of negation *a-* < **n̥-*.

10) The postulation of PIE **$h_1$es-* leads to an adequate understanding of the Vedic imperfect and, in so doing, confirms its correctness as in the case of *ā́sant-* in § 9. It was namely always noticeable that the Vedic singular and plural augmented forms exhibited equally lengthened *ās-*, although the language-internal comparison does not at first lead one to expect this, and, in the plural, should lead to a short initial vowel, see above, the table in E 502 § 12 with the analysis of the 1 sg. *ā́sam* < **á-as-m̥* and the 3 pl. *ā́san* < **á-s-ant*, in which the reconstruction cannot explain the long initial vowel. — While in the case of a postulated Proto-Indo-European root form **es-* / **s-* one could expect a first grade Proto-Indo-European singular **e-es-* / plural **e-s-* or rather Proto-Indo-Iranian singular *ās-* / plural **as-* and an analogous transfer of length into the plural, the PIE **$h_1$es-* / **h_1s-* produces directly the attested,

unified paradigm: PIE **é-*h_1*es-* > Proto-Indo-Iranian **á-Has-*[3] > **á.as-* > *ās-* and the plural **e-*h_1*s-* > Proto-Indo-Iranian **a-Hs-* > *ās-*.

11) Contrary to today's research and its laryngeal *h_1*es-*, earlier research, with its postulation of the simple non-larygeal **es-* /**s-*, had considerable argumentative difficulties. As representative of the *communis opinio* of the time, one may cite Thumb / Hauschild *Handbuch des Sanskrit* I / 2 1959 § 488 (as well as Leumann LLFL 1977 p. 522 § 400.A.1b). Thumb and Hauschild draw a direct parallel between the Vedic *sánti* and the Doric Greek ἐντί and trace it via **henti* back to **sénti*. Through analogy to the singular, the expected aspiration is eliminated. Correspondingly, Ionic/Attic Greek εἰσί would be traced back to **hensi* or rather **sensi* (with Southern Greek *-si* instead of *-ti*). But in the case of the 1st person plural **smén* and the 2nd person plural **ste* the initial *e-* would be analogously introduced. But the extension of the analogous *e-* to the stems of the optative and the participle cannot be explained. Further, the Mycenaean *-e-o-te*, i.e. *-ehontes*, known since 1952, forces the pushing forward of the analogy in question into the 2nd millenium BC. The *communis opinio* leaves one utterly helpless before the Mycenaean *e-* of the 3 pl. *e-e-si*, i.e. *ehensi*, particularly if one, in the cases of Ionic/Attic εἰσί and Doric ἐντί, believed he could succeed with the use of **senti*.

But despite all evidence: Even today there are researchers who happily continue to use **es-* / **s-* as a starting point and build hypotheses from there: → K. Shields *"On the Origin of Dialectal Ablaut Patterns of the Present Active Indicative of PIE *es 'To Be'"* in HS 110 1997 p. 176-180.

E 505. As a result of the first three steps of E 502-504, both of the following paradigms may with certainty be attributed to Proto-Indo-European:

Proto-Indo-European *h_1*es-* 'to exist'	Proto-Indo-European *h_1*ei̯-* 'to go'
*h_1*és-mi*	*h_1*éi̯-mi*
*h_1*ési* < * h_1*és-si*	*h_1*éi̯-si*
*h_1*és-ti*	*h_1*éi̯-ti*
*h_1*s-mé-*	*h_1*i-mé-*
*h_1*s-té-*	*h_1*i-té-*
*h_1*s-énti*	*h_1*i̯-énti*

3 *Nota bene*: Because the laryngeal quality of Indo-Iranian laryngeals is no longer recognizeable, I note it normally with H.

1) To the given meaning of the PIE *$h_1$es- 'to exist, to be there' may be added that this verb must have had this strong meaning in the Proto-Indo-European period. Nominal sentences of the type, 'the floor is dry' were thus not, as we would expect from the standpoint of German, formed with 'is,' which developed as a helping verb, but rather the simple series of PIE **d^{h}éǵ^{h}ōm* with **t̥rstéh$_2$* was enough. See below, S 206 on the nominal sentence. Proto-Indo-European *$h_1$es- was often clarified with local particles of the type, '*ab-wesend*,' cf. Latin *ab-sent-*, Mycenaean Greek *a-pe-o-te* i.e. *ap-ehontes*.

2) One further remark on **ei̯-*: It may not be omitted here that the root originally contained a word inital laryngeal, and was thus *$h_1$ei̯-: → LIV 1999 p. 207. This renders plausible the surprising notion that, as in the case of *as-* in the imperfect singular as well as in the plural, despite the ablaut **ei̯-* : **i-*, both begin in Vedic with a long vowel (cf. 1 sg. *ā́yam* and 3 pl. *ā́yan*): 1 sg. *ā́yam* < **á-Hai̯-am* < **é-h$_1$ei̯-m̥*, 3 pl. *ā́yan* < **á-Hi̯-ant* < **é-h$_1$i̯-ent*.

3) Information on the continuity of *$h_1$es- in other ancient Indo-European languages: — On Hittite: → Tischler HEG I p. 109f.; Friedrich / Kammenhuber HW II (E) p. 93ff.; further see below, L 414. — On Germanic → A. Bammesberger in Graz 2000 p. 11-19. — On Tocharian: → Pinault *Tokharien* 1989 p. 132ff.; C. Batke in TIES 8 1999 p. 1ff.

E 506. The third and last example of reconstruction is the PIE *(h_1)éḱu̯o- masculine and feminine, 'horse, steed, mare.'

1) I shall begin this time directly with correspondence sets (cf. E 507): PIE *(h_1)éḱu̯o- = Vedic *áśva-* masculin, *áśvā-* feminin = Old Avestan and Later Avestan *aspā-* feminine, Later Avestan *aspa-* masculine = Old Persian *asa-* masculine = Greek ἵππος (already Mycenaean *i-qo* i.e. *ik^{w}k^{w}os*) masculine/feminine = Latin *equus* = Old English *eoh* = Old Norse *jór* = Lithuanian (only Bretke) *ešva* 'mare' (the usual word for 'horse' is *arklỹs*!) = Old Iranian *ech* = Tocharian B *yakwe*, Tocharian A *yuk*. The list is not exhaustive, but can easily be completed: → Mayrhofer EWAia I p. 139f.; Chantraine DELG I p. 467f.; Vries AnordEW 1962 p. 293; Buck *A Dictionary of Selected Synonyms in the Principal Indo-European Languages*. 1949 p. 167f.; de Lamberterie in BSL 73 / 1 1978 p. 262ff. (On the etymological affiliation of the Armenian *ēš* [genitive singular *išoy*] 'Donkey').

2) Vedic *áśva-* may be traced back to **áḱu̯a-* without any problems (Concerning the phonetic shift of the satem languages from *ḱ* to *ś*, see below L 339 § 3.); in Iranian, *sp*, which comes from *śu̯*, results from *ḱu̯*: → Hoffmann /

Forssman *Avestische Laut- und Flexionslehre* 1996 p. 86. If one were to undo the Indo-Iranian vowel shift of *a*, *e*, and *o* to *a*, one would find (from **áḱu̯a-*) in the result **éḱu̯o-* or **(h₁)éḱu̯o-* a clear relation to the Latin *equus*. And this leads without problem to the forms of the Germanic languages and to those of Lithuanian, Old Iranian, and Tocharian.

3) The labiovelar of the Latin *equus* requires a comment. — As is commonly known, the labiovelar k^w merged with, and belongs to the same phonetic group as *ku̯*. Controversial however, is whether the result marked *qu* represents the single-value k^w, or the double-value *ku̯*: → Sommer / Pfister *Lautlehre* 1977 p. 143 ("...for the initially guttural Latin + u̯"); Meiser *Laut- und Formenlehre* 1998 p. 52 (single-value *qu*, because it does not represent a position). In the case of *equus*, this means that from the standpoint of Latin one cannot know whether *-qu-* developed from **-*k^w*-* or from **-ḱu̯-*. Indo-Iranian however, offers clear evidence in favor of **-ḱu̯-*. — In the transition from Old to Classical Latin, one expects (according to phonetic rules) to find, preceding endings with initial *-o-* or *-u-* the modified stem **ec-* (having dropped its labial element); however, preceding endings that begin with *-e-*, *-i-*, or -a-, one expects to find the unmodified stem *equ-*. Although the expected *ecus* is attested, *equ-* gained acceptance before *o* and *u* under the pressure of analogy from declined forms that retain *equ-*, see below L 106 and L 217 § 2 (on *novus*).

4) The most problematic case is the Greek ἵππος, the *i*-vocalism of which is best understood as an inheritance from the Mycenaean period. At that time, *e* in a particular phonetic situation must have been pronounced in a more closed manner, cf. *di-pa* i.e. *dipas* neuter 'lidded container for drinking' vs. the later δέπας (since Homer): → Risch *Kleine Schriften* 1981 p. 455 and p. 536 with comment 16; O. Panagl in *FS Zaic* 1989 p. 129-135. That the *-i*-form extended to the entire Greek region may be explained in that the word, very central during Mycenaean rule of the entire region (2nd millenium BC), spread and suppressed the *e*-form that had certainly been present at one time. — On the *-pp-*: The original double-consonance *-ku̯-* was likely replaced by *-*k^wk^w*-* in the pre-Mycenaean period, and again, in turn by *-pp-* after the disappearance of the labiovelars, see below L 343 § 4. Suggestions of an ancient *-*k^wk^w*-* are already given by the Mycenaean form as *i-qo* (a possible **i-ko-wo* does not appear) and the noted double-consonance in alphabetic Greek. — The aspiration of the word at the beginning remains a riddle. C. J. Ruijgh suggests, perhaps correctly, a borrowing in the expression ἅρμα καὶ ἵππους 'wagon and horse': → Coll. Myc. 1975 [1979] p. 207 and p. 220.

5) A word on the construction of the feminine ‘mare.’ Along with the choice of words of different origins to express masculinity and femininity (e.g. ‘mother,’ ‘father’), another option is inflection, i.e. the changing or extention of the masculine ending by means of suffixes. For example: the Vedic *áśvā-* feminine = Old Vedic and Late Vedic *aspā-* feminine. So-called *communia* present another possibility. “Thus are called … such substantives, which denote animated, sexually characterized beings, in the case of which both the masculine and the feminine specimen can be denoted such that the substantive form does not change, but rather, according to the gender of the specimen, the corresponding pronoun (or adjective) is in masculine or feminine form.” (For example, ὁ/ἡ ἵππος and Old Latin *lupus fēmina* ‘she-wolf’): → Wackernagel *Vorlesungen* II 1926 p. 23f., further p. 10 and p. 315. As a rule, the *communia* prove to be older than the corresponding feminine inflected forms. For that reason it is advisable to ascribe the *commune* for ‘mare’ (*éku̯o- m./f.) to Proto-Indo-European, but the formation of the feminine *éku̯eh_2- from the Vedic word *áśvā-* to post-PIE languages. — See below L 421 § 2 on *snusó- f. ‘daughter-in-law.’

6) The further analysis of *(h_1)éḱu̯o- is uncertain. It is often grouped together with the word family of PIE *h_1eḱ- ‘quick’ (Compare Greek ὠκύς, Vedic *āśú-*, Latin *acu-*, *ōcior* ‘quick(er),’ and *ōḱ- from the PIE *h_1oh_1ḱ-?) and then analyzed as PIE *h_1éḱu̯-o- ‘provided with *h_1éḱu̯- (‘quickness’)’: → Mayrhofer EWAia I p. 140 and p. 179f.; Rix *Termini der Unfreiheit* 1994 p. 10 and by the same author, in *Kratylos* 41 1996 p. 156 (on Latin *acu-*); I. Balles in HS 110 1997 p. 220 note 8. However, this cannot be rigorously proven.

7) Concerning concrete facts, e.g. whether the wild horse living in the forests is meant, see below E 512 § 3 and 4b.

2. Fundamentals of Reconstruction

E 507. The individual Indo-European languages provide the point of departure for Indo-European linguistics. All of these languages show equivalences in great number in all possible sub-areas. The equivalences are often very extensive: As a rule, individual lexemes and morphemes not only exhibit similar or even identical forms, their content is just as similar or even identical, for example Vedic *ás-t-i*, Greek ἐσ-τ-ί and Latin *es-t* (above E 502ff.), in which not only the external form and construction are unmistakably similar, but also the meaning (‘to be’) and position of the forms in the paradigm (present, strong, third person, singular) are the same. Vedic *ásti*, Greek ἐστί and Latin *est* offer only one example among countless others. With the help of phonetic rules, the equivalences may be proven even where the individual words are outwardly very different. For example, compare the Vedic *śrómata* 'honor, good reputation' with Old High German *hliumunt* 'reputation, rumor,' where both evidently, according to rules of phonetics, come from the PIE **ḱléu̯-mn̥t-*: → Mayrhofer EWAia II p. 667

1) The presence of numerous firmly established commonalities within the individual Indo-European languages can in no way be explained as if the commonalities were universal aspects of human language. Indeed, there are surely universal givens, of which the future-oriented linearity of speaking is an example: On the axis of time, one may only speak in a forward/future oriented manner, and not in a backward/past oriented manner. The linguistic signs are, as a rule, not universal, but rather are arbitrary, created through convention within each linguistic community. In the case of 'to be,' the *verbum existentiae* is fully different in Semitic languages, for example, Hebrew *hāi̯āh* 'to happen, to become, to be,' etc.

2) Coïncidence is equally unsuitable as an explanation. Of course there are astounding coïncidences, such as the apparent similarity of classical Latin *deus* 'God' to Greek θεός 'God.' A short examination of the older and oldest occurrences of both words (Old Latin *deivos* and Mycenaean *t^hehós*) clearly shows that both *nomina* are different from their inception: *deivos* is derived from PIE **di̯eu̯-* '(God of the daytime) heavens' in the sense of 'heavenly (being),' *t^hehós* (< **$d^h h_1 s$-ó-*) is derived from PIE **$d^h e h_1 s$-* 'God, divine': → Meiser, *Laut- und Formenlehre* 1998 p. 107. Contrarily, the tonal similarity of the Vedic *ás-t-i*, Greek ἐσ-τ-ί and Latin *es-t* excludes the possibility of coïncidence. Accordingly, the older the examples, the more their content and form are similar.

3) Borrowing is also not valid as an explanation. Borrowing takes place of course, in the lexical area, for example Latin *māchina* and Doric Greek μαχανά or German *Kaiser* and Latin *Caesar*. In both cases the routes of the borrowings are known; in the former case, *māchina* was taken by the Romans from Doric Greeks of Lower Italy. The original **mācana* was integrated into the Latin lexicon and later, through the typical Latin vowel weakening, changed to **mācina*, and finally established as *māchina*, with the *h* to indicate the aspiration of the original Greek. In the latter case, *Kaiser* was given by the Roman dictator Caligula (officially C. Caesar) around 37 to 41 AD to the Germanic peoples, from which came his bodyguards at that time. (→ H. Rix

"*Latein - wie wurde es ausgesprochen?*" in *Beiträge zur mündlichen Kultur der Römer*, edited by G. Vogt-Spira. Tübingen 1993. p. 14).

4) Alone the hypothesis of the derivation from a common preliminary phase of the language groups in question is a suitable explanation of the numerous equivalences in the areas of phonetics, construction, and semantics. In other words: Vedic *ás-t-i*, Greek ἐσ-τ-ι and Latin *es-t* are related to one another and are based upon the reconstructible common preliminary PIE **$h_1$ésti* (see above, E 505). This language was spoken by the Proto-Indo-European linguistic community. No system of writing was known to this community. From the Proto-Indo-European form **$h_1$ésti* follow individual routes through a continuum of tradition and generations of speakers to Latin, to Greek, and to Vedic forms:

Proto-Indo-European **$h_1$ésti*

Vedic *ásti* Greek ἐστί Latin *est*

5) For the sake of simplicity in representation no tree tables are used, but rather a correspondence set is used in its place as an abbreviation: PIE **$h_1$ésti* = Vedic *ás-t-i* = Greek ἐσ-τ-ί = Latin *es-t*. One must not misunderstand and draw the conclusion that the Vedic *ásti* comes from the Greek ἐστί, or that the Latin *est* comes from Greek.

E 508. Since the time of Bopp (see above, E 302), Indo-European linguistics has been a methodically established and functional science. Its primary method is the internal and external comparison within, and among the Indo-European languages, as well as the constant review of the relation of the Indo-European languages to the original language and vice versa.

1) The specialized knowledge in all questions of Indo-European linguistics and in the reconstruction of assertions about the original language gained through comparison has in the meantime become very comprehensive and comes from the work of generations of Indo-European linguists. Owing to the dialogue in the international community of researchers, this specialized knowledge is subjected to an ongoing process of review. New finds and new ideas continually show that we are on the correct path with our specialized knowledge. Time and time again, new pieces, some larger, some smaller, can be

added to the puzzle of Indo-European linguistics. It attests to the accuracy of our progress when a form that had been unclear on the basis of earlier research suddenly is understood without problem.

A small example from my research: The Epic Homeric verb form ἐάφθη (in ἀσπὶς ἐάφθη Iliad N 543 and Ξ 419) has been unclear since antiquity and has given occasion to untenable speculations (→ Chantraine DELG *sub voce*: "*rien de clair*"). In another context entirely, I asked myself one day, what the Greek equivalent of German *singen* is. Known to me from textbooks was the associated nominative active-voice ὀμφή (Epic-Poetic Greek since Homer) '(divine) voice' (< **song*^{wh}*ā́*). The underlying verb is believed to be lost. (→ Frisk GEW *s.v.*: "*das zugrunde liegende primäre Verb ist nur im Germanischen erhalten*"). An idea struck me: as an aorist, ἐάφθη belongs to this lost verb (< **e-sn̥g*^{wh}*-*). The meaning (the word occurs in two battle scenes) fits remarkably well: "(upon him) sounded the shield." For the verbal form in question, this means that it was translated from the Homeric singers in the correct context, but was very early no longer understood. On the details of the explanation, see below, L 345 §1.

2) Thanks to the numerous comparisons of equivalent forms we are the best and most accurately informed in the problems of phonetics. Thus, the form of the Indo-European root **snei̯g*^{wh}*-* is for certain correctly determined, see above E 501. However, while the determination of its meaning as 'to snow' is rather certain, the question of how this relates to the Vedic meaning 'to be sticky' cannot be answered with certainty. The degree of certainty of assertions varies in semantics just as it does in morphology and still more in syntax, see below S 101. Each case must be checked individually. For example, PIE ***h_1*es-* (see above E 505), of which the reconstructed 3 sg. ***h_1*ésti* is quite probably the form of the original language, whereas in the 1 pl. ***h_1*s-mé-* the exact form of the present ending cannot be ascertained.

E 509. The reality of the linguistic continuity of traditions from the postulated Proto-Indo-European original language to the known individual Indo-European languages of historical times cannot be doubted. To what extent linguistic relation implies familial clan and a common genetic origin of the dispersing groups of speakers remains to be discovered. Concerning necessary information as to the location, time and culture of this original language, as well as ideas on the 'how' of the genesis of the individual languages, see below E 511ff.

1) However, our reconstruction has its very clear limits. We are decisively dependent on extant attestations of the individual languages. This varies widely, see above E 400. Just imagine the situation if we had only contemporary Greek and the first Middle Greek/Byzantine attestations after the fall of Constantinople in 1453. Greek, which is extremely well documented, would hold a position similar to that of Albanian within the Indo-European realm, and would not have the weight that it has long been accorded, owing to ist unique documentation in the Mycenaean and Ancient Greek periods.

2) Our reconstructions are not fixed for all time. Depending on argumentation, judgements may differ from researcher to researcher. Further, new information and finds can certainly require one to make corrections. However, corrections of both kinds do not mean that the postulated language has changed, rather only that we have adapted our assertions to the latest level of research.

3) Our reconstructions lead us indeed directly from the lexical offspring in question to the underlying uniform phase of language that last unified them. But the route from the last uniform language phase to the individual language was not as straight as is necessarily suggested by the existing forms, which have prevailed in the process of linguistic development. "(One can) say that comparative reconstruction determines the average quantity and not the common quantity … of the linguistic phenomena concerned, and thus only grasps a part of reality.": → H. Eichner in *Akten 13. Österreich. Linguistentagung* 1988 p. 15. "We must not delude ourselves into believing that our retrogressive method of reconstruction matches, step by step, the real progression of linguistic history": → E. Pulgram "Proto-Indo-European Reality and Reconstruction" in *Language* 35 1959 p. 423. Time and time again, there must have been forms, for example, that were once a part of the lexicon or grammar, but then became uncommon and disappeared. Only in the best case do we have knowledge of them, such as when, for example, they are handed down in lexicalized form. We can reconstruct, for example, that there was a Proto-Indo-European nominal root **$h_2$ent-* '(side of) forehead.' While it is still alive in Hittite, other Indo-European languages such as Greek only show it in lexicalized forms, e.g. ἀντί 'in face of/towards' (which is used not only as a preverb and preposition, but also as a prefix in compound forms and is formally a fossilized locative singular form of the former nominal root: → Friedrich / Kammenhuber HW III p.158ff. See also L 322 § 2.

Further literature on reconstruction: → M. Mayrhofer *Über sprachliche Rekonstruktionsmethoden* in AÖAW 117 1980 [1981] p. 357-366; D. M. Job *Zur Bewertung von Rekonstrukten* in *GS Kronasser* 1982 p. 46-71;

Akten 13. Österreich. Linguistentagung 1988 (p. 7ff. Contributions to the podium discussion: "*Sprachwandel und Rekonstruktion,*" among which that of H. Eichner [p. 10-40] is particularly fruitful); *Language Typology* 1988 [1991] (among others, H. M. Hoenigswald *'Morphemic Change, Typology, and Uniformitarianism: A study in reconstruction'* p. 17-26; E. P. Hamp *"On Reconstructing Morphology and Syntax"* p. 105-110). For more information see below, end of § 4.

4) It is important to recognize that linguistic change is not a planned process, according to which a language is constructed in an orderly fashion. "A language such as German, Swahili, or Italian is a spontaneous system. It is the non-intended result of human interaction": → R. Keller "*Sprachwandel, ein Zerrspiegel des Kulturwandels?*" in *Kulturwandel im Spiegel des Sprachwandels, Achtes Partnerschaftskolloquium* 1991 in Düsseldorf, edited by K.-E. Lönne. Tübingen / Basel 1995 (= Culture and Knowledge 11) p. 213; by the same author, "*Zur Erklärungskraft der Natürlichkeitstheorie*" in *Sprachwandel and Sprachgeschichte*. Commemorative publication for H. Lüdtke, edited by J. Schmidt-Radefeldt and A. Harder, Tübingen 1993, p. 109-116; see also by the same author, *Sprachwandel* 1994 (subtitle: *Von der unsichtbaren Hand in der Sprache*).

Further literature on linguistic change and reconstruction: → H. Eichner (For title, see above at end of § 3); *Linguistic Change and Reconstruction Methodology* 1990 (which includes, among others, H. M. Hoenigswald *"Is the 'comparative' method general or family-specific?"* p. 375-383; *Diachrony within Synchrony* 1990 [1992] (which includes, among others, A. Bammesberger *"Phonology, analogy, and how languages change: Notes on the development of some grammatical categories in English"* p. 359-375; H. M. Hoenigswald *"Semantic change and 'regularity': A legacy of the past"* p. 85-105); *"Explanation in Historical Linguistics"* 1992 (which includes, among others, R. Anttila "Historical explanation and historical linguistics" p. 17-39; B. D. Joseph *"Diachronic explanation: Putting speakers back into the picture"* p. 123-144); *Historical Linguistics* 1993 (which includes J. Anderson *"Parameters of syntactic change: a notional view"* p. 1ff.; B. Comrie *"Typology and reconstruction"* p. 74ff.); R. Gusmani, "*Ursprache, Rekonstrukt, hermeneutische Modelle*" in *FS Meid* *60 1989 p. 69-77 (further literature may be found in note 1.)

E 510. The language that is analyzed with the help of reconstruction, the Indo-European mother language, called Proto-Indo-European, should not be considered a 'primitive' original language. Rather, it was a fully 'normal' language, with its own long prior history, and was spoken, to our knowledge, by a linguistic community that had no system of writing.

1) The resulting reconstructions of Proto-Indo-European lay on a uniform line and may necessarily provide only a one-sided portrait, without spatial and historical perspectives (see above, E 509 § 3). "It is the nature of every reconstruction, that in it all diachronic, dialectal and other qualified differences be neglected": → B. Schlerath in ZVS 95 1981 p. 180. Of course, whereas Proto-Indo-European was concretely a living language with dialects and a complex structure , the only Proto-Indo-European that we can attain, i.e. the reconstructed language, can furnish us with no clues about this. It is thus methodologically erroneous to equate the reconstructed Proto-Indo-European to the concrete Proto-Indo-European, and to place it in a time/space model. I direct this negative conclusion toward the discussion surrounding the 'time/space model' proposed by W. Meid and shall not conceal that the counter-argument by B. Schlerath has convinced me: → W. Meid "*Probleme der räumlichen und zeitlichen Gliederung des Indogermanischen*" in *Fachtagung Regensburg* 1973 [1975] p. 204-219; B. Schlerath "*Ist ein Raum/Zeit-Modell für eine rekonstruierte Sprache möglich?*" in ZVS 95 1981 p. 175-202; by the same author, "*Sprachvergleich und Rekonstruktion: Methoden und Möglichkeiten*" in *Incontri Linguistici* 8 1982-1983 p. 53-69; *Incontri Linguistici* 9 1984, which includes on p. 63ff. a debate on the subject, sketched by B. Schlerath in Volume 8 (written by E. Campanile, F. Crevatin, M. Doria, R. Gusmani, R. Lazzeroni, E. Neu, P. Ramat, K. H. Schmidt and K. Strunk.); *Incontri Linguistici* 10 1985 yields on pages p. 11-18 the conclusion of B. Schlerath, "*Probleme der Rekonstruktion: Schlußwort und Ausblick*"; J. Tischler, "*Bemerkungen zum 'Raum-Zeit-Modell'*" in *FS Meid* *60 1989 p. 407-429; W. P. Lehmann "*Earlier stages of Proto-Indo-European*" in *FS Meid* *60 1989 p. 109-131; F. R. Adrados "*The new Image of Indo-European*" in IF 97 1992 p. 1-28; E. Seebold in RGA 15 2000 under the heading, *Indogermanische Sprache und Sprachfamilien*.

2) The concrete Proto-Indo-European must itself be the product of a long historical development. Several assertions about early phases of Proto-Indo-European may be gained from language-internal comparison (→ H. Rix *Modussystem* 1986 p. 6f.):

> "Whereby comparative reconstruction is based upon a group of similar forms in a number of languages, internal reconstruction takes its point of departure from irregularities or inhomogeneities of the system of a single language. ... The fundamental supposition of language-internal reconstruction is that such an irregularity or inhomogeneity in the grammar of a lan-

guage is the result of a diachronic process, in which an older pattern, or homogeneity is eclipsed, but not fully supressed. ... There is no reason to renounce the use of language-internal reconstruction, which was developed particularly in corpus linguistics, on knowledge of Proto-Indo-European gained through comparative reconstruction. The use of the epithet, 'glottogonic speculation,' a term occasionally used to defame language-internal reconstruction, is, even in the case of Proto-Indo-European, not merited, because the process neither can nor purports to investigate the creation of human language."

Rix works back from Late Proto-Indo-European Phase B (reconstructible Proto-Indo-European) using deducible information about an Early Proto-Indo-European Phase A, and gathers in his work related evidence on the Proto-Indo-European verbal system.

The organizers of the *Fachtagung Zürich* 1992 [1994] planned to research the route from Proto-Indo-European to Early Proto-Indo-European, but the subject was not treated sufficiently: → G. E. Dunkel, p. VIIIf.; by the same author, *"Early, Middle, Late Indo-European: Doing it My Way"* in *Incontri Linguistici* 20 1997 p. 29-44.

3. The Time, Place, and Culture of the Proto-Indo-Europeans

E 511. No precise statement concerning the exact time period of the Proto-Indo-European linguistic community is possible. One may only state that the ancient Indo-European languages that we know, which date from the 2nd millenium B.C., already exhibit characteristics of their respective linguistic groups in their earliest occurrences, thus allowing one to presume the existence of a separate and long pre-history. For example, *te-o*, i.e. *t^hehós*, 'God' was already common in Mycenaean Greek. Based upon finds in Indo-Iranian and Italic, one must conclude that **dei̯u̯ó-* was one of the Proto-Indo-European terms for 'divinity' (see below, W 202 §2), which was replaced in Ancient Greek by θεός. The period of 5,000 BC to 3,000 BC is suggested as a possible timeframe of a Proto-Indo-European language.

E 512. Efforts to determine the region and culture of the Proto-Indo-European community offer special difficulties. In the case of both questions, assertions in pre- and early history play a decisive role. Further information may come from the reconstructible lexicon, as well as from potential conclusions drawn from the later geographical region of the linguistic communities of the individual Indo-European languages: → J. Untermann, "*Ursprache und historische Realität*" in *Ethnogenese* 1985 p. 133-164 (which includes the chapters: "*Die theoretischen Grundlagen der historisch-vergleichenden Sprachwissenschaft und das Stammbaummodell*"; "*Indogermanistik und Vorgeschichtsforschung*"; "*Innersprachliche Evidenz für vorgeschichtliche Ereignisse*" with the subtitles "*Die Kritik am Stammbaummodell,*" "*Wortinhalte als Gegenstand der Sprachvergleichung*" and "*Ethnische Strukturen im Wortschatz der indogermanischen Grundsprache?*"); by the same author, in *Kratylos* 34 1989 p. 48ff. ("*Forderungen und Bedenken, die meines Erachtens bei der Erschließung der 'indogermanischen' Kultur, Geisteswelt oder Gesellschaft zu beachten sind*" in the context of the review of *Studien zum Indogermanischen Wortschatz*, 1987). Further basic information: → A. Scherer "*Hauptprobleme der indogermanischen Altertumskunde (seit 1940)*" in *Kratylos 1* 1956 p. 3-21; by the same author, *Indogermanische Altertumskunde (seit 1956)*, loc. cit. 10 1965 p. 1-24; W. Dressler "*Methodische Vorfragen bei der Bestimmung der 'Urheimat'*" in *Sprache* 11 1965 p. 25-60; Zimmer *Ursprache* 1990.

1) As a rule, the early historic and Prehistoric finds do not coïncide with the linguistic facts: → B. Hänsel in *FS Schlerath* 1992 [1994] p. 26f.:

> "Linguistic development may be described in steps that, although logically comprehensible, are not precisely analyzable without a timescale. The archaeologist pursues certain areas of cultural development, the logic of which (if one exists) remains a mystery to him, or is only accessible in a few aspects of its complex causality." On the other hand, he is provided with concrete ideas with regard to time, as vague as these may be, and works with a concept of culture that the Indo-European linguist cannot attain. For the archaeologist, culture is understood in the sense of a sociological definition, as W. E. Mühlmann puts it (→ *Wörterbuch der Soziologie*, edited by W. Bernsdorf. Stuttgart 1969. p. 598f.): "the totality of typical ways of life in a population, including the mentality upon which they rest, and in particular, the value system, whereby the typical ways of life include … even the technical bases of existence, including a material substrate of clothing, shelter, tools, equipment, etc." The archaeologist has direct access to the latter areas, and indirect access to the former. The definition of our concept of culture in archaeology is far too open and imprecise in its borders in order for us to equate archaeological culture with 'a people' or 'a closed linguistic community,' in the sense of a politically unified group.

Their concurrence is at best imaginable, but *a priori* unlikely. — We archaeologists know about the instability and ephemeral quality of early societies, we know of the most diverse factors of social coherence, among which language is but one – an important one – yet one from the realm of communications. We archeologists pursue only sub-areas of cultural development within open, changing communities without clear borders. — Cultural contexts, as they are understood for example in marriage communities of particular upper classes, or with regard to burial customs, have very different borders from, for example, contemporaneous types of settlements and their relation to their landscapes. But which of these two aspects of culture and which others are relevant to language? Limited to our current methods, we shall never be able to answer this question. — The archaeological concept of culture is composed of so many components, that by its very nature its contours must remain blurred. But languages are quite different. Of course there are connections; no one can imagine cultural connections without any possibility of verbal communication. But it is too much to ask that archaeologists equate their concept of culture, which is open and incorporates references on various levels, to the single dimension of linguistic community. Archaeology and linguistics are so fundamentally different that, while points of agreement may be expected, parallels and congruency may not. The advantage of linguistic research is its ability to precisely distinguish between individual languages and the regularity of developments. The strength of archaeology is its precision in developing timelines. What one can do, the other cannot. They could complement each other beautifully, if only there were enough commonality."

2) Nothing more precise may be said regarding the localization of the Proto-Indo-European linguistic community. Based upon the localization of later languages such as Greek, Anatolian, and Indo-Iranian, a swathe of land in southern Russia north of the Black Sea is often proposed as the native area of the speakers of Proto-Indo-European: → *Urheimat* 1968 (Views of various authors from the years 1892-1963). On the region south of the Caucasus: → Gamkrelidze / Ivanov *IE and IEs* I 1995 p. 850f.; Th. V. Gamkrelidze, "*Neueres zum Problem der indogermanischen Ursprache und der indogermanischen Urheimat*" in ZVS 100 1987 p. 366-377.

3) The reconstructible lexicon permits several assertions about the culture of the speakers of Proto-Indo-European. For example, they kept and bred livestock (For example, the Proto-Indo-European words *g^{w}óu̯-* 'cow,' *$h_2$óu̯i-* 'sheep,' *peh$_2$-* 'to lead to pasture, to shepherd' and *poh$_2$i-mén-*

[Details on the research: → Hackstein, *Sigmatische Präsensstammbildungen* 1995 p. 176f.] 'shepherd,' **k̑(u)u̯ón-* 'dog,' among others).

B. Forssman offers an accurate summary: → *Sprache - Fünf Vorträge* 1991 p. 63f. (The bracketed text in the following quotation is my addition and refers to corresponding Proto-Indo-European forms.):

"The keeping of cows yielded 'milk' [Compare Greek, γ(ά)λα(κ)(τ)- and Latin *lact-*] and 'to milk' [Compare PIE **d^heu̯g^h-*: → *LIV* 1998 p. 129]; the keeping of sheep yielded 'wool' [Proto-Indo-European **h_2u̯l̥h_1-neh_2-*: → M. Peters in *Sprache* 33 1987 p. 114f.] and 'to process wool' [Compare PIE **pek̑-* 'to pluck (wool or hair)' and **kes-* 'to comb wool': → N. Oettinger in MSS 53 1992 p. 149f.]. The horse [Proto-Indo-European **(h_1)ék̑u̯o-*, see above, E 506] pulled the chariot [Proto-Indo-European **rot-h_2-o-*: → Mayrhofer EWAia II p. 429f.] ... Like other societies that bred livestock, the speakers of Proto-Indo-European lived with extended family [Compare PIE **dem-* 'house clan/community' and **u̯ik̑-* 'settling clan/community': → Mayrhofer EWAia I p. 697 and II p. 561; cp. also below L 217 § 1]. At the head of the extended family was a master of the house [Proto-Indo-European **déms póti-*: → Mayrhofer EWAia I p. 699; cp. also below W 211]; the married sons [Proto-Indo-European **suH-i̯u-*, or **suH-nu-*: → Mayrhofer EWAia II p. 741] also belonged to the extended family and were, with their respective families, subordinated to the master of the house. ... But a purely male-dominated hierarchy surely did not apply. Alone the fact that the wife of the master was called 'mistress' [Proto-Indo-European **potnih_2-*: → Mayrhofer EWAia II p. 74f.; cp. also L 211 § 4], confers respect to her position. ... In their polytheistic religion, they worshiped many gods, including forces of nature such as the 'father' god of the heavens [Proto-Indo-European vocative, **d(i)i̯éu̯ p$h_2$ter*: → Mayrhofer EWAia I p. 751; cp. also F 318 § 6a] ..., the 'mother' earth [Proto-Indo-European **d^hé$\acute{g}^h$om-*, see below F 321 § 1], and the dawn [Proto-Indo-European **$h_2$éu̯s-os-*: → Mayrhofer EWAia I p. 236; cp. also L 310, F 321 § 2 and W 303]. ... Man considered himself ... a counterpart to the gods; he named things such as himself 'earthly' [compare the PIE **$d^h\acute{g}^h$óm-ii̯o-*: → Meid *Gaulish inscriptions* 1992 p. 22] and "mortal" [Proto-Indo-European **mr̥-tó-*: → Mayrhofer EWAia II p. 327]. But death [Proto-Indo-European **mr̥-ti-*, see below F 317 § 7] could be ... overcome by indestructible fame. Our distant linguistic ancestors clearly believed such things. Thus, one can reconstruct the Proto-Indo-European expression **k̑léu̯os ń̥$d^h$$g^{wh}$itom* 'indestructible fame,' in which **k̑léu̯os* actually means the 'heard news' ... In a society completely without writing ... fame spreads principally through oral retelling on the part of a creative singer and through auditive reception on the part of other people, for example, at a festival of the Gods. Of what was the fame of men composed, of which the singers then ... spoke and sang? Surely, to a large extent of men's [Compare PIE **u̯iH-ró-*: → Mayrhofer EWAia II 569f.] deeds of battle. The community of speakers of Proto-Indo-European declared their support for heroism and thus fundamentally for the subjugation of the weak. Peoples of Indo-European languages have conquered, in the course of time, large parts of the world..."

4) Following is a small selection of literature on individual themes among those mentioned. — a) On several areas: → Buck *A Dictionary of Selected Synonyms in the Principal Indo-European Languages.* 1949; Hehn *Cultivated Plants and Domesticated Animals* (1885) 1976; *Studien zum indogermanischen Wortschatz* 1987; Scardigli *Weg zur Deutschen Sprache* 1994 p. 43ff.; Gamkrelidze / Ivanov *IE and IEs* I 1995 p. 377ff. (Part Two: Semantic Dictionary of the Proto-Indo-European Language and Reconstruction of the Indo-European Proto-Culture); Mallory / Adams *Encyclopedia* 1997; A. Häusler in *RGA* 15 2000 under the heading *Indogermanische Altertumskunde.* — b) Focused on problems concerning the horse: → *FS Schlerath* 1992 [1994]; P. Raulwing, "*Pferd, Wagen und Indogermanen: Grundlagen, Probleme und Methoden der Streitwagenforschung*" in *Fachtagung Innsbruck* 1996 [1998] p. 523ff.; by the same author, *Horses* 2000; also by the same author, in DNP 9 2000 under the heading *Pferd.* — c) On the social structure: → Benveniste *Institutions* I + II 1969; B. Schlerath, "*Können wir die urindogermanische Sozialstruktur rekonstruieren?*" *Methodologische Erwägungen* in *Studien zum indogermanischen Wortschatz* 1987 p. 249-264; S. Zimmer, "*Linguistische Rekonstruktion und Geschichte*" in *Bopp-Symposium* 1992 [1994] p. 302-313. — d) On religion: → G. E. Dunkel, "*Vater Himmels Gattin*" in *Sprache* 34 1988-1990 [1992] p. 1-26 and *Sprache* 35 1991-1993 p. 1; B. Schlerath, *Religion der Indogermanen* in *Fachtagung Innsbruck* 1996 [1998] p. 87ff. — e) On poetic language: → Schmitt *Dichtersprache* 1967; *Indogermanische Dichtersprache* 1968; Watkins *How to Kill a Dragon* 1995.

E 513. That the various Indo-European languages have developed from a prior unified language is certain (see above, E 435). Questionable is, however, the concrete 'how' of this process of differentiation. Various hypotheses have been formulated on this subject.

1) The most suitable model for our understanding of our reconstructions remains the tree diagram first proposed by A. Schleicher: → Schleicher *Compendium* 1866 p. 9. While all other models (including those of J. Schmidt and O. Höfler) give a good account of observable linguistic development, they are lacking in that they are not usable and verifiable in the context of uniform reconstructions as we receive them in our work. See above E 507 § 4, further H. Rix cited in E 426 § 1. — J. Schmidt opposed the tree diagram with a wave image "which spreads itself in concentric rings and becomes weaker as the distance from the center increases": → Schmidt (J.) *Verwandtschaftsverhältnisse* 1872 p. 27f. — O. Höfler "*Stammbaumtheorie, Wellentheorie, Entfaltungstheorie*" in PBB 77 1955 p. 30ff goes beyond J. Schmidt. On the whole complex in the light of numeric-taxonomic processes of classification: → H. Goebl "'*Stammbaum' und 'Welle'*" in *Zeitschrift für Sprachwissenschaft* 2 1983 p. 3-44.

2) As little certainty as may be gained concerning the localization of the native land and determining of the time period of Proto-Indo-European (see above, E 511 and E 512 § 2), it may in fact be possible to reveal how the Proto-Indo-European community dispersed and developed. Several models are conceivable: Thus, for example the gain of new land through campaigns of conquest, or expansion of the region of the language in the wake of a perfectly peaceable spread of agriculture. Much speaks for the former, i.e. conquest, in my opinion. (See above, E 512 § 3, at the end, on heroism.) In the words of B. Schlerath (→ B. Schlerath in ZVS 95 1981 p. 199.):

> "The belligerent operations for the spread of the Indo-Europeans seem to me far more important than the relocation of farming populations that occurred in that context, or rather in their wake. I thus achieve an immediate connection with that which we must accept from the Indo-European conquest of Asia Minor, Iran, and Greece, and I may consider the Celtic and Germanic migrations as immediate continuations of this process under very similar conditions":

The vital question of why the campaigns of conquest are not archaeologically documented remains unanswered.

3) We have quite clearly voiced our support of the 'diverging tree model,' i.e. of a uniform Proto-Indo-European language, with later division in daughter languages. However, one may not ignore that our model is opposed by a 'converging association of languages model,' in which

languages that are in spatial and temporal contact [and are not necessarily related to each other] exchange linguistic elements and rules, thus developing and acquiring from each other. Among the prominent advocates is N. S. Trubetzkoy (→ A text from 1939 is printed in *Urheimat* 1968 p. 214f.):

> "The supposition of an original Indo-European language is not totally impossible. However, it is not at all important; and one can very well do without it. The term, 'language family' does not presuppose the common descent of a quantity of languages from a single original language. We consider a 'language family' a group of languages, in which a considerable quantity of lexical and morphological elements exhibit regular equivalences. In order to clarify the regularity of the phonetic equivalences it is not necessary for one to suppose common descent, since such regularity may also originate through borrowings between neighboring unrelated languages (so-called *Fremdlautgesetze*). Neither is agreement in rudimentary lexical and morphological elements a proof of common descent, since all elements of human language may be borrowed. ... Thus there is in fact no compelling reason for the acceptance of a uniform original Indo-European language, from which individual Indo-European languages might have descended. It is just as conceivable that the ancestors of the Indo-European language branches were originally different from each other, but through constant contact, mutual influence, and borrowings, approached each other, without however ever becoming identical to one another."

Compare further: A. Häusler "*Archäologie, das Indogermanenproblem und der Ursprung der Hellenen*" in Ohlstadt 1996 [1998] p. 79-123.

However, the thesis of a 'converging association of languages' may immediately be dismissed, given that all Indo-European languages are based upon the same Proto-Indo-European flexion morphology. As H. Rix makes clear, it is precisely this morphological congruence that speaks against the language association model, and for the diverging tree model (→ InL 17 1994 1994 18f.; G. Neumann argues similarly in Ohlstadt 1996 [1998] 262f.):

"Linguistic elements and rules are not exchanged *ad libitum*, at least not in the *langue*. There is always a motive for borrowings from another language: in phonetics, the imitation of an idiom with higher prestige or exotic attraction; in vocabulary, the naming of a borrowed thing, or again the use of a more prestigeous language; in syntax, a rule that seems fitting or exemplary, etc.; this motive must be investigated. ... Understandably, borrowings take place more easily in open sub-systems of language than in closed sub-systems, in which it is more difficult to insert new elements. Open sub-systems include phonems and vocabulary, and to a lesser extent syntax. Flexion morphology, on the other hand, is the closed sub-system par excellence. Thus, if one wishes to investigate 'Proto-Italic,' he or she must first investigate the flexion morphology in languages of typologically Indo-European structure. Even the connection between the Indo-European languages was not discovered through phonetics, vocabulary, and syntax, but rather through the system of conjugation."

Since H. Krahe there have been efforts to formulate assertions, through linguistic analysis of ancient European hydronomy, about the language (presumably Proto-Indo-European) of its creators: → W. P. Schmid "*Alteuropäische Gewässernamen*" in *Onomastik* 1995 p. 756-762; by the same author, *Schriften* 1994 *passim*. However, the material is very problematic. The controversial thesis of a 'converging language association' plays a central role here. Criticism: → Th. Andersson *Zur Geschichte der Theorie einer alteuropäischen Hydronymie in Probleme der Namenbildung* 1986 [1988] p. 59-90. For more information, see W 305 § 3.

II. Proto-Indo-European Phonology

A. General Information

L 100. In anticipation of the individual sections below, the following table of relevant Proto-Indo-European phonemes may be reconstructed:

vowels (see below, L 200ff.):	*i	*e	*a	*o	*u
	*ī	*ē	*ā	*ō	*ū
semivowels (see below, L 212ff.):	*i̯	*u̯			
diphthongs (see below, L 219ff.):	*ei̯	*ai̯	*oi̯		
	*eu̯	*au̯	*ou̯		
liquids, nasals (see below, L 300ff.):	*l [*l̥]		*r [*r̥]		
	*m [*m̥]		*n [*n̥]		
continuants (see below, L 308ff.):	*s				
laryngeals (see below, L 314ff.):	*h_1	*h_2	*h_3		
dentals (see below, L 336):	*t	*d	*d^h		
labials (see below, L 337):	*p	*b	*b^h		
palatals (see below, L 339ff.):	*ḱ	*ǵ	*$ǵ^h$		
velars (see below, L 339ff.):	*k	*g	*g^h		
labiovelars (see below, L 343f.):	*k^w	*g^w	*g^{wh}		

L 101. The system of denotation used in L 100, including the ^{h} as superscript to indicate an aspirated occlusive that is a single phoneme, follows the recommendations of B. Forssman in *Kratylos* 33 1988 p. 61 (with note 30) on the occasion of his review of Mayrhofer *Lautlehre* 1986. This system is used consistently throughout the present work.

L 102. The present description of the Proto-Indo-European inventory of phonemes is consciously phonological and not phonetic. Giving priority to phonemes elevates indeed the transparency of reconstructions, but only at the cost of their presumably concrete phonetic realization, e.g., PIE **ni-sd-ó-* 'nest,' and not [**nizdó-*] (surely with a voiced *z* before the voiced *d*); PIE **steh₂-* 'to walk, to position oneself,' and not [**stah₂-*] (with vowel quality assimilation in the following laryngeals); PIE $*d^hh_1$*tó-*, and not [$*d^hh_1$°*tó-*] (with weak vowel, see below, L 103); Proto-Indo-European accusative plural **-ms*, and not [**-ns*] (with assimilation, see below, F 104; but in this case one is not consistent and **-ns* can also easily be found); PIE **dems-poti-*, and not [**dens-poti-*] (see below W 211).

L 103. The Proto-Indo-European continuant 'thorn,' which features voiceless **þ*, and voiced **ð* , was often reconstructed in older research, and is considered here, as in J. Schindler, to be a secondary product that appeared in tautosyllabic position in initial consonant groups such as **tk* and $*d^h\acute{g}^h$, see below, L 313. I thus write PIE $*d^h\acute{g}^h$*em-* 'earth' and not $*\acute{g}^h$*ð em-*, and further, PIE **tḱei̯-* 'inhabit, settle' and not PIE **kþei̯-*.

Laryngeals are here considered as consonants. According to this approach, their postulated Proto-Indo-European allophones $*ə_1$, $*ə_2$, $*ə_3$ are the result of the development of an initially phonologically irrelevant weak vowel between a laryngeal and a consonant: Since the laryngeal is positioned immediately before a weak vowel, the existence of which it brought about, it disappears in accordance with phonetic rules. For example, compare the PIE $*d^hh_1$*-tó-* 'placed' with the spoken [$*d^hh_1$°*tó-*] or rather [$*d^hə_1$*tó-*] and the descendents from individual Indo-European languages, such as Latin **datus* (in *conditus* < **con-datus*, and also in its simplex, *fac-tus*), Greek θετός and Vedic *hitá-*. That which remains after the disappearance of the laryngeal is the weak vowel, which in Greek gets the quality of the laryngeal by assimilation (thus *e*, *a*, or *o*), or receives another sole bias independent of its quality (Latin *a*, Vedic *i*, etc., see below L 325).

The series of occlusives are expressly not written in glottal form. See below, L 335 § 3.

L 104. One must be aware that we are entirely dependent on written records for our knowledge of ancient Indo-European languages. The step from the grapheme (of the letter or character) to the phoneme, which is as a rule what the grapheme denotes, must be respected. Statements such as *i̯- > Greek ζ- are in error, because the suggested phonetic change is first described on the level of the phoneme, and then is completed as ζ on the level of the grapheme. Objectively correct is in this case alone the statement, that PIE *i̯- > Greek *d*^{j}-, or rather *dz*-. On problems of phonetics (which is interested in phonemes in relation to their articulation) and phonology (which depicts language on the level of its relevant sounds or phonemes): → M. Leumann "*Phonologie der toten Sprachen*" in *Kleine Schriften* 1959 p. 398-407. On the history of the origins of the terms 'grapheme' and 'phoneme' (and also on the confusion of sounds and letters as well as the difference between written and spoken language): → Kohrt *Problemgeschichte* 1985 p. 4ff.

L 105. I shall here discuss only briefly universal observations and causes of diachronic phonological evolution (which concerns all areas of language in varying degrees).

Language is subject to constant change. As an example, compare the Old Latin *deivos* 'divinity' > Classical Latin *deus*, see below L 217 § 3. Since the neogrammarians (see above, E 306) it is established that phonological evolution takes place according to certain laws. Thanks to more precise empirical investigation, among which research performed in the region of Frankfurt and Cologne (i.e. in the *Rheinische Fächer*) is well-known, today one can better describe and understand the processes and spread of phonetic developments: Initially, changed and unchanged forms coexist; the variant applies at the beginning to few words; during the process of spread of the new feature, there is variance and irregularity; if there is no social pressure that resists the spread, the new feature can spread to the entire vocabulary in the entire community of speakers. For further details: → Bynon *Historical Linguistics* 1977 p. 173ff.

Further literature: → Boretzky *Historische Linguistik* 1977 p. 79ff.; Szemerényi *Einführung* 1990 p. 14ff. (Language in transformation); Hock *Language History* 1996 p. 126ff. ('Some types of sound change'), p. 143ff. ('Why sounds change?') and p. 541f. ('Chapter notes and suggested readings'). Further, see above, E 509 § 4.

L 106. Development according to rules of phonetics may be disturbed through the use of analogies. Thus, the development proceeds, not according to the given phonetic pattern, but rather takes as its model another pattern, one which already existed within the specific language. That is why the key expression '*Lautgesetz und Analogie*' was chosen at the time of the neogrammarians. — Compare as an example the Latin *equos* / *equus* 'horse': According to phonetic rules, one expects in the nominative singular *ecus* < **ecos* < *equos*. However, the normal paradigm of Classical Latin does not yield a nominative singular *ecus*, but rather *equus*: The analogical pressure of the *equ*-forms such as genitive singular *equī* (phonetic rules here yielding the form *equ-*) was clearly so strong that even the nominative singular *equos* (> Classical Latin *equus*) was preserved, even though *u̯*, when it is before *o*/*u* and not at the beginning of a word, normally disappeared in the 3rd century B.C. See above, E 506 § 3.

Literature on analogy: → Szemerényi *Einführung* 1990 p. 29f.

L 107. The absolute dating of phonetic, and other linguistic changes is only possible in rare cases. Approximative assertions as to dates are the rule. Compare as an example the formulation of M. Leumann LLFL 1977 p. 62 on the dating of the phonetic change in Latin from *ei* > *ī*:

> "The *ī* of Classical Latin appears sometimes as *i* and sometimes as *ei* in the Old Latin of inscriptions , and indeed until 150 B.C., the phoneme, which is based upon one of the *i*-diphthongs, is written as *i* or perhaps *ei*, but the ancient monophthong *ī* only as *i*; then, there appears variance in the orthography between *ei* and *i*, until finally only *i* remains. Thus, around 150 B.C., a phonetic fusion of the older *ei* and *ī* took place, producing *ī*."

The information necessary to precisely determine a date is most often missing. Nonetheless, we are sometimes in a position to chronologically place a dubious change A in relation to a verified change B, and thus to classify A chronologically before B, or vice versa.

For examples of relative chronology, see the notes on the palatal law in L 206 § 2 and the comments on Germanic accents in L 421 § 4.

Literature: → R. Gusmani, "*Marginalien zum Problem der relativen Chronologie*" in *FS* Szemerényi *75 I 1992 p. 143-152.

L 108. In the following description, it is important to distinguish between context-independent and context-dependent development. The former represents the normal case, which is unaffected by its phonetic context. In the case of the latter, the phonemes or accents in its context lead to greater or lesser deviations from the norm.

An example from Latin: PIE *e* is context-independent and remains in Latin *est* 'is.' PIE **e* followed **u̯*, appearing as *o*, as in the Latin *novo-* 'new,' on the other hand, is context-dependent in contrast to the Greek context-independent *neu̯o-* (Mycenaean *ne-wo* in the sense of 'of the current year'). However, when followed by **ng*, PIE **e* becomes Latin *i* (example: Latin *tingō* 'to moisten') whereas the context-independent Greek τέγγω 'that' the **e* remains unchanged. The case of Latin *in* 'in, into' in relation to the Greek ἐν 'that' is more complex: According to the Greek, the Proto-Indo-European form of the local particle was **en*. Therefore, we must accept that an early phase of Latin featured variation of the particle (according to the beginning of the following word) from the unchanged *en* to the changed (phonetically context-dependent) *in* and that in the following period this double representation *en/in* was decided in favor of *in*. Incidentally, the same explanation applies in the case of the *e* in the negation **en-* < Proto-Indo-European**n̥-*: The original double representation **en-/in-* is simplified to *in-*. In the case of Latin *sedeō* 'to sit,' compared with *obsideō* 'to besiege,' *sed-* is context-independent, whereas *-sid-*, in an initial secondary position is a weakened form of *-sed-*. (For information on vowel weakening in short middle syllables, see below, L 204.) For more information on the Latin examples above: → Leumann *LLFL* 1977 p. 45ff.; Sommer / Pfister *Lautlehre* 1977 p. 53ff.

L 109. In order to more fully document the descendents of Proto-Indo-European phonemes, comparisons not only of the habitual Latin, Greek, and Vedic are treated in the section on phonology, but also of Hittite, Lithuanian, Old Church Slavic, and the Old Germanic languages.

B. Proto-Indo-European Vowels

1. Vowels

L 200. A methodical comparison of Indo-European languages yields a Proto-Indo-European system of five short vowels and five long vowels:

**i*				**u*	**ī*				**ū*
	**e*		**o*			**ē*		**ō*	
		**a*					**ā*		

L 201. In this chapter, only those occurrences of the vowels, **a*, **o*, **ā* and **ō*, are treated that are not the products of laryngeal influence. Developments such as **a* < **h_2a* < PIE **h_2e*; **o* < **h_3o* < PIE **h_3e*; **ā* < **ah_2* < PIE **eh_2*; and **ō* < **oh_3* < PIE **eh_3* are discussed in the context of laryngeals. — Likewise, **ē* < PIE **eh_1* is missing, see below, L 323 § 1a. — Neither are the long vowels **ī* and **ū* unproblematic, since some of the occurrences may equally be traced back to *i+H* or *u+H.* See below, L 211 § 7.

Short commentaries on the equivalents in various Indo-European languages follow in L 202-210. Examples follow in L 211.

L 202. According to the view represented here, weak vowels (sometimes called anaptyctic vowels) had at the beginning no phonologically relevant value in Proto-Indo-European. — In older Indo-European research, a weak vowel (usually indicated by *ə*) appears there, where we would now, in light of progress in the understanding of individual Indo-European languages, place a laryngeal. For example, in the case of Latin *pater*, Greek πατήρ, Vedic *pitā́,* the older representation, **pətḗr* has been replaced by **ph_2tḗr*. For details, see above, L 103. Because this *ə* was considered having the status of a phoneme, it received the name 'schwa *indogermanicum*' or 'schwa *primum*': → Brugmann *Grundriß* I 1897 § 193; Thumb / Hauschild *Handbuch des Sanskrit* I / 1 1958 § 69; Schmitt-Brandt *Indogermanistik* 1998 p. 119f. For more information on the history of research, see below, L 318. For more information on 'father,' see below, L 324 § 3.

L 203. Phonologically irrelevant Proto-Indo-European weak vowels (here indicated by °) may further be observed in zero grade ablaut forms. In order to distinguish them from zero grade, one speaks of reduction grade. These vowels carry the name 'schwa *secundum*' for historical reasons: They were classed in second position next to the schwa *indogermanicum.* — The ablaut of full grade PIE **k^{w}et-* 'four' (compare Doric Greek τέτορες, Vedic *catvā́ras*, Old Church Slavic *četyre*) includes both zero grade **k^{w}t-* (compare Later Avestan *ā-xt-ūirīm* 'four times') and reduction grade **k^{w}°t-*. This weak vowel appears in Greek as *-i-*, in Latin as *-a-*, and in Slavic as **-ъ-*. Compare the Aeolic Homeric πίσυρες, Latin *quattuor*, Czech *čtyři* < **čъtyr-* (On the IE treaments of the PIE labiovelar **k^w*- cf. L 343). — A similar relationship exists between full grade PIE **pet-* (compare Greek πετάννυμι) and reduction grade PIE **p°t-* (compare Greek πίτνημι 'to spread out,' and Latin *pat-ēre* 'to stand open') and between full grade PIE **meǵh_2-* 'large' (Greek μέγας) and reduction grade PIE **m°ǵh$_2$-* (Latin *mag-nus*). That which one would in this case expect, namely **m̥ǵh$_2$-*, is avoided for paradigmatic reasons, but likely may be detected in the Latin *ingēns* 'violent.' (If, in fact *ing-* < **eng-* < **n̥ǵ-* < **m̥ǵ-*.). — Further, compare the Greek ναίω 'inhabit,' if, in fact < **n°s-i̯e-*: → G.-L. García-Ramón in *FS Narten* 2000 p. 67 note 13. The verb would then be an *-i̯e*-present of the PIE **nes-* 'to come away, to come home safely.' The reduction grade **n°s-i̯e-* would be there in place of the now unclear **as-i̯e-* < **n̥s-i̯e-*. For more information: → Mayrhofer *Lautlehre* 1986 p. 175ff.; B. Vine, "Greek ῥίζα and 'Schwa *secundum*" in *UCLA IE Studies* I 1999 p. 5-30. See also L 503 § 5.

L 204. Where development remained undisturbed, the Proto-Indo-European long and short vowel systems are preserved without great changes in Latin: → Leumann *LLFL* 1977 p. 44. For information on problems with short vowels in word-internal syllables which were affected by syncope and vowel weakening around 450 B.C. compare on the subject of syncope the example of *opifex* 'handworker' versus *officīna* [*off-*< *opif-*] 'workshop,' and on the vowel weakening, the example *f-a-cere* 'to do, to make' versus *conf-i-cere* [*-i-* being the result in an open syllable] 'to end' versus *dēf-e-ctiō* [*-e-* being the result in a closed syllable] 'failure, renunciation'): → H. Rix "*Die lateinische Synkope als historisches und phonologisches Problem*" in *Kratylos* 11 1966 p. 156-165 (= *Probleme der lateinischen Grammatik*, edited by K. Strunk. Darmstadt 1973. p. 90-102).

A conspicuous and typical quality of Latin is the frequent appearance of *a* in place of *e* or *o*. For example, *quattuor* 'four' (with *-a-* in place of *-e-*, compare PIE **k^{w}et-u̯or-*) and *canis* 'dog' (with *-a-* in place of *-o-*, compare PIE **ḱu̯on-*). The reasons for this are in part phonological in nature, but are also linked to context: → Leumann *LLFL* 1977 § 48; Schrijver *Laryngeals* 1991 p. 420ff.; H. Rix in *Kratylos* 41 1996 p. 162.

L 205. Even the most ancient Greek exhibited the unchanged Proto-Indo-European vowels. Dialects, however deviate to some extent.

The Ionic-Attic dialect exhibits further developments in two cases: — In place of PIE **ā, ē* <η> appears in Ionic since the 8th century B.C. In Attic, *ā* is found in the position following *e, i,* and *r*, otherwise *ē* as in Ionic: → Meier-Brügger *Griechische Sprachwissenschaft* II 1992 L 400 § 1. — Instead of PIE **u / ū* , Ionic-Attic *ü / ǖ* appears since antiquity. This change is as a rule not detectible in the writen records because the graphem υ remains still the same. Writers of Boetian texts from the 4th century B.C. on preserved however the difference between the native *u* <ου> and the Ionic-Attic *ü* <υ>. For example, cp. Boetian <τούχα> [$tuk^{h}\bar{a}$] in comparison with Attic <τύχη> [$t\ddot{u}k^{h}\bar{e}$]: → Lejeune *Phonétique* 1972 § 252.

L 206. Vedic, on the other hand, exhibits a simplification (dephonologization) that took place already in the Indo-Iranian period. PIE *e, *o, *a become a single Indo-Iranian *a, PIE *ē, *ō, *ā a single Indo-Iranian *ā. We are indebted to F. de Saussure for this insight: → Saussure *Mémoire* 1879 (prior to which, one considered precisely this uniform vocality of Indo-Iranian as if it were originally Proto-Indo-European, thus assuming, for example, that the Greek and Latin *e, o, a* were secondary developments). Concerning the special case of PIE *o > Vedic *ā*, see below, L 412. Thus, a loosely-woven three part system in Indo-Iranian corresponds to the five-part system of Proto-Indo-European:

*i		*u		*ī		*ū
	*a		or		*ā	

1) Whereas the diphthongs *ai̯ and *au̯ are preserved as *ay* and *av* when they precede vowels, they become either *ē* (in linguistics, traditionally transcribed as short *e*) or *ō* (traditionally written as short *o*), see below L 220 § 3. A system of five long-vowels is thus once more completed. In addition, in the Middle Indian period, *e* and *o* appear as shortened forms of *ē* and *ō* before multiple consonants and complet thus also the system of five short vowels: → Geiger *Pāli* 1916 p. 43 § 6.

2) It is affirmed by the law of palatals that the vowel diversity of Proto-Indo-European *e/ē, *o/ō and *a/ā continued until an early phase of Indo-Iranian. The word initial difference between Vedic *kád* 'what' and *ca* 'and' (cf. Latin *quod* 'what' and *que* 'and') requires that the delabialization of Indo-Iranian labiovelars (here from *k^{w}ód to *kód and from *k^{w}e to *ke) and the palatization before palatal vowels (*kód remains, but *ke becomes *če) must have preceded the simplification of *o*, *e* and *a* to *a* (which resulted in *kád*, and *ca*):

I	PIE	*k^{w}ód	*k^{w}e
		↓ a)	↓ a)
II	Indo-Iranian A	*kód	*ke
			↓ b)
III	Indo-Iranian B		*če
		↓ c)	↓ c)
IV	Vedic	*kád*	*ca*

Key: a) = delabialization; b) = palatalization; c) = simplification of vowel quality.

3) In the years between 1875 and 1877, six researchers succeeded in demonstrating this independently of one another: → Wackernagel / Debrunner *Altindische Grammatik I* 1957 § 124; Mayrhofer *Sanskrit und die Sprachen Alteuropas* 1983 p. 132ff. (p. 137ff. an excursus: "*Das Palatalgesetz und seine Entdecker*"; in addition, J. Gippert in MSS 54 1993 [1994] p. 69ff.); Collinge *Laws* 1985 p. 133 ff.

L 207. The cuneiform script of Hittite is phonetically and phonologically far less transparent than the alphabets that were introduced in Italy, Greece, and India: → H. Eichner "*Phonetik und Lautgesetz des Hethitischen - ein Weg zu ihrer Entschlüsselung*" in *Fachtagung Wien* 1978 [1980] p. 120-165; Melchert *Anatolian Historical Phonology* 1994 p. 12ff. — Cuneiform accounts reveal that the Proto-Indo-European short vowels *i, *u and *e are preserved in Hittite. PIE *o became *a* in Hittite, thus homophone with *a* < PIE *a and with the *a* in the sequences *ḫa* and *aḫ* < PIE *h_2e and *eh_2: → Melchert *Anatolian Historical Phonology* 1994 p. 105. — One may presume an analogous process concerning long vowels.

In addition, in the context of accents, the vowel quantities were altered in such a way that, while in open syllables the accented vowel is lengthened, in syllables in an unstressed position, the accented vowel is shortened. The case of closed syllables is more complex: → Melchert *ibid.*, p. 107f.

L 208. In the case of the Germanic languages, the PIE short vowels *o and *a were simplified to *a in Proto-Germanic. PIE *i, *u and *e remain undisturbed. Individual Old Germanic dialects undergo context-sensitive developments with results that sometimes vary: Thus, from *i* > *e* (which in the case of Gothic, when directly preceding *h*, *ƕ* and *r* [called breaking], was preserved as the grapheme <*ai*>; and which in North and West Germanic, among others, preceding *a* in the following syllable [so-called *a*-umlaut]) and in analogous conditions from *u* to *o* (Gothic <*au*>), otherwise from *e* > *i* (as in Gothic with the exception of the 'break-position,' North and West Germanic preceding *nK* or *i*, *i̯* and to some extent also preceding *u* in the following syllable). — Among the long vowels, PIE **ō* and **ā* are simplified to Old Germanic **ō* (which, in stem syllables, in turn became Old High German *uo*, or New High German *ū*). In North Germanic, and in a large part of West Germanic, PIE **ē* became *ā* relatively late: → Krahe / Meid *Germanische Sprachwissenschaft* I 1969 pp. 42, 51, 57ff.

L 209. Lithuanian, to which other Baltic languages correspond in terms of short vowels, exhibits, like Hittite, Germanic, and Slavic, a simplification of PIE **a* and **o* in *a*, whereas PIE **e*, **i* and **u* are retained. — The long-vowels PIE **ī* (Lithuanian <*y*>) and PIE **ū* are retained in Lithuanian, as is PIE **ē* (Lithuanian <*ė*>). The development of PIE **ō* (Lithuanian > *uo*) is different in comparison with that of PIE **ā* (Lithuanian > *ō*, but which is retained as *ā* in Old Prussian): → Stang *Vergleichende Grammatik der baltischen Sprachen* 1966 p. 22ff.

L 210. In Old Church Slavic, PIE **i* and **u* are retained as ь and ъ, respectively; PIE **e* remains *e*; and **o* and **a* are simplified as *o*. — The replacement of PIE **ī* is Old Church Slavic *i*; that of PIE **ū* is Old Church Slavic *y*; PIE **ē* became Old Church Slavic *ě*, PIE **ō* and PIE **ā* both produced Old Church Slavic *a*. The discussion of the extent to which older Proto-Slavic preliminary phases precede the established Old Church Slavic phonological data has not as yet been resolved. Much speaks in favor of the theory that before the consolidation of PIE **o* and **a* to *o* and of PIE **ō* and **ā* to *a*, there existed a Proto-Slavic intermediate phase with **a* and **ā*:

PIE	**o*	**a*	**ō*	**ā*
	\	/	\	/
Proto-Slavic	**a*		**ā*	
	↓		↓	
OCS	*o*		*a*	

Early Slavic loan-words in Finnish potentially offer evidence of this Proto-Slavic intermediate phase. Compare, for example, Finnish *akkuna* with Old Church Slavic *okъno* 'window' < PIE 'containing *o*' **h*$_3$*k*^{w}-: → Aitzetmüller *Altbulgarische Grammatik* 1991 p. 8ff., p. 19ff.; J. Udolph in *IF* 87 1982 [1983] p. 366f.; M. Trummer in *Die slawischen Sprachen* 7 1984 p. 117ff.; by the same author, *Aus der älteren slavischen und balkanischen Sprachgeschichte I. Fragen des urslavischen Vokalismus*. Graz 1985 (*non vidi*: short reference in *Indogermanische Chronik* 32a Nr.1084).

L 211. Following is a list of correspondence sets for the individual vowel phonemes.

1) Proto-Indo-European **i*: — PIE **k*^{w}*i-s* 'who?,' PIE **k*^{w}*i-d* 'what?' = Latin *quis, quid,* Greek τίς, τί, Hittite *ku-iš, ku-it* i.e. *k̯uis, k̯uit*; further, cf. Vedic *cit* 'sogar, selbst'; Gothic *ƕi-leiks*, Old English *hwi-lc*, 'which'; Old Church Slavic *čь-to* 'what?.' — PIE **ni-sd-ó-* masculine or neuter 'nest' (on the problem of phonetic realization, cf. L 102) = Latin *nīdus* and Vedic *nīḍá-* (with -*ī*- as compensatory lengthening from Early Latin *-*iz*- or Early Vedic *-*iž*-), Old English, Old High German *nest* (Proto-Germanic **nista*- n.). — PIE **dik̑*- (the zero grade of PIE **dei̯k̑*-) 'to indicate, announce' = Latin *dicāre* 'formally announce,' Cretan Greek προ-δίκ-νυτι (2nd century B.C. in an epigram: → Bile *Crétois* 1988 note 297 b) 'he/she/it shows,' Vedic *diś-áti* 'he/she/it shows, explains,' Gothic *ga-taih-un* 'they announced' (with breaking, cf. L 208), Old High German *bi-zih-t* f. 'accusation.' — PIE **h*$_2$*óu̯i*- m. f. 'sheep' = Latin *ovis*, Greek ὄϊς, in dialect ὀϝις, Vedic *ávi*-, Luwian *ḫa-a-ú-i-iš* i.e. *ḫāu̯īs* < **ḫáu̯i*-, Lithuanian *avìs*; further, cf. Old Church Slavic *ovь-ca* f. 'sheep'; Old High German *awi-st* m. 'sheep stall.'

2) Proto-Indo-European **u*: — PIE **i̯ugó*- n. 'yoke' (For information about the word beginning in Proto-Indo-European and Greek, cf. L 213 § 1) = Latin *iugum*, Greek ζυγόν, Vedic *yugám*, Hittite *i-ú-kán* in the sense of *i̯ugan*, Proto-Germanic **i̯uka*- (compare Gothic *juk*, Old High German *joh*). — PIE **d*^{h}*ugh*$_2$*tér*- f. 'daughter' = Greek θυγατέρ-α accusative singular, Vedic *duhitár*-, Gothic *dauhtar* (for more information on *o* <*au*> cf. L 208), Lithuanian *duktė̃*, Old Church Slavic *dъšti*. For more information on this word: → Mayrhofer EWAia I p. 737f. — PIE **h*$_1$*rud*^{h}*ró*- 'red, blood-colored' = Latin *ruber* < Proto-Italic **ruþro*-; Greek ἐρυθρός; Vedic *rudh-irá*- (→ Mayrhofer EWAia II p. 453f.); cf. further, Lithuanian *rùdas* 'redish, red-brown'; Old English *rudian* 'to be red.'

3) Proto-Indo-European **e*: — PIE **néb*^{h}*eleh*$_2$- f. and **néb*^{h}*-es-* n. 'cloud' = Latin *nebula* f., Greek νεφέλη f., νέφος n., Vedic *nábhas-* n., Hittite *ne-pí-ši* i.e. *nepis-i* locative singular 'in the sky' (< * 'in the clouds'), Old Church Slavic *nebo* n. 'sky'; cf. also Old High German *nebul* m. 'Nebel,' Lithuanian *debes-es* nominative plural 'clouds..' For further information on this word family: → Mayrhofer EWAia II p. 13. — PIE **b*^{h}*er-* 'to carry' = Latin *fer-ō*, Greek φέρω, Vedic *bhárati*, Gothic *bairan*, Old High German *beran* (New High German *ge-bären* in the sense of 'to deliver'). — PIE **g*^{wh}*en-* 'to strike, to kill' = Greek θεν-ῶ future (on the word beginning, cf. L 345 Abs. 1), Vedic *hán-ti*, Hittite *ku-en-zi* i.e. *ku̯en-t*^{s}*i* 'to beat to death, to kill,' Lithuanian *gen-ù* 'to hunt, to herd,' Old Church Slavic *žen-ǫ* 'I herd, I pursue.'

4) Proto-Indo-European **o*: — PIE **póti-* m. 'sir, spouse,' PIE **pótnih*$_2$- f. 'madam, (female) spouse' = Greek πόσις (with Southern Greek *-si-* < *-ti-*), πότνια; Vedic *páti-*, *pátnī-*; Gothic *brūþ-faþs* 'groom'; Lithuanian *patìs* 'spouse,' *vieš-patni* 'wife'; Latin *potis* 'wealthy, powerful.' — PIE **u̯oséi̯onti* 'they cloth, cover someone' (the causative of PIE **u̯es-* 'to wear, to be clothed,' also cf. the root of Latin *ves-ti-* 'gown') = Hittite *u̯a-aš-ša-an-zi* i.e. *u̯assant*^{s}*i* (For details: → Melchert *Hittite Historical Phonology* 1984 p. 31f.); cf. also Gothic *wasjan* 'to clothe' and L 310. — PIE **g*^{h}*osti-* m. 'stranger' = Latin *hostis* m. [and f.] 'stranger' (also 'enemy'), Gothic *gasts* m. 'foreigner,' Old High German *gast* m. 'stranger, guest,' Old Church Slavic *gostь* m. 'guest'.

5) Proto-Indo-European **a*: — This short vowel is shown to have predominently been adjacent to PIE **h*$_2$, cf. L 322 § 2. Reconstruction leads however, to occurrences of PIE **a* that may not be attributed to the influence of the second laryngeal. They are simply far less common than PIE **e* and PIE **o* and appear to be limited to particular phonetic contexts: → Mayrhofer *Lautlehre* 1986 p. 169f.; H. Eichner in *Laryngaltheorie* 1988 p . 133. A critical perspective: → A. Lubotsky *"Against a Proto-Indo-European Phoneme *a"* in *New Sound of Indo-European* 1989 p. 53-66. — The following examples may perhaps have a claim to the age of Proto-Indo-European. (Concerning *ai̯*, cf. further below, L 221 § 3; for information on *au̯*, L 223 § 3): — **ḱas-* 'gray,' and in addition **ḱas-ó-*, **ḱas-en-* 'hare' (< *'gray [fur]'), cf. Latin *cānus* 'gray, gray from aging' < Early Latin **kas-no-*, Latin *cascus* 'old,' Vedic *śaśá-* m. 'hare' < **śasá-* = Khotanese *saha-*, Old High German *hasan* 'gray,' *haso* 'hare,' Old Prussian *sasins*. — **ǵ*^{h}*ans-* 'goose' = Latin *ānser* < **hans-*, Mycenaean Greek TH *ka-si* i.e. *k*^{h}*ansi* dative/locative plural Ionic-Attic χῆνες nominative plural <* *k*^{h}*ans-es*, Vedic *haṃsá-*, Old High German *gans*, Lithuanian *žąsìs*. — κάπτω < **kap-i̯e-* 'to snatch, to swallow.' —

**kápro-*, used to designate various animals as 'snappers' (applied in Latin to the goat, in Greek, to the male pig): → Meier-Brügger in *Minos* 23 1988 [1989] p. 206) = Latin *caper* 'billy goat' (< **kapro-* with Old Latin *-ros* > *-er*: → Leumann LLFL 1977 § 106), Old Norse *hafr*; Greek κάπρος 'boar.' — For information on PIE *g^hlad^h-* cf. L 342 § 2.

6) An example of PIE *ī is found in PIE **u̯īs-* 'poison.' It is the lengthened grade form of the nominative singular of the root noun **u̯is-*, cf. Later Avestan *vīš*. Vedic *viṣá-* n. 'poison' is constructed from the short vowel form **u̯is-+-o-* (→ Mayrhofer EWAia II p. 563f.), Greek ἰός m. and Latin *vīrus* n., on the other hand, are constructed from the long vowel form **u̯īs-+-o-*. (The unique Lat. neuter *-o*-stem is likely old and must have been established at a time when the speakers had a choice of classification of nouns among objective or personal classes, cf. F 303 § 2). — More often, however, (as in the case of PIE *ū) *ī originates from PIE **iH*, cf. PIE *g^wih$_3$-u̯ó-* 'alive' = Latin *vīvus*, Vedic *jīvá-*, Lithuanian *gývas*, Old Church Slavic *živъ* (For information on the Proto-Indo-European root word *g^wi̯eh$_3$-* 'to live': → LIV 1998 p. 192f.).

7) Proto-Indo-European **nū(n)* 'well, now' contains PIE *ū, cf. Greek νῦν, Vedic *nū́* (along with PIE **nu* = Greek νυ, Vedic *nú*; from which PIE **néu̯o-* is derived: → Darms *Vr̥ddhi* 1978 p. 392ff.). — A further example is probably PIE **mūs-* 'mouse' = Latin *mūs*, Greek μῦς (possibly evidenced in the Mycenaean proper noun *mu-ka-ra* i.e. *mūkárā(s)* 'mouse-head': → Meier-Brügger in *Glotta* 67 1989 p. 45), Vedic *mūṣ-*, Old High German *mūs*, Old Church Slavic *myšь*. However, a *ū* < **uH* may not be ruled out. In a manner analogous to PIE *ī, most of the occurrences of *ū*, may be traced to PIE **uH*. — In the case of PIE *uh$_2$*, the sequence *uḫ*, is still attested in Hittite, cf. PIE *d^huh$_2$-* 'to breath, to steam' and PIE *d^huh$_2$mó-* 'smoke' with Hittite *túḫ-ḫa-an-da-at* i.e. *tuḫḫandat* 'they panted, were short of breath' and *tuḫ-ḫu-u̯a-i-* i.e. *tuḫḫu(u̯a)i-* 'smoke'; compared with *ū* < **uh$_2$* in Latin *fūmus* m. 'steam, smoke,' Vedic *dhūmá-* m., Lithuanian *dū́mai* m. plural, Old Church Slavic *dymъ* m. 'smoke,' Greek θυμός 'vital energy' (→ Meier-Brügger in MH 46 1989 p. 243ff.; S. Zeilfelder in *Graz 2000* p. 497-508).

8) PIE *ē is to be distinguished from *ē*, which derives from **eh$_1$*, cf. L 323 § 1a. The long vowel is most often found in the lengthened grade of morphemes that include *e*, cf. L 409ff. — Examples: — PIE **ph$_2$tḗ(r)* (cf. F 310 § 3) nominative singular 'father' = Greek πατήρ, Vedic *pitā́* (along with full grade in accusative singular Greek πατέρ-α = Vedic *pitár-am*). — PIE **(H)i̯ḗk^{w}r̥-* 'Leber' = Greek ἧπαρ, Later Avestan *yākarə* (along with full grade in genitive singular PIE **Hi̯ek^{w}n-és* = Vedic *yaknás*, cf.

Latin *iecinoris* and F 314 § 6; for information on the word beginning, cf. L 213). — PIE ***h_2*stḗr* nominative singular 'Stern' = Greek ἀστήρ. — An ancient PIE **ē* is presumed to underly the connection of Latin *rēx, rēg-is* 'king' to Vedic *rā́j-*.

An excursus: It is appropriate here to refer to the typically Celtic phonetic rule, *ē* > *ī*. It reveals the Gallic names ending in *-rīx* (*Vercingetorix* etc.; cf. Old Irish *rīg* 'of the king') as genuine and proves that common words in Germanic languages are borrowings from Celtic, including, New High German *reich, Reich* and (*Fried-*)*rich*, Gothic (with *<ei>* in place of *ī*) *reiks* m. 'ruler,' *reiki* n. '*Reich*,' Old High German *rīhhi* 'powerful,' *rīhhi* n. '*Reich*,': → W. Meid in *Althochdeutsch* I 1987 p. 10f. — For information on Hittite-Luwian *ḫe* and *eḫ*, derived from PIE ***h_2*ē* and **ē*h_2, in which the *ē* was conserved intact, cf. L 331.

9) PIE **ō*, like PIE **ē* (cf. § 8), appears predominantly in lengthened grade constructions. In individual IE language constructions it is merged with **e*h_3 (cf. L 323 § 3). — Examples: — PIE **u̯édōr* n. 'body of water' = Hittite *ú-i-da-a-ar* i.e. *u̯idā́r*, Greek ὕδωρ (On its flexion, cf. F 314 § 6). — The Proto-Indo-European root word **dom- / dem-* 'house' had an accusative singular of PIE **dōm* (cf. L 303 and F 320 § 1a), cf. Armenian *town* 'house' and Greek δῶμ-α n. 'house, apartment, temple': → Mayrhofer *Lautlehre* 1986 p. 172 and note 312.

10) Primary PIE **ā* is rare, as is PIE **a*. — The usual IE *ā* developed from PIE **a*h_2 (older PIE **e*h_2). — Although an original **e*h_2 may not be ruled out, the Proto-Indo-European word for 'mother,' which was preserved in some form in most IE languages, possibly contained the primary PIE **ā*: Latin *māter-*; Mycenaean Greek *ma-te* i.e. *mātēr*, Doric μᾱ́τηρ, Ionic-Attic μήτηρ, Vedic *mātár-*; Old Norse *mōđer*, Old English *mōdor*; Old Church Slavic *mati* (genitive singular *mater-e*); Lithuanian *mótė* 'wife' (genitive singular, *móter-s*). Indeed, along with the problem of determining the vowel quality of the first syllable (*-ā-* = Proto-Indo-European **-ā-* or < **-e*h_2*-*), the indications regarding flexion and accentuation of the word 'mother' are equally ambiguous. Two possibilities are thinkable: — a) PIE **méh*$_2$*ter-* (or **mā́ter-*) originally (as in Ancient Greek μήτηρ), secondarily adapted to the paradigm of **ph*$_2$*tér-* (thus Vedic *mātár-*; also represented in Proto-Germanic **mōđér-*, as shown in Old Norse *mōđer* and Old English *mōdor,* cf. L 421 § 1). — b) PIE **meh*$_2$*tér-* (or **mātér-*) = Vedic and Germanic (the Greek stress on the beginning of the word in the nominative comes from the vocative; the suffixal stress in cases other than the nominative is older, for instance in the accusative singular μητέρα: → Mayrhofer EWAia II p. 345).

2. Semivowels

L 212. For the two high vowels, PIE **i* and **u*, reconstruction yields the non-syllabic equivalents PIE **i̯* and **u̯*. At first glance, PIE **i* and **i̯*, and **u* and **u̯* appear to be two pairs of allophones, each of a single phoneme (with complementary distribution of PIE **i* before consonants and PIE **i̯* before vowels, cf. Vedic *i-más* 'we go,' compared with *y-ánti* 'they go'), cf. L 218. Whether this impression is misleading and each of PIE **i* and **i̯*, and **u* and **u̯*, do in fact possess the property of a phoneme is open to discussion: → This is affirmed by Mayrhofer in *Lautlehre* 1986 p. 160f., while B. Forssman voices criticism in *Kratylos* 33 1988 p. 63.

However, independently of these phonological considerations, the assessment of PIE **i̯* and **u̯* is important for the comparative method. PIE **i̯* and **u̯* are also included as secondary components of diphthongs, cf. L 221 and L 223.

L 213. In the languages presently considered, PIE **i̯* is, as a rule, preserved in context-free development. Graphemically, it appears in Latin as <*i*>, in Vedic as <*y*>, and in Germanic, Lithuanian, and OCS as <*j*>. Preceding *a*, Hittite cuneiform employs *i̯a*, otherwise, *i*.

1) Since the 8th century B.C., Greek exhibits as a rule *h-* <῾> in place of *i̯-* (compare ὅς and Vedic *yá-*); in a small group of words, however, *dz-* (older *d*^{j}) <ζ> is found in place of the expected *h-*. Consider the following examples: nom. sg. ζεῦγος 'team (of livestock), couple' in comparison with the Latin nom. pl. *iūgera* 'a morning's worth of land,' i.e. 'that which may be plowed with the help of a pair of oxen in a certain period of time' or poetic Greek ζείδωρος (Homeric and later) 'yielding grain' (with the prefix ζει- < * *d*^{j}*éu̯e-*) in comparison with Vedic *yáva-* m. 'grain.' — Mycenaean, attested c. 1400 B.C. – 1200 B.C., features, in the predominating *h*-group, notations both with word-initial *i̯-*, and without: compare sentence-initial <*jo-*> and <*o-*>. The small *dz*-group is also already established. Compare *ze-u-ke-si* i.e. *d*^{j}*éu̯gesi* dat. pl. 'oxteam.' — The causes for the appearance of these two different groups within Greek are not fully known. Quite a lot seems to indicate that the Greek *h*-group contains remnants that descend from PIE **Hi̯-*, but it is also possible that they descend from PIE *h_1*i̯-* or *h_2*i̯-*. In consequence, Greek *d*^{j}-, or rather *dz-* <ζ-> would be a descendant of PIE **i̯-* (and possibly of PIE *h_3*i̯-* as well).

2) The Greek ὑσμίνη f. 'battle, encounter' (*husmin-* < **hut*^{h}*smin-* < **i̯ud*^{h}*-smin-*) may suggest the origin of Greek *h-* < PIE **Hi̯-*, which I shall call here

thesis 1. According to Indo-Iranian evidence, the verbal root *$\underset{\frown}{i}e\underset{\frown}{u}d^h$-, which underlies the noun, likely featured a word-initial laryngeal and would thus be *$H\underset{\frown}{i}e\underset{\frown}{u}d^h$- 'to enter in motion.' Compare Vedic *yúdh-* f. 'fight' with the composite *amitrāyúdh-* 'fighting enemies' < **amitra-*$H\underset{\frown}{i}ud^h$-, characterized by a long linking vowel *-ā-* < *-aH-*: → LIV 1998 p. 201f. with note 1; see also L 323. — A further example is provided by PIE *$H\underset{\frown}{i}eh_1$- 'to throw' and Attic Greek ἵημι 'I throw': → LIV 1998 p. 201. — Further, compare ὑγιής < *$h_2\underset{\frown}{i}u$-, cf. L 344.

3) The situation is contradictory, for one may equally argue the contrary (which I refer to as thesis 2) and in the case of PIE *$\underset{\frown}{i}e\underset{\frown}{u}g$-, appeal to Greek ζυγόν and ζεῦγος (see above, § 1), tracing the related Vedic imperfect form *āyunak* 'he harnessed (an animal)' with its unexpectedly lengthened augment *ā* back to the apparent form **a-*$H\underset{\frown}{i}ug$-, and thus deduce that in fact the Greek *dz-* (older d^j) < PIE *$H\underset{\frown}{i}$-.

4) Literature for thesis 1: → Peters *Laryngale* 1980 p. 321; J. Schindler in Mayrhofer EWAia II p. 406; J. L. García-Ramón in *GS Schindler* 1999 p. 93f.. — Literature for thesis 2: → B. Forssman in F*S Hoenigswald* 1987 p. 118. — A socio-linguistic explanation, without the help of laryngeals, of the small *dz*-group which comes from the agricultural realm: → C. Brixhe in BSL 74 / 1 1979 p. 249ff.; by the same author, *Phonétique et Phonologie* 1996 p. 18ff.

5) As I have no intention of making a definitive decision on the subject in the present work, the question concerning PIE *$H\underset{\frown}{i}$- / *$\underset{\frown}{i}$- shall no longer be pursued here, and, for the sake of simplicity, when presented with Greek *h-*, PIE *$H\underset{\frown}{i}$- shall be assumed, and when presented with either Greek *dz-* or d^j-, PIE *$\underset{\frown}{i}$- shall be assumed.

L 214. Correspondence sets for word-initial *$H\underset{\frown}{i}$- / *$\underset{\frown}{i}$- (cf. L 213): — PIE *$\underset{\frown}{i}es$- 'to boil' = Myc. *ze-so-me-no* i.e. d^j*esoménōi̯* fut. part. dat. sg., Gr. ζέω 'to boil,' Ved. *yásyati* 'it boils, becomes hot,' OHG *jesan* 'to ferment.' — PIE *$\underset{\frown}{i}\bar{u}s$- (or is, in place of *$\bar{u}$, perhaps *$uH$ better here?, cf. L 211 § 7 the example of PIE *d^huh_2-) 'broth' = Lat. *iūs* n. 'broth,' Gr. ζῦμη (with *-ū-m-* < **-ūs-m-*) 'sourdough,' Ved. *yū̃ṣ-* n. 'soup, broth,' Lith. *jū̃šė* 'fish soup,' OCS *jucha* 'broth, soup' (with *-ch-* < *-s-*, cf. L 309 § 6). — PIE *$H\underset{\frown}{i}e/oh_1$-*r-* 'year, season' = Gr. ὥρα 'season, time of day, hour,' Later Avestan *yār* n. 'year,' Got. *jer*, NHG *Jahr*, Russian-CS *jara* 'spring.' — For information on PIE *$\underset{\frown}{i}ug\acute{o}$- and *$H\underset{\frown}{i}e\underset{\frown}{u}d^h$-, cf. L 213.

L 215. The most important phonetic rules of IE languages have to do with the disappearance of PIE **i̯* between vowels (for example, in Latin, Greek, Hittite, and, under certain conditions, in Germanic) and its assimilations with consonants that it immediately follows. (For examples in Greek: → Lejeune *Phonétique* 1972 §§ 68f., 93ff.)

1) Examples of PIE **i̯* between vowels: — PIE **tréi̯-es* 'three' with *i̯* preserved in Vedic *tráyas*, OCS *trьje*, and without *i̯* in Latin **tre.es* (NB: The period indicates the separation of syllables.) > *trēs*, Cretan Greek τρεες, Lesbian τρης, Ionic-Attic Greek τρεῖς, Old Norse *þrír* < Proto-Germanic **þrii̯iz*: → H. Eichner in *Althochdeutsch* I 1987 p. 190ff. — PIE **$h_2$ei̯es-* (or **ai̯es-*?) n. 'metal' with the preserved *i̯* in Vedic *áyas-* n. 'usable metal, copper, iron,' but no longer with *i̯* in Latin *aer-is* gen. sg. n. < **ái̯es-es* (the nom. sg. *aes* is an analogical formation, based upon the genitive, and not the expected **a.us* < **ai̯os*: → Leumann LLFL 1977 p. 378) and in Latin *aēnus* 'made of bronze' < **a.ez-no-* < **ai̯es-no-*.

2) Examples of PIE **i̯* assimilation with preceding consonants: — PIE **áli̯o-* (or rather **$h_2$éli̯o-*?) 'other' = Ionic-Attic Greek ἄλλος with *li̯* > *ll* (also compare Cypriot *a-i-lo-*, i.e. *ai̯lo-* < **ali̯o-*). This is in contrast to Latin *alius* i.e. [*alii̯o-*] with secondary vocalically formed *i* + transitional sound *i̯*. The consonant grade is attested in Latin, e.g. *veniō* < **g^weni̯ō* < **g^wem-i̯ō* < **g^wm̥-* (The assimilation of *-mi̯-* to *-ni̯-* is only understandable before *i̯* ; a *-mii̯-* would have been preserved.), cf. W 202 § 1. — PIE **méd^{h}i̯o-* 'middle' = Proto-Greek **mét^{h}i̯o-* > Attic μέσος, Doric, Lesbian μέσσος, Boetian, Cretan μέττος with *t^hi̯* > *s(s)* / *t(t)*, but Latin *medius* i.e. [*medii̯o-*] with secondary vocalically formed *i* + transitional sound *i̯*. (For information on word-internal Lat. *d* < PIE **d^h*, see L 336 § 3 below.) — PIE **pédi̯o-* 'belonging to the foot' = Ved. *pádya-* (However, the frequently cited connection to the Greek πεζός 'on foot' [with *-dz-* < *-di̯-*] is problematic because of the final accent; perhaps the Greek word is not at all directly related, but rather based upon the old verbal objective compound **ped-(h_1)i̯-ó-* 'going on foot': → Schwyzer *Griechische Grammatik* I 1939 p. 472). Or, as I. Balles asserts in *Sprache* 39 1997 p. 162, πεζός < **pedi-ó-* 'being on foot' (as opposed to riding).

L 216. IE *u̯* is adopted without change in the presently considered languages. However, the graphemes vary: Lat. <*u/v*>, Ved. <*v*>, Germ. <*w*> etc. In Hittite one finds notations analogous to *i̯*, with *u̯a* (and *u*), *ú*, and seldom *u̯i₅*.

Even in the oldest Greek, *u̯* is preserved: It may be recognized in the graphism of Mycenaean syllables that contain *w* and is noted in several Post-

Mycenaean dialects with the digamma <Ϝ>. However, *u̯* disappeared in Ionic-Attic dialects before the introduction of the alphabet and before the Homeric epics took their final form. Although the Attic-Ionic alphabet, like all Greek alphabets, includes the digamma in sixth position, it is only used to indicate the numerical value six.

Many Homeric words and phrases presume the existence of *u̯*, and must have belonged to the Epic language at a period when *u̯* was still an integral part of the Epic phonetic system, cf. among many examples (another of which is found in L 217 § 1) the regular hiatus before ἄναξ 'lord.' This is only understandable if it is caused by the disappearance of a word-initial *u̯*. In fact, the word is preserved in Mycenaean as *wa-na-ka*, i.e. *u̯anaks* 'king' (For information on Post-Mycenaean semantic development: → LfgrE II *s.v.* βασιλεύς; P. Carlier *La royauté en Grèce avant Alexandre*. Strasbourg 1984). Concerning the digamma in Homer: → B. Forssman in *Colloquium Rauricum* II 1992 p. 283f. § 73.

L 217. Correspondence sets for PIE *u̯*:

1) Word-initial: — PIE **u̯óik̑o-* m. 'settlement, dwelling' = Lat. *vīcus* 'village, settlement,' Myc. Gr. *wo-(i-)ko-de* i.e. *u̯oi̯kon-de*, Arcadian-Thessalian Ϝοικος, Ionic-attic οἶκος (Compare Homer, *Ilias* A 606 and its formulaic ἔβαν οἶκόνδε, with a metrically long (owing to its position) -αν before οἶκον, which is understandable when we accept that while the singers of epics no longer knew the *u̯* from their mother language, they learned from their scholarly oral tradition to pronounce οἶκος with a word-initial vowel insertion [< *u̯*-] in order to furnish the correct position, cf. L 216. Compare also Gothic *weihs* n., OCS *vьsь* f. 'village.' — PIE **u̯ei̯d-* 'to see,' in addition **u̯ói̯d-e* (perfect tense: 'he has seen' >) 'knows,' cf. Latin *vid-ēre*, Lithuanian *veizdḗti*, OCS *viděti* 'to see'; Greek (Ϝ)οἶδε, Ved. *véda*, Got. *wait* 'he knows.' — PIE **u̯ét-es-* n. 'year' = Gr. ἔτος, Ϝετος, Myc. acc. sg. *we-to* i.e. *u̯étos*; Ved. *tri-vat-s-á-* 'lasting three years' (derivation compound with the suffix *-á-*: prefix *tri-*, the subsequent syllable *vat-s-* with zero grade *-s-* of the suffix and not *-as-*); further, compare Lat. *vetus* 'old' (On the origin [by deduction] of the adjective on the basis of the former neuter form *vetus-tāt-* 'age': → M. Leumann in CFS 31 1977 p.127-130), Lithuanian *vẽtušas*, OCS *vetъxъ* 'old.' The root noun **u̯et-*, which exists along with its neuter form **u̯ét-es-*, is still attested in Hittite, compare *ú-it-ti* i.e. *u̯iti* 'year (dat.).'

2) Between vowels: — PIE **néu̯o-* 'new' = Greek dialect νεϜος (Myc. *ne-wo* 'of the current year'), Ved. *náva-* 'new,' Hitt. *néu̯a-* 'fresh' (cf. the instrumental sg. *ne-e-u-it* '[employing] fresh (things)'), OCS *novъ*; Latin *novus* al-

ready with Proto-Italic *-ou̯- < *-eu̯-, cf. L 222 § 2. — In the case of this word, the situation in Latin is all the more complex that the form *novus* itself with its intervocalic *-v-* is a phonetic exception. Expected is rather the disappearance of non-word-initial *u̯* followed by *o/u* in the course of the 2nd to 3rd centuries B.C. However, the *-v-* was able to establish itself in the entire paradigm through analogy to forms which preserve the *-v-* preceding *e/i/a* (cf. genitive sg. *novī*): → Leumann LLFL 1977 p. 137f.; further, cf. E 506 § 3 on the subject of *equus*.

3) Excursus on the Latin *deus* / *dīvus*:

	nom. sg.		gen. sing.
a) Old Latin	*deivos*	and	**deivī*
b) 3rd cent. B.C.	> **dẹ̄vos*	and	> **dẹ̄vī*
c) 3rd/2nd cent. B.C.	**dẹ̄.os* > *dĕ.us*	but	*dīvī*

Commentary: In individual cases, the phonetic situations described in § 2 have led to the disintegration of paradigms. Thus, *deus* 'god/divinity' vs. *dīvus* 'as a divinity, worshiped.' (Several of the forms featured on the table are not attested; although they are marked with *, their assertion is non-controversial.) The 'a' level shows a uniform Old Latin paradigm of the root *dei̯u̯o-* 'divinity' < 'heavenly.' (For more information on this word, cf. W 202 § 2.) On level 'b' is shown the monophthongization of *ei̯* > *ē*, cf. L 220 § 1. A divergent development is shown in level 'c': disappearance of *u̯* when followed by *o/u* (on **dẹ̄.os* > *dĕ.us* cp. Leumann LLFL 1977 p. 105f.), retention when followed by *e/i/a*. From the last stage (c) of development began the formation of two new paradigms: On the one hand, *deus* with the new genitive sg. *deī* 'god'; on the other hand, *dīvī* with the new nom. sg. *dīvus* 'as a divinity, worshiped.' — Compare equally the Classical Latin words *oleum* 'olive oil' vs. *olīva* 'olive, olive tree': The initial forms are **elai̯u̯om* (from which, in a first step, the phenomenon of vowel weakening of middle syllables yields **olei̯u̯om*, and in a second *-ē̯u̯om* > *-e.om* > *-eum*) and **elai̯u̯ā* (from which comes first **olei̯u̯ā*, then *-ẹ̄u̯a* > *-īu̯a*).

4) Postconsonantal *u̯* is also for the most part preserved. However, several phonetic rules of Latin have obscured important correspondence sets. Com-

pare the following examples with **su̯e-* > *suo-* > *so-* (→ Leumann LLFL 1977 p. 47): — PIE **su̯ésor-* f. 'sister' (compare Ved. *svásar-*, Got. *swistar*) = Lat. *soror* (concerning *-r-* < *-s-*, cf. L 309 §1). — PIE **su̯ep-n-* 'sleep' (→ Mayrhofer EWAia II p. 791f., compare Ved. *svápna-*, Old Norse *svefn*) = Lat. *somnus*. — PIE **su̯éḱru-*h_2*-* (itself probably derived from **su̯eḱu̯r̥-*h_2*-* [cf. L 304 § 3] **su̯éḱur-o-* m. 'stepfather') f. 'mother-in-law' (compare Ved. *śvaś-* < **svaś-*, OHG *swigar*, OCS *svekry*; for further information: → Mayrhofer EWAia II p. 675f.) = Lat. *socrus*. — PIE **su̯ói̯do-* 'sweat' (compare Ved. *svéda-*, NHG *Schweiß*) = Lat. *sūdor* (→ H. Rix in *FS Knobloch* 1985 p. 339ff.).

L 218. Independently of syllabic structure, the semivowels PIE **i̯* and **u̯* change allophonically with their corresponding full vowels PIE **i* and **u*, cf. L 212. PIE **i̯* and **u̯* share this allophony with PIE **r*, **l*, **n* and **m*, cf. L 304 and the following. The allophones **i* and **u* are connected to subsequent vowels by means of homorganic glides, resulting in **ii̯* and **uu̯*.

1) The variant forms *-i̯-V-*/*-ii̯-V-* exhibit derivative suffixes with elements containing *-i̯-* on a larger scale, for example *-i̯o*-adjectives (cp. W 202), *-i̯os*-comparatives (cp. F 325 § 1a), and *-i̯e-* present stems (cp. F 203 § 1 LIV type 1q and 1r). — Consideration of Germanic material offers first clues as to the distribution of the variant forms: *-i̯-* follows a light sequence *KV.K* (NB: The period indicates a syllable change.) Cf. Proto-Germanic **χar-i̯a-* = Got. *harjis* 'of the army,' Proto-Germanic **lag-i̯e-* = Got. *us-lagjiþ* 'he/she/it lay.' On the other hand, *-ii̯-* follows a heavy sequence: *KVK.K* or *KV̄.K*. Compare Proto-Germanic **χerð-ii̯a-* = Got. *hairdeis* 'shepherd,' Proto-Germanic **stōđ-ii̯e-* = Got. *ana-stodeiþ* 'he / she / it lifts.' — This phenomenon may be considered, with certain limitations (including the change only from *i̯* to *ii̯*, but not from *ii̯* to *i̯*; no *ii̯*, after *KVKK*), to be PIE and is associated with the name of E. Sievers (Sievers' law). — General literature on Proto-Indo-European and especially Vedic: → Seebold *Halbvokale* 1972 (further, by the same author, in *Kratylos* 46 2001 p. 138-151); J. Schindler in *Sprache* 23 1977 p. 56ff.; Mayrhofer *Lautlehre* 1986 p. 164ff.; Collinge *Laws* 1985 p. 159ff.; Rubio Orecilla *Sufijo de derivación nominal* 1995; cf. W 202 § 1. — On Latin: → Meiser *Laut- und Formenlehre* 1998 p. 89f. — On Greek: C. J. Ruijgh in *Fachtagung Leiden* 1987 [1992] p. 75-99 (published again in Ruijgh *Scripta Minora* II 1996 p. 353-377). — On Celtic: → J. Uhlich "*Die Reflexe der keltischen Suffixvarianten *-i̯o- vs. *-ii̯o- im Altirischen*" in *Deutschsprachige Keltologen* 1992 [1993] p. 353-370. — On Tocharian: → D. Ringe, "*Laryngeals and Sievers' law in Tocharian*" in MSS 52 1991 p. 137-168 .

2) There are also one-syllable variant forms of this type. Compare PIE **k̑u̯ō* ‘dog’ (= Ved. *śvā́*) with the sub-form PIE **k̑uu̯ō* (= Ved. *śuvā́*, Gr. κύων) which appears under certain conditions. Compare also PIE **di̯eu̯-* to **dii̯eu̯-* (cf. F 318 § 6a). For more information on this subject, called the Lindeman Law: → Mayrhofer *Lautlehre* 1986 p. 166f. As J. Schindler so impressively shows (*Sprache* 23 1977 p. 56ff.), the Lindeman law is merely the sandhi variant of Sievers’ law, cf. L 405.

3) For information on the assimilation of *-u̯-* with a following nasal of the PIE type **di̯éu̯m* > **di̯ḗm*, cf. L 303.

3. Diphthongs

L 219. The three vowels PIE **e*, **o* and **a* combine with the semivowels PIE **i̯* and **u̯* and form what are called ‘falling’ or ‘true’ diphthongs such as PIE **ai̯* and **au̯*, compare as an example NHG *Baum* [*báom*]. ‘Climbing’ or ‘false’ diphthongs, for example the French *roi* [*ru̯á*] ‘king,’ are not attested in Proto-Indo-European

The expected, and, in correspondence sets widely attested diphthongs are:

**ei̯*   **oi̯*   **eu̯*   **ou̯*

**ai̯*   **au̯*

In addition it may be asserted that under certain conditions long diphthongs such as PIE **ōi̯* or **ēu̯* may have existed, cf. L 224.

L 220. Information regarding the fate of *-i̯*-diphthongs in Indo-European languages:

1) The three short *-i̯-* diphthongs are preserved as *<ei>*, *<ai>* and *<oi>* in pre-Classical Latin. — In the course of development of Classical Latin in the 2nd century, *ei̯* became the monophthong *ī*, after a transitory *ę̄* phase. — Unaffected by the phonetic circumstances, *oi̯* became *ū*; however, in certain positions, the diphthong *oi̯* was preserved in the slightly modified form *oe <oe>*. For example: *poena* ‘punishment’ vs. *pūnīre* ‘to punish’ and *Poenus* ‘inhabitant of Carthage’ vs. *Pūnicus* ‘Punic.’ Important correspondence sets such as Lat. *vīcus* (= Myc. Gr./ dialect *u̯oi̯ko-*) show the phonetic transformation *u̯oi̯-* > *u̯ei̯-* > *u̯ī-*, influenced by the phonetic environment, in this case, by *u̯-*. — Since the 2nd century B.C., *ai̯* is replaced by *<ae>*, which denotes a diphthong

just as *oe* above. An attestation of this is *Caesar*. As the New High German loanword *Kaiser* shows, the pronunciaton of the word at the time of the borrowing was [*Ka.esar*], cf. E 507 § 3. The pronunciation of *ae* as a monophthong is a post-Classical development.

For further information on all aspects of monophthongization in Latin: → Leumann LLFL 1977 p. 60ff.; Wachter, *Altlateinische Inschriften* 1987 p. 477ff.; H. Rix, "*Latein - wie wurde es ausgesprochen?*" in *Beiträge zur mündlichen Kultur der Römer*, edited by G. Vogt-Spira. Tübingen 1993 p. 11ff.; Meiser *Laut- u. Formenlehre* 1998 p. 57ff.

2) The PIE -*i̯*- short diphthongs are preserved unchanged in Greek as ει, αι, οι.

3) In the case of Indo-Iranian, in which PIE **e*, **o* and **a* merged (cf. L 206), of the three PIE short -*i̯*- diphthongs, one would expect *ai̯* alone to have been preserved, and, that the PIE short -*u̯*- diphthongs would have developed in an analogous way (cf. L 222 § 3). This aspect is preserved in the Old Iranian languages and must also be postulated for the Early Vedic period. In extant Indo-Aryan records, *ai̯* becomes the monophthong *ē* when it precedes a consonant. In traditional Indological transcription practices, this is denoted as <*e*>, since there is no <*ē*> in Old Indo-Aryan (→ Wackernagel / Debrunner *Altindische Grammatik* I 1957 p. 35ff.; Thumb / Hauschild *Handbuch des Sanskrit* I/1 1958 p. 228f.), compare prevocalic *áy-āni* 'I want to go,' but preconsonantal *é-mi* 'I go.' On the other hand, Ved. *ē* <*e*> may be traced to Indo-Iranian *az*, compare Ved. *néd-iṣṭha-* 'the next' with Old Avestan/Later Avestan *nazd-išta-*; Ved. *e-dhi* 'be!' < **as-dhi* [$azd^{h}i$] with *ás-ti* '[you] are': → Wackernagel / Debrunner *Ai. Grammatik* I / 1 1957 p. 37ff.

4) A tendency toward monophthongization is discernible in Hittite – whereas initial PIE **oi̯* and **ai̯* became an open *ę*, PIE **ei̯* became a closed *ẹ*. The latter could become *ī* following a velar. Where open and closed versions are preserved, they both appear (at least in terms of graphical notation) to be denoted as *e*: → H. Eichner in MSS 31 1972 p. 76ff.; Melchert *Anatolian Historical Phonology* 1994 p. 148f.; S. E. Kimball in *Sprache* 36 1994 p. 1ff.

5) In Germanic, PIE **oi̯* and **ai̯* merged to form **ai̯* (as in the case of PIE **o* and **a*, which became **a*, cf. L 206). PIE **ei̯* appears in all ancient Germanic languages as *ī* (Got. <*ei*>, OE, OHG, etc. <*ī*>). Attestations in non-Germanic sources, in which Germanic **ei̯* < PIE **ei̯* should be preserved, are insufficient.

6) In the case of Lithuanian, *ai* represents PIE **oi̯* and **ai̯*; *ei*, on the other hand, represents PIE **ei̯*. In addition, under certain conditions Lithuanian *ie* appears for all three short *-i̯-* diphthongs: → Stang *Vgl. Gramm.* 1966 p. 52ff. — In OCS, PIE **oi̯* and **ai̯* merge to form *ě*, and PIE **ei̯* becomes *i*.

L 221. Following are correspondence sets for the individual diphthongs:

1) Correspondence sets for PIE **ei̯*: — PIE **dei̯u̯ó-* 'heavenly, from the heavens' = OL *deivos* (> Classical Lat. *deus / dīvus*, cf. L 217 § 3), Ved. *devá-* m., Lith. *diẽvas* m. 'god,' ON *tív-ar* nom. plural 'gods.' For more information on this subject, cf. W 202 § 2. — PIE **dei̯ḱ-* 'to point, indicate' (For examples of zero grade PIE **diḱ-*, see above L 211 § 1.) = Lat. *dīcere* 'to announce, determine, speak' (*ex-deic-endum* is preserved in Old Latin), Gr. δείκνῡμι 'I show,' Ved. *deśá-* m. 'area' (< *'direction'), Got. *ga-teihan* 'to report, proclaim,' OHG *zīhan* = NHG *zeihen*. — PIE **ǵ^{h}ei̯-m-* 'winter' = Gr. χεῖμα n. 'winter (storm),' Ved. *hé-man* loc. sg. 'in the winter,' Hitt. *gimmant-* (→ Melchert *Anatolian Historical Phonology* 1994 p. 102, p. 145), Lith. *žie-mà* f., OCS *zi-ma* f. 'winter.'

2) Correspondence sets for PIE **oi̯*: — PIE **(H)ói̯-no-* 'one' = OL *oino(m)* m. 'the one (acc.)' (Classical *ūnus*), Gr. οἴνη f. 'one (as on a die)' (→ Chantraine DELG *s.v.*), Got. *ains* 'one,' Old Prussian *ains* 'alone, only,' cf. F 502 § 1. — PIE **loi̯k^{w}-o-* 'remaining, left over' (with *-o-* ablaut, changes to PIE **lei̯k^{w}-*, Gr. λείπω etc.) = Gr. λοιπός 'remaining,' Lith. *ãt-laikas*, OCS *otъ-lěkъ* 'remnant,' compare Ved. *rék-n̥as-* n. 'inheritance, property,' Proto-Germ. **lai̯χ^{w}-na-* > OHG *lēhan* 'fief.' – Also compare PIE **u̯ói̯ḱo-* and **u̯ói̯de* in L 217 § 1.

3) Correspondence sets for **ai̯*: — PIE **lai̯u̯o-* 'left' = Gr. λαιός, Lat. *laevus*, OCS *lěvъ* 'left.' — PIE **kai̯ko-* 'blind (in one eye)' = Lat. *caecus* 'blind,' Got. *haihs* 'one-eyed.' — For information on problems concerning Proto-Indo-European *a*, cf. L 211 § 5.

L 222. The fate of short *-u̯-* diphthongs in the IE languages:

1) The Proto-Indo-European short *-u̯-* diphthongs **eu̯*, **ou̯* and **au̯*, which are analog to the short *-i̯-* diphthongs are preserved in Greek as ευ ου, and αυ.

2) While <*au*> is preserved in Latin until the classical period, PIE **eu̯* and **ou̯* are already unified as **ou̯* in Proto-Italian; it has been suggested that isolated attestations of OL correspond to *eu̯* (compare *Leucesie*, attested in a *Carmen Saliare*): → Leumann *LLFL* 1977 p. 71; Meiser *Laut- u. Formenle-*

hre 1998 p. 59 § 47,5. Old Latin _ou_ became the monophthong _ū_ in the formation of Classic Latin. But, between word-initial _l_ and a labial, a Latino-Faliscan _ou̯_ appears as _oi̯_ (from which _ei̯_ and _ī_ develop according to phonetic rules. Cf. L 223 § 1 and the example of *_$h_1$léu̯d^hero-_).

3) In a manner parallel to the assimilation of all Proto-Indo-European short -_i̯_- diphthongs in Vedic to _ē_ (<e>, cf. L 220 § 3), the preconsonantal short PIE -_u̯_- diphthongs were assimilated in Vedic to _ō_ (<o>). Compare prevocalic -_hav_- in _ju-hav-āma_ 'we want to pour' vs. preconsonantal -_ho_- in _ju-ho-mi_ 'I pour.' In addition, Vedic _ō_ results from _az̧_, _az_. Compare Vedic _ṣó-ḍaśa_ 'sixteen, _ṣo-ḍhā́_ 'six times' vs. _ṣáṣ_ 'six'; further, _dveṣo-yút_- 'averting enmity (_dvéṣas_-).'

4) Monophthongization, at least of PIE *_eu̯_ to _u_ is discernible as well in Hittite. The case of _ou̯_ and _au̯_ is similar: → Melchert _Anatolian Historical Phonology_ 1994 p. 56 § 8, p. 148f.; S. E. Kimball in _Sprache_ 36 1994 p. 1ff.

5) In Proto-Germanic, *_ou̯_ and *_au̯_ are fused to form *_au̯_ (= Got. <au>, OHG _ou_ and [preceding dentals and Germanic χ] _o_). PIE *_eu̯_ was retained in Proto-Germanic (= Got. _iu_, OHG _eo_ / _io_ / _iu_). For information on Got. <áu> (as a diphthong): → K. Dietz "_Die gotischen Lehnwörter mit au im Altprovenzalischen und die Rekonstruktion des gotischen Lautsystems_" in _Sprachwissenschaft_ 24 1999 p. 129-156.

6) PIE *_ou̯_ and *_au̯_ appear in Lithuanian as _au_, while for *_eu̯_ appear _iu_ and _au_. — The case of OCS is analogous: PIE *_ou̯_ and *_au̯_ > OCS _u_, PIE *_eu̯_ > _ju_.

L 223. Following are correspondence sets for the individual diphthongs:

1) Correspondence sets for PIE *_eu̯_: — PIE *_leu̯k_- 'to light' = Lat. _lūc_-root word (nom. sg. _lūx_) 'light,' _Lūcius_ (OL _Loucios_: the gentile name that derives from the proper noun *_Leu̯kos_), Gr. λευκός 'light, white,' Ved. _rocá_- 'lighting' (concerning _r_, cf. L 301 § 1), Got. _liuhaþ_ n. 'light.' — PIE *_$h_1$leu̯d^h-e-_ Präs.-St. 'to climb, grow' (the Ved. _upā-rúh_- f. 'upward growth' refers, with -_ā_- < *-_a-Hrudh_-, to the initial part of the root, which contains a laryngeal; for information on Gr., cf. § 2; for information on semantics: → LIV 1998 p. 221 note 2) = _ródhati_ 'he/she/it grows'; the nominal PIE *_$h_1$léu̯d^hero-_ 'offspring, freemen, men of the people, people' = Lat. _līberī_ 'children,' _līber_ 'free' (_lībero_- < *_lei̯bero_- < *_loi̯bero_- <Proto-Ital. *_lou̯bero_- < PIE *_$h_1$léu̯d^hero-_: For information on this special phonetic development: → Leumann LLFL 1977 p. 61), Gr. ἐλεύθερος 'free' , OHG _liuti_ 'people,' Old Russian _ljudinъ_ 'free man.' — PIE *_téu̯teh₂_- f. 'people' = Oscan _touto_ and

Umbrian *tota* 'state' (→ Meiser *Umbrisch* 1986 p. 66 and p. 123), Got. *þiuda*, OHG *deot(a), diot(a)* 'people,' Lith. *tautà* 'people, nation, country.'

2) Correspondence sets for PIE **ou̯*: — PIE **lou̯k-ó-* m. 'clearing, clear space' (the nominal form of PIE **leu̯k-* 'to light,' cf. §1) = Lat. *lūcus* (OL acc. sg. m. *loucom*) 'grove, forest' (< *'clearing'), Ved. *loká-* m. 'clear space, world' (no doubt < 'clear[ing]': → Mayrhofer EWAia II p. 481), OHG *lōh* m. 'a grown-over clearing'), Lith. *laũkas* m. 'field, farmland, land.' — Also included are causative stems of the type PIE **b^hou̯dhéi̯e-* 'to awaken' (related to PIE **b^heu̯d^h-* 'to awaken, to become attentive') = Ved. *bodháyati* , OCS *buditi* 'to wake' and PIE **lou̯kéi̯e-* (related to PIE **leu̯k-*, cf. §1) = OL *lūcēre*, Hitt. *lu-uk-ki-iz-zi* i.e. *luk-iṭˢi* 'to ignite' (Further information on the appraisal of both of these forms: → LIV 1998 p. 376f.). — Further included are perfect forms (acc. sg.) with qualitative *o*-ablaut: Compare Gr. εἰλήλουθα (for information on PIE **h₁leu̯d^h-* cf. §1; concerning its meaning, 'to go, come': → LIV 1998 p. 221 note 2; as well as Gr. fut. ἐλευσομαι with *-eu̯s-* < **-eu̯t^h-s-*, aorist, zero grade ἤλυθον).

3) Correspondence set for PIE **au̯*: — PIE **tau̯ro-* m. 'steer' = Gr. ταῦρος, Lat. *taurus*, Lith. *taũras* ('steer, buffalo, aurochs'), OCS *turъ* 'aurochs.' — For information on problems concerning PIE *a*, cf. L 211 § 5.

L 224. Isolated cases of long PIE diphthongs also appear: For example, PIE **ōi̯* and **ēu̯*. They are clearly identifiable in Indo-Iranian (Avest. *āi, āu* = Ved. *ai, au*, contrarily to Ved. *ē, ō* from short diphthongs, cf. L 220 § 3), and in Greek, owing to the Ionic alphabet with the letters η and ω, compare dat. sg. *-ōi̯* <-ῳ>. In individual languages there appear contractions adjacent to closing semivowels (compare PIE **-ōi̯* > Lat. *-ō*), which may also produce the corresponding short diphthong (compare PIE **-ēu̯-* > Gr. -ευ- in the paradigm of *-ēu̯-* derivatives of the type gen. sg. βασιλέως < *-ēu̯-os* [in the Mycenaean period] vs. nom. sg. βασιλεύς).

Examples: — Compare the Proto-Indo-European thematic dat. sg. *-ōi̯*, which was formed through contraction by *-o-* [stem closing] + *-ei̯* [dat. sg. ending]= Gr. -ῳ, Lat. *-ō*, OAv. *-āi*; cf. F 311 § 1. — An example of PIE **-ēu̯-* presumably found in nom. sg. **di̯ḗu̯s* m. 'heavens, god of the heavens, day,' compare Ved. *dyáus* and (when shortened as above) Gr. Ζεύς. For more information on this word, cf. F 318 § 6a. For more information on problems involving diphthongs: → Mayrhofer *Lautlehre* 1986 p. 173ff. On the secondary νηῦς cf. F 318 § 6c.

C. Proto-Indo-European Consonants

1. Liquids and Nasals

L 300. While the PIE liquid consonants *r and *l, and the PIE nasals *m and *n are related to the PIE semivowels *i̯ and *u̯, their syllabic allophones, PIE *[r̥], *[l̥], *[m̥] and *[n̥], are related to full vowels. In their normal, non-syllabic quality they remain unchanged in most Indo-European languages.

L 301. Individual Languages:

1) In the case of Indo-Iranian languages, one observes the phenomenon of dialects that assimilate PIE *r and *l, forming r (e.g.Ved. *rih-*, Avest. *riz-* 'to lick' as opposed to OCS *lizati*; Ved. *rocá-* as opposed to Gr. λευκός, cf. L 223 § 1) as well the phenomenon of those that retain PIE *l (e.g. Late Ved. *lih-*, Mod. Pers. *lištan* 'to lick'; Ved. *loká-* [cf. L 223 § 2]), and finally that of those dialects in which PIE *r and PIE *l are assimilated to become l (e.g. Ved. *lup-* 'to break apart' along with the original Ved. *rup-* 'to tear apart,' Lat. *rumpere* 'to break'; Mid. Indo-Aryan [Aśoka] *lāja* 'king' as opposed to Ved. *rā́jā*, Lat. *rēx* 'king'). See also L 306 § 3 below, with PIE *l̥ representing Ved. *r̥*.

2) The Mycenaean Linear B alphabet does not differentiate l and r, a feature attributable to the fact that the creators of Linear B spoke a non-Indo-European language. Although the difference between l and r was phonologically anchored in their language, the Mycenaean Greeks adopted this peculiar quality in their writing system: → Heubeck in *Res Mycenaeae* 1983 p. 163 f.

3) A final position PIE *-m becomes *-n* in Greek, Hittite, Germanic, and in Baltic as well. (In Lithuanian, postvocalic *-n* is only discernible in the purely graphical nasalization). — Final PIE *-ēr and *-ōr and PIE *-ēn and *-ōn appear in several languages less the final *-r* (or *-n*). Compare Gr. πατήρ 'father' and θυγάτηρ 'daughter' with Ved. *pitā́* 'father' and *duhitā́* (= Lith. *duktė̃*, OCS *dъšti* < **duktē*). Compare Gr. κύων with Ved. *ś(u)vā́* 'dog' and Gr. ἄκμων 'anvil' with Lith. *akmuõ* 'stone.'

L 302. Correspondence sets:

1) PIE *r: — PIE *dóru- n. 'wood' (For declension, cf. F 317 § 8) = Gr. δόρυ, Ved. dā́ru, Hitt. ta-ru-u-i, i.e. taru̯i dat. loc. sg.; compare Got. triu, OCS drěvo 'tree.' — PIE *tréi̯es 'three' (Lat. trēs etc., cf. L 215 § 1).

2) PIE *l: — PIE *melit- 'honey' = Lat. mel, Gr. μέλιτ-ος gen. sg., Hitt. mi-li-it i.e. milit, Got. miliþ. — PIE *leu̯k- 'to shine' (Lat. lūx etc., cf. above L 223 § 1).

3) PIE *m: — PIE *melH- 'to crumble, grind' (→ LIV 1998 p. 388f.; H. Rix in *GS Schindler* 1999 p. 517) = Lat. *molere*, Hitt. *malla-*, Got. *malan*, OCS *mlěti* 'to grind,' compare Ved. (ŚB) *mr̥ṇántas* 'grinding.' — PIE *melit-, cf. §2. — PIE *méh₂ter- (or *mā́ter) 'mother' = Lat. *māter* etc., cf. L 211 § 10. — In final position: PIE *tó-m acc. sg. 'this' = Lat. *is-tum*, Gr. τόν, Ved. *tám*, Got. *þan-a*; PIE *kʷi-m acc. sg. 'which' = Hitt. *ku̯in*; PIE *-o-* stem acc. sg. *-o-m = Lat. *-om* / *-um*, Gr. -ον, Ved. *-am*, Hitt. *-an*, Old Prussian *-an*, Lith. *-ą* etc.

4) PIE *n: — PIE *sen- 'old' = Lat. *senex* with gen. sg. *senis*, Gr. ἕνος, Ved. *sána-*, Got. *sin-ista* 'oldest (m.),' Lith. *sẽnas* 'old.' — PIE *néu̯o- 'new' = Lat. *novus* etc., cf. L 217 § 2.

L 303. In several morphologically important cases, semivowels and laryngeals are assimilated to post-positioned *-m*(-), which is associated with the compensatory lengthening of a pre-positioned short vowel.. The phenomenon is known as Stang's law, or Lex Stang: → Szemerényi *Scripta Minora* II 1987 (in an essay from 1956) p. 801ff; Chr. S. Stang in *FS Kuryłowicz* 1965 p. 292ff. = Stang *Opuscula* 1970 p. 40ff; Mayrhofer *Lautlehre* 1986 p. 163f.

Prime examples: — Pre-PIE *d(i)i̯éu̯m acc. sg. 'heavens, god of the heavens, day' > Pre-PIE *d(i)i̯émm > PIE *d(i)i̯ḗm = Ved. *dyā́m*, Epic Gr. Ζῆν (with secondary interpretation as Ζῆν' in the sense of Ζῆνα), Lat. *diem* (On the shortening of long vowels: → Leumann LLFL 1977 p. 225). For more information on this word, cf. F 318 § 6a. — Pre-PIE *gʷóu̯-m acc. sg. 'cow' > Pre-PIE *gʷómm > PIE *gʷṓm = Ved. *gā́m*, Ep. Gr. βῶν in the sense of 'a shield of bovine leather' (the usual acc. sg. βοῦν is reconstructed in an analogous manner). — The acc. sg. fem. of *-eh₂*-stems leads to Pre-PIE *-ah₂m (cf. L 323 § 2) > Pre-PIE *-amm > PIE *-ām (Gr. -ᾱν/-ην; Lat. *-am* [with shortening of the long vowel preceding *m*, as in the case of *diem*]). — A further problem: — In the case of accusative plural forms of *-eh₂-* stems, Pre-PIE *-ah₂ns (based upon *-eh₂-m-s, but affected by *eh₂* > *ah₂* and the assimilation of *-ms* > *-ns*) leads to Pre-PIE *-āns, and from there, > PIE *-ās. Compare Ved. *-ās*, Got. *-ōs*. (→ J.

Schindler in *GS Kronasser* 1982 p. 194 note 42; initially as a sandhi variant?) Analogously, the acc. pl. of Pre-PIE *g^w*o*u̯-m-s* leads via Pre-PIE *g^w*ou̯ns* > Pre-PIE *g^w*onns* > Pre-PIE *g^w*ōns*, and from there, just as the preceding > PIE *g^w*ōs*, compare Ved. *gā́s*, Doric Gr. βῶς. For more information on PIE *g^w*ou̯-*, cf. F 318 § 6b. — On the PIE acc. sg. **dōm* 'house' < pre-PIE **dom-m*, cf. F 320 § 1a; on the PIE acc. sg. *d^h*éǵ*^{h}*ōm* < pre-PIE *d^h*éǵ*^{h}*om-m* cf. F 321 § 1.

L 304. In many positions, but particularly between consonants (*KRK*) and in final position following a consonant (*-KR#*), the so-called sonorants, PIE **r*, **l*, **m* or **n* (which includes PIE **i̯* and *u̯*, cf. L 212) become the syllabic allophones *[*r̥*], *[*l̥*], *[*m̥*], and *[*n̥*] (with the vowels **i* and **u*). Compare PIE *b^h*er-* 'to carry': The *-tó-* verbal adjective requires the zero grade form of the root, which thus appears phonetically as PIE *b^h*r̥-tó-*.

1) The fundamental rule for the production of syllabic allophones functions iteratively (nonsyllabic-syllabic-nonsyllabic, etc.). Further, in the series *KRRK*, the second sonant is affected first. On the subject of the iterative quality, compare PIE **ḱu̯n-és* gen. sg. 'dog' => **ḱun-és* (the ending *-és* remains, the preceding *-n-* is non-syllabic and includes syllabic *u* with itself) = Ved. *śúnas*. Concerning the use of the second sonant before the first, compare PIE **ḱu̯n-*b^h*-* with *-*b^h*-* case => **ḱu̯n̥-*b^h*-* (and not **ḱun-*b^h*-*) = Ved. *śvábhis*.

2) Several exceptions to this fundamental rule are known, for example the word-initial PIE **mn-eh*$_2$*-* 'to think of' (as opposed to the expected **m̥n-eh*$_2$*-*), or the *-n-*present form PIE **i̯ung-* 'to harness' (as opposed to the expected form **i̯u̯n̥g-*), or the paradigm of PIE **tréi̯-es* 'three' the genitive plural **trii̯ōm* with syllabic *i* + transitional sound *i̯* (cf. L 218; according to the rule, one would expect **tr̥i̯ōm* with syllabic *r* and non-syllabic *i̯*). For further information: → J. Schindler in *Sprache* 23 1977 p. 56f. Further, for information on PIE **m°ǵ-*, cf. L 203.

3) The metathesis of PIE **u̯r̥* before *K/#* > **ru* presents an interesting special case. Compare the example of Gr. ἱδρύω 'to seat, to install a place of worship < *to create the seat of a divinity' < Proto-Gr. **s°du̯r̥-i̯e-* (On the subject of the weak vowel °, the so-called schwa secundum, cf. L 203; for information on *s-* > *h-* cf. L 309 § 2.): The verb represents a factitive *-i̯e-* present form of **séd-u̯r̥* n. 'seat'; compare the parallel Attic construction βλίττω 'to harvest honey, to cut honeycombs' < **mlit-i̯e-* from **melit-* 'honey' (cf. L 302 § 2 above). From whom it was that I first learned of the example ἱδρύω, I can no longer say, although perhaps it came up in a course

given by J. Schindler at Harvard in the Fall Term of 1980. The excellence of the questionable analysis of ἱδρύω is shown by dubious efforts such as "obvious derivation from *ἱδρῦς" (→ Peters *Laryngale* 1980 p. 98). A treatment that approaches a solution, however without bringing metathesis into account, is: → C. J. Ruijgh in *GS Kuryłowicz* I 1995 p. 353 note 34 with the remark "dérivé de **séd-ru-*?" — Further examples: → Mayrhofer *Lautlehre* 1986 p. 161f.; concerning PIE **su̯éḱu̯r̥-*h_2- also cf. L 217 § 4 above; for information on PIE **k*^{w}*tru-K-* < **k*^{w}*tu̯r̥-K-* 'four' also cf. F 501 below. For a derivation of 'four' with metathesis, bringing Hittite *kutruen-* 'witness' into account: → Rieken *Nom. Stammbildung* 1999 p. 289 note 1385.

Perhaps the juxtapositioning of PIE **u̯l̥k*^{w}*o-* (= Ved. *vŕ̥ka-* etc., cf. L 307 § 2) and **luk*^{w}*o-* may be explained by the same process. Concerning **luk*^{w}*o-*, compare Lat. *lupus* and Gr. λύκος. The Latin *lupus* is likely a loanword from Oscan. The development of *-p-* < *-k*^{w}*-* is not Latin. **luk*^{w}*o-* is dissimilated to *luko-* in Greek.

L 305. In constrast to the clarity of the state of affairs concerning liquids, only through the astute combination of comparative and language-internal methods could the syllabic nasals *[*m̥*] and *[*n̥*] be designated as allophones of PIE **m* and **n*. Since the relationship Ved. *man-* 'to think': *matá-* 'thought' corresponded perfectly to that of Ved. *bhar-* : *bhr̥tá-*, it was possible, given the relation *bhar-* : *bhr̥-* = *man-* : *x* for *x* (= Ved. *ma-*), to postulate **mn̥-*. The language comparison shows that the *-a-* of the Vedic *ma-(tá-)* and *ma-tí-* f. 'thinking' corresponds only in Greek to an *-a-* (cf. the compound, αὐτό-ματος 'it/himself striving, of its/his own volition,' attested since Homer), but in Latin corresponds rather to an *-en-* (cf. *menti-* 'thought power, thought technique, thought' with the nom. sg. *mēns*, gen. sg. *mentis*: → Reichler-Béguelin *Typ mēns* 1986 p. 19ff.), in Germanic to *-un-* (Got. *ga-munds* 'remembrance'), in Lithuanian, *-in-* (*mintìs* 'thoughts'), and in Old Church Slavic *-ę-* (*pa-mętь* 'memory'). These disparities led precisely to the common denominator *-*n̥*-, which was originally taken from Old Indian material.

The existing knowledge of *nasalis sonans* may be traced to Karl Brugmann "*Nasalis sonans in der indogermanischen Grundsprache*" in *Studien zur griechischen und lateinischen Grammatik* (edited by G. Curtius and, starting with volume 9, together with K. Brugman[n]) 9 1876 p. 285ff. Brugmann had predecessors, including the fifteen year old pupil Ferdinand de Saussure (1857-1913). According to his own account, he revealed Gr. -α- < *-*n̥*-:

Nous lûmes ... un texte d'Hérodote ... [qui] contenait la forme τετάχαται. La forme τετάχαται était pour moi complètement nouvelle ... A l'instant où je vis la forme τετάχαται, mon attention, extrêmement distraite en général ... fut subitement attirée d'une manière extraordinaire, car je venais de faire ce raisonnement, qui est encore présent à mon esprit à l'heure qu'il est: λεγόμεθα : λέγονται, par conséquent τετάγμεθα : τετάχΝται, et par conséquent N = α

→ C. Watkins *Remarques sur la méthode de Ferdinand de Saussure comparatiste* in CFS 32 1978 [1979] p. 61 (= Watkins *Selected Writings* I 1994 p. 266); Kohrt *Problemgeschichte* 1985 p. 112ff.

L 306. The remnants of the PIE allophones *[*r̥*], *[*l̥*], *[*m̥*] and *[*n̥*] vary in nearly all of the IE languages. Only in the case of Old Indo-Iranian is the relationship between *bhar-* and *bhr̥tá-* still quite clear. That is why the Old Indian grammarians were able to develop an ingenious ablaut system, cf. L 413 § 1 below. For example, the Ved. [*r̥*] is represented in Latin by *-or-* (cf. *fors*, *for-ti-* 'chance' < **b^{h}r̥-ti-*), in Germanic, by *-ur-* (cf. NHG *Ge-bur-t*) etc.

1) Latin retains the PIE syllabic liquids *[*r̥*] and *[*l̥*] as *or* and *ol*, and the PIE syllabic nasals *[*m̥*] and *[*n̥*] as *em* and *en* (and secondarily as *in*, cf. L 108).

2) In Greek, PIE *[*r̥*] and *[*l̥*] became ρα/αρ and λα/αλ; in dialects, ρο/ορ, λο/ολ as well. For details: → Lejeune *Phonétique* 1972 § 201; Risch *Kl. Schr.* 1981 (in an essay from 1966) p. 266ff. PIE *[*m̥*] and *[*n̥*] yielded α; in dialects, also ο: → Risch l.c. Preceding vowels, semivowels, and laryngeal/vowel combinations, αμ and αν represent the normal case. On the subject of **R̥H* in Greek, cf. L 332 below.

3) IE *[*r̥*] and *[*l̥*] are preserved as syllabic liquids in Old Indo-Aryan (not to mention Indo-Iranian), and as *r̥* (which corresponds to Avestan *ərə*) in Vedic. The only Vedic root containing *-l̥-* in its zero grade, *kalp- / kl̥p-* 'to add, equip' has no sure explanation. (Perhaps PIE **k^{w}erp-*, if it corresponds to Vedic *kr̥p-* 'figure' and Latin *corpus*: → Mayrhofer EWAia I p. 324). The syllabic PIE nasals *[*m̥*] and *[*n̥*] appear as *a*, preceding vowels and semivowels, as *am* or *an*.

4) In Hittite, PIE *[*r̥*] and *[*l̥*] developed into *ar* and *al*. The PIE syllabic nasals are presumably represented by *an*: → Melchert *Anatolian Historical Phonology* 1994 p. 125f., which contains further details.

5) The remaining three language families that are treated here have in common, that in each of them corresponding non-syllabic *r*, *l*, *m*/*n* formed from PIE *[*r̥*], *[*l̥*], and *[*m̥*] (or *[*n̥*]). Cf. in Germanic, the sequence *ur*, *ul*, *um*, and, *un* (with consequent developments in IE languages), in Lithuanian *ir*, *il*, *im*, and, *in* (for information on the intonation, cf. L 332 § 4d), and in Proto-Slavic, **ьr*, **ьl*, **ьm* and **ьn* (= OCS [*rь*/*rъ*], [*lь*/*lъ*] and *ę*).

L 307. Correspondence sets:

1) PIE *[*r̥*]:— PIE **ḱr̥d-* 'heart' (full grade **ḱerd-* in OSax. *herta*, NHG *Herz*) = Lat. *cor* (stem: *cord-*), Epic Gr. κραδίη, Attic καρδία, Hitt. *kard-*, Lith. *širdìs*, OCS *srъdь-ce*. — PIE **ḱr̥-n-* 'horn' = Lat. *cornū*, Ved. *śr̥ṅga-*, Proto-Germ. **χurna-* = Runic *horna*, ON, OHG *horn* with *o* through *-a-*umlaut and Got. *haurn* through breaking, cf. L 208. — PIE **mr̥-tó-* 'dead' = Epic Gr. βροτός 'immortal' (the pronunciation -ρο- < *-r̥-* betrays the Aeolic origin of this word; the Greek meaning 'mortal' must be secondary in comparison to 'dead' and was probably attained through back derivation from the negated verbal adjective ἄμβροτος 'immortal = not mortal' [< PIE **n̥-mr̥-to-*]: → Seiler *Sprache und Sprachen* 1977 [in an essay from 1952] p. 81 note 8), Ved. *mr̥tá-* (Avest. *mərəta-*) 'dead' (equally here mentioned, OHG *mord* 'murder' < **murþa-* was probably abstracted within the Germanic realm from **murþra-*, compare OHG *murdr-eo* 'murderer': → Bammesberger *Urgerm. Nomen* 1990 p. 85f. and p. 182). Further, compare the corresponding nominative active **mr̥-tí-* 'dead' = Lat. *mors* (stem: *morti-*), Lith. *mirtìs*, OCS *sъ-mrьtь* 'dead,' cf. F 317 § 7. — PIE **str̥-tó-* 'struck down' = Gr. στρατός (Lesbian and Boetian στροτός) 'army' (concerning the subject of semantics: → Strunk *Nasalpräsentien und Aoriste* 1967 p. 111 with note 109), Ved. *á-str̥ta-* (Avest. *a-stərəta-*) 'insuperable.'

2) PIE *[*l̥*]: — PIE **ml̥dú-* with f. **ml̥du̯-íh*$_2$*-* 'soft' = Lat. *mollis* < **moldu̯i-* (however, the tracing of *-ol-* < *-*l̥*- is not necessarily the case; equally possible is the *-e-* grade form [with the secondary development of *-eld-* to *-old-*], as may be shown in the case of other Latin adjectives. Compare *brevis* 'short' < **mreǵ*^{h}*u̯i-* 'short': → H. Fischer in MSS 52 1991 p. 7), Gr. βλαδύς 'slack,' Ved. *mr̥dú-* f. *mr̥dvī́-* 'soft.' — PIE **u̯l̥k*^{w}*o-* m. 'wolf' = Ved. *vŕ̥ka-*, Proto-Germ. **u̯ulχ*^{w}*a-* (= Got. *wulfs* with the assimilation of **u̯* - *χ*^{w} to **u̯* - *f*), Lith. *vil̃kas*, OCS *vlьkъ* (to **lúk*^{w}*os* > Gr. λύκος cf. L 304 § 3). — PIE **pl̥h*$_2$*-i-* 'wide' = Hitt. *palḫi-*; with another suffix, PIE **pl̥h*$_2$*-nó-* = Lat. *plānus*, cf. L 332 § 4e.

3) PIE *[*m̥*]: — PIE **dḱm̥-tó-* (On the initial dissimilation > **h*$_1$*ḱm̥-tó-* cp. F 502 § 13 below.) 'hundred' = Lat. *centum*, Gr. ἑκατόν (Arcadian ἑκοτόν),

Ved. *śatám* (Avest. *satəm*), Got. *hund-* 'hundred,' Lith. *šim̃ta-s* 'hundred'; PIE **déḱm̥-to-* 'the tenth' = Gr. δέκατος (Arcadian/Lesbian δέκοτος), Got. *taihunda*, Lith. *dešim̃tas*, OCS *desętъ*.

4) PIE *[n̥]: — On PIE **mn̥-tó-*, **mn̥-tí-* (Ved. *matá-*, *matí-* etc.), cf. L 305. — The PIE negation **n̥-* 'un-, non-, -less' = Lat. *in-* (< **en-*, cf. L 108) in *in-somnis* 'sleepless' etc., Gr. (οὐκ) ἀ-θεεί; '(not) without a God,' ἄν-υδρος 'without water,' Ved. *a-pútra-* 'without a son,' *an-udrá-* 'without water,' NHG *un-schön*, etc. — PIE **b^{h}n̥ǵ^{h}ú-* 'abundant' = Gr. παχύς 'well-nourished,' Ved. *bahú-* (~ full grade in the superlative *báṃh-iṣṭha-* 'most dense'), in addition, probably Hitt. *pangu-* 'entirety,' OHG *bungo* 'nodule.' Cf. L 348 § 2; on the verbal root **b^{h}eug^h-* see LIV 1998 p. 61. — PIE **n̥s-* 'us' (compare the Latin lengthened grade *nōs*) = NHG *uns*, Hitt. *an-za-a-aš* i.e. *ant^s-ās* 'us' (On *t^s* in place of *s* cf. L 309 § 4), further, compare the expanded **n̥s-mé* in Ved. *asmā́n* 'us'; in Gr. **n̥s-mé* > **asmé* > **ammé* = Aeolic/Homeric ἄμμε (with Lesbian retraction of the accent), in Doric, in place of **ammé*, with disposal of the double-consonant through compensatory lengthening ἀμέ, in Ionic-Attic again compensatory lengthening **āmé* with secondary aspiration and the additional nom. pl. ending *–es* > ἡμεῖς and the accusative plural ending *-n̥s* > ἡμέ+ας > ἡμᾶς 'us.' Cf. also F 401 § 2 below.

2. Continuants *s* (and *þ*?)

L 308. Proto-Indo-European contained the voiceless dental-alveolar fricative **s*, to which no voiced counterpart (the phoneme **z*) corresponded. It is possible however that when **s* was followed by a voiced plosive, it became the allophone *[*z*]. Although the accuracy of the allophone *z* is certain, for practical reasons the phonetically correct notation is generally avoided in favor of the phonemically correct notation. For example, PIE **h_2ó-sd-o-* 'branch' is reconstructed in place of *[*h_2ó-zd-o-*], cf. L 102 and L 310.

L 309. The situation in the Indo-European languages:

1) In the very oldest Latin, Indo-European **s* was preserved in all positions. A decisive change, rhotacism, indicating the development of *VrV* from *VsV*, took place in the course of the documented history of Latin, probably around 350 B.C. Old Latin *ESED*, known from inscriptions, corresponds to Classical Latin *erit*. L. Papirius Crassus (*praetor* 340 B.C.) writes his given name, formerly *Papīsius*, for the first time without *-s-*. Rhotacism clarifies the

frequent variations of *s*/*r* within paradigms and word families. — Example: Cf. *es-se* 'to be' with *es-t* and *es-set* as opposed to *er-at* and *er-it*; cf. *ges-tus* (past participle) as opposed to *ger-ō* < **ges-ō* (present stem) 'to carry, lead'; cf. *flōs* nom. sg. 'flower, bloom' as opposed to gen. sg. *flōr-is*; cf. *hones-tus* 'honored, honorable,' *honōs* 'honor' (an old nom. sg., used as an archaism and in poetry) as opposed to *honor* (a nom. sg. obtained from the gen. sg. *honōr-is*): → Leumann LLFL 1977 § 180. See also E 503 § 4.

2) In Greek, PIE **s* is preserved when adjacent to plosives or in word-final position. Word-initially, it becomes *h-* (i.e. *spiritus asper* < ῾->). It is subject to what is called Grassmann's Law, cf. L 348 § 2. In Aeolic and parts of Ionic the word-initial aspirate disappears, a feature which is called psilosis. This development explains, for example, why one says *India* and not **Hindia*: For the non-aspirated word we have the Ionic Greeks to thank, who learned of the region from the Persians initially as *Hindu-* [< *Sind*^{h}*u-* 'Indus region']. — Word-internal *-s-* between vowels becomes *-ø-*, cf. θεός 'god' < *t^hh_1s*-ó-* (cf. E 507 § 2). — For more information on this subject: → Lejeune *Phonétique* 1972 § 82ff.; Brixhe *Phonétique et phonologie* 1996 p. 43. — On dialectal *-si-* < *-ti-* cp. L 336 § 2.

3) In Vedic, PIE **s* is generally preserved. — In what is known as the *ruki*-rule, **s* becomes *ṣ* when it follows *r* [*r̥*], *u*, *k*, *i*, and also after *e* or *o* that developed from original *ai̯* and *au̯* (cf. L 220 § 3), cf. E 502 § 6 with the example of *éṣi*. For more information: → M. Hale "Postlexical RUKI and the *tisrá*-Rule" in *FS Watkins* 1998 p. 213ff. — In Old Indian texts, word-final *-s* (and *-r*) appear only as such in certain phonetic positions; in the pausal form they appear as *ḥ*, which is called *visarga*. In today's Indo-European linguistics, the pausal form is avoided in citing individual forms in favor of inserting the simple stem. For example, *ávi-* 'sheep' and not *áviḥ* (cf. p. XX). When the entire form is needed, it is noted without sandhi with the underlying *-s* or *-r*. (For example, voc. sg. *bhrā́tar* and not *bhrā́taḥ*).

4) In general, PIE **s* is preserved in Hittite. In special cases, however, it is replaced by t^s. Compare PIE **n̥s-* with Hitt. *an*t^s*-*, cf. L 307 § 4: → Melchert *Anatolian Historical Phonology* 1994 p. 121.

5) PIE **s* is preserved in Germanic. However, along with the Germanic voiced fricatives, it is subject to Verner's Law, according to which it becomes *z* (= Got. *z*, ON, OHG *r*), cf. L 421 § 2.

6) In Baltic and Slavic, PIE **s* is preserved in most positions. In the case of Slavic, a process similar to the Vedic (Indo-Iranian) *ruki*-rule of § 3 changed pre-vocalic PIE **s* following *i, u, r, k* (probably via **š*) to Old Church Slavic *x*.

A similar $s > š$ change in Lithuanian affects only a part of the cases that come into question: → Stang *Vergleichende Grammatik* 1966 p. 94ff.

L 310. Correspondence sets for PIE **s*: — PIE **seǵʰ-* (zero grade **sǵʰ-*) 'to overpower' = Ved. *sáhate*, OHG *sigu* m. 'victory,' Gr. zero grade thematic aor. ἔ-σχ-ον of the full grade thematic pres. ἔχω 'to hold, to posess' (ἔχω by aspirate dissimilation [cf. L 348 § 2] < **hekʰ-* < **seǵʰ-* [with the typically Greek transformation of *mediae aspiratae* into *tenues aspiratae*, cf. L 336 § 2]) and the Fut. ἕξω (here *heks-* without aspirate dissimilation < **hekʰs-*: The consonant group *–ks-* < *-kʰs-* was formed just early, and thus, during the period of activity of Grassmann's Law, could no longer play a dissimulative role: → Meier-Brügger *Gr. Sprachw.* I 1992 p. 59 § E 211.4; also cf. Ved. *bandh-* vs. Fut. *bhantsyati*, cf. L 348 § 3). — PIE **h₂eu̯s-* 'ear' = Lat. *auris* (~ *aus-cultō* 'eavesdrop'), Got. *auso*, OHG *ōra* n. 'ear' = Lith. *ausìs* f., OCS *uxo* n. 'ear.' — PIE **h₁és-ti* 'he is' and PIE **h₁esi* 'you are' (For information on the simplification, during the PIE period, of original **h₁es-si*, cf. L 312) = Lat. *est, es,* Gr. ἐστί, εἶ, Ved. *ásti, ási*, Hitt. *ēs-tˢi, ēsi* (for information on the lengthening of stressed vowels in Hitt., cf. L 207), Got. *ist, is*, Lith. *ẽsti, esì.* — PIE **h₂ó-sd-o-* m. 'branch' (concerning phonetic pronunciation **[ózdo-]*, cf. L 102; on word-initial sounds: → H. C. Melchert in HS 101 1988 p. 223 note 16 with the comparison, already made by E. H. Sturtevant, with Hitt., *ḫasdu̯er* 'timber, brushwood') = Gr. ὄζος (with <ζ> = [*zd*]), Got. *asts.* — PIE **ǵénh₁-os* nom. sg. 'gender' with gen. sg. **ǵénh₁-es-os* 'gender' = Lat. *genus*, *generis* (with *-eri-* < **-ese-*), Ionic-Epic Gr. γένος, γένευς (with *-eu̯-* < *-e.o-* < *-eho-* < **-eso-*). — PIE **u̯es-* 'to wear, to be clothed' = Ved. *vás-te*, Hitt. *ú-e-eš-ta* i.e. *u̯ēs-ta* 'wears,' compare Gr. ἕννυμι (present stem **u̯es-nu-* along with Aor. ἕσ-σαι) 'I dress (myself),' Lat. *ves-ti-s* 'robe,' Got. *wasjan* 'to clothe' and cf. L 211 § 4. — PIE **pis-tó-* 'he crushes' = Lat. *pistus*, Ved. *piṣṭá-*, compare OCS *pьxati* 'to push.' — PIE **steh₂-* (> **stah₂-*, cf. L 323 § 2) 'to stand' = Lat. *stāre* (which is not directly traced to a root aorist as is the *communis opinio*, but is rather contracted from **steh₂-i̯e-*: → Meiser *Laut- und Formenlehre* 1998 p. 187), Dor. Gr. ἵστᾱμι (<**si-stah₂-*), cf. Ved. *sthā-trá-* n. 'location,' OHG *stān* 'to stand,' Lith. *stóti*, OCS *stati* 'to place oneself.' — PIE **h₂eu̯s-* (> **h₂au̯s-*, cf. the examples in L 323 § 2) 'to light up (sunrise),' compare Lat. *aurōra* (< **au̯sōs-ā*), Proto-Gr. **au̯sōs* > **au̯u̯ōs* > Lesbian Aeolic αὔως, Ion. ἠώς and Att. ἕως (on the phonetic developments in Greek, with **au̯.u̯ōs* vs. **au̯u̯.ōs* > **āu̯ōs*: → Ruipérez *Opuscula* 1989 p. 237 and p.

247), Ved. *uṣ-ás-* f., Lith. *auš-rà* f. 'sunrise.' — Also compare NHG *uns*, Hitt. *ant^s^-*, cf. L 307 § 4.

L 311. In ancient Indo-European languages there are indisputable cases in which *s-* alternates with *ø-*, often within the same language. For example, Gr. στέγος n. (in tragedies, Hellenic Greek, and in later prose) alongside τέγος (occurring as early as the Odyssey, but not in tragedies) 'roof'; Ved. *spaś-* (< **speḱ-* = Lat. *speciō*, NHG *spähen*) alongside *paś-* 'to see': → Mayrhofer EWAia II p. 107f.; NHG *schlecken* (< mhd. *sl-*) alongside *lecken*. In this context, one speaks of the phenomenon of the moveable *s*. — It remains open to question whether or not **steh₂-* was formed with such a moveable *s*: → M. V. Southern in MSS 60 2000 p. 100ff. (He argues that Lat. *tabula* should be included in this group). — For more information on the interpretation of this phenomenon and on literature treating it: → Mayrhofer *Lautlehre* 1986 p. 119f.; Szemerényi *Einführung* 1990 p. 98f. and cf. L 405.

L 312. In practice, the pre-PIE geminate simplification rule concerns primarily PIE **s*. Thus, the association of the PIE root **h₁es-* 'to exist,' with the Proto-Indo-European 2nd person singular morpheme, yielded, via **h₁és-si*, to PIE **h₁ési* 'you are' (= Gr. εἶ; in forms such as the Epic-Homeric ἐσσί, the more transparent form developed secondarily; For more information on the conjugation of this verb, cf. E 502-505). In the same fashion, the simplification of *-s.s-* in the dat./loc. pl. of **ǵénes-su* must have occurred at a pre-Proto-Indo-European period. The dative plural forms of the type γένεσι are thus old: → A. Morpurgo Davies in *FS Palmer* 1976 p. 188.

L 313. In many treatments, a further PIE fricative is taught: '**þ*' with an allophone **[ð]* that is both voiced and aspirated. Called 'thorn,' this should clarify some uncontroversial correspondence sets in which some IE languages show a retained *-t-* sound and others show a retained *-s-* sound.

1) Examples: — 'bear' with Gr. ἄρκ-τ-ος in comparison with Ved. *ŕ̥k-ṣ-a-*, Lat. *ur-s-us*. (For more details on this word: → Mayrhofer EWAia I p. 247f.) — 'earth' with Gr. χ-θ-ών in comparison to Ved. *k-ṣ-ám-* (For more details on this word: → Mayrhofer EWAia I p. 424f. For information on declension cf. F 321 § 1). — 'to reside' with Myc. Gr. *ki-ti-je-si*, i.e. *ktii̯ensi* 'they reside' in comparison with Ved. *kṣiyánti*, Lat. *situs* 'situated' (Further details: → Mayrhofer EWAia I p. 427; concerning the same root as *si-tus*, including Lat. *pōnō* < **po-si-nō*: → H. Rix in *Kratylos* 38 1993 p. 87).

2) First researched in the twentieth century, the IE languages Hittite (cf. E 410) and Tocharian (cf. E 408) have contributed significantly to examples of this type: The sequence $k^{(h)}$-$t^{(h)}$, attested in Greek, corresponds to an inverse sequence ($t^{(h)}$-$k^{(h)}$) in Hittite and Tocharian. In Hittite, 'earth' appears in nom./acc. sg. as *te-e-kán* i.e. *tēgan* (further attestations in Tischler, *HEG* III p. 292ff.), and in Tocharian A as *tkaṃ*. The Hittite nom. sg. *ḫar-tág-ga-aš* i.e. *ḫartkas*, appears to mean 'bear' (further attestations, including suggestions for further reading: → Puhvel HED III p. 201f.).

3) Thus, in place of PIE $*g^h\eth\ m$- ('earth'), a reconstruction of a paradigm with conventional consonants appears correct: Hitt. strong stem with nom. sg. *tēkan* < PIE $*d^h\acute{e}\acute{g}^h\bar{o}m$ and weak stem with gen. sg. *takn-* < Proto-Anat. $*d^{h\circ}g^hm$- < PIE $*d^h\acute{g}^hm$-. While Anatolian, thanks to the schwa secundum, was able to keep the sound group paradigm-internal, elsewhere PIE $*d^h\acute{g}^hm$- was simplified to $*\acute{g}^hm$-. Compare: Gr. χαμαί 'on the earth,' Lat. *humī* 'on the ground' (from which, secondarily, *humus* f. 'ground' developed: → Wackernagel *Vorlesungen* II 1928 p. 32), Lith. *žẽmė*, OCS *zemlja* 'earth.' Finally, in such a case as that of the loc. sg. PIE $*d^h\acute{g}^h\acute{e}m$, the tautosyllabic $*d^h\acute{g}^h$- was transformed to $*\acute{g}^hd^h$-, upon the basis of which both Gr. k^ht^h <χθ> and Ved. *kṣ* may be understood. For more information on the paradigm of 'earth', cf. F 321 § 1.

4) The exemplary treatment of the subject is that of J. Schindler, "A Thorny Problem" in *Sprache* 23 1977 p. 25-35. Further: → Mayrhofer *Kleine Schriften* II 1996 p. 255-270 (in a report from 1982); Lipp *Palatale* 1994.

3. Laryngeals

L 314. The use of the term 'laryngeal' for the pronunciation of three Proto-Indo-European consonants (fricatives) finds its cause in the history of the field, cf. L 315 § 1. The algebraic notation for laryngeals as PIE $*h_1$, $*h_2$, and $*h_3$ has become common. Where a phoneme is determined to be a laryngeal, the nature of which cannot be further described, the cover-symbol *H* is used. — The symbol *H* is further used in the notation of the various Indo-European languages, especially in Indo-Iranian, in which the types of laryngeals may no longer be distinguished, but in which, with the help of Greek, the PIE reconstruction may still be determined, cf. among others, the examples in L 323 § 1b and in L 334 § 1.

1) The primarily consonantal character of these PIE phonemes is uncontroversial, cf. L 329. The supposition of a phonetically unmarked aspirate [*h*] for PIE $*h_1$, a marked aspirated *ach* phoneme [χ] for PIE $*h_2$ and a voiced velar (or labiovelar) fricative [γ], [γ^w] for PIE $*h_3$ is in all probability accurate: → Mayrhofer *Lautlehre* 1986 p. 121 Note 101, p. 122 note 103f.; H. Rix in HS 104 1991 p. 191 with note 27; by the same author, in IF 96 1991 p. 271f.; J. Gippert in *Kolloquium Pedersen* Copenhagen 1993 [1994] p. 464f.; further cf. L 329 § 1.

2) The following introduction to laryngeals is limited in scope. As a rule, special cases are not discussed.

3) The bibliography is long. Because space limitations only allow the mention of a couple of helpful titles, it is worth the trouble in this case to consult the corresponding critical reviews: → *Evidence for Laryngeals* 1965 (with a bibliography and research report by E. Polomé p. 9-78); Beekes *Laryngeals* 1969; Rix *Hist. Gramm. d. Gr.* 1976 p. 36-39, p. 68-76 (a good synopsis of the material in Greek); Mayrhofer *Lautlehre* 1986 p. 121-150; *Laryngaltheorie* 1988 (which includes p. 130-135 a good overview of PIE laryngeals with nine points [*Ennealogie*] by H. Eichner); *Laryngales* 1990; Schrijver *Laryngeals in Latin* 1991; Lindeman *Introduction* 1997; *Kolloquium Pedersen Copenhagen* 1993 [1994] (which includes the round table discussion: "*Zur Phonetik der Laryngale*" with contributions by R. S. P. Beekes, J. Gippert, J. E. Rasmussen and M. Job).

4) What every reader should know: The existence of three laryngeals in Proto-Indo-European is asserted today by a large majority of researchers. There is not, however, unanimity. The supposition of a larger number of laryngeals (reaching ten in a research paper mentioned in Szemerényi *Einführung* 1990 p. 132) recurs even in a contemporary standard work: Puhvel HED takes six as a basis. Lindeman *Laryngeal Theory* 1997 uses three unvoiced and three voiced laryngeals. — On the other hand, Szemerényi *Einführung* 1990 (Cf. among others p. 127ff.; p. 147): "*nur ein Laryngal anzunehmen*") and Bammesberger (*Laryngaltheorie* 1984) assert a PIE phoneme system with only one **h* (along with **ə* further **n̥̄*, **m̥̄*, **l̥̄*, **r̥̄*).

L 315. The inclusion of the three laryngeals in reconstructions of contemporary Indo-European linguistics may be clarified by a brief look at the history of the field.

1) The beginnings of these reconstructions are to be found in the brilliant *Mémoire sur le système primitif des voyelles dans les langues indo-*

européennes by Ferdinand de Saussure, written as a student at age 21 (Leipzig 1879, first appeared 1878; published again in Saussure *Recueil* 1922 p. 1ff). Among his credits, he adopted the organization, by Indian grammarians, of Sanskrit roots into *aniṭ*- and *seṭ*- roots, for modern comparative linguistics. — The sages of ancient India had observed that some roots, when followed by certain grammatical elements, did not exhibit the *-i-* (thus called *an-i-ṭ*, i.e. 'without *-i-*') that other roots did exhibit (which were thus called *seṭ* < **sa-i-ṭ* i.e. 'with *-i-*'). Thus, Vedic *man-* 'to think' is an *aniṭ*- root: Compare Ved. *man-tár-* m. 'thinker,' *mán-tra-* m. 'speech, suggestion' without *-i-* when preceding *-tar-*, *-tra-*. In contrast, Ved. *jan-* 'to create' and *san-* 'to gain,' (which are in modern IE linguistics more accurately noted as *jan*^{i}- and *san*^{i}-, respectively) are *seṭ*-roots. They exhibit *-i-* preceding the suffixes *-tar-*, *-tra-*. Compare: Ved. *jani-tár-* m. 'creator,' *janí-tra-* n. 'place of birth,' *sani-tár-* m. 'winner, one that benefits,' *saní-tra-* n. 'gain, wage.' The Indians also distinguish among their zero grade roots those that exhibit *-i-* from those that exhibit *-ø-* preceding certain suffixes. They represent the verbal root *pū-* (full grade *pav*^{i}-) as heavy (= *seṭ*): Compare *pavi-tár-* m. 'purifier,' *paví-tra-* n. 'sieve.' The verb *śru-* 'to hear' (full grade *śrav-*), on the other hand, is considered light (= *aniṭ*). Compare *śrótar-* m. 'listener' and *śró-tra-* n. 'hearing (sense),' both with preconsonantal *śro-* < **śrau̯-*, cf. L 222 § 3. Further, compare the light Vedic verbal root *bhr̥-* (full grade *bhar-*) 'to carry,' Ved. *bhár-tu-m* 'to be carried,' and *bhar-tár-* m. 'porter' with the heavy Ved. full grade *tar*$^{\breve{\bar{\imath}}}$- 'to overcome,' Ved. *duṣ-ṭárī-tu-* 'insuperable.' (Here, as elsewhere, the *-i-* is sometimes lengthened: → Wackernagel / Debrunner *Ai. Gr. I* 1957 § 18; Hirt *Idg. Gr.* II 1921 § 135.)

2) It is possible that the connection of *seṭ*-roots such as Ved. *pū-* (*pav*$^{\breve{\bar{\imath}}}$-) 'to purify' (cf. the participle *pū-tá-* 'purified') with present stems of the Old Indian ninth class (cf. Ved. *pu-nā́-ti* 'he purifies,' *pu-nī-tá* imperative plural 'purify!') was already discernible in Vedic grammar. Saussure's great achievement was the abstraction of comparing nasal present forms with the more transparent *-n-* infix verb type of the Old Indian seventh class. Comparing Ved. *yu-ṅ-k-tá* 'harness!' with the participle *yuk-tá-* 'harnessed,' the insertion of *-n-* before the final phoneme of the root *yuk-* was clearly visible. Saussure recognized this nasal infix present pattern not only in verbs of the Old Indian fifth class (Ved. *śr̥-ṇ-u-tá* 'hear!' [imperative, pl.] and *śru-tá-* 'heard'; on the *aniṭ*-root *śru-*, cf. §1), but also in the relation of Ved. *pu-n-ī-tá* 'purify!' to *pū-tá-* 'purified.' In fact, he arrived at the correspondence set: Ved. *yók-tra-* n. 'harness' (with *yok-* < **yau̯k-*, cf. L 222 § 3) : *yu-ṅ-k-tá* : *yuk-tá-* = *śró-tra-* (above §1) : *śr̥-ṇ-u-tá* : *śru-tá-* = *paví-tra-* : *pu-nī-tá* : *pū-tá-*. If this was true, then the *seṭ*-root must have contained a root-final feature, which we shall call *X* (not corre-

sponding to Saussure's term) for the time being. It appeared following consonants (*-v-*, *-n-*) as *-i-* (and is sometimes also lengthened, cf. §1: *duṣ-ṭárī-tu-*), following short vowels, as *-u-*; but in both cases as a lengthening. If one formulates accordingly the last series, the analogy to the first series is conspicuous:

pávi(tra-)	*pu-n-ī(tá)*	*pū(tá-)*
< **páu̯X(tra-)*	< **pu-n-X(tá)*	< **puX(tá-)*

3) That Indian grammarians, in proposing the presence of an additional *-i-* in *seṭ*-roots, recognized an immanent linguistic trait, is evidenced by roots with liquid and nasal sounds. If the *aniṭ*-root *man-* (cf. *man-tár-*, above §1) had **mn̥-* as its zero grade (cf. Ved. *ma-tá-*), then the zero grade forms of the *seṭ*-root *jan*^{i}- (cf. Ved. *jani-tár-*) may be traced back to an *-n̥-* + *-X-* (cf. Ved. *jātá-* 'create' with *-ā-* < **-aX-* < **-n̥X-*). Likewise, only *aniṭ*-roots such as *har-/bhṛ-* 'to carry' have a zero grade form with *-ṛ-* (cf. *bhṛ-tá-* 'carried'). However, in the case of *seṭ*-root forms such as full grade *tar*$^{ī̆}$- 'to overcome' or full grade *par*^{i}- 'to fill,' *-r̥-* + *-X-*, and *-l̥-* + *-X-* must be added with the result *-īr-*, and *-ūr-*, cf. Ved. *tīr-thá-* 'ford' and *pūr-ṇá-* 'filled').

L 316. To summarize, while this *X* is only preserved following consonants (and non-syllabic sonants) as Ved. *-ī̆-* (corresponding to the *i-ṭ* from Old Indian grammar), after vowels and syllabic nasals and liquids it has caused a lengthening, cf. PIE **peu̯X-* > Ved. *pav*^{i}- compared with PIE **puX-* > Ved. *pū-*; PIE **ǵenX-* > Ved. *jan*^{i}- compared with PIE **ǵn̥X-* (corresponding to **ǵn̥̄-* in older transcriptions) > Ved. *jā-*; PIE **terX-* > Ved. *tar*$^{ī̆}$- compared with PIE **tr̥X-* (corresponding to *tr̥̄-* in older transcriptions) > Ved. *tīr-*. However, where this element was preserved as the vowel Ved. *-ī̆-*, it largely corresponded to *-a-* in non-Indo-Iranian languages. Thus the verb type of the Old Indian ninth class, with zero grade *-nī-* in *pu-nī-té* 'is purified' and full grade *-nā-* in *pu-nā́-ti* 'he/she/it purifies' (cf. L 315 § 2), may be compared with the zero grade Gr. -να- in δάμ-να-ται 'to control' and the full grade Ion.-Att. -νη- (< *-nā-*) in δάμ-νη-σι 'controlled.' — The equating of Ved. *sthitá-* to Gr. στατός 'arranged' further indicates that even the zero grade of long vowel roots such as Ved. *sthā-* and Gr. (non-Ion.-Att.) *stā-* (in Ion.-Att. ἵ-στη-μι < **si-stā-*) 'to stand' contain this *X*, which would tend to indicate that roots of the *sthā-* type in fact ended in *-a-X-*, cf. L 417 § 2. Thus, **sthaX-* (= Ved. *sthā-*) : **sthX-tá-* (= Ved. *sthitá-*) should be regarded as parallel to Ved. *bhar-* : *bhṛ-tá-*. In addition, the phonetic equivalence Ved. *-i-* = Gr. -α- is repeated in such clear correspondence sets as Ved. *pitár-* = Gr. πατήρ 'father': The element *X* is thus present even here.

L 317. Not only did Ferdinand de Saussure identify the element here referred to as *X*, he also postulated two such values, to which a third would later be added by researchers. Thus, today's view of three different laryngeals underlying the Gr. *tʰē-*, *stā-* and *dō-*: Gr. *tʰē-* 'to place, lay, sit' (cf. τί-θη-μι) < PIE *d^heh_1-*; non-Ion.-Att. *stā-* (cf. Ion.-Att. ἵ-στη-μι with *ē* < *ā*) < PIE *$steh_2$-*; *dō-* 'to give' (cf. δί-δω-μι) < PIE *deh_3-*. De Saussure had seen vocalic elements (*coefficients sonantiques*) in these values.

L 318. Classical Indo-European linguistics of the period followed de Saussure in many ways, but not in all. For example, in place of the *X*, for which he had postulated two values, and for which his laryngealist successors even proposed a third, a single schwa, *ə*, the schwa *indogermanicum* was postulated. The field further adopted his assertion that the *seṭ*-roots could be traced to Proto-Indo-European. An example such as the Ved. *janⁱ-* was traced (with the denotation of the period) back to PIE **ǵenə-*. In the case of the corresponding zero grade in *jā-tá-* , *jā-* was traced to a heavy PIE **ǵn̥̄-*, which was thus denoted at the time.

On the history of the reception of de Saussure's early work in classical Indo-European linguistics: → M. Mayrhofer, "A hundred years after the work of de Saussure," in SbHAW 1981 *Bericht 8* p. 26ff. (review: O. Szemerényi in *Kratylos* 28 1983 [1984] p. 54-59 = *Scripta Minora I* 1987 p. 557-562).

L 319. In 1912, Albert Cuny contributed significantly by refuting the insight, universally accepted around the turn of the century, that the zero grade of *seṭ-* roots containing *-n-* and *-r-*, were *-n̥̄-* and *-r̥̄-*, respectively: → A. Cuny "*Indo-européen et sémitique*" in *Revue de phonétique* 2 1912 p. 101ff.

1) His argumentation was the following: If the full grade of *seṭ-* roots in fact were to end in PIE *-*ə*, as the understanding at that time of full grade PIE **ǵenə-* > Ved. *janⁱ-* (cf. L 318) suggested, then one should expect the zero grade PIE **ǵnə*, with vocalic *-ə-* following consonantal *-n-*. This would have been preserved as Ved. **jñi-*. However, this form does not exist. Instead, we find Ved. *jā(-tá-)*, which may be traced via the pre-historic transitory form **jaX-tá-* to PIE **ǵn̥X-tó-*.

2) Cuny's treatment contains a suggestion of the consonantal nature of *X*, which, in the case of de Saussure's '*coefficients*,' had already been accepted by Hermann Möller in 1879 / 1880. Möller thought of laryngeals as they are

familiar in Semitic languages: → H. Möller *Semitisch und Indogermanisch, Teil I (Konsonanten)*, Copenhagen 1906, p.VI:

> "When Ferdinand de Saussure made his brilliant discovery of, as he called them, the '*phonèmes*' *A* and *O* (*Mémoire* ...), I immediately voiced the supposition (1879) that these fundamental elements, to which I added a third, were consonantal, and indeed glottals ... and claimed in 1880 that 'they were probably gutturals as exist in Semitic languages'"

L 320. Current insights concerning laryngeals take into account that the meaning and use of the term 'laryngeal' have developed throughout the history of Indo-European linguistics without a precise phonetic connotation. It is fundamental, firstly, that the existence of three consonantal values is assumed, and secondly, that the majority of their effects, as they are taught in the present introduction, already appeared in Cuny's essay of 1912. At that time, Hittite and its *ḫ* phoneme had not yet been discovered.

The basis of what is called 'laryngeal theory,' i.e. the continuation of de Saussure's insights, was already complete in 1912 and relied upon the comparative analysis of root structure and ablauts, particularly in Ancient Greek and Vedic. For information on the early history of laryngeal theory with pertinent information on Cuny, Möller, and other researchers, see the exciting portrayal by O. Szemerényi: *La théorie des laryngales de Saussure à Kuryłowicz et à Benveniste* in BSL 68 / 1 1973 p. 1ff. (= by the same author, *Scripta Minora I* 1987 p. 191ff.).

The assertion by Jerzy Kuryłowicz in 1927 that the Hittite *ḫ* corresponds perfectly to Cuny's second laryngeal had as its chief consequence that the consonantal understanding of de Saussure's *coefficients*, initially considered heretical, finally gained acceptance. It is certainly of importance that the earliest attested Indo-European branch confirms the consonantal character of laryngeals. Nonetheless, it is worth emphasizing that the conclusions reached by de Saussure and Cuny based upon the non-Anatolian languages, owing to their eminent logic, would have found acceptance even if Anatolian texts had never come out of the earth: → Mayrhofer *Kleine Schriften* II 1996 (in an essay from 1987) p. 416.

L 321. The following effects of PIE $*h_1$, $*h_2$ and $*h_3$ are important for the central IE languages and their early phases.

The usual PIE root structure, as it is found in Latin and Greek forms such as *leg-ō*, *fer-ō*, *cap-iō*, *clep-ō*, λείπ-ω, κεῖ-μαι, is composed of one or more non-syllabic word-initial phonemes, for example *l-*, *kl-*, *k-*, followed by a middle *-e-* (or, seldom, *-a-*) and finally one or more non-syllabic phonemes, for example *-g*, *-i̯*, *-i̯kʷ*. PIE roots, with an initial (cf. L 322 on *He-*) or final (cf. L 323 on *-eH-*) sound that must be traced to $*h_1$, $*h_2$ or $*h_3$, easily fit into this root type thanks to their non-syllabic nature. For more information on PIE root structure: → Szemerényi *Einführung* 1990 p. 102-104; LIV 1998 p. 5ff. (on verbal roots).

L 322. Roots of the type **He-* with initial laryngeal:

1) An example for PIE $*h_1e$-: — PIE $*h_1es$- 'to exist' = Lat. *es-t* etc. The initial position $*h_1$- is evidenced in forms containing the zero grade $*h_1s$-, cf. E 504 § 9. The $*h_1$ in the full grade PIE $*h_1es$- seems to have disappeared in all known IE languages.

2) Examples for PIE $*h_2e$-: — PIE $*h_2ent$- 'face.' Even into the Proto-Indo-European period, $*h_2$ contributed to the evolution of PIE $*h_2e$ to $*h_2a$; the lexeme thus became $*h_2ant$-. The former presence of PIE $*h_2e$ is still reflected in the lengthened grade, PIE $*h_2\bar{e}$, in which the *ē* is preserved despite the preceding $*h_2$, cf. L 331. The same conclusion may be drawn from the presence of forms containing the ablaut *-oh_2- (cf. ὄγμος below): These forms are best understood if they are traced back to a time when *-eh_2-, with its *e*, provided the starting point for the ablauts *-e-* : *-o-* and *-e-* : *-ē-*. The initial position *H* of $*h_2a$ is preserved in Anatolian, cf. Hitt. *ḫant-s* 'face, front.' The other languages conserve **ant-* directly, cf. PIE loc. sg. $*h_2\acute{e}nt$-*i* = Lat. *ant-e* (cf. L 423 § 1) 'before,' Gr. ἀντ-ί (the original Gr. *ἄντι is not attested; the actual accent is abstracted from the usual unstressed proclitical ἀντὶ before the corresponding genetive) 'in the face of,' Ved. *ánt-i* 'before.' — PIE $*h_2e\acute{g}$- (> $*h_2a\acute{g}$-; along with the form PIE $*h_2o\acute{g}$- with –*o*-ablaut) 'to drive, lead' = Lat. *ag-ere*, Gr. ἄγ-ειν (also compare the *-o-* full grade noun ὄγ-μος 'a strip of mown grass'), Ved. *ájati* 'he/she/it drives.'

3) Example for PIE $*h_3e$-: — PIE $*h_3ek^w$- 'to see,' among others with the primary full grade *-mn̥*-formation $*h_3\acute{e}k^w$-*mn̥* (of the same type as Gr. σπέρ-μα, δέρ-μα) 'eye': $*h_3e$ becomes $*h_3o$ already in the PIE period, which, in all certain examples, in turn is assimilated with PIE **o*. Compare the initial positions of Gr. ὄμ-μα 'eye,' Lat. *oculus*, Ved. *ákṣi-* 'eye' which all come from the root in question. — For information on Anatolian, cf. L 334.

L 323. Roots of the type *-*eH-* with a closing laryngeal followed by a consonant or a vowel:

1) Examples for PIE *-eh_1-: In the case of *-eh_1-, h_1 does not effect a transformation of *e*; neither does it in the case of PIE $*h_1e$- (cf. L 322 § 1).

1a) When *-*eh*$_1$- precedes a consonant, *h*$_1$ effects compensatory lengthening, creating -*ē*-. As a rule, the long vowel is assimilated in PIE*-*ē*-. — PIE *d^heh_1- 'to place, erect, make' = Gr. τί-θη-μι, Lat. *fē-cī*, Ved. *á-dhāt*, Lith. *dė̃-ti* 'to lay'. — PIE *$h_2\underset{\frown}{u}eh_1$- 'to blow' = Gr. ἄησι, Ved. *vā́-ti*, OCS *vě-jati*. — PIE *reh_1- 'to grant, to give' = Ved. *rā́-si* 'you give, you lend.'

1b) But when *-*eh*$_1$- precedes a vowel or a syllabic sonorant, an *e* that precedes *h_1 retains its properties and is treated as PIE **e*; *h_1 disappears later in a hiatus. — Cf. PIE *$h_2\underset{\frown}{u}\acute{e}h_1$-*n̥t-o*- 'wind' > Indo-Iranian **Hu̯áHata*- > **u̯á.ata*- > OAv. LAv. *vāta*- m. 'wind' (OAv. Yasna 44,4 was possibly treated as *va'ata*- having three syllables) = Ved. *vā́-ta*-, Lat. (with *-*eh*$_1$*nt*- > -*ent*-) *ventus* (Thus, cf. Hitt. *ḫuu̯ant*- 'wind' <**ḫu-ant*- < PIE *h_2uh_1-*ent*-). — PIE *reh_1-*í*- 'property' > Indo-Iranian **raHí*- > **ra.í*- (cf. Ved. *rayí-m* acc. sg. with the transitional sound -*y*- and Ved. *re-vánt*- 'rich' < **rai̯-u̯ánt*- < **ra.i-u̯ánt*- < **raHi-u̯ánt*-); in contrast, in the same paradigm (following consonantal *i̯*) PIE *reh_1-*i̯-és* gen. sg. 'of the property' > Indo-Iranian **raHi̯-ás* > Ved. *rāyás*. — For further information on both of these examples: → Mayrhofer EWAia II p. 438 (on *rayí*-) and p. 542 (concerning *vā́ta*-); further, concerning *vā́ta*-: → B. Vine *"Rig-Vedic VÁATA- and the Analysis of Metrical Distractions"* in IIJ 33 1990 p. 267-275.

2) Examples for PIE *-*eh*$_2$- preceding a consonant: — PIE *h_2 effects a transformation in *eh_2 (as well as in *h_2e) from *e* to *a*. Evidence of the prior existence of *eh_2 comes, as in the case of *eh_1 (see above, §1), from the lengthened grades with*$\bar{e}h_2$ that are based upon it (see below, L 331 §1) as well as from examples of *oh_2 with ablaut (cf. Gr. φω-νή below). Thus, already in the pre-PIE period, *eh_2 became *ah_2 (cf. L 303 on the acc. sg. Pre-PIE *-*eh*$_2$*m* > *-*ah*$_2$*m* > *-*amm* > PIE *-*ām*, in which the transformation takes place before the Pre-PIE assimilation). The *ah_2 grade is preserved in the Anatolian languages. In non-Anatolian languages, *ah_2 preceding a consonant was assimilated into PIE **ā*. — Concerning PIE *$steh_2$-, becoming *$stah_2$- 'to go somewhere, to put oneself somewhere,' cf. Ion.-Att. Gr. (with *ā* > *ē*) ἵ-στη-μι , Ved. *á-sthā-t*, OHG *stān* 'to stand,' OCS *sta-jǫ* 'I position myself'. — Concerning PIE *peh_2- becoming *pah_2- 'to look after, to graze' (On the problems regarding this root: → LIV 1998 p. 415) cf. Hitt. *paḫ-s*- 'to protect' (On its graphism and form: → Oettinger *Verbum* 1979 p. 210), Lat. *pā-scō*. — Concerning PIE *b^heh_2-, becoming *b^hah_2- 'to speak, say' cf. Ion.-Att. Gr. (with *ā* > *ē*) φημί, Lat. *fā-rī* 'to speak,' Russ.-CS *ba-jati* 'to recount' (IE *b^heh_2-

has as an ablaut $*b^h oh_2$- with its preserved *-o-* preceding $-h_2$-, cf. Gr. φω-νή 'voice').

3) Examples for PIE $*\text{-}eh_3$- preceding a consonant: Already in the PIE period, $*h_3$ effected the transformation of $*eh_3$ to $*oh_3$. Preceding a consonant, $*\text{-}oh_3$- assimilates into **-ō-*. — Concerning PIE $*deh_3$- 'to give' cf. Gr. δί-δω-μι, Lat. *dōs dō-t-* 'gift, dowry,' Ved. *á-dā-t* 'he/she/it gave,' Lith. *dúo-mi* 'he/she/it give (subj.),' OCS *da-mь* 'I will give.' In the Latin present stem, 2 sg. *dās* vs. 1 pl. *damus* (< $*dh_3\text{-}mos$) the full grade *dās* replaces an older **dōs* (< $*deh_3\text{-}s$); the vocalic quality *ā* instead of *ō* is adopted by analogy to the plural: → Meiser *Laut- und Formenlehre* 1998 p. 188. — Concerning PIE $*peh_3$-, cf. Gr. πῶ-μα 'beverage,' Lat. *pō-tus* 'drunk,' Ved. *pā-hí* 'drink!,' Hitt. *pā-s-* 'swallow.'

L 324. The zero grade that corresponds to the full grade forms PIE $*h_1e$ and $*eh_1$ is PIE $*h_1$; the zero grade form corresponding to PIE $*h_2e$ and $*eh_2$ is PIE $*h_2$; the form PIE $*h_3$ corresponds to PIE $*h_3e$ and $*eh_3$.

1) Positioned between consonants, PIE $*h_1$, $*h_2$ and $*h_3$ are most often retained as vowels, but occasionally also as *-ø-*. The vocalic variant may be explained phonetically by the development of a weak vowel between the *H* and the consonant that follows it. The product, $*H^\circ$ leads to the disappearance of **H* according to phonetic rules, leaving only the vocalic °, cf. L 103. For more information on its properties, see the following paragraphs.

2) The above description of the vocalic development of laryngeals between consonants is not evident at first glance. This is the reason why the field of classical Indo-European linguistics erroneously fixed itself upon the special phoneme *ə*, the schwa indogermanicum, also called the schwa primum. Cf. in L 319 A. Cuny's refutation of this approach.

3) The case of *ø*, which occurs less often than $*H^\circ$, may in part be understood as a simplification of consonant groups. For both of these resultant forms, cf. the initial position of PIE $*ph_2t$- 'father': derivative forms such as Gr. πατήρ and Ved. *pitā́* exhibit complete vocalization and may be traced back to PIE $*ph_2{}^\circ t$-. The case of Avestan is of greater complexity, cf. nom. sg. OAv. *ptā, tā*, LAv. *ptā, pita* and dat. sg. OAv. *fᵊδrōi, piθrē*, LAv. *piθre*. The dative *fᵊδrōi* i.e. *fθrái̯* is traced back to **pt-* < PIE $*ph_2t$-. For information on vocalization, for example when $*ph_2{}^\circ t$- or $*ph_2t$- is the case: → Kuiper *Vedic Noun-Inflexion* 1942 p. 20ff.; E. Tichy in MSS 45 1985 p. 229ff. (The author argues convincingly that vocalization occurred in the voc. sg. form $*ph_2{}^\circ ter$ [with stressed first syllable] already in the Proto-Indo-European era. The new

vowel subsequently spread in paradigms of individual IE languages.) Mayrhofer EWAia II p. 128f. (with suggestions for further reading). The situation is different in the non-laryngeal approach toward **patér-* by H. Schmeja in *FS Meid* *70 1999 p. 413-423. For further information on the paradigm of 'father,' cf. F 318 § 3.

L 325. Interconsonantal PIE *h_1 yields, via **H°*, *e* in Greek, *ĭ̄* in Vedic, Indo-Iranian (on the occasional *ø*, cf. L 324 § 3), and in the other languages, insofar as they are observable, *a* or its continuation. In Classical Latin, for example, an *e* or an *i* takes its place because of vowel weakening in short middle syllables (cf. L 204). Cf. F 101 § 2 for *gene-trīx* and *genitor* < **gena-* < **ǵenh*$_1$-.

Examples: — For PIE **d*^{h}*eh*$_1$- 'to place, lay' cf. PIE **d*^{h}*h*$_1$*-tó-* passive perfect participle 'placed,' reflected in Greek by θετός 'placed,' Ved. *hitá-* (< **dhi-tá-*), Lat. *ab-ditus* (< **ab-dato-*) 'removed, hidden,' further, cf. PIE **é-d*^{h}*h*$_1$*-to* aor. 'he placed' with Gr. ἔ-θε-το = Ved. *a-dhi-ta* (with *ø* PIE *-*d*^{h}*h*$_1$*-més* in Ved. *da-dh-más* 'we place'). — PIE **ǵenh*$_1$*-tor-* 'creator' = Gr. γενέ-τωρ, Ved. *jani-tár-*, Lat. *geni-tor* (with vowel weakening <**gena-tor-*). — PIE **h*$_2$*n̥h*$_1$*-mo-* = Gr. ἄνε-μος 'wind,' Osc. *anamúm* 'animam' (Lat. *animus* with vowel weakening < **anamo-*), Ved. *áni-ti* 'he breathes.' — PIE **u̯emh*$_1$- = Gr. ἐμέ-ω 'I spit out,' Lat. *vomit* 'he vomits' (< **u̯éma-ti* [however as a starting point, an *o*-grade **u̯óm-* is also not out of the question]. Already in the Proto-Italic era, the initially expected **u̯émati* likely became **u̯émeti* through the addition of a thematic vowel: → H. Rix in *GS Schindler* 1999 p. 516f.), Ved. *vámi-ti* 'he spits out,' Lith. *vém-ti* 'to have nausea' (with *-ém-K-* < *-*emH-K-*).

L 326. Interconsonantal PIE *h_2 yielded *a* in Greek, *ĭ̄* (and occasionally *ø*) in Vedic (Indo-Iranian), and otherwise **a* as in the case of PIE *h_1. — Cf. above L 324 concerning PIE **ph*$_2$*tér-* = Gr. πατήρ (Lat. *pater*, Got. *fadar*), Ved. *pitár-* (but **ptr-* in OAv. *f*^{ə}*δrōi*). — PIE **sth*$_2$*-tó-* 'placed (participle)' (concerning PIE **steh*$_2$-, becoming PIE **stah*$_2$- 'to stand,' cf. L 323 § 2) = Gr. στατός 'standing,' Lat. *status* 'placed (participle),' Ved. *sthitá-* 'standing,' cf. OHG *stat* f. 'place (locality).' — PIE **senh*$_2$- 'to gain' = Ved. *seṭ-* root (cf. L 315 § 1) with nom. ag. *sani-tár-*, Hitt. *sanḫ-* 'to search, to intend to do' (with retained *ḫ* < PIE *h_2).

L 327. Interconsonantal PIE *h_3 appears in Greek as *o*. In other languages it is reflected just as PIE *h_1 and *h_2: In Vedic, as a rule, as *ĭ̄* (seldom *ø*), Lat. *a*, etc. — Cf. PIE **é-dh*$_3$*-to* 'he gave,' **dh*$_3$*-tó-* 'given' (concerning the root PIE **deh₃-* 'to give' with the development, already in the PIE era > **doh₃-*, cf. L 323 § 3) = Gr. ἔ-δο-το, Ved. *a-di-ta* and Gr. δοτός, Lat. *datus*, but (with *ø*) Ved. *(devá-)tta-* 'given (by the gods)' (concerning the early replacement by *-dattá-* and *dātá-* of *-tta-*: → Mayrhofer EWAia I p. 715). — PIE **ph₃-tó-* 'drunk' (PIE root **peh₃-* becoming **poh₃-*; sometimes **peh₃-* appears, with the addition of *-i̯-*, which comes from the present stem, cf. Gr. ἔπιον < **é pih₃-ont* with **pih₃-* < **ph₃-i-* by metathesis in special contexts) = Gr. ποτόν n. 'beverage.' — PIE **h₂erh₃-* 'to plow' in Gr. ἄρο-τρον n. 'plow' = Lith. *ár-klas* 'plow' (with *ár-* < *arH-*).

L 328. When PIE $*h_1$, $*h_2$, or $*h_3$ appear word-initially followed by a consonant, they are most often represented in the ancient IE languages as *ø*. — In Greek however, preconsonantal PIE $*h_1$- appears as *e-*, PIE $*h_2$- as *a-*, and PIE $*h_3$- as *o-*. — In Hittite, a preconsonantal $*h_1$- is represented by *a*, whereas $*h_2$- is sometimes preserved as *ḫ-*. The situation is in fact more complex than the present description: → Melchert *Anatolian Historical Phonology* 1994 p. 66ff. — In Armenian and Old Phrygian, preconsonantal **H-* is vocalized. — In Indo-Iranian, an original preconsonantal **H-* may be identified by its lengthening, which may be observed when the final position of an initial element is occupied by a vowel, followed by an element with an original initial **H-*, cf. § 1 Ved. *ā́sat-* and § 2 Ved. *viśvā́nara-* above.

1) Examples for PIE $*h_1K$-: — PIE $*h_1s$-*énti* 'they are' (pres. act. 3rd person pl. with zero grade root becomes PIE $*h_1es$- 'to exist,' cf. L 322 § 1) = Ved. *s-ánti*, Got. *s-ind*, Myc. *e-e-si* i.e. *eh-ensi* = ion.-att εἰσί, Hitt. *as-ant^{s}i*. — PIE $*h_1s$-*ont-/-n̥t-* part. 'being' = Myc. Gr. *ap-eh-ontes*, Ion. ἐ-ών among others; Ved. *sánt-/sat-*. Original word-initial $*h_1s$- is yet visible in the negated participle Ved. *ā́sat-* 'not being' with long-vocalic *ās-* < **a-Hs-* < PIE $*n̥-h_1s$-. Otherwise, short vowel forms are usual in the formation of negations: *a-K-* < PIE **n̥-K-*, cf. E 504 § 9.

2) Examples for PIE $*h_2K$-: — PIE $*h_2nér$- 'man' = Gr. ἀνήρ nom. sg., Arm. *ayr* (< **anīr*) , Phryg. αναρ; Ved. *nár-* 'man,' Umbr. *ner-um* gen. pl. 'the men's.' However, in Indo-Iranian original $*h_2nar$- is still discernable, cf. Ved. *viśvā́nara-* 'all having manpower' and OAv. *kamnā.nar-* 'having few men,' both with *-ānar-* < **-a-Hnar-*. — PIE $*h_2stér$- 'star' = Gr. ἀστήρ, Arm. *astł*, Hitt. *ḫaster-*, Ved. *stár-*, NHG *Stern*. — PIE $*h_2u̯eh_1$- 'to blow' = Gr. ἄησι, Hitt. *ḫuu̯ant-*, Lat. *ventus*, cf. L 323 § 1b.

3) Example for PIE *h_3K-: — PIE *h_3*neịd*- 'to malign, reprimand' = Gr. ὄνειδος subst. 'reprimand,' Arm. *anicanem* 'I curse'; Ved. *nidānā́*- part. 'reprimanded,' Got. *naiteins* f. 'blasphemy.'

L 329. When *H is in a post-plosive, prevocalic position, the consonantal nature of the laryngeal values is further shown, as they were described briefly above:

1) From PIE **(s)tí-sth*$_2$*-e-ti* (root **steh*$_2$- becoming **stah*$_2$-, cf. L 323 § 2) > Ved. *tí-ṣṭh-a-ti* we learn that PIE **t* becomes in Vedic the tenuis aspirata *th* (as de Saussure already perceived: → Saussure *Recueil* 1922 p. 603 in a note from 1891). By analogy, this Vedic *th* has also found its way into other forms. In place of **stā*- < PIE **steh*$_2$- which one would normally expect, one finds the generalized *sthā*-. — Further examples demonstrate that PIE *h_2, because of its fricative nature, when followed by a vowel and preceded by a plosive, can transform the latter into an aspirate: — When word-final prevocalic *-*th*$_2$- precedes *-*u*- in the case of PIE **pleth*$_2$- 'to become wide,' the product, PIE **pl̥th*$_2$*ú*-, becomes in turn Ved. *pr̥thú*- 'far, wide' (Note: In preconsonantal position, this *-*th*$_2$- appears in Greek as -τα-, cf. πλατα-μών 'flat stone'). — If an h_2, at the origin of which is an ablaut, appears in the paradigm of PIE **pént-oh*$_2$*-s* nom. sg. 'path' directly following *t* (cf. gen. sg. **pn̥t-h*$_2$*-és*), then one should expect the Indo-Iranian result nom. sg. **pántās* (and gen. sg. **pathás*): Avest. *pantā̊*, *paθō* carries on this pattern consistently, whereas in Vedic, *panth*- is generalized from *pathás* and is also found in nom. sg. *pánthās*. — In the case of PIE **rotah*$_2$- 'wheel' (= Lat. *rota*) there exists a derivation already in the PIE era: **rot-h*$_2$*-o*- 'wheeled object > wagon' = Ved. *rátha*-. — Also compare the Vedic suffix -*tha*- < PIE *-*th*$_2$*-o*-, cf. F 503. — Based upon such clear examples and others, the supposition is justified that the origin of the Indo-Iranian tenues aspiratae is to be found in this sequence of two phonemes. — For information on the material: → Hiersche *Tenues Aspiratae* 1964. For information on its interpretation: → Mayrhofer *Kleine Schriften* II 1996 (in an essay of 1981) p. 298, note 17. — Several Indo-Iranian mediae aspiratae may be explained as originating from media + *h_2 + vowel. Compare, for example, the paradigm of PIE **még̑-oh*$_2$- and **még̑-h*$_2$ 'large,' in which the direct contact of *g̑* and h_2 in forms such as gen. sg. **m̥g̑-h*$_2$*-és* may explain the Vedic aspirate. Compare also *mah-ás* (containing *mah*- and not **ah*-, cf. L 203 concerning Lat. *mag*-; based upon *mah*-, also in the case of -*oh*$_2$- forms, *mah*- is formed through analogy, and not **maj*-), but Gr. μέγας. For further information on the subject: → Mayrhofer *Lautlehre* 1986 p. 135ff.

2) The present tense of the PIE root *peh_3- (with change > *poh_3-) 'to drink' (cf. L 323 § 3) should be postulated as *pí-ph_3-e-ti. Ved. *píbati*, Old Iranian *ibid* < *pibeti 'drink!' (imperative, pl.) and Lat. *bibit* may be traced, in a first step, to *píbeti. Both forms, *píbeti and *píp$h_3$eti are accounted for when we assume that PIE *h_3 (in this case prevocalic) lent the characteristic [+voiced] to the preceding unvoiced plosive and thus, that already in the PIE period, *ph_3 became *b. — In the case of PIE *$h_2$ep- 'water' (= Ved. *áp-* RV+ 'water' with *apás apā́ ádbhis* and others, cp. Gr. εὔριπος 'inlet,' probably already represented in Mycenaean as *e-wi-ri-po* i.e. *eu̯rīpo-* < *eu̯rūpo- < *h_1u̯ru-h_2p-o-: → B. Forssman "*Mykenisch e-wi-ri-po und εὔριπος*" in MSS 49 1988 p. 5-12) there exists the alternative form *$h_2$eb-, cf. Hitt. *ḫa-ap-pa*, *ḫa-pa-a* i.e. *ḫab-ā* 'to the / at the river' (→ Friedrich / Kammenhuber HW III Lief.13 1998 p. 197ff.) and Cymric *afon* 'river' (Lat. *amnis* 'river' is ambiguous: < *ap-n- or < *ab-n-). According to E. P. Hamp, PIE *$h_2$ép-$h_3$on- '(river) with flowing water,' built upon *$h_2$ep- with what is called the Hoffmann suffix (→ K. Hoffmann "*Ein grundsprachliches Possessivsuffix*" in MSS 6 1955 p. 35-40 = Hoffmann *Aufsätze* II 1976 p. 378-383), may be considered the basis of the voiced variant *$h_2$eb-, via the intermediary step of *ab-on-/*ab-en-: → E. P. Hamp "*Palaic ha-a-ap-na-aš 'river'*" in MSS 30 1972 p. 35-37. If true, these assertions would permit the establishment of the suffix as *-$h_3$on-, whereas Hoffmann himself could assert the presence of an undetermined laryngeal. According to M. Mayrhofer however, Hamp's argument is not convincing, since there is proof of voiced *$h_2$eb- elsewhere than in the suffix: → Mayrhofer *Lautlehre* 1986 p. 144. That is why, as a reason for the coexistence of *$h_2$ep- and *$h_2$eb-, the paradigm itself comes into question: A dat. pl. *$h_2$eb-b^hi with an assimilated *-b-* preceding -b^h- may have been the reason for including *$h_2$eb- even before a vowel (thus, in the gen. sg. the new *h_2b-és is reconstructed in place of *h_2p-és). If this is the case, the above suffix must not necessarily have been *-$h_3$on-; rather, *-$h_1$on- is just as likely. For more information on the Hoffmann suffix, cf. W 204 § 4.

L 330. Special cases: — One special case, already described by de Saussure, is the disappearance of a laryngeal in the position *KoRHK*, cf. Gr. τόλμη (Note: The prime example fem. τόλμη is declined in Ionic/Attic Greek according to the schema nom. sg. τόλμα, acc. sg. τόλμαν, gen. sg. τόλμης etc.; the nom. sg. τόλμη is quite seldom.) 'daring' < *tólh_2-meh_2- and PIE *telh_2- 'to pick up, to take upon oneself': → Saussure *Recueil* 1922 (in a contribution of 1905) p. 582 note 2; A. J. Nussbaum "The 'Saussure Effect' in Latin and Italic" in *FS Beekes* 1997 p. 181-203; compare further R. Lipp in LIV 1998 p. 98 note 1 (in which he suggests that

PIE *dom-s* 'house' may be derived from *$domh_2$-s*); see also Melchert *Anatolian Historical Phonology* 1994 p. 49ff. — PIE *$h_2n̥h_1$-os-* 'nose' presents another special case. According to M. Fritz, it is a fem. -*s*- stem of the type PIE *$h_2éu̯s$-$ōs$* 'red dawn' [cf. F 321 § 2] and is derived from PIE *h_2enh_1-* 'to breathe.' The declension is holodynamic (cf. F 321) with nom. sg. *$h_2énh_1ōs$*, but gen. sg. *h_2n-$és$* < *$h_2n̥h_1$-$és$*, etc.: → M. Fritz, "*Das urindogermanische Wort für 'Nase' und das grundsprachliche Lautgesetz* *R̥HV > *RV" in HS 109 1996 p. 1-20. According to Fritz (p. 17), "...in a strong case, the root-final laryngeal falls into a prevocalic position following an open syllable… and disappears in accordance with rules of phonetics." — Cases such as the PIE thematic present stem *$gí$-$gn̥h_1$-e-ti* (of the root *$ǵenh_1$-/*$ǵn̥h_1$-* 'to create') which produces Lat. part. *gignit* 'produced' fall under the same rubric: → H. Rix in *GS Kuryłowicz I* 1995 p. 407 ("disappearance of h_1 between resonant and vowel in the reduplicated root"). — Further, compare compound words of the type Gr. νεογνός (Homeric, hymns) 'newborn' with second member -*gnó*- < *-*$ǵn̥h_1$-ó-*. Further reading: → Fritz, loc. cit. p. 7; I. Balles in *Sprache* 39 1997 [2000] p. 160 (-*R̥HV*- > -*R̥RV*- and -*N̥HV*- > -*N̥NV*-, suppression of the syllabic resonant preceding a homorganic glide in the long compound form.)

L 331. A full grade -*o*- ablaut and lengthened grades with -*ē*- are also expected in the case of roots, of which the basic vowel *e* precedes or follows a laryngeal. Directly adjacent, PIE *h_2 and h_3 transformed the short vowel -*e*- at a very early period, cf. L 323 § 2 and 3.

1) That lengthened grades with -*ē*- (which evolved further into -*e*-), unlike those with short vowels, withstood transformation under the influence of *h_2 and *h_3, shows that in these cases there must have been a period before the transformation in which the -*e*- vowel was still present. The first detailed treatment of this problem is by H. Eichner "*Die Etymologie von heth. mēhur*" in MSS 31 1972 p. 53-107. (The following phenomenon, cited as Lex Eichner, is thus formulated on p. 78: "Preservation of the timbre of lengthened grade *ē* in the vicinity of H_2.")

2) Two levels may be distinguished diachronically:

Level I before transformation:

a)	*h_2e- : *h_2o-	and	*-eh_2- : *-oh_2-
	*h_3e- : *h_3o-		*-eh_3- : *-oh_3-
b)	*h_2e- : *$h_2ē$-	and	*-eh_2- : *-$ēh_2$-
	*h_3e- : *$h_3ē$-		*-eh_3- : *-$ēh_3$-

Level II after transformation:

a) $*h_2a$- : $*h_2o$- and $*$-ah_2- : $*$-oh_2-
$*h_3o$- : $*h_3o$- $*$-oh_3- : $*$-oh_3-

b) $*h_2a$- : $*h_2\bar{e}$- and $*$-ah_2- : $*$-$\bar{e}h_2$-
$*h_3o$- : $*h_3\bar{e}$- $*$-oh_3- : $*$-$\bar{e}h_3$-

3) Examples: — For Hitt. *mēḫ-ur* 'appropriate, correct time' < PIE *$*m\bar{e}h_2$-u̥r̥*: → Eichner in §1. — For PIE $*h_2e\acute{k}$- (becoming $*h_2a\acute{k}$-) 'pointed' and $*h_2o\acute{k}$- with ablaut, one may cite Gr. ἄκ-ρος 'located on the point' and ὄκ-ρις 'point, sharp edge,' further Hitt. *ḫé-kur* i.e. *ḫēk-ur* 'clifftop' (However, this interpretation by H. Eichner [in MSS 31 1973 p. 71] is not uncontroversial: → Melchert *Anatolian Historical Phonology* 1994 p. 144; Rieken *Nominale Stammbildung* 1999 p. 287-289). — Along with PIE $*seh_2$*u̯el*-, becoming $*sah_2$*u̯el*- 'sun' (> Proto-Gr. **hāu̯el-ii̯o-* = Cret. [Hesychius] ἀβέλιος, Epic-Ionic ἠέλιος, Att. ἥλιος) one may also be able to ascertain, via Luwian *si(ḫ)u̯al* 'lamp,' a Vr̥ddhi derivation, $*s\bar{e}h_2$*u̯ol-ó*- (including Luwian *ē* > *i* and disappearance of *ḫ* preceding *u̯*): → Starke *Keilschr.-luw. Nomen* 1990 p. 342f. — Along with PIE $*\acute{g}neh_3$- (becoming $*\acute{g}noh_3$-) 'to discern' (compare with the zero grade $*\acute{g}\mathring{n}h_3$- Lat. [*g*]*nō-scō*, OCS *zna-ti*) there appears to exist in Hittite *gnē-s-* 'he discerns' a lengthened grade $*\acute{g}n\bar{e}h_3$-: → J. Jasanoff in *Laryngaltheorie* 1988 p. 227ff. — Formerly unclear ablaut relationships, such as that between Lat. *aqua* 'water' and ON *ægir* 'sea' < PIE $*\bar{e}k^w$- now reveal themselves to be simple quantity ablauts with full grade $*h_2ek^w$- (becoming $*h_2ak^w$-) and lengthened grade $*h_2\bar{e}k^w$-. — Further examples and suggestions for further reading: → Mayrhofer *Lautlehre* 1986 p. 132ff., p. 141f.; Melchert *Anatolian Historical Phonology* 1994 p. 68.

L 332. For *set*-roots PIE $*\acute{g}enh_1$- 'to create' = Ved. jan^i- and PIE $*terh_2$- 'to cross' = Ved. tar^i-, one would expect zero grade forms with $*$-$\mathring{n}h_1$- , and $*$-$\mathring{r}h_2$- (in older notation: $*$-$\bar{\mathring{n}}$-, $*\bar{\mathring{r}}$-), cf. L 315 § 3. For information on the significance of these zero grade forms with regard to the consonantal character of **-H-*, cf. L 319 § 1. They confirm the accuracy of the use of PIE $*h_1$, $*h_2$, and $*h_3$:

1) In Greek, while preconsonantal PIE $*\mathring{n}h_1$ becomes νη, PIE $*\mathring{n}h_2$ becomes νᾱ, PIE $*\mathring{n}h_3$ becomes νω. Correspondingly, preconsonantal PIE $*\mathring{r}h_{1\text{-}3}$ > Gr. ρη /ρᾱ / ρω etc.

2) Additionally, there are a number of two syllable examples in Greek of the type θάνατος 'death' alongside the regular θνητός 'mortal.' The explanation of this appearance of two syllables is disputed. One possible reason is the ac-

cent: Thus, the development of PIE *-$\acute{\mathring{n}}h_2$- > *-°nh_2- > *-*ana*- etc. would be conceivable (with assimilation of the weak vowel from the series °*n* [itself having originated in *n̥*] into the quality of the laryngeal that immediately follows): → Rix *Historische Grammatik des Griechischen* 1976 p. 73; Vine *"Deverbative *-etó-"* 1998 p. 12ff. (including the suggestion of another solution); C. Rico in *IF* 105 2000 p. 161-200; H. Rix in *Kratylos* 41 1996 p. 158 (concerning Latin).

3) Further languages that are not treated here, such as Armenian and Tocharian, exhibit developments that vary according to the nature of the laryngeal. Compare the material for IE*$\mathring{r}h_1$ vs. IE*$\mathring{r}h_2$ and *$\mathring{r}h_3$. Further reading: → Mayrhofer *Lautlehre* 1986 p. 128.

4) Correspondence sets for preconsonantal PIE *n̥*H*, PIE *m̥*H*, PIE *l̥*H* and PIE *r̥*H*:

4a) PIE *$\mathring{n}h_1$ = Gr. *nē*. In the other languages that are more thoroughly treated here, PIE *n̥*H* has in each case only one result: Lat. *nā* < *n̥*H*, Ved. *ā* < **aH* < *n̥*H* (concerning *m̥*H*: → M. Mayrhofer in *Quaderni dell'Istituto di Glottologia* 6 1994 [1995] p. 197ff.), Germ. *unK* < **unHK* (with interconsonantal laryngeal disappearance) < *n̥*HK*. For information on Lithuanian and Slavic, cf. 4d). — Cf. PIE *$\acute{g}\mathring{n}h_1$-*tó*- part. 'created, born' = Gr. κασί-γνητος 'brother,' Lat. (*g*)*nātus*, Ved. *jātá*-, Got. (*airþa-*)*kunds* 'of earthly origin' (cf. L 334 § 4). — Also compare Ved. *ā́sat*- < PIE *$\acute{\mathring{n}}$-h_1s-$\mathring{n}t$- above E 504 § 9.

4b) PIE *$\mathring{n}h_2$ = Gr. *nā* (ion.-Att. > *nē*), otherwise as in 4a (Ved. *ā*, Lat. *nā*, Germ. *un* etc.). — Cf. PIE *$d^h u̯\mathring{n}h_2$-*tó*- 'filled with smoke' = Ion. Gr. θνητός (with *ē* < *ā*) 'mortal' (older *'breathed out,' *'dead'; the meaning 'mortal' is a secondary development from ἀθάνατος 'immortal' [< *'having no death'] cf. semantic parallels with βροτός above in L 307 § 1). However, this long-held etymology of θνητός is not phonetically unproblematic. One would expect to find echoes of *t^h*u̯ánato*- in this case; however, traces of *u̯* are not attested in the Homeric θάνατος: → J.-L. Perpillou in *RPh* 50 1976 p. 50ff.

4c) PIE *$\mathring{n}h_3$ = Gr. *nō*; otherwise as in 4a (Ved. *ā*, Lat. *nā*, Germ. *un* etc.). — Compare PIE zero grade *$\acute{g}\mathring{n}h_3$- (from PIE *$\acute{g}neh_3$- 'discern') = Lat. *gnā-rus* 'knowledgeable' (as well as *narrāre* < **gnārāre* according to the so-called *littera*-rule for the type *Iuppiter* < *Iūpiter*. → H. Rix in *FS Watkins* 1998 p. 625f.), OHG *kun-d* 'well-known,' Lith. *pa-žìntinas* 'worth knowing'; as well as phonetically Gr. γνω-τός 'well-known' (→ Mayrhofer Lautlehre 1986 p. 144 with suggestions for further reading). — Also compare the negation PIE *n̥*- + PIE *h_3b^hel- (cf. Gr. ὄφελος n.

'use'): PIE _*n̥-h$_3$p^h-_ > Gr. _nōp^h-_ yet in Myc. _no-pe-re-ha_ i.e. _nōp^{h}ele^{h}a_ acc. pl. n. 'useless' (the same word appears later with a clearer negation as ἀνωφελής).

4d) PIE _*l̥h$_1$_, _*r̥h$_1$_ = Gr. _lē_ / _rē_, Lat. _lā_ / _rā_, Ved. _īr_ (in a labial context _ūr_), Germ. _ul_ / _ur_; in the Baltic and Slavic languages, _*il_ / _ir_ / _im_ / _in_ distinguish themselves from _*l̥H_ / _r̥H_ / _m̥H_ / _n̥H_ through intonation (for example, Lith. _ìl_) of _il_ / _ir_ / _im_ / _in_ from non-laryngeal _*l̥_ / _r̥_ / _m̥_ / _n̥_ (Lith. _il̃_ etc.): → Schrijver _Laryngeals in Latin_ 1991 p. 5ff. — Zero grade PIE _*pl̥h$_1$-_ (Concerning the full grade _*pleh$_1$-_ 'to fill,' cf. Gr. πίμ-πλη-μι; the full grade _*pelh$_1$-_ is only reflected in Ved. _párī-ṇas-_ n. 'fullness' and Gr. πολύς < _*polh$_1$u-_: → LIV 1998 p. 434 note 1. For more information on Gr. πολύς → Nussbaum _Two Studies_ 1998 p. 149; for more information on the two full grades, cf. L 417 § 3) = Gr. πλη-θύς f. 'fullness,' Ved. _pūr-ṇá-_ 'full,' Proto-Germ. _*fulH-na-_ (with simplification of the consonant group > _*fulna-_ = Got. _fulls_), Lith. _pìlnas_ (in comparison with Lith. _vil̃kas_ 'wolf' < _*u̯l̥k^{w}o-_ = Ved. _vŕ̥ka-_).

4e) PIE _*r̥h$_2$_ / _*l̥h$_2$_ = Gr. _rā_ / _lā_, otherwise as _*h$_1$_ in 4d: — PIE _*k̑r̥h$_2$-tó-_ part. 'mixed' (IE root _*k̑erh$_2$-_ with Gr. aorist κερά-σ[σ]αι) = Gr. ἄ-κρᾱτος 'unmixed,' Ved. _ā́-śīrta-_ part. 'mixed.' — PIE _*tl̥h$_2$-_ (IE root _*telh$_2$-_ 'to carry, bear' in Gr. τελα-μών 'straps for carrying') = Dor. Gr. τλᾱτός (> Att. τλητός) 'bearable,' Lat. _lātus_ < _*tlātos_ 'carried'; PIE _*pl̥h$_2$-nó-_ 'flat, even' = Lat. _plānus_ (also PIE * _pl̥h$_2$-i-_ = Hitt. _palḫi-_ 'wide'), cf. L 307 § 2.

4f) PIE _*r̥h$_3$_ = Gr. _rō_; otherwise analogous to _*h$_1$_ in 4d: — PIE _*str̥h$_3$-tó-/*str̥h$_3$-nó-_ 'spread out' (concerning full grade PIE _*sterh$_3$-_, cf. Ved. _stárī-man-_ 'spread') = Gr. στρωτός, Lat. _strātus_, Ved. _stīrṇá-_, cf. also Lith. _stìrta_ '(hay)stack.'

L 333. The triple character of the PIE laryngeals is also shown in the various representations of preconsonantal PIE _*#HR̥_ in Greek and perhaps also in Latin. The classical treatment of this subject is: → H. Rix "_Anlautender Laryngal vor Liquida oder Nasalis sonans im Griechischen_" in MSS 27 1970 p. 79-110. According to what is called the Lex Rix, preconsonantal PIE _*#h$_1$r̥-_ (= Ved. _r̥-_) becomes, in Greek for example ἐρ-, PIE _#h$_2$r̥-_ (= Ved. _r̥-_) becomes ἀρ-, PIE _*#h$_3$r̥-_ (= Ved. _r̥-_ and Avest. _ərə-_]) becomes ὀρ-.

1) Evidence: — PIE _*h$_1$r̥sk̑e-_ 'to come, to reach' = Gr. ἔρχεται, Ved. part. _r̥ccháti_ 'reached,' Hitt. _arski-t^{s}i_ 'he arrives.' — PIE _*h$_2$r̥ǵ-(r)ó-_ (along with the _-i-_ stem [originally substantive] _*h$_2$r̥ǵ-i-_) 'shining, flashing, white' = Gr. ἀργός along with ἀργί-πους, Ved. _r̥jrá-_ along with the proper noun _R̥jí-śvan-_

(Translated into Greek, one may find the Homeric expression κύνες ἀργοί: → W. Schulze *Kleine Schriften* 1966 p. 124); Hitt. *ḫarki-* 'white.' For more information on the juxtapositioning of the suffixes *-ro-* / *-i-* cf. W 206. — PIE **h₂r̥K-* also in Gr. ἄρκτος = Ved. *ŕ̥kṣa-* 'bear,' and Hitt. *ḫartka-*, cf. L 313 § 2. — For more details (including examples for other representations including PIE **h₂r̥-*, **h₂l̥-*, **h₃r̥-* etc.): → H. Rix above.

2) Whether the situation in Latin resembled that of Greek is still discussed. Any remnants of this, as in Greek, seem to be lost. Concerning PIE *#*h₂n̥-*, see the example *amb*(*i*)- 'around, about' < **h₂n̥bʰ-*; for PIE *#*h₃n̥K-* see the examples *umbilīcus* 'navel' < **h₃n̥bʰel-* and *unguis* 'nail' < **h₃n̥gʷʰ-*: → Rix *Termini der Unfreiheit* 1994 p. 14ff.; by the same author, in *Kratylos* 41 1996 p. 155 note 3 (also concerning *ēnsis* 'sword' < *'knife'; it belongs with Ved. *así-* 'battle knife' and may be traced to **n̥s-i-* 'knife'; while Palaic *ḫasira-* 'dagger' is different; for a more thorough treatment of these problems in terms of content: → B. Schlerath "*Metallgegenstände in vedischer Zeit*" in *Χρόνος, Beiträge zur prähistorischen Archäologie zwischen Nord- und Südosteuropa, Festschrift für B. Hänsel*, edited by C. Becker et al. Espelkamp 1997, p. 823ff.).

3) For information on the representation of laryngeals in Tocharian: O. Hackstein in *Fachtagung Innsbruck* 1996 [1998] p. 220ff.

L 334. As a rule, the laryngeals were disposed of only after the Proto-Indo-European era.

1) With its *ḫ*, Anatolian retains direct traces of PIE **h₂*, cf. among others, *ḫant-* 'face' in L 322 § 2 above and *ḫaster-* 'star' in L 328 § 2 above. The extent to which *h₃* is also reflected by *ḫ* is currently discussed: → Melchert *Anatolian Historical Phonology* 1994 p. 72-74.

2) Indo-Iranian also contains direct traces: — The initially conspicuous metrical measurement of *devī́* in the Vedic phrase RV I 40,3 *devyètu* i.e. *deví etu* as — ⏑ is best understandable if we suppose that *devī́* 'goddess' still contained the laryngeal form **deu̯íH* (with **-íH* < **-ih₂*) at the time of formulation of the verse in question. In the phase **-íH* it was possible for the laryngeal simply to disappear before a vowel (in this case, *e-* <**ai̯-*) as a sandhi phenomenon: **-íH#V-* = **-í.HV-* > **-í.V-*. In the case of **-aH* (< **-eh₂*) stems, which are formed in a parallel manner, confirmed clues as to a sandhi variant with *-ă* (from **-aH#V-* = **-a.HV-* > **-ă.V-*) are missing. The source of the preceding material is F. B. J. Kuiper: → *Sprache* 7 1961 p. 14ff. (= Kuiper *Selected Writings* 1997 p. 359ff.).

3) The sandhi variant that is no longer attested in Vedic appears to be furnished by Greek and Old Church Slavic. The PIE *-ah_2- (<*-eh_2-) stems also have, along with a uniform nom. sg. -ah_2 > -*ā* (cf. Gr. νύμφη 'young woman' and OCS *žena* 'woman'), voc. sg. -*ă* forms (cf. Gr. νύμφα and OCS *ženo*). Clear traces are missing that would confirm a PIE ablaut with *full grade* *-eh_2- and zero grade *-h_2-. (For potential clues in Mycenaean: → I. Hajnal in *Floreant Studia Mycenaea I* 1995 [1999] p. 265-276). That is why it appears as if the differentiation between the nominative and vocative singular in this case could be traced to sandhi-influenced double forms that were common at a time when the stems were still composed of *-ah_2, and the contraction *-ah_2- > *-*ā*- had not yet occurred. The form *-ah_2, at the time situated in the position -*VH#K*-, with the later development *-ah_2.*K*- > -*ā.K*-, became the normal nominative form; while -*ă* (with actual *-*a.*h_2 *V*- > *-*ă.V*-), which occurred in the position -*VH#V*-, was assigned to the vocative.

4) Another example of the individuality of the various IE languages in their reception of the then extant laryngeal is furnished by a past participle participle such as PIE *ǵn̥h_1-*tó*- 'created, born' (cf. L 332 § 4a), in which various IE language forms of PIE *n̥ first appear, and only afterward is PIE *h_1 eliminated: The laryngeal is retained in Vedic until the conclusion of the *n̥ > *ă vocalization process, after which it lengthens the short vowel which it produces, forming *jātá*-. In the case of Greek, the same basic form develops via *gn°h_1-*tó*- > *gnētó*- (cf. κασί-γνητος), in Latin, via the same intermediate grade > *(g)nātus*. In a similar fashion as in Vedic, a **kunHda*- with –*un*- < -n̥- is created in Proto-Germanic via *ǵn̥h_1*tó*-, with the simplification of the consonant group *-*nHd*- to *-*nd*-. Cf. Got. *airþa-kunds* 'of earthly origin.' — On the possibly two-syllable Old Avestan *va.ata*- < **Hu̯áHata*- cf. L 323 § 1b. — On Vedic 1 sg. **ca-kar-Ha* (the *H* still preserved in the period of the activity of Brugmann's law), cf. L 412. — On Ved. *náuṣ* < **naHus*, cf. F 318 § 6c.

4. Occlusives

L 335. The faithful phonetic handing down of the Vedic language reveals a group of four plosives, also called occlusives. For example, in the realm of dentals Vedic contains the phonemes *t*, *th*, *d* and *dh*. The transcription of simple symbols in Indian script into the digraphs *th*, *dh*, etc. is established in Indology. However, these are in fact single phoneme values that distinguish themselves from *t*, and *d*, for example, only by the characteristic [+ aspirated]. Thus, equivalents such as t^h, d^h or *t*,' *d*ʿ would be more appropriate.

1) This Vedic group of four provided the model for Proto-Indo-European reconstructions. The Proto-Indo-European preliminary phase of the Vedic phonemes was reconstructed (here, for the sake of simplicity, dentals are used) from unchanged **t*, $*t^h$, **d*, $*d^h$.

2) Several reconstruction approaches for the tenuis aspirata $*t^h$ must be abandoned in light of current knowledge of laryngeals, according to which Vedic *th* might have originated from PIE **t* + $*h_2$, cf. L 329 § 1. Thus, reconstructions which include the true PIE tenuis aspirata are seldom. For example, compare PIE $*skeh_1t^h$- with Gr. ἀσκηθής 'undamaged' and Got. *skaþis* n. 'damage' and PIE $*\acute{k}onk^ho$- and Gr. κόγχος and Ved. *śaṅkhá-* m. 'mussel.' For the sake of clarity, in the following depiction, only tenuis, media, and media aspirata shall be taken as points of departure.

3) Because of the extreme deficit of correspondence sets with tenues aspiratae, as well as other typological reasons (including the rarity of correspondence sets for PIE *b*: → W. Meid *Das Problem von idg. /b/.* Innsbruck 1989), replacement systems for the PIE occlusive series have been suggested, for example (among others) the glottalization theory, represented by Th.V. Gamkrelidze and V.V. Ivanov in Gamkrelidze / Ivanov *IE and IEs* 1995, which asserts the existence of glottalized (*p*', *t*', *k*'), voiced (*bh*/*b*, *dh*/*d*, *gh*/*g*) and voiceless (*ph*/*p*, *th*/*t*, *kh*/*k*) in place of the traditional triads, media (*b*, *d*, *g*), media aspirata (b^h, d^h, g^h) and tenuis (*p*, *t*, *k*).

The reaction to this in the field is split: — A new statement from the pen of Th. V. Gamkrelidze: → *"A Relative Chronology of the Shifts of the Three Stop Series in Indo-European"* in *FS Hamp* I 1997 p. 67-82; by the same author, "*Neue Wege in der Indogermanistik in der zweiten Hälfte des 20. Jahrhunderts*" in Graz 2000 p. 153-158. — Reports and positions on glottal theory: → Mayrhofer *Lautlehre* 1986 p. 92 ff.; W. Cowgill in *Kratylos* 29 1984 [1985] p. 4-6 (Concerning contributions by P. J. Hopper, G. Dunkel and Th. V. Gamkrelidze, he reports: "it looks to me as if a pre-Proto-Indo-European system **t*(*h*), **t*,' **d*(*h*) shifted ... to a highly unstable PIE system **t*, **d*, **dh*, which was replaced everywhere before our earliest written documents by a more stable configuration"); Szemerényi *Scripta Minora I* 1987 (in an essay from 1985) p. 400-410 and Szemerényi *Einführung* 1990 p. 159-162 (p. 160: "The new interpretation ... has already found a considerable following ..., while the refusal appears rather sheepish for the time being"; p. 160f. "perhaps it will be useful to call attention to a few disturbing moments"); W. Meid "*Germanische oder* *indogermanische Lautverschiebung?*" in *Althochdeutsch I* 1987 p. 3-11 (p. 11: "The explanation of a loanword such as the Germanic **rīk-* within the context of a 'new' theory bumps against so many problems that the appropriateness of the theory must be seriously questioned"); *New Sound of Indo-European* 1989 (The complete spectrum of glottal theory is discussed broadly by various researchers, p. 83ff.); J. Gippert "*Die Glottaltheorie und die Frage urindogermanisch-kaukasischer Sprachkontakte*" in *Kolloquium Pedersen Copenhagen* 1993 [1994] p. 107-123; by the same author, in BNF 33 1998 p. 41-45 (p. 43 "serious reservations," p. 45 "such argumentative weaknesses"); M. Job, "Did Proto-Indo-European have Glottalized Stops?" in *Diachronica* 12 1995 p. 237ff.; Lamberterie, *Armenien classique* 1992 p. 251-255 (p. 255: "*Le traitement du groupe *dw- (> Arm. erk-) ... oblige en outre à partir d'une sonore *d, non d'une sourde glottalisée *t*"'); Ch. de Lamberterie "*Latin pignus et la théorie glottalique*" in *Aspects of Latin* 1993 [1996] p. 135-151; F. Kammerzell in *IF* 104 1999 p. 234ff.

In the opinion of the authors of the present work, doubts as to the justification of the glottal approach to Proto-Indo-European have not been dismissed. Thus, glottals shall not be taken into account in present reconstructions.

4) Along with the dentals presented above, there are labials (cf. L 337f.) and tectals (cf. L 339ff.). The latter are composed of palatals, velars and labiovelars. Following the example of H. Eichner in *Kolloquium Lat. u. Idg.* Salzburg 1992 p. 65, the inventory of PIE occlusives may thus be displayed:

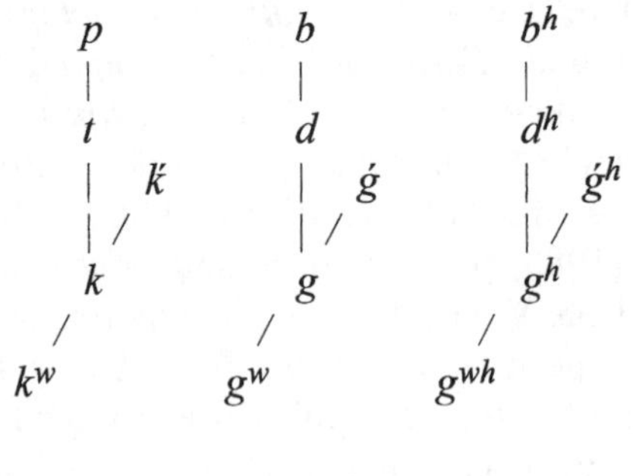

5. Dentals

L 336. In the Indo-European languages:

1) The PIE tenuis *t, media *d and media aspirata *d^h reconstructions are, in their articulation type, preserved in Vedic. The point of articulation also remains the same in the case of dentals, in contrast to PIE *$\acute{k}$ > Ved. *ś* and PIE *k^w > Ved. *k*, cf. L 339 § 2: — Compare PIE **tréi̯es* 'three' = Ved. *tráyas*; PIE **déḱm̥* 'ten' = Ved. *dáśa-*; PIE *$d^h uh_2 m\acute{o}$- 'smoke' = Ved. *dhūmá-*, PIE *$m\acute{e}d^h i̯o$- adj. 'middle' = Ved. *mádhya-*, PIE *$h_1 rud^h r\acute{o}$- 'red' = Ved. *rud-hirá-*.

2) Only the articulation type of the PIE mediae aspiratae changes in Greek. Already in the pre-Mycenaean period, they lose their [+ voiced] characteristic. Thus, Gr. t^h <θ> takes the place of PIE *d^h. Concerning the examples in § 1, compare τρεῖς and δέκα, but θυμός and ἐρυθρός (already in the Mycenaean period *e-ru-ta-ra* i.e. *eruthrā́*). Also compare PIE *$med^h i̯o$- with Gr. μέσ(σ)ος, cf. L 215 § 2. – On the so called assibilation with *-t(h)i-* > *-si-* see Lejeune *Phonétique* 1972 p. 63-65; cf. § 5 below for a similar development in Hittite.

3) In the case of Latin, only the preservation of tenuis and media can generally be ascertained (cf. *trēs*, *decem*). The continuations of media aspirata must be separately described in each case. Thus, PIE *d^h becomes *f-* (cf. *fūmus*) when it is word-initial, *-d-* (cf. *medius*) when word-internal, and *-b-* under special conditions (e.g. following *-u-* and near *-r-*, as in the case of *ruber* < PIE *$h_1 rud^h r\acute{o}$-): → Leumann LLFL 1977 p. 163ff.

4) In the case of Germanic, in principle one rule may be advanced which is called the first consonant shift or Grimm's Law and concerns all articulation types: The tenuis becomes an unvoiced fricative, cf. PIE **tréi̯es* 'three' vs. ON *þrír* 'three'; the media becomes a tenuis, cf. PIE **déḱm̥* 'ten' vs. Got. *tai-hun* 'ten'; the media aspirata becomes a voiced fricative, cf. PIE *$h_1 rud^h r\acute{o}$- 'red' vs. ON *rauðr* 'red'). — However, the unvoiced fricatives that are produced by this process are only preserved (as is the case of word-internal PIE **s* [cf. L 308ff.] in a voiced context), when they directly follow the PIE accent. They otherwise become voiced fricatives (Verner's Law), cf. L 421 § 1 ff. For information on later developments, particularly the second consonant shift: → Schwerdt *2. LV* 2000.

5) The media and media aspirata having merged, the tenuis : media dichotomy was probably preserved in the Hittite language, however cuneiform allows the difference to be discerned in only a few cases. Thus, in the present case, the same *t/d-* symbols for PIE **t* (cf. *e-eš-du* along with Ved. *ás-tu* 'he should be'), **d* (cf. *e-it-mi* 'I eat,' *e-du-un* 'I ate' alongside Lat. *edere*) and PIE *d^h are presented (cf. L 211 § 7 concerning *túḫ-ḫu-u̯a-i-* and Ved.

dhūmá-; further cf. L 313 § 3 concerning PIE *d^h*eǵ^h*- = Hitt. *te-e-kán*, loc. sg. *da-ga-an* 'earth'). — Yet there exists what is called the Sturtevant Rule in order to distinguish tenuis particularly between vowels through doubling of the media, cf. *ú-it-ti* = Lat. *vet-us*, cf. L 217 § 1. — Rules of lenition must also be taken into account: → H. Eichner in MSS 31 1973 p. 79-83 and p. 100 note 56; Melchert *Anatolian Historical Phonology* 1994 p. 60f. (A tenuis following an accented long vowel changed to a lenis articulation already in the Proto-Anatolian era, cf. PIE *d^héh$_1$ti* 'stellt' > Proto-Anatolian **dḗdi* = Lycian *tadi*). — Finally, what is called assibilation of *t* > t^s (common notation: *z*) preceding *i* cf. 3rd pers. sg. *e-eš-zi* i.e. *ēs*t^s*i* = Ved. *ásti* 'he is'. In the case of *th$_2$* (= Ved. *th*), the assibilation is stopped preceding *i*. On a similar development in Gr. dialects see § 2 above. — Concerning Hitt. *tst* < PIE **tt*, cf. L 347 § 1.

6) The tenuis is preserved in Baltic and Slavic (thus, PIE **t* as *t*); while media and media aspirata merge into media (PIE **d* and PIE *d^h > *d*). Compare Lith. *trỹs*, OCS *trьje* 'three'; Lith. *dešimtìs*, OCS *desętь* 'ten'; Lith. *dū́mai*, OCS *dymъ* 'smoke' (cf. L 211 § 7); Lith. *rùdas* 'reddish,' Russ. *rudyj* 'red-haired.' The existence of a Baltic or a Slavic version of the media/media aspirata dichotomy has not been confirmed: → Mayrhofer *Lautlehre* 1986 p. 96 note 21.

6. Labials

L 337. The labial tenuis and media, PIE **p* and PIE **b*, are retained in most of the IE languages. In Germanic, however, PIE **p* led to *f* (and, in cases where lex Verner applies, to *ƀ*, cf. L 421) and PIE **b* led to *p*. In Celtic, PIE **p* first becomes **f*, then, when preceding *s* and *t*, it appears as *x*, and otherwise as *h* (preceding a disappearance), cf. Irish *athir* 'father' < PIE **ph$_2$ter-*, cf. Old Irish *ibim* 'I drink' < PIE **pi-ph$_3$-e-*, cf. *Ver-cingeto-rix*, the Celtic leader known from Caesar, in whose name the first element *u̯er-* may be traced to **u(p)er-*, or cf. the place name *Mailand* = Lat. *Mediolānum* < **Medio-(p)lānum*.

1) Correspondence sets for PIE **p*: — PIE **pod-*/**ped-* = Lat. *pēs, ped-* 'foot,' Gr. πούς, ποδ-, Ved. *pád-*, Luwian *pa-da- pa-ta-* 'foot,' Lith. *pėdà* 'foot bottom,' Slovenian *pòd* 'floor'; Got. *fotus*, NHG *Fuß*. — PIE **su̯ep-*/**sup-* = Lat. *sopor* (< **su̯ep-*) 'deep sleep,' Gr. ὕπνος m. (< **sup-no-*), Ved. *svápna-* m. 'sleep,' Hitt. *šu-up-pa-ri-i̯a-* i.e. *supari̯a-* 'to sleep,' Lith. *sãpnas* 'dream,' OCS *sъpati* 'to sleep'; ON *svefn* subs. 'sleep.' Concerning Lat. *somnus*, cf. L 217 § 4. — PIE *(*s*)*up-* with Gr. ὑπέρ 'over,' Ved. *upári*

'over to,' OHG *ubir* 'over' (Proto-Germ. **uf-´,* concerning the accent, cf. L 421 § 1), celtic **u̯er-* (cf. § 1 above).

2) Correspondence sets for PIE **b*: — PIE **bel-* with Lat. *dē-bil-is* (*-bil-* < **-bel-*) 'powerless,' Gr. βελ-τίων 'better' (< *'stronger'), Ved. *bála-* n. 'power,' OCS *bolijь* 'larger.' — PIE **dʰeu̯b-* with Lith. *dubùs* 'deep, hollow,' OCS *dъbrъ* 'gorge,' Toch. A *tpär* 'high'; Got. *diups*, NHG *tief*. For more information: → Mayrhofer *Lautlehre* 1986 p. 99f.; Meid /b/ 1989.

L 338. As expected, the labial media aspirata PIE **bʰ* corresponds to Ved. *bh*, Gr. *pʰ* <φ>, Proto-Germ. **ƀ*, Hitt. *b* <*p,b*>, Lith. and OCS *b*. Word-initially, Latin features *f-*; word-internally, *-b-*.

Correspondence sets: — PIE **bʰer-* = Lat. *ferō*, Gr. φέρω, Ved. *bhárāmi* 'I carry,' Got. *bairan* 'to carry,' OCS *berǫ* 'I take, I collect.' — PIE **bʰréh₂ter-* becoming **bʰráh₂ter-* = Lat. *frāter* 'brother,' Gr. φρᾱ́τηρ 'member of a brotherhood,' Ved. *bhrā́tar-* m., Got. *broþar*, OCS *brat(r)ъ* 'brother,' cf. Lith. *bróterautis* 'to fraternize.' — PIE **nebʰ-* = Lat. *nebula* f. 'haze, fog,' Gr. νεφέλη f. 'cloud,' νέφος n. 'cloud, cloud mass,' Ved. *nábhas-* n. 'cloud, fog,' Hitt. *ne-pí-ša-aš* gen. 'of the sky,' OCS *nebo, -ese* 'sky.'

7. Tectals

L 339. Under the heading 'tectals' are included palatals, velars, and labiovelars.

1) All three types are retained in Luwian, cf. Luw. *kar-š-* < PIE **(s)ker-* 'to cut' (→ LIV 1998 p. 503), *kui-* < PIE **kʷi-* 'who' and *zārt-* < PIE **ḱr̥d-* 'heart': → Melchert *Anatolian Historical Phonology* 1994 p. 251f. Albanian and Armenian provide similar clues, cf. J. Tischler in § 4; further cf. L 343 § 3. However, a reduction to only two sorts is the rule.

2) In the centum languages (Italic [including Latin], Greek, Hittite, Germanic, Celtic, Tocharian, and Phrygian) palatals and velars produce the same results. One may thus assume that the tenues PIE **ḱ* (palatal) and PIE **k* (velar) lead to only one continuation in these languages. In Latin this is *k* (<c>), in Greek, *k* (<κ>), in Hittite, *k* (denoted as *k* or *g*), and in Proto-Germanic, *χ* (where Verner's Law applies, however: *g*, cf. L 421). The heading for this group, the Latin <*centum*>, i.e. *kentum* < PIE **dḱm̥tó-* 'hundred,' is purposely sometimes spelled '*kentum*' in order that the Classical Latin *c* not be falsely taken as a palatal.

3) The satem languages (Indo-Iranian, Baltic, Slavic, Armenian and Albanian) feature two separate developments of the PIE phonemes *k̑ and *k. The palatal *k̑ becomes an unvoiced sibilant (Ved. ś, Lith. š, OCS s); while the velar k remains unchanged (Ved. k, Lith. k, OCS k). — In the satem languages, the velars lead to the same results as the labiovelars, as a rule. — Just as occurred most often in later Roman Latin, where a k preceding e or i was palatized (indeed centum [i.e. kentum] > Logudorian [of Sardinia] kentu, but Italian cento, French cent, etc.), k-phonemes of satem languages are subjected to secondary palatizations preceding front vowels. It should be noted that also in Indo-Iranian, *ĕ caused the palatization of a preceding k phoneme. Only after this process did *ĕ become ă, cf. L 206 § 2. Parallel to the heading centum, the Later Avestan satəm 'hundred,' usually written in the simplified satem form, provided the name for this group of languages.

4) The categorization of IE languages into centum and satem languages bore too much emphasis in earlier research. The affiliation of IE languages as centum and satem languages cannot have played a decisive role in the evolution of IE languages. Consider, for example the centum language Greek and the satem language Armenian: Despite this difference, they both must be considered quite near to one another, cf. E 435 § 1.

An overview of research: → J. Tischler "Hundert Jahre kentum-satem Theorie" in IF 95 1990 p. 63-98. Cf. particularly p. 94:

"The centum-satem isogloss is not to be equated with a division of Indo-European, but rather represents simply one isogloss among many ... examples of 'centum-like aspects' in satem languages and of 'satem-like aspects' in centum languages that may be evaluated as relics of the original three-part plosive system, which otherwise was reduced everywhere to a two-part system."

Cf. further G. van Driem and S. R. Sharmā, "In Search of Kentum Indo-Europeans in the Himalayas" in IF 101 1996 p. 107-146; Lipp Palatale 1994.

L 340. Correspondence sets:

1) For PIE *k̑: — PIE *k̑erd- / *k̑r̥d- 'heart,' PIE *k̑r̥-n- 'horn,' PIE *(d)k̑m̥tó- 'hundred,' PIE *dek̑m̥to- 'the tenth,' cf. L 307 § 1 and 3. — PIE *k̑leu̯- 'to hear' with the participle PIE *k̑lu-tó- 'famed' = Lat. in-clutus, Gr. κλυτός 'famed,' Proto-Germ. *χluda- (cf. the name of the Frankish king Chlodo-meris, among others) alongside Ved. śrutá- 'heard, named, famed,'

Lith. *šlóvinti* 'to prize, to praise,' OCS *sluti* 'to name.' — PIE **k̑u̯on-* / **k̑un-* 'dog' = Gr. κύων, gen. sg. κυνός, Got. *hun-d-s* 'dog' alongside Ved. *śvā́*, gen. sg. *śúnas*, Lith. *šuõ*, gen. sg. *šuñs* (or, older *šunès*) 'dog' (On this word, cf. L 218 § 2 above). — Concerning PIE **k̑ei̯-* 'to lay' (related to PIE **k̑éi̯-u̯o-* 'dear, familiar,' substantivized as 'home') cf. Lat. *cīvis* (Old Latin *ceivis* 'citizen': the *-i-* stem is conspicuous; perhaps it developed from a compound such as the Early Latin **kon-kei̯u̯i-* 'which has the same homeland,' cf. the type adj. *biennis* 'two-years old' < **du̯i-anni-* with *-anni-* for *-anno-*: → Rix *Termini der Unfreiheit* 1994 p. 78 with note 89), Gr. κεῖμαι 'I lay,' Hitt. *ki-it-ta(-ri)* 'he lay,' Got. *heiwa-frauja* 'head of the household' alongside Ved. *śáye* 'he lay,' *śéva-* 'dear, familiar,' *śivá-* 'goodly, friendly' (Cf. also name of a divinity *Śiva*), cf. Lith. *šeimà* 'family,' Russ. *semьja* 'family.'

2) For PIE **k*: — Concerning PIE **kreu̯h₂-* / **kruh₂-* 'raw, bloody, raw meat' cf. Lat. *cruor* m. 'raw blood,' Gr. κρυερός 'terrible,' κρέας n. 'meat,' OHG *hrō* 'raw,' Ved. *kravíṣ-* n. 'raw meat,' *krūrá-* 'bloody, raw,' Lith. *kraũjas* m. 'blood,' OCS *krъvь* f. 'blood.' — PIE **leu̯k-* 'to light' with PIE subst. **lou̯k-o-* 'clearing' (cf. L 223 § 2), cf. Ved. *lok-á-*; with secondary palatization Ved. *róc-ate* 'he/she/it lights' (< **leu̯k-e-*), *rúci-* f. 'light,' Russ. *lučь* m. 'ray.'

L 341. According to L 339 § 2, the palatal and velar media PIE **ǵ* and **g* only have one retained form in the centum languages: Latin, Greek, and Hittite *g*, and Germanic *k*. In the satem languages, PIE **ǵ* becomes Ved. *j* (= Avest. *z*), Lith. *ž*, OCS *z*. PIE **g* remains *g* but is subjected to secondary palatization.

1) Correspondence sets for PIE **ǵ*: — PIE **ǵneh₃-* /**ǵenh₃-* 'to discern' with the participle PIE **ǵn̥h₃-tó-* (cf. L 332 § 4c), cf. Lat. *(g)nō-scō*, Gr. γι-γνώ-σκω, OHG *kun-d* 'known'; in the satem language Ved. *(*r̥ta-)jñā́-* 'knowing the R̥ta,' Lith. *žén-klas* m. 'symbol' (with *-én-K-* < **-enh₃-K-*), OCS *zna-ti* 'to discern.' — PIE **ǵonu-* / **ǵnu-* 'knee,' cf. Lat. *genū-*, Gr. γόνυ, Hitt. *ge-e-nu*, Got. *kniu* 'knee' alongside Ved. *jā́nu* n. 'knee,' Later Avestan *zānu(-drājah-)* 'showing knee-length.' For more information on this word: → Mayrhofer EWAia I p. 584f.

2) Correspondence sets for PIE **g*: — PIE **h₂eu̯g-* becoming **h₂au̯g-* / **h₂ug-* 'to increase, to grow,' cf. Lat. *augēre* (→ LIV 1998 p. 245 with note 3). The *-g-*, retained in satem languages, (cf. among others Ved. *ug-rá-* 'powerful') is subjected to secondary palatization when it precedes an original front vowel. This is easily observable in the change of (velar) *-g-* and (palatalized) *-j-* as a reflection of the qualitative ablaut (cf. L 412) in the Old Avestan acc.

sg. *aogō* 'the power' (< PIE **$h_2$au̯gos*) alongside instr. sg. *aojaŋh-ā* 'by means of power' (< PIE **$h_2$au̯ges-*). In Vedic, the palatized form *ójas-* n. 'power' (which corresponds to Old Avestan *aojaŋh-*) was formed in an analogous manner. Taking evidence from Iranian into account, the PIE velar **g* with secondary palatization (= Ved. and Avest. *j*) may clearly be distinguished from the PIE palatal **ǵ* (= Ved. *j*, but Avest. *z*). — PIE **i̯ugó-* n. 'yoke' (cf. L 213 § 1) with the verbal **i̯eu̯g-* 'to yoke, to harness,' cf. Lat. *iungere* 'to connect,' Gr. ζεύγνῡμι 'I yoke' along with Ved. *yóga-* m. 'the harnessing' (with the palatized *-j-*, however *yój-ana-* n. 'team (of draft animals)' and Old Avestan *yaoj-ā* 'I want to yoke'), Lith. *jùngiu* 'I harness to the yoke,' OCS *igo* n. 'yoke.'

L 342. Only one retained form is expected in the centum languages for palatal and velar media aspirata PIE **ǵ^h* and **g^h*. In Greek, this is the tenuis aspirata *k^h* <*χ*>; in Hittite, *g* (denoted as *k* or *g*); and in Germanic, **g*. Latin retains both word-initial prevocalic, and intervocalic **g^h* as *h*, while postconsonantal **g^h* is retained as *g*: → Sommer / Pfister *Lautlehre* 1977 p. 141 (below). — In the satem languages: Vedic retains PIE **ǵ^h* as *h* (Avest. *z*), and PIE **g^h* as *gh* (secondarily palatalized *h* [Avest. *j*]). In Baltic and Slavic the results of PIE **ǵ^h* and PIE **g^h* are identical with those of PIE **ǵ* and PIE **g*: Lith. *ž*, OCS *z*, and Lith., OCS *g*.

1) Correspondence sets for PIE **ǵ^h*: — PIE **ǵ^{h}i̯em-* / **ǵ^{h}im-* (partially **ǵ^{h}ei̯m-*) 'winter,' cf. Lat. *hiems* f., Gr. χειμών m. 'winter,' Hitt. *gi-im-ma-an-t-*, i.e. *gemmant-* 'wintertime,' in satem languages Ved. *himá-* m. 'cold' (Avest. *ziiam-* 'winter'; cf. the Old Indian name of the mountain range *Himālaya-*), Lith. *žiemà*, OCS *zima* f. 'winter.' — PIE **$h_2$enǵ^h-* becoming **$h_2$anǵ^h-* 'to lace up, to narrow in' (older **$h_2$emǵ^h-*: → LIV 1998 p. 236 with note 1), cf. Lat. *angor* (older **angōs*) m. 'constriction,' *angustus* 'narrow,' Gr. ἄγχω 'to strangle,' NHG *eng*; in satem languages Ved. *áṃhas-* n. 'fear' (Avest. *ązah-* n. 'difficulty'), OCS *ǫzъkъ* 'narrow.'

2) Correspondence sets for PIE **g^h*: — PIE **stei̯g^h-* 'to stride,' cf. Gr. στείχω 'I stride,' Got. *steigan* 'to climb'; in satem languages Ved. *pra-stigh-nuyāt* 'he climb (subjunctive),' Lith. *steĩgti* 'to hurry,' OCS *po-stig-nǫ* 'I attain, reach.' — PIE **g^{h}osti-* 'foreigner' = Lat. *hostis* m./f. 'stranger' (later 'warring enemy'), Got. *gasts* m. 'foreigner,' OHG *gast* m. 'stranger, guest'; OCS *gostь* m. 'friendly guest.' — PIE **g^{h}lad^h-* 'smooth,' cf. Lat. *glaber* 'smooth, hairless,' NHG *glatt*; Lith. *glodnùs, glodùs, glõdnas* 'smoothly lying upon,' OCS *gladъkъ* 'smooth, even.' Concerning the problem of PIE *a*, cf. L 211 § 5. — PIE *(h_3)mei̯g^h-* 'cloud, fog,' (which must be distinguished from

the verbal form *$h_3$meig̑^{h}- 'to urinate' [with palatal *ǵ^h]: → Mayrhofer EWAia II p. 381; LIV 1998 p. 268), cf. Gr. ὀμίχλη f. 'fog,' Ved. *meghá-* m. 'cloud,' *míh-* f. 'fog, mist,' Lith. *miglà*, OCS *mьgla* f. 'fog.'

L 343. In contrast to velars, labiovelars have the characteristic of lip-rounding. They are single-phoneme values. Appearing in many languages around the world, labiovelars are commonly denoted in Indo-European linguistics as k^u (more seldom as q^u, k^w or q^w), g^u, etc. The notation k^w, g^w, etc. is preferred in the present work, because of the potential for confusion with *ku̯* in writing k^u: → B. Forssman in *Kratylos* 33 1988 p. 61 note 30.

As a rule, and in the interest of simplification, only examples of labiovelar tenues shall be mentioned in this section. The labiovelar media and media aspirata are treated particularly in L 344ff.

1) The descendents of Proto-Indo-European permit us to reconstruct labiovelars in the mother language with certainty. This is demonstrated in the graphem <*qu*> in the Latin word for the number 'four,' *quattuor*. In Greek, the word-initial sounds vary among the dialects: Ionic, τέσσαρες; Attic, τέτταρες; but Lesbian (Balbilla, Hesychius), πέσ(σ)υρες; Boetian, πέτταρες 'four' among others. Thus, the conclusion was drawn quite early that the variation τ- : π- must be based upon an older *k^w-, (similar to the Latin) with secondary development, following a dark vowel, to a labial; following a bright vowel, to a dental, cf. § 4. Mycenaean has since shown, through *qe-to-ro-*, i.e. *k^wetro-* 'four,' not only that this was in fact true, but also that the elimination of k^w occurred only after the Mycenaean period. — Another correspondence set with Latin *qu-* is the interrogative stem *quo-d* 'what?,' Gr. πό-θεν '(from) where?' In the case of Germanic, the labiovelar tenuis shift completely to their corresponding unvoiced fricatives, compare Got. *ƕa-s* 'who?' with <*ƕ*>, i.e. h^w. — Further, compare *qui-s*, Gr. τίς, Hitt. *ku̯i-* , Got. *ƕi-* (cf. L 211 § 1 above). Also cf. E 506 § 3 and 4, concerning PIE *(h_1)*éku̯o-*.

2) While the centum languages exhibit labiovelars (Lat. <*qu*>, Myc. k^w <*q-*> Hitt. *ku̯*, Got. <*ƕ*> etc.) or their retained forms (Gr. *p* / *t*, Umbr. *p* [*petur-* 'four'], etc.), it is characteristic of satem languages, along with the exceptional development of palatals to sibilants (cf. L 339 § 2), that they eliminate the labial characteristic of labiovelars. Thus, the labiovelars in satem languages merged, as a rule, with the velars. Word-initial *-k-* (Lith. *keturì* 'four,' *kàs* 'who?,' Ved. *kás*, OCS *kъto* 'who?'), or its palatalized equivalents (Ved. *catvā́ras* 'four' [<*k^wet-, but *k^wt- > *kt- in contrast in LAv. *ā-xt-ūirīm* 'four

times', cp. L 203], OCS *četyre* 'four'), correspond to word-initial PIE *k^w- in *k^w*etu̯er-* 'four,' and *k^w*o-* 'who?.'

3) In a few cases it appears that the merging of velars and labiovelars in satem languages did not take place. This is important insofar as the simultaneous existence of the three tectal groups is thus proven, cf. L 339 § 1 concerning Luwian.

Other examples are disputed, however. The various types of vocalization for PIE **-r̥H(V)-* might thus indicate that, while the *g-* in *gir-ás* 'of the ode (gen.)' may be traced back to the velar PIE **gr̥H-és* (cf. Gr. γῆρυς 'voice'), the *g-* in Ved. *gur-ú-* 'heavy' is traced back to the labiovelar PIE **g^wr̥H-ú-* (cf. Gr. βαρύς). However, the different types of vocalization cannot be interpreted as a proof of phonetic difference: The root *gir-* also probably featured a labiovelar and would thus be reconstructed as PIE **g^werH-* (cf. Lat. *grā-t-* in nom. pl. *grātēs*, Osc. *brā-t-* in gen. sg. *brateis*): → Mayrhofer EWAia I p. 469 (with the corrections contained in Mayrhofer *Lautlehre* 1986 p. 104f.); H. Rix in *FS Narten* 2000 p. 216ff.

4) In most of the Greek dialects, PIE *k^w preceding *ŏ̄* and *ă̄*, and also preceding consonants, is represented as a labial by *p*; preceding *ĕ̄* and *ĭ̄*, it is represented as a dental by *t*; and when located near *ŭ̄* or *u̯*, it is represented by the loss of the labial characteristic as the tectal *k*. Aeolic also features *p* preceding front vowels.

Examples: — Cf. PIE **pénk^u̯e* 'five' with Ion., Att., etc. πέν-τ-ε, but πέμ-π-τος, πεμ-π-άς, Aeol. πέμ-π-ε. — PIE **lúk^{w}o-* 'wolf' (along with PIE **u̯l̥k^{w}o-* with Ved. *vŕ̥ka-*, cf. L 304 § 3) > Gr. λύκος (with *k* < *k^w*). — PIE **-k^{w}olh$_1$ó-* 'herdsman' (root PIE **k^{w}elh$_1$-* 'to make a turn, to turn around, to turn to': → LIV 1998 p. 345-347) in αἰπόλος (< **ai̯.k^{w}ólo-* < **ai̯.k^{w}oló-* [Concerning the typically Greek accent displacement, cf. L 420 § 3] < **ai̯.kk^{w}oló-* < **ai̯k-k^{w}oló-* < **ai̯g-k^{w}oló-*: → K. Strunk in *FS Szemerényi* *75 II 1992 p. 77-83) '(goat-)herdsman' (but following the prefix **g^{w}ou̯-* 'cow' already Myc. *qo-u-ko-ro* i.e. *g^{w}ou̯kolos* 'cow herdsman' with dissimulation of *-u̯k-* < *-u̯k^w-*). For a more detailed treatment: → Lejeune *Phonétique* 1972 § 26.

L 344. In many ways analogous to the development of PIE *g^w (cf. L 343) is that of PIE *g^w: Myc. g^w <*q-*>, Gr. <β>, <δ>, <γ>; Hitt. g^w (denoted as *ku*), Proto-Germ. *k^w (Got. *q*). In Latin, PIE *g^w- (<*gu-*>) is only retained following nasals; in other positions it has become *u̯* <*v*>. Satem languages feature delabialized *g* or its retained variant forms.

Examples: — PIE *neg^w- / *nog^w- 'naked' with Hitt. *ne-ku-ma-an-za*, Got. *naqaþs*, Ved. *nagná-*, Lith. *nuógas*, OCS *nagъ* 'naked.' — PIE *$n̥g^w en$- 'bulge' with Lat. *inguen* n. 'bulge in the genital region, genitals,' Gr. ἀδήν f. m. 'gland.' — PIE *$g^w ih_3$-*u̯o*- 'living' = Lat. *vīvus*, Got. *qiwans* acc. pl. 'the living,' Lith. *gývas* 'living'; further Ved. *jīvá-*; Old Persian *jīva-* and OCS *živъ* 'living' (all three with palatalization of *g- [< *g^w-] before -*ĭ*-); the case of Gr. βίος m. 'life' is more complicated, because preceding a bright vowel, one should expect to find **díos*: → Lejeune *Phonétique* 1972 § 37; in the case of ὑ-γιής 'healthy, undamaged' dissimilation is exhibited: *-u-$g^w i$- > *-u-gi-* (< PIE *h_2*i̯u*-$g^w ih_3$-*ḗs* in the sense of 'having a powerful, long life'; instead of the traditionally supposed *h_1*su*- 'good,' *h_2*i̯u*- [For more information on the nominals *h_2*ói̯u*- / *h_2*éi̯u*- / *h_2*i̯u*- 'life power, life duration' cf. F 317 § 8] in the suffix is the better suggestion: → M. Weiss in MSS 55 1994 p. 150f. [The author discusses the entire subject and shows that de Saussure had already weighed this solution as one of three possibilities.]).

L 345. Even the continuation of labiovelar media aspirata PIE *g^{wh} may be derived in various ways. While Mycenaean k^{wh} <*q*-> must be postulated, one expects in later developments a tenuis aspirata, the distribution of which is determined through position: <ϑ> (before *ĕ*), <φ> (before *ŏ*, *ă* and before a consonant), <χ> (near *ŭ*). In Hittite, one expects g^w (<*ku*>); in Germanic, *g^w. Latin offers postnasal -g^w- <-*gu*-> , word-initial *f*-, and otherwise, *u̯* <*v*>. Vedic exhibits delabialized *gh* (or its palatalization to *h* = Avest. *j*). Baltic and Slavic both have *g*, but lose their labialization and aspiration.

1) Correspondence sets for PIE *g^{wh}: — PIE *$g^{wh}en$- 'to strike' (→ LIV 1998 p. 194f.) with the ablaut grades *$g^{wh}on$- and *$g^{wh}n$- in Gr. ϑείνω 'I strike,' fut. ϑεν-ῶ, nom. act. φόνος m. 'manslaughter,' aorist πε-φν-εῖν, perf. pass. πέ-φα-ται; Hitt. *ku-en-zi* i.e. *ku̯en-tˢi* 'he/she/it kills'; Ved. *hánti* 'he/she/it strikes, kills' (= Avest. *jaiṇti*) < *j^h*án-ti* < *j^h*én-ti* < *g^h*én-ti* < PIE *g^{wh}*én-ti*, however *ghn-ánti* 'they strike' directly <*g^h*n-énti* < IE*g^{wh}*n-énti*; even more complex *jahí* 'strike!' (= Avest. *jaiδī*) <*$j^h ad^h i$ (with dissimilation of j^h to *j*, directly before d^h; word-initial *j^h- originates from the singular *j^h*an-ti*, which originally contained -*e*-; one would normally expect, namely, in the imperative *$g^h a$-$d^h i$ < PIE *g^{wh}*n̥*-$d^h i$); Lith. *genù* and OCS *goniti* 'I hunt and drive' (< 'to repeatedly strike'). — PIE *$h_1 l n̥ g^{wh}$-*ú*- / *$h_1 l n̥ g^{wh}$-*ró*- > Gr. ἐλαχύς 'low,' Ved. *raghú-* 'quick, swift,' *laghú-* 'light, low,' and Gr. ἐλαφρός 'quick, light' = OHG *lungar* 'fast.' — PIE *$g^{wh}er$- 'to burn' with the adj. *g^{wh}*er-mó*- 'warm' and nom. ag. *g^{wh}*or-mó*- m. 'heat,' cf. Gr. ϑερμός, Lat. *formus* 'warm'; Ved. *gharmá-* m. 'heat' (~ *háras* n. 'flame'), Lith. *garẽti*

'to burn,' OCS *gorěti* 'to burn,' Russ. *žar* m. 'heat, embers.' — Further, cf. verbal PIE *$séng^{wh}$-e-* with the nom. act. *$song^{wh}$-$éh_2$-*: The former is continued in Got. *siggwan* 'to sing, to recite'; the latter in Gr. ὀμφή f. 'divine voice, oracle' (< *$homp^h\acute{\bar{a}}$*). The verbal zero grade form *-$s\mathring{n}g^{wh}$-* is apparently evident in the Homeric form ἀσπὶς ἐάφθη in the sense of 'the shield sounded (upon him),' the lineage of which is to this day unclear: → M. Meier-Brügger in MSS 50 1989 p. 91ff. and cf. E 508 § 1. — Concerning Latin *nix niv-is* 'snow' and *ninguit* 'it snows' < PIE *$snei̯g^{wh}$-* cf. E 501.

2) The Germanic form *-g^w-* is only preserved in Gothic in a post-nasal position as g^w, compare Got. *siggwan* in § 1. Concerning OHG *snīwan* 'to snow' < PIE *$snei̯g^{wh}$-* cf. E 501 § 2. Correspondence sets for the word-initial Germanic *g^w-* < PIE *g^{wh}-* are only given when they show *g-*, *w-*, or even *b-* as continuations. Thus, as an example, PIE *g^{wh}er-* 'to burn' [above § 1] is connected with the Germanic families of NHG *gar, warm*, and *brennen*. However, only one of these three groups can be the correct one: → E. Seebold "*Die Vertretung von anlautend idg. $g^{u}h$ und ghu̯ im Germanischen*" in *Fachtagung Wien* 1978 [1980] p. 450-484.

8. Assimilations and Dissimilations

L 346. Direct contact between occlusives leads to assimilation. Thus, a tenuis preceding a media results in a media; a media preceding a tenuis results in a tenuis. Assimilations are also otherwise produced, cf. L 215 § 2 and L 303.

Examples: — The zero grade of PIE **ped-* 'foot,' namely **pd-*, becomes **-bd-*, cf. LAv. acc. sg. *fra-bd-əm* 'front foot,' cf. Gr. ἔπι-βδ-α f. in the sense of 'the day following (* at the foot of) the celebration.' However, the Greek term is only superficially formed from *-bd-*; it is more precisely based upon the *-i̯a-* feminine **epi-bd-i̯ă*. An exceptional phonetic development **-bdi̯- > -bd-* would thus be suggested: → Schwyzer *Gr. Gr.* I 1939 p. 475 and Frisk GEW *s.v.* — The zero grade root form PIE *nig^w-* 'to wash' (Ved. *nir-ṇih-ānā́-* 'which is cleaned,' Gr. νίζω 'I wash [myself]' < *nig^w-i̯ō*, Old Irish *nigim* 'I wash') is combined with the suffix *-tó-* to form the participle *nik^w-tó-* 'washed': Ved. *niktá-* 'washed,' Gr. ἄ-νιπτος 'unwashed,' Old Irish *necht* 'pure.'

L 347. Special cases:

1) The first special case concerns dental sequences, which sometimes are formed due to assimilation rules: PIE **-t-t-*, and PIE **-d-d$^{(h)}$-*. This case is important with regard to several dental-initial elements (such as **-to-*, **-ti-*, **-tor-*) and endings (such as the 3rd person singular primary ending **-ti*, the imperative endings **-d^{h}i, *-tu*). As early as the Proto-Indo-European period, the closure in the sequences **-t-t-*, **-d-d$^{(h)}$-* was interrupted by the insertion of an **-s-*. — Example: — PIE **sed-* 'to sit' and PIE **h$_1$ed-* 'to eat,' with the addition of *-t-* morphemes, produced **s(e)t-s-t-* and **h$_1$(e)t-s-t-*. In Hittite, **-tst-* is retained, cf. *e-ez-du* i.e. *et^{s}tu* 'he should eat.' The phonetic sequence *-tst-* was simplified to *-st-* in Greek, Baltic, Slavic and Iranian, and to *-ss-* in Latin and Germanic, cf. Lith. *sė̃sti*, OCS *sěsti* 'to sit,' Avest. *aiβi-šasta* 'to sit upon,' Lat. *sessiō* f. 'sitting,' ON *sess* m. 'seat, rowing bench,' Lith. *ė̃sti* 'to feed.' In Indo-Aryan, *-s-* is expelled from **-tst-*, as is the case of ancient **s*, cf. *ud-* + *sthā-* > **utsthā->* *ut-thā-* 'to stand up'). For that reason, it is true that PIE **u̯oi̯d-th$_2$e* 'you know' > **u̯oi̯tsth$_2$e* = Gr. οἶσθα, OAv. *vōistā*, in contrast to Ved. *vét-tha*. — Also compare **-dsd^h-* (phonet. **[-dzd^h-]*), which developed from **-d-d^h-* in the Indo-Iranian imperative **da-d-dhí* 'give!' > **dadzdhí* > LAv. *dazdi*. In accordance with the Ved. *véttha*, one would expect from **dadzdhi* the Ved. **daddhi*. Instead, one finds **dazdhi* (resulting in *dehí* 'give'; concerning *-e-* <**-az-* cf. L 220 § 3), which is explained if we accept that when **dadzdhi* existed, the **-d-* following **da-* and preceding **-dhí* disappeared through dissimilation. On this and other questions: → Mayrhofer *Lautlehre* 1986 p. 110f. Cf. L 407 below.

2) The immediate sequence media aspirata + tenuis in Vedic resulted in media + media aspirata. — Example: — Zero grade Ved. *budh-* 'to awaken' + suffix *-tá-* resulted in *buddhá-* 'awakened, enlightened' (cf. *Buddha*); full grade Ved. *yodh-* 'to fight' + Suffix *-tar-* resulted in *(a-)yoddhár-* '(bad) fighter'; also cf. Indo-Iranian **dhrugh-* and **drugh-* 'to betray, to damage' (Ved. *druh-* ~ *drógha-* 'deceitful') + *-tá-* > *drugdhá-* 'deceitful, injurious.'

This law, presented in 1882 by Christian Bartholomae, is for sure Indo-Iranian since it is reflected in Old Avestan (cf. **au̯g^h-* 'to say' + 3rd person sg. ending *-ta* > **au̯gd^{h}a*, OAv. *aogədā* 'said'); however Bartholomae's Law, with the exception of a few inheritances (cf. LAv. *ubdaēna-* 'made of weaved material': **ubda-* < **ubd^{h}a-* < **ub^h-tá-* from PIE **u̯eb^h-* 'to weave') no longer applies in Later Avestan. This fact is due to the renewed production of morphemes by analogy (cf. LAv. *aux-ta* 'said' compared with the above mentioned OAv. *aogədā*; cf. LAv. *-druxta-*, OPers. *duruxta-* 'lied' compared with Ved. *drugdhá-*). — It is difficult to judge the extent to which Bartholomae's Law might have been valid as early as the Proto-Indo-European era. Although attestations outside of Indo-

Iranian are rare, they can be seen as certain. Thus, the juxtaposition of suffixes such as **-tlo-* (in OHG *sta-dal* 'barn' < Proto-Germ. **sta-þla-*) and **-d^h^lo-* (cf. Lat. *sta-bulum* 'location, stable' with *-bul-* < *-bl-* < **-d^h^l-* or Gr. χύτλον 'container for pouring,' dissimilated from the older **k^h^u-t^h^lo-*, and Pre-Proto-Gr. **g^h^u-d^h^lo-*) may be explained in that suffixes of the latter type were formed from 'Bartholomae contexts,' in which phonetically **-d^h^lo-* < **-dd^h^lo-* (concerning the consonant simplification of *dd^h^.l* > *d^h^.l*, cf. L 407) < **-d^h^-tlo-*. In other words, **-d^h^lo-* can be explained as a suffix that first appears as a *-tlo-* derivation of roots with final-position *d^h^* but then also found use elsewhere. Cf. also W 205 § 3.

Literature and discussion: → Mayrhofer *Lautlehre* 1986 p. 115ff.; H. Scharfe *"Bartholomae's Law Revisited or how the Ṛgveda is dialectally divided"* in *Studien zur Indologie und Iranistik* 20 1996 p. 351-377.

L 348. A rule of dissimilation that concerns Vedic and Greek is connected with the name of the mathematician, Veda-researcher, and linguist Hermann Grassmann. The rule applies independently to each of these two languages as a natural process of dissimilation that also is evidenced outside of the Indo-European language family. Efforts to assert a hereditary relationship linking the effects of Grassmann's Law in both Greek and Vedic have not been convincing: → Mayrhofer *Lautlehre* 1986 p. 113ff.

1) Concerning Vedic material: Grassmann's Law says that, in the case of an indirect sequence of two aspirated plosives (or *-h-*), the first of them loses its aspirated quality. According to the example of Ved. *dá-dā-mi* 'I give' (root *dā-* 'to give') one should expect from Ved. *dhā-* 'to lay, to place,' a present stem **dhá-dhā-mi*. The resulting form, however, is Ved. *dádhāmi* 'I lay.' The 2 sg. mid. *dhátse* shows that **dha-dh-* was the initial form: In this case *-dh-* preceding *-s-* lost its voiced and aspirated qualities (**-dhs-* > **-ds-* > *-ts-*); the *dh-* in the initial position retained its aspirated quality since no more an aspirated phoneme followed. — Cf. also the root word formed from the root **dhrugh-* 'to deceive, to injure,' with the nom. sg. *dhrúk* 'damaging' (with final-position **-g^h^s* > *-k*[*ṣ*]), but the gen. sg. *druh-ás* (< **drugh-ás* < **dhrugh-ás*). — Further, cf. the regular Ved. *budh-* 'to awaken' (< **bhudh-*), but 1 sg. aor. *á-bhut-s-i*.

2) A rule of the same type affects Greek. It applies to the tenues aspiratae (cf. L 336 § 2), which developed within Greek from media aspiratae –a fact which excludes the possibility of a causal relationship with the analogous development in Vedic. Thus, according to the model of δί-δω-μι 'I give' in the case of PIE **d^h^eh$_1$-* one should expect **d^h^id^h^eh$_1$mi*. The Greek τίθημι re-

veals that the PIE *$d^hid^heh_1mi$ became in a first step, as yet unaffected, *$t^hit^h\bar{e}mi$ and only afterward was subjected to aspirate dissimilation. A PIE *$did^h\bar{e}mi$ should have resulted in the Greek *$dit^h\bar{e}mi$. — PIE *$b^h\underset{\circ}{n}\acute{g}^h\acute{u}$- 'abundant' > Ved. *$b^hag^h\acute{u}$- and Gr. *$p^hak^h\acute{u}$-, and afterward with dissimilation rule of individual IE languages Ved. *baghú-, becoming *bahú-* and Gr. *pakhú-* (παχύς). See also L 307 § 4. — 'Hair' has the Greek stem *t^hrik^h-. In the nom. sg. *$t^hr\acute{i}k^h$-s, the -k^h- lost its aspirate quality before –s so early that the initial t^h- was not any more affected (= θρίξ). In the gen. sg. *t^hrik^h-ós > $trik^h$ós (τριχός),the initial t^h- had to lose the aspiration qualitiy because of the following still aspirated -k^h-. — Grassmann's Law also affects indirect sequences of Gr. *h-* (generally < PIE *s-) and aspirates, cf. the present stem *$h\acute{e}k^h\bar{o}$ (< PIE *$se\acute{g}^h$-) > $ek^h\bar{o}$ <ἔχω> compared with the fut. *héksō* <ἕξω>, cf. L 310.

3) Only with the help of Grassmann's Law can we understand the initial-position differences between Lat. *fingere* 'to knead, to form' vs. Got. *daigs* vs. NHG *Teig* vs. Gr. τεῖχος n. 'wall' vs. Ved. *dehī́-* f. 'dam, embankment.' The point of departure is PIE *d^hei̯$\acute{g}^h$- (with present stem *$d^hin\acute{g}^h$-e- with nasal infix): Lat. without Grassmann's Law *$d^hin\acute{g}^h$-e- > *þinχe- > *finge-*, Proto-Gr. first without Grassmann *d^hei̯g^h- > *t^hei̯k^h-, and afterward with Grassmann > tei̯k^h- <τειχ->; Ved. with Grassmann *d^hai̯j^h- > *dai̯jh- > *deh-*.

Grassmann's proof of 1862 helped at the time to resolve an apparent discrepancy in the Germanic consonant shift: → Szemerényi *Einführung* 1990 p. 20. The PIE *b^hend^h- 'to bind' serves as a good example: That Gothic *bindan* and not *pindan corresponds to the Vedic *bandh-* 'to bind' is explained by the fact that the basic PIE is the not yet dissimulated *b^hend^h- and not (as researchers earlier believed) the dissimulated *$bend^h$-. Working from basis of PIE *b^hend^h-, Proto-Germanic *bend- is understandable. — However, *bhandh- leads to the dissimulated form *bandh-* in the case of Vedic. In contrast, the initial position of the future form *bhantsyati* remained untouched, because the phonetic sequence *-dhsya- of the form *bhandh-sya- resulted immediately in non-aspirated *-tsya-*, through exclusion of the aspirated quality in the group *-dhsya- and through assimilation of *-dsya- > *-tsya-, cf. also *dhatse* and *ábhutsi* in § 1. — In Greek, the development of *b^hend^h- may be traced via *p^hent^h- to $pent^h$-, cf. πενθ-ερός 'father-in-law' (this term for a familial relationship belongs, via the image of relational 'fastening,' to 'to bind,' cf. the similar Ved. *bándhu-* 'family member').

D. Larger Phonetic Unities

1. Word, Sentence, Text

L 400. The word: Although the word is the most important element of a language (cf. W 100), it exists in the larger context of sentences and text and receives from these only then its legitimation and definition. "The unit 'word' must exist, in order that on this basis the signals of sentence hierarchy or sentence perspective may be ... realized." : → Hj. Seiler in Seiler *Sprache und Sprachen* 1977 (in a contribution of 1962) p. 39; cf. by the same author, "On defining the word" loc. cit. (in a contribution of 1964) p. 70-73.

However, the definitions of what words really are, are even more multilayered: → Bussmann *Lexikon d. Sprachw.* 1990 p. 849f. under the heading 'Wort.' In this context, the following contributions are interesting: → A. Morpurgo Davies *"Folk-linguistics and the Greek word"* in *FS Hoenigswald* 1987 p. 263-280 (for example, for information on word-separators in Mycenaean ["mainly determined by accentual criteria"], and on literary and grammatical opinions); LALIES 10 1992 with different contributions regarding '*Le mot*' (Cf, among others, J. Lallot "*Le mot dans la tradition prégrammaticale et grammaticale en Grèce*"; M.-J. Reichler-Béguelin "*Perception du mot graphique dans quelques systèmes syllabiques et alphabétiques*"; G.-J. Pinault "*Le mot et l'analyse morphologique selon la grammaire indienne*").

L 401. The sentence: Following are a couple of cross-references regarding the sentence level and the possibility of syntactical reconstruction, cf. S 102; regarding sentence accent and sentence-initial position, cf. S 209; further, cf. F 214.

L 402. Text: For information on the text level and its syntax, cf. S 200. R. Barthes goes beyond the text level. He emphasizes correctly that in addition to sentence syntax, the discourse has its own syntax (→ Meier-Brügger *Gr. Sprachw.* I 1992 p. 97f.):

> "le discours lui-même (comme ensemble de phrases) est organisé ... le discours a ses unités, ses règles, sa 'grammaire' ... Cette linguistique

du discours, elle a eu pendant très longtemps un nom glorieux: la Rhétorique"

2. Accent; Word-initial, Word-final and Sandhi Phenomena

L 403. Word accent is a central characteristic of the word. Assertions regarding Proto-Indo European word accent are possible, cf. L 419.

Further, individual Indo-European languages exhibit more or less high degrees of restriction and simplification in word endings: — Latin: Consonant groups are simplified for the most part, cf. nom. sg. n. *cor* 'heart' < **cord* (which remains visible in forms such as gen. sg. *cord-is*, in which the word-internal consonant group *rd* remains possible): → Leumann LLFL 1977 p. 219ff. (with further information). — Greek: Classical Greek only tolerates *-s*, *-n* and *-r* among consonants in final position; *-t* for example, is not possible: → Meier-Brügger *Gr. Sprachw.* II 1992 p. 102f. — It is difficult to ascertain the extent to which final-position simplifications and changes took place already in Proto-Indo-European.

Although there is a greater freedom regarding changes to the initial position as compared with changes to the word ending, such restrictions must be taken into account in each language.

L 404. The reciprocal influence of word-initial and word-final phonemes of adjacent words in oral language is common in every language. The extent to which this sandhi phenomenon (the term, meaning, "uniting, composition" owes its origin to the ancient Indians) is reflected in the written language, or whether the pausal form in absolute position has priority in the clear denotation of the individual word, is a question in itself. The IE languages and their systems of writing reveal various evaluations.

Greek: → Meier-Brügger *Gr. Sprachw.* II 1992 p. 103f. — On Vedic sandhi: J. Wackernagel in Wackernagel / Debrunner *Ai. Gramm.* I 1903 p. 306ff. — Avestan sandhi: → Hoffmann / Forssman *Avest. Laut- u. Flexionslehre* 1996 p. 110-112.

L 405. Sandhi phenomena are so common in all spoken languages that their existence in Proto-Indo-European must be asserted.

Additionally, the supposition of PIE sandhi phenomena permits us to understand a couple of Proto-Indo-European phonetic phenomena. — The first example is Lindemann's Law, which is the sandhi equivalent to Sievers' Law. According to Sievers' rule, the variant PIE **dii̯éu̯s* of PIE **di̯éu̯s* is determined by the final position of the preceding word: On the one hand, we have *##...V̄#dii̯éu̯s ##* and *##...VR#dii̯éu̯s##*, on the other *##...K#*di̯éu̯s##*, cf. L 218. — Another possible example is the mobile *-s-* of the type PIE **(s)teg-* 'to cover, to spread over' (→ LIV 1998 p. 535), cf. Lat. *tegō* vs. Gr. στέγω: → Mayrhofer Lautlehre 1986 p. 120 ("in other cases, sandhi *-s# #K-* may have led to *#sK-*") and cf. L 311.

Occasionally the supposition of prehistoric sandhi can be helpful in the understanding of phenomena in individual IE languages. — Cf. the diverging initial position of the Greek pronoun μ-ιν vs. ν-ιν (cf. F 406), on the subject of which J. Wackernagel in Wackernagel *Kleine Schriften* I 1969 (in a contribution of 1892) p. 10) comments: "It seems to me ... easiest to attribute μ- and ν- to sandhi." — In the case of the problematic Greek initial position *p*(*t*)- (cf. πόλις / πτόλις 'city'; which, according to the evidence of the proper noun *po-to-ri-jo* i.e. *Ptolii̯ōn* including the element 'city,' dates from Mycenaean) O. Szemerényi also appeals to prehistoric sandhi phenomena, considering exemplary phrases such as **ḗlut^{h}et pólin* 'he came into the city' [with the preserved *-t* in the Greek final position] and its regrouping to *ḗlut^{h}e *tpolin*, and then, with consonant position reversal, *ptólin*): → Szemerényi *Scripta Minora* III 1987 (in a contribution of 1975 [1979]) p. 1491f. Whether his supposition is correct, is disputable.

On further sandhi phenomena, cf. L 334 § 2-3.

3. Syllable

L 406. Between the levels of entire words and individual phonemes, there are syllables. General information: → Bussmann *Lexikon d. Sprachw.* 1990 p. 684f.

In Ternes' *Phonologie* 1987 p. 170-172, it is claimed:

> "A syllable is composed of an obligatory syllable core and a (facultative) syllable margin. ... The syllable margin is composed, as a rule, of one or more consonants that precede and/or follow the syllable core. The syllable margin is facultative insofar as a word can also be composed of only a vocalic syllable core. ... The description of the syllabic structure of a language is hardly less important than the determining of its phoneme system."

The limits and division of syllables is handled variously depending on perspectives and approaches, including those of orthography, pronunciation, metrics, and theory.

A syllable is considered open when the syllable limit is placed immediately after the vocalic syllable core. A syllable is considered (naturally) metrically long or short according to the long or short quality of the core. Word internal syllables are 'closed' when the syllable limit immediately follows one or more consonants, which would then form the syllable margin. The vocalic syllable core may then be long or short, but for the sake of metrics, every closed syllable is long (by position).

The consonant group muta (i.e. occlusive) cum liquida plays a special role. It can be shown that in prehistoric times and in Proto-Indo-European in particular, the syllable division was made between muta and liquida, and that in Latin and Greek it could be before the muta and liquida, and thus no longer represented a position that could affect the length of a vowel (i.e. *correptio attica*). Cf. the Latin nom. pl. *integrī* 'undamaged,' of which the syllabification is attested in poetry as *in.te.grī* as well as *in.teg.rī*. The word *integrī* may be traced back to **in-tag-ro-*. The vowel weakening of *-tag-* to *-teg-* shows that at the time it took place *.tag.* was a closed syllable: Had the syllable been open at the time, a *.ta.* would have led to *.ti.*, yielding **intigrī*. However, no traces of this exist.

Further sources: — Latin: → Leumann LLFL 1977 p. 21f. — Greek: Changes in syllabification are possible, cf. again the muta cum liquida group, in which both πατ.ρός and πα.τρός are attested. Compare further genitive singulars ending in *-oi̯i̯o* < **-osi̯o*, in which likely both *-oi̯.i̯o* (= Myc. *-o-jo* and Aeol. -οιο) and *-o.i̯i̯o* / *-o.i̯o* are evidenced (the latter following the disappearance of *i̯* in the Ionic/Attic contraction to -ου, and the Doric contraction to -ω). However, the facts are not indisputable. Literature: → Meier-Brügger *Gr. Sprachw.* II 1992 p. 105f. and p. 79f.

L 407. Clues as to the syllabic structure of Proto-Indo-European may be discovered indirectly. Thus, Gr. μέτρον (attested from Homer on) 'measure' can be understood as a *-tro-* derivation from PIE **med-* 'to measure' (→ LIV 1998 p. 380f.), if PIE **med-tro-* or, assimilated, **met-tro-* i.e. **mett.ro-* (with simplification from **mett.* to **met.*) was valid. B. Forssman remains skeptical: → *Kratylos* 33 1988 p. 63). Similarly, (→ Gotō I. Präsensklasse 1987 p. 218 note 454) the Vedic imperative *bodhi* (RV) is often traced to PIE *b^{h}eu̯d-d^{h}i, i.e. *b^{h}eu̯.d^{h}d^{h}i, with .d^{h}d^h simplified to .d^{h}i. But the facts in this case are deceptive. The questionable form *bodhi* may be better understood as originating from Vedic *bháva* (> *bho*) +*dhi*:

→ St. W. Jamison "*Syntactic Constraints on Morphological Change: The Vedic Imperatives bodhí, dehí, and dhehí*" in *Syntaxe des langues indo-iraniennes anciennes* 1993 [1997] p. 63-80.

If the explanation of the type **mett.ro-* is correct, then the instances of syllabification of the type *VKK.RV* and *VR.KKV* may be traced to the Proto-Indo-European period: → Saussure *Recueil* 1922 (in an essay from 1889) p. 420ff. (with further examples); Mayrhofer *Lautlehre* 1986 p. 111f.

Further information on PIE syllabification may be derived from the variant forms of the type *-i̯-V-* and *-ii̯-V-*. J. Schindler makes this clear (→ *Sprache* 23 1977 p. 56-65 in his review of Seebold *Halbvokale* 1972; cf. L 218). Namely, Sievers' Law was valid in the following context: R > R̥ / #....*V̄.K_VK₀*# and #...*VR.K_VK₀*#, compare with the conspicuously constant consonantal sonant, Ved. *mát.sya-* (RV +) 'fish' and *ūr.dhvá-* (RV +) 'upright' (< **u̯r̥H.dʰu̯ó-*). Further reading: → Szemerényi *Einführung* 1990 p. 110ff.

The detailed discussion by J. Schindler of problems surrounding the apparent PIE fricative **þ* (cf. L 313) secondarily include further assertions concerning PIE syllabic structures: → "*A Thorny Problem*" in *Sprache* 23 1977 p.33f. (with discussion of the example of PIE **h₂ér.tḱo-* vs. **h₂r̥t.ḱó-* 'bear' among others).

4. Ablaut

L 408. All ancient IE languages exhibit regularly a quantitative or qualitative vowel change in certain groups of forms, such as in different cases of a substantive, or derivations from a common root.

An example: The suffixal element -τερ- in the Greek word for 'father' appears with *-e-* in the accusative singular πα-τέρ-α, but with *-o-* in the compound accusative singular ἀ-πά-τορ-α 'someone who has no father.' The vowel is absent in the dative singular πα-τρ-ί. The dative plural πα-τρά-σι '(to) our forefathers' contains the continuation of *-tr̥-* (cf. Ved. *pi-tŕ̥-ṣu* '[with] the ancestors'), the expected syllabic allophone of **-tr-* that one expects to find before the consonant-initial -σι. The nominative singular πα-τήρ reveals a quantitative 'increase' of *-e-* to the corresponding long vowel; the nominative singular ἀ-πά-τωρ reveals the same, but with the corresponding *-o-* form.

This change clearly did not initiate in Greek, but rather reveals itself as a PIE inheritance through parallels in other IE languages. Compare πατέρ-α, πατρί, πατήρ with Ved. acc. sg. *pi-tár-am* 'father,' dat. sg. *pi-tr-é*, nom. sg. *pi-tā́* (with *-tā́* < **-tā́r*, cf. L 301 § 3).

L 409. Two facts are essential concerning this change: The change is datable to the PIE period and is limited to a few formal possibilities which are used in morphology. The above case of πατήρ / ἀπάτωρ includes only the qualitative changes of *e* and *o*, and the three quantities *e* / *o*, *ē* / *ō* and zero (*ø*).

In a language that, in terms of vowel quality and vowel quantity, has changed as little as Greek, this consistent regularity may be demonstrated by citing just a few phonological-historical examples. This regular change of vowel quantity and quality, called ablaut, may be subdivided on two further levels: qualitatively as *e*/*o*- alternation; and qualitatively as full, or 'normal' grade, lengthened grade, and zero or *ø* grade.

Compare the following schematic depiction:

	full grade	lengthened grade	zero grade
e	πα-τέρ-α	πα-τήρ	πα-τρ-ί πα-τρά-σι
o	ἀπά-τορ-α	ἀπά-τωρ	

L 410. The table in L 409 shows five grades, all of which are represented in a single word family in a very few cases, such as that of πατέρ- / ἀπάτορ-: *F(e)* = full grade with *-e-*; *F(o)* = full grade with *-o-* nuancing; *L(ē)* = lengthened grade with *-ē-*; *L(ō)* = lengthened grade with *-ō-*; *Z (ø)* = zero grade. — Examples: — In Greek, compare the evidence of four grades in πέτ-ομαι 'I fly' = *F(e)*, ποτ-έομαι 'I fly, flap' = *F(o)*, πωτ-ήεις 'flapping' = *L(ō)* and πτ-έσθαι 'flying up' = *Z(ø)*; the fifth formal possibility *L(ē)* = *πητ- was not used in any known form.

The changes *e*/*o*, *ē*/*ō* and *ø* may be demonstrated in many further roots with internal *-e-*, also in those in which *-i̯-* or *-n-* follows *-e-*, or in which *-r-* precedes the *-e-*. — Examples: — Cf. Gr. λείπ-ω 'I leave behind' = *F(e)*, λοιπ-ός 'staying behind' = *F(o)*, (ἔ)-λιπ-ε 'he left' = *Z(ø)*. — Cf. τεν-ῶ 'I will harness' = *F(e)*; τόν-ος m. 'tension, string, note' = *F(o)*; τά-σις f. 'tension, stretching' with *ta-* < **tn̥-* = *Z(ø)* (concerning *n̥*, cf. L 305). — Cf. τρέπ-ω 'I turn' = *F(e)*; τρόπ-ος m. 'turn' = *F(o)*; τρωπ-άω 'I twist, turn, change' = *L(ō)*; εὐ-τράπ-ελος '(lightly) twisting, moveable' with *-tra-* < **-tr̥-* = *Z(ø)*.

L 411. The changes between *e* / *o* / *ē* / *ō* / *ø* are also visible in other IE languages. However, one must expect much greater phonetic changes than in Greek.

Following are examples from Latin, in which phonetic changes among vowels and diphthongs have obscured the original ablaut relationships: — Ideal cases with unchanged PIE values include, for example, Lat. *teg-ō* 'I cover, hide' = *F(e)*, *tēg-ula* f. 'rooftile' = *L(ē)* and *tog-a* f. 'article of clothing, toga' = *F(o)*. On the other hand, along with *foedus* n. 'alliance' (cf. Old Latin *foideratei* 'allied') = *F(o)* and *fīdēs* f. 'faith' = *Z(ø)*, *feid-* = *F(e)* is only by chance attested in early Latin (cf. *di[f]feidens* from inscriptions): In 150 B.C., the normal development led from *ei̯* via *ē* to *ī* and thus to *fīdō* 'I trust.' A simultaneous *fīdō* is no longer identifiable as *F(e)*. — Cf. as a further example Lat. *fer-ō* 'I carry' = *F(e)*, *fors, for-ti-* f. 'chance, providence' = *Z(ø)* with *-or-* < **-r̥-* (a simultaneous ablaut change *fer-* / *for-* appears; however, *-ti-* derivations traditionally have zero grade roots, cf. Ved. *bhr̥-tí-* f. 'maintenance' and NHG *Ge-bur-t*; thus, all seems to indicate the presence of a former **-r̥-*). Also, in the case of the related root word *fūr* m. 'thief,' the *L(ō)* is no longer recognizable, because in the phonetically expected **fōr* = Gr. φώρ 'thief, one who carries away' *ō* has been replaced by *ū*.

The case of Latin *me-min-ī* 'I bear something in mind' is also not immediately clear: Although *mon-eō* 'I warn' attests *F(o)* in the first syllable, the middle-syllable *F(o)* of **me-mon-* (cf. Gr. μέμον-α 'I commemorate') is changed through vowel weakening to *-min-* (cf. L 204). — Further, the ablaut change **-en-* : **-n̥-* is no longer discernible because every **-n̥-* became *-en-*: Cf. the *-ti-* abstractum *men-ti-* (*mēns*) f. 'thought,' in which it is no longer clear whether the stem may be traced to an *Z(ø)* of **mn̥-ti-* as expected, or whether the *F(e)* of **men-ti* provides the basis, cf. F 317 § 7.

L 412. In Vedic and its Indo-Iranian preliminary phase, since the difference between PIE **e*, **o* and **a* as well as that between PIE **ē*, **ō* and **ā* was eliminated, only the quantitative ablaut is clearly discernible, cf. L 206.

Through linguistic comparison, however, one may detect in some developments the pre-Proto-Indo-Iranian passage of the qualitative ablaut from PIE **ĕ̄* to PIE **ŏ̄*. An example of this may be found in the effects of the palatal law, cf. L 206 § 2. Thus, the ablaut PIE **-ge-* : **-go-* is reflected in Old Avestan as *-ja-* : *-ga-*, cf. L 341 § 2. Other example: The Vedic 3 sg. perfect form *ca-kār-a* 'has done,' with its *ca-*, suggests **-e-* in the reduplication syllable, but with *-kār-*, suggests **-o-* in the root syllable, as do the Greek perfect forms λέ-λοιπ-ε and δέ-δορκ-ε.

Further information on Vedic *-kār-*: In this case, PIE **-o-* clearly became Indo-Iranian *-ā-*, and thus reveals its contrast to PIE **-e-* > Indo-Iranian *-a-*. Called Brugmann's Law, this assertion explains the difference between the Vedic acc. sg. *dā-tā́r-am* 'donor' and acc. sg. *pi-tár-am* 'father' as a reflection of the PIE qualitative vowel difference **-tor-* : **-ter-*, compare Greek δώ-τορ-α with πα-τέρ-α. However, the details are more complex. As a rule, this affected open syllables. Proof of this is provided by the 1st person singular of the same perfect form, *cakára*, in which the original vowel in the middle syllable can only have been *-o-*. However, the *-a* ending of the 1st person singular, unlike the 3rd person singular (with PIE **-e*), may be traced back to **-Ha* < PIE **-h₂e*. In the period of activity of Brugmann's Law, the 1st person singular with its **-Ha* formed a closed middle syllable, thus **-kar.Ha*. While in the 3 sg. **-ka.ra* became *-kā-ra*, **-kar.Ha* remained intact and did not even change when the laryngeal *H* disappeared.

Further literature: → Mayrhofer *Lautlehre* 1986 p. 146 ff; Collinge *Laws* 1985 p. 13ff.; Volkart *Brugmanns Gesetz* 1994; I. Hajnal "*Das Brugmannsche Gesetz in diachroner Sicht und seine Gültigkeit innerhalb der arischen a-Stämme*" in HS 107 1994 p. 194-221.

L 413. The insightful Indian grammarians brought the quantitative ablaut, the only one known to them, into a system, of which the zero grade (such as *bhr̥-* 'to carry,' for example in the participle *bhr̥-tá-* 'carried') was the starting point.

1) To the zero grade basic forms, *-a-* is added a first grade, called Guṇa (presumably in the sense of 'high grade'), cf. *bhár-aṇa-* n. 'burden.' The highest grade, called Vr̥ddhi (in the sense of 'increase, growth'), adds *-ā-* to the root, cf. *bhār-ía-* 'to be carried, to be cared for.' A further prime example: — Concerning *ji-* 'to be victorious over' (cf. Ved. *ji-tá-* 'conquers') compare with the Guṇa **jai̯-* (= prevocalic Ved. *jay-*, but preconsonantal *je-*, cf. L 220 § 3; cf. *jay-úṣ-* 'victorious,' *je-tár-* m. 'victor') and Vr̥ddhi *jāi̯-* (= Ved. prevocalic *jāy-*, preconsonantal *jai-*; cf. *jāy-ú-* 'victorious,' *jái-tra-* 'victory-bringing'). — Corresponding to *śru-* 'to hear' (Ved. *śrutá-*) compare with Guṇa **śrau̯-* (= Ved. prevocalic *śrav-*, preconsonantal *śro-*; cf. *śráv-as-* n. 'fame,' *śró-tar-* 'Hörer') and 'Vr̥ddhi' **śrāu̯-* (= Ved. prevocalic *śrāv-*, preconsonantal *śrau-*; cf. *śrāv-áyati* 'renders audible,' *á-śrau-ṣīṣ* aor. 'you heard').

2) But because of its adoption of the zero grade as the fundamental root form, this astute observation of the Indian ablaut grade system was not always successful. In instances such as *man-* ‘to think’ or *pat-* ‘to fly,’ because the zero grade forms in cases like **mn̥-* > *ma-* (cf. L 306 § 3) or *pt-* (in the aorist form *a-pa-pt-at*) were not discernible to the Indian grammarians, they were forced to assert full grades as root forms. The case *svap-* ‘to sleep’ (with *sváp-na-* m. ‘sleep’) is similar, in which a gradation based upon the zero grade *sup-* (*sup-tá-* ‘slept,’ Gr. ὕπ-νος etc.) led the Indian grammarians astray. Indo-European linguistics corrected the Indian system by adopting as a starting point the *full grade* (as in PIE **k̑leu̯-*, PIE **su̯ep-*), the weakening of which (= minus *-e-*) > PIE **k̑lu-* and > PIE **sup-*, produces no problems.

L 414. In Hittite, the set of rules regarding the quantitive ablaut is quite clear, for example the change between *e* vs. *ø* in verbal paradigms, cf. 3 sg. *ku-en-zi* i.e. *ku̯en-*t^s*i* ‘he kills’ vs. 3 pl. *ku-na-an-zi* i.e. *kun-ant*^{s}*i* ‘they kill’ (= Ved. *hán-ti* vs. *ghn-ánti*, cf. L 345 § 1). — Laryngeal effects also play a role (cf. L 314ff.): Cf. concerning PIE *h_1*és-ti* ‘he is’ (= Lat. *est* etc., Hitt. *e-eš-zi* i.e. *ēs-*t^s*i* < **és-*t^s*i*; the so-called plene-spelling is explained as a lengthening due to the accent) the zero grade plural *h_1*s-énti* = *a-ša-an-zi* i.e. *as-ant*^{s}*i* ‘they are’ = Myc. *e-e-si* i.e. *ehénsi*, but Ved. *sánti*, NHG *sind*, cf. E 504 § 11 and cf. L 419 § 3 below. — Concerning the important statements in Hittite (Anatolian) on the lengthened grades PIE *$h_2\bar{e}$ and *$\bar{e}h_2$, cf. L 331.

L 415. In Germanic, the ablaut was retained and expanded as a central means of expression in the realm of morphology. An old Germanic language without ablaut (i.e. strong) verbs is unimaginable. In new Germanic languages such as English, there are form series (e.g. *sing* : *sang* : *sung* : *song*) in which the ablaut is the only remaining difference. Along with revelations in the Indian grade system (cf. L 413), it was through work in Germanic that helped early Indo-European linguistics in its understanding of the ablaut system.

The uniform PIE ablaut schema was transformed by the numerous phonetic changes that took place concerning vowels, diphthongs, and also *r̥, l̥, m̥,* and *n̥*. For instance, NHG *binden* : *band* : *ge-bunden* may be traced back to PIE *b^hend^h- : *b^hond^h- : *$b^h\text{n̥}d^h$- and may be associated with the grades *F(e)*, *F(o)* and *Z(ø)*, cf. L 410.

Further examples: — Got. *niman* ‘to take, to take up’ < PIE **nem-* = *F(e)*, Got. *nam* ‘took’ < **nom-* = *F(o)*, Got. *nemun* ‘they took’ with <e> for *ē* = *L(ē)*, Got. *in-numan* ‘taken in’ < **nm̥-* = *Z(ø)*. — Got. *wairþan* ‘to become' < PIE *$\underset{^}{u}$ert- = *F(e)*, *warþ* 'became' < *$\underset{^}{u}$ort- = *F(o)*, *waurþun* 'they became' < *$\underset{^}{u}\underset{\circ}{r}$t- = *Z(ø)* (concerning Gothic *-or-* < Proto-Germ. **-ur-*, cf. L 208). — Got. *tiuhan* 'to pull, to lead' < PIE **deu̯k-* = *F(e)*, *ga-tauhans* part. 'pulled' < **duk-* = *Z(ø)* (concerning Gothic *-oh-* < Germ. **-uh-*, cf. L 208).

The various Germanic continuations of the uniform PIE ablaut types such as **er *or *r̥* or **eu̯ *ou̯ *u* are the major reason for the differences between the first five series of strong verbs in the Old Germanic languages.

L 416. Many instances of inherited ablauts are also attested in the Baltic and Slavic languages: — Cf. Lith. *tekù*, OCS *teko* 'I run, flow' = *F(e)*; Lith. *tãkas* m. 'canal, pipe, barrel,' OCS *tokъ* 'run, flow, threshing floor' *F(o)*; Lith. *tėkẽ* 'deep place in a river,' OCS *těxъ* 'ran' < **tēk[-s-]* = *L(ē)*; Russ.-CS *takati* 'to drive an animal' = *L(ō)*. — Cf. Lith. *merë́ti* 'to starve,' OCS *mrěti* 'to die' < PIE **mer-* = *F(e)*; Lith. *mãras* 'epidemic,' OCS *morъ* 'plague' = *F(o)*; Lith. *mirtìs*, OCS *sъ-mrьtь* f. 'death' < **mr̥-* = *Z(ø)*. — Slavic even exhibits the ideal case: all five possible ablaut grades,cf. L 410: OCS *greb-o* 'I dig, scratch' = *F(e)*, *grobъ* m. 'grave' = *F(o)*, *grěsъ* 'dug' < **grěb-s-* = *L(ē)*, *grabiti* 'to steal' = *L(ō)*, Cz. *po-hřbiti* 'buried' < Proto-Sl. **gьrb-* = *Z(ø)*; and Lith. *grë́b-ti* ' to grab violently' ~ *grób-ti* 'to grab.' Following established patterns, the ablaut remained productive: → Stang *Vgl. Gramm.* 1966 p. 121ff.; Arumaa *Urslav. Grammatik* I 1964 p. 172ff.

L 417. Further ablaut series, which are most often considered as an extra group in older treatments, may, in light of laryngeal theory (cf. L 314ff.), be included in the *e o ē ō ø* schema.

1) Thus, the apparent '*a*/*o*-ablaut' is explained by the observation that word-initial *a-*, in most IE languages, originates from PIE **h_2e-* becoming * *h_2a-* (in Hittite retained as *ḫa-*), cf. L 322 § 2. Ablaut relationships such as that of Gr. ἄγω 'I drive, I pull' (Lat. *agō* among others) with Gr. ὄγμος m. 'a row of mowed grass, a strip of land' (cf. ὄγμον ἄγειν in Theocrates) may be assigned to the normal type (as in Gr. πετ- vs. ποτ- = *F(e)* vs. *F(o)*) through the reconstruction PIE **h_2eǵ-* (becoming **h_2aǵ-*) vs. **h_2oǵ-*. — PIE **h_2eḱ-* (becoming **h_2aḱ-*), **h_2oḱ-* and **h_2ēḱ-* and thus the vowel grades *F(e)*, *F(o)* and *L(ē)* are retained in the Gr. ἄκρις f. 'mountain peak' along with ὄκρις m. 'point, corner' (Lat. *ocris* m. 'rocky mountain') and Hitt. *hēkur* 'clifftop' (cf. L 331 § 3). — Also cf. Gr. ἀγκάλη f. 'bent arm' along with ὄγκος m. 'hook' and Hitt. *hēnk-* 'to bend' (*ḫi-in-g-*) < PIE **$h_2$enk-* vs. **$h_2$onk-* vs. **h_2ēnk-*. —

Further, Ved. *ī́jate* 'drives' comes from PIE *h_2eǵ- (Gr. ἄγω etc.), if in fact it may be traced to the reduplicated present stem *h_2i-h_2ǵ-e-*: → K. Strunk in Mayrhofer EWAia I p. 51.

2) The understanding presented above (L 323) of roots such as Gr. (τί-)θη(-μι), (ἵ-)στᾱ(-μι) and (δί-)δω(-μι) as originating from PIE *d^heh_1-, *$steh_2$- and *deh_3- leads one to abandon the hypothesis of a separate ablaut type with primary long vowel endings, the zero grade of which would be -*ə*-, cf. ἵ-στᾱ-μι : στα-τός (= Ved. *sthi-tá-*). In fact, the ablaut *e* / *o* / *ē* / *ō* / *ø* is present even here. — Examples: — PIE *d^heh_1- > Gr. -θη- = *F(e)*, PIE *d^hoh_1- > Gr. θω-ή f. 'punishment, sentencing' = *F(o)* and PIE *d^hh_1- > Gr. ἔ-θε-το 'has sat,' Ved. *a-dhi-ta* = *Z(ø)* (concerning the vowels, cf. L 325). — PIE *b^heh_2- 'to speak' (becoming PIE *b^hah_2-) = Myc. Gr. 3 sg. *pa-si* i.e. *p^hāsi* 'he claims'= *F(e)*; PIE *b^hoh_2- = Gr. φω-νή 'voice' = *F(o)*; PIE *b^hh_2- = Gr. ἄ-φα-τος 'unmentioned' (cf. Lat. *fatērī*) = *Z(ø)*. — PIE *ǵneh_3- 'discern': PIE *ǵn̥h_3- = Gr. (γι)γνώ-σκω = *Z(ø)*; PIE *ǵnēh_3- = Hitt. *ga-ne-eš-* i.e. *gnēs-* = *L(ē)*, cf. L 331 § 3.

3) An unusual form of ablaut concerns roots that feature a closing postconsonantal laryngeal such as PIE *pelh_1- 'to fill' (cf. Ved. *párī-ṇas-* n. 'fullness'). They are those that the Indian grammarians had already designated as '*seṭ*'- roots (cf. L 315). This group includes not only the zero grade *pl̥h_1- (cf. Ved. *pūr-ṇá-* = Lith. *pìl-nas*), designated as "minus -*e*-," but also the second *full grade* PIE *pleh_1- (cf. Gr. πίμ-πλη-μι). — This swaying *-*e*- in PIE *p-e-lh_1- vs. *pl-e-h_1- is called a fluctuating ablaut (Schwebeablaut). The most probable explanation of the phenomenon is the postulation of a Pre-PIE form with two vowels capable of exhibiting full grade, thus *peleh_1- in this case. In the Pre-PIE period, during which*-*e*- was dropped in positions of secondary stress, there were three possibilities: a) Pre-PIE *péleh_1- > PIE *pélh_1- (= full grade I); b) Pre-PIE *peléh_1- > PIE *pléh_1- (= full grade II); c) Pre-PIE *peleh_1- (both syllables unstressed) > PIE *pl̥h_1-. It is also conceivable that from *pelh_1- a new full grade *pleh_1- was formed via the zero grade *pl̥h_1-. In any case there exists a juxtaposition of two full grades, most clearly in the laryngeal-closing *seṭ*-roots: full grade I with *pelh_1- = Ved. *parī-* vs. full grade II with *pleh_1- = Gr. -πλη-. The same zero grade *pl̥h_1- = Ved. *pūr-* corresponds equally to both full grade forms. The full grade *ǵneh_3- = Lat. [*g*]*nō-vī* (full grade II) also falls into this category. One would have expected the full grade I, *ǵenh_3-, which is in fact exhibited in Lithuanian *žénklas* m. 'mark, characteristic' (with *-én-K-* < *-*énh_3-K*-). The zero grade *ǵn̥h_3- is reflected in OHG *kund* etc., cf. L 332 § 4c. Literature: → Anttila *PIE Schwebeablaut* 1969.

L 418. The ablaut was already an important morphological means in Proto-Indo-European. However, as controversial as this may be in individual cases, the origin of ablaut variants is most certainly found on the phonological level, cf. E 502 § 2. It is thus with good reason that the ablaut assigned to an area between phonology and morphology: morphonology.

The use of ablaut grades, which originated in phonology, in morphological categories is, among other things, comparable to the New High German Rule, according to which the comparative morpheme *-er* causes vowel mutation, cf. NHG *läng-er* with *lang*. The phenomenon, actually an assimilation, is no longer a general phonetic development (*-a-* preceding *-er* is retained in *langer Weg*), but rather a rule that is limited to the morphological comparative, which, however has a phonetic origin, cf. OHG *lengiro* 'longer' < **lang-iro* vs. *lang*. NHG *Gäste* vs. *Gast* also has a phonological-historical cause, cf. OHG *gesti* vs. *gast*. The plural *Generäl-e* vs. *General*, which certainly cannot be traced as far back as this period, is simply the application of a morphological rule.

1) Among the phonological causes of the ablaut, the appearance of a zero grade through loss of **-e-* in an unstressed syllable seems most likely: — Cf. Gr. πατρ-ί with πατέρ-α. — Cf. Ved. *ghn-ánti* 'they kill' and Hitt. *kun-anťi* < PIE**g^wh^n-énti* in comparison to Ved. *hán-ti* 'he kills' and Hitt. *ku̯en-ťi* < PIE **g^wh^én-ti*. — Cf. Ved. *i-más* 'we go' < PIE **h₁i-més* compared with *é-mi* 'I go' < *PIE *h₁éi̯-mi*.

2) However, already in Proto-Indo-European the combination of zero grade and lack of stress is not always present. Reconstructions such as PIE **u̯ĺ̥k^w-o-* m. 'wolf' (with *-*ĺ̥*-!) are indisputable. Also, in Gr. πατράσι = Ved. *pitŕ̥ṣu* (cf. L 408) zero grade (*-*r̥*-) and accent placement are no longer two mutually exclusive characteristics of a case form. Secondary morphological processes could be the cause of such irregularities. Thus, **u̯ĺ̥k^wo-* is perhaps the nominal form of a former adjective **u̯l̥k^wó-*. For further information on Ved. *pitŕ̥ṣu* and Gr. πατράσι: → M. Meier-Brügger in *Fachtagung Leiden* 1987 [1992] p. 288. — On the other hand, there exist inherited PIE combinations of normal grade and lack of stress, cf. Ved. *roká-* m. 'light,' *rocá-* 'lighting' = Gr. λευκός 'light, white' or cf. PIE **dei̯u̯ó-*, cf. W 202 § 2. See also the verbal morphology with a PIE form like loc. pl. **bhéromenoi̯su*.

3) Concerning the origins of the remaining ablaut grades there are only assumptions. The lengthened grade may, at least in some cases, have originated through compensatory lengthening. Thus, PIE **ph₂tér-* 'father' + nom. sg. *-s* > **ph₂térs* > **ph₂térr* > **ph₂tḗr* (= Gr. πατήρ) is thinkable, cf. F 310 § 3.

4) The nuancing of *-*e*- to *-*o*- (cf. Gr. πα-τέρ-, but -πά-τορ-, cf. L 408) may no longer be, as was for a long time suggested, traced back to an effect of accent that is separate from the origin of the zero grade. Nevertheless, it may have phonetic causes. Thus, the game of qualitative ablauts in thematic verbs (cf. Gr. φέρ-ο-μεν, but φέρ-ε-τε) creates the impression that post-tonic -*e*- preceding *r* (and *l m n*) might have become -*o*-: Cf. in addition to Gr. ἀπά-τορ-α also PIE **de-dórḱ*- 'have seen' = Ved. *dadárś*- (Gr. with secondary stress δέδορκ-): It is explained by Pre-PIE 1st person sg. **dedérk-h_2e* with *-*e*- > *-*o*- preceding -*h_2e*: → W. Mańczak in *Lingua* 9 p. 1960 277ff. For information on the history of research on this subject, cf. Szemerényi *Einführung* 1990 p. 124-127.

5. Accent

L 419. Only the independent word accent is discussed here. For information on nominal accent classes, cf. F 314ff. For information on verbal accents cf. F 214. On sentence accent, cf. S 209.

1) Among the IE languages, some of those whose surviving documents do reveal information about accent placement show free accent stress, i.e. accent stress that is independent of word structure. A Greek word such as φορος may carry the word accent on the first syllable (φόρος: 'tribute, gift') or on the second syllable (φορός: 'useful, profitable'). In Vedic, the gen. sg. *brahmaṇas* occurs with stress on the first syllable (*bráhmaṇas*: 'the prayer formula') as well as on the second syllable (*brahmáṇas*: in the sense of 'of one who prays, of the priest'). These examples show that the supra-segmental phenomenon of accents placed above phonemic segments is the only means of distinguishing such pairs of cognates.

2) It is important for the historical comparative observation of word accents that these free accents correspond in several languages, a fact which can only be explained by the existence of a common preliminary phase. However, the agreements with word structure independent accents have been obscured by language-internal rules. Research by Karl Verner on the effects of PIE accent placement on the Germanic fricative system has revealed Germanic as a further essential source of information on the original accents, cf. L 421. The free accent systems of Baltic and several Slavic languages may be traced to subsequent developments of the inherited status, cf. L 422. Among the languages that have exchanged the PIE accent in favor of a secondary accent system, Latin is the most important, cf. L 423.

3) Concerning the efforts to ascertain PIE accents from the basis of phonetic results in IE languages that have no certain graphic representation of accent positions, a few hints shall have to suffice. — For information on Hittite, cf. L 207. Further, cf. L 414 above, where in the example *e-eš-zi* i.e. *ēs-tˢi*, the singular plene-spelling may be understood as the result of *$h_1$és-*, above which is placed the accent; cf. L 336 § 5 above, in which the lenition rule requires the presence of a preceding accented long vowel. Literature: → Melchert *Anatolian Historical Phonology* 1994 p. 106f. — For information on implications from Avestan and Paštō: → M. Mayrhofer in *Compendium Ling. Iran.* 1989 p. 12f.

L 420. Many Greek – Vedic word pairs show full agreement in accent placement.

1) Cf. the familial terms Gr. πατέρ-α = Ved. *pitár-am* 'father,' φρᾱ́τερ-α = Ved. *bhrā́tar-am* 'brother,' θυγατέρ-α = Ved. *duhitár-am* 'daughter,' μητέρ-α = Ved. *mātár-am* 'mother' (in each case acc. sg.); Gr. νέφος n. = Ved. *nábhas-* n. 'cloud'; Gr. θῡμός m. 'surge, courage, anger'= Ved. *dhūmá-* m. 'smoke'; Gr. (Dor.) φέροντι 'they carry' = Ved. *bháranti*, Gr. ἔφερον 'they carried' = Ved. *ábharan.*

2) However, in Greek the inherited freedom of accent placement is limited by what is called the 'three-syllable rule.' As a result, accents that were originally placed on the fourth to last syllable or further forward in the word were moved to the third to last syllable: Additionally, it was determined that the accent could only stay on the third to last syllable when the last syllable was short. Unstressed words were also subjected to the rule when they comported three or more syllables.

While Greek ἔφερον (⏑⏑⏑) remains possible as an equivalent to the Vedic *ábharan*, as a result of the three syllable rule the Greek ἐφέρομεν (= ⏑⏑⏑⏑) and ἐφερέτην (= ⏑⏑⏑–) do not any more correspond to the accentuation of the Vedic verbal forms *á-bharāma* 'we carried' and *ábharatām* 'they both carried.' For more information, cf. F 214 § 1.

3) A further change in Greek of the inherited accent positions is a product of the dactylos rule, also referred to, owing to B. I. Wheeler's classical description in his book *Nominalaccent* of 1885, as Wheeler's Law: It states that all final position stressed dactylic forms in Greek move the accent to the next to last syllable. This may be demonstrated just as well within Greek (in the group of traditionally final position stressed verbal government compound forms of the type ψῡχο-πομπός 'leading the souls of the dead' the examples that end with a dactylos receive the accent

on the next to last syllable, cf. πατροκτόνος 'killing the father') as in an external comparison (the form, **poi̯kiló-* 'colorful,' similar in morphology to Ved. *peśalá-* 'beautiful, decorated' becomes, according to the dactylos rule, ποικίλος). Literature: → Meier-Brügger *Gr. Sprachw.* II 1992 p. 39.

4) For further information on the accent in Greek and its peculiarities: → Risch *Kl. Schr.* 1981 (in an essay from 1975) p. 187ff.; M. Meier-Brügger in *Fachtagung Leiden* 1987 [1992] p. 283ff.

L 421. According to Verner's Law, published in 1876, the retention of an unvoiced word-internal fricative in Germanic proves that in an accentuation, similar to that of Vedic and Greek, and which was still present in the oldest Germanic, the stress was placed immediately before the fricatives: → K. Verner "*Eine Ausnahme der ersten Lautverschiebung*" in KZ 23 1876 p. 97-130. According to an account by O. Jespersen (→ *Portraits* I 1966 p. 539), Verner made his discovery shortly before taking a nap, as he briefly leafed through *Comparative Grammar* by F. Bopp. His glance fell upon *pitár-* vs. *bhrā́tar-*: "It struck me that it was strange that the one word had a *t* in the Germanic languages and the other a *th* ... and then I noticed the accent-marks on the Sanscrit words": Further reading: → A. Calabrese and M. Halle, "*Grimm's and Verner's Laws: A New Perspective*" in *FS Watkins* 1998 p. 47-62; K.-H. Mottausch in IF 104 1999 p. 46ff.

1) Proto-Germanic *f, þ, χ, χʷ, s* < PIE *p, t, k, kʷ, s* were only retained when they immediately followed a word-internal accent in a voiced context, cf. L 336 § 4. In all other cases they became voiced fricatives (*ƀ, đ, g, gʷ, z*). The retained Germanic *-þ-* in the Gothic *broþar* 'brother' thus suggests Proto-Germanic **ƀrṓþer-*, the accent position of which agrees with that of Ved. *bhrā́tar-*, Gr. φράτερ-. In contrast, Got. *fadar* and ON *móðer* 'mother' originate with the Proto-Germanic **faþér-*, **mōþér-*, the accent position of which corresponds to that of *pitár-* = Gr. πατέρ- cf. Ved. *mātár-* = Gr. μητέρ-. For further information on 'mother' cf. L 211 § 10. — A retained Germanic **-χ-* immediately following an accent is shown in the word for 'father-in-law': According to the evidence of Ved. *śváśura-*, its accent position resulted in PIE **su̯éḱuro-*, from which came **su̯éχura-* = OHG *swehur*, NHG *Schwäher*. In contrast, the word for 'mother-in-law,' PIE **su̯eḱrúh₂-* (cf. L 304 § 3) exhibits, according to the evidence of Ved. *śvaśrū́-* a post-tectal accent position: Proto-Germ. **su̯eχrū́-* thus develops further to become **su̯egrū́-* = OHG *swigur*, NHG *Schwieger(mutter)*.

2) That *-*s*- was retained in Germanic only immediately following the accented syllable, and elsewhere became *-*z*-, is not only shown by individual word pairs such as Ved. *áyas*- 'precious metal' = Proto-Germ. **á̯ies*- > **ai̯ez*- (Got. *aiz*, OHG *ēr* 'ore') or Ved. *snuṣā́*- = Gr. νυός 'daughter-in-law' (thematic **snusó*- f., incidentally, is older than **snusā́*-, cf. E 506 § 5, which is clearly marked as feminine through inflection) = Proto-Germ. **snuzṓ* (OHG *snora, snur*, Early NHG *Schnur* 'daughter-in-law'). It is also demonstrated by a consequence of Verner's Law, according to which a common accent (and ablaut) difference in Vedic grammar between perfect singular and perfect plural (and dual) is echoed in the change between*-*s*- (< *-*s*-) and *-*z*- (< *-*s*-). This effect of the PIE accent change in Germanic grammatical morphology is known as the "Grammatical Change." Just as in the Veda the singular *ju-jóṣ-a* 'he has enjoyed' relates to the plural *ju-juṣ-úr* 'they have enjoyed,' the Proto-Germanic **káu̯s-e* (= Ved. *-jóṣ-a*) with its retained *-s-*, relates to the OHG *kōs* 'he chose,' but **kuz*- (= Ved. *-juṣ-úr*) in OHG *kur-un* 'they chose.' Likewise in the case of original PIE tenues: OHG *ward* 'he became' < Proto-Germ. **wárþ-e* (= Ved. [*va*-]*várt-a* 'has turned'), but *wurtun* 'they became' < Proto-Germ. **wurđ*- (= Ved. 3 pl. [*va*-]*vr̥t-úr*).

3) Although Germanic, as it has been handed down, has abandoned the PIE accent in favor of word-initial stress in independent words, the results arrived at by K. Verner thus require accent positions for distinctively Germanic words that are equivalent to those of Greek and Vedic equivalents: Thus Proto-Germ. **ƀrṓþer*- = Ved. *bhrā́tar*-, Proto-Germ. **faþér*- = Ved. *pitár*-, Proto-Germ. **mōþér*- = Ved. *mātár*-, Proto-Germ. **snusṓ* = Ved. *snuṣā́*-, Proto-Germ. **sweχrū́*- = Ved. *śvaśrū́*-, Proto-Germ. **káu̯se*- / **kus*-′ = Ved. *-jóṣa -juṣúr* etc. Owing to these effects of Verner's Law, Germanic is the third most important reference for PIE word accent following Vedic and Greek. Verner's discovery, which explained hundreds of exceptions to the Germanic consonant shift through the supposition of the existence of Proto-Indo-European accent positions in post-consonant shift Germanic, thus clearing the way for a more precise application of phonetic laws, was a watershed in the development of diachronic comparative linguistics.

4) In conclusion, the following relative chronology may be established for Germanic: a) PIE accent positions are fixed; b) the Germanic consonant shift takes place; c) Verner's Law operates; d) change of accent position and appearance of typical Germanic first-syllable stress.

L 422. The Baltic and several Slavic languages have accents that are free and movable, i.e. that change position within paradigms. In his

Akzent.Ablaut 1968 p. III, Kuryłowicz writes "It is this mobility and relative freedom that inspire the comparative linguist to search for a historical context [which relates the Balto-Slavic and Vedic-Greek (Germanic) accent positions]." However the inherited situation in Balto-Slavic was subjected to several changes, concerning the dimensions of which as yet no unanimity has been achieved.

Thus, it remains disputed whether the accent position variations in Lith. *duktẽ* 'daughter,' gen. sg. (old) *dukterès*, and acc. sg. *dùkteri* are an echo of the PIE (Ved.) accent positions: compare *-tẽ* with Ved. *duhitā́* 'daughter,' compare *-terès* (for **duktr-ès*) with the weak case of the type Ved. dat. sg. *duhitr-é* and Gr. gen. pl. θυγατρ-ῶν, compare *dùkteri* (with regular accent **duktẽri*) with Ved. *duhitár-am* and Gr. θυγατέρ-α. Nevertheless, in most cases one must expect further developments that in principle will be traceable to Proto-Indo-European forms. Accent positions that remain the same, such as Russ. *nébo*, Serbo-Croatian *nȅbo* 'sky' = PIE **$néb^hos$* (Gr. νέφος, Ved. *nábhas* 'cloud,' cf. L 338), resemble curious coïncidences. One is tempted to formulate rules, for instance that a syllable containing a laryngeal, followed by a stressed syllable in Proto-Indo-European, pulled the accent upon itself in Baltic and Slavic: for example, PIE **d^huh_2-mó-* (Ved. *dhūmá-*, Gr. θῦμός, cf. L 211 § 7) = Baltic and Slavic *dū́m-*, Lith. *dū́mai*, Russ. *dym* (gen. sg. *dým-a*), Serbo-Croatian *dȉm* 'smoke'; PIE **g^wriH-u̯éh$_2$-* (Ved. *grīvā́-* f. 'neck') = Latvian *grĩva* 'river mouth,' Russ. *gríva*, Serbo-Croatian *grȉva* 'mane.' If such a result were combined with the continuation of the PIE accent position in syllables that contain laryngeals (cf. PIE **u̯ĺ̥H-nah$_2$-* 'wool' [Ved. *ū́rṇā-*] > Latvian *vil̃na*, Russ. *vólna*, Serbo-Croatian *vȕna* 'wool'), the value of assertions based on Baltic and Slavic regarding PIE accent positions would be relativized. Although the movable and free accents in Baltic and Slavic have the PIE accent positions as a starting point, at the most they can serve to confirm in a case by case manner the assertions already made based on the evidence in Vedic, Greek, and Germanic.

Further reading: → Kuryłowicz *Akzent.Ablaut* 1968 p. 111f., p. 123; Stang *Vgl. Gramm.* 1966 p. 134f.; Kortlandt *Slavic Accentuation* 1975; Illič-Svityč *Nominal Accentuation* 1979; Collinge *Laws* 1985; I. Hajnal in HS 109 1996 p. 314-316 (a review of R. Derksen, *Metatony in Baltic* Amsterdam / Atlanta 1996).

L 423. In the case of Latin, no obvious traces of PIE (i.e. Vedic and Greek) accent positions remain. At most is found indirect evidence, cf §1.

The original PIE accent positions were replaced in a first step by the initial accent (cf. § 3), from which Classical Latin then broke away (cf. § 2).

1) The fate of word-final *-i* may provide a clue as to the original PIE accent position: In non-stressed cases such as *est* < PIE *$*h_1$ésti* the *-i* is dropped, whereas in cases such as the final stressed loc. sg. *pede* < PIE **ped-í*, it may be preserved: → H. Rix in *Kratylos* 41 1996 p. 158 note 7 (based upon cases such as **ped-í* , the locative *-e* is generalized, even when [as in the case of *ante* < *$*h_2$ént-i*, cf. L 322 § 2] in the paradigm it was not accented).

2) Classical Latin is subjected to a rule that is dependent on the form of the word, according to which two-syllable words that are stressed carry the accent on the second to last syllable (*paenultima*), while words with more than two syllables carry the accent on the *paenultima* when it is long (either by position or by nature), otherwise the accent is on the third to last syllable, or *antepaenultima*: *régit, régunt; regḗbat, regúntur; régitur*.

3) However this system of accent placement must have been preceded by an older one, which was equally restricted, but which fixed the accent on the first syllable of the word. Word stress in the very oldest Latin was thus: **fáciō, *cón-faciō, *cón-factom*. Since word internal short *-*a*- in an open syllable becomes *-i-*, and in a closed syllable becomes *-e-* (see L 204), the two latter forms resulted in Lat. *conficiō* and *confectum*. As further examples, cf. *agō* : *ex-igō* (< **éx-agō*), *sedeō* : *ob-sideō* (**ób-sed-*, cf. L 108), *talentum* (< **tálantom*, a loanword from the Greek τάλαντον), and finally *igitur* 'thus, because' (separated from the question formula *quid igitur* < *quid agitur* 'what is it about, what then?)' — Information about the prehistoric initial accent (which reached into the historical era) as well as its effects is important for linguistic comparison since the results that one would expect are often affected by the initial accent: PIE *$*\acute{g}enh_1tor$-* (cf. F 101 § 2) becomes, in the earliest Latin, **génator*, which then becomes *genitor* (cp. **éxagō* > *exigō*). That Lat. short *-*a*-, in a closed syllable becomes *-e-*, is illustrated by the feminine form *genetrīx* < **génatrīk-* (= Ved. *jánitrī-* f. 'one that gives birth'). The Lat. *(*áb-*), *(*cón*)*-datos* (< PIE *$*d^h h_1$tó-*, cf. L 325), which corresponds to the Greek θετός, accordingly appears as *ab-ditus, con-ditus*. — Aliterative formulae from religious and juridical texts that have been handed down are final allusions from the classical period to this older epoch of word-initial accents, cf. Cato's *Pastores pecuaque salva servassis duisque duonam salutem* "(Father Mars, I bid you, that you) keep herdsmen and herds unharmed and give guard well" in *De Agricultura* 141,2).

4) The first step away from the Proto-Indo-European accent system toward the word-initial accent was necessarily influenced by the Middle-Italian coine, to which belonged, in addition to Latin, also Sabellic and Etruscan. Further reading: → H. Rix "*Die lateinische Synkope als historisches und phonologisches Problem*" in *Kratylos* 11 1966 p. 156-165; Leumann LLFL 1977 p. 235-254; Meiser *Laut- u. Formenlehre* 1998 p.53.

III. Proto-Indo-European Morphology

A. General Information

F 100. In traditional grammar, morphology, in the broadest sense, is situated between phonology (see part II, above) and syntax (see part IV, below).

1) A verb form such as Lat. ind. pres. 3 sg. act. *gignit* 'creates, brings about' is composed of a word stem (or, more precisely, of a verbal stem, or more precisely yet, of the indicative present stem), in this case, *gignV-* and the 3rd person sg. active ending *-t*. A substantive form such as the Lat. nom. sg. *genetrīx* (*'creator [f.]' >) 'mother' is based upon the word stem (or, more precisely, the nominal stem) *genetrīc-* and the nom. sg. ending *-s* (the character *x* indicates the double consonance *c+s*, the character *c* indicates a voiceless *k*). The initial, unchanged part of both forms, the word stem, carries the signification, and includes the lexeme. The latter part, the ending, is part of a larger interchangeable set, or paradigm (cf. in the case of *gignV-* among others, the pres. ind. act. endings *-ō -is -it -imus -itis -unt*, cf. in the case of *genetrīc-* among others, the sg. endings *-s -is -ī -em -e*). The endings indicate the grammatical category of the word form in question, or morpheme.

2) The summary in § 1 outlines the general tasks of morphology. The branches etymology, word formation, and semantics are concerned with word stems, which shall in the present work be treated under the heading 'Vocabulary' in part V.

The presently discussed, more narrow sense of morphology (French *morphologie*; German, *Formenlehre*) is concerned with paradigms and their endings. Since the structure of a verb combines various tense stems (compare the above present stem *gi-gn-V-*, and perfect stem **gena-u̯-* with the classical Latin 1 sg. *genuī* etc.), they shall also be discussed here.

3) Concerning the definition of inflection and morphology: → Bussmann *Lexikon der Sprachwissenschaft* 1990 p. 244f. and p. 504f.; Lewandowski *Linguist. Wörterbuch* 2 1994 p. 306 and p. 729f.

F 101. As a rule, every verbal or nominal word stem may be subdivided.

1) A first example: The Greek verb form ἐρητύσασκε (Hom., poetic) 'to hinder' contains, along with the ending *-ø* (< **-t*; which here indicates 3 sg. Aor.) the elements ἐρητυ+σα+σκε-. The nominal stem ἐρητυ- serves as the basis to which both of the suffixes *-sa-* (which indicates the aorist stem), and *-ske-* (which indicates an iterative quality) are added. The nominal stem may be further subdivided into the verbal root ἐρ- (< PIE **u̯er-* 'to hinder,' cf. Ved. *vár-tave* 'to be hindered,' *vár-tra-* 'protective embankment') and the complex nominal suffix -ητυ- (which belongs to the group of Greek verbal abstracta with *-tu-*; the secondary form, with the addition of *-ē-*, and *-ā-*, is comparable to the familiar substantives of the type ἀγορητύ- [Hom. Od.] 'speech'; my suggested analysis is supported by the Homeric substantive ἐδητύ- 'food,' which is constructed in a parallel manner, and is clearly based upon the verbal stem ἐδ- 'to eat' < PIE **$h_1$ed-*).

2) A second example: The two Latin nominal stems *gene-tr-ī-c-* f. 'mother' (older [from before the short vowel weakening in middle syllables: → Leumann LLFL 1977 p. 82f.; see L 204] **gena-tr-ī-c-*) and *genitōr-* m. 'father' (older **gena-tōr-*) are both composed of the full grade verbal root **gena-* (< PIE **ǵenh_1-*) and the suffix *-t(V)r-* (which is indicative of the nomina agentis, cf. W 205 § 1). In the case of the masculine, the suffix form is the lengthened grade *-tōr-*, in that of the feminine, it is the zero grade *-tr-* with the addition of the complex suffiix *-ī-c-* (i.e. *-ī-k-*) in order to clearly mark the feminine (on *-ī-* < **-ih_2-*, cf. W 204 § 1).

3) Along with the countless word stems that may be divided into the root (the core that is left after removing all suffixes) and its suffixes, there are also those that are solely composed of the root, cf. from the verbal realm, the root presents of the type Ved. *ás-mi* (< PIE **$h_1$és-mi*, cf. E 502 § 4) and the root aorists of the type Gr. ἔφυν (< PIE **é b^huh_1-m*), or, from the realm of substantives, the root nouns of the type Lat. *vōc-* 'voice' (< PIE **u̯ōk^w-* / **u̯ok^w-*, which corresponds to the verbal form PIE **u̯ek^w-* 'to say').

4) Among word stems, one may distinguish athematic from thematic word stems. The criterion for this distinction is the presence or absence of the thematic vowel *-e-* at the end of the stem, just before the ending. The ablaut of the thematic vowel is *-o-*. In the case of substantives, the *-o-* takes prece-

dence; however, the *-e-* ablaut is found in the vocative singular (in masculine and neuter with *-e*) and in a part of the locative singular and instrumental singular forms (along with *-o̯i̯* and *-oh₁* there are indications of *-e̯i̯-* and *-eh₁-* forms), cf. F 311 § 1. In the case of verbs, *-e-* and *-o-* alternate. The phonetic context appears to play a role here. Namely, the *-o-* vowel is only found before endings that begin with *-m-*, *-nt-* , *-h₂-*, or *-ih₁-*, cf. F 209 and cf. L 418 § 4. For more information on the subject in general: → Rasmussen *Morphophonemik* 1989 p. 136ff.

As a rule, in order to simplify reconstructions, thematic nominal forms are given an *-o-* and thematic verbal forms are given *-e-*. A nominal stem such as PIE **u̯érǵ-o-* 'work' is thus determined to be every bit as thematic as the verbal stem PIE **bʰér-e-*. The nominal stem PIE **ḱ(u)u̯on-* 'dog,' for example or the verbal stem PIE **h₁es-* 'to exist' are, in contrast, athematic. In the course of the development of the individual IE languages, the quantity of thematic substantives and verbs has increased, while the quantity of athematic nouns and verbs has decreased. The endings of thematic verbal and nominal stems are somewhat different from those of the athematic forms, cf. F 209 for information on the verb, and F 311 for information on the noun.

F 102. Verbal inflection (conjugation) and nominal inflection (declension) shall be treated separately; the verb, below in F 200ff., the noun, below in F 300ff. A couple of characteristics, however, are common to both inflections.

1) Paradigms may be defined for conjugation and declension, for example the paradigm for the Latin present stems of the type *gignV-* (namely, in the indicative, present, active, 1 sg. *-ō*, 2 sg. *-is*, 3 sg. *-it*, etc.) or the masculine singular paradigm for Greek *-o-* stems (nom. sg. -ος, acc. sg. -ον, loc. sg. -οι, etc.). These paradigms, familiar to all from textbooks and grammars, are not simply the inventions of schoolmasters, they are based upon immanent linguistic criteria: → Hj. Seiler "*Das Paradigma in alter und neuer Sicht*" in *Kratylos* 11 1966 p. 190-205.

2) One tends to regard paradigms as fixed values, complete in their formation, an assertion which, however, does not correspond to the everyday realities of language. Thus, not all positions must at all times be occupied by forms. There are substantives that may only be used in the singular (*singularia tantum*) and also those that are only used in the plural (*pluralia tantum*). Further, nominal paradigms reveal structural differences, cf. F 310. Various requirements must be met in the use of place names, proper nouns, and things:

For example, place names require a locative; proper nouns, a vocative; things require an instrumental, etc.: → Risch *Kleine Schriften* 1981 p. 736; concerning Anatolian, E. Neu in HS 102 1989 p. 13f. ("Much evidence indicates that the construction and extension of case inflection for nouns of the personal and object type did not develop uniformly and simultaneously").

For further information on changes in the nominal paradigms, cf. F 302.

F 103. As a rule, a single root forms the basis of the entire diversity of forms of a word: Compare, for example, the Latin present stem *laud-ā-i̯e-* with the slightly varied perfect stem *laudā-u̯-*; as well as the Latin *dominus* m. 'head of the household, owner' (from the nominal stem *dom-ino-*), *domina* f. 'mistress of the houshold, wife' (from the nominal stem *dom-inā-*), *dominūre* 'to be the head of the houshold' (from the verbal stem **domin-ā-i̯e-*), *dominātiō* f. 'rule' (from the nominal stem *dominā-ti-ōn-*), and others.

In a few old examples, genetically different stems complete each other through suppletion. In contrast to the above-mentioned examples, compare the Latin present stem *esse* (*sum*) 'to be,' which has the perfect stem *fuī* (a perfect stem **eruī* or the like is not attested); or compare Gr. ἀνήρ m. 'man,' to which the corresponding feminine is γυνή f. 'woman' (*ἀνδρία does not exist). For information on the subject of suppletion: → K. Strunk, "*Überlegungen zu Defektivität und Suppletion im Griechischen und Indogermanischen*" in *Glotta* 55 1977 p. 2-34.

F 104. Nominal endings give information regarding the paradigmatic categories of casus, numerus, and genus. Their verbal counterparts give information regarding numerus, person, voice, aspect, mode, and tempus. The description in terms of content of these categories is part of syntax, cf. part IV, with C on the morphosyntax of the verb, and D on the morphosyntax of the noun. However, mention of content shall be included in cases in which it is important for the understanding of the formal side.

It is characteristic of the Indo-European languages that there is not a *formans* that is analytically proper to each grammatical category, but rather that the individual endings combine, synthetically and cumulatively, two, three, or more statements concerning content in the same bundel. For instance, compare, from the verbal realm, the Latin ending *-tur* (in, for example, *laudātur* 'he/one is praised'), in which the qualities 3rd person, singular, present, and passive are all expressed. Another example from the verbal realm is the PIE ending **-ént-i* (in, for example PIE **h_1s-énti* 'they exist,' cf. E 505), which includes the information: 3rd person, plural, active, and present. From the nominal realm, consider the example of Lat. *-us* (in the example *dominus*) which expresses: nominative, singular, and masculine.

An indication that the analytical process too was known in Pre-Proto-Indo-European is found in the accusative plural **-ns*: Assuming the comparison of the PIE acc. sg. **-m* is not misleading, the accusative plural **-ns* resulted from the combination of **-m* (acc.) and -(*e*)*s* (pl.).

B. Verbs

1. General Information

F 200. The verb is the center of the verbal phrase. It offers a much greater wealth of forms and contents than the substantive. For information on syntax, cf. S 300ff.

Occasionally the reproach is voiced that reconstructions of the PIE verbal system are disproportionately based upon knowledge of Greek and Indo-Iranian. Critics of the 'graeco-aryan' reconstruction model often point out the differentness of Anatolian, Tocharian, and Celtic. However, alternative models could not be offered. In fact, where exact data is available, it is again and again shown to be the case, that this differentness may be seen as a secondary variation from the model as it is offered in Greek and Indo-Iranian. Thus, the privileged place of Greek and Indo-Iranian seems not to be attributable to any bias in the research, but rather to the history of Greek and Indo-Iranian: → H. Rix "*Das keltische Verbalsystem auf dem Hintergrund des indo-iranisch-griechischen Rekonstruktionsmodells*" in *Kolloquium Keltisch* Bonn 1976 [1977] p. 132-158.

F 201. Literature: — a) Concerning the verb in general: → Bussmann *Lexikon d. Sprachw.* 1990 p. 828f. *s.v.* '*Verb*'; *Metzler Lexikon Sprache* 1993 p. 675 *s.v.* '*Verb*'; Lewandowski *Linguist. Wörterbuch 3* 1994 p. 1221f. *s.v.* '*Verb*'; R. Stempel "*Aspekt und Aktionsart, Tempus und Modus: Zur Strukturierung von Verbalsystemen*" in IF 104 1999 p. 23ff. — b) Concerning the verb in Proto-Indo-European: → LIV 1998; Brugmann *Grundriß* II-3 1916; Krahe *Idg. Sprachw.* II 1969 p. 50-89; Watkins *Verbalflexion* 1969; Jasanoff *Stative and Middle* 1978; Szemerényi *Ein-*

führung 1990 p. 244-370 (see *Einleitendes über das idg. Verbalsystem*; *Personalendungen, Themavokal, Diathesen*; *Modusbildungen*; *Tempusstämme*; *Synthese: Paradigmen mit Anmerkungen*; *Verbum infinitum*; *Vorgeschichte*); J. H. Jasanoff "*Aspects of the Internal History of the PIE Verbal System*" in *Fachtagung* Zürich 1992 [1994] p. 149-168. — c) Concerning the Latin verb: → Leumann LLFL 1977 p. 505-624 (see *Das Verbalsystem und seine Formen*; *Praesenssystem mit Praesensstämmen und Flexionsformen*; *Perfektsystem mit Perfektstämmen und Flexionsformen*); Meiser *Perfekt* 1991; Meiser *Laut- und Formenlehre* 1998 p. 178-228 (see the sections: *Flexion des Verbums*; *Aufbau des Paradigmas*; *Die Bildung des Präsensstamms*; *Tempora und Modi des Präsensstamms*; *Der Perfektstamm*; *Die Endungen*; *Unregelmäßige Paradigmen*; *Infinite Verbalformen*). — d) Concerning the Greek verb: → Meier-Brügger *Gr. Sprachw.* II 1992 p. 46-63; Hauri *Futur* 1975; Tucker *Early Greek Verbs* 1990; Rijksbaron *Verb in Class. Greek* 1994. — e) Concerning Vedic and Indo-Iranian verbs: → Gotō *Materialien* Nr. 1-29 1990-1997; *Werba Verba IndoArica* I 1997; Kellens *Verbe avestique* 1984 + 1994; Further: → Hoffmann *Aufsätze* I-III 1975-1992 and Narten *Kleine Schriften* I 1994 with numerous and methodically exemplary treatments of Indo-Iranian and PIE verbal systems; Narten *Sigmatische Aoriste* 1964; Schaefer *Intensivum* 1994; Kümmel *Stativ und Passivaorist* 1996. — f) Concerning Hittite and Anatolian verbs: → Oettinger *Verbum* 1979. — g) Concerning the Germanic verb: → Seebold *Germ. starke Verben* 1970; Bammesberger *Germ. Verbalsystem* 1986; R. Lühr "*Reste der athematischen Konjugation in den germanischen Sprachen*" in *Kolloquium Germanisch* Freiburg 1981 [1984] p. 25-90. — h) Concerning Balto-Slavic verbs: → Koch *Aksl. Verbum* I / II 1990; Petit *Lituanien* 1999 p. 75ff. — i) Concerning the Celtic verb: → H. Rix "*Das keltische Verbalsystem auf dem Hintergrund des indo-iranisch-griechischen Rekonstruktionsmodells*" in *Kolloquium Keltisch* Bonn 1976 [1977] p. 132-158. — k) Concerning the Armenian verb: → Klingenschmitt *Altarm. Verbum* 1982; Lamberterie *Arménien classique* 1992 p. 269-276 (see *morphologie verbale*). — l) Concerning the Tocharian verb: → Pinault *Tokharien* 1989 p. 123-162 (see *morphologie verbale*); Hackstein *Sigmat. Präsensstammbildungen* 1995.

2. Verbal Stem Formation

F 202. Every PIE verbal form may be split into parts. The first central division separates the verbal ending from the verbal stem that follows it, cf.

F 101. — Verbal stems are, according to their form, either athematic (e.g. PIE *h_1*es*-) or thematic (e.g. PIE *b^h*ere*-), with final -*e*- (with ablaut -*o*-), cf. F 101 § 4 and F 203 below, toward the end of the introductory text. The increase in the number of thematic verbs, and the corresponding decrease in the number of athematic verbs may be observed in all IE languages: → LIV 1998 p. 12f.

1) Each verbal stem without an ending is initially considered a tempus-modus stem (called a secondary stem in H. Rix's terminology). After the elimination of the tempus-modus suffixes (which Rix correspondingly names secondary suffixes: suffix -*ø*- for indicative, and in present and aorist, also for imperative and injunctive; suffix -*e*- for the subjunctive; suffix -*i̯eh*$_1$-/-*ih*$_1$- for the optative) remains only the actual verbal stem (called the primary stem by Rix). Rix's terminology is explained, for example in Rix *Hist. Gramm. d. Gr.* 1976 p. 190ff. The common terminology is non-uniform. It allows itself to be led astray from the realities of the IE languages. Depending on the presence or absence of an aspect system or a tempus system (the latter being derived from the former), one speaks either of the aspect or the tempus stem.

2) The actual verbal stem is either composed of the verbal root (as is the case of root present and root aorist forms), or is further divisible into the verbal root and one or more suffixes.

The actual verbal stem is in use either as the present stem, the aorist stem, or the perfect stem. The terms present, aorist, and perfect all indicate aspect, which is a grammatical dimension. The aorist stem indicates the perfective aspect. The present stem indicates the imperfective aspect. The perfect stem indicates a sort of resultative aspect. For further information, cf. S 304 and S 306-308. The formation types of present, aorist, and perfect stems, which are demonstrable in Proto-Indo-European, are discussed in F 203, with reference to LIV 1998 p. 14ff.

Along with aspect, the lexical aspect (i.e. the manner of action, or *Aktionsart*) also plays a role. The manner of action (or *Aktionsart*) is a quality of the verbal meaning which relates both to the process of taking place of the action that the verb describes, and to the verb's *agens* or *patiens*. For more information, cf. S 305. The action types, which are demonstrable in Proto-Indo-European are discussed in F 204 below, with reference to LIV 1998 p. 22ff.

3) The present, aorist, or perfect stem forms the basis of the tempus-modus stem, which serves in the expression of the categories of tempus and modus, and is created through the addition of tempus-modus suffixes:

	athematic	thematic
indicative suffix	*-ø-*	*-e-+-ø- = -e-* in alternance with *-o-+-ø- = -o-*
subjunctive suffix	*-e-* in alternance with *-o-*	*-e-+-e- = -ē-* in alternance with *-o-+-o- = -ō-*
optative suffix	*-i̯eh₁-* in ablaut with *-ih₁-*	*-o-+-ih₁- = -oi̯-*

The stem with the suffix *-ø-* is automatically the indicative stem. In the present and aorist systems, the injunctive and the imperative are both formed from, and attributed to, the indicative stem. With his use of the indicative stem, the speaker indicates that he attributes validity to the contents of his statement, cf. S 310. Stems that are marked with the addition of *-e-* (in alternance with *-o-*) indicate the subjunctive; while those featuring the suffix *-i̯eh₁-* (ablaut *-ih₁-*) indicate the optative, cf. F 207. For further information on *modi* and considerations of content, cf. S 313.

4) To the modus-tempus stem are affixed endings. These endings serve, with the help of accent and ablaut differences in the verbal stem, to express the categories of person, numerus, and diathesis.

However, the endings contribute more than just this. On the one hand, thanks to characteristic ending sets, they help to distinguish the present/aorist, imperative, and perfect systems from one another. — Further, owing to the existence of two sets of endings (primary and secondary), the two additional tempus types present and preterit/past (non-present) are formed. The primary endings indicate the present tense, the here and now. In contrast, the secondary endings are unmarked in relation to tense. They indicate freedom from temporality, and further, in the case of concious refusal of a present form, clearly the past. The choice of the two sets of endings is partially dependent on the desired aspect, and partially dependent on the desired mode. For reasons of aspect, only secondary endings may be combined with aorist stems. When combined with present stems, primary endings indicate the present tense, and secondary endings the past tense (or imperfect). While the subjunctive accepts both primary and secondary endings, the optative, owing to its content, may only accept secondary endings.

5) In order to clearly indicate the past tense, using secondary endings, the facultative use of a temporal adverb PIE **h_1é* 'at that time' could achieve this emphasis. For more information on the augment, cf. F 213. In contrast, in order to mention an action without temporal precision (injunctive), the secondary endings may be used, but not the temporal adverb, cf. F 213 and S 311.

6) Ancient IE languages employ various methods in order to indicate the future tense. For example, *-se-* formations in Greek, *-s(i)i̯e-* formations in Baltic and Indo-Iranian: → Szemerényi *Einführung* 1990 p. 307-312. The subjunctive mode of the aorist stem was also a possibility, cf. S 306.

F 203. Through the presentation of a large amount of data, this section contains an overview of present, aorist, and perfect stem formation. The reference on this subject is LIV 1998 p. 14ff. with the numbers 1(a-v) for present, 2(a-c) for aorist, and 3(a) for perfect. Also worthy of mention is the list of reconstructed stems on pp. 649-661. Also helpful are two works by H. Rix: → "*Einige lateinische Präsensstammbildungen zu Seṭ-Wurzeln*" in *GS* Kuryłowicz I 1995 p. 399-408; "*Schwach charakterisierte lateinische Präsensstämme zu Seṭ-Wurzeln mit Vollstufe*" in *GS Schindler* 1999 p. 515-535. Szemerényi's *Einführung* 1990 p. 244ff. contains an abundance of suggestions for further reading.

As I depend upon LIV 1998 for my treatment, and thus follow the precedent set by Rix, it should be clear that I consider this approach adequate and capable of creating a consensus. Most other treatments and works on the PIE verb system lack a clear image. My fundamental agreement with the approach of LIV 1998, however, does not imply that I recognize every analysis featured in LIV. For example: PIE **g^wi̯eh_3-* 'to live' with the Latin present *vīvō* = Ved. *jī́vati* is traced back to the PIE present stem **g^wi̯éh_3/*g^wih_3-u-* (= LIV-Typ 1e) on page 192. In this case I rather follow Rix, in his *Termini der Unfreiheit* 1994 p. 79, in which PIE **g^wíh_3-u̯e-ti* 'he lives' is directly connected with the (verbal) adjective **g^wih_3-u̯ó-* 'lively.' The verb in question is presumably nothing other than a very archaic denominative formation with a *ø* suffix. The nominal *-u̯o-* stem is used directly as a basis of verbal inflexion, yielding the nominal inflections nom. sg. **g^wih_3u̯ó-s*, acc. sg. **g^wih_3u̯ó-m* etc., and the verbal inflections Präs. 3 sg. **g^wíh_3u̯e-ti*, 3 pl. **g^wíh_3u̯o-nti*, etc.

Meanwhile a second improved edition of LIV has appeared 2001, which, unfortunately could not be assimilated here.

In the case of the present stem formations (nr. 1) I shall not comment on all of the types a-v, from LIV, equally. I shall rather limit myself to the most common and most interesting, giving examples (always the indicative 3rd person singular, active, and sometimes the 3rd person plural) and possibly suggestions for additional reading. In order to simplify comparison with the Vedic and Old Indian verbal system, I shall also mention the corresponding Old Indian indication of verb class.

Among the formations mentioned in F 204 and F 205, the majority are deverbative (of verbal origin), some however are denominative (of nominal origin), cf. comments on the types 1r and 4a. — Included among the denominative formations are the archaic _*-eh_$_2$_-_ denominatives, cf. the nominal PIE _*néu̯-o-_ 'new,' from which the verbal formation _*néu̯-eh_$_2$_-ti_ 'to renew' is derived, cf. Hitt. 3 pl. _ne-wa-aḫ-ḫa-an-zi_ i.e. _neu̯aḫḫ-ant^{s}i_. The basis for derivation is the collective formation _*néu̯-e-h_$_2$_-_, which is simply conjugated from the aforementioned schema _*g^{w}ih$_3$u̯ó-s_ : _*g^{w}íh$_3$u̯e-ti_. Further reading: → Rix _Modussystem_ 1986 p. 13; Steinbauer _Denominativa_ 1989 p. 85-90; H. C. Melchert _"Denominative Verbs in Anatolian"_ in _FS Puhvel_ 1997 p. 131-138.

Concerning the differentiation of thematic and athematic verbs, cf. F 101 § 3 and 4. The athematic formation of active verbs shows ablaut between singular and plural. More particularly, this is most often an _e_ grade singular with an accent on the root syllable vs. a zero grade plural with an accent on the ending [cf. E 505 with the example _*h$_1$és-ti_ vs. _*h$_1$s-énti_], and relatively seldom a case of a singular lengthened grade vs. _e_ grade plural. The athematic middle voice uses the ablaut of the corresponding plural. In contrast, thematic formations show no difference between singular and plural. The alternation of _-e-_ with _-o-_ is of phonetic origin, cf. F 101 § 4.

Terminology: concerning the technical terms 'amphidynamic' and 'acrodynamic,' cf. F 315 § 4. Concerning the terms 'root present' and 'root aorist,' cf. cf. F 202 § 2 and F 101 § 3. — The accents of Greek and Vedic verb forms pose their own problems, cf. F 214.

1) The most important present stem formations (→ LIV p. 14-20; N.B.: All references to LIV refer to LIV 1998, even when 1998 is not always named.).

LIV type 1a — is the amphidynamic, athematic root present (which corresponds in Old Indian to the 2nd class). LIV offers 139 sample root reconstructions (of which, 102 cases are certain). — A prime example is PIE _*g^{wh}en-_ 'to strike (down)' (→ LIV p. 194-196) with the active 3 sg. _*g^{wh}én-ti_ vs. 3 pl. _*g^{wh}n-énti_, cf. L 345 § 1. The middle voice forms that correspond in terms of formation are treated separately as zero grade root statives (type 1c).

LIV type 1b — is the acrodynamic, athematic root present, also called the Narten present. LIV offers 46 sample roots, of which 31 are certain. — Consider the prime example, PIE **steu̯-* 'to be/to make manifest, to prize' (→ LIV p. 546; concerning its meaning in Greek and Indo-Iranian: → Puhvel HED 2 1984 p. 483-485 *s.v. istuwa-*) with the active 3 sg. **stḗu̯-ti* vs. 3 pl. **stéu̯-n̥ti*. — The middle voice forms that correspond in terms of formation are treated separately as *e* grade root statives (type 1d). I shall include them here. A prime example is PIE middle voice 3 sg. **stéu̯-o(-i̯)* (the *-o* ending is archaic and is most often replaced by *-to-*, cf. **k̑ei̯-*, in which case the Vedic alludes to *-o*, but the Greek only alludes to *-to*, or to *-tai̯*, which came yet later) 'was/is manifest' = Gr. στεῦτο / στεῦται 'was/is clearly present'= Ved. *stáve* (< **stéu̯-o-i̯*) 'is prized.' — Cf. PIE middle voice 3 sg. **k̑éi̯-o-(i̯)* 'lay/lies' (→ LIV p. 284; Mayrhofer EWAia II p. 613f.) = Gr. κεῖ-ται (Mycenaean and Cypriot feature *-toi̯*, in place of the later *-tai̯*) = Ved. *áśayat* (in place of **á-śay-a* < **é-k̑ei̯-o*) and *śáy-e* (< **k̑éi̯-oi̯*). — Further reading: → J. Narten "*Zum 'proterodynamischen' Wurzelpräsens*" in *Kleine Schriften* I 1995 (an essay from *FS Kuiper* 1969) p. 97-101; M. J. Kümmel "*Wurzelpräsens neben Wurzelaorist im Indogermanischen*" in HS 111 1998 p. 191-208.

LIV type 1g — is the athematic present with *-e-* reduplication, which corresponds to the Old Indian 3rd class. LIV gives 49 roots, of which 25 are certain. — Cf. the prime example PIE *d^heh_1- 'to place, to lie, to sit, to produce, to make' (→ LIV p. 117-119) with the 3 sg. active *$d^hé$-d^hoh_1-ti* vs. 3 pl. *$d^hé$-d^hh_1-n̥ti* = Ved. *dádhāti* (→ Mayrhofer EWAia I p. 786 with further information). The Greek τίθημι, which corresponds to this, is secondarily adapted to fit the LIV type 1h. However, the plural form ending τιθέασι may provide a last indication of the affiliation of τίθημι to the LIV type 1g, cf. E 504 § 5.

LIV type 1h — is the athematic present with *-i-* reduplication. LIV gives 47 instances, of which 35 are certain. — A prime example is PIE *$steh_2$- 'to walk somewhere, to put oneself somewhere' (→ LIV p. 536-538) with the 3 sg. active *sti-$stéh_2$-ti* vs. 3 pl. *sti-sth_2-énti* = Gr. 3 sg. ἵστησι vs. 3 pl. ἱστᾶσι. The Homeric 3 sg. τίθησι (with typical southern Greek *-si* < *-ti*) and the 3 pl. form τιθεῖσι corresponds to τίθημι. Concerning the plural form τιθέασι, see above — Further reading on Greek: → Giannakis *Reduplicated Presents* 1997 p. 61ff.

LIV type 1i — is the thematic present with *-i-* reduplication. This type, of which LIV offers 9 roots (7 are certain) is clearly a secondary development from the LIV type 1h: — A prime example is PIE **ǵenh₁*- 'to produce' (→ LIV p. 144-146) with the 3 sg. active form **ǵi-ǵn̥h₁-é-ti* = Lat. *gignō* = Gr. γίγνομαι (for information on the phonetics of which, cf. L 330). — Further examples of Seṭ- roots in Latin are offered in: → H. Rix in *GS Kuryłowicz* I 1995 p. 406f. — Examples of Seṭ- roots in Greek may be found in: → Giannakis *Reduplicated Presents* 1997 p. 122ff.

LIV type 1k — is the athematic nasal infix present, which includes the Old Indian classes 5, 6, 8, and 9. LIV gives 237 roots, of which 170 are certain: — A prime example is PIE **lei̯kʷ*- 'to leave (behind)' (→ LIV p. 365f.) with the 3 sg. active form **li-né-kʷ-ti* vs. 3 pl. **li-n-kʷ-énti* = Ved. 3 sg. *riṇák-ti* (→ Mayrhofer EWAia II p. 457f.) = Lat. 3 pl. *linqu(-unt)*. — Cf. PIE **peu̯H*- 'to clean, to reform' (→ LIV p. 432) with the 3 sg. active form **pu-né-H-ti* = Ved. *pu-nā́-ti* (cf. L 315 § 2). — Cf. PIE **demh₂*- 'to tame, to make compliant' (→ LIV p. 99f.) with the 3 sg. active form **dm̥-né-h₂-ti* (cf. L 316). — The type *-néu̯-/-nu-*, which has as a basis roots with final position *-u-*, is included in the LIV under 1l (with 51 roots, 35 certain), cf. PIE **ḱleu̯*- 'to hear' with the 3 sg. active **ḱl̥-né-u̯-ti* = Ved. *śr̥ṇóti* (older **śr̥-ná-u̯-ti* [with Proto-Vedic *ś* < *ḱ*, *r̥* < *l̥* and *a* < *e*], cf. L 315 § 2). — For examples of Seṭ- roots in Latin: → H. Rix in *GS Kuryłowicz* I 1995 p. 401-406. — Nasal infix present formations (or parts of it) has been treated several times, sometimes controversially: → Kuiper *Nasalpräsentia* 1937; Strunk *Nasalpräsentien und Aoriste* 1967; K. Strunk "*Anhaltspunkte für ursprüngliche Wurzelabstufung bei den indogermanischen Nasalpräsentien*" in InL 5 1979 [1980] p. 85-102; by the same author, *Reflexions sur l'infixe nasal* in *Colloque E. Benveniste* II 1983 p. 151-160; McCone *Old Irish Nasal Presents* 1991; G. Meiser "*Zur Funktion des Nasalpräsens im Urindogermanischen*" in *FS Rix* 1993 p. 280-313; (concerning Hittite:) S. Luraghi *I verbi derivati in -nu e il loro valore causativo in Grammatica ittita* 1992 p. 153-180.

LIV type 1n — is the *e* grade present with the thematic suffix *-e-*, and is represented in the LIV in 425 roots, of which 231 are certain. — A prime example is PIE **bʰer*- 'to carry, to bring' (→ LIV p. 61f.) with the 3 sg. active form **bʰér-e-ti* = Lat. *fert* (< **fereti* with syncope: → Meiser *Laut- und Formenlehre* 1998 p. 224 § 3) = Gr. φέρει (concerning the ending *-ei̯*: → M. Kümmel in PFU 2-3 1996-1997 p. 121f.; see also F 209) = Ved. *bhárati*. — Further reading: → Gotō *I. Präsensklasse* 1987; J. H. Jasanoff "The Thematic Conjugation Revisited" in *FS Watkins* 1998 p. 301-316.

LIV type 1o — is a present with a zero grade root and thematic suffix *-é-*, and corresponds to the Old Indian 6th class. The LIV cites 47 roots, of which 20 are certain. — A prime example PIE **gʷerh₃*- 'to devour' (→

LIV p. 189) with the 3 sg. active form *g^wr̥h_3-é-ti = Ved. *giráti* (→ Mayrhofer EWAia I p. 469f.).

LIV type 1p — is a present form with a zero grade root and the stressed suffix -sḱé-, and is cited in LIV with 70 roots (50 certain). — A prime example is PIE *g^wem- 'to go (somewhere), to come' (→ LIV p. 187f.) with the 3 sg. active form *g^wm̥-sḱé-ti = Hom. Gr. (in its simplex [non-compound] form, found only in the imperative) βάσκε 'go!,' in the compound form παρέβασκε 'has taken the adjacent place (in the chariot)' = Ved. *gácchati* 'to move, to go, to come.' — Cf. PIE *preḱ- 'to ask' (→ LIV p. 442f.) with the 3 sg. form *pr̥ḱ-sḱé-ti or rather (already simplified in Proto-Indo-European) *pr̥-sḱé-ti = Lat. *poscit* = Ved. *pr̥ccháti* = Germ. *forsce- (which led to the noun *forsca-, of verbal origin, then, in a further step, led to a new verb of nominal origin, cf. OHG *forscōn*). — Examples of Seṭ- roots in Latin: → H. Rix in *GS Kuryłowicz* I 1995 p. 400f. — Further reading on -sḱe- present forms: → Dressler *Verb. Pluralität* 1968; M. Keller *Verbes latins à infectum -sc-* 1992; Rix *Modussystem* 1986 p. 19 (concerning the Epic-Ionic iteratives with -σκον); Haverling *Sco-Verbs* 2000.

LIV type 1q — are present forms with zero grade roots and the stressed thematic suffix -i̯é-, which includes the Old Indian 4th class. LIV cites 190 roots, of which 98 are certain. — A prime example is PIE *ǵenh_1- 'to produce' (→ LIV p. 144-146) with the 3 sg. middle voice form *ǵn̥h_1-i̯é-toi̯ = Ved. *jā́yate* 'is born.' — Also consider the commentary on the Latin *fugiō* at the end of type 1r.

LIV type 1r — is a present form with an *e* grade root and the thematic suffix -i̯e-. LIV gives 49 roots, of which 21 are certain. — A prime example is PIE *(s)peḱ- 'to look (at)/to peer' (→ LIV p. 524) with the 3 sg. active form *spéḱ-i̯e-ti = Lat. *specit* = Gr. Med. σκέπτεται (phonetically, *skepte-* < *skepi̯e- < *spek-i̯e-) = Ved. *páśyati*. — H. Rix (→ *Modussystem* 1986 p. 13; by the same author, *Termini der Unfreiheit* 1994 p. 71) is in all probability correct, if he considers this type more precisely as a derivation of a nomen agentis, in the sense of 'those who perform the action described in the noun.' Accordingly, cf. *spéḱ-i̯e- 'I am a peerer' and the nominal root *speḱ- 'peerer.' Thus, the type 1q becomes understandable: cf. *b^hug-i̯é- 'I conduct the escape' along with the nominal root *b^hug- 'escape' (cf. PIE *b^heug- 'to flee, to come free' → LIV p. 68) = Lat. *fugiō*. — Concerning the problems in Latin with the semi-thematic inflection (here common) of the type *capiō* vs. *capit* cf. E 503 § 11.

2) Aorist stem formation (→ LIV p. 20f.).

LIV type 2a — is an athematic root aorist which sometimes became thematic in IE languages. LIV gives 392 roots, of which 265 are certain. — A prime example is PIE *g^wem- 'to come' (→ LIV p. 187f.) with the 3 sg. active form *(é) g^wem-t vs. 3 pl. *(é) g^wm-ent = Ved. *á-gan* (with *-an* < **-an-t* < **-am-t*) vs. *á-gm-an* (For more information on Vedic and Indo-Iranian: → Mayrhofer EWAia I p. 465f.). — Further reading: → Harðarson *Wurzelaorist* 1993.

LIV type 2b — is an athematic aorist with the suffix *-s-*, which, for this reason is also called the sigmatic aorist. LIV gives 174 roots, of which 79 are certain. — A prime example is PIE **preḱ-* 'to ask' (→ LIV p. 442f.) with the 3 sg. active form **é prēḱ-s-t* vs. 3 pl. **é preḱ-s-n̥t* = Ved. *áprāṭ*; for the present stem cp. § 1 LIV type 1p. — For information on the fate of the *-s-* aorist in the IE languages: → Meiser *Laut- und Formenlehre* 1998 p. 207f. (concerning Latin); Risch *Kleine Schriften* 1981 p. 125-132 and p. 762 (concerning the secondary expansion in Greek to the *-sa-* aorist); Narten *Sigmatische Aoriste* 1964 (concerning Vedic).

LIV type 2c — is a reduplicated thematic aorist, which, in a Post-Proto-Indo-European phase, was partially athematically inflected. LIV gives 14 roots, of which 5 are certain. — A prime example is PIE **u̯ek^w-* 'to say' (→ LIV p. 614f.) with the 3 sg. active form **é u̯e-u̯k^w-e-t* = Gr. εἶπε (phonetically, *e-u̯ei̯k^w-* < *e-u̯eu̯k^w-* by dissimilation: → Meier-Brügger in ZVS 100 1987 p. 314 note 5) = Ved. *ávocat* (in which *o* < *au*; thus, **á-u̯a-u̯c-at* is older). — Further reading: J. A. Harðarson "*Bemerkungen zum reduplizierten Präteritum II im Tocharischen und zum Kausativaorist im Altindischen*" in *FS Beekes* 1997 p. 95-102.

3) Perfect stem formation (→ LIV p. 21f.).

LIV type 3a — is a reduplicated perfect, of which 259 examples (143 certain) are given in LIV. — A prime example is PIE **g^{w}em-* 'to come' with the singular active **g^{w}e-g^{w}om-* vs. the plural **g^{w}e-g^{w}m-* = Ved. *ja-gā́m-a* (concerning *ā* < *o*, cf. L 412) vs. *ja-gm-úr*. — Further reading: → Giovine *Perfetto* I-III 1990-1996. — Concerning perfect stem formation in Latin: → Meiser *Laut- und Formenlehre* 1998 p. 202-215. — Concerning perfect stem formation in Greek: → Meier-Brügger *Gr. Sprachw.* II 1992 p. 57f. — Concerning perfect stem formation in Vedic: → Krisch *Perfekta mit langem Reduplikationsvokal* 1996; M. J. Kümmel *Das Perfekt im Indoiranischen* Wiesbaden 2000.

F 204. Along with the stem formations of present, aorist, and perfect forms, Proto-Indo-European stem formations of the manner of action (or *Aktionsart*) have also been determined. The present overview of the manners of action (or *Aktionsart*) (causative/iterative, desiderative, intensive, fientive, and essive) finds its orientation in LIV 1998 p. 22ff. with the LIV numbers 4-8. The terms fientive and essive are not well established since the discussion and assessment of *fientiva* and *essiva* have not been completed.

There is information in LIV on each type. I shall limit myself here to citing a few excerpts, giving a few examples and a few suggestions for further reading. I shall also adhere to the numbering 4-8 from LIV.

1) The stem formation of the causative/iterative action type conveys the meaning "A cause of bringing about a state of affairs, or the repeated bringing about of a state of affairs" (LIV p. 22f.).

LIV type 4a — is a causative/iterative stem with an *-o-* grade root and the thematic suffix *-éi̯e-*. LIV presents 424 roots (232 certain). — The double meaning of this formation type is best explained when we postulate a nominal origin: Cf. PIE **men-* 'to hold a thought' (→ LIV p. 391-393) with the abstract noun **móno-* 'the holding of a thought.' From the basis of **móno-*, and with the addition of the denominative *-i̯e-*, the form **moné-i̯e-ti* 'bringing about the holding of thoughts' is formed, in the sense of 'to make to think about' = Lat. *moneō* = Ved. *mānáyati* 'honors, esteems.' — For further reading: → Jamison -áya- 1983 (in which the author comes to the conclusion that there are two types of forms in Indo-Iranian: A causative form with transitive meaning in the *-o-* grade root *-éi̯e-*, and a zero grade form with intransitive meaning).

LIV type 4b — is causative/iterative with a stressed, lengthened grade *ō* in in its root and the thematic suffix *-i̯e-*. LIV gives 25 forms, 12 of which are certain. — A prime example is PIE **su̯ep-* 'to sleep' (→ LIV p. 556f.) with the 3 sg. active form **su̯ṓp-i̯e-ti* 'to lull to sleep' = Lat. *sōpiō*. — Further reading: → G. Klingenschmitt, "*Zum Ablaut des indogermanischen Kausativs*" in ZVS 92 1978 p. 1-13.

2) The stem formation of the desiderative action type conveys "the subject's desire to bring about a state of affairs" (→ LIV p. 23f.). — In liquid and nasal roots, the desiderative suffix carries an initial suffix. A point of departure is provided by roots containing laryngeals such as PIE **kʷelh₁-* 'to make a turn, to turn around,' **terh₂-* 'to come through, to cross over,' **k̑emh₂-* 'to become tired, to try hard' or **senh₂-* 'to reach, to catch.' Following the re-analysis of *KVRH-s-* and *KVNH-s-* as *KVR-Hs-*

and *KVN-Hs-*, it appears that complex suffix *-Hs-* must have also found its way into the non-laryngeal stems with final *-l-*, *-r-*, *-m-*, and *-n-*.

LIV type 5a — is a desiderative form with the suffix *-(H)s-*, of which LIV cites 72 examples (28 certain): — A prime example is PIE **u̯ei̯d-* 'to see, catch sight of' (→ LIV p. 606-608) with **u̯ei̯d-s-* 'to wish to see' = Lat. *vīsere* 'to visite.'

LIV type 5b — is a reduplicated desiderative with the thematic suffix *-(H)sé-*. LIV cites 36 roots, of which 9 are certain: — A prime example is PIE **u̯en-* 'to overpower, to win' (→ LIV p. 622) with **u̯i-u̯n̥-Hsé-* = Ved. *vívāsati* 'would like to win.'

3) The stem formation of the action type 'intensive' carries the connotation of "repeated bringing about of a state of affairs" (→ LIV p. 24f.).

LIV type 6a — is a reduplicated athematic *intensivum*, of which LIV cites 14 roots (5 certain). — A prime example is PIE **k^wer-* 'to cut (off), to carve' (→ LIV p. 350f.) with **k^wérk^{w}r-* = Ved. participle *kári-kr-at-* 'doing again and again.' — Further reading: → Schaefer *Intensivum* 1994; M. Fritz, "*Keine Spuren von Laryngalen im Vedischen: Die Laryngalkürzung beim Intensivum*" in *FS Narten* 2000 p. 55-61.

4) The stem formation of the action type 'fientive indicates "the entry of the subject into a new state of being" (→ LIV p. 25).

LIV type 7a — is a fientive stem with a suffix *-éh*$_1$*-/-h*$_1$*-*, of which LIV cites 58 roots (19 certain): — A prime example is PIE **men-* 'to hold a thought' (→ LIV p.) with **mn-eh*$_1$*-* = Gr. ἐμάνην 'became furious.' — Further reading: → LIV 1998 p. 25; J. A. Harđarson in *Fachtagung Innsbruck* 1996 [1998] p. 323ff.

5) The stem formation of the action type 'essive' conveys "a subject's state of being ... without stressing the entry of the subject into the state of being" (→ LIV p. 25).

LIV type 8a — is an essive with the thematic suffix *-h*$_1$*i̯é-*. LIV offers 94 roots, of which 44 are certain. As a derivative of *-i̯é-*, the compound suffix *-h*$_1$*i̯é-* is based upon the fientives with *-eh*$_1$*-/-h*$_1$*-*. — A prime example is PIE **ten-* 'to tighten, to twist' (→ LIV p. 569) with **tn̥-h*$_1$*i̯é-* = Lat. *tenēre* 'halten.' — For further reading, see § 4 type 7a.

F 205. The majority of the stem forms mentioned in F 203 and F 204 are, according to their aspect, present stems. However, if the speaker wants to switch from the present to the aorist, or the perfect, or from the aorist to the present, or to the perfect, or from the perfect to the aorist or the present, he must add to the given present, aorist, or perfect stem, a new 'aspect' stem.

Either the speaker uses what is called a regular stem form series of the type as in the Greek παιδεύω παιδεύειν (present stem) 'to raise' vs. ἐπαίδευσα παιδεῦσαι (aorist stem) vs. πεπαίδευκα πεπαιδευκέναι (perfect stem) or, as in rarer cases, he uses a suppletive stem form series of the type as in the Greek ἔρχομαι ἔρχεσθαι (present stem) 'about to go, to just now be going' vs. ἦλθον ἐλθεῖν (aorist stem) 'to come to someone, to come to the goal' vs. ἐλήλυθα ἐληλυθέναι (perfect stem) 'to have come,' in which case two or three different stems with similar meaning are combined. (The meanings cited here are Homeric: → LfgrE II col. 535f. and col. 726f.). The verbal stem form series are not predictable with the same certainty, with which the verbal and nominal ending paradigms could be predicted. That, for example, Gr. ἔρχομαι is paired in aspect with ἦλθον, the speaker must simply know, or deduce from the context.

It is possible to describe rather well the stem form series of the individual IE languages. In fact, one may suspect that Proto-Indo-European already featured both types of stem form series. For example, on the one hand, PIE **gʷem-* 'to come' (→ LIV p. 187f.) with the present stems **gʷm̥-sḱé-* and **gʷm̥-i̯é-* vs. the aorist stem *gʷém-* vs. the perfect stem **gʷe-gʷóm-*, and on the other hand PIE **h₁es-* 'to be, to exist' with the present stem **h₁es-* vs. the aorist stem **bʰuH-* (Gr. ἔφυν). However, the extent to which the concrete examples originate from the Proto-Indo-European period must be determined on a case-by-case basis: → Bloch *Suppletive Verba* 1940; K. Strunk "*Überlegungen zu Defektivität und Suppletion im Griechischen und Indogermanischen*" in *Glotta* 55 1977 p. 2-34; by the same author, *'Vorhersagbarer' Sprachwandel* 1991 p. 34ff..

F 206. It is conspicuous that among the stem formations in F 203 the aorist and perfect stems only feature 4 types, while the present stems feature up to 21 (→ LIV p. 14-20). If one adds to that the stem forms of the action types (which are all present!), it is in all probability not false to suppose that the PIE verbal system developed from a highly developed system of action types. Aorist and perfect stem forms were also originally action types. Only secondarily did they become aspect stems, a development which made possible an aspect system in which an aorist or perfect stem may be juxtapositioned with a particular present stem to which it refers. H. Rix presents the following development model (in *Modussystem* 1986 p. 11ff), in which he also includes the subjunctive and optative:

1) In the Pre-PIE period (phase A) there existed only stem forms for the manner of action (or *Aktionsart*), including subjunctive and optative stems, the meanings of which were the same as later: Subjunctive indicating a voluntative/prospective quality; optative indicating a cupitive/potential quality.

2) Moving from the Pre-PIE phase A to the PIE phase B, two decisive innovations developed: a) The introduction and application of the present stem/aorist stem aspectual dichotomy (s. § 3); and b) the polar reorientation of subjunctives and optatives to create forms that could then modally determine all present and aorist stems (cf. F 207).

3) The initial impetus to form this aspectual dichotomy originated with the root present forms which, being action-type neutral, according to their meaning could be durative or punctual, for example the durative PIE *h_1*es*- 'to exist' vs. the punctual PIE **g*^{w}*em*- 'to go (somewhere), to come.' The durative quality permitted both primary and secondary endings, while the punctual quality only allowed the secondary endings. The decisive break in the development of the aspect system was the spread of the possibility of forming a punctual *s*-stem from every possible present stem. — Further reading on the origin of the aspectual dichotomy: → K. Strunk *"Relative Chronology and Indo-European Verb-System: The Case of Present- and Aorist-Stems"* in JIES 22 1994 p. 417-434. Note the synopsis on p. 417:

> "Some evidence will be discussed in favour of the preliminary conclusion that 'Aktionsarten' expressed by different types of present-stems [occurring both in Hittite and other IE languages] already existed in early PIE, whereas the category of aspects expressed by contrastive present- and aorist-stems [lacking in Hittite] did not develop before a later period of the PIE verb-system."

4) The aspect system of most early IE languages was largely replaced by a tense system which is based upon time relationships: → R. Stempel, "*Zur Vorgeschichte und Entwicklung des lateinischen Tempus- und Modussystems*" in HS 111 1998 p. 270-285; E. Tichy "*Vom indogermanischen Tempus/Aspekt-System zum vedischen Zeitstufensystem*" in *Kolloquium Delbrück* Madrid 1994 [1997] p. 589-609; H. C. Melchert *"Traces of a PIE Aspectual Contrast in Anatolian?"* in InL 20 1997 p. 83-92.

F 207. Concerning the reorientation of the subjunctive and optative action type stems to tempus/modus stems (cf. F 206):

1) The subjuctive suffix is PIE *-*e*-. In the case of athematic verbal stems, the rule is -*K*+*ø*- (indicative stem), -*K*+*e*- (subjunctive stem); corre-

spondingly, that of thematic verbs is _-e+ø-_ (indicative stem), _-e+e-_ (subjunctive stem) cf. F 202 § 3.

The formal identity of the athematic subjunctive stem (e.g. PIE _*h$_1$és-e-_) to the thematic indicative stem (e.g. the type PIE _*b^{h}ér-e-_ from F 203 § 1n) is no coïncidence. This identity may be understood if we suppose that the subjunctive with _-e-_ was first an action type. The voluntative/prospective meaning was neutralized when the primary endings, which emphasized the present tense, and thus the immediacy of the action type, were used and could give the impetus for the formation of indicative _-e-_ stems. At the same time, the _-e-_ stem voluntative/prospectives proved very lasting and established themselves, together with the optatives, as a mode which could be attached to every stem, lastly even the indicative _-e-_ stems.

For details on the present description: → Rix _Modussystem_ 1986 p. 14f. with note 20. — Further reading on related problems: → E. Risch "_Zum Problem der thematischen Konjugation_" in Risch _Kleine Schriften_ 1981 (in a contribution from 1965) p. 702-709; B. Barschel "_Zu δέρκομαι und einigen anderen thematischen Wurzelpräsentien des Griechischen_" in _Beiträge zur historischen und vergleichenden Sprachwissenschaft Jena_ 1990 p. 4-8 (which discusses the Greek form as a subjunctive aorist); K. Strunk "_Zur diachronischen Morphosyntax des Konjunktivs_" in _Kolloquium Kühner Amsterdam 1986_ [1988] p. 291-312.

2) One may presume an origin for the optative that is similar to that of the subjunctive. — In terms of form, the suffix in athematic formations is PIE _*-i̯eh$_1$-_ in the full grade, and _*-ih$_1$-_ in the zero grade. — A PIE _*-o-ih$_1$-_ or _*-o-i̯h$_1$-_ must be the starting point for thematic stems. According to K. Hoffmann (→ Aufsätze II 1976 p. 615 note 12) a 3 sg. _*-o-ih$_1$-t_ leads, in the case of laryngeal disappearance, via _*-o-īt_ > _*-oït_ and _*-oi̯t_, a 1 sg. _*-o-ih$_1$-m̥_ via _*-oïa_ > _*-oïi̯a_ > _*-oi̯i̯a_. In contrast, H. Rix (→ _Hist. Gramm. d. Gr._ 1976 p. 233) uses _*-o-i̯h$_1$-_ as a basis. I share Hoffmann's position in accepting _*-o-ih$_1$-_ and postulate that, as in the case of Gr. θεῖμεν < _*t^{h}é-ī-men_ < _*d^{h}eh$_1$-ih$_1$-me-_ (→ Risch _Kleine Schriften_ 1981 [in an essay of 1975] p. 193) there was originally a morpheme division between _-o-_ and _-ih$_1$-_. — Further reading: → J. H. Jasanoff "The Ablaut of the Root Aorist Optative in Proto-Indo-European" in MSS 52 1991 p. 101-122; H. Eichner in _Bopp-Symposium_ 1992 [1994] p. 80ff. (where he considers, in light of F. Bopp, whether the optative should be understood as a periphrastic formation, cf. Lat. _edim_ < Pre-PIE _*h$_1$ed+i̯eh$_1$-m_ 'I ask for food' in the sense of 'I would like to eat').

3) Anatolian and Hittite feature neither optative nor subjunctive modes. It appears that Anatolian left the community of IE languages before the reorientation of the action types voluntative/prospective and cupitive/potential to the modes subjunctive and optative, respectively. While no traces of the action type cupitive/potential may be found, perhaps there do exist traces of the voluntative/prospective action type (→ Rix *Modussystem* 1986 p. 20f.).

Further reading on the subject: → K. Strunk "*Probleme der Sprachrekonstruktion und das Fehlen zweier Modi im Hethitischen*" in InL 9 1984 [1985] p. 135-153; J. A. Harđarson "*Der Verlust der Moduskategorie Optativ*" in HS 107 1994 p. 31f. (It is argued that the loss of the optative did not take place at the stage of action type, but rather after it had already become a mode.)

3. The Verb Ending

F 208. The following descriptions are intentionally kept quite short. The established facts concerning Proto-Indo-European are named, whereas for details concerning the individual IE languages the mention of further sources shall have to suffice.

Sources concerning endings in general: → E. Neu "*Zum Verhältnis der grammatischen Kategorien Person und Modus im Indogermanischen*" in *FS Polomé* 1988 p. 461-473; Szemerényi *Einführung* 1990 p. 247ff.

Concerning the differentiation of the primary and secondary endings, cf. E 502 § 11 and F 202 § 4. — 'Dual' forms are not discussed here, cf. F 304 § 1.

F 209. The active endings of the present/aorist system:

	secondary endings		primary endings	
	a) athem.	b) them.	a) athem.	b) them.
1 sg.	*-m*	*-o-m*	*-m-i*	*-ō* or *-o-h₂*
2 sg.	*-s*	*-e-s*	*-s-i*	*-e-s-i*
3 sg.	*-t*	*-e-t*	*-t-i*	*-e-t-i*
1 pl.	*-me*	*-o-me*	*-mes / -mos*	*-o-me-*
2 pl.	*-te*	*-e-te*	*-te*	*-e-te*
3 pl.	*-n̥t / -ént*	*-o-nt*	*-n̥t-i / -ént-i*	*-o-nt-i*

Comment: — The endings shown above are divided into athematic and thematic endings. The endings a) and b) are the same, with the exception of the 1 sg. thematic primary ending. Otherwise, the only difference is the presence or absence of the thematic vowel. — The thematic vowel: — In the case of indicative stems and the subjunctive stems (formed from athematic stems) that are formally and genetically (cf. F 207 § 1) identical to them, the thematic vowel *-e-* is exchanged with *-o-* (preceding *-m-*, *-nt-*, and possibly *-h_2*; *-o-* is also used before *-ih_1-* in the optative), see F 101 § 4. — Endings: — In the case of the 1 sg., the secondary ending is **-o-m* (as determined by the athematic *-m*), however, the primary ending is surprisingly not **-o-m-i*, but rather **-ō* (or possibly **-o-h_2*: → Rix *Hist. Gramm. d. Gr.* 1976 p. 250; K. Strunk in *Kolloquium Kühner* Amsterdam 1986 [1988] p. 304f.). — In the 1 and 2 pl., the IE language attestations are not clear enough to clarify the differentiation of the primary and secondary endings in terms of form (1 pl. probably *-mes*, secondary *–me*, or *-men*?).

Further reading: — a) General IE: → Rix *Hist. Gramm. d. Gr.* 1976 p. 239ff. (endings) and p. 206 (thematic vowel); Szemerényi *Einführung* 1990 p. 247-252 (endings) and p. 266-268 (thematic vowel); Meiser *Laut- und Formenlehre* 1998 p. 40f.; M. Kümmel in *PFU* 2-3 1996-1997 p. 120-122. — b) Particularly Latin: → Leumann *LLFL* 1977 p. 512ff.; Meiser *Laut- und Formenlehre* 1998 p. 216f. — c) Particularly Greek: Meier-Brügger *Gr. Sprachw.* II 1992 p. 53f.; E. Risch "*Ein Problem des griechischen Verbalparadigmas: Die verschiedenen Formen der 3. Person Plural*" in *FS Neumann* 1982 p. 321-334; F. Kortlandt *"The Greek third person plural endings"* in MSS 49 1988 p. 63-69. Concerning the thematic present endings 2 sg. -εις, 3 sg. -ει: → H. M. Hoenigswald in *FS Hamp* I 1997 p. 93ff.; see also M. Kümmel in F 203 § 1 (LIV type 1n). — d) Particularly Vedic and Indo-Aryan: Hoffmann / Forssman *Avest. Laut- und Flexionslehre* 1996 p. 179f. (offering a good tabular overview of the active endings) and p. 190ff. (active paradigm). — e) Particularly Celtic: F. Kortlandt *"Absolute and Conjunct Again"* in MSS 1994 p. 61-68.

F 210. The middle voice endings of the present/aorist system:

	secondary endings		primary endings	
	a)	b)	a)	b)
1 sg.		*-h_2e*	*-mai̯* and	*-h_2e-i̯*
2 sg.	*-so* and	*-th_2e-*	*-so-i̯*	
3 sg.	*-to* and	*-o*	*-to-i̯*	*-o-i̯*
1 pl.	*-med^hh_2*		*-mesd^hh_2*	

	a)	b)
2 pl.	*-d^hu̯e*	*-(s)d^hu̯e*
3 pl.	*-nto*	*-nto-i̯*

Comment: — The PIE middle voice endings (or secondarily passive) are those in column a). They are formed presumably in the Pre-PIE era from the basis of the active voice endings, cf., in the case of the secondary endings 2 sg. *-s-o*, 3 sg. *-t-o* and 3 pl. *-nt-o*. In several ancient IE languages (e.g. Italic, Celtic, Hittite, Tocharian, and Phrygian), the middle/passive endings are marked with a special *-r(i)*. — The endings in column b) (as well as the *-r-* forms) show forms that are identical to perfect forms, cf. F 211. They are usually said to be the output of the 'stative voice'. On the whole problem see now J. H. Jasanoff *Hittite and the IE verb* Oxford 2003.

Further reading: — a) General: Rix *Hist. Gramm. d. Gr.* 1976 p. 246-249; Jasanoff *Stative and Middle* 1978; H. Rix "The Proto-Indo-European Middle: Content, Forms and Origin" in MSS 49 1988 p. 101-119 (proposes that one see, in the *-o* ending, an anaphoric pronoun); Szemerényi *Einführung* 1990 p. 257-259; J. H. Jasanoff in *Fachtagung Zürich* 1992 [1994] p. 152ff. — b) Particularly Latin and Italic: Leumann LLFL 1977 p.515ff. (concerning the *-r-* forms); H. Rix "*Zur Entstehung des lateinischen Perfektparadigmas*" in *Kolloquium Lat. u. Idg.* Salzburg 1986 [1992] p. 221-240; Meiser *Laut- und Formenlehre* 1998 p. 218f.; G. Meiser "*Die sabellischen Medialendungen der 3. Person*" in *Fachtagung Leiden* 1987 [1992] p. 291-305; J. H. Jasanoff *"An Italic-Celtic Isogloss: The 3 pl. Mediopassive in *-ntro"* in *FS Hamp* I 1997 p. 146-161. — c) Particularly Greek: Meier-Brügger *Gr. Sprachw.* II 1992 p. 54. In the case of the verb κεῖμαι 'to lie,' the replacement of the older middle voice endings *-mai -toi* (as is still the case in Cypriot: → Egetmeyer *Wörterbuch* 1992 p. 66) by the newer (Homeric) *-mai -tai* directly attested. — d) Particularly Vedic and Indo-Iranian: Hoffmann / Forssman *Avest. Laut- und Flexionslehre* 1996 p. 180f. (with a tabular overview of the middle voice endings) and p. 194ff. (middle voice paradigm). — e) Hittite: *Neu Mediopassiv* 1968 and *Neu Interpret. Mediopassiv* 1968; Yoshida *Endings in -ri* 1990, G.-J. Pinault (in his review of Yoshida) in BSL 86 / 2 1991 p. 134-141.

F 211. Perfect endings:

1 sg.	$-h_2e$
2 sg.	$-th_2e$
3 sg.	*-e*

1 pl.	*-me*
2 pl.	
3 pl.	*-r*

Comment: — The perfect endings represent a system of their own. The differentiations between athematic and thematic forms, primary ending and secondary endings, and active and middle voices are missing. However, the middle voice of the present/aorist system shows individual sub-forms that are identical to perfect forms, cf. F 210 column b. — The Hittite *-ḫi-* conjugation poses problems of its own, but is part of the whole business. An adequat insight is now given by J. H. Jasanoff *Hittite and the IE verb* Oxford 2003.

Bearing in mind that a *communis opinio* is not on the horizon, following are some further sources of information on the perfect and the stative: — a) General IE: Rix *Hist. Gramm. d. Gr.* 1976 p. 255-257 (concerning the perfect); Szemerényi *Einführung* 1990 p. 259f. (concerning the perfect); LIV 1998 p. 22 (concerning the stative). — b) Particularly on the Latin perfect: → Leumann LLFL 1977 p. 606ff.; Meiser *Laut- und Formenlehre* 1998 p. 217f. — c) Particularly on the Greek perfect: → Meier-Brügger *Gr. Sprachw.* II 1992 p. 54f.. — d) Particularly on Vedic and Indo-Iranian: → Hoffmann / Forssman *Avest. Laut- und Flexionslehre* 1996 p. 179f. and p. 236ff.; T. Gotō "*Überlegungen zum urindogermanischen 'Stativ'*" in *Kolloquium Delbrück* Madrid 1994 [1997] p. 165-192.

F 212. The imperative: The basis upon which the PIE imperative is formed is the bare verbal stem, used in the 2 sg. For example, PIE thematic *$*b^hér$-e* 'carry,' but athematic PIE *$*h_1s$-$d^hí$* 'sei,' with a particle that characterizes the imperative. The thematic form 3 sg. *$*b^hér$-e-tōd* 'he should carry' is also Proto-Indo-European. The expansion of further forms was Post-Proto-Indo-European. For information on syntax, cf. S 312.

Further reading: → B. Forssman "*Der Imperativ im urindogermanischen Verbalsystem*" in *Fachtagung Berlin* 1983 [1985] p. 181-197; E. Neu "*Betrachtungen zum indogermanischen Imperativ*" in *FS Schmeja* 1998 p. 119-127. Concerning details: → K. Strunk in *FS Dihle* 1993 p. 486-472 (Gr. θές, ἕς and δός); B. Forssman p. 185 note 12 (A reference to Th. Benfey, who was the first to suggest that the Vedic imperative type *neṣi* 'lead' could be traced back to the 2 sg. subjunctive aorist *neṣasi*).

4. The Augment

F 213. The augment *(h_1)*é* is common to Greek, Phrygian, Armenian, and Indo-Aryan as an indication of the past tense, e.g. PIE *(h_1)*é b*^{h}*eret* = Gr. ἔ-φερε = Ved. *á-bharat*. The PIE augment *(h_1)*é* was quite probably an adverb with the meaning 'at that time' and could be employed facultatively where indicative forms of present and aorist stems were combined with secondary endings to produce a clear past tense, cf. F 202 § 5. The establishment of the augment as a norm in the indicative aorist, indicative imperfect, and indicative pluperfect took place in a post-Proto-Indo-European phase. Other IE languages such as Latin or Germanic developed their own suffixal means of indicating past tense forms, e.g. Lat. pres. 3 sg. *es-t* 'is,' but imperfect 3 sg. *er-a-t* (< **es-ā-t*) 'was': → Meiser *Laut- und Formenlehre* 1998 p. 197.

K. Brugmann gave the impulse to call the Vedic indicative forms that do not feature an augment 'injunctive.' Vedic features the injunctive as a mode of its own, with a 'memorative' semantic connotation.

Suggestions for further reading: → K. Strunk "*Der Ursprung des verbalen Augmentes - Ein Problem Franz Bopps aus heutiger Sicht*" in Bopp-Symposium 1992 [1994] p. 270-284. — Particularly concerning Vedic and its memorative: → Hoffmann *Injunktiv* 1967. — Concerning Greek, in which the augment was facultative in poetic language and Mycenaean, but in the Classical language was, as a rule, non-facultative: → I. Hajnal in MSS 51 1990 p. 50-55; Meier-Brügger *Gr. Sprachw.* II 1992 p. 50-52; E. J. Bakker "Pointing to the Past: Verbal Augment and Temporal Deixis in Homer" in *Euphrosyne, FS Dimitris N. Maronitis*, Stuttgart 1999, p. 50-65. On the New Greek situation see at the end of the paragraph. — In Armenian, the augment is only found as a functionless element in single-syllable verb forms that permits phonetic reinforcement, e.g. aor. ind. act. 1 sg. *beri* 'I carried,' but 3 sg. *e-ber*: → J. Wackernagel in *Wackernagel Kleine Schriften* I 1969 (in a contribution from 1906) p. 148-155 (Wackernagel refers to the phenomenon of the Homeric ἔσχον '(they) had,' in which *σχόν is missing). — Further, compare the characteristics of New Greek verbs of the type of 3 sg. έδεσε 'he has bound' vs. 1 pl. δέσαμε 'we have bound,' in which the augment is preserved when it was stressed.

5. The Verbal Accent

F 214. The finite verb of an PIE main clause was normally placed following the subject and the object, at the end of the sentence, where the sentence accent usually decreases. However, when the verb was stressed at the beginning of the sentence, or in a subordinate clause, it carried its normal accent.

1) Researchers agree that Vedic generally reflects the fundamental characteristics of Proto-Indo-European, and thus, that the finite verb in a main clause was unstressed: → Wackernagel / Debrunner *Ai. Grammatik* I 1957 p. 290; Klein *Verbal Accentuation* 1992 p. 90; Hettrich *Hypotaxe* 1988 p. 779.

2) It may also be shown that this assertion about Proto-Indo-European also at one time held for Greek. The characteristics of Greek may best be understood if we start from the premise of an unstressed finite verb as an established norm. Finite verbal forms also featured normal word accents that were used in case the word was in a position of emphasis. — The introduction of the typically Greek restriction of all accents to the last three syllables brought a significant change, forcing all unstressed finite verb forms, which formed accent unity with the preceding word and had generally three or more syllables, to be accented according to the schema [x́ x ⏑], and [x x́ –], cf. L 420 § 2. The new accent was often used as a word accent, and the old (which often differed), often dropped. This explains, among other things, why a verb form such as βαίνομεν 'we go' carries its accent on the first syllable, although its origin of PIE **g^wm̥-i̯ó-mes* would suggest rather *βαινόμεν. Only the two-syllable root presents εἰμί and φημί escaped the effects of the radical new accentuation. Not least owing to their shortness, they remained enclitical. For further details: → Meier-Brügger *Gr. Sprachw.* II 1992 p. 48-50.

3) It remains disputed whether the second position of the finite verb, common to the modern Germanic languages such as German, originated from the inherited phenomenon of enclitics, or whether it appeared secondarily: → J. Wackernagel in *Wackernagel Kleine Schriften 1* 1969 (in an essay of 1892) p. 427 ("the german rule of word order was already valid in the mother language"); Th. Eythórsson "*Zur Historisch-vergleichenden Syntax des Verbums im Germanischen*" in *Fachtagung Innsbruck* 1996 [1998] p. 407 note 16: ("The hypothesis [is] … not supported by findings").

6. Infinitive Verb Forms

F 215. Alongside the finite, or conjugated verb forms, which, thanks to their endings are marked (grammarians of antiquity speak of 'limited' forms), and specify qualities among the verbal categories of aspect-action type, tempus-modus, person-number, and voice, there are also infinite verb forms that are not conjugated and, in comparison with the finite forms, are not as strongly marked (grammarians of antiquity speak of 'unlimited' forms). In the case of infinite verb forms, for example, no information is given with regard to person. Among the infinite verb forms are the infinitives and the participles.

F 216. Infinitives are verbal nominal forms, which are based on generalized case forms of verbal abstract nouns. It is doubtful that Proto-Indo-European featured a specific infinitive suffix. The development of means of differentiation of voice, aspect, and tempus in the infinitive formations is post-Proto-Indo-European. For information on syntax, cf. S 202.

Further sources of information on the infinitive: — a) Proto-Indo-European: → H. Rix "*Die umbrischen Infinitive auf -fi und die Urindogermanische Infinitivendung -d*^{h}*i̯ōi̯*" in *FS Palmer* 1976 p. 319-331; Disterheft *Infinitive* 1977; Gippert *Infinitive* 1978; H. Rix in *FS Szemerényi* *65 II 1979 p. 736ff. (containing a list of PIE verbal abstract nouns); J.-L. García-Ramón "*Infinitive im Indogermanischen? Zur Typologie der Infinitivbildungen und zu ihrer Entwicklung in den älteren indogermanischen Sprachen*" in InL 20 1997 p. 45-69; . — b) Particularly concerning Latin: → Leumann LLFL 1977 p. 580-582; Risch *Gerund.* 1984 p. 26f. (for a general characterization of the Latin infinitive); Meiser *Laut- und Formenlehre* 1998 p. 225; for information on Umbrian, cf. Rix. — c) Particularly concerning Greek: → Meier-Brügger *Gr. Sprachw.* II 1992 p. 60f.; K. Stüber in MSS 60 2000 p. 138f. (containing information on -ειν < **-esen* i.e. **-es-en* as an *-en-* locative form of the type of *-es-* neuter forms). — d) Particularly concerning Avestan: → J. Kellens "*Retour à l'infinitif avestique*" in MSS 55 1994 p. 45-59.

F 217. Because of their quality of being between a nominal form and a verbal form, participles were said by grammarians of antiquity to be 'participating.' In German grammar, one sometimes uses the term *Mittelwort* to indicate a participle. For information on syntax, see S 202 below.

In a bold move, H. Rix includes participles in the tempus-modus dimension, including them in the same category as the subjunctive and optative.

He defines their contents as "temporal or causal subordination," pointing out that the subject is indicated, not through the categorie 'person,' but rather with the help of congruence of nominal categories (cases): → H. Rix in *Kolloquium Keltisch* Bonn 1976 [1977] p. 139.

Further general sources concerning the participle: → Risch *Gerund.* 1984 p. 6ff. (including a general characterization of the Latin participle, including participial formations).

1) The PIE suffix indicating that a participle is present tense and active voice is **-nt-*, with the feminine **-nt-ih$_2$-*. — The inflection of athematic participles appears to have been holodynamic of the type PIE **u̯ék̑ont-* (strong) vs. **uk̑n̥t-´* (weak). For more information on inflection, see F 321 § 2. For example, the present participle of PIE **h$_1$es-* 'to exist' was originally **h$_1$és-ont- / *h$_1$s-n̥t-* (the zero grade stem being most often generalized; apparent traces of full grade *-ent-* forms do not exist: → A. Morpurgo Davies in *FS Lejeune* 1978 p. 159: "As far as we know, there is no reason to attribute **h$_1$s-ent-* to Proto-Greek") = Lat. *(ab)sent-* (with *-en-* < **-n̥-*; the Latin participle is indifferent to gender) = Myc. Gr. nom. pl. m. *(a-p)e-o-te* i.e. *ap-ehont-es* and nom. pl. f. *(a-p)e-a-sa* i.e. *ap-ehassai̯* (with *-assa-* < **-n̥t-i̯h$_2$-*) = Ved. *sánt-* m.n. and *sa-t-ī́-* f. (with *-a-* < **-n̥-*). — The thematic form is **-o-nt-*. It remains to be seen whether the thematic forms as well were originally declined as **-ont- / *-n̥t-* (as in Vedic) and were only secondarily reinterpreted as **-o-nt-*. — Further sources:→ Rix *Hist. Gramm. d. Gr.* 1976 p. 233f.; Szemerényi *Einführung* 1990 p. 345-347.

2) The PIE suffix indicating that a participle is perfective in aspect and active in voice is **-u̯os-* with the feminine **-us-ih$_2$-*. Here, as well, the inflection seems to have been of the holodynamic type, cp. F 321 § 2. — Examples include Myc. Gr. nom. pl. n. *a-ra-ru-wo-a* i.e. *arar-u̯oh-a* 'added' with *-u̯oh-* < **-u̯os-* and nom. pl. f. *a-ra-ru-ja* i.e. *arar-ui̯i̯a* with *-ui̯i̯a* < **-us-i̯h$_2$-* and Ved. *ca-kr̥-vás- / ca-kr-us-* of *kar-* 'to do, to make, to bring about,' etc. Further sources: → Szemerényi *Einführung* 1990 p. 347f.; Meier-Brügger *Gr. Sprachw.* II 1992 p. 62f. (Including, on the subject of Mycenaean and Homeric Greek, the Post-Mycenaean replacement of *-u̯oh-* with *-u̯ot-*). — Only formal traces are attested in Latin and Italic, e.g. Lat. *memor-* 'remembering, bearing in mind' < **me-mn-us-* from the perfect stem *me-min-ī* < **me-mon-* 'to remember, to commemorate'): → Leumann LLFL 1977 p. 610; H. Rix in *Kolloquium Lat. u. Idg.* Salzburg 1986 [1992] p. 229 (H. Rix traces the Latin perfect stems of the type

laudāv- back to periphrastic expressions of the active perfect participle and substantivized verb *esse*).

3) The PIE suffix of the middle voice participle is **-mXno-* (athematic) and **-o-mXno-* (thematic), where X = *V* or *H*, or even *HV*. The exact form is uncertain. G. Klingenschmitt makes a case for PIE **-mh₁no-* (*Fachtagung Regensburg* 1973 [1975] p. 159-163 f.). The field is not united regarding this assertion: → H. C. Melchert supports *-mn-o-* (in *Sprache* 29 1983 p. 24f.); Mayrhofer finds the suggestion significant, but points out that even proponents of the triple-laryngeal theory share doubts about it (in *Lautlehre* 1986 p. 130f.); Szemerényi remains with *-mn-o-* (*Einführung* 1990 p. 349f.); further, see B. Forssman in *Kratylos* 45 2000 p. 69f., where he comments on the treatment of suffixes from Lindeman *Laryngeal Theory* 1997. As M. Fritz indicated to me, the two competing zero grade suffix variants **-mh₁no-* and **-mno-* may be combined via the full grade **-mh₁eno-*, provided the laryngeal in the suffix disappears when the suffix is added to a root or stem with a non-syllabic final position preceding the full vowel *e*. The non-laryngeal full grade form **-meno-* would then have the newly constructed zero grade form **-mno-*. — Examples include, Myc. Gr. nom. sg. f. *ki-ti-me-na* i.e. *kti-men-ā* 'cultivated, built-upon (and thus inhabited)' and Ved. *kr̥ṇv-ān-á-* to *kar-* 'to do, to make, to bring about' with the present stem *kr̥ṇau̯- / kr̥ṇu-* (one must admit the elegance of Klingenschmitt's explanation *-ān-* < **-aHn-* < **-m̥h₁n-*; the alternative with *-mn-* has its difficulties, cf. Szemerényi: "the origin of this formation is not certain"). — The differentiation of the perfect **-m̥h₁n-ó-* vs. the present **'-o-mh₁no-* in the various IE languages may be traced back to the athematic/thematic dichotomy: → Rix *Hist. Gramm. d. Gr.* 1976 p. 236.

4) The verbal adjectives **-to-* and **-no-* function as past participles in individual IE languages, cf. W 203.

7. Periphrastic Constructions

F 218. Relative to the ancient IE languages, periphrastic constructions of the type Lat. *quid futūrum est* 'what should that become' or *quod habeō tollere* 'what I intend to take' are considered new. However such forms are attested in the Hittite of the 2nd millenium B.C., e.g. the *ḫark-* constructions for the perfect and pluperfect. If in fact the Latin perfect of the type *portāvī* may be traced to the periphrase **portāu̯osis esom* (i.e. an active perfect participle with *-u̯os-* + *verbum substantivum* [cp. F 217 § 2]), then also it must date from prehistoric period. Thus, it may not be ruled out that Proto-Indo-European already featured several periphrastic constructions.

I also consider cases such as the following to be similar to paraphrases: Lat. *vēndere* < *vēnum* **dide-* 'to put up for sale,' in the sense of 'to sell' vs. *venīre* < *vēnum īre* 'to go for sale' in the sense of 'to be sold' (*dide-* must here be traced to PIE *d^heh_1- and not to *deh_3-!: → Meiser *Laut- u. Formenlehre* 1998 p. 192). Or, similarly, *interficere* 'to separate (from life), to make disappear' in the sense of 'to kill' vs. *interīre* 'to go and disappear' in the sense of 'to decline' (For details relative to *inter*: → H. Hettrich in MSS 54 1993 p. 169-172; *-facere* makes clear that this is a case of PIE *d^heh_1-). This combination of substantivized verb or preverb and *d^heh_1- (in the active sense), or *$h_1ei̯$- 'to go' (in the passive sense) certainly dates from a pre-individual language period. For a further example, cf. F 207 § 2 with H. Eichner's reflections on the optative.

Further sources: → Rosén *Periphrase* 1992; Boley *Hittite hark-construction* 1984; Cotticelli-Kurras *Hitt. 'sein'* 1991; by the same authors *"The Hittite periphrastic constructions"* in *Grammatica ittita* 1992 p. 33-59; S. Luraghi "*I verbi ausiliari in ittita*" in *FS Ramat* 1998 p. 299-322.

C. Nouns and Adjectives

1. General Information

F 300. Nouns as nominal members expand, complete, and clarify the content of the central verb form of the sentence. In contrast to verbs, nouns have a relatively limited number of forms. Through the basic meaning of the word, which is contained in its nominal stem, the endings communicate information about the number and genre of the content, as well as information about the role of the noun, which is assigned to it by the speaker in the syntactical context, cf. S 400ff.

F 301. Substantives and adjectives are closely related. This closeness is demonstrated by the fact that an adjective can take the place of a substantive, e.g. Classical Gr. τὸ κακόν 'the bad' and Lat. *lūna* 'moon' (< Proto-

Ital. **louk-snā* 'the shining'). Substantives and adjectives are exchangeable in nominal sentences.

Adjectives often qualify substantives and, in order to externally mark association, often use congruence in genre, number, and case. The dimension of genre is particularly variable. Unlike the noun, the adjective has no fixed association with a particular genre, cf. S 400. Reading: → J. Untermann "*L'aggettivo, Forma e funzione*" in *Quaderni Patavini di Linguistica* 7 1988 p. 3-21.

Formal peculiarities of the adjective are discussed in F 323ff.

F 302. The peculiarities of nominal paradigms in IE languages may in general be traced to Proto-Indo-European. However, every family of Indo-European languages and its individual languages has undergone in the course of time a greater or lesser quantity of changes that are characteristic of itself. In the area of gender, a history may be written of coexistence and replacements among the masculina, feminina, and neutra, cf. F 303. In the area of number, the rise and fall of the dual must be noted, cf. F 304. In that of case, individual forms are changed over time or even fully disposed of, cf. F 305.

Reading: → E. Risch "*Betrachtungen zur indogermanischen Nominalflexion*" in *Kleine Schriften* 1981 p. 730-738; by the same author, "*Die mykenische Nominalflexion als Problem der indogermanischen und griechischen Sprachwissenschaft*" in *Sprache* 32 1986 p. 63-77.

F 303. Gender developments:

1) Ancient IE languages generally feature three genders: masculine, feminine, and neuter, cf. S 416. On the subject of the term 'neuter,' cf. p. XVII. Although the three-part system is well attested, one should not be misled into regarding it as a fixed triad. For example, in the Romance languages and in Lithuanian, the neuter gender was abandoned, being replaced by a new masculine/feminine dichotomy. Today's English makes do without any genders. — For information on gender in the transformation from Latin to the Romance languages: → Schön *Neutrum und Kollektivum* 1971. — For information on English: → Leisi *Streiflichter* 1995 p. 107-111 (*How English rejected sexism*).

2) Anatolian features a two-part system, separating 'animate' (common gender) from 'inanimate' (neuter gender). Whether a feminine gender never really developed, or developed and vanished without leaving clear traces, is currently discussed by researchers. If the former theory is correct (which evidence seems to suggest), it would indicate that the speakers of Proto-

Anatolian left the PIE language community before the three-part masculine/feminine/neuter system had been established. A consequence of this would be that a two-part system had existed in Proto-Indo-European much like that preserved in Anatolian. This two-part system was composed, on the one hand, of a class A, in which a nominative and accusative were differentiated[4], on the other hand, a class B, in which this differentiation was ruled out[5], cf. S 416. — See also L 211 § 6 (on Lat. *vīrus* n.) and F 403 (on PIE *k^wi-* with no distinction between masculine and feminine)

3) The impulse which led to the change from a two class system to a three-gender system occurred with the inclusion of natural gender in class A. The first step consisted, in all likelihood, of the naming of individual natural feminina (in families and among the animals) clearly as such. The first such developments may well have taken place in Proto-Indo-European. However, only after the migratory departure of the Proto-Anatolians from the community of PIE language speakers did the change pick up momentum. By the end of this development, all nouns of the class A had been firmly assigned a masculine or feminine gender that was often unrelated to natural sexus.

4) How did the speakers of the ancient IE languages proceed concretely in the formal marking of the feminine gender? — A first possibility (called heteronymy; concerning this and the following information: → Wackernagel *Vorlesungen* II 1928 p. 9-11) is shown by examples such as PIE **ph$_2$tér-* 'father' vs. PIE **méh$_2$ter-* (or **mā́ter-*, cf. L 211 § 10) 'mother,' in which the gender differentiation is performed by inserting two different lexemes. — Concerning the second possibility, that of the *communia* of the type Lat. *lupus fēmina*, see E 506 § 5. — The third and most often used possibility is the alteration or extension of the word ending. The suffixes used for this were **-h$_2$-*, as well as the complex suffixes **-e-h$_2$-* and **-i-h$_2$-*, the latter of which was as a rule expanded to *-ī-k-* in Latin, e.g. Lat. **gena-tor-* 'creator, i.e. father' vs. **gena-tr-ī-k-* 'female creator, i.e. mother,' cf. F 101 § 2. This **-h$_2$-* may not be separated from the *-h$_2$-* forms of class B (indicative of collectiva), cf. F 313. In Proto-Indo-European, the *-h$_2$-* suffix supposedly had the function of forming abstract/collective derived forms: From there, one lineage leads to the PIE collective nouns of B, which function in the case of neuter forms as

[4] This topic is discussed by researchers under various headings which indicate that the objects in question are conceivable to the speaker as operators in a verbal discourse: *commune*, *genus animatum*, *genus distinctum*, personal class.

[5] Further headings for this group of objects which are conceivable to the speaker as not operating in a verbal discourse: neuter, *genus inanimatum*, object class.

plurals of the type Lat. *iuga* vs. sg. *iugum* 'yoke'; the other lineage leads to the PIE feminine forms of A (which include, along with the true inflected feminine forms, abstract nouns of the type Lat. *fuga* 'escape,' *iūstitia* 'justice,' etc.). Pronominal forms such as masc./fem. sg. PIE **se-h_2-* 'this' (class A) vs. n. PIE **te-h_2-* 'this' (class B) must have played a central role in these development processes.

5) Roughly stated, the masculine and feminine nouns of ancient IE languages are thus the continuation of IE class A, while the neuter forms are the continuation of class B. While neuter forms reveal more or less the contents of the ancient PIE class B, the question of sexus, including the formation of feminine forms on the basis of the suffix *-h_2-* (which comes from class B) obscures the content of the ancient class A considerably.

6) Bearing in mind that a *communis opinio* will not be reached in the immediate future, the following are sources of further information on various related subjects: — a) General information: → K. Strunk "*Grammatisches und natürliches Geschlecht in sprachwissenschaftlicher Sicht*" in *Frau und Mann, Geschlechterdifferenzierung in Natur und Menschenwelt*, edited by V. Schubert, St. Ottilien 1994, p. 141-164; Leisi *Streiflichter* 1995 p. 112-116 ("*The description and naming of women as a linguistic problem*"). — b) Proto-Indo-European: → E. Tichy Kollektiva, "*Genus femininum und relative Chronologie*" in HS 106 1993 p. 1-19; M. Fritz "*Die urindogermanischen s-Stämme und die Genese des dritten Genus*" in *Fachtagung Innsbruck* 1996 [1998] p. 255-264. — c) Anatolian: → E. Neu "*Zum Alter der personifizierenden -ant-Bildung des Hethitischen, Ein Beitrag zur Geschichte der indogermanischen Genuskategorie*" in HS 102 1989 p. 1-15; J. A. Harđarson "*Der Verlust des Genus femininum*" in HS 107 1994 p. 32-35.

F 304. Number developments:

1) While singular and plural are relatively fixed values, the dual has proven to be unstable. Generally speaking, the rise and decline of the dual may be directly investigated in individual IE languages, for example in Greek, in which the dual is a fixed component of the language, while it is missing altogether in Ionic and Lesbian. Attic inscriptions attest its presence in Attic through the 4th century B.C.: → Meier-Brügger *Gr. Sprachw.* I 1992 p. 144f.

The dual shall not be further discussed in the present work. As yet, the field lacks a monography on the subject. Matthias Fritz is in the process of filling this gap with his "*Untersuchungen zum indogermanischen Dual, Vom Werden und Schwinden einer grammatischen Kategorie*," on the subject of which he added:

"The externally reconstructible Proto-Indo-European *numerus* category 'dual,' which includes all gramatically inflectable forms and is thus firmly anchored in the linguistic system, developed in the course of Proto-Indo-European history first to a systematic *numerus* category. The origins of the dual are contained in two word types: On the one hand, the personal pronoun is a starting point of the *numerus* dual; on the other, among nouns, terms for paired body parts are of great importance. While pronouns in the first and second person feature the dual as grammatical category as far back as they can be traced, the dual category initially does not exist among substantives. In the case of the terms for paired body parts the duality is lexically founded. To these terms for body parts was added a particular suffix, that probably did not initially have the meaning 'pair,' which of course was already provided in the terms for paired body parts. Instead, this meaning would perform a deictic function, emphasizing the inalienability of the body parts. While inalienability is a property of all body parts, since most body parts are present in pairs, a reinterpretation of the suffix from an indication of inalienability to one of a paired quality could take place. The symbol PIE **-i* is a stem suffix for terms for body parts. Since the dual meaning is also contained in the dual forms of personal pronouns, which are indicated by PIE **-*h_1, this clear indicator is transferred to body parts, where, combined with the existing suffix, it continues to serve as a stem suffix. This is primarily caused by the fact that further cases are formed, based on the nominative/accusative type, and that several of the concerned body part terms retain the stem element as such yet in the individual IE language. The formation of verbal dual forms based upon the first person personal pronoun takes place where the formation was no longer completed in the Proto-Indo-European period, which then does not take place in the language branches. Thus, the secondary endings may be reconstructed. In the case of syntagmata, using the substantive as a basis, a dual form and the number word for 'two' transferred the dual inflection over to the numera, thus echoing the relation of syntagmata to pronouns and adjectives."

Suggestions for further reading (a small selection): — Proto-Indo-European: → M. Fritz "*Der urindogermanische Dual - eine Klasse für sich?*" in *Graz 2000* p. 133-137; M. Malzahn "*Die nominalen Flexionsendungen des idg. Duals*" in HS 112 2000 p. 204-226; by the same author "*Die Genese des idg. Numerus Dual*" in *Graz 2000* p. 291-315. — Greek → Meier-Brügger *Gr. Spr.* II 1992 p. 68f. — Germanic: → K.

Strunk "*War auch das andere Horn gemeint? Horn B von Gallehus und Fragen des Duals*" in PBB 114 1992 p. 179-211. — Tocharian: → J. Hilmarsson *"The Dual Forms of Nouns and Pronouns in Tocharian"* Reykjavík 1989 (= TIES, Suppl. Series 1); O. Hackstein *"On the Prehistory of Dual Inflection in the Tocharian Verb"* in *Sprache* 35 1993 p. 47-70; M. Malzahn in TIES 9 2000 p. 45-52.

2) A word on the singular and plural: Singular and plural are grammatical categories that are common to the verb and the noun. They permit one to indicate by means of congruence the association of the noun with the subject of the action, indicated by the verb form employed. The relationship of singular to plural is a question of syntax. Differentiations in terms of content may effect formal changes: In the case of plurality the attention may be focused on the distributive-additive aspect (cf. Hom. Gr. λαοί 'people, men, warriors': → M. Schmidt in LfgrE II Sp. 1634, 60ff.; cf. Hom. Gr. μηροί 'the individual thigh parts'), but one may also emphasize the comprehensive-collective aspect of plurality, seeing in the *collectivum* a singular unity, e.g. (corresponding to the examples above) Hom. Gr. λαός 'people as a collective unity' and μῆρα 'all thigh pieces as a unified mass.' The distributive-additive forms belong to class A; the comprehensive-collective forms belong to class B, cf. F 303 § 2. For further information, cf. F 313. See also E 504 § 4.

Suggestions for further reading: → Schmidt (J.) *Neutra* 1889; H. Eichner "*Das Problem des Ansatzes eines urindogermanischen Numerus 'Kollektiv' ('Komprehensiv')*" in *Fachtagung Berlin* 1983 [1985] p. 134-169; J. A. Harðarson "*Zum urindogermanischen Kollektiv*" in MSS 48 1987 p. 71-113; E. Neu "*Zum Kollektivum im Hethitischen*" in *Grammatica Ittita* 1992 p. 197ff.; Prins *Hittite neuter* 1997; H. Craig Melchert *"Tocharian Plurals in -nt- and Related Phenomena"* in TIES 9 2000 p. 53-75.

F 305. Developments in case:

1) External changes may be caused by phonemic changes, e.g. the attested change from Old Latin to Classical Latin in the nominative plural ending from *-oi̯ > -ei̯ > -ẹ̄ > -ī*.

2) Changes may also take place through mutual influence of forms within a single paradigm, or between two paradigms. For example, the typical Greek replacement of the loc. pl. PIE **-su* by *-si*, which took place in a pre-Mycenaean period. The immediate cause of this paradigm-internal straighten-

ing is the loc. sg. ending with *-i* in combination with the instr. pl. ending *-p^hi*, which also contains *-i-*.

3) Formal changes may also be understood against the backdrop of content-shifts. Thus, it is possible that paradigmatic categories that were once clearly distinct became unified to form one single category. As a rule, this 'casual syncretism' leads to an excess of inflected forms, because at the time of each differentiation a separate form was in use. In a first phase, the forms in question become allomorphs. In a second phase, one of the allomorphs generally asserts itself as a norm, while the other(s) become disused. It ages and is generally forgotten by the speakers. — Concerning casual syncretism, cf. S 404 and F 324 (with a Latin exemple). — Further: → H. Rix "*Morphologische Konsequenzen des Synkretismus*" in *Proceedings of the Fourteenth International Congress of Linguists* II, edited by W. Bahner, J. Schildt and D. Viehweger, Berlin 1990, p. 1437-1441; by the same author, *Hist. Gramm. d. Gr.* 1976 §121f. Essential information is also offered in: Wackernagel *Vorlesungen* I 1926 p. 302f. Concerning the term 'syncretism,' which comes from the Greek for 'mix': → *Kl. Pauly* 5 Sp. 1648ff.

2. Nominal Stem Formation

F 306. The formation of nominal stems, and further the history of the suffixes and suffix groups involved, is part of morphology, cf. W 200ff.

The stem ending is of primordial importance for the understanding of noun inflection in ancient IE languages. It is thus important whether a noun stem ends in a vowel or a consonant. In the case of the acc. sg., depending on the ending one finds the variants **-m* or **-m̥*. Compare for example the Greek acc. sg. *-a* that one finds following consonantal stem ending (the type κήρυκ-α with *-a* < **-m̥*), but *-n* that is found following a vocalic stem ending (the type πόλι-ν with *-n* < **-m*). A further ancient PIE distinction is made between athematic and thematic stems, cf. F 101 § 4.

In contrast, for an understanding of PIE inflection quite another thing is of importance, namely, the assignment of a nominal stem to an accent, or ablaut class.

F 307. In the organization and presentation of nominal stems, current manuals on ancient IE languages used the stem class principle. Stems are classed according to stem ending and additionally differentiated according to individual differences in the ending or the gender.

1) Classical Latin declension is traditionally presented in grammars in terms of five declension types: 1st declension with the type *capra* f. 'goat' (*-ā-* stems), 2nd declension with the type *lupus* m. 'wolf' and *iugum* n. 'yoke' (*-o*-stems), 3rd declension with the type 3A *rēx* m. 'king' and *nōmen* n. 'name' (consonant stems) and type 3B *ignis* m. 'fire' and *mare* n. 'sea' (*-i-* stems), 4th declension with the type *manus* f. 'hand, flock' and *genu* n. 'knee' (*-u-* stems), 5th declension with the type *diēs* m. '(light of) day' (*-ē*-stems). — The 5th declension was modeled according to *diēs diem*. In the case of type 3B of the 3rd declension, various inherited consonant stems were inserted, e.g. Lat. *cani-s* m. f. 'dog' < PIE **k̑u̯on-*, cf. Lat. *iuveni-s* m./f. 'young; young man, young woman' < PIE *$*h_2i̯éu̯-h_3on-$* (→ Mayrhofer EWAia II p. 413f.; H. Rix in *Etrusci e Roma* 1981 p. 108; for information on suffixes, cf. W 204 § 4), cf. Lat. *nāvi-s* f. 'ship' < PIE *$*néh_2u-$* (cf. F 318 § 6c). — For more information: → Leumann LLFL 1977 § 347; E. Risch "*Das System der lateinischen Deklinationen*" (published in 1977) in *Kleine Schriften* 1981 p. 599ff.; Meiser *Laut- und Formenlehre* 1998 p. 129ff.

2) Classical Greek is presented with the following declensions: The first declension with the type 1A, τιμή τιμῆς f. 'honor' and type 1B τράπεζα τραπέζης f. 'table,' 2nd declension with the type ἵππος m. 'horse' and ζυγόν n. 'yoke,' and the 3rd declension which includes various subgroups. Among them, there are those with, following the stem ending, an occlusive such as αἰγ- f. 'goat,' those with *-r-* such as πατήρ πατρ- m. 'father,' those with a nasal of the type ποιμήν m. 'herdsman,' those with *-i-* and *-u-* such as πόλις f. 'city' and ἡδύς. adj. 'sweet,' those with *-ēu̯-* such as βασιλεύς βασιλέως (-έως Ion.-Att with metathesis of the older -ῆος [as in Homer], Myc. and Cypr. *-ēu̯-os*) m. 'king,' those with *-s-* such as γένος n. 'gender,' etc. — For more information: → Rix *Hist. Gramm. d. Gr.* 1976 p. 127ff.; Meier-Brügger *Gr. Sprachw.* II 1992 p. 72ff.

3) For the Old Indian corpus, Thumb / Hauschild *Handbuch des Sanskrit* I/2 1959 p. 30ff. presents declensions for the *-a-* and *-ā-* stems, *-i-*, *-u-* and diphthong stems, *-r-* and *-n-* stems, and further plosive stems, sibilants, and, as a separate group, the heteroclites.

4) Concerning Anatolian: → Rieken *Nom. Stammbildung* 1999. — Concerning Germanic, including its stems with *-a-*, *-ō-*, *-i-*, *-u-*, *-n-*, root nouns and further consonant stems: → Bammesberger *Urgerm. Nomen* 1990 p. 13ff. —

For information on Old Church Slavic stem classes: → Aitzetmüller *Abulg. Gramm.* 1991 p. 68ff.

F 308. Efforts to describe Proto-Indo-European declension are usually based upon the principles of stem class, which are commonly applied in the individual IE languages: → Szemerényi *Einführung* 1990 p. 173ff. (which classifies plosive stems, nasal and liquid stems, *s*-stems, *i*-, *u*- and diphthong stems, and thematic stems).

However, a view that is becoming more and more prevalent proposes accent and ablaut as the two most relevant criteria determining declension class in Proto-Indo-European: → H. Eichner in *Sprache* 20 1974 p. 27f. with notes 1-2.

In the present treatment, the sets of endings that are common to all substantives shall first be listed (cf. F 309ff.), followed by information on PIE accent and ablaut classes (cf. F 314ff.).

3. Nominal Endings

F 309. Substantives are generally composed of a nominal stem and an ending, cf. F 101.

The differentiation of thematic and athematic stems is a problem in itself, cf. F 101 § 4. It may be demonstrated that nominal endings were initially uniform, including for the thematic -*o*- stems, e.g. PIE athem. dat. sg. *ph$_2$tr-éi̯ 'father' vs. PIE them. dat. sg. *u̯érĝōi̯ 'work.' The latter may best be understood as the product of contraction of Pre-PIE *u̯érĝo-ei̯. In contrast to the vocalic -*i*- and -*u*- stems, in which the allophones -*i*- and -*u*- may alternate from being syllabic to non-syllabic (cf. L 212), thematic stems followed by vowel-initial endings were contracted. Further, some of the -*o*- stems formed qualifying adjectives and thus came into relation with pronouns. Under the influence of these -*o*- stems, the -*o*- stem paradigm developed into an independent inflection, cf. F 311.

Each substantive of an ancient IE language must belong to a gender category, whether it be masculine, feminine, or neuter. In terms of their development, masculine and feminine may be grouped together, cf. F 303 § 2. Neuter forms must be distinguished from the others, cf. F 313.

For information on nominal morphosyntax and casual categories, cf. S 401ff.

F 310. Proto-Indo-European athematic nominal endings (excluding neuter endings) may thus be presented in tabular form:

	sg.	pl.	du.
voc.	*-ø*	as nom.	
nom.	*-s / -ø*	*-es*	*-h_1*
acc.	*-m / -m̥*	*-ns / -n̥s < -m+s*	
gen.	⎤ *-és / -os / -s*	*-om*	
abl.	⎦	⎤ *-m-*	
dat.	*-ei̯*	⎦	
instr.	*-éh_1 / -h_1*	⎦ *-b^h-*	
loc.	*-ø / -i*	*-su*	

1) The set of endings above is the norm for substantives with root-final consontants. The substantives may be of masculine or feminine gender. A special formal mark for this distinction is not necessary, e.g. PIE m. **p$h_2$tér-* 'father' vs. PIE f. **mé$h_2$ter-* 'mother,' cf. F 303 § 4. The best means of distinguishing the gender of a noun is offered by adjectives and pronouns with three endings that reveal congruence with the concerned noun, cf. F 301.

2) The ending *-ø*, which appears equally in the vocative, nominative, and locative, reveals that this ending alone cannot have served to differentiate the cases in question. Differences in accent and ablaut must have provided decisive criteria.

3) While vowel and plosive stems are characterized by the ending *-s* in the nominative singular, the ending *-ø*, combined with a long vowel, is the norm with nasal, liquid, or *-s-* stems, e.g. PIE **ph_2tḗr* 'father' or PIE **k̑(u)u̯ṓn* 'dog.' This conspicuous distribution may best be understood if we suppose that the *-s-* ending was initially used in the nominative singular of all stems, and that this ending was dropped under certain circumstances. Compare, in the case of the *-r-* stems, the presumably Pre-PIE starting point **-V̆rs*, which was simplified to PIE **-V̄r* via the transitory phase **-V̆rr*. → Szemerényi *Einführung* 1990 p. 121f.; E. P. Hamp in *Baltistica* 31 / 2 1996 (1998) p. 139f.

4) The various genitive singular and instrumental singular endings may be explained by the effects of accent and ablaut, e.g. in the stressed full grade gen. sg. *-és* in PIE **p$h_2$tr-és* 'father' in contrast to the unstressed zero grade *-s* in gen. sg. PIE **mn̥t-éi̯-s* 'thought.'

5) In superficially comparing dative singulars featuring PIE *-ei̯* with locative singulars featuring PIE *-i* one is tempted, as in the case of § 4, to think of an old ablaut difference. However, full grade dative *-ei̯* and zero grade locative *-i*

were, according to all evidence established differentiated values already in Proto-Indo-European. For this reason, full grade *-ei̯* could certainly be placed before a stressed full grade suffix, e.g. PIE dat. sg. **mn̥t-éi̯-ei̯* 'thought.' — Concerning the Mycenaean coexistence of *-ei̯* and *-i*: → Hajnal *Sprachschichten* 1997 p. 21ff. (p. 60ff. includes information on the Vedic type *divédive* 'day for day'). — The locative had a special status with regard to the accent and ablaut types, cf. F 318 § 6a and F 321 § 1.

6) The accusative singular with PIE *-m* / *-m̥* and the accusative plural with PIE *-ns* / *-n̥s* are examples of ending variants that are determined by nominal stems with a consonant or a vowel in final position: *-V-m* and *-V-ns* vs. *-K-m̥* and *-K-n̥s*, cf. F 306.

Concerning the origin of the accusative plural, cf. F 104 (end). Concerning various accusative plural forms in IE languages (cf. among others, the *-u-* stem PIE *-u-ns* and its three descendents in early IE languages *-uns*; *-ūns*; *-ūs*): → H. Rix in *FS Risch* 1986 p. 586-590.

7) While the singular forms of the cases genitive and ablative are formally not differentiated, both showing the endings (*-es*/*-os*/*-s*), they are in fact differentiated in the plural. The genitive features the separate ending *-om*, while the ablative is linked to the dative:

	Lat.	Gr.	Indo-Ir.	Proto-Germ.	Balto-Slav.
abl.	*-bus*		*-bhi̯as*	*-m-*	*-mos*
dat.	*-bus*		*-bhi̯as*	*-m-*	*-mos*
instr.		*-p^hi*		*-m-*	*-mi(s)*

8) According to evidence in the individual IE languages, the instrumental plural is linked with the dative and ablative plurals. Evidence seems to indicate that while the dative and ablative plural were marked with *-mos*, the instrumental plural was marked with *-b^hi*: → J. Katz *Personal Pronouns* 1998 p. 248f. Thus, *-b^h-* would have established itself in Italic and Indo-Iranian as the sole initial consonant, replacing *-m-*. Conversely, *-m-* would have established itself in Balto-Slavic and Germanic. Indo-Iranian *-b^hi̯as* can thus be regarded as a cross between the instrumental *-b^hi* and the dative/ablative *-mos*. See also J. Matzinger "*Die "m-Kasus" des Balto-Slawischen und Germanischen*" in *GS Hartmut Katz* 2001 p. 183-208. — Concerning the problem of whether and to what extent the Greek *-p^hi* (< *b^hi*) bears singular traits (cf. Hom. dat. ἶφι '(with) force' [already in Myc. as *wi-pi-* in the prefixes of two proper nouns]): → Meier-Brügger *Gr. Sprachw.* II 1992 F 302 § 2.

F 311. The thematic, or _-o-_ stem substantives form a group that is separate from all other substantives (cf. F 309) and features several formal peculiarities. Its range of forms reveals close connections to the pronouns.

1) The following Proto-Indo-European schema was established based upon endings in the various ancient IE languages:

	sg.	pl.
voc.	_*-e_	as nom.
nom.	_*-o-s_	_*-ōs_ < _*-o-es_ / _*-oi̯_
acc.	_*-o-m_	_*-o-ns_ < _*-o-m-s_
gen.	_*-o-si̯o_ / adj.	_*-ōm_ < _*-o-om_
abl.	_*-ōt_ < _*-o-et_	_*-ōi̯s_ < _*-o-oi̯s_
dat.	_*-ōi̯_ < _*-o-ei̯_	as instr.
instr.	_*-o-_h_1 / _*-e-_h_1	_*-o-mos_ / _*-o-_b^h_(i̯)os_
loc.	_*-o-i_ / _*-e-i_	_*-oi̯-su_ < _*-oi̯s-su?_

2) It is clear that thematic substantives generally use the athematic endings, which is contracted with the thematic vowel _-o-_. The contractions presumably took place at a Pre-PIE stage, cf. F 309.

3) Influences of pronouns that may be dated to the Proto-Indo-European period are revealed in the genitive singular, in which one finds pronominal _-o-si̯o_ in place of the expected _*-o-s_ or _*-o-es_ (N.B.: the genitive is sometimes replaced by a possessive adjective); the ablative singular, in which the genitive and ablative are differentiated through the addition of the pronominal ablative _-et_; the nominative plural, where _-ōs_ is often replaced by _-oi̯_; the ablative plural, where pronominal _-oi̯s_ is inserted; and the locative plural, where one finds pronominal _-oi̯[s]-_ in place of simple _-o-_. For more information, cf. F 405.

4) The genitive singular: — Concerning _*-osi̯o_: Literature regarding the genitive singular is difficult to assess. Newer sources are: → H. Rix in MSS 49 1988 p. 107 (H. Rix makes the case that _*-o-s_ is the expected genitive singular and that _*-os-i̯o_, and _*-os-o_ was formed in the Pre-PIE period on the basis of nominal syntagmata such as _*pódds_ h_1_éḱu̯os-i̯o_ and h_1_éḱu̯os-o_ 'the foot, that of the horse': _-(H)i̯o_ or _-o_ should then be considered a relative pronoun, or an anaphoric demonstrative pronoun, which could be added to the substantive in question in the Pre-PIE period; concerning nominal relative clauses, cf. Chr. Koch in S 205 at the end of § 2); L. A. Prosdocimi in _Studi Etruschi_ 57 1991 p. 152ff. (which concerns the Lepontic _χosiosio_); A. Nikolaev _"PIE Ergativity and the Genitive in *-osyo"_ in _UCLA IE Conference 1999_ [2000] p. 293-309. — In place of

*-*osi̯o*, sometimes the ending *-*ī* is found in ancient IE languages. The ending *-*ī* is the only genitive singular ending in Celtic. Although a couple of *-osi̯o-* forms are attested in Latino-Faliscan (e.g. the incription from Satricum, 500 B.C.: *Popliosio Valesiosio suodales* 'the comrades of Publius Valerius'), starting in the 5th century B.C. the *-ī-* genitives are the norm. In Osco-Umbrian one finds *-eis* in place of *-ī-*. Concerning *-*ī* in Proto-Indo-European: → G. Klingenschmitt in *Kolloquium Lat. u. Idg.* Salzburg 1986 [1992] p. 98-104. The author proposes an 'appertinentive' featuring PIE *-*iH-*, the chief purpose of which would have been to indicate familial possession. This would explain the perceptible competition in ancient IE languages between *-*ī* and the genitive *-*os(i̯)o*. — An adjective may be used in place of a genitive to indicate possession. A significant treatment: → J. Wackernagel "*Genetiv und Adjektiv*" in *Kleine Schriften* II 1969 (an essay of 1908) p. 1346-1373. Suggestions for further reading: → F. Bader "*Les génitifs-adjectifs déterminés et le problème de l'article: comparaison typologique entre l'étrusque et les langues indo-européennes*" in *FS Rix* 1993 p. 12-45; I. Hajnal "*Der adjektivische Genetivausdruck der luwischen Sprachen*" in *Graz 2000* p. 159-184.

5) For more information on *-o-* stem paradigms in ancient IE languages (including plural forms): → Rix *Hist. Gramm. d. Gr.* 1976 p. 135ff. (2nd declension); G. Klingenschmitt in *Kolloquium Lat. u. Idg.* Salzburg 1986 [1992] p. 93ff.; Sihler *New Comparative Grammar* 1995 p. 256ff. — Concerning the Vedic *-ena*: → Hauri *-ena* 1963.

F 312. The PIE feminine *-*e-*h_2-stems (becoming *-*a*h_2- and then *–ā-* stems) are, from their origins with final h_2, athematic consonant stems. The complex suffix *-*e-*h_2- must be seen as an *-h_2- derivation from thematic stems, cf. W 204 § 1. For more information on the understanding of *-h_2- and *-*e-*h_2-, cf. F 303 § 4. The *-*e-*h_2- suffix originally belonged to the PIE class B described in F 303 § 2. This explains why the ending *-s*, which marks a subject, is strangely missing in the feminine nominative singular, cf. F 313.

Under pressure from the *-*o-* stem adjectives, which included feminine *-*e-*h_2- in order to mark gender congruence, the athematic paradigm of *-*e-*h_2- was adapted to the thematic paradigm of the masculine *-*o*-stems, particularly since *-*e*h_2- was inflected usually without an ablaut (cp. F 322) and the *-*e*h_2-, followed by vowel-initial endings, contracted after disappearance of *-h_2-, making the new forms externally similar to the *-*o*-stems, which were themselves already contracted. Compare the Latin *-ā-* stems of the 1st declension, which, in traditional grammars, are grouped with the *-o-* stems of the 2nd declension, and at the same time separated from the nouns of the 3rd declension. Further, compare (in the nominative plural) PIE **-e-h$_2$-es* (> **-ās*), retained in Vedic (as *sénās*) and Gothic (as *gibōs*) vs. renewed fem. *-ai̯* in Latin (e.g. *terrae*) and in Greek (e.g. τιμαί) following the example of thematic pronominal **-oi̯*.

Further references: For information on the vocative singular, cf. L 334 § 3; concerning the accusative singular and plural, cf. L 303.

Suggestions for further reading: For information concerning problems associated with *-eh$_2$-* stems: → Rix *Hist. Gramm. d. Gr.* 1976 p. 129ff.; G. Klingenschmitt in *Kolloquium Lat. u. Idg.* Salzburg 1986 [1992] p. 89ff.; Sihler *New Comparative Grammar* 1995 p. 266ff.; I. Hajnal "*Die lykischen a-Stämme: Zum Werdegang einer Nominalklasse*" in *Kolloquium Pedersen* Copenhagen 1993 [1994] p. 135-171; by the same author, see L 334 § 3 above.

F 313. Neuter forms generally feature the same endings as masculine forms, but reveal different in the nominative and accusative cases: The formal identity of nominative and accusative may be explained by the fact that a main characteristic of PIE neuter forms (and of their underlying PIE class B) was to identify things that were not conceivable as agents in a verbal phrase, cf. F 303 § 2. Thus, the formation of a nominative case (in the sg. with the ending *-*s* to mark the subject) did not initially come into question.

Nominative/accusative neuter singular: While athematic substantives have no endings (zero) in the nominative and accusative, thematic substantives feature the single *-*m* ending, e.g. PIE athem. nom./acc. **spérmn̥-ø* 'the planted' vs. PIE them. nom./acc. **u̯érĝo-m* 'the work.'

Nominative/accusative neuter plural: In terms of content, the idea of a collective mass is certainly dominant. Therefore, the collective suffix (= athematic *-h$_2$-* and thematic *-e-h$_2$-*) is used, no ending (zero) added. If, however, the distributive/additive aspect were to be stressed, a plural of class A could have been used. Cf. F 304 § 2.

The understanding of the neuter plural as collective explains the ancient IE characteristic, observable in isolated cases, of combination of the neuter plural and the singular of a verb: → J. A. Harðarson in MSS 48 1987 p. 81ff. with mention of the practice in Attic Greek (A good example is the sentence: πάντα ῥεῖ 'everything flows': → Meier-Brügger *Gr. Sprachw.* I 1992 p. 157), in Vedic (the RV only contains three attestations, which are not necessarily based on old formations), Old Avestan, in which it is regular, and in Hittite, in which it is exclusively used. — Further sources: → H.

Craig Melchert in TIES 9 2000 p. 53-75 (p. 61ff. “Collective vs. Count Plural in PIE and in Anatolian”).

4. Inflection Paradigms and their Ablaut Classes

F 314. As a quick glance in the research history shows, it was only gradually that the insight became established that the fundamental organization of PIE nominal inflection is defined by the accent classes, or more precisely stated, by the ablaut classes that guide them. — The following depiction is oriented according to research history, culminating in the current understanding of the subject in F 319. Research in this area is very much in progress.

1) As is generally known, the athematic nominal paradigm shows a change between the strong and the weak stem. The weak stem may be distinguished from the strong by a different accent behavior, e.g. in the case of the paradigm of ‘father’ PIE strong **ph_2-tér-* (the suffix is full grade) vs. PIE weak **ph_2-tr-´* (the suffix is zero grade). Accordingly, in Greek there is nom. sg. strong πα-τήρ, gen. sg. weak πα-τρ-ός; in Vedic nom. sg. strong *pi-tā́* (< **pi-tā́r*), dat. sg. weak *pi-tr-é*. As shown in the example (and as is continually confirmed in practice), the change from weak to strong moves the accent toward the end of the word by one syllable. — Compare further, from the paradigm of Vedic ‘son,’ the nom. sg. strong *sūn-ú-s* (with zero grade suffix; the accent was originally on the root, but is transferred to the suffix, cf. § 4), gen. sg. weak *sūn-ó-s* i.e. **sūn-áu̯-s* (with full grade suffix). — The distinction between strong and weak was already made in Old Indian grammar: → Rix *Hist. Gramm. d. Gr.* 1976 p. 121. The terms ‘strong’ and ‘weak’ must not be confused with the differentiation between casus rectus (nominative) and casus obliquus (all cases other than nominative), cf. p. XVII.

2) The Proto-Indo-European cases which certainly featured a strong stem are: in the singular, the vocative, the nominative, the accusative, and sometimes also the locative; in the dual, the vocative, the nominative and the accusative; in the plural, the nominative, and sometimes also the accusative. All remaining declensions are formed with the weak stem.

3) A milestone in research on nominal stems is the work by Pedersen, *Cinquième déclinaison* 1926. He discovered two different types of nominal ablaut. — As the author finds, the key examples, Ved. dat. sg. weak *pi-tr-é* i.e. **pi-tr-ái̯*, and Ved. gen. sg. weak *sūnós* i.e. **sūn-áu̯-s* differ in their ablauts.

In the case of the former, the suffix in the weak stem is zero grade and the ending full grade; in that of the former, the suffix of the weak stem is full grade, and the ending is zero grade. Pedersen uses the terms (p. 24 note 1): "*'Flexion forte' et 'flexion faible' de F. de Saussure*" (→ Saussure *Mémoire* 1879 = *Recueil* 1922 p. 187, 194ff., 205ff.).

> "*Mais ces termes prêtent à la confusion avec les expressions 'stark' et 'schwach' de la grammaire des langues germaniques, et en soi ils n'expriment pas la vraie nature du contraste entre les deux types. En adoptant le mot δύναμις au sens de 'degré vocalique fort' on pourrait peut-être forger les termes 'flexion hystérodyname'* [of the type πατήρ, or *pitā́*] *et 'flexion protérodyname'* [of the type *sūnú-s*]."

In other words, Pedersen distinguishes on the one hand what he calls the hysterodynamic inflection type with its strong stem (according to the schema: zero grade unstressed root, full grade stressed suffix, and zero grade unstressed ending) and weak stem (according to the schema: zero grade unstressed root, zero grade unstressed suffix, and full grade stressed ending), and on the other hand, what he calls the proterodynamic inflection type with a strong stem (according to the schema: full grade stressed root, zero grade unstressed suffix and zero grade unstressed ending) and weak stem (according to the schema: zero grade unstressed root, full grade stressed suffix, and zero grade unstressed ending).

4) Pedersen makes clear that the original combinations of stressed full grade and unstressed zero grade[6] are only rarely preserved in the IE languages. Thus, a large number of analogies and innovations have taken place in extant IE paradigms. In the case of nom. sg. *sūnú*s, for example, neither the zero grade stem, nor the stressed zero grade suffix correspond with the postulated proterodynamic ending form **séu̯H-nu-s*. In that of the Vedic gen. sg. *pi-tur* (with *-tur* <* *-tŕ̥-s*) the zero grade and stressed suffix contradict each other with regard to the postulated hysterodynamic ending form **ph₂-tr-és*. The ending *-tur* is clearly old and originates from a pattern such as Ved. *bhrā́tr-*, in which the root syllable always carries the accent. Although the zero grade suffix in Ved. dat./abl. pl. *pi-tŕ̥-bhyas* corresponds to expectations, the accent does not: In place of the accent on the zero grade suffix, one should expect a stressed **-bhyás*. Just the opposite is true in Ved. dat. abl. pl. *sūnú-bhyas*:

---

[6] Compare the zero grade unstressed root, the full grade stressed suffix, and the zero grade unstressed ending in the example *sūnós* i.e. **sū-náu̯-s* (cp. L 222 § 3) and the zero grade unstressed root, the zero grade unstressed suffix, and the full grade stressed ending in the example πα-τρ-ός

The accented suffix is expected, but not its zero grade. Pedersen *Ibid* p. 25: "*Bref, on ne saurait maintenir l'hypothèse indiquée ci-dessus sur le caractère primitif du contraste entre les types πατήρ et sūnús qu' à condition de supposer une longue série d'actions analogiques et d'innovations.*"

5) While Kuryłowicz *Études* I 1935 p. 131ff. (*Remarques sur la flexion nominale*) adopts the established terminology of Saussure, Kuiper *Ved. Noun-Inflexion* 1942 directly builds upon Pedersen's work. In his ground-breaking work on *-i-* and *-u-* stems (p. 1ff.) and on Vedic words of the type *go-ṣā́s* 'cattle-producing' (p. 71ff.), Kuiper uses the categories proterodynamic and hysterodynamic as a point of departure. Cf. p. 4: "The terms are a little pompous to my taste, but it will be best to retain them."

6) Kuiper's research fell on particularly fertile ground in K. Hoffmann's department in Erlangen. As H. Rix reports (MSS 18 1965 p. 86 note 18), a colloquium was held in 1964 on the subject of *-r/n-* heteroclitica. His pioneering contribution "Latin iecur iocineris," printed by Rix (l.c. p. 79-92), handles formal paradigm problems. The form *iecur iecoris* n. 'liver,' common in Cicero, is structurally earlier than *iecur iocineris*, which has become established since Livy. Regarding the disputed source of the *o*-grade *ioc-*, Rix comes to the conclusion that it was inherited. The related nouns Gr. ἧπαρ ἥπατος n. 'liver' (< PIE **i̯ḗkʷ-*) and Ved. *yákr̥t yaknás* (< PIE **i̯ekʷ-*) are unfortunately of little help since a single ablaut grade (whether *-ē-* or *-e-*) became generalized in them both. The word for 'water,' namely PIE n. **u̯édōr*, constructed in a parallel manner, clearly has retained an older schema with a paradigmatically based *o*-grade. Rix thus reconstructed, according to the state of research at that time, the following 'water' paradigm and traced *ioc-* through analogy back to the locative **i̯okʷ-*:

strong st. nom. acc.	**u̯éd-ōr*	~	**i̯ékʷ- r̥t*
weak stem	** ud-n-*	~	**ikʷ - n- '*
loc. sg	**u̯od-én*	~	**i̯okʷ- én*

7) It became clear only later that the paradigm for the Proto-Indo-European word 'water' is even more complex and must be divided into a singular, or acrodynamic paradigm (cf. F 320) and a collective, or holodynamic paradigm (cf. F 321): → J. Schindler "*L'apophonie des thèmes indo-européens en -r/n*" in BSL 70 / 1 1975 p. 1-10; by the same author, in *Kolloquium Pedersen* Copenhagen 1993 [1994] p. 398f.:

	singular	collective
strong stem nom. acc.	**u̯ód-r̥*	**u̯éd-ōr*
weak stem	**u̯éd-n-*	**ud-n-´*
loc. sg.	**ud-én(i)*	

8) Further, in contrast to the singular form **u̯ódr-*, PIE **i̯ḗkʷr-* perhaps had the weak stem **i̯ókʷr-* (→ Nussbaum *Two Studies* 1998 p. 150 note 179), from which the Latin *ioc-* might have received its *-o-*. But this is not the last word on this subject: → Meiser *Laut- und Formenlehre* 1998 p. 142.

F 315. Various authors have dealt with accent and ablaut paradigms in recent years.

1) The first to be named is J. Schindler. Concerning his life's work: → R. Schmitt in AlmÖAW [*Almanach der Österreichischen Akademie der Wissenschaften*] 145 1994 / 1995 p. 584ff.). Following are his major essays: → "*Das indogermanische Wort für 'Erde' und die dentalen Spiranten*" in *Sprache* 13 1967 p. 191-205; "*Zu hethitisch nekuz*" in ZVS 81 1967 p. 290-303; "*L'apophonie des noms racines indo-européens*" in BSL 67/1 1972 p. 31-38; "*Zum Ablaut der neutralen s-Stämme des Indogermanischen*" in *Fachtagung Regensburg* 1973 [1975] p. 259-267 (p. 262f. on the four PIE ablaut classes); "*L'apophonie des thèmes indo-européens en -r/n*" in BSL 70/1 1975 p. 1-10; "*Alte und neue Fragen zum indogermanischen Nomen*" in *Kolloquium Pedersen* Copenhagen 1993 [1994] p. 397-400.

2) From the abundance of other sources, I shall name: — a) H. Eichner "*Die Etymologie von Hitt. mehur*" in MSS 31 1973 p. 91 (in note 33 regarding terminology, cf. § 3 and 4); by the same author, "*Zu Etymologie und Flexion von vedisch str̥̄́ und púmān*" in *Sprache* 20 1974 p. 26-42. — b) Rix *Hist. Gramm. d. Gr.* 1976 p. 121ff. — c) Beekes *IE Nominal Inflection* 1985. (Among other things, Beekes postulates boldly the existence of a hysterodynamic type with nom. sg. *KéK-K*, acc. sg. *KK-éK-m̥* and gen. sg. *KK-ós*, as well as various sub-paradigms. Neuter forms, on the other hand, use a proterodynamic paradigm); Lubotsky *Nominal Accentuation* 1988. — d) On various related subjects: W. Hock "*Der urindogermanische Flexionsakzent und die morphologische Akzentologiekonzeption*" in MSS 53 1992 p. 177-205; N. Oettinger "*Der Akzent des indogermanischen Kollektivums im Lichte des Hethitischen*" in MSS 53 1992 p. 207-214; by the same author, "*Der Ablaut von 'Ahorn' im Indogermanischen*" in HS 107 1994 p. 77-86. — e) X. Tremblay "*Un nouveau type apophonique des noms athématiques suffixaux*

de l'indo-européen" in BSL 91 / 1 1996 p. 97-145. The author tries to establish the additional 'anakinetic' inflection type according to the model, nom. sg. *Kek-ṓs* and **Kek-tór-* and gen. sg. *Kék-s-s* and *Kék-tr-*. However, this theory is clearly contradicted by the fact that in all provable paradigms, in changing from a strong case to a weak case, the accent always moves toward the end of the word and never the opposite. In the case of **Kek-tór-*, the author forces (p. 104), despite evidence to the contrary, the accentuation into conformity with his theory, noting simply "*l'absence d'attestation de l'oxytonie de *-tór- n'est pas significative*."

3) Unfortunately, research has not yet produced a uniform terminology. It is important to note that accent and ablaut patterns are distinguished from one another, the latter being the immediate consequence of the former.

In his *Hist. Gramm. d. Gr.* 1976 p. 122f., Rix expressly draws the connection from 'dynamic' to 'accent' ("*von* δύναμις *'Akzent'*"), placing himself in opposition to Pedersen's definition, which, as described in F 314 § 3 above, associates δύναμις in the sense of '*degré vocalique fort*' rather with the ablaut. H. Eichner also insists (MSS 31 1972 p. 91 note 33) on the importance of the accent patterns, suggesting that an accent that remains on a single word element as 'static.' If the accent does not stay in the same place in the word, Eichner considers it 'kinetic.'

Researchers such as J. Schindler (→ in *Fachtagung Regensburg* 1973 [1975] p. 262f.), N. Oettinger (→ in HS 107 1994 p. 83) and W. Hock (→ in MSS 53 1992 p. 177ff.) follow the example of Eichner. Rieken follows Rix in his *Nom. Stammbildung* 1999 p. 6.

4) Concerning ablaut paradigms, I shall follow the example of Pedersen and Kuiper in using the term 'dynamic.' However, in focusing on the accent, I shall employ Eichner's 'kinetic' and 'static.'

The following compilation (taken from Harđarson *Wurzelaorist* 1993 p. 26, and also used in: → W. Hock in MSS 53 1992 p. 177f.) refers to accent, but may be converted to apply to ablauts by simply replacing 'static' and 'kinetic' with 'dynamic.'

Static accent
1. acrostatic (constant root stress)
2. mesostatic (constant suffix stress)
3. teleutostatic (constant ending stress)

Mobile accent
1. proterokinetic (transfer of accent from the root to the suffix)

2. hysterokinetic (transfer of accent from the suffix to the ending)
3. amphikinetic (transfer of accent from the root to the ending)
4. holokinetic (transfer of accent between root, suffix, and ending)

F 316. In PIE nominal inflection, the ablaut classes proterodynamic and hysterodynamic were on the one hand well established, cf. F 314 § 3ff. As shall be shown in F 319, the additional categories acrodynamic and amphi/holodynamic must also be included.

In the following depiction, I shall use the abbreviations W (= root), S (= suffix) and E (= ending), and *z* (zero grade; borrowing from J. Schindler, I shall use *z* [= zéro] and not *ø*: → *Sprache* 15 1969 p. 144; by the same author, *Fachtagung Regensburg* 1973 [1975] p. 262ff.), *é* (stressed, *e-grade*), *ó* (stressed, *o*-grade) and *o* (unstressed, *o*-grade). 'Strong' stands for 'strong stem'; 'weak' stands for 'weak stem.'

The appropriate accent pattern is primary. The ablaut pattern associated with it is originally only the product of the accent circumstances, according to the principle, 'stressed syllable = *e*-grade,' 'unstressed syllable = zero grade or *o*-grade.'

In the evolution of Proto-Indo-European into the individual IE languages, the ablaut was more often retained than the accent. Among the ablauts, the circumstances in the suffix and at the ending remained the most stable. Ablauts in the root were most often dropped in favor of formal uniformity.

F 317. The proterokinetic/proterodynamic nominal class:

1) A schematic depiction of the Proto-Indo-European proterokinetic accent pattern (the underlined elements carry an accent):

	W	S	E
strong	$\underline{W}$	*S*	*E*
weak	*W*	$\underline{S}$	*E*

2) A schematic depiction of the Proto-Indo-European proterodynamic ablaut pattern:

	W	S	E
strong	*é*	*z*	*z*
weak	*z*	*é*	*z*

3) Consider the model example Ved. 'son' (cf. F 314 § 3; for further details: → Mayrhofer *EWAia* II p. 741):

strong	nom. sg. Ved. *sū-nú-s*	instead of PIE **séu̯H-nu-s*
weak	gen. sg. Ved. *sū-nó-s* < **sū-náu̯-s*	< PIE **suH-néu̯-s*

4) Commentary on § 3: While the suffixal ablaut change is attested in Vedic, such evidence is missing for the ablaut change in the root syllable *sū-*. Thus, the reconstruction must remain uncertain in this regard. As an alternative to full grade **séu̯H-*, stressed, zero grade **súH-* cannot be ruled out. — The paradigm of Ved. *sūnú-* consistently exhibits a stable suffixal accent. However, this state may not be very old. The accent is expected on the full grade suffix of the weak stem, but not on the zero grade suffix of the strong stem. In other words: The ablaut behavior of the suffix may only be explained if an older proterokinetic accent preceded the newer static accent.

5) The various PIE *-i-* and *-u-* stems are distinctively proterodynamic:

IE strong	nom. sg.	**KéK-i-s*	**KéK-u-s*
IE weak	gen. sg.	**KzK-éi̯-s*	**KzK-éu̯-s*

6) As a rule, IE languages have retained the *–i-* and *–u-*suffixal ablaut marker. However, in root ablaut formation and accentuation, simplification is the rule: Starting from the weak stems, zero grade roots were generalized and accents became static on the root or the suffix.

7) As examples of § 5, I shall name a few abstract *-ti-/-tei̯-* nouns: — Latin: *mors mortis* f. 'dying, death' < PIE weak **mr̥-téi̯-* (which is an abstract *-ti-* noun from PIE **mer-* 'to disappear, to die') with the generalized zero grade *mor-* < **mr̥-*. For information on other Latin descendents of abstract *-ti-* nouns: → Leumann LLF 1977 p. 344f.; Reichler-Béguelin *Type mēns* 1986 p. 23. — Greek: Hom. πόσις f. 'drinking' < PIE weak **ph₃-téi̯-* (which is an abstract *-ti-* noun from PIE **peh₃-* 'to drink') with generalization both of the weak stem's zero grade root, and of the strong stem's accent, which is on the root. In the case of ablaut in the suffix, most Greek dialects exhibit generalized zero grade *-si-* (i.e. nom. sg. *-si-s*, gen. sg. *-si-os* etc.; the assibilated Southern Greek *–si*-form may be traced back to *-ti-*, cp. L 336 § 2; however, thanks to the dominance of the Early Ionic scientific language within the whole of Greece, the abstract nouns became established with the form *-si-*). As an archaism, the Attic paradigm offers gen. sg. -σεως < **tēi̯-os* (*-tēi̯-* probably originates in the loc. sg. *-tēi̯*) and dat. sg. -σει < **-téi̯-i*. For more information on abstract *-ti-* / *-si*-nouns: → Risch *Wortbildung* 1974 §16. Note also that Attic πόλις

'city' shows the same pattern as the *–si*-abstracts. — Vedic: *matí-* f. 'thinking, thought, sense' < PIE weak **mn̥-téi̯-* with generalization of the weak stem's zero grade in the root, and of the weak stem's accent on the suffix. A genitive singular form such as *puṣṭés* 'flourishing, growth' < **-tái̯-s* < PIE **-téi̯-s* is to be expected. In contrast, forms such as acc. pl. *matī́s* and instr. pl. *matíbhis* (the suffixes of which are indeed zero grade, but are also stressed) constitute exceptions to the rule. — In examining the *-ti-* stems of IE languages it is conspicuous that the full grade that is expected in a strong stem's root is hardly attested, cf. Ion. ἄμπωτις 'low tide' (if < **-peh₃-ti-*). Thus, B. Vine, in a lecture given in Copenhagen in 2000, considered the idea of explaining the strange behavior of abstract *-ti-* nouns by the well-known fact that they were often compound formations. One would then have to draw the conclusion that in the formation of simplicia, the ablaut conditions of word composition were respected.

8) The two nouns PIE **dóru-* n. 'wood' and PIE **h₂ói̯u-* n. 'life power, lifespan' are considered proterodynamic because of their weak forms of the type gen. sg. **dréu̯-s* and **h₂i̯éu̯-s*: → Kuiper *Vedic Noun-Inflexion* 1942 p. 30ff. For that reason they are also discussed here. As we now know, they were initially acrodynamically inflected (cf. F 320): strong stem **dór-u-* and **h₂ói̯-u-* vs. weak stem **dér-u-* and **h₂éi̯-u-*. Only later on, the weak forms were restructured. In place of **dér-u-* and **h₂éi̯-u-*, the new forms **dr-éu̯-* and **h₂i̯-éu̯-* entered into use. — Details concerning **dóru-*: Cf. Ved. nom. acc. sg. n. *dā́ru* (= jAvest. *dāᵘru*) 'wood' < PIE strong **dóru-* with gen. sg. *dróṣ* (= LAv. *draoš*) < restructured PIE weak **dréu̯-*. For more information, also on Gr. n. δόρυ 'tree trunk, wood' and the form f. δρυ- 'tree, oak' (gen. sg. δρυ-ός and nom. sg. δρῦς): → K. Strunk in *GS Kuryłowicz* I 1995 p. 357f.; Janda *Stock und Stein* 1997 p. 143ff. — Details concerning PIE **h₂ói̯u-* 'life power, lifespan': On the strong stem **h₂ói̯u-* cf. Ved. *ā́yu-* and OAv., LAv. *āiiu*; further, cf. W. Cowgill (→ *Language* 36 1960 p. 347ff.), who derives the Greek negation οὐ (already Myc. as *o-u-* i.e. *ohu-* < **oi̯u* < **h₂ói̯u*) from the pre-Proto-Greek negative formulation **ne ...*h₂ói̯u-*, in the sense of 'not a duration of time' thus asserting the existence of the strong stem in Greek too. Concerning the weak stem **h₂i̯-éu̯-* or **h₂i̯-u̯-* cf., on the one hand, full grade OAv. gen. sg. *yaoš* n. 'life,' and on the other hand, zero grade Gr. αἰϝ-εί and αἰ-ές. Suggestions for further reading: → Kuiper *Ved. Noun-Inflexion* 1942 § 6; Peters *Laryngale* 1980 p. 76f.

9) In contrast to § 8, the neuter *-men-* and *-r/n-* stems were without any doubt proterodynamic. The PIE schema is:

PIE strong st.	nom. acc. sg.	**KéK-mn̥*	**KéK-r̥*
PIE weak st.	gen. sg.	**KzK-mén-s*	**KzK-én-s*

10) The paradigms of the IE language neuter *-men-* stems only show isolated traces of the postulated initial state of affairs. Avestan is in this case the most conservative. It is important to note that there were also *-men-* stems that signified animate objects and were thus not neuter. These belong to the holodynamic class, cf. F 321 § 2. — Latin: Cf. strong nom. acc. sg. *sē-men* 'seed,' and its weak gen. sg. *sē-min-is*: While the root *sē-* < **seh₁-* retained the full grade, the suffix most probably shows ablaut with zero grade nom.acc. *-men* < **-mn̥* and full grade weak *-min-* < PIE **-mén-* (the gen. sg. ending *-is* < *-es* is secondary). — Greek: In the nominative and accusative singular, the suffix shows the expected form *-ma* (in a labial context in Mycenaean, sometimes also *-mo*). In contrast, in the weak forms such as the genitive singular, the suffix form is, in place of **-men-*, already in the Mycenaean period (with dental extension) *-ma-t-* < **-mn̥-t-*, cf. instr. sg. *e-ka-ma-te* i.e. *hekʰ-mat-ē* PY 'holder.' An *-i̯e-* present form such as ὀνομαίνω (Homeric and later) 'to name' is a very old structure, originating at a time when the dental extension was not yet established. Further information on this complex of problems in Greek: → Risch *Wortbildung* 1974 § 21; N. Oettinger "*Die Dentalerweiterung von n-Stämmen und Heteroklitika im Griechischen, Anatolischen und Altindischen*" in *FS Neumann* 1982 p. 233ff. (To which H. Rix responds critically in *Kratylos* 30 1985 p. 70f.). — Vedic: Cf. strong nom.acc. sg. *nā́ma* 'name,' weak gen. sg. *nā́mnas*. The zero grade suffix form *-mn-* (and not **-man-*) was altered in IE languages according to the model of the *-mn-* forms of the non-neuter *-men-* stems, cf. F 321 § 2. — Avestan: Cf. LAv. strong nom. acc. sg. *nąma* 'name' < PIE **-mn̥*; OAv. weak gen. sg. *cašmə̄ŋg* 'field of vision,' LAv. weak gen. sg. *dā-mąn* 'place, creation,' both of which have the extended genitive singular ending < PIE **-mén-s* (Details and further forms: → Hoffmann / Forssman *Avest. Laut- und Flexionslehre* 1996 p. 143). — For more information on Proto-Indo-European 'name': → I. Hajnal in IF 92 1987 p. 83 note 51 (which concerns Greek material. He supports the assertion of **h₁néh₃-mn̥*); Mayrhofer EWAia II p. 35-37; Puhvel HED 5 2001 p. 51-56.

11) Concerning the neuter *-r/n-* stems cf. the prime example 'fire' with the PIE singular paradigm strong nom.acc. **péh₂-u̯r̥*, weak gen. sg. **ph₂(u)-u̯én-s* (direct evidence for which is provided by Hitt. nom.acc. sg. *pa-aḫ-ḫur*, gen. sg. *pa-aḫ-ḫu-e-na-aš*). On details of the PIE paradigm:

→ J. Schindler in BSL 70/1 1975 p. 10. Concerning Hittite: → CHD P-1 1994 p. 12-16; Rieken *Nom. Stammbildung* 1999 p. 331-333.

F 318. The hysterokinetic/hysterodynamic nominal class:

1) A schematic depiction of the Proto-Indo-European hysterokinetic accent pattern (the underlined elements carry an accent):

	W	S	E
strong	*W*	*S* (underlined)	*E*
weak	*W*	*S*	*E* (underlined)

2) A schematic depiction of the corresponding Proto-Indo-European hysterodynamic ablaut pattern:

	W	S	E
strong	*z*	*é*	*z*
weak	*z*	*z*	*é*

3) Cf. the prime example, Ved. 'father' (cf. F 314 § 1ff.; on phonetics, cf. L 324 § 3):

strong	Ved. nom. sg.	*pi-tā́*	< PIE **p*h_2*-tḗr* <**-tér-s*
	Ved. acc. sg.	*pi-tár-am*	< PIE **p*h_2*-tér-m̥*
weak	Ved. dat. sg.	*pi-tr-é*	< PIE **p*h_2*-tr-éi̯*

4) Further classic examples are the Vedic compounds of the type strong nom. sg. *-sthā́s* < PIE **-stéh*$_2$*-s*, weak gen. sg. *-sthás* < PIE **-sth*$_2$*-és* (with secondary generalization of *-sth-* in Vedic, also in the strong stem). However, according to Scarlata (*Wurzelkomposita im R̥g-Veda* 1999 p. 659) the evidence concerning the weak stem is uncertain. — More complex are the Vedic compounds built from the root *san*^{i}- 'to obtain, to gain' < PIE **senh*$_2$- 'to obtain, to catch': strong nom. sg. *-sánis* < PIE **-sénh*$_2$*-s*. On the other hand, forms such as strong nom. sg. *-sā́s* and weak gen. sg. *-sás* must be considered secondary: → Kuiper *Ved. Noun-Inflexion* 1942 p. 83ff.; Scarlata *Wurzelkomposita im R̥g-Veda* 1999 p. 586.

5) The non-neuter nouns with *-r-* and *-n-* suffixes also suggest a hysterodynamic pattern. Cf. the prime example of PIE 'star': strong nom. sg. **h*$_2$*s-tḗr* vs. weak gen. sg. **h*$_2$*s-tr-és* = Hom. Gr. nom. sg. ἀστήρ, dat. pl. ἀστράσι < **h*$_2$*s-tr̥̄́-si* = Ved. *s-tr̥̄́-bhis* and PIE 'young steer': strong nom. sg. **h*$_2$*uk*^{w}*s-ḗn* vs. weak gen. sg. **h*$_2$*uk*^{w}*s-n-és* = Ved. *ukṣán-* (→ Mayrhofer *EWAia I* p. 210).

6) The Proto-Indo-European nouns *di̯eu̯- 'sky, god of the sky, day,' *g^{w}ou̯- 'cow' and *neh$_2$u- 'barge, bark' form a group of their own. I consider them in this context because in prior research, owing to their weak stems with stressed endings (e.g. gen. sg. *diu̯-és), they were included in the hysterodynamic class: → Kuiper *Ved. Noun-Inflexion* 1942 p. 39. — According to the evidence of IE languages, *di̯eu̯- was always inflected with the strong stem *di̯eu̯- vs. weak stem *diu̯-. The important question today is whether this is really a hysterodynamic -u- stem of the type *di̯-éu̯- vs. *di-u̯-ʹ, or perhaps rather an amphidynamic root noun of the type -é- vs. -z-, cf. F 320 § 3. The evidence suggests the latter: → Rieken *Nom. Stammbildung* 1999 p. 39. — Both nouns PIE *g^{w}ou̯- 'cow' and PIE *neh$_2$u- 'barge, bark' have come to resemble the paradigm of *di̯eu̯- in the IE languages. But they differ from *di̯eu̯- in their origin. PIE *g^{w}ou̯- is presumably an acrodynamic root word of the type -o- vs. -e- with strong stem *g^{w}ou̯- vs. weak stem *g^{w}eu̯- (cf. § 6b); PIE *néh$_2$u- is presumably an acrodynamic noun with a weak stem *néh$_2$u- (cf. the supposition in § 6c).

6a) The Proto-Indo-European paradigm for *di̯eu̯- 'sky, sky god, day' is presumably:

strong voc. sg.	*d(i)i̯éu̯ (+ *ph$_2$ter)	
strong nom. sg.	*d(i)i̯ḗu̯-s or *d(i)i̯éu̯-s	
strong acc. sg.	*d(i)i̯ḗ-m < *d(i)i̯éu̯-m	
weak gen./abl. sg.		*diu̯-és
weak gen./abl. sg.		*diu̯-éi̯
weak instr.sg.		*diu̯-éh$_1$
loc.sg.	*di̯éu̯-i	

Commentary on details: — Concerning PIE inflection: → J. Schindler "*Bemerkungen zur Herkunft der idg. Diphthongstämme und zu den Eigentümlichkeiten ihrer Kasusformen*" in *Sprache* 19 1973 p. 148-157; by the same author, *s.v. Zeus* in RE Suppl. 15 1978 Sp. 999-1001; Szemerényi *Einführung* 1990 p. 191-193. — Concerning the syllabification of *d(i)i̯-, cf. L 218 § 2. — Concerning the relationship between PIE * di̯éu̯- and *dei̯-h$_2$-: → Mayrhofer EWAia I p. 701 *s.v. DAY*$^{i\,2}$ ('to shine, to beam') and p. 752 *s.v. dyáv-* 'sky, divinity of the sky, father sky, day'; F. Bader "*Formes de la racine *dei- 'briller avec rotation'*" in *FS Szemerényi* *75 III 1993 p. 3-59. — Concerning nominative singular forms: → See Wachter below, under Latin and Italic. — Concerning the accusative singular form, cf. L 303. — Concerning Latin and Italic: → Leumann LLFL 1977 § 318. Wachter *AltLat. Inschriften* 1987 p. 150ff. asserts instead of nom. sg. **di̯ēu̯s* a well established Proto-Italic nom. sg. *diēs*, attested particularly in *Diēspiter.* This may best be understood when we presume that the form was very early restructured, in analogy to acc. sg. **di̯ēm*. Concerning the pre-Lucian form *dipoteres*: → H. Rix in *FS Hamp* II 1997 p. 146-149 (< **Dīī pater* < **Diē pater*). — Concerning the Greek and Mycenaean paradigms (note: Mycenaean Dat. sg. *Diu̯ei̯* is parallel to *Hērāi̯*): → Aura Jorro *DMic.* I 1985 p. 180 *s.v. di-we*; E. Risch "*Die mykenischen Personennamen auf -e*" in *Tractata Mycenaea* 1987 p. 281- 298 (on the type *ku-ne* / *ku-ne-u*, among others); Hl. Hagen "*Die Diskussion um die Schreibweise von Ζῆν (') im homerischen Epos*" in *Glotta* 72 1995 p. 98-104; J. Martínez García "*Quod licet Ioui, non licet boui, Zum griechischen Namen Ζεύς*" in HS 110 1997 p. 211-214 (He asserts that the accentuation of βοῦς is regular; that of Ζεύς is secondary); Concerning διόσδοτος: → LfgrE *s.v.* — On the Vedic paradigm: → Mayrhofer EWAia I *s.v. dyáv-* (the singular accented form *divám* RV VIII 34, 1-15 in Aufrecht *Hymnen des RV* 1877 erroneous for *dívam*: → Wackernagel / Debrunner *Ai. Gramm.* II / 2 1954 p. 142; Oldenberg *Noten 1909-1912* ad loc.) — Concerning what is called an *Āmreḍita*-compound, *divédive*: → W. Dressler in *GS Brandenstein* 1968 p. 39ff. (with Greek and Armenian parallels); further, cf. Hajnal in F 310 § 5. — Concerning Anatolian (including whether *-eu̯-* is preserved or reproduced): → Neu *AHitt. Glossar* 1983 p. 168 with note 496; Rieken *Nom. Stammbildung* 1999 p. 35-39.

6b) Concerning **gʷóu̯-* 'cow': — PIE: **gʷou̯-* was initially an acrodynamic root with a strong stem **gʷou̯-* vs. weak stem **gʷeu̯-*: → Mayrhofer EWAia p. 478-480 (with the discussion in fine print). Only in the post-Proto-Indo-European period did **gʷou̯-* approach **di̯eu̯-* in terms of form, a fact which gave weight to the idea that **gʷóu̯-* should be categorized as a second Proto-Indo-European diphthong stem along with **di̯eu̯-*. The reconstruction **gʷéh₃u-*, which competes with **gʷou̯-*, was not least inspired by **néh₂u-* (→ Rix *Hist. Gramm. d. Gr.* 1976 p. 147; further, cf. Leukart *Frühgr. Nomina* 1994 p. 49 note 7), but the old and well-documented acc. sg. **gʷōm* betrays the true origin of **gʷou̯-*: → J. Schindler in *Sprache* 19 1973 p. 155. — Latin: → Leumann LLFL 1977 p. 357. — Greek: The classical paradigm is βοῦς βοῦν / βοός etc. On the accent in βοῦς vs. Ζεύς, cf. J. Martínez García in § 6a. In Homer, cf. also βῶν (1x) 'leather shield' and εὔβων (from Homeric hymns) 'having a wealth of cows': → Meier-Brügger *Gr. Sprachw.* II 1992 p. 75. Concerning Mycenaean: → Aura Jorro *DMic.* II 1993 p. 207. — Vedic: → Mayrhofer EWAia I p. 478-480 *s.v. gáv-*.

6c) In the case of PIE *$néh_2u$- 'barge, bark' a paradigm is often asserted with strong nom. sg. *$néh_2u$-s, strong acc. sg. *$néh_2u$-m (secondarily also *$néh_2$u̯-m̥) vs. weak gen. sg. *n̥h_2u̯-és or rather *n°h_2u̯-és. One should also consider the possibility of an initially acrodynamic paradigm with strong *$nóh_2u$- vs. weak *$néh_2u$-: → B. Vine in *Kratylos* 45 2000 p. 67. The weak stem *neh_2u- (the genitive singular of which must originally have been *$néh_2u$-s) would then have been secondarily inflected with a stressed ending, producing the new gen. sg. *neh_2u̯-és. — The Proto-Indo-European *-u-* stem behaves, in the individual languages after the dropping of the laryngeal before *u* (but not before *u̯*), to some degree like a diphthong. That is why the *-u-* stem *$néh_2u$- formally joined to some extent with the two nominal forms *di̯eu̯- and *g^wou̯-. Taking this secondary optic as a starting point, older research often argues contrary to the reality. — Greek: The classical paradigm is: nom. sg. ναῦς acc. sg. ναῦν dat. pl. ναυσί (all these forms < *neh_2u-) vs. gen. sg. Dor. νᾱός / Ion. νηός (Epic-Ionic also features the secondary nom. sg. νηῦς) / Att. (with quantitative metathesis) νεώς (all forms < *neh_2u̯-). However, the secondary Ionic nominative form νηῦς may not, as was earlier believed, be traced back to *nā́u̯s. — Vedic: nom. sg. *náuṣ* is not derived from *nā́us, but rather from < *ná.us <*náHus < *$néh_2us$; the meter of RV V 59.2 suggests a two-syllable quality (→ Oldenberg *Noten*); the oblique cases, including the accusative singular, are constructed from the stem *nāv-*. For further information on this problem in Vedic: → Mayrhofer EWAia II p. 59 *s.v. náu-*.

F 319. In addition to the two PIE nominal classes of the proterodynamic or hysterodynamic pattern, at least two others may be discerned using evidence in IE languages, namely an acrodynamic and a holodynamic pattern, cf. F 320-322. The first depiction and classical account of these four classes is: → J. Schindler in *Fachtagung Regensburg* 1973 [1975] p. 262f.; Rix *Hist. Gramm. d. Gr.* 1976 p. 123. For current discussion: → Rieken *Nom. Stammbildung* 1999 p. 5-7. The following depiction is based upon A. J. Nussbaum's Berlin *Blockseminar* of March, 2001.

As has been shown above, the individual facts can only be adequately assessed from an overal nominal concept, cf. F 317 § 8 (with *dóru- and *$h_2$ói̯u-) and F 318 § 6 (with *g^wóu̯- and *$néh_2u$-), in which the facts lead to contradictory assessments. It is important to recognize that individual paradigms were restructured in the course of time.

I shall first give an overview of all four Proto-Indo-European classes, using, for the sake of simplification only the 'dynamic' ablaut patterns. The exceptional status of the locative has to be noted.

I) The acrodynamic nominal class (cf. F 320):

	W	S	E
strong	*ó* or *ḗ*	*z*	*z*
weak	*é*	*z*	*z*
loc.	*z*	*é*	

II) The proterodynamic nominal class (cf. F 317):

	W	S	E
strong	*é*	*z*	*z*
weak	*z*	*é*	*z*
loc.	*z*	*ḗ*	

III) The hysterodynamic nominal class (cf. F 318):

	W	S	E
strong	*z*	*é*	*z*
weak	*z*	*z*	*é*
loc.	*z*	*é*	

IV) The amphi- or holodynamic nominal class (cf. F 321):

	W	S	E
strong	*é*	*o*	*z*
weak	*z*	*z*	*é*
loc.	*z*	*é*	

F 320. The acrostatic, or acrodynamic nominal class I.

This class reveals the following accent schema:

	W	S	E
strong	*W̲*	*S*	*E*
weak	*W̲*	*S*	*E*

The ablaut in the root syllable produces the differentiation between strong and weak stems. — The normal schema is strong *-ó-* vs. weak *-é-*. J. Schindler showed (→ BSL 67/1 1972 p. 32-36) that a part of the root nouns belongs to this class, namely the type with the strong stem **dóm-*

vs. weak stem *_dém-_, cf. § 1 below. Depending upon their content, these root nouns may be considered, according to Schindler p. 36, partially as "_substantifs féminins à valeur résultative ou passive_," and partially as "_noms d'agent (substantifs et adjectifs), souvent avec une nuance itérative_." The amphidynamic root nouns may be distinguished from these acrostatic root nouns, cf. § 3 below. It is worth noting that individual acrostatic root nouns secondarily became amphidynamic, cf. PIE *_ḱu̯on-_ vs. weak *_ḱun-'_ instead of exspected *_ḱu̯én-_ 'dog' (details on the subject in Schindler, _ibid._ p. 33-36). — In addition to the class with root vowel _-ó-_ vs. _-é-_, a separate sub-class may be distinguished with the schema root vowel strong _-ḗ-_ vs. weak _-é-_ (or _-ó-_), cf. § 2 below.

1a) A prime example for the type _-ó-_ vs. _-é-_ in the root syllable: — PIE *_dom-_ 'house' (details: → Mayrhofer EWAia I p. 697 _s.v. dám-_ and 699 _s.v. dámpati-_; R. Lipp in LIV 1998 p. 98 note 1 suggests tracing *_dom-_ back to *_dom_h_2_-_, because of the verbal form *_dem_h_2_-_ 'to unite, to build', cf. L 330; however the addition of h_2 is not mandatory; on the acc. sg. see also L 303):

		PIE	ancient IE languages
strong	nom. sg. acc. sg.	*_dóm-s_ *_dṓm_ < *_dóm-m_	 Arm. _tun_; Gr. δῶ
weak	gen. sg.	*_dém-s_ ⇒ *_dm̥-és_	used in Gr. δεσ(πότης) and in Ved. _dámpati-_ Arm. _tan_
	loc. sg.	*_dém-i_	Ved. _dáme_ (with athematic _-e_?)

1b) A further example for the type with _-ó-_ vs. _-é-_ in the root syllable: — PIE *_nó_k^{w}_-t-_ 'night' (for details: → Rieken _Nom. Stammbildung_ 1999 p. 128f.; the noun represents the verbal abstract noun corresponding to PIE *_ne_k^{w}_-_ 'to dawn': → Mayrhofer EWAia II p. 2f.):

		PIE	IE
strong	nom. sg. acc. sg.	*_nó_k^{w}_-t- s_ *_nó_k^{w}_-t-m̥_	Lat. _nox_
weak	gen. sg.	*_né_k^{w}_-t-s_	Hitt. _nekut_^{s}
loc.	loc. sg.	*_né_k^{w}_-t_	

2) PIE strong *_i̯ḗ_k^{w}_-r̥_ vs. weak *_i̯ó_k^{w}_-n̥-_ 'liver' suggest a separate sub-class, cf. F 314 § 6 and 8.

3) In addition to the acrodynamic root nouns of the type strong *-ó-* vs. weak *-é-* in the root syllable (cf. § 1), a second group of root nouns of the type strong *-é-* vs. weak *-z-* may be demonstrated: → J. Schindler in BSL 67/1 1972 p. 36-38. This type falls under the category of 'amphidynamic' nouns, cf. F 321 § 3. A prime example is **di̯eu̯-* 'sky, sky god, day' with the strong stem **di̯éu̯-* vs. weak stem **diu̯-´*, cf. F 318 § 6. In terms of content, according to Schindler (p. 38) one finds "*noms d'actions*" and "*noms d'agent tirés de verbes d'état*."

F 321. The amphidynamic and the holodynamic nominal class IV.

The amphidynamic paradigm is characterized by its direct accent transfer from the root to the ending: The full grade root with zero grade ending is correspondingly exchanged with the zero grade root and its full grade ending. This exchange is typical for a part of the root nouns. However, when, along with the root, a suffix is also added, and thus a locative singular with a stressed full grade suffix, then the whole is to be considered a holodynamic ablaut pattern: → J. Schindler in *Fachtagung Regensburg* 1973 [1975] p. 262f.

A schematic depiction of the amphi- and holokinetic accent pattern (the former with W+E; the latter with W+S+E):

	W	S	E
strong	$\underline{W}$	*S*	*E*
weak	*W*	*S*	$\underline{E}$
loc. sg.	*W*	$\underline{S}$	*E*

1) The Proto-Indo-European word for 'earth' furnishes the classic example of a holodynamic ablaut paradigm (→ Mayrhofer EWAia I p. 424f. with further information on details; a central work concerning all issues associated with this word is given by J. Schindler in *Sprache* 23 1977 p. 31; on the acc. sg. see L 303):

		PIE	IE
strong	nom. sg. acc. sg.	**d*^{h}*éǵ*^{h}*ōm* **d*^{h}*éǵ*^{h}*ōm* < **d*^{h}*éǵ*^{h}*om-m*	Hitt. *te-e-kán*; Gr. χθ-ών Ved. *kṣā́m*
weak	gen. sg.	**d*^{h}*ǵ*^{h}*m-és* ⇒**d*$^{h\circ}$*ǵ*^{h}*m-és* ⇒**ǵ*^{h}*m̥-és* ⇒**ǵ*^{h}*m-és*	 Hitt. *ták-na-a-aš* cf. Gr. χαμ-αί Ved. *jmás*

loc. sg.	*$d^h$$\acute{g}^h$*ém* ⇒ *$\acute{g}^h$*ð ém*	
		Ved. *kṣámi*; Gr. initial χθ-

2) Further examples of the holodynamic class are furnished by non-neuter (animate) simplicia of the type PIE fem. **$h_2$eu̯s-os-* 'dawn redness' with PIE strong nom. sg. **$h_2$éu̯s-ōs* (cf. Hom. Gr. ἠώς f., cf. L 310) and weak gen. sg. **$h_2$us-s-és* (cf. Ved. *uṣás*) 'dawn redness,' and further similar *-r/n-* and *-men-* stems, e.g. Ved. *áśman-* m. 'stone, stone for slinging' < PIE **h_2éḱ-mon-* the archaic weak gen. abl. sg. *áś-n-as* 'stone' < IE**h_2ḱ-mn-és* (secondarily with simplification of the medial triple consonance and with stable accent on the first syllable; details: → Mayrhofer EWAia I p. 137f.). Concerning the neuter *-r/n-* and *-men-* stems, cf. F 317 § 10. — In addition to the neuter collective paradigm (cf. **u̯édōr* 'water' in F 314 § 7), the active present/aorist *-nt-* participles also belong to the holodynamic nominal class, cf. **u̯éḱ-ont-* vs. **uḱ-n̥t-´* in F 217 § 1. — Cf. also *-u̯os-* in F 217 § 2 and *-i̯os-* in F 325 § 1a.

3) In contrast, the amphidynamic root nouns (i.e. root nouns consisting of a root and an ending, but not suffix) have a stressed full grade root and a zero grade unstressed ending when the stem is strong, and an unstressed zero grade root and stressed full grade ending when the stem is weak, cf. **di̯éu̯-* vs. **diu̯-´* in F 320 § 3.

F 322. A mesodynamic ablaut paradigm should have the following schema:

	W	S	E
strong	*W*	*<u>S</u>*	*E*
weak	*W*	*<u>S</u>*	*E*

It is possible that the PIE fem. of the type **-é-h_2-* = Gr. τιμ-ή 'honor' = Ved. (AV) *īṣ-ā́-* 'rule' may be traced to this schema: → Rix *Hist. Gramm. d. Gr.* 1976 p. 123. However, the possibility may not be excluded that these feminine forms featured in fact suffixal ablauts too, cf. I. Hajnal in L 334 § 3.

The four nominal classes compiled in F 319 have yet to be thoroughly researched. — An interesting question concerns the importance of the change from one class to another, cf. 'water' in F 314 § 7 above. The change clearly serves what is called 'internal derivation.' In contrast to what is called 'external suffixal derivation,' this takes place without affecting the word other than changing the accent position, e.g. Gr. adj. γλαυκός 'light blue, sparkling' vs. the proper noun Γλαῦκος. — Since

Schindler's research (→ *Wurzelnomen* 1972 and cf. F 315 § 1 above), the root nouns featuring both PIE accent types (acrostatic and amphikinetic) represent a particularly interesting group, cf. F 320. Lastly: → K.-H. Mottausch in *HS* 113 2000 p. 29-52. — The classes are further important for the understanding of the suffix system named after W. Caland, cf. W 206.

5. Formal Characteristics of the Adjective

F 323. The dimension of gender is not connected with the lexeme in the case of adjectives. On the contrary, adjectives are capable of forming masculine, feminine, and neuter forms in order to show congruence, cf. F 301.

As a rule, adjectives may accept all three sets of endings. However, in IE languages, there are also adjectives with only two endings, cf. § 3 below.

1) The majority of adjectives have the *-o*-stem, among which I include verbal adjectives and compound adjectives, e.g. PIE **dei̯u̯-ó-* 'belonging to the sky(god), heavenly,' cf. PIE **k̑lu-tó-* 'hear, heard named, famous,' cf. Ved. *an-udr-á-* 'waterless.' The corresponding feminine forms feature PIE **-eh$_2$-* (>*-ā-* in the IE languages), cf. F 312.

2) But there are also adjectives (again, including verbal adjectives and compound adjectives) with *-i-* and *-u-* stems, and also with consonant stems, e.g. PIE **su̯éh$_2$du-* 'sweet' (= Lat. *svāvis* < **su̯ādu̯-i-*; Gr. ἡδύς; Ved. *svādú-*) and PIE **bʰér-o-nt-* 'carrying.' — In this group, the suffix **-ih$_2$-* (in weak cases, **-i̯éh$_2$-*) is applied to the feminine forms. The complex suffix **-ih$_2$-* is taken from *-h$_2$-* forms of *-i-* stems, cf. W 204 § 1. The exact Proto-Indo-European form of these feminina is not clear. Cf. the contradiction: Gr. ἡδεῖα < **-éu̯-ih$_2$* vs. Ved. *svādvī́* < **-u̯-ih$_2$*. The isolated Greek fem. πίειρα = Ved. *pī́varī-* < **piH-u̯ér-ih$_2$-* form, which belongs to Gr. πίων = Ved. *pī́van-* 'fat' is evidence for the advanced age of the Gr. -ειᾰ- form and thus for an ancient feminine form with a strong stem **-éu̯-ih$_2$* vs. weak stem **-u-i̯éh$_2$-*. The Vedic strong *-vī́* < **-u̯-ih$_2$* would then have developed secondarily from the weak stem.

3) Individual ancient IE *-o*-stem adjectives and compounds conspicuously avoid the feminine marker **-e-h$_2$-*, e.g. the Greek adjectives with two endings. For an introductory overview of the examples (I shall name

here only πάτριος 'fatherly,' which usually has three endings, but sometimes also has only two, e.g. with a feminine in Euripides *Helena* 222 χθόνα πάτριον): → Kühner / Blass *Ausführliche Gramm. d. Gr. Sprache* I / 1 1890 p. 535ff. Also helpful is Wackernagel *Kl. Schr.* I 1969 (in a work from 1919) p. 488 and Kastner *Adjektive* 1967 (in which the auther depicts the general issues of the subject).

F 324. Adjectives form the basis for modal adverbs: In ancient IE languages, modal adverbs are generally instrumental singular forms, but also sometimes adverbial fossilized nominative or accusative forms.

Latin: — Cf. the type *ben-e* 'good' < **du̯en-ēd*. However, the further pre-history of **-ēd* is not clear, because in Proto-Italic the ablative and intrumental cases merged syncretically, with the better characterized ablative form becoming dominant. From the point of view of content, however, an understanding of the adverbial form **-ēd* as an old instrumental **-ē* (<**-eh₁*) seems likely, which secondarily received the additional *-d* from the ablative in the course of the Proto-Italic syncretism mentioned above. In contrast, the type *aliter* < **aliteros* 'otherwise' is a fossilized nominative singular form. For more information: → Leumann LLFL 1977 p. 499ff.; Meiser *Laut- und Formenlehre* 1998 p. 155.

Greek: — Cf. the type δικαίως 'according to use and custom, appropriate,' which is usually understood as an *s*-extension of the instrumental case with *-ō*: → Risch *Wortbildung* 1974 p. 362; further: → Rix *Hist. Gramm. d. Gr.* 1976 p. 170.

Vedic (concerning the type *badhrám jī́vantas* 'happily living,' among others, as an adverb that is actually a fixed accusative singular neuter form): → Delbrück *Ai. Syntax* 1888 p. 185f.; further: → Thumb / Hauschild *Handbuch des Sanskrit* I / 2 1959 p. 173ff.

F 325. The adjective in its natural, or 'positive' state may be made comparative and superlative by the addition of suffixes.

The Proto-Indo-European suffixes **-i̯os-* (sometimes with the ablaut **-is-*) and **-tero-* mark the comparative, or a difference of grade between two compared values: → *Metzler Lexikon Sprache* 1993 p. 318f. *s.vv. Komparation* and *Komparativ*. PIE **-i̯os-* is the basis for what is called the primary comparative forms (cf. § 1a-1d); PIE **-tero-* is the basis for the secondary comparative forms.

The superlative marks the highest grade among two compared values: → *Metzler Lexikon Sprache* 1993 p. 620. Proto-Indo-European features no proper suffix for the superlative. Ancient PIE forms such as *-to-*, *-th₂o-*

and *-m̥h₂o-* recall the ordinal numbers (cf. F 503) as they developed from them. The ordinal numbers were often used to mark the concluding, and most important elements of a series, thus receiving superlative traits: → Benveniste *Noms d'agent* 1948 p. 144ff.; Risch *Kleine Schriften* 1981 p. 684ff. — Each of the individual IE languages reveals its own typical characteristics. Suggestions for further reading: → Seiler *Steigerungsformen* 1950; Szemerényi *Einführung* 1990 p. 203-214.

1a) In the primary comparative form, the comparative suffix PIE **-i̯os-* (with ablaut **-is-*; the ablaut pattern is holodynamic, cp. F 321 § 2) replaces the positive suffix directly following the (generally) *full grade* root of the adjective stem, e.g. Lat. positive *magnus* (i.e. *mag-no-*) 'great' with comparative *maior* (< **mag-i̯ōs-*; while the *a* in the root is short, the syllable is counted as long because of its double consonant; clever school books thus often cite *māior* 'greater,' although it is not completely correct) and *mag-is* 'more'; Gr. positive κακ-ό- 'bad' with the comparative κακ-ίων 'worse'; Ved. positive *náv-a-* 'new, fresh, young' with the comparative *náv-yas-* / *náv-īyas-* 'new, newer, newest (in case forms such as the accusative singular neuter, instrumental, and dative) anew.' — The form PIE **-i̯os-* varies allophonically with PIE **-ii̯ō̆s* (which replaces it in nominative singular masculine and feminine forms with the structure *KV̄.K-* and *KVR.K-*; whereas, according to rules of phonetics, **-i̯os-* is expected in forms with three or more syllables), cf. L 218 § 1 on Siever's Law. — Evidence seems to suggest that the suffix *-i̯os-* belongs to the group of forms derived from *-es*-stems, which feature masculine/feminine and neuter forms, e.g. Lat. m. *dolor* (stem **dolh₁-ōs-*: from the PIE verbal root **delh₁-* 'to hew, to split') 'pain' vs. n. *genus* (stem **genh₁-es-*) 'gender.' The form in question, *-i̯os-* should then be considered a complex suffix, which was initially in pre-PIE time formed as *-es*-derivative from *-i̯e-* verbal stems, but then, when newly re-analyzed, could be linked directly to the verbal root: root-*i̯e-* + *-es-* > root- + *-i̯es-*. If Gr. κάλλος n. 'beauty' may be traced back to **kal-i̯es-*, then it is possible that καλλίων 'more beautiful' is a remnant form of m./f. **kal-i̯os-*. (However, one must then accept that the expected 'normal' comparative form **kallos-* also brought about the initial *kall-* in the case of the variant form **kal-ii̯os-*.) Indeed, from the starting point of nominal sentences of the type '*X *még-i̯os-*,' 'X is greatness,' comparative forms such as 'X is greater than,' or 'X is as great as' may have developed: → N. Berg "*Einige Betrachtungen über den indogermanischen Komparationskasus*" in NTS 18 1958 p. 202-230; P. K. Andersen in *Kolloquium Syntax Pavia* 1979 [1980] p. 225ff. — In the superlative, the zero grade **-is-* is connected with slightly varying complex suffixes such as **-is-to-*, **-is-th₂o-* oder **-is-m̥h₂o-*, which originate from the ordinal numbers, cf. § 2c.

1b) A prime example in Latin is furnished by the positive *magnus* 'great,' the comparative *maior* and the superlative *maximus*. — A few remarks: The lengthened grade *-i̯ōs-* is generalized in Latin, with the exception of the nominative/accusative neuter form with *-ius* < *-i̯os*, cf. *maius*. The paradigm changes its appearance through rhotacism (cf. L 309 § 1): From forms such as nom. sg. m. **maiōs* and gen. sg. m. **maiōsis* first developped **maiōs* and *maiōris* (the latter with *-r-* < *-s-*). Through analogy to the gen. *-ōr-is*, to the nominative form was added *-ōr* (and subsequently shortened around 200 B.C. to *-ŏr*: → Leumann LLFL 1977 p. 111). — The superlative form then becomes **-is-m̥(h₂)o-* (cf. among others *maximus* < **mag-isemo-*) in Italic (and Celtic): → Leumann LLFL 1977 p. 497f.; Meiser *Laut- und Formenlehre* 1998 p. 152f.

1c) Prime examples in Greek: — positive κρατύς (thus, in Homer, among others; but in prose, most often κρατερός instead) 'strong' with the comparatives Ion. κρέσσων, Att. κρείττων and superlative κράτιστος. — A few remarks: Mycenaean comparatives are purely based on the *s*-stem. In intervocalic position, the *s* becomes aspirated as *-h-*, e.g. nom. pl. m./f. *me-zo-e* i.e. *meg-ʲoh-es* 'greater.' Alphabetic Greek, on the other hand, reveals an *-n-* paradigm that is mixed with *-s-* forms, e.g. Att. nom. sg. m./f. κακ-τ̓ων, gen. sg. m./f. κακ-τ̓ον-ος, dat. sg. m./f. κακ-τ̓ον-ι, but acc. sg. m./f. κακ-τ̓ω (*-s*-stem: < **-ī́i̯oh-a*; nom./acc. pl. m./f. κακ-τ̓ους (again *-s-* stem: < **-ī́i̯oh-es*), gen. pl. m./f. κακτ̓όνων, dat. pl. m./f. κακ-τ̓οσι (which may be interpreted both as an old *-s-* stem form of the type dat. pl. γένεσι [*-es-* stem with *-esi* < *-es-si*] and also as an *-n-* stem of the type δαίμοσι [*-mon-* stem with *-mosi*; contains analogously formed *-osi* in place of **-asi* < **-n̥-si*]). For more information concerning the Attic Greek paradigm: → Threatte *Attic* II 1996 p. 311f. — Researchers are split on the origin of the Greek *-n-* forms: They are either a post-Mycenaean Greek-internal innovation, or the result of a long-standing coexistence of *-i̯os-* and *-is-on-* stems. For information on the former theory (to which I subscribe): → Risch *Wortbildung* 1974 p. 89 which refers to the research of O. Szemerényi; for information on the latter theory: → Rix *Hist. Gramm. d. Gr.* 1976 p. 167: M. Peters in *Festschrift Risch* 1986 p. 312 note 36. — The active coexistence of *-i̯os-* and *-ii̯ŏs* (Sievers' Rule, cf. L 218 § 1) was disposed of in Greek, however the suffix pair *-i̯os-* and *-ii̯os-* may be traced back to them, cf. indeed Myc. nom. pl. *ka-zo-e* i.e. *kak-ʲoh-es* 'worse,' but Att. κακ-τ̓ον-ες, cf. indeed γλύσσων

(Xenophanes) with *-ssōn* < *-k-i̯ōn* 'sweeter,' but γλυκ-ίων (in Homer's Odyssey). Material for further discussion: → J.-L. Perpillou in BSL 69 / 1 1974 p. 99ff. — A further problem, specific to Attic Greek, is the lengthening of the syllable preceding *-i̯os-*, e.g. Att. *-īi̯on-* vs. Ion. *-ii̯on-*, cf. Att. μείζων vs. Ion. μέζων 'better', cf. Att. κρείττων vs. Ion. κρέσσων 'stronger' (where Ion. *-ss-* and Att. *-tt-* < *-ti̯-*: → Risch *Kleine Schriften* 1981 p. 506). According to information provided by forms like ἆσσον 'nearer' and μᾶλλον 'more, rather' with Attic *-ā-* and not *-ē-*, the development cannot be ancient (an old Ionic-Attic *-ā-* would have been affected by the *ā* > *ē* vowel shift, cf. L 205). Risch (*Wortbildung* 1974 p. 89) sees a replacement for the initially common full grade of the root in this lengthening. Other full grade forms are κρέσσων (< **krét-i̯ōn*: but superlative κράτ-ισ-το-ς < **kr̥t-is-to-*) and ὀλείζων (concerning Attic inscriptions: → Threatte Attic II 1996 p. 309) 'smaller in number' (< **-lei̯g-i̯ōn*: but positive ὀλίγ-ο-). — In the superlative, the Greek is *-is-to-*. The form is attested as early as the Mycenaean period, cf. nom. pl. n. *me-ki-ta* i.e. *meg-ista*.

1d) A prime example in Vedic: — positive *tavás-* 'strong, powerful' with comparative *táv-īyas-*, and *táv-yas-* 'stronger, more powerful.' For the superlative, cf. *yáv-iṣṭha-* 'recently, recently born' from *yúv-an-* (< PIE **h_2i̯éu̯-$h_3$on-*. For details: → Mayrhofer EWAia II p. 413; concerning the suffix, cf. W 204 § 4) 'young.' — Comparative: While the coexistence of *-īyas-* and *-yas-* is of post-PIE origin, it can (as can Greek) in its essentials be traced back to PIE allophonic arrangement mentioned at the beginning (1a). The cause of the lengthening of *ī* is not clear, although one reason could be an origin in seṭ-roots, cf. just above *távīyas-* < **táu̯iHi̯as-* with laryngeal metathesis < **táu̯Hii̯as-* < PIE **téu̯h_2-ii̯os-*. — The superlative in Vedic is *-iṣ-ṭha-* < **-is-th$_2$o-*.

2a) The secondary comparative form uses the PIE suffix **-(t)ero-*. — Good examples include Gr. δίκαιος 'just' with δικαιό-τερος and δικαιό-τατος and Ved. *tavás-* 'strong, powerful' with *tavás-tara-* and *tavás-tama-*. For information on Latin, cf. § 1b above.

2b) The PIE suffix **-(t)ero-* is the *-o-* adjective form of adverbs ending in PIE **-(t)r̥* and **-(t)er*: → Risch *Wortbildung* 1974 p. 91f.; G. Pinault in *Dialectes indo-aryennes* 1986 [1989] p. 42f. (concerning the type Ved. *sanu-tár* 'gone'). Examples from IE languages include Lat. *sub* (< **supV*) 'under,' *sup-er* 'over' and *sup-er-o-* 'found above' (cf. *superī* 'the higher gods, the gods in heaven'); Gr. πρό 'at the front, forward' and πρό-τερο-ς 'toward the front, earlier'; Ved. *úpa* 'to, up, upon, etc.,' *upár-i* 'over, above, upward' and *úpar-a-* 'beneath, nearer, further back, later.' Adverbs and adjectives that were derived from them were capable of marking relative contrasts (e.g. in the case of opposites or selection from a pair), cf. Gr. πότερος 'which (of two),' cf. Myc. Gr., *a-te-ro* i.e. *hateron* 'the other of two in a unity' (< PIE **sm̥-ter-o-* from PIE **sem-* 'one'; Cf. Gr. ἕτερος 'other' with an assimilated word-initial vowel; the vocalism that is still visible in Mycenaean is retained, for example, in Att. ἅτερος, i.e. ὁ ἅτερος: → Threatte *Attic* II 1996 p. 345f.). One can only then presume that individual local and temporal formations gave the impulse for the development of **-tero-* as a common suffix for comparative forms in both Greek and Vedic: → Risch *Wortbildung* 1974 p. 94f.

2c) In the case of the superlative of the secondary comparative form, one finds again formations from among the ordinal numbers, see the beginning of F 325. — Latin: — In Latin and Celtic, one finds **-m̥(h₂)o-*. Details: → Meiser *Laut- und Formenlehre* 1998 p. 152f. — Greek: — Cf. already in Mycenaean nom. pl. *me-sa-to* i.e. *mes-atoi̯* 'of intermediate measure' from the positive **mes(s)o-* < **medʰi̯o-*. The model here is *dekato-* 'tenth' < **dék̑m̥to-*. However, the Greek *-tato-* is common. — Vedic: — Cf. Ved. *madhy-amá-* 'intermediate, most intermediate.' The model is *saptamá-* 'seventh.' However, the Vedic *-tama-* is common.

3) While in the cases mentioned in § 1 and § 2 the same adjective stem is generally used, there was also the possibility, also in Proto-Indo-European, of using stems for positive forms that were different from those for comparative and superlative forms. Sometimes, positive, comparative, and superlative forms each used a different form with a similar meaning by suppletion, e.g. Lat. *bonus* (OL *du̯enos*) vs. *melior* (from which was lexicalized *mulier* 'woman' < **ml̥-i̯es-* 'better' [original term for mistress: → Meiser *Laut- und Formenlehre* 1998 p. 64]; In Greek, *mel-* corresponds to the word group μάλα 'very,' μᾶλλον 'more, rather,' μάλιστα 'most') vs. *optimus* (root *op-* 'power, strength'), cf. on the one hand ἀγαθός vs. βελτίων / βέλτιστος, on the other ἀγαθός vs. ἀμείνων vs. ἄριστος. Suggestions for further reading: → Seiler *Steigerungsformen* 1950 p. 27ff.; W. Hock "*Zur Suppletion beim Adjektiv im Altgriechischen und Germanischen*" in *FS Seebold* 1999 p. 207-223.

4) Further sources: — General: → P. K. Andersen *Word Order Typology* 1983. — Germanic: → Bammesberger *Urgerm. Nomen* 1990 p. 230ff. — Hittite: → P. Cotticelli-Kurras in Graz 2000 p. 33-45. — Celtic: → W. Cowgill in *IE and IEs* 1970 p. 114ff.

D. Pronouns

1. General Information

F 400. Pronouns are among the most important deictic and anaphoric elements of the sentence. Only pronouns share the important grammatical category 'person' with the verb, cf. S 301. Contrarily to the 3rd person "*celui qui est absent, la non-personne,*" the 1st person marks "*le 'je' qui énonce*" and the 2nd person, "*le 'tu' auquel 'je' s'adresse.*" The corresponding plural forms are more complex. Whereas the 3rd person permits a true plural, the 1st person plural "*nous*" is either to be interpreted as "*moi + vous*" or as "*moi + eux*"; "*le 'nous' annexe au 'je' une globalité indistincte d'autres personnes.*" And for the 2nd person plural: "*'vous,' qu'il s'agisse du 'vous' collectif ou du 'vous' de politesse, on reconnaît une généralisation du 'tu'*": → E. Benveniste "*Structure des relations de personne dans le verbe*" in Benveniste *Problèmes* I 1966 (essay from 1946) p. 225ff.

1) It has been shown that Proto-Indo-European had, on the one hand, what are called single-gender personal pronouns, including the possessive pronouns derived from them, and, on the other hand, what are called the double-gender interrogative and indefinite pronouns as well as, in ancient IE languages, the triple-gender demonstrative and relative pronouns. The conservation of the original forms in the IE languages varies. The most changes affected demonstrative pronouns, which could lose their referential effect, and then must be newly determined.

2) In comparison with the normal order and enclisis in a nominal or verbal syntagma, the position of emphasis at the beginning of a sentence increases the pronominal information. The difference between enclisis and emphasis (orthotony) was not manifested exclusively by the presence (or absence) of the accent, but rather also morphologically, i.e. through the shortened form in the case of enclitica as opposed to the longer stressed form.

3) Pronouns played an important role in the development of nominal inflection. Their influence on the *o*-stems is unmistakable, cf. F 311.

4) Suggestions for further reading: — a) general: Benveniste (see above); Wackernagel *Vorlesungen* II 1928 p. 75ff.; *Metzler Lexikon Sprache* 1993 Sp. 487 *s.v.* '*Pronomen.*' — b) Proto-Indo-European: → Krahe *Idg. Sprachw.* II

1969 p. 38-46; Szemerényi *Einführung* 1990 p. 215-234; R. S. P. Beekes *"The origin of the Indo-European pronominal inflection"* in *FS Polomé* 1988 p. 73-87; F. Bader "*Les pronoms dans les langues indo-européennes*" in *Mémoires de la Société de Linguistique de Paris* N.S. 1 1990 p. 23-35.— c) Latin: → Leumann LLFL 1977 p. 460-484; Meiser *Laut- und Formenlehre* 1998 p.156-169. — d) Greek: → Rix *Hist. Gramm. d. Gr.* 1976 p. 174-189: Meier-Brügger *Gr. Sprachw.* II 1992 p. 85-93. — e) Vedic: → J. Wackernagel in Wackernagel / Debrunner *Ai. Grammatik* III 1930 p. 431-594. — f) Anatolian: E. Neu "*Zu einigen Pronominalformen des Hethitischen*" in *FS Puhvel* I 1997 p. 139-169. — g) Celtic: → Schrijver *Celtic Pronouns and Particles* 1997. — For more information, see the sections on the individual groups below, particularly in F 401 § 4.

2. Personal and Possessive Pronouns

F 401. Personal pronouns are part of the hereditary lexicon of the IE languages. For information on syntax, cf. S 400.

1) However incomplete, the following table shows the most important characteristics of PIE personal pronouns, which do not distinguish between genders. — Thus, in the case of 'I' (speaker) and 'you' (interlocutor) there is no distinction between masculine and feminine gender. — The nominative is distinguished from other cases in having its own stem, cf. PIE nom. sg. *eǵ-óh$_2$ vs. acc. sg. PIE *m-ḗ. — Since every finite verb form automatically indicates the 'person' of the verb, the nominal pronoun forms are already adequately marked. — In comparison with the orthotonic forms, which are often strengthened by particles, the enclitic forms feature the minimal word stem and may be used in multiple cases, cf. orthotonic PIE nom. sg. *eǵ- with suffix -oh$_2$ or -h$_2$-óm vs. enclitic *m-oi̯ for gen. and dat. sg. — For the 3rd person, several demonstrative pronouns are possible. These are presented in F 405f. Only the 3 sg. reflexive pronoun is treated in § 3 below. Even externally, one may discern that PIE acc. sg. *se belongs to 1 sg. *me and 2 sg. *te.

	1 sg.	2 sg.	1 pl.	2 pl.
nom. sg.	*eǵ-óh$_2$	*túh$_2$	*u̯éi̯s	*i̯úHs
only stressed	*eǵh$_2$-óm			
acc. sg. encl.	*me	*te / *tu̯e	*nos	*u̯os
acc. sg. stressed	*mḗ	*tḗ	*n̥s-mé	*us-mé

gen. dat. sg. encl.	**moi̯*	**toi̯*		
gen. sg. stressed	**méne*	**téu̯e*		
dat. sg. stressed	**me-ǵ^{h}ei̯* **me-ǵ^{h}i̯-om*	**te-b^{h}ei̯* **te-b^{h}i̯-o*	**n̥s-mé-i*	**us-mé-i*

2) Details concerning Proto-Indo-European: — J. T. Katz (→ "*Archaische keltische Personalpronomina aus indogermanischer Sicht*" in *Fachtagung Innsbruck* 1996 [1998] p. 265-291;) asserts, based on oblique cases in Celtic material, the existence of an ending **-me* for the 1st person and an ending **-u̯e* for the 2nd person: In place of the commonly reconstructed 1 pl. **n̥s-mé* and 2 pl. **us-mé*, the author thus suggests a new 1 pl. **n̥s-me* vs. 2 pl. **us-u̯é* and consequently holds the balance in favor of **-me* in the 2nd person plural for secondary; thus, from this perspective the 2nd person singular form **tu̯e* is old (the *u̯* from **tu̯e* is generally seen as coming from the nominative **tu-H-*), and further **me* < **m-me*. — Latin: → Leumann LLFL 1977 p. 461ff.; Meiser *Laut- und Formenlehre* 1998 p. 156ff. (concerning dissimilation in Pre-PIE dat. sg. **me-b^{h}ei̯* to PIE **me-ǵ^{h}ei̯* etc.). — Details on Greek: → Rix *Hist. Gramm. d. Gr.* 1976 p. 176ff. The forms of the 1st and 2nd person plural are in Proto-Greek newly constructed on the basis of the acc. **n̥s-mé* and **us-mé*. For the 1 pl. cf. Aeol. nom. and acc. ἄμμε; in Att. cf. nom. ἡμεῖς <**hāmé+es* and acc. ἡμᾶς < ἡμέας < **hāme+as* (*-as* < **-n̥s*) (on **hāmé* and **ammé* <**n̥s-mé* cf. L 307 § 4). For the 2 pl. cf. Aeol. nom. and acc. ὔμμε and Att. nom. ὑμεῖς and acc. ὑμᾶς. Greek must also have featured the enclitic **nos-* at some point, evidence of which is the lexicalized adverb νόσ-φι 'separate from' < *'apart from us': → M. Meier-Brügger in MSS 48 1987 p. 179ff. — Details on Vedic: → J. Wackernagel in Wackernagel/ Debrunner *Ai. Gramm.* III 1930 p. 448ff.

3) The dative singular form of the reflexive pronoun is PIE **soi̯*, in accusative singular PIE **se* (encl.) 'himself,' cf. Latin *sē* (originating from the stressed form), Got. *si-k*. Particular IE languages have **su̯oi̯* and **su̯e*, cf. Gr. ἕ, Lesb. ϝε. According to J. T. Katz precisely this **s-u̯e* is regarded as ancien and **se* as secondary. In contrast, G. E. Dunkel connects **soi̯* / **se*, which he considers more ancient, with the demonstrative pronoun **so*: → *Fachtagung Leiden* 1987 [1992] p. 171ff. — PIE encl. **s-b^{h}i* > Gr. σ-φι; creation of a new paradigm with σφε and σφεῖς < *σφέ+ες etc.; already Myc. loc. pl. *me-ta-qe pe-i* i.e. *meta-k^{w}e sp^{h}ehi* 'in their

midst'. For more information on the Greek sp^h-: → Katz *Personal Pronouns* 1998 p. 226ff.

4) Further sources, particularly on personal pronouns (of course, see also the suggestions for further reading in F 400 § 4): → G. Schmidt *Personalpronomina* 1978; Seebold *Personalpronomina* 1984; S. Howe "The Personal Pronouns in the Germanic Languages, a study of personal pronoun morphology and change in the Germanic languages from the first records to the present day." Berlin / New York 1996 (= *Studia Linguistica Germanica* 43); J. Matzinger "*Zum Lokativ sg. des Personalpronomens der ersten Person im Altarmenischen*" in MSS 57 1997 p. 65-80; by the same author, "*Zu armenisch mek' 'wir'*" in HS 110 1997 p. 83-92; Katz *Personal Pronouns* 1998.

F 402. Already in the Proto-Indo-European period, possessive pronouns could be formed as *-o*-stem adjectives from personal pronouns. Contrary to the banal **-o*-suffix, the also used *-tero*-suffix originates from the comparative form, cf. F 325 § 2.

The following may be reconstructed: — For the 1 sg. PIE **m-o-* 'my' (cf. Greek ἐ-μός, in which *e-* comes from ἐ-γώ), but perhaps additionally **mei̯-o-* (derived from the locative, cf. Lat. *meus*). — For the 2 sg. PIE **tu̯-o-* 'your' (cf. Gr. Ion. Att. σός) and **teu̯-o-* (cf. Lat. *tuus*). — For the 1 pl. PIE **nos-tero-* 'our' (cf. Lat. *noster*) and **n̥s-mó-* (cf. Gr. ἁμός [Hom.: → LfgrE I Sp. 640f.] and ἡμέτερος [< **n̥smé-tero-*]). — For the 2 pl. PIE **u̯os-tero-* 'your' (cf. Lat. *vester* with *ve-* from *vo-*) and **us-mó-* (cf. Gr. ὑμός [Hom.] and ὑμέτερος [< **usmé-tero-*]). — For the 3 sg. reflexive PIE **su̯o-* 'his' (cf. Gr. ὅς) and **seu̯-o-* (cf. Lat. *suus*).

Further details: → Leumann LLFL 1977 p. 465f.; Meiser *Laut- und Formenlehre* 1998 p. 159; Rix *Hist. Gramm. d. Gr.* 1976 p. 181; J. Wackernagel in Wackernagel / Debrunner *Ai. Gramm.* III 1930 p. 492-494; Petit *Su̯e-* 1999.

3. Interrogative and Indefinite Pronouns

F 403. The substantive interrogative pronoun in Proto-Indo-European was $*k^wi$- (also with ablaut, $*k^wei̯$-). The *o*-stem $*k^wo$- (or, with ablaut, $*k^we$-) was used to fill adjectival functions. While the difference between 'who' and 'what' was central for the PIE substantive pronoun, within the meaning of 'who' there was no distinction between masculine and feminine. This absence is ancient and particularly plausible in Proto-Indo-European, in which presumably the feminine was only firmly established after the splitting off of Anatolian, cf. F 303 § 2.

While the sentence-initial orthotone forms mark questions such as 'who?,' 'what?,' 'from whom?,' 'whose?,' etc., the enclitic forms could be 'moderated' to form indefinite pronouns meaning, for example, 'whoever' or 'anyone,' etc.

The situation in IE languages varies. The range of application of *k^wi-* vs. *k^wo-* is difficult to determine, particularly since *k^wi-* and *k^wo-* were also used in restrictive relative clauses just as the appositive **Hi̯o*-. For information on the apparent connection of *k^wo-* with the copula *k^we*, cf. G. Dunkel in *FS Narten* 2000 p. 9-29. For further information, cf. F 404.

The following table serves to clarify a few points concerning the inflection of the substantive interrogative pronoun. The reconstructed forms are taken from Rix *Hist. Gramm. d. Gr.* 1976 p. 187. The present work is inappropriate for a discussion of the extent to which Rix's postulated differentiation of m./f. *k^wo-* (cf. Lat. *cuius* < *$k^wosi̯o$-*) from n. *k^we-* (cf. Avest. *cahiiā* mit *ca-* < **će-* < **ke-* <*k^we-*; concerning phonetic, cf. L 206 § 2) in the genitive and dative is conclusive. The genitive and dative forms are unthinkable without the influence of demonstrative pronoun inflection, cf. F 405.

	sg. m./f.	sg. n.	pl. m./f.	pl. n.
nom.	*k^wi-s*	*k^wi-d*	*$k^wéi̯$-es*	*k^wi-h_2*
acc.	*k^wi-m*	*k^wi-d*		
gen.	*$k^wó$-s(i̯)o*	*$k^wé$-s(i̯)o*		
dat.	*$k^wó$-sm-ōi̯*	*$k^wé$-sm-ōi̯*		
instr.	*k^wi-h_1*			

4. Relatives, Demonstratives, and Pronominals

F 404. The PIE relative pronoun *k^wo-* (also *k^wi-*) originates with interrogative pronouns, cf. F 403. It initially reveals restrictive meaning, i.e. meaning that reduces the reference span of the referent. The appositive (parenthetic) **Hi̯o*- on the other hand, has an entirely other origin. For more information on issues of content and syntax: → Hettrich *Hypotaxe* 1988 p. 776ff.; I. Hajnal "*Definite nominale Determination im Indogermanischen*" in IF 102 1997 p. 38-73. Concerning word-initial **Hi̯*-, cf. L 213 § 5. Concerning its sytactical properties, cf. S 205.

Suggestions for further reading on the IE languages and their individual characteristics: — a) PIE: → Szemerényi *Einführung* 1990 p. 220-224; ferner cf. F 311 § 4. — b) Latin (traces of PIE *$H\underset{\frown}{i}o$- are no longer attested in Proto-Italic; Latin interrogative/indefinite *quis quae quid* <*k^wi- vs. relative *quī quae quod* <*k^wo-): → Meiser *Laut- und Formenlehre* 1998 p. 164-167 (on p. 164, the terms 'appositive' and 'restrictive' are presumably falsely exchanged). — c) Greek (interrogative and indefinite τίς τί < *k^wi- [via acc. sg. τίν, i.e. τίν' = τίν-α formation of a secondary -*n*- stem] vs. relative ὅς ἥ ὅ < *$H\underset{\frown}{i}o$-): → Rix *Hist. Gramm. d. Gr.* 1976 p. 186f.; Meier-Brügger *Gr. Sprachw.* II 1992 p. 87 (concerning *$H\underset{\frown}{i}o$-) and p. 89f. (on the origin of τιν-); E. Risch in MSS 46 1985 p. 173-191 (on the Greek paradigm of *$H\underset{\frown}{i}o$-). — d) Vedic (interrogative/indefinite *ka*- and *ki*- vs. relative *ya*-): → Mayrhofer EWAia I p. 284f. concerning *ka*-, p. 347f. concerning *ki*-, p. 359 concerning *ku*- and Mayrhofer EWAia II p. 390 concerning *ya*-. — e) *$H\underset{\frown}{i}o$- and *k^wi- in further IE languages such as Balto-Slavic, Hittite, Luwian, Lycian, and Carian: → I. Hajnal l.c. at the beginning of the section; cf. also Chr. Koch in S 205 § 2.

F 405. Among demonstrative pronouns there are both those with a deictic function and those with an anaphoric function. Despite formal changes in individual IE languages, the situation in Proto-Indo-European is recognizable: → G. Klingenschmitt "*Erbe und Neuerung beim germanischen Demonstrativpronomen*" in *Althochdeutsch* I 1987 p. 169-189. Demonstrative pronouns formed the basis upon which articles were formed, cf. Classical Greek ὁ ἄνθρωπος, NHG *der Mensch.*

Literature on this complex of issues is quite involved: → Szemerényi *Einführung* 1990 p. 216-218; EWAhd II Sp. 589-599 *s.v.* '*der*' (featuring an amazing wealth of material on the IE field). Concerning the article in Greek: → Meillet *Aperçu* 1975 p. 187ff.; concerning the article in Armenian: → Ch. de Lamberterie in *Kolloquium Delbrück* Madrid 1994 [1997] p. 311ff.

One well-founded Proto-Indo-European demonstrative pronoun is **to*-, which features all three genders. The stem (with *e*-vocalism) for all feminine forms and for the neuter plural is PIE *$t\acute{e}$-h_2. A notable development in the nominative is the appearance of **s*- in place of **t*- in nom. sg. m. **so* and nom. sg. f. *$s\acute{e}$-h_2. The nominative marker, compared with the markers for other cases, is reminiscent of the situation of personal pronouns, cf. F 401 § 1. Regarding issues of gender, cf. F 303 § 2 (near the end of the fourth section).

The following table illustrates the most important masculine and neuter forms:

	sg. m.	sg. n.	pl. m.	pl. n.
nom.	**só*	**tó-d*	**tó-i̯*	**té-h_2*
acc.	**tó-m*	**tó-d*	**tó-ns*	**té-h_2*
gen.	**tó-s(i̯)o*		**tói̯s-om*	
dat.	**tó-smōi̯*			
loc.			**tói̯su* < **tói̯s-su?*	
instr.	**tó-h_1*		**tōi̯s*	

The inflection of pronouns reveals characteristics that distinguish it from nominal inflection: cf. *-d* (and not *-m*) in nom. acc. sg. n., cf. *-i̯* in nom. pl. m. (and not *-es*), cf. *-s(i̯)o* in gen. sg., cf. *-sm-* in dat. sg. and cf. stem *toi̯(s)-* in gen. and loc. pl. The *-o-* stem nominal forms show this influence, cf. F 311 § 3. Concerning the much discussed problem of gen. sg. *-s(i̯)o*, cf. F 311 § 4.

Further sources: — Concerning the dubious invariable **só* (called the "*sá-figé*" in Vedic, Greek, and Anatolian): → G. E. Dunkel in *Kolloquium Wackernagel* Basel 1988 [1990] p. 100ff.; S. W. Jamison *Vedic 'sá-figé': "An inherited sentence connective?"* in HS 105 1992 p. 213-239: J. S. Klein *'sá-figé' and Indo-European Deixis"* in HS 109 1996 p. 21-39; G. E. Dunkel in IF 102 1997 p. 176f.; C. Watkins in *FS Narten* 2000 p. 263-281. — Concerning the coexistence of **so* / **to-*: → K. Strunk in *Glotta* 55 1977 p. 7-9.

F 406. A further demonstrative pronoun with a Proto-Indo-European basis is PIE **i-* (or, with ablaut, **ei̯-*): cf. in Latin, anaphoric *is*, *ea*, *id*, and *ī-dem*, *ea-dem*, *id-em* (→ Meiser *Laut- und Formenlehre* 1998 p. 159-161); cf. in Greek the formal remnants μ-ιν (already *min* as early as Mycenaean) and ν-ιν (→ Wackernagel *Kleine Schriften* I 1969 p. 10); cf. Ved. m. *ay-ám*, f. *iy-ám*, n. *i-d-ám* (→ Mayrhofer EWAia I p. 103). Concerning the entire body of issues: → Szemerényi *Einführung* 1990 p. 218-220.

The form *(*h_1*)*é* (unstressed *-*o*) is also datable to the Proto-Indo-European period. It found use as an augment (cf. F 213); and further presumably played a decisive role in the formation of middle voice endings (cf. F 210), as in the genitive *-*os-o* (cf. F 311 § 4).

The individual IE languages developed (mostly on the basis of Proto-Indo-European material) an entire series of new pronouns, cf. Lat. *hic haec hoc*, *iste ista istud*, and *ipse ipsa ipsum*, cf. Gr. ὅδε, οὗτος, ἐκεῖνος and αὐτός; etc.: → Meiser *Laut- und Formenlehre* 1998 p. 162f.; Rix *Hist. Gramm. d. Gr.* 1976 p.184f.

F 407. Nominal forms such as PIE *(h_2)*al-i̯o*- and *(h_2)*an-i̯o*- 'other' are properly categorized as vaguely belonging to the field of pronouns. Due to this understandable proximity, they equally receive pronominal inflection: → J. Wackernagel in Wackernagel / Debrunner *Ai. Grammatik* III 1930 p. 579ff. (concerning Ved. *anyá-*, *víśva-* etc.).

5. Correlative Pronouns

F 408. In Proto-Indo-European sentence formation, the insertion of the relative pronoun PIE **kʷo-*, and **(H)i̯o-* through the demonstrative **to-* must have been quite common. Echos of this PIE phenomenon (correlation) are the IE pairs such as Lat. *cum* (older *quo-m*) 'when' vs. *tum* (older **to-m*) 'then, at that time' and *qu-ālis* 'how constituted' vs. *t-ālis* 'so constituted,' Gr. ὅσος 'how much, how large' vs. τόσος 'so much, so large' (< PIE **kʷo-ti̯o-* and **Hi̯o-ti̯o-* vs. **to-ti̯o-*) etc.: → Leumann LLFL 1977 p. 483f.; Meiser *Laut- und Formenlehre* 1998 p. 167.

D. Numerals

1. General Information

F 500. The following treatment can only aim to offer a small part of the complex and involved issues of Proto-Indo-European and Indo-European numerals.

1) An excellent treatement of the comprehensive subject from the point of view of Old Indian is offered by J. Wackernagel in Wackernagel / Debrunner *Ai. Grammatik* III 1930 p. 329ff. Proto-Indo-European featured cardinal numbers, ordinal numbers that were derived from them, as well as a few attested numerical adverbs.

2) For information on the writing of numbers: → *Metzler Lexikon Sprache* 1993 p. 706 *s.v.* '*Ziffer.*' — Concerning the numerals of the Middle Italian

coine of the Oscians, Latins, and Etruscians: → H. Rix "*Buchstabe, Zahlwort und Ziffer im Alten Mittelitalien*" in *FS Pisani* II 1969 p. 845-856; by the same author, "*Die Altersangabe in der oskischen Inschrift Ve. 70 und Oscan-Umbrian akno- 'Jahr'*" in MSS 37 1978 p. 149-163. As Rix is able to show, the presumption of older research that Middle Italian numerals were in fact re-interpreted writing symbols must be corrected.

3) Further sources: — a) General: → *Metzler Lexikon Sprache* 1993 p. 430 *s.v.* '*Numerale*.' — b) Proto-Indo-European: → Krahe *Idg. Sprachw.* II 1969 p. 46-49; Szemerényi *Numerals* 1960; Eichner *Numeralia* 1982 (on 2-5); Szemerényi *Einführung* 1990 p. 234-243; *Numerals* 1992 (an anthology with a complex history; the foreword gives details; the individual books refer to the volume that was left for a considerable time unpublished, cf. Lewandowski *Linguist. Wörterbuch* 2 1994 p. 754 *s.v.* '*Numerale*' with the entry by Ross A. C., ed., "Indo-European numerals." 1981 and Metzler *Lexikon* l.c. in section A J. Grozdanovic [sic] (Gvozdanović) (ed.), "Indo-European Numerals." Berlin, 1988; contains descriptions of the situation in various IE languages: cf. R. Coleman 'Italic,' F. M. J. Waanders 'Greek,' R. Emmerick 'Old Indian,' H. Eichner 'Anatolian,' A. S. C. Ross and J. Berns 'Germanic' and B. Comrie 'Balto-Slavonic'); Blažek *Numerals* 1999. — c) Particularly concerning Latin: → Leumann LLFL 1977 p. 484-495; Meiser *Laut- und Formenlehre* 1998 p. 170-177. — d) Particularly concerning Greek: → Rix *Hist. Gramm. d. Gr.* 1976 p. 171-173; Meier-Brügger *Gr. Sprachw.* II 1992 p. 93-98; F. Kortlandt "Greek numerals and PIE glottalic consonants" in MSS 42 1983 p. 97-104. — e) Particularly on Vedic: → J. Wackernagel in Wackernagel / Debrunner *Ai. Grammatik* III 1930 p. 329-430; Thumb / Hauschild *Handbuch des Sanskrit* I / 2 1959 p.154-166. — f) Particularly on Anatolian: → H. Eichner in *Numerals* 1992 p. 29-96; O. Carruba "*Betrachtungen zu den anatolischen und indogermanischen Zahlwörtern*" in *Fachtagung Innsbruck* 1996 [1998] p. 505-519. — g) Particularly on Germanic languages: → Krahe / Meid *Germ. Sprachw.* II 1969 p. 87-94. — h) Balto-Slavic: → B. Comrie in *Numerals* 1992 p. 717-833. — i) Armenian, Tocharian: → F. *Kortlandt "Proto-Armenian numerals"* in *Kolloquium Pedersen* Copenhagen 1993 [1994] p. 253-257; W. Winter "*Tocharian*" in *Numerals* 1992 p. 97-161.

2. Cardinal Numbers

F 501. The cardinal numbers are part of the inherited lexicon quite like the terms for familial relationships of the type PIE *$*ph_2tér$-* 'father.' —

Presumably, the cardinal numbers were not declined initially in pre-PIE time. — The genitive was used to communicate quantities, as is the case in individual IE languages from the number 'five' on (e.g. Old Church Slavic). — In order to mark congruence, in Proto-Indo-European the nominal endings are included for the lower numbers. The paradigms for the numbers 'one' to 'four' presumably featured a single set of endings for masculine and feminine forms with additional forms for neuter, and sometimes also for feminine forms. — Numerals were often inserted as prefixes of possessive compound forms, cf. the type Gr. τρι-ποδ- 'tripod' in W 208. In this case they are generally zero grade, cf. PIE **sm̥-* 'one' = Lat. **sem-* > *sim-* in *sim-plex* 'simple,' Gr. ἁ- in ἅ-παξ 'one time'; Ved. *sa-* in *sa-kr̥t* 'one time' or cf. PIE *$*k^w$tu̯r̥-* 'four' in Homeric Greek τρυ-φάλεια 'with four helmet decorations' (in this case with the variant form *$*k^w$tru-* preceding *K*, cf. L 304 § 3; in addition simplification of the initial consonant group *$*k^w$tru-* > *tru-*, cf. also τρά-πεζα p. XX above)

F 502. Following are general indications on cardinal numbers. Although strictly speaking the following treatment belongs in the section on the PIE lexicon, traditionally it is included here in 'morphology.'

1) 'one': — PIE **sem-* (= Myc. instr. sg. *e-me* i.e. *hem-ē*; Class. Gr. gen. sg. ἑν-ός etc.) and PIE **(H)oi̯-* (in OL *oi-no-* = Class. Lat. *ūnus*; Ved. *éka-* < *ai̯-ka-* [already in 'Mitanni-Indian,' cf. E 404 § 1] < **oi̯-ko-*). — For further information on **sem-*: → G. Darms in MSS 34 1976 p. 13f.; on continuations in Greek: Meier-Brügger *Gr. Sprachw.* I 1992 p. 60. — For more information on **(H)oi̯-*: → Mayrhofer EWAia I p. 262f. *s.v. éka-* 'one'; EWAhd II Sp. 989ff. *s.v.* '*ein.*' — On **sm̥-* as prefix of compounds cf. F 501.

2) 'two': — PIE **d(u)u̯o-* = Lat. *duo*; Gr. δύω and δύο, cf. also Myc. instr. pl. *du-wo-u-pi* i.e. *du̯ou̯-p^hi*; Ved. *d(u)vā́* and *d(u)váu*; etc.: → Mayrhofer EWAia I p. 761-763. The inflection of 'two' is connected to issues concerning the dual, cf. F 304 § 1. — On Mycenaean *du̯ou̯-p^hi* (which has a parallel in Ep.-Hom. adv. ἀμφου-δίς 'with both [hands]'): → M. Meier-Brügger in *Glotta* 71 1993 [1994] p. 137-142. — On the Armenian *erku* with the consonant shift *erk-* < **du̯-* (Meillet's Law): → Ch. de Lamberterie in *Histoire, Épistémologie, Langage* 10 / II 1988 (= *Antoine Meillet et la linguistique de son temps*, edited by S. Auroux) p. 222ff.

3) 'three': On continuations of PIE **tréi̯-es*, cf. L 215 § 1. — On **tri-* as prefix of compounds cf. F 501.

4) 'four': — PIE *k^wétu̯or- = Lat. *quattuor*; Gr. Att. τέτταρες (< *k^wétu̯r̥-es) and others; Ved. nom. pl. *catvā́r-as*, acc. pl. *catúr-as-* and others; etc.: → Mayrhofer EWAia I p. 526f. (p. 527 below, also on f. *k^wetesr-es* in Indo-Iranian). — On Latin *quattuor*: → Meiser *Laut- und Formenlehre* 1998 p. 171; further, cf. L 203f. — On 'four' as prefix of compounds cf. F 501.

5) 'five': — PIE *pénk^{w}e* = Lat. *quīnque*; Gr. πέντε; Ved. *páñca*; etc.: → Mayrhofer EWAia II p. 65f.; V. Blažek in IF 105 2000 p. 101-119. — On Latin *quīnque*: → H. Eichner in *Kolloquium Lat. u. Idg. Salzburg* 1986 [1992] p. 70-72.

6) 'six': — PIE **s(u)u̯éḱs* = Lat. *sex*; Myc. Gr. *we-pe-za* i.e. *hu̯es-ped^{j}a* 'composed of six feet' (in which *hu̯es-p-* is simplified from **hu̯eks-p-*); Ved. *ṣáṣ-*; etc.: → Mayrhofer EWAia II 680f.; R. Virédaz "*'Six' en indo-européen*" in IF 102 1997 p. 112-150. — On Indo-Iranian: → A. Lubotsky in Graz 2000 p. 255-261.— Particularly on the Armenian *vecʻ* < **su̯u̯eḱs*: → G. Klingenschmitt and J. Schindler in *Fachtagung Wien* 1978 [1980] p. 419 note 25a.

7) 'seven': — PIE **septḿ̥* = Lat. *septem*; Gr. ἑπτά; Ved. *saptá*; etc.: → Mayrhofer EWAia II p. 700. — On Hittite: → E. Neu in *FS Meid* *70 1999 p. 249-254.

8) 'eight': — PIE **oḱt-* = Lat. *octō*; Gr. ὀκτώ; Ved. *aṣṭā́* and *aṣṭáu*; etc.: → Mayrhofer EWAia I p. 142; EWAhd I Sp. 121ff. *s.v.* '*ahto*.' Whether the ending may be associated with the dual (compare 'eight' with 'two') is doubtful.

9) 'nine': — PIE *$h_1$néu̯n̥ = Lat. *novem* (the initial *-n-* in the ending attests the ordinal *nōnus*); Gr. ἐννέα; Ved. *náva*; etc.:→ Mayrhofer EWAia II p. 24f.; M. Peters "*Idg. '9' im Armenischen und Griechischen*" in *Zeitschrift für Phonetik, Sprachwissenschaft und Kommunikationsforschung* 44 1991 p. 301-310; V. Blažek in HS 112 2000 p. 188-203.

10) 'ten': — PIE **déḱm̥* = Lat. *decem*; Gr. δέκα; Ved. *dáśa*; etc.: → Mayrhofer EWAia I p. 708f.

11) 'eleven' to 'nineteen': — All evidence indicates a Proto-Indo-European habit of simply placing the 'ten' before the 'one' without any copulative particle. For information on the various IE strategies of word order in numerals: → Wackernagel *Kleine Schriften* I 1969 (in an essay of 1935) p. 236-256. — On the Latin type *ūndēvīgintī*: → M. Lejeune "*Procédures soustractives dans les numérations étrusque et latine*" in BSL 76 / 1 1981 p. 241-248 (concerning the adaptation of the Etruscan method to Latin). — On Indo-Iranian: → R. Schmitt "*Die Zählreihe zwischen "10" und "20," zum Beispiel im Iranis-*

chen” in HS 107 1994 p. 12-29. — For information on the formation of ‘eleven’ and ‘twelve’ in Germanic: → EWAhd II Sp. 1008ff. _s.v._ ‘_einlif._’

12) ‘Twenty’ to ‘ninety’: — PIE compound forms with the suffix _*-dḱm̥-t-_ /_*-dḱom-t-_ (or _*-_h_1_ḱm̥t-_ / _*-_h_1_ḱomt-_ which developed from it) ‘group of ten, decade,’ cf. for ‘twenty’ PIE _*(d)u̯i-_h_1_ḱm̥-ti-_h_2, for ‘thirty’ PIE _*tri-_h_1_ḱm̥-t-_h_2, etc. — Latin: → Meiser _Laut- und Formenlehre_ 1998 p. 172f. — Greek: πεντήκοντα < _*pente-_h_1_ḱomt-_: → F. Kortlandt in MSS 42 1983 p. 98. — Germanic: → R. Lühr “_Die Dekaden ‘70-120’ im Germanischen_” in MSS 36 1977 p. 59-71; G. Schuppener “_Einschnitte bei den indogermanischen Zehnerzahlen_” in _Fachtagung Innsbruck_ 1996 [1998] p. 293-321 (concerning, among other issues, the fact that in various Germanic dialects, there is a break in the word formation after 60).

13) ‘hundred’: — PIE _*dḱm̥-tó-_ understood as ordinal ‘the tenth of ten decads’ (= Lat. _centum_, gr. ἑκατόν, Ved. _śatám_): → Risch _Kleine Schriften_ 1981 (in an essay of 1962) p. 677-689. — Particularly concerning the Greek ἑ-κατόν: The word-initial _e_ is at first a laryngeal-like echo of the original initial _d_ and may be traced via _*_h_1_ḱm̥tó-_ to PIE _*d-ḱm̥tó-_. Only secondarily was _e-_ interpreted as belonging to _*sem-_ and accordingly aspirated: → F. Kortlandt in MSS 42 1983 p. 98; H. Rix voices agreement in _GS van Windekens_ 1991 p. 225 note 1.

14) ‘200’-‘900’: — PIE compound forms with the main root _*-dḱm̥tó-_ in the sense of ‘100.’ — For information on the Latin _-centī_ (also _-gentī_): → Meiser _Laut- und Formenlehre_ 1998 p. 173f. — For information on the Greek type διακόσιοι vs. διακατιοι: → E. Risch in _Kleine Schriften_ 1981 (in an essay from 1966) p. 265ff.

15) ‘1000’: — For information on formations with PIE _*ǵʰes-lo-_ ‘a hand-full (of grain)’ (cf. Lat. _mille_ and _mīlia_ < _*smi_h_2_-ǵʰsl-i_h_2_-_, Gr. χῑλιοι, Ved. _sa-hásra-_): → H. Rix in _GS van Windekens_ 1991 p. 225ff.; _ibid, Termini der Unfreiheit_ 1994 p. 61 note 16. — For information on the Germanic _*þ ūsont-_ and corresponding Balto-Slavic forms: → R. Lühr. “_Zur Semantifizierung von Zahlwörtern: Das Wort ‘tausend’ - eine germanisch-baltoslavische Isoglosse?_” in _Linguistica_ XXXIII (= _FS Čop_) 1993 p. 117-136.

16) ‘countless’: — For information on the Greek μῡρίοι ‘countless, immeasurable,’ also ‘ten thousand’: → M. Weiss in HS 109 1996 p. 199-204 (The author compares the Hittite _mūri-_ ‘grape’ and reconstructs the PIE root _*meu̯H-_ ‘abundant, reproductively powerful’).

3. Ordinal Numbers

F 503. In Proto-Indo-European, and naturally also later, ordinal numbers had the function of signaling the end of a series, e.g. 'We traveled for nine days. But on the tenth...: → J. Wackernagel in Wackernagel / Debrunner *Ai. Gramm.* III 1930 p. 400ff.; Risch *Kleine Schriften* 1981 (in an essay of 1962) p. 684ff. (including many examples from ancient IE languages). As is otherwise common in ancient IE languages, ordinal numbers are *–o*-stem adjectivs derived from the cardinal numbers. In the case of 'first' and 'second,' non-cardinal derived formations were possible too, cf. Lat. *prīmus* 'foremost' in the sense of 'first' and *secundus* 'following (adj.)' in the sense of 'second.' The ordinal numbers are the starting point for superlative formations, cf. F 325.

The common PIE ordinal suffixes are *-to-* and _-th$_2$o-_. One also finds the more ancient *-o-*, sometimes alternating with the complex form _-h$_2$o-_, cf. PIE _*septm̥-(h$_2$)o-_'seventh.' The old *-o*-stem formation _*déḱm̥-th$_2$-o-_ 'belonging to the decad', derived from the PIE abstract noun _*déḱm̥-teh$_2$-_ is a potential starting point for the ordinal suffix variant PIE _*-h$_2$o-_ and also for the PIE variant _*-th$_2$o-_ of _*-to-_[7]: Concerning the understanding of the abstract noun _*-t(e)h$_2$-_: → Kuryłowicz *Études* I 1935 p. 49; the Vedic suffix *-tha-* can indeed best be traced back to PIE _*-th$_2$-o-_, cf. L 329 § 1 with further examples for Ved. *-th* - < PIE _*-th$_2$-_. — Concerning details in Latin: → Leumann LLFL 1977 p. 491ff. and Meiser *Laut- und Formenlehre* 1998 p. 174f.; — Greek: → Rix *Hist. Gramm. d. Gr.* 1976 p. 170f.; — Vedic: → J. Wackernagel l.c. — On the subject as a whole: → G. Schmidt "*Indogermanische Ordinalzahlen*" in IF 97 1992 p. 197-235.

4. Numerical Adverbs

F 504. In the case of the numerical adverbs of the type of multiplicatives 'once,' 'twice,' the word formations of the lowest numbers have their origins in Proto-Indo-European, cf. PIE _*du̯i-s_ 'twice' (= Lat. *bis* with the consonant shift *du̯-* > *b-*) and PIE _*tri-s_ 'thrice' (= Gr. τρίς). To express 'once' there existed a compound form with the prefix _*sm̥-_, cf. in F 501 the three PIE representatives with varying suffixes. For further informa-

[7]The h_2 in _*déḱm̥th$_2$-o-_ is primarily part of the abstract noun formatiom, but is then added by the speakers to the suffix through a restructuration from _*déḱm̥th$_2$-o-_ to _*déḱm̥-th$_2$o-_ and to _*déḱm̥t-h$_2$o-_.

tion: → Leumann LLFL 1977 p. 494f.; Wackernagel / Debrunner *Ai. Gramm.* III 1930 p. 422ff.

IV. Proto-Indo-European Syntax

— by Matthias Fritz —

A. General Information

S 100. Berthold Delbrück's *Vergleichende Syntax der indogermanischen Sprachen* was the first comprehensive and fundamental treatment of the field and has not been replaced in the hundred years since its appearance: → Delbrück *Vgl. Syntax* I-III 1893-1900. The importance of this work was underscored by a conference dedicated to its author on the hundredth anniversary of its publication: → *Kolloquium Delbrück Madrid* 1994 [1997]. For information on the role of this work in the history of the field, cf. K. Strunk p. 571ff.

1) Whereas since the time of A. Schleicher efforts have been made to reconstruct the phonology and morphology of Proto-Indo-European (see E 305), B. Delbrück does not reconstruct the syntax of Proto-Indo-European, but rather compares and analyzes phenomena of the individual IE languages. Only the future may tell whether or not this 'pre-Schleicherian' approach to research on syntax, particularly on that concerning larger parts of sentences, is insurmountable. Only those sentence parts may be reconstructed which reveal comparable information in both content and expression. However, it is often difficult to decide whether these comparable phenomena are present in Proto-Indo-European, or Proto-Indo-European merely provided the conditions for related developments in various individual languages.

2) Alongside B. Delbrück's work, the comprehensive treatments of syntax by Karl Brugmann (→ Brugmann *Einfacher Satz* 1925, by the same author, *Kurze Vgl. Gramm.* 1902-1904; *Grundriß* II-3 1916 on particles in the simple sentence) and Hermann Hirt (→ Hirt *Idg. Gramm.* VI 1934 and VII 1937) are worth naming. Although a contemporary equivalent of these works does not exist, one is planned within the scope of the *Indogermanischen Grammatik* by

J. Kuryłowicz and M. Mayrhofer and is presently being prepared by a numerous staff led by José Luis García Ramón, Heinrich Hettrich, and Oswald Panagl (→ For more information, see the web sites of the universities of Würzburg and Salzburg. See links on our web site [see E 100], under the heading 'Indo-European linguistics in Europe'). The *Indogermanische Gesellschaft* held a conference on this subject Würzburg from 29 September to 3 October 1999: → *Indogermanische Syntax, - Fragen und Perspektiven -*, H. Hettrich ed., Wiesbaden 2002.

3) Winfred P. Lehmann (→ Lehmann *PIE Syntax* 1974) and Paul Friedrich (→ P. Friedrich *Syntax* 1975) offer manageable treatments which, however, are more concerned with the more narrow syntactical question of word order in view of typology and which, owing to their limited scale, cannot offer a comprehensive treatment. For an in-depth discussion of the subordinated importance of word order in Proto-Indo-European with its wealth of inflected forms, see C. Watkins "Towards Proto-Indo-European Syntax: problems and pseudo-problems" in *Watkins Selected Writings* I 1994 (in a contribution from 1976) p. 242-263.

4) A reconstruction of Proto-Indo-European syntax is dependent on an idealized notion of a standard Proto-Indo-European. Questions of style, to which particularly O. Panagl has dedicated himself, demand particular sensitivity. The language of poetry is of particular importance due to its traditional formulas: → R. Schmitt *Dichtersprache* 1967; Watkins *How to kill a dragon* 1995. Owing to the very nature of the coexistence of oral innovations and written tradition, colloquial language is only with difficulty accessible. Potential sources include above all texts in which dialogues occur, of either dramatic, philosophical, or lyrical nature: → Hofmann *Lat. Umgangssprache* 1978.

5) Basic literature on Proto-Indo-European and Indo-European syntax includes: → Brugmann *Grundriß* II-2 1911 and II-3 1916; by the same author, *Einfacher Satz* 1925; Bühler *Sprachtheorie* 1934; Chantraine *Gramm. hom.* II 1953; Delbrück *Vgl. Syntax* I-III 1893-1900; by the same author, Gr. Syntax 1879; by the same author, *Ai. Syntax* 1888; Havers *Erklärende Syntax* 1931; Hirt *Idg. Gramm.* VI - VII 1934-1937; Hofmann / Szantyr *Syntax* 1965; *Kieckers Gr. Gr.* III-IV 1926; Krahe *Vergl. Syntax* 1972; Kühner / Gerth II 1898-1904; Kühner / Stegmann II 1955; Kuryłowicz *Inflectional Categories* 1964; Matthews *Syntax* 1981; Meier-Brügger *Gr. Sprachw.* I 1992; Miklosich *Vergl. Syntax* 1868-1874; Monro *Homer. Dialect* 1891; Pinkster *Lateinische Syntax* 1988; Scherer *Lat. Syntax* 1975; Schwyzer / Debrunner *Gr. Gr.* II

1950; Sommer *Vergl. Syntax* 1931; Speyer *Syntax* 1896; Wackernagel *Vorlesungen* I-II 1926-1928.

S 101. Given their dependence on questions of that which signifies and that which is signified, efforts at reconstructing Proto-Indo-European syntax are necessarily more reliant on hypotheses and probabilities than are the realms of morphology and phonology. Internal syntactical reconstruction goes even one step further, since the observation of divergences ascertained through external reconstruction is based upon preconceived notions of a syntactical system and also because the target idea that results from the comparison of historical syntactical systems ('cleansing' them) can only be made plausible in terms of typology.

The problematic nature of syntax reconstruction is comparable to that of semantics insofar as syntactic meanings, like semantic meanings, belong to the linguistic realm of content: Thus, morphemes, like lexemes, consist of *significans* and *significatum* and are used by the speaker to indicate his conceptual idea (conceptual level: *designatum*) of the language-external world. As in the case of lexemes, morphemes may be assigned basic meanings that are not dependent on context: Thus, the functions of a morpheme may vary according to the lexemes that appear in a sentence. The linguistic code employed by the speaker directly refers to his conceptual idea which, in turn, is dependent on his interpretation of the actual situation such that various speakers may discuss the same real situation with varying linguistic codes.

The following schematic diagram describes the relationship of linguistic code to conceptuality and reality in different terms:

	signifiant	significans
semantic level	signifié	significatum
conceptual level		designatum
language-external reality		

S 102. Syntax is the scientific description of sentences. From the outset, questions must be addressed as to the nature of a sentence and the criteria that a sentence must fulfill in order to be considered as such. In the case of prehistoric linguistic research it becomes important to address the additional question of how sentences may be reconstructed.

Even from the standpoint of contemporary languages, the question of what constitutes a sentence is not simple to answer. It may in any case only be clearly and definitively answered, if sentences in themselves reveal the prerequisites to such an answer; i.e., when sentences contain certain characteristics which make them sentences, and without which they would not be sentences. If sentences do not contain these characteristics, the question of the fundamental criteria of the sentence becomes a matter of definition.

Taking, for example, the sentence criterion of the pairing of a subject with a predicate, then, along with such sentences as '*The cat caught a bird,*' we may also accept as sentences phrases that are quite different, for example the use of the German noun, '*Hilfe!*' The latter type may of course be explained in such a way that the predication of a subject takes place in such cases as well, as it does in another formulation that could be chosen in the same situation: '*Hilf mir!*' Thus, the differences are limited to the *signifiant*.

One might suggest that in order for a sentence to be taken as such, it must be complete and meaningful. Of course, incomplete sentences are not necessarily meaningless, and complete sentences are not necessarily meaningful. Examples give the impression that complete sentences are more or less meaningful, or rather, in themselves meaningful. However, sentence examples are not linguistic reality. In the natural linguistic reality, each expression exists within a larger context and serves the goal of communication. Errors of execution, i.e. miscommunication, are natural in this as in any other human activity. However, miscommunication may occur in complete sentences as well as in incomplete ones. On the other hand, the incomplete sentence may fulfill its purpose in a larger context just as well as the complete sentence, and is, of course, omnipresent in daily speech. The decisive factor is understandability in context. Thus, understandability and completeness of an individual sentence apart from its context cannot be considered fundamental and essential qualities of a sentence.

With regard to syntactical reconstruction, the assertion that real sentences, i.e. sentences in their full context, cannot be reconstructed, is self-evident. This is not a failing of syntactical reconstruction, for, as we have just seen, individual sentences without a context, like individual words and sounds, are not linguistic reality. That which cannot be reconstructed is the linguistic reality; that which can be reconstructed is the system of a language. Individual examples can only serve to illustrate the reconstructed system. Whether or not the system of an entire language can be reconstructed is quite another question, the answer to which is more dependent on the state of research than on research methods. Also dependent on the state of research is the ability to formulate reconstructed sentences, for the formulation of a sentence, which has no claim to linguistic reality, is hindered not by the fact that sentences cannot be reconstructed, but rather by the fact that one may not be able to verify that the reconstructed elements all belong to the same historical phase of language. If the historical contemporaneousness of all of the elements in a formulation were assured, nothing would be left to hinder its assertion. While this in no way guarantees that the formulated sentence existed in its given form, this limitation affects all reconstructions.

Suggestions for further reading: → C. Watkins "Preliminaries to the reconstruction of Indo-European sentence structure" in *Proceedings of the 9th International Congress of Linguists Cambridge Massachusetts*, edited by H. G. Lunt. The Hague 1964 p. 1035-1042; by the same author, *"Towards Proto-Indo-European Syntax: Problems and Pseudo-Problems"* in *Watkins Selected Writings* I 1994 (in a contribution from 1976) p. 242-263; W. Dressler "*Über die Rekonstruktion der indogermanischen Syntax*" in ZVS 85 1971 p. 5-22; W. Winter *"Reconstructional Comparative Linguistics and the Reconstruction of the Syntax of Undocumented Stages in the Development of Languages and Language Families"* in *Historical Syntax* 1984 p. 613-625; S. Jamison *"Determining the Synchronic Syntax of a Dead Language"* in *Historical Linguistics* 1989 p. 211-220.

B. Sentence Syntax

1. General Information

S 200. Whether compound or simple, the individual sentence is not the largest unit of syntax. Also included in syntax are the syntactical and semantic relations that go beyond the limits of the single sentence. Hence, one speaks of 'text syntax' in current research. In the appearance of hypotaxis from parataxis in main clauses and subordinate clauses, the direct connection between text syntax and sentence syntax becomes clear, owing to the supra-sentential effect of pronouns. This is illustrated in Latin by the use of sentence-initial relative pronouns.

S 201. Phrases may be divided into hypotactic and paratactic phrases according to whether or not they are included within other phrases. According to whether they are independent in terms of content, they can be divided into main and subordinate clauses. According to the intention of the speaker they may be divided into statements, questions, and imperative sentences. According to whether or not they contain a finite verb, they may be divided into verbal and nominal sentences.

S 202. There are infinitive and participial constructions that may be traced to the use of verbal nouns in certain Proto-Indo-European cases. Among the verbal nouns in Proto-Indo-European are included those verbal substantives and verbal adjectives that are included in verbal paradigms of IE languages as infinitives and participles. While it is as yet unclear whether one may postulate the use of particular infinitive or participial constructions in Proto-Indo-European, the existence of participles may safely be asserted. Additionally, infinitive constructions with final dative, accusative of direction, and the locative of destination are presumed to have existed. While infinitives are defined by syntax, the very presence of participles reveals that there were participial constructions in Proto-Indo-European. According to J. L. García Ramón, "[the assertion] of a true Proto-Indo-European infinitive ending in **-sén(i)* is justified,"[8] which could be traced to a locative form, which, according to K. Stüber, appears in the case of *s*-stem abstract nouns with the locative forms ending in **en.*[9] Even in what are known as absolute constructions, there was the possibility in Proto-Indo-European of employing various cases to insert a phrase in a sentence. According to Keydana the locative was used in such cases. For more information of morphology, cf. F 216[10].

Suggestions for further reading: → Gippert *Infinitive* 1978; by the same author, "*Zum 'prädikativen' Infinitiv*" in ZVS 97 1984 p. 205-220; by the same author, "*Ein keltischer Beitrag zur indogermanischen Morphosyntax: Das altirische Verbalnomen*" in Kolloquium Delbrück Madrid 1994 [1997] p. 143-164; H. Hettrich "*Zur historischen Syntax der nomina actionis im Ṛgveda: Der 'doppelte Dativ'*" in MSS 43 1984 p. 55-106; by the same author, "*Nochmals zu Gerundium und Gerundivum*" in *FS Rix* 1993 p. 190-208; Risch *Gerund.* 1984; J. L. García Ramón "*Zur Konkurrenz von Dativ und Akkusativ von Nomina actionis und Abstrakta im Indogermanischen*" in *GS Kuryłowicz* 1995 [1996] p. 101-113; by the same

---

[8] *Infinitive im Indogermanischen? Zur Typologie der Infinitivbildungen und zu ihrer Entwicklung in den älteren indogermanischen Sprachen* in InL 20 1997 p. 45-69

[9] K. Stüber Zur Herkunft der altindischen Infinitive auf *-sáni* in MSS 60 2000 p. 135-167

[10] *Absolute Konstruktionen* 1997 p. 33

author, "*Infinitive im Indogermanischen? Zur Typologie der Infinitivbildungen und zu ihrer Entwicklung in den älteren indogermanischen Sprachen*" in InL 20 1997 p. 45-69; Keydana *Absol. Konstr.* 1997; K. Stüber "*Zur Herkunft der altindischen Infinitive auf -sáni*" in MSS 60 2000 p. 135-167.

2. Parataxis and Hypotaxis

S 203. Parataxis is the coordination of sentence clauses, which may themselves be statements, questions, or imperative sentences. Statements and questions may contain the same elements, differing only slightly in word order and intonation, such that the one can easily be transformed into the other. Imperative sentences, on the other hand, like the imperative mode, constitute a special case.

1) In statements, the speaker takes a position regarding the validity he attaches to the content of his expression; for example, whether the validity is presupposed (injunctive) or claimed (indicative), or whether he regards the statement as a possibility (optative), or as taking place in the future (subjunctive). Only with the perfective aspect could the indicative mood be used to describe future events, since the perfective aspect does not permit statements about the immediate present. However, in Proto-Indo-European the perfective aspect of the indicative aorist, paired with the augment and secondary ending, is only used to describe past events. When paired with the primary ending without the augment, the perfective aspect only appears in the subjunctive aorist, revealing the probable origin of the association of the future tense and the subjunctive mood.

2) Unlike statements, questions express the incomplete or uncertain idea of the speaker. Accordingly, one may distinguish completive questions from yes-or-no questions. In completive questions, interrogative pronouns and pronominal adverbs take the places of nominal (including pronominal) and adverbial syntagmata, respectively. In yes-or-no questions, no replacement of word type takes place; rather the entire verbal action of the sentence is put in question. This may be accomplished through variation of the word order and intonation of the statement form. However, the thematization of a finite verb may not be confirmed on the basis of evidence from individual languages.

For information on the Proto-Indo-European questions *$*k^wís$ $h_1ési$?* 'Who are you?' and *$*k^wósi̯o$ $h_1ési$?* 'Whose (son) are you?': → R. Schmitt *Dichtersprache* 1967 p. 136f.

S 204. Along with parataxis (coordination), there is also evidence of hypotaxis (subordination) in Proto-Indo-European. Hypotaxis may be understood as the insertion of one phrase into another. The essential characteristic of hypotaxis is the possibility of including one phrase with a finite verb form in another such phrase, i.e. the integration of one verbal clause into another.

The insertion of one clause into another is accompanied by variations in the form of the subordinate clause from the form that it had as a main clause. Subordinate clauses are thus differentiated from main clauses in that their *significans* is of a form that is not found in coordinated clauses, whereby the formal difference may in fact be limited to suprasegmental phonology. In terms of content, given that a subordinate clause only represents a completion of, or additional information about, a main clause, a paratactic relationship may exist between independent sentences that is similar to the hypotaxis between main and subordinate clauses. However, one can speak of hypotaxis only when this relationship is expressed through the formal integration of the subordinate clause in the main clause as in the case of adverbs, attributes, and appositions. The formal characteristics of subordinate clauses vary among the individual IE languages. In Proto-Indo-European, the accentuation of the finite verb is accepted as a formal characteristic of the subordinate clause as opposed to the main clause, in which the finite verb is not accentuated, except when it establishes the theme at the beginning of the sentence.A summary of the criteria that distinguish main clauses from subordinate clauses may be found in E. Hermann "*Gab es im Indogermanischen Nebensätze?*" in KZ 33 1895 p. 481-535.

In *Syntax* III 1900, Delbrück asserts, "that … originally all sentences were coordinated alongside one another." (p. 411) He continues: "The historical view, as it is generally accepted today, must have as its point of departure the hypothesis that there was a time at which there were only main clauses." (p. 412) Further, speaking of his time, Delbrück states: "The assertion that hypotaxis developed from parataxis has become the common heritage of the field." (p. 413) In order to systematize subordinate clauses, Delbrück proposes, (1900, 413f.) their division into *a priori* and *a posteriori* subordinate clauses according to "thought relationship."

S 205. In Proto-Indo-European, the existence of subordinate clauses with relative pronouns may be asserted, which, in addition to filling the role of a relative clause, may also serve as adverbial phrases. The comparison of IE languages does not support the existence of special conjunctions for the introduction of adverbial phrases. Adverbial phrases that are introduced by conjunctions have their origin in relative clauses. This is evidenced by the fact that conjunctions may be traced to certain cases of relative pronouns, e.g. Lat. *cum* < *quom* = acc. sg. m. of the relative pronoun *k^wo-*. Following the origin of adverbial phrases, whereby conjunctions found their origins in relative pronouns, other parts of speech were also transformed into conjunctions. Thus, subordinated clauses that are introduced by relative pronouns can perform the function of subject, object, adverbial phrase, appositional phrase, and attribute.

1) Proto-Indo-European features two types of relative clauses: attributive and appositive. These are distinguished from one another by sentence-initial pronouns: The attributive relative clause is introduced by the pronoun *k^wi- / *k^wo-*; the appositive, by the pronoun **Hi̯o-*. There is one semantic difference between the two types of relative clause: While the attributive relative clause describes an additional quality, the appositive relative clause states a known quality of that to which the relative pronoun refers, i.e. the referent. The attributive relative clause may thus appear without a referent, while the appositive relative clause may only be used in connection with a referent. In the post-Proto-Indo-European period, this formal characteristic of the two types of relative clause was abandoned, such that the individual IE languages each use just one of these relative pronouns.

2) According to Ch. Lehmann, Proto-Indo-European features only postnominal and sentence-initial relative clauses, and none that are prenominal and sentence-final.[11] 'Postnominal' and 'prenominal' indicate the placement of the relative clause relative to the referent; 'sentence-initial' and 'sentence-final' indicate the placement of the relative clause in relation to the main clause. In Lehmann's view, the **Hi̯o-* relative clause occurs only in a postnominal position and originates either from an attribute that was added to **Hi̯o-*, or from an independent sentence introduced by **Hi̯o-*. In fact, **Hi̯o-* fulfills an anaphoric function. The sentence-initial *k^wi-/k^wo-* phrase, according to Lehmann, serves to indicate a theme, to which the following main clause refers: "The nucleus of a restrictive relative clause [sic] is necessarily semantically indefinite; thus, the relative pronoun that determines it must be indefinite. The use of a relative pronoun that is closely related both to the interrogative pronoun and to the indefinite pronoun is thus explained ..." (p. 163). According to Hettrich (*Hypotaxe*, 1988 p. 776-778), following a linguistic phase which fea-

[11] Ch. Lehmann "*Der indogermanische *kwi-/kwo-Relativsatz im typologischen Vergleich*", *Kolloquium Syntax Pavia* 1979 [1980] p. 155-169

tures relative participles, relative clauses develop from paratactically coordinated clauses with anaphoric pronouns, a process which leads in turn to the formation of appositive-explicative relative sentences (from sentences with anaphoric **Hi̯o-*) and attributive-restrictive relative clauses (from sentences with anaphoric **kʷi-*/**kʷo-*). For information on morphology, cf. F 404.

For more information regarding the terminology 'appositive vs. attributive': → Seiler *Relativsatz* 1960; concerning appositive vs. restrictive: → Lehmann *Relativsatz* 1984 and Hettrich *Hypotaxe* 1988. According to Ch. Koch, there was no relative attribute in Proto-Indo-European, but rather it developed in individual IE languages upon the basis of nominal relative clauses.[12]

3. Verbal and Nominal Phrases

S 206. In a verbal phrase, the finite verb determines the actants, which are governed by rules of dependence. In the nominal phrase, there is no finite verb to determine the actants. Nominal phrases are not simply verbal phrases without a finite verb (with what is called elipsis of the copula), but rather constitute an independent type of clause. Thus, the predicate noun in nominal phrases is always stressed, unlike the verbal predicate in verbal phrases. In fact the term 'elipsis' is not exact, since the copula is not essential. Contrarily, the use of the copula should rather be seen as an adaptation to the common pattern of verbal phrases, which always feature a finite verb form. This use of the copula is in fact a sort of explicative signification, in which the content of the copula is expressed through the connection of the various sentence elements and is given particular emphasis alone through an independent linguistic symbol of comparable meaning.

S 207. For more information on parataxis: → Kieckers *Stellung des Verbs* 1911; Ammann *Untersuchungen* I 1922; by the same author, "*Untersuchungen zur homerischen Wortfolge und Satzstruktur. 2. Teil: Die Stellung des Verbums, im Einzelnen untersucht*" in IF 42 1924 p. 149-171 and 300-322; W. Dressler "*Eine textsyntaktische Regel der idg. Wortstellung*" in ZVS 83 1969 p. 1-25; R. Harweg "*Zum Verhältnis von Satz, Hauptsatz und Nebensatz*" in ZDL 38 1971 p. 16-46; C. Watkins "*Some Indo-European verb-phrases and their transformations*" in *Selected*

---

[12] "*Zur Vorgeschichte des relativen Attributivkonnexes im Baltischen und Slavischen*" in *Kolloquium Idg., Slaw. u. Balt.* Jena 1989 [1992] p. 45-88

Writings I 1994 (in a contribution from 1975) p. 189-209; K. Heger *Parataxe und Hypotaxe* in *Kwartalnik Neofilologiczny* 24 1977 p. 279-286; A. Scherer "*Rekonstruktion grundsprachlicher Satzbaupläne*" in *FS Szemerényi* 1979 p. 755-762; Andersen *Word Order Typology* 1983; F. Bader "*Structure de l'énoncé indo-européen*" in *Historical Linguistics* 1987 p. 13-34; Luraghi *Old Hittite Sentence Structure* 1990; A. Hintze "Parataxis and Hypotaxis in the Avesta" in *Syntaxe des langues indo-iraniennes anciennes* 1993 [1997] p. 51-62.

S 208. For more information on hypotaxis: → Seiler *Relativsatz* 1960; R. Sternemann "*Temporale und konditionale Nebensätze des Hethitischen*" in *Mitteilungen des Instituts für Orientforschung* 11 1965 p. 231-274 and 377-415; R. Schmitt-Brandt "*Vergleich der indogermanischen Nebensatzkonstruktionen*" in *Fachtagung Bern* 1969 [1973] p. 125-141; G. Bossong "*Typologie der Hypotaxe*" in FoL 13 1979 p. 33-54; H. Rix "*Abstrakte Komplemente im Urindogermanischen*" in *FS Szemerényi* 1979 p. 725-747; H. Hettrich "*Zur Entwicklung der Finalsätze altindogermanischer Sprachen*" in ZVS 100 1987 p. 219-237; by the same author, "*Lateinische Konditionalsätze in sprachvergleichender Sicht*" in *Kolloquium Lat. u. Idg.* Salzburg 1986 [1992] p. 263-284; by the same author, *Hypotaxe* 1988; Lehmann *Relativsatz* 1984; Krisch *Konditionalsätze* 1986.

S 209. With regard to sentence accent, one may note that the word that begins the sentence is stressed. Sentence-initial position implies the function of establishing the topic: In nominative language, the subject in sentence-initial position is considered the normal, unmarked type. In interrogative sentences, the nominal element, about which the question is asked, establishes the theme. It is thus the interrogative pronoun that begins the sentence.

An enclitic is added as a second word in the sentence; a further enclitic is added as a third word. This is known as the (Delbrück-)Wackernagel Law: → J. Wackernagel "*Über ein Gesetz der indogermanischen Wortstellung*" in *Wackernagel Kleine Schriften* I 1969 (in a contribution from 1892) p. 1-104; Collinge *Laws* 1985 p. 217-219; T. Krisch "*B. Delbrücks Arbeiten zur Wortstellung aus heutiger Sicht*" in *Kolloquium Delbrück* Madrid 1994 [1997] p. 283-309.

S 210. Syntactical relations

In relations of dependence there is a dominant component and a dependent component. The dominant component creates a syntactical opening for the dependent component, which the latter fills. Phrasal elements that fill the openings left by finite verbs are actants; phrasal elements that do not fill openings left by the finite verb are circumstants.

Suggestions for further reading: → Tesnière *Syntaxe structurale* 1959; Happ *Grundfragen* 1976; Pinkster *Lat. Syntax* 1990; Haudry *Cas en védique* 1977.

1) Agreement and government have in common that they appear in dependency relations. This does not mean that components that participate in agreement and government are thus equivalent to each other; rather, the one is independent and the other dependent. In addition, the components are not equivalent to each other within the realms of agreement and government: → Matthews *Syntax* 1981 p. 249: "(...) that government and agreement are directional relations." However, agreement and government are not equal in their accordance with the dependency relation: → Matthews *Syntax* 1981 p. 249: "But the direction does not always match that of dependency."

2) By 'agreement' is only meant the accordance of a declined form of one grammatical category with another: → Matthews *Syntax* 1981 p. 246: "Agreement (or concord) is usually described as a relation between words that share a morphosyntactic feature." However, the agreement may also take place between a lexical and a grammatical category, which is then evidenced in a syntactical incongruence, such as when a singular quantity is given as a subject of a verb that is in a plural form. For example: Caesar *Bellum Gallicum* 2, 6, 3 *cum tanta multitudo lapides ac tela conicerent* "when such a large group (of people) hurled stones and projectiles" Syntactical disagreement is thus possible when, in place of syntactical agreement, agreement between a grammatical and a lexical category takes place. A similar relationship also exists between personal pronouns and the verbal category of person.

3) Agreement is not dependent upon the fact that an identical (morphologically) linguistic symbol is used to express the category of agreement. As Scherer puts it in his *Lat. Syntax* 1975 p. 97, "...it is characteristic of ancient IE languages that morphological elements, which are equivalent to each other, are not generally phonetically equivalent...." In a main clause, the category of agreement may also remain fully unexpressed.

4) Various gradations among the various categories of agreement may be observed: → Ch. Lehmann *Kongruenz in Syntax* 1993 1 p. 725a: "the essential is that it is more probable that a category in a language functions in agree-

ment, the more the category is grammaticized (…) Gender and nominal class only appear in the context of agreement. But precisely they are the more grammaticized variants of other processes of nominal classification, such as the possessive or number classification, which themselves are not bound by agreement." In the case of internal agreement (i.e. within the nominal syntagma), both parts of the agreement have the same referent. In the case of external agreement, the predicate is in agreement: → Matthews *Syntax* 1981 p. 250: "It appears that agreement follows the direction of dependency when the dependant is a modifier or a determiner (...) but is the opposite when it is a complement, or at least the complement of a predicator."

5) Ch. Lehmann, to the origin of affixes of agreement, asserts ("*Kongruenz*" in *Syntax* 1993 1 p. 729a): "Affixes of agreement ultimately originate from pronouns (...) In internal agreement, demonstratives, and in external agreement, pronouns are the basis (...) In a diachronic perspective, reference is thus the primary function of agreement."

6) Government is a syntactical relation in which the subordinated compontent of a dependence relation fills a semantic blank created by the dominant component: → Matthews *Syntax* 1981 p. 250: "Government, which is traditionally recognized only in complement constructions, follows the direction of dependency throughout." On the other hand, when the dominant component fills the semantic role of the subordinate component, there exists what is called a relation of modification. Government and modification may thus be defined with precision in relation to one another: If, in a sentence, an element r_1 is semantically relational and syntactically dominant, and, another element r_2 is semantically absolute and syntactically dependent, while filling the syntactical blank left by r_1, then government occurs, with r_1 governing r_2. If, in a sentence, an element m_1 is semantically relational and syntactically dependent, and another element m_2 is semantically absolute and syntactically dominant, and each of these fills a blank left by the other, then modification occurs, with m_1 modifying m_2.

C. Verbal Morphosyntax

1. General Information

S 300. In addition to its lexical meaning, the finite verb consists of grammatical categories, which are in turn composed of the following five dimensions: person, number, mode, tense-aspect, and diathesis. For information on morphology, cf. F 200ff.

1) The categories in themselves are three categories of number (singular, dual, and plural), the five modes (indicative, injunctive, imperative, conjunctive, and optative), the three tense-aspects (present, aorist, perfect), and the three diatheses (active, middle, passive).

Suggestions for further reading: → K. Hoffmann "*Das Kategoriensystem des indogermanischen Verbums*" in Hoffmann *Aufsätze* II 1976 (in a contribution from 1970) p. 523-540.

2) Transitivity is not marked morphologically, but rather is expressed through the presence of an accusative morpheme in the complement. In his "*Zur Funktion des Nasalpräsens im Urindogermanischen*" (in *FS Rix* 1993 p. 280-313), G. Meiser tries to show that the nasal infix of nasal presents was the original expression of transitivity.

2. Person and Number

S 301. Within the dimension of person, PIE features three categories which are normally numbered following the example of grammarians of antiquity, a practice which should not be understood as a statement about the meanings of these categories. In the singular, the first person indicates the speaker; the second, the person to whom he speaks; and the third, that about which one speaks. Thus, the first person refers in every case to a human being, or rather to an object that is thought of as animated. The second person essentially refers to a being that is thought of as listening, or an accordingly conceived object. The third person, on the other hand, has no natural tendency to indicate either living beings, or objects, and can indicate the one just as well as the other. For more information, cf. F 400.

The plural of the first or second person does not necessarily indicate that there is more than one speaker, or people, to whom one speaks, but may simply indicate that the speaker and listener represent groups. The distinction between the inclusive first person plural ('we,' i.e. including the speaker, his group, and the listener) and exclusive first person plural ('we,' i.e. the speaker and his group, without the inclusion of the listener) cannot be reconstructed in Proto-Indo-European. That which is true of the plural, also applies to the dual: separate subcategories for the inclusive dual ('we two,' i.e. the speaker including the listener) and the exclusive dual ('we two,' i.e. the speaker and his group without the listener) have not yet been observed.

S 302. In the verbal as in the nominal number categories, Proto-Indo-European features a singular, a plural, and a dual.

In the case of the verb, number refers to the number of living beings or things that are indicated by the subject noun. The number plural does not indicate that the verbal activity takes place repeatedly or over a longer duration; this is expressed by the activity type of the verb: → Dressler *Verb. Pluralität* 1968.

Number is the dimension in which, in general, agreement exists between verbal and nominal inflection, namely the agreement between the finite verbal form of the predicate and nominal form of the nominative subject.The verbal aspect of 'person' must, with regard to agreement, be considered in another light: Aside from its reflection in the verb form, 'person' is not a grammatical category, but rather a lexical one, one that is firmly linked to the personal pronoun.

3. Tense-Aspect and Mood

S 303. The dimensions 'tense-aspect' and 'mood' are linked in their functions and appear together. While tense and aspect are represented within a single morpheme and are thus connected with each other in terms of content, the category of 'mood' is sometimes expressed using a proper modal morpheme, as in the cases of the subjunctive and optative, and is sometimes expressed through the use of different endings (indicative, injunctive, imperative).

Suggestions for further reading: → Mutzbauer *Gr. Tempuslehre* 1893-1909; Mutzbauer *Konjunktiv und Optativ* 1908; P. Kiparsky "Tense and Mood in Indo-European Syntax" in FL 4, 30-57; Rix *Modussystem* 1986; K. Strunk "*A propos de quelques catégories marquées et non-marquées dans la grammaire du grec et de l'indo-européen*" in *Colloque P. Chantraine* 1989 [1992] p. 29-42.

S 304. Using aspect, the speaker places the verbal action in a chronological relationship, whereby he specifies whether the the verbal action is completed (perfective aspect), or in course (imperfective aspect). When the grammar of a language includes this distinction, the language in question is considered an aspectual language. Aspect is a grammatical dimension.

H. Rix theorizes that an earlier phase of Proto-Indo-European featured a larger number of categories within the aspect dimension, and otherwise no longer distinguished between grammatical aspect and lexical aspect, rather uniting the two under the rubric 'aspect-action type': → H. Rix in LIV 1998 p. 10: "Aorist, present, perfect, as well as, departing more or less from the *communis opinio*, in causative-iterative, desiderative, intensive, fientive and essive." For further information, cf. F 206. For further information: → Rix *Modussystem* 1986.

S 305. Unlike grammatical aspect, lexical aspect (i.e. manner of action, or *Aktionsart*) is a property of the verbal meaning, and thus belongs to the lexical realm. Lexical aspects are not uniform in terms of content: They sometimes refer to the process of verbal activity, sometimes to the subject. Lexical aspects that refer to the process of verbal activity may be divided into telic and atelic lexical aspects, the former being those that only last a moment, the latter, those of more significant duration. Telic lexical aspect may be the result of the verbal activity as a whole (momentative), of its beginning (initial-terminative), or of its end (final-terminative). Atelic lexical aspect is a feature of verbal activities that last longer (durative), or are repeated (iterative). Lexical aspects that refer to the subject may concern a desire of that subject (desiderative), or the bringing about of a state of affairs (factitive), or the cause of an event (causative). In terms of contents, lexical aspects are sometimes similar to grammatical categories, e.g. the desiderative lexical aspect and the optative mood, which overlap in the first person singular when the speaker and subject are one and the same. The factitive and the causative lexical aspects correspond to the active voice. Because lexical aspect and aspect are sometimes similar, the lexical aspect system can be carried over into the grammatical aspect system and vice versa, as may be observed in the evolution of Proto-Indo-European into the individual IE languages. Evidence of the change from lexical aspect to a grammatical aspect system may be even be observed in suppletive verbal paradigms with stem forms of different verbal roots, e.g. 'carry,' 'bring': Lat. pres. *ferō* vs. perf. *tulī*; Gr. pres. φέρω vs. aor. ἤνεγκον.

S 306. Proto-Indo-European features three tense-aspect stems for expressing tense and aspect: aorist stem, present stem, and imperfect stem. The imperfect stem is formed from the present stem. The indicative forms of the tense stem only indicate the present (indicative present, perfect) and past (indicative aorist, imperfect); future actions are expressed through the subjunctive mood.

In the post-Proto-Indo-European period, there are, aside from the languages that continue the use of the subjunctive, various other means of expressing future actions, for example the Latin *-b-* future (→ Leumann LLFL 1977 p. 577-580; Meiser *Laut- und Formenlehre* 1998 p. 199f.), cf. Hitt. *uu̯ami* ("to come") / *paimi* ("to go") + present (→ E. Neu "*Futur im Hethitischen?*" in *FS Strunk* 1993 p. 195-202), cf. Ved. *-tar-* (*nomen agentis*) + copula (→ E. Tichy "*Wozu braucht das Altindische ein periphrastisches Futur?*" in *ZDMG* 142 1992 p. 334-342).

S 307. In its task as an indicator of tense, the present stem reveals a similarity to both the perfect stem and the aorist stem. The perfect, like the present indicative, refers to the present tense, indicating a state of affairs to which the verbal action led, e.g. 'the goat has eaten,' i.e. 'the goat is sated.' On the other hand, the imperfect, which derives from the present stem, has in common with the aorist a reference to the past tense: The imperfect and the indicative aorist differ only in their stem forms and are otherwise formally identical. The indicative aorist cannot be used to indicate the present tense, since the indicative aorist paradigms do not feature primary endings that indicate the 'here and now' of the communication process. This is due to the perfective aspect, which in the indicative excludes the possibility of referring to the present and has more of a future meaning. The Proto-Indo-European aorist and perfect categories fused into the perfect in Latin.

S 308. Examples: — a) present: Plautus *Trinummus* 400, *aperiuntur aedes* "the house is opened"; λ 100 νόστον δίζηαι μελιηδέα "You seek honey-sweet homecoming"; RV 10, 107, 7 *dákṣiṇā́śvaṃ dákṣiṇā gā́ṃ dadāti* "the Dakṣiṇā gives a steed, the Dakṣiṇā gives a cow." — b) imperfect: Plautus *Casina* 178, *nam ego ibam ad te* "for I came to you"; M 152 μάλα γὰρ κρατερῶς ἐμάχοντο, "for they fought very hard." — c) aorist: Δ 459 τόν ῥ' ἔβαλε πρῶτος, "It was him that he hit first"; RV 10, 85, 41 *rayíṃ ca putrā́m̐ś cādād*, "He gave riches and sons. — d) perfect: Plautus *Captivi*, 575 *servos es, liber fuisti* "A slave you are; free you have been";

τ 72 κακὰ δὲ χροῒ εἵματα εἶμαι "I have bad clothing on my skin"; RV 4, 16, 6 *apó rireca* "he released the water."

S 309. Aside from the category of tense, the aorist stem indicates the perfective aspect, the present stem the imperfective aspect, and the perfect stem a sort of resultative aspect. While the present and the aorist form a dichotomy, the perfect is isolated outside of this dichotomy. The isolated position of the perfect is also shown by the fact that the perfect, unlike the aorist and the present, has no moods other than the indicative, while it is precisely in the moods other than the indicative that the aspectual opposition of aorist and present is relevant. It thus remains questionable whether or not one may speak of aspect in the case of the perfect. In any case, the perfect is situated outside of the aspectual opposition of the present and the aorist.

H. Rix thus describes the qualities of the perfect: "Primary affixes as reduplication, mark, among other things, modes of action in Proto-I.-E., and differences of the endings distinguish, among other things, voices. The Proto-I.-E. perfect, therefore, is to be defined as a certain mode of action that appears in a certain voice only."[13] For information on morphology, cf. F 211.

S 310. The indicative is used for statements to which the speaker lends validity: By using the indicative, the speaker gives his statement the character of a true statement. Whether or not the contents of the statement in fact correspond to reality, is of course uncertain. Examples: Δ 443 ἐπὶ χθονὶ βαίνει "she runs on the earth"; RV 1, 105, 1 *candrámā apsv àntár ā́ suparṇó dhāvate diví* "the beautifully winged moon runs in the waters across the sky."

S 311. According to K. Hoffmann (K. Hoffmann *Injunktiv* 1967), the injunctive serves to mention an action, without specifying chronology. In P. A. Mumm's "*Verbale Definitheit und der vedische Injunktiv*" (*FS Strunk* 1993 p. 169-193), he asserts that the injunctive in Vedic expresses verbal definiteness (p. 190), or the presumed validity of an action (p. 177). The injunctive in Vedic receives a special function in prohibitive phrases in which it is then used in combination with the negation *mā́* in order to express that something is forbidden. The injunctive of the perfective aorist stem is used to express 'preventive' interdictions; the injunctive of the im-

[13] MSS 49 1988 p. 103

perfect present stem is used to express 'inhibitive' interdictions. Preventive interdictions avoid an event from the outset; inhibitive interdictions halt an event that is in course. The common term for these phrases is 'prohibitive'; a useful terminological differentiation of the two types of interdiction is that between prohibitive and inhibitive interdictions.

Examples: a) prohibitive: RV 3, 53, 2 *mā́ párā gāḥ* "don't go away" — b) inhibitive: AV 10, 1, 26 *mā́ tiṣṭhaḥ* "don't stay (standing)."

Suggestions for further reading: → Hoffmann *Injunktiv* 1967; H. Ammann "*Die ältesten Formen des Prohibitivsatzes im Griechischen und Lateinischen*" in IF 45 1927 p. 328-344.

S 312. The imperative, particularly the true, 2nd person imperative, holds a special place in the verbal paradigm, similar to that in the nominal paradigm occupied by the vocative, which is equally directed to a listener, and with which the imperative shares the formal characteristic of having a singular form which is composed of the stem without an ending, with no sign of its connection to the sentence.

Examples: — Plautus, *Mostellaria*, 387 *habe bonum animum* "have good courage"; B 331 ἀλλ' ἄγε μίμνετε πάντες "come now, stay"; RV 1, 16, 6 *tám̐ indra sáhase piba* "Drink this, oh Indra, for strength."

For further information: → B. Forssman "*Der Imperativ im urindogermanischen Verbalsystem*" in *Fachtagung Berlin* 1983 [1985] p. 181-197. For information on morphology, cf. F 212.

In addition to the true imperative, which expresses a request or an order that demands the immediate execution of the verbal activity, another form of expression for instructions and requests with a temporal function developed from the association of this imperative form with the ablative of the demonstrative pronoun PIE **tōd*. While these instructions and requests have the immediate validity of the true imperative, they do not bring about the immediate execution of the verbal activity.

Interdictions, or negative orders or requests, are, unlike positive orders and requests, not expressed with the imperative, but rather with the injunctive in connection with the negation PIE **meh*$_1$. The use of the infinitive to name the prohibited verbal activity in IE languages is comparable.

S 313. According to Delbrück's investigations of fundamental notions (*Ai. Syntax* 1888 p. 302), the subjunctive mood expresses a will, while the optative mood expresses a wish. It is important to note that the will or the wish (as the case may be) that is meant is that of the speaker, and not that of the subject, or, more precisely stated, that of the actor that is designated by the nominative form. The wish of the subject was originally expressed through its own derivational verbal form, namely, the desiderative. For Gonda (*Character of the Moods* 1956), the characteristic properties are 'visualization' for the subjunctive (p. 69ff.), and 'eventuality' for the optative (p. 52). According to A. Scherer ("*Die ursprüngliche Funktion des Konjunktivs*" in *Fachtagung Bern* 1969 [1973] p. 99-106), the subjunctive draws the conclusion from a given situation" (p. 101). "The subjunctive would then indicate a state of affairs, which *according to the relevant facts*, may be accepted as factual (i.e. concluded from the circumstances to be *necessarily* true), while the indicative reports what the speaker *knows* (or believes to know), or asserts as a fact. The optative characterizes merely that the state of affairs was thought." (p. 101). The original Proto-Indo-European categories 'optative' and 'subjunctive' fused in Latin.

Suggestions for further reading: → Delbrück *Conjunctiv und Optativ* 1871; Hahn *Subjunctive and Optative* 1953; Gonda *Indo-European Moods* 1956; K. Strunk "*Zur diachronischen Morphosyntax des Konjunktivs*" in *Kolloquium Kühner* Amsterdam 1986 [1988] p. 291-312. For information on morphology, cf. F 206f.

1) The subjunctive, which originally indicates the future, has two functions: In its prospective function, it serves to express things that happen in the future, while in its voluntative function, it indicates the will of the speaker. The subjunctive is used to express his will when he considers that it is within his power to bring about the verbal action. A declaration of will in a strict sense is only possible when the speaker has direct influence on events, such that that which is desired may also be executed. This means that a true expression of will may only be in the first person singular, while all other cases are equally requests. If the first person subjunctive is taken as a request made of oneself, a connection to the second and third person subjunctive is possible in which the speaker has no direct influence on the realization of the verbal action, so that the statement may only be understood as a request. A further connection may be made with the 1st person plural, in which the speaker communicates his own will, and at the same time directs a request to others.

2) Examples: — a) 1 sg.: Plautus *Bacchides* 1049 *quod perdundumst properem perdere* "what may be lost, I will/want to hurry up and lose"; υ 296 ἀλλ' ἄγε οἱ καὶ ἐγὼ δῶ ξείνιον "thus I will/want to give a gift of welcome also to him"; RV 10, 39, 5 *purāṇā́ vāṃ vīryā̀ prá bravā jáne* "your earlier heroic deeds I will/want to announce to all people"; RV 6, 59, 1 *prá nú vocā sutéṣu vām* "On the occasion of the pressing, I thus will/want to announce the heroic deeds of both of you." — b) 1 pl.: Ω 601 νῦν δὲ μνησώμεθα δόρπου

"now we will/want to think about the meal"; RV 5, 51, 12 *svastáye vāyúm úpa bravāmahai* "We will/want to call to Vāyu for the sake of welfare." — c) 2nd person: Plautus, *Mostellaria*, 388 *taceas* "you should remain silent"; RV 4, 31, 3 *abhī́ ṣú ṇaḥ sákhīnām avitā́ jaritr̥̄ṇā́m śatám bhavāsi ūtíbhiḥ* "you, oh helper of the singer's friends, will/should protect us well with a hundred helps." — d) 3rd person: Plautus, *Captivi* 115 *sed uti adserventur magna diligentia* "but they should be guarded with great care"; H 197 οὐ γάρ τίς με βίῃ γε ἑκὼν ἀέκοντα δίηται." For none will/should force me to leave against my own will"; H 87 καί ποτέ τις εἴπῃσι καὶ ὀψιγόνων ἀνθρώπων "and one day, even one of the descendants will say"; RV 8, 1, 22 *sá sunvaté ca stuvaté ca rāsate* "who will/should give both to him who presses, and to him who prizes"; RV 10, 81, 7 *sá no víśvāni hávanāni joṣad* "That man will/should be friendly and take receipt of all our sacrifices."

3) The optative, which originally indicates possibility, has two functions, either expressing the wish of the speaker (desiderative function), or expressing possibility (potential function). When the optative is used to express a wish, the speaker indicates that he is not directly able to bring about the verbal action. The optative proves to be more uniform than the subjunctive, given that in its cupitive function, the optative, independently of the category of person, always indicates a simple wish of the speaker, regardless of his influence on the realization of the verbal action.

Examples of the potential function: — Plautus, *Amphitruo*, 1060 *nec me miserior femina est neque ulla videatur magis* "a more miserable woman than myself does not exist, and will most probably never be seen."; Terence, *Eunuchus*, 511 *roget quis* "one might ask"; ξ 122f. οὔ τις κεῖνον ἀνὴρ ἀλαλήμενος ἐλθὼν' ἀγγέλλων πείσειε γυναῖκά τε κ αὶ φίλον υἱόν "a man, who comes traveling with news of that, could not convince his son and the woman"; RV 5, 50, 1 *víśvo devásya netúr márto vurīta sakhyám* "each mortal will likely desire the friendship of the leading god."

Examples of the desiderative function: — a) 1st person: Σ 121 νῦν δὲ κλέος ἐσθλὸν ἀροίμην "and now I would like to wrest noble fame"; RV 6, 13, 6 *víśvābhir gīrbhír abhí pūrtím aśyām* "by all songs, I would like to obtain fulfillment"; RV 1, 4, 6 *syā́méd índrasya śármaṇi* "we would like to be under Indras's protection". — b) 3rd person: Terence, *Eunuchus*, 302 *ut illum di deaeque senium perdant* "that elder is the one that the gods and goddesses would like to ruin"; A 18 ὑμῖν μὲν θεοὶ δοῖεν "to you indeed, the gods like to give"; P 416f. ἀλλ' αὐτοῦ γαῖα μέλαινα' πᾶσι χάνοι "the black earth should open to all precisely here"; RV 5, 21, 4 *devám̥ vo devayajyáyāgnim īḷīta mártyaḥ* "the mortal should praise your god Agni through worship."

4) In terms of content, the similarity between the prospective function of the subjunctive and the potential function of the optative is evident in the comparison of Z 459 καί ποτέ τις εἴπῃσιν "one day, someone will say" and Z 479 καί ποτέ τις εἴποι "one day, someone will in all likelihood say."

5) J. E. Rasmussen considers the possibility of a further mood in Proto-Indo-European, a proper prospective mood, for which there is little evidence: → "*Der Prospektiv – eine verkannte indogermanische Verbalkategorie*" in *Fachtagung Berlin* 1983 [1985] p. 384-399.

4. Diathesis

S 314. Within the dimension of diathesis, three categories may initially be reconstructed: active, middle, and stative.

1) Active and middle voices may be distinguished formally by their endings, cf. F 209f. However, in terms of content, the attribution of agentivity to the active voice and patientivity to the middle voice is not tenable: Lexemes with active contents are not always used in the active voice, just the same as lexemes with patientive content are not always used in the middle voice. Owing to the incompatibility of lexical meanings with one or the other voice, some verbs only occur in either the active or the middle voice.

2) Originally, the middle voice had a reflexive meaning, thus incorporating the function of the passive voice. The middle voice appears when the verbal action affects the subject directly or indirectly, or, when the verbal action does not have an affect beyond the subject. When the subject is plural or dual, the middle voice also expresses reciprocity.

3) In addition to the active and middle voices, a third diathesis category may be distinguished, the stative, indicating a state of being. For information on morphology, cf. F 211. The stative voice expresses the subject's state of being. In Proto-Indo-European, the stative merges on the one hand with the middle voice, which, in addition to its original reflexive meaning, takes on the additional 'state of being' meaning of the stative, and on the other hand, forms the basis for the perfect, which formally differs from the stative by its reduplication. H. Rix describes the earlier distribution of functions that became the

middle voice in the following way: "It is quite obvious how to distribute the two functions of the more recent middle voice among these two older voices: the content of the middle was the reflexive along with the passive, and the content of the stative was the deponent."[14] Rix emphasizes that the middle voice is more related to the stative voice than to the perfect mood: "It is this voice 'stative' and not the mode of action 'perfect,' that is the partner of the voice middle." (p. 104).

Examples: — RV 4, 21, 4 *rāyó bṛható yá ī́śe* "who has great wealth at his disposal"; RV 7, 101, 2 *yó víśvasya jágato devá ī́śe* "the god, which has the entire world at his disposal."

Suggestions for further reading: → Neu *Mediopassiv* 1968; C. Watkins in *Selected Writings* I 1994 (in a contribution from 1971 [1973]) p. 146-188; N. Oettinger "*Der indogermanische Stativ*" in MSS 34 1976 p. 109-149; by the same author, "*Zur Funktion des indogermanischen Stativs*" in *FS Rix* 347-361; Jasanoff *Stative and Middle* 1976; K. Strunk "*Zum idg. Medium und konkurrierenden Kategorien*" in *FS Seiler* 1980 p. 321-337; H. Rix "The Proto-Indo-European Middle: Content, Forms and Origin" in MSS 49 1988 p. 101-119; Kümmel *Stativ und Passivaorist* 1996; T. Gotō "*Überlegungen zum urindogermanischen 'Stativ'*" in *Kolloquium Delbrück Madrid* 1994 [1997] p. 165-192; R. Stempel "*Stativ, Perfekt und Medium: Eine vergleichende Analyse für das Indogermanische und Semitische*" in *GS Kuryłowicz* 1995 p. 517-528.

4) The function of the category 'passive,' which appears in many IE languages, but did not exist as a grammatical category in Proto-Indo-European, was performed by the middle voice. The various IE languages that feature a passive voice each formed it independently from each other. Suggestions for further reading: → E. Schwyzer "*Zum persönlichen Agens beim Passiv, besonders im Griechischen*" in *Schwyzer Kleine Schriften* 1983 (in a contribution from 1943) p. 3-79; H. Jankuhn *Passive Bedeutung* 1969; Hettrich *Agens* 1990.

5) According to I. Mel'čuk, there is a difference between 'diathesis' and 'voice.'[15] According to his view, one speaks of 'diathesis' in cases in which forms of the same verb that are commonly said to differ in voice cannot be used to describe the same real situation. Such is the case of

[14] *"The Proto-Indo-European Middle: Content, Forms and Origin"* in MSS 49 1988 p. 105.

[15] I. Mel'čuk *"The inflectional category of voice: towards a more rigorous definition"* in *Causatives and Transitivity* 1993 p. 1-46

middle voice forms and their corresponding active forms. On the other hand, the possibility of referring to the same real situation exists in the case of the passive forms that correspond to active forms. In this case, one speaks of 'voice.'

D. Nominal Morphosyntax

1. Nominal Properties

S 400. The verb, with its system of categories, presents a contrast with all other inflectable parts of speech, which share a common system of categories. For this reason, one speaks of nominal categories when speaking not only of the noun, which includes substantives and adjectives, but also when speaking of pronouns. The commonalities that combine these word types are the case and number categories.

In the case of adjectives and gendered pronouns, the dimension of gender is not directly linked to the lexeme, cf. F 323.

The personal pronoun plays a special role among the pronouns and nouns, not just because it does not distinguish between gender, but also because personal pronouns, unlike other pronouns, do not in fact take the place of nouns, which is why it would be better to use the term 'personals.' Unlike the case of verbs, the dimension 'person' in personal pronouns is lexical. For information on morphology, cf. F 401.

a) Case (S 401 - S 414)

S 401. To each case may be attributed a certain meaning. To be certain, the meaning may vary from the central meaning in certain cases. Meanings of cases vary as do lexical meanings, according to context. However, two opposing meanings may not be unified in a single linguistic symbol. The meaning of a case is generally independent of context, while the various functions are determined by the context. H. Hettrich proposes a process for the description of meaning and function of IE casual categories: → "*Zur funktionalen Variationsbreite altindogermanischer Kasus: Der Ablativ im R̥gveda*" in *FS Strunk* 1993 p. 53-55. In the wider context of a sentence, there are certain roles that may be assigned to the various nominal forms that appear in the sentence. These roles, however, are independent of the linguistic symbol and concern the actual situation, which may be described quite variously by the speaker. The same actual situation may thus be described in an active construction, or in a passive construction: *The cat ate the mouse. – The mouse was eaten by the cat.* In the one case, the nominative form 'cat' corresponds to the *agens*, in the other, the nominative form 'mouse' corresponds to the *patiens*. *Agens* and *patiens* are two opposing roles, which may neither be assigned as different meanings of a single linguistic symbol, nor classified as functions of a single meaning. As roles, *agens* and *patiens* are separated from the linguistic symbol of the nominative and may not be indicated by the nominative. Rather, the nominative indicates that which is in the foreground, thus, the theme; whether the *agens* or the *patiens* provides the theme is unimportant.

For further information: → E. Tichy "*Transponierte Rollen und Ergänzungen beim vedischen Kausativ*" in *FS Rix* 1993 p. 436-459.

S 402. The claim is often made that case meaning is least distinct in the case of complements, and most distinct in the case of extensions. According to W. U. Dressler: .'..case forms are obligatory completions of verbs ... subjects and objects are automatic results of the use of verbs, which, in their dependence schemes, present corresponding fillable spaces[16]," and further: "...there remains the function of case in the facultative extension of the sentence. Here, the case has syntactical value of its own.[17]"; → Haudry: "As a general rule, one may assert that government tends to deprive the case of its own semantic contents; a governed use is defined by a function. Positive semantic contents may only appear in free uses."[18]; → Pinkster: "...the semantic relations within a sentence are revealed by the cases only to a very limited extent, because: – within the nuclear predication the predicate determines the possibility of lexemes to occur as arguments with the predicate; the number and nature of the semantic functions are fixed for each verb; – outside the nuclear predication the lexical meaning itself determines to a high degree whether a lexeme may be used with a given semantic function."[19] However, the claim may

[16] „*Über die Rekonstruktion der indogermanischen Syntax*" in ZVS 85 1971 p. 10f.

[17] „*Über die Rekonstruktion der indogermanischen Syntax*" in ZVS 85 1971 p. 12.

[18] *Cas en védique* 1977 p. 14

[19] *Lat. Syntax* 1990 p. 47f.

not be made with such comprehensive validity: → H. Hettrich "*Rektionaler und autonomer Kasusgebrauch*" in *Kolloquium Wackernagel Basel* 1988 [1990] p. 82-99; by the same author, "*Semantische und syntaktische Betrachtungen zum doppelten Akkusativ*" in *Fachtagung Zürich* 1992 [1994] p. 111-134. Because the nominative does not occur as an extension, its meaning as a complement cannot be compared with that of an extension. The locative, on the other hand, may always indicate a spatial relationship, regardless of whether it is a complement or a given.

Suggestions for further reading: → Fraenkel *Syntax der Lith. Kasus* 1928; E. Risch "*Betrachtungen zur indogermanischen Nominalflexion*" in *Risch Kleine Schriften* 1981 p. 730- 738; S. Luraghi "*Der semantische und funktionelle Bau des althethitischen Kasussystems*" in ZVS 99 1986 p. 23-42.

S 403. Although they have meanings that sometimes vary greatly, different cases fit into a single paradigm: Thus, in terms of content, the nominative case, when used to indicate a grammatical subject, is completely different from the locative case when it is used to indicate the spatial aspects of the verbal action.

1) The order in which cases are listed originates in Sanskrit grammar, in which the cases in the paradigm that were formally identical were grouped together in each of the three numbers. However, this formal criterion is not a purely external characteristic. This formal identity is also generally defensible in relation to meaning, just as the partial formal fusion of various case forms may be seen as a preliminary phase of case syncretism.

2) Proto-Indo-European cases may be classified into groups according to aspects of content: There are cases with rather abstract meaning, that cross-reference within the language system, and others that have rather concrete meaning, referring primarily to language-external reality. This differentiation is not new, but must not be seen as an absolute classification, since individual cases are situated between the two poles, able to be used concretely or syntactically.

Cases assume particular meanings in the establishment of spatial relations of the verbal action: The spatial cases are the locative (where?), the accusative (where…to?), and the ablative (where…from?). The noun that indicates the place to which the verbal action refers is declined in one of these cases, allowing that which is signified by the subject (in the case of intransitive verbs), or that which is signified by the object (in the case of transitive verbs), to be spatially situated. That which is spatially situated is referred to as the *locatum*; that which refers to the place of reference, is the *relatum*.

Suggestions for further reading: → Fraenkel *Syntax der Lith. Postpositionen und Präpositionen* 1929; *Starke Kasus und Adv. im AHitt.* 1977; Luraghi *Casi e preposizioni* 1996.

S 404. A common phenomenon of the linguistic development from Proto-Indo-European to the IE languages is case syncretism, which means that cases which were originally separate from each other and distinguishable by their endings, were subsumed into a single ending. The spectrum of meaning of the resulting case becomes correspondingly broad, rendering the task of discerning a basic meaning of the case more difficult. For information on morphology, cf. F 305 § 3.

An intermediate stage in the fusion of one or more cases may be observed in which, according to number, or the context of gender or stem formation, the number of endings is smaller than the number of cases, and thus, within one and the same paradigm, not all cases are formally different from each other in all numbers. The differentiation of cases is no longer paradigmatic, but rather syntactic. Thus, already in Proto-Indo-European, all eight of the cases may be differentiated only in the singular of non-neuter thematic nominal stems. The plural and dual of the same paradigm no longer permit the reconstruction of eight different case endings.

In Latin, the ablative represents the merger of three cases: instrumental, ablative, and locative. In Greek, the PIE instrumental and locative cases merged to form the dative, and the ablative was subsumed in the genitive.

Suggestions for further reading: → Delbrück *Synkretismus* 1907; H. Hettrich "*Zum Kasussynkretismus im Mykenischen*" in MSS 46 1985 p. 111-122; M. Meier-Brügger "*Zum Verhältnis von Form und Funktion grammatischer Kategorien*" in *Fachtagung Berlin* 1983 [1985] p. 271-274.

S 405. Nominative

The nominative occupies a special position within the nominal paradigms of IE languages. This position is revealed by, among other things, the fact that in Old Indian -apart from neuter forms- all three numbers are formed on the basis of the strong stem and that the columnal nominal accent in Greek follows the accent position in the nominative case. Within the realm of syntax as well, the nominative traditionally plays a special role as the *casus rectus*, which contrasts with all the other *casus obliqui* of the paradigm.

The nominative indicates the theme of the sentence which, in a non-marked sentence, is placed in sentence-initial position. Other sentence elements are also thematized in taking the sentence-initial position, which, in the non-marked sentence, is reserved for the subject.

"The Proto-Indo-European nominative does not indicate the subject of an action in the logical sense, but rather in the sense that appears to the observer to be bearer and middle-point of the action that is expressed by the verb." (→ Delbrück *Gr. Syntax* 1879 p. 78). However, this does not apply to the interrogative pronoun, which places its referent in the middle-point, even when it does not take the subject position and is not the bearer of the verbal action. The concept of the subject is itself difficult to grasp; for H.-J. Sasse it is, "...a syntactical relation with semantic and pragmatic functions ... [the] sentence element that is indicated as the subject has a doubled function as it is both pragmatic (as an indicator of the topic of the sentence) and semantic (as an identifier of the agent). This double-function finds expression in its syntactical characteristics."[20]

For further information: → G. Serbat "*Der Nominativ und seine Funktion als Subjektkasus im Lichte moderner Sprachtheorien*" in *Glotta* 59 1981 p. 119-136.

S 406. Vocative

The vocative is the nominal form that is used for addressing a listener. There is only a distinct vocative in the singular, and even then, not all nominal paradigms feature a separate vocative form. Where there is no vocative, its function is taken by the nominative. The same occurs when two actions of addressing are linked: While the first is in the vocative, the second is in the nominative. — Examples: Γ 276f. Ζεῦ πάτερ ... Ἠέλιός θ' "Oh father Zeus and Helios"; RV 3, 25, 4 *ágna índraś ca* "Oh Agni and Indra"

Suggestions for further reading: → Svennung *Anredeformen* 1958; Zwolanek *Anrufungsformen* 1970.

1) The vocative element in the sentence receives no accent. —Example: RV 1, 184, 2 *asmé ū ṣú vr̥ṣaṇā mādayethām* "Enjoy yourselves nicely, you two heroes, in our company."

2) In Old Indian, when the vocative forms a sentence of its own, and is thus in sentence-initial position, it receives stress, regardless of its normal nominal accent, on its first syllable, i.e. on the first syllable of the sentence. In this case,

---

[20] *Subjektprominenz* in *FS Stimm* 1982 p. 270

sentence stress is meant and not word stress. — Example: AV 19, 70, 1 *dévā jī́vata* "Gods! Live!"

S 407. Accusative

The accusative has two apparently very different functions: On the one hand, it indicates the direct object in the case of transitive verbs (i.e. accusative object), on the other hand, it expresses that the verbal action bears an orientation in terms of space (i.e. directional accusative). The accusative is further used to express spatial or chronological expanse (i.e. accusative of expanse). In addition, it expresses the relation of the verbal action to a referent in a non-spatial sense (relational accusative). Finally, the accusative is also used when the contents of a verb are additionally expressed through a noun which appears in the accusative (i.e. accusative of contents): The technical term for this use of a substantive and a verb with the same lexical contents is *figura etymologica*. The original meaning of the accusative is probably that of direction, in the sense of spatial relation. The additional meanings that developed upon this basis include extent, relation, object and contents.

1) According to Hübschmann (*Casuslehre* 1875), the accusative indicates the "completion or narrower definition of the verbal concept" (p. 133), distinguishing an obligatory accusative, i.e. the object accusative, from a facultative accusative. Delbrück (*Gr. Syntax* 1879) thus describes the use of the accusative: "Originally, it served neither to indicate the object, nor the destination, nor the relation, etc., but rather simply to complement the verb. The choice of senses in which this complement was to be understood was left to the listener." (p. 29). He further asserts that there were "different types of uses ... already in the Proto-Indo-European period" (p. 29).

2) As an indicator of place, the accusative is similar to the locative, which is also used to indicate the arrival at a destination toward which a movement was oriented. In contrast, although the accusative does not exclude the arrival at a destination, it is semantically indifferent to the question of arrival at a destination: → J. L. García Ramón "*Zum Akkusativ der Richtung im Vedischen und im Indogermanischen*" in *FS Strunk* 1995 p. 33-52.

It remains disputed whether the local or grammatical meaning of the accusative is original. According to G. De Boel (*"The Homeric accusative of limit of motion revisited"* in *Kolloquium Kühner Amsterdam* 1986 [1988] p. 53-65), the directional accusative is not inherited, but rather newly created:

"With causative motion verbs, first of all, the accumulation of accusatives is clearly caused by the addition of a secondary goal accusative to an object accusative that was already present in the construction. Similarly the accusative with intransitive motion verbs cannot be shown to reflect original use. It is restricted to a lexical subclass, in which such a use of the accusative seems likely to develop spontaneously, as happened again in Modern Greek." (p. 64f.).

For further information: → De Boel *Goal accusative* 1988.

3) Equally unclear is the relationship in Proto-Indo-European of a specialized directional case, the 'directive,' which was continued in Anatolian, to the directional accusative. According to G. Dunkel (*"The IE Directive"* in *Fachtagung Zürich* 1992 [1994] p. 17-36), the directive only indicates the direction: "It expressed only the aim or direction of a movement." (p. 34). In comparison, the accusative and the locative have additional meanings: the accusative indicates "attainment of the goal and entering it" (p. 34); and the locative, "attainment of the goal ... and ... state of rest" (p. 34).

Suggestions for further reading: → W. P. Schmid *"Sprachwissenschaftliche Bemerkungen zum hethitischen "Direktiv""* in *FS Otten* 1973 p. 291-301; *Neu Lokativ* 1980.

4) Only miscellaneous remnants of the accusative of direction without the use of a preposition are extant in Latin, e.g. *domum* "(to) home," *rus* "to the countryside."

Examples: — a) Accusative of direction: A 322 ἔρχεσθον κλισίην "go both of you to your tent"; K 195 ὅσοι κεκλήατο βουλήν "who were summoned for consultation"; TS 6, 2, 11, 4 *yadā́ múkhaṃ gachaty, áthodáraṃ gachati* "if it goes to the mouth, then it goes to the stomach." — b) accusative of extent: Plautus, *Truculentus* 278 *noctem in stramentis pernoctare* "to pass one night in the straw"; Ψ 529 δουρὸς ἐρωήν "at a spear throw's distance"; λ 190 χεῖμα "in the winter"; TB 1, 3, 6, 3 *saptádaśa pravyādhā́n ājíṃ dhāvanti* "they run a race for a distance of seventeen times the range of one shot"; TB 1, 1, 3, 9 *só aśvatthé saṃvatsarám atiṣṭhat* "he remained in the tree for one year." — c) accusative of relation: Plautus, *Menaechmi* 511f. *indutum ... pallam* "clothed in a dress"; E 354 μελαίνετο δὲ χρόα καλόν "and she was reddened on her beautiful skin"; ŚB 14, 7, 2, 27 *nàinaṃ kr̥tākr̥té tapataḥ* "neither things done, nor things undone hurt this one." — d) object accusative: ŚB 14, 7, 1, 24 *jíghran vái tád ghrātávyaṃ ná jighrati* "truly smelling, he smells not what is to be smelled." — e) accusative of content: Plautus, *Captivi* 358 *quod bonis bene fit beneficium* "which charitable act is well directed to the good"; O 414 ἄλλοι δ' ἀμφ' ἄλλῃσι μάχην ἐμά-χοντο νέεσσιν "here and there they fought the fight for the ships"; RV 8, 7, 4 *yád yā́maṃ yā́nti vāyúbhiḥ* "when they go the way with the winds."

5) Suggestions for further reading: → La Roche *Accusativ* 1861; Gaedicke *Accusativ im Veda* 1880; Müller *Nominativ und Akkusativ* 1908; Jacquinod *Double accusatif en grec* 1989; H. Hettrich "*Semantische und syntaktische Betrachtungen zum doppelten Akkusativ*" in *Fachtagung Zürich* 1992 [1994] p. 111-134;

S 408. Instrumental

The instrumental case indicates that which accompanies the verbal activity. This meaning forms the basis from which other meanings have developed: In the case of inanimate objects, the instrumental indicates the means by which the verbal action is executed; in the case of a person, it indicates that the person executes, or helps to execute the action; in the case of places, it indicates where movement takes place. The instrumental further indicates constitution, accompanying circumstances, a reason, and in comparisons, the distinguishing characteristic. The function of the instrumental that relates to people, or 'sociative' function may be reconstructed in Late Proto-Indo-European. However, this function presumably finds its origins in a use that is purely related to inanimate objects: → K. Strunk "*Syntaktische Bemerkungen zum hethitischen und indogermanischen Instrumental in Istoričeskaja lingvistika i tipologija*" edited by G. A. Klimov et al. Moscow 1993 p. 81-91. In the indication of temporal circumstances, the instrumental bears a resemblance to the temporal locative. In Latin, the instrumental, like the locative, has merged into the ablative. In Greek, the instrumental has merged with the dative, cf. S 404.

Examples: — a) Instrumental of accompaniment: Plautus, *Amphitruo* 219 *postquam utrimque exitum est maxuma copia* "after they marched up in great numbers on both sides"; λ 160f. ἐνθάδ' ἱκάνεις νηί τε καὶ ἑτάροισι "you arrive here with the ship and the companions"; RV 1, 1, 5 *devó devébhir ā́ gamat* "the god should come here with the gods" RV 5, 51, 1 *víśvair ū́mebhir ā́ gahi* "come here with all helpers"; RV 1, 92, 7 *divá stave duhitā́ gótamebhiḥ* "the daughter of the heavens is prized by the Gotamas." — b) Instrumental of means: Plautus, *Truculentus* 526f. *neque etiam queo / pedibus mea sponte ambulare* "and I cannot even walk around independently on my own feet"; Lucretius 4, 387 *vehimur navi* "we sail with the ship"; A 527 κεφαλῇ κατανεύσω "I will nod with my head"; M 207 πέτετο πνοιῇς ἀνέμοιο "he flew with a breath of the wind"; RV 1, 128, 3 *śatáṃ cákṣāṇo akṣábhiḥ* "the god that sees with a hundred eyes"; RV 3, 32, 14 *nāvéva yā́ntam* "as to those who go with the ship." — c) Instrumental of route: Plautus, *Curculio*, 35 *nemo ire quemquam publica prohibet via* "no one hinders another from walking on a public street"; Plautus, *Poenulus*, 1105 *terra marique* "on earth and sea"; RV 1, 25, 7 *antárikṣeṇa pátatām* "which fly in the air"; RV 3, 58, 5 *éhá yātam pathíbhir devayā́naiḥ* "comes this way on divine paths"; RV 5, 64, 3 *mitrásya yāyām pathā́* "I would walk on Mitra's path." — d) Instrumental of constitution: Cato, *De agricultura* 88, 1 *amphoram defracto collo* "an amphora with a broken neck"; PY Ta 641.1 *ti-ri-po e-me po-de* i.e. *tripos hemē podē* "a tripod with one leg"; RV 4, 7, 3 *dyā́m iva stṛ́bhiḥ* "like the heavens with the stars." — e) Instrumental of accompanying circumstances: Λ 555 τετιηότι θυμῷ "with a worried temperament"; σ 199 φθόγγῳ ἐπερχόμεναι "coming forward with noise"; RV 4, 13, 1 *út sū́ryo jyótiṣā devá éti* "up comes the divine sun with light"; RV 9, 97, 36 *índram ā́ viśa bṛhatā́ rávenạ* "go to Indra with great noise." — f) Instrumental of reason: Plautus, *Amphitruo* 1118 *nam mihi horror membra misero percipit dictis tuis* "for fright seizes from poor me my limbs because of your words"; Φ 390 γηθοσύνῃ "out of joy"; ŚB 1, 2, 3, 1 *sá bhīṣā́ ní lilye* "he hid himself out of fear." — g) Instrumental of comparison: Plautus, *Cistellaria* 205 *qui omnes homines supero antideo cruciabilitatibus animi* "I, who supercede all men, surpass in tortures of the heart"; Γ 194 εὐρύτερος δ' ὤμοισιν "wider, however, than the shoulders."

Suggestions for further reading: → W. Schulze *Kleine Schriften* (in a contribution from 1896) p. 652.

S 409. Dative

When used to indicate people, the dative indicates an actor or actors who receive (action; [indirect] object dative) or possess (state; possessive dative). Further, while the dative is used to indicate one who is positively or negatively affected (*dativus commodi/incommodi*), only the quality of being affected is expressed by the dative; the positive or negative connotations themselves remain outside of the domain of the dative. When applied to abstract nouns, the dative indicates that the noun is the goal of an action (*dativus finalis*). This function is important for the formation of infinitive constructions.

Examples: — a) relational dative: Plautus, *Stichus* 260 *nullan tibi lingua est*? "have you no tongue?"; Plautus, *Mostellaria* 293 *tibi me exorno ut placeam* "I adorn myself for you, in order to please"; Plautus, *Rudens*

229 *quoniam vox mihi prope hic sonat*? "what voice thus sounds for me so near?"; Plautus, *Rudens* 274 *nunc tibi amplectimur genua* "now we shall seize your knees"; Plautus, *Truculentus* 378 *mihi quidem atque oculis meis* "indeed for me and my eyes"; H 423 οἳ δ' ἤντεον ἀλλήλοισιν "and they met one another"; H 101 τῷδε δ' ἐγὼν αὐτὸς θωρήξομαι "and for this one I will arm myself"; A 4 αὐτοὺς δὲ ἑλώρια τεῦχε κύνεσσιν "and he gave them to the dogs as prey"; E 249f. μηδέ μοι οὕτως θῦνε "do not rage so to me"; B 142 τοῖσι δὲ θυμὸν ἐνὶ στήθεσσιν ὄρινε "and he stirred the soul in their chests"; Ψ 595 δαίμοσιν εἶναι ἀλιτρός "to be a sinner to the gods"; RV 4, 12, 3 *dádhāti rátnaṃ vidhaté ... mártyāya* "he distributed wealth to the devoted mortal"; RV 1, 15, 12 *devā́n devayaté yaja* "sacrifice to the gods for the worshipper of gods"; RV 2, 2, 8 *átithiś cā́rur āyáve* "a dear guest for the sohn of Āyu." — b) *dativus finalis*: Plautus, *Poenulus* 626 *ut quaestui habeant male loqui melioribus* "that they have it as a gain, that they speak badly of their betters"; H 285 χάρμῃ προκαλέσσατο "he called out to battle"; RV 1, 30, 6 *ūrdhvás tiṣṭhā na ūtáye* "be there upright to support us."

For further information: → Havers *Kasussyntax* 1911; Oertel *Dativi finales* 1941.

S 410. Ablative

The ablative expresses the place of origin of the verbal action. Accordingly, the ablative is principally featured when a *locatum* moves, or is moved, away from a *relatum*. To this central meaning may be traced the ablative functions relating to origin, which refers to a spatial idea, relating to separation, which is accompanied by a movement away, relating to comparisons, in which the ablative is used to indicate the object in relation to which a compared object differs. In Greek, the ablative was subsumed within the genitive, cf. S 404.

Examples: — a) Ablative of place of origin: Cato, *De agricultura* 5 *primus cubitu surgat* "he gets up out of bed first"; Plautus, *Trinummus* 805 *cunctos exturba aedibus* "drive all from the house"; O 655 νεῶν μὲν ἐχώρησαν "they retreated from the ships"; E 456 οὐκ ἂν δὴ τόνδ' ἄνδρα μάχης ἐρύσαιο" "could you not push this man from the fight?; RV 7, 18, 10 *īyúr gā́vo ná yávasād ágopāḥ* "they went like cows from the field without a herdsman"; RV 7, 5, 6 *tváṃ dásyū́m̐r ókasa agna ājaḥ* "you, oh Agni, drive the Dasyus from their homeland." — b) *Ablativus originis*: Plautus, *Captivi* 277 *quo de genere natust* "from which family he originates"; RV 1, 123, 9 *śukrā́ kr̥ṣṇā́d ajaniṣṭa* "the shining one was born from the darkness"; RV 10, 72, 3 *ásataḥ sád ajāyata* "from the non-being came the being forth." — c) *Ablativus separativus*: ζ 192 οὔτ' οὖν ἐσθῆτος δευήσεαι "and you will not lack in clothing"; Σ 126 μηδέ μ' ἔρυκε μάχης "do not hold me back from battle." — d) *Ablativus comparationis*: Plautus, *Poenulus* 812 *levior pluma est gratia* "thanks is lighter than a feather"; Δ 400 εἷο χέρηα μάχῃ "worse than he in battle"; Σ 109 πολὺ γλυκίων μέλιτος "much sweeter than honey"; RV 1, 114, 6 *svādóḥ svā́dīyo* "sweeter than sweets"; RV 10, 176, 4 *sáhasaś cid sáhīyān* "stronger even than the strong."

S 411. Genitive

In its partitive root meaning the genitive expresses that a part is meant of the noun in the genitive case. Originally, the genitive relates only to the contents of the lexeme, a noun featuring the genitive ending. Various functions have developed from this root meaning, including indications of composition, possession, and relation. According to G. Serbat ("*Zum Ursprung des indogermanischen Genitivs und seiner lateinischen Verwendung*" in *Kolloquium Lat. u. Idg. Salzburg* 1986 [1992] p. 285-291), "(...) the sense is asserted of a certain, limited quantity, which is of a smaller scale than the term indicated by the stem. ... In other words, the ending only affects the word stem. At the same time, the ending plays no syntactical role." (p. 288) "As a result, this partitive form may not be classified among the syntactically significant characteristics, but rather among the forms that have no syntactical value, the quantitative forms ... singular, dual, and plural." (p. 289) The genitive may often replace other cases without expressing their meaning; it lends an additional partitive meaning to the meaning that the expected case would have brought. According to Scherer (Lat. *Syntax* p. 50), three realms of use may be distinguished for the genitive, namely: the indication of possession, quality, and relation. The genitive is also used in comparisons to indicate that with which something is compared. For information on competing roles of genitives and adjectives, cf. F 311 § 4.

Examples: — a) partitive: Plautus, *Casina* 538 *modius ... salis* "a scoop of salt"; ι 102 λωτοῖο φαγών "eating of lotus"; Θ 470 ἠοῦς "in the morning." — b) *Genitivus qualitatis*: Cato, *De agricultura* 121 *lauri folia* "leaves of the laurel"; φ 7 κώπη δ' ἐλέφαντος ἐπῆεν "a handle of ivory was on it." — c) *Genitivus possessivus*: Plautus, *Mostellaria* 980 *patris amicus* "the father's friend"; Sophocles, *Aias mastigophoros* 172 Διὸς Ἄρτεμις "Artemis (daughter of) Zeus" Φ 109 πατρὸς δ' εἴμ' ἀγαθοῖο "and I am (the son) of a noble father." — d) *Genetivus relationis*: Terence, *Phormio* 954 *monstri ... simile* "similar to a miracle";

Ψ 485 ἢ τρίποδος περιδώμεθον ἠὲ λέβητος "both of us are betting a tripod and a basin"; A 512 ἥψατο γούνων "she touched the knee."

Suggestions for further reading: → Yoshida (D.) *Old Hittite Genitive* 1987; J. Kellens "*Les fonctions du génitif en vieil-avestique*" in *Syntaxe des langues indo-iraniennes anciennes* 1993 [1997] p. 81-90.

S 412. Locative

By expressing that the verbal action takes place in spatial relation to the object that is indicated by the referent, the locative serves primarily to situate the verbal action spatially, and secondarily to situate the verbal action temporally. The extent to which the idea of space is expressed is also dependent upon the lexical meaning of the noun. If the noun indicates something that has spatial extent –which may include concrete as well as abstract nouns-, the spatial idea may thus be quite evident. However, when the noun indicates, e.g. a unit of time, the use of the locative only reveals the original spatial metaphor that underlies the concept of a temporal relation, at the same time without requiring that the metaphor predominates. In addition, the spatial idea may be carried over to the most various circumstances. Thus, the realm of use of the locative includes local, temporal, and modal expressions. The local meaning of the locative is not limited to a certain part of the object, but rather may just as well pertain to its interior, exterior, or environment. This is sometimes dependent on the object that is designated and its form. Depending in turn on the nature of the verbal action, the locative may have the function of indicating the goal of a movement that is coming to completion. In Latin, the locative was subsumed within the ablative. There exist only miscellaneous inherited locative forms, such as *domi* "at home" and *ruri* "in the countryside." In Greek, the locative was subsumed in the dative, cf. S 404.

Examples: — a) Locative of place: Plautus, *Amphitruo* 568 *homo idem duobus locis ut simul sit* "that the same man should be in two places at the same time"; Δ 166 αἰθέρι ναίων "living in the heavens"; δ 844 ἔστι δέ τις νῆσος μέσσῃ ἁλί "there is an island in the middle of the sea"; N 179 ὄρεος κορυφῇ "on the peak of the mountain"; Γ 10 εὖτ' ὄρεος κορυφῇσι Νότος κατέχευεν ὀμίχλην "as when the south wind pours fog down from the mountain top"; RV 7, 68, 7 *mádhye ... samudré* "in the middle of the sea"; RV 9, 18, 4 *ā́ yó víśvāni vā́ryā vásūni hástayor dadhé* "who holds all treasures that one could desire to have in his two hands"; RV 1, 32, 2 *áhann áhim párvate śiśriyāṇám* "he smote the dragon that had occupied the mountain"; RV 5, 36, 2 *párvatasya pṛṣṭhé* "on the back of the mountain"; RV 3, 23, 4 *sárasvatyāṃ revád agne didīhi* "shine beautifully on the Sarasvati, oh Agni"; RV 7, 18, 18 *tásmin ní jahi vájram* "Strike him with the cudgel!" — b) *Locativus temporalis*: Plautus, *Amphitruo* 568 *tempore uno* "at one time"; B 468 ὥρῃ "in the spring"; Γ 189 ἤματι τῷ "on this day"; RV 3, 4, 2 *yáṃ devā́sas trír áhann āyájante* "whom the gods summon three times a day." — c) *locativus conditionis*: RV 3, 56, 8 *vidáthe santu devā́ḥ* "the gods should be present at the sacrifice"; RV 6, 52, 17 *víśve devā havíṣi mādayadhvam* "all of you gods amuse yourselves at the pouring of libations."

Suggestions for further reading: → M. Holzman "*Der sogenannte Locativ des Zieles im Rigveda und in den homerischen Gedichten*" in *Zeitschrift für Völkerpsychologie und Sprachwissenschaft* 10 1878 p. 182-230; *Neu Lokativ* 1980.

S 413. Local cases and local particles; case, adverb, and adposition.

The Proto-Indo-European cases with local meaning are the locative, accusative, and the ablative. These cases designate a general spatial relationship between two objects, which include places (which are concrete objects) and actions (in which concrete persons or objects participate). The locative simply organizes spatially. With the accusative and the ablative, the concept of direction enters into play, with each indicating an opposing direction: The accusative indicates that the verbal action is oriented toward the object referent; the ablative indicates that the verbal action is oriented away from the object referent. These local dimensions then serve –in a process of transfer that is itself the result of cognitive reflection– equally to describe temporal relations and other circumstances. Because in the case of local cases the spatial relation of intransitive verbs exists between the *locatum* (indicated by the nominative subject) and the *relatum*, while in the case of transitive verbs it exists between the *locatum* (indicated by the accusative object) and the *relatum*, one may also observe, in comparing such a means of designating spatial relations with the designation of subject and object in ergative languages, an ergative trait: → Ch. Lehmann "Latin Preverbs and Cases" in *Latin Linguistics and Linguistic Theory* in ICLL I 1981 [1983] p 145-161.

S 414. Adpositions, like adverbs, modify their referents semantically; indeed, while the adposition features the characteristic of government, the adverb does not: While the adposition is distinguished by the additional characteristic of government, this syntactical connection to the referent is missing in the case of the adverb, which is why the semantic connection through modification comes to the fore.

	adposition	adverb
government	+	–
modification	+	+

The adverbs in IE languages that correspond to adpositions are positioned following their referents: → Benfey *Vedica et Linguistica*, Strasbourg / London 1880 p. 101-114.

Suggestions for further reading: → *Starke Kasus und Adv. im AHitt.* 1977; G. Dunkel "Preverb repetition" in MSS 38 1979 p. 41-82; by the same author, "*Die Grammatik der Partikeln*" in *Fachtagung Leiden* 1987 [1992] p. 153-177; Horrocks, *Space and Time* 1981; Ch. Lehmann "Latin Preverbs and Cases" in *Latin Linguistics and Linguistic Theory. Proceedings of the 1st International Colloquium on Latin Linguistics* 1981 in Amsterdam, edited by H. Pinkster. Amsterdam / Philadelphia 1983 p. 145-161; Krisch *Konstruktionsmuster* 1984; J. Boley *"Hittite and Indo-European Place Word Syntax"* in *Sprache* 31 1985 p. 229-241.; by the same author, *Sentence Particles* 1989; H. Hettrich "*Syntax und Wortarten der Lokalpartikeln des R̥gveda. I: ádhi*" in MSS 52 1991 p. 27-76; G.-J. Pinault "*Le problème du préverbe en indo-européen in Les préverbes dans les langues d'Europe, Introduction à l'étude de la préverbation,*" edited by A. Rousseau. Villeneuve d'Ascq (Nord) 1995 p. 35-59.

b) Number

S 415. The dimension 'number' in Proto-Indo-European includes three categories: singular, dual, and plural. Number is a verbal as well as a nominal dimension: Thus, the finite verb of the predicate corresponds in number with the nominative form of the subject.

In the case of the noun, the singular indicates that a single unit of that which is indicated by the nominal lexeme is concerned, whereby the nominal lexeme may either indicate a single unit from a group (singulative), or a collectivity (collective). The dual number indicates duality, and the plural, plurality. The Late Proto-Indo-European nominal category 'dual' may be traced to an Early Proto-Indo-European lexical category which could be found in terms for body parts that exist in pairs. R. Lühr tries to explain the connection of dual forms with singular or plural forms (incongruence) by citing the difference among individual word categories in referentiality, which is greatest in the case of substantives and smallest in the case of verbs.[21] For information on the possibility of a further category of number, which, however, would not be a category of inflection, but rather a category of derivation: → H. Eichner "*Das Problem des Ansatzes eines urindogermanischen Numerus 'Kollektiv' ('Komprehensiv')*" in *Fachtagung Berlin* 1983 [1985] p. 134-169; J. A. Harðarson "*Zum urindogermanischen Kollektivum*" in MSS 48 1987 p. 71-115; R. Lühr "*Zum Gebrauch des Duals in der Indogermania*" in Graz 2000 p. 263-274. For further information on the dual number, cf. S 301 and F 304 § 1.

c) Gender

S 416. Proto-Indo-European includes three categories within the dimension 'gender': masculine, feminine, and neuter. However, since the gender of the substantive need not correspond to the sex of that which it indicates, this terminology, taken from grammarians of antiquity, does not adequately describe the contents of the categories. Masculine substantives need not refer to masculine subjects, just as feminine substantives need not refer to feminine subjects.

1) While internal reconstruction enables one to trace the three gender system (masculine/feminine/neuter) back to a two gender system (common/neuter), the attribution in terms of meaning is not clear at this early stage. Various underlying principles of distribution are conceivable: animate vs. inanimate, agent vs. non-agent, with subject marking vs. without subject marking. The breadth of the spectrum from lexical to grammatical contents becomes clear. For more information, cf. F 303.

Suggestions for further reading: → E. Tichy Kollektiva, "*Genus femininum und relative Chronologie im Indogermanischen*" in HS 106 1993 p. 1-19, M. Fritz "*Die urindogermanischen s-Stämme und die Genese des dritten Genus*" in *Fachtagung Innsbruck* 1996 [1998] p. 255-264.
The classification of an earlier PIE language phase that is internally reconstructed as an ergative language or an active language is linked with the question of gender in connection with, as the case may be, the existing (masculine/feminine), or missing (neuter) characteristics of the nominative:

---

[21] R. Lühr "*Zum Gebrauch des Duals in der Indogermania*" in Graz 2000 p. 263-274.

→ K. H. Schmidt "*Probleme der Ergativkonstruktion*" in MSS 36 1977 p. 97-116; F. Villar "*Ergativity and animate/inanimate gender in Indo-European*" ZVS 97 1984 p. 167-196.

V. The Proto-Indo-European Lexicon

A. General Information

W 100. The most important element of a language is the word, in which are represented phonetic, phonological, morphological, syntactic, lexical, and stylistic aspects.

All words in a language compose the lexicon of that language. Each participant in a community of speakers acquires a more or less large part of the lexicon, and is capable of using these words in a manner consistent with the common practice of his time. A mistaken use of a word stem is more consequential than a mistaken inflexion. The former immediately renders comprehension impossible.

As a rule, most words are acquired by the child from his immediate family, whose members, in turn, have acquired words from their parents. Because of this tradition, most words may be traced back for generations.

According to conventional thinking, the lexicon is presumably organized in the brain according to themes, model phrases, and chains of association. While organization of entries according to letters of the alphabet does not correspond to linguistic reality, this concept is practical and effective.

A lexicon is not a static quantity. It is, like human life itself, subjected to ongoing fluctuations. It is dependent upon consensus in the community of speakers. The lexicon is always open to the expression of new meanings.

On the one hand, new words may be formed analogically, based upon existing models and elements, cp. for example the Gr. model βασιλεύς 'king' with βασιλεύω 'I am king' and the analogical new formation ἀρχεύω 'I am ἀρχός' (a form *ἀρχεύς is unknown). Further, the meaning of an existing word may be expanded (figuratively) or even replaced by a new meaning, cf. Lat. *ariēs* 'ram,' with the figurative sense '(battering) ram' (the item of battle equipment is comparable in its effect to the animal) and Lat. *testa* 'earthenware, pot, jug, shard,' becoming 'head' in the Romance languages. In place of the elegant *caput*, *testa* was later used to indicate the skull, eventually developing into the standard term for head. The Latin examples are taken from H. Rix: → *Gentilnamensystem* 1972 p. 714.

On the other hand, foreign words can at any time be incorporated into the lexicon. As soon as the orthography, pronunciation and inflection are adapted to the receiving language, one considers the word a loan-word: → Bussmann *Lexikon der Sprachw.* 1990 p. 253. In Latin, for example, the loan word **ampora* 'two-handled clay container with a narrow neck with a pointed bottom' < Gr. acc. sg. ἀμφορέα (the Lat. *-a* is presumably best explained if we assume instead of *–éa* a spoken form *amp^{h}oreá* with consonantal *e*; the accusative form serves here for the speakers as a basis because it was in daily use for inventories and recipes, etc.). The phoneme p^h, uncommon in Latin, was replaced by *p* and the word integrated into the typical Latin *-ā-* declension). Proof of the complete integration of the loan word in the language is the purely Latin-internal diminutive *ampulla* 'ointment flask, bottle.' Finally, the basis word **ampora* was recognized again as a foreign term in the Classical Latin form *amphora*, with *ph* replacing *p*, this time following the Greek. On an other example see above E 507 § 3 (*māchina*).

Each word was re-created at a certain time with a certain meaning. Once created, each word has its own history: It may find daily use; it may be limited to a certain style or level of language; it may one day fall into disuse and disappear from the lexicon, etc. Etymology and word history may not be separated from each other: → Seebold *Etymologie* 1981 p. 58. The explicit goal of etymology is to determine the 'true' first meaning (motivation) of a word, and to thus gain information about the 'true' nature of that which it indicates. But this is naïvely optimistic. Language is always arbitrary and, as such, information about 'true' nature cannot thus be attained, but rather, in the best case, one may find information about the motivations of the speakers in naming the object, etc., as they did and not otherwise: → Rix *Termini der Unfreiheit* 1994 p. 9f with suggestions for further reading in note 21.

In most cases, one cannot trace a word all the way back to its creation, cf. e.g. PIE **ḱ(u)u̯ṓn* 'dog,' which, owing to correspondence sets in the IE languages (cf. E 507 § 5), may with certainty be traced to Proto-Indo-European. What we can no longer determine, is how the 'dog' received its name in pre-Proto-Indo-European. E. P. Hamp proposes a relationship to PIE **péḱu-* 'livestock,' deriving **ḱu̯on-* from a basic form **peḱu̯-on-*

'responsible for herds' (evidence to the contrary: → Mayrhofer *Lautlehre* 1986 p. 118). On the other hand, the word for 'tooth,' which, again owing to IE correspondence sets, may be traced to PIE *h_1*d-ont-*. However, the verbal root PIE *h_1*ed-* 'to bite, to eat' allows us in this case to understand PIE *h_1*d-ont-* as a participial derivation, in the sense of 'biter.'

Even though the age and/or motivation of a term are no longer ascertainable, the possibility remains, within the limits of documentation, of tracing back the lifespan of a concerned word in IE languages.

Suggestions for further reading: — a) General: → *Wörterbücher* 1-3 1989-1991. — b) Specific to Proto-Indo-European: → Pokorny IEW 1959; C. Watkins, et al., Indo-European roots in *The American Heritage Dictionary of the English Language*, edited by W. Morris. Boston, et al. 1969 [1980] p. 1505-1550; R. S. P. Beekes "*Een nieuw Indo-Europees etymologisch woordenboek*" in MKNA (= *Mededelingen van de Koninklijke Nederlandse Akademie van Wetenschappen, afdeling Letterkunde*) 61 / 9 1998 (see also the presentation of the project TITUS / Frankfurt in *Actualia / Projekte / Leiden*: There is a link to the Frankfurt page on our web site [cf. E 100] *s.v.* 'Indo-European linguistics in Europe'). — c) Individual perspectives on the reconstruction of the PIE lexicon: → *Stud. z. idg. Wortschatz* 1987; R. Wachter "*Wortschatzrekonstruktion auf der Basis von Ersatzbildungen*" in *Fachtagung Innsbruck* 1996 [1998] p. 199-207. — d) Latin: → Leumann / Hofmann / Szantyr *Allg. Teil* 1965 p. 74*ff.; Szemerényi *Lat. Wortschatz* 1989. — e) Greek: → Meier-Brügger *Gr. Sprachw.* II 1992 p. 7ff.

W 101. While synchronic semantic research varies among the individual IE languages according to the availability of documentation, the reconstruction of Proto-Indo-European word semantics is particularly limited.

Assertions may however be made concerning groups of words, for example, names of familial relations, body parts, natural elements (fire, water, light, etc.), home, and family, etc., cf. E 512 § 4, which includes suggestions for further reading.

W 102. Etymology and word history have always been the focus of great interest. All single-language etymological dictionaries offer information on Proto-Indo-European, including statements to the effect that a term is 'inherited' or ex. gr. 'pre-Greek' which are termed 'etymology,' although strictly speaking only statements concerning the concret creation of a word have etymological value.

Suggestions for further reading: → A. Bammesberger "*Geschichte der etymologischen Forschung seit dem Beginn des 19. Jahrhunderts*" in *Sprachgeschichte* 1 1998 p. 755-786. — Concerning the individual IE languages, see (among many others): → *Etymologisches Wörterbuch* 1983 (including contributions on various IE languages); Walde / Hofmann LEW 1965; Ernout / Meillet DELL 1959; Frisk GEW 1960-1972; Chantraine DELG 1968-1980; Mayrhofer EWAia; Tischler HEG; CHD; Kluge / Seebold 1995; Seebold *Etymologie* 1981; Vries AnordEW 1962; EWAhd; Vasmer REW 1953-1958; Fraenkel *Lit. etym. Wörterbuch* 1962-1965; Demiraj Alban. *Etymologien* 1997; etc. — The 'checklist' by K. Hoffmann and E. Tichy regarding the assertion, or appraisal of etymological interpretations: → Hoffmann *Aufsätze* III 1992 (first published, 1980) p. 761ff.

W 103. Whether or not the Proto-Indo-European lexicon contained foreign or loan words is unknown, but, as in the case of any living language, quite possible. If yes, it remains to be known from what language the borrowings might have taken place: The Finno-Hungarians (cf. E 436) and Hamito-Semites (cf. E 437) have been suggested as possibilities.

B. Word Formation

1. General Information

W 200. As a rule, the creation of new words only takes place according to models. Normally, the speaker takes existing material from his own lexicon as a model from which to abstract the basis for rules of word formation, cf. the example from Greek, ἀρχεύω in W 100.

An unlimited number of relationships can be created and re-established in word formation by analogy, which is not confined to the real historical developments. Latin substance adjectives of the type *-no-* present an example of this, including *īlignus* 'made of oak' and *aēnus* 'made of bronze' (< **ai̯es-no-*, cf. L 215 § 1): A substance adjective that would correspond to *terra* 'earth,' should thus be **terrā-no-* 'made of earth.' The attested form *terr-ēnus* 'made of earth' shows that the historically inaccurate reanalysis of *aēnus* as *a-ēnus* was so common as to make possible the transmission of the new suffix *-ēnus*. — Through such transformations, new suffixes and entire conglomerates of suffixes are created, cf. ex. gr. Lat. *-tōrium*: Starting from a regular series of examples, e.g. *audīre* 'to listen' > *audītor* 'listener' > *audītōrium* 'room for listeners' a direct connection was later drawn from *audīre* to *audītōrium* 'a place for listening' (called a suffix shift). Later, based upon this example, the word *dormītōrium*, 'room for sleeping,' was formed from *dormīre* 'to sleep,' regardless of the fact that the requisite step *dormītor* was in this case uncommon: → Leumann / Hofmann / Szantyr *Allg. Teil* 1965 p. 72*. — Suffix conglomerates such as **-ih₂* and **-eh₂-* have been shown to date from the Proto-Indo-European period, cf. W 204 § 1. For an other example see above F 507 with note 7.

W 201. Word formation of the ancient IE languages has been quite thoroughly researched. Following are fundamental recommendations for all areas of word formation: — a) Latin: → M. Leumann "*Gruppierung und Funktionen der Wortbildungssuffixe des Lateins*" in *Leumann Kleine Schriften* 1959 (in an essay dated 1944) p. 84-107; Leumann LLFL 1977 p. 273ff. (nominal stem formation), p. 383ff. (nominal composition). — b) Greek: → Debrunner *Gr. Wortbildung* 1917; Chantraine *Formation des noms* 1933; Schwyzer *Gr. Gr.* I 1939 p. 415-544 (including introductory material and information on root nouns, composite nouns, and nominal suffixes); Risch *Wortbildung* 1974. — c) Vedic: → J. Wackernagel *Einleitung zur Wortlehre, Nominalkomposition*, A. Debrunner "*Die Nominalsuffixe*" in Wackernagel / Debrunner *Ai. Gramm.* II / 1 1957 and II / 2 1954. — d) Hittite: → Rieken *Nom. Stammbildung* 1999. Further bibliographical suggestions may be found at appropriate places in the text.

In the following section, individual suffixes and compounds shall be presented that can be traced to Proto-Indo-European. With this purpose in mind, I shall permit myself to follow the overview offered in Meier-Brügger *Gr. Sprachw.* II 1992 p. 20ff. and shall limit myself to referring to the Proto-Indo-European core of suffixes and types of composite nouns.

2. Word Formation Using Suffixes; Suffix Systems

W 202. Adjectives that are derived from substantives:

1) Concerning possessive adjectives, in the sense of 'belonging to,' or 'in relation to': — The suffix that is most widespread among the IE languages is **-io-*.

1a) However, this reconstruction, common in older treatments, is not sufficiently precise. The following three endings are theoretically conceivable: I) *-i̯o-; II) *-i(i̯)-o-, III) -iH-o-. To all appearances, the forms vary in their individual uses: → Peters *Laryngale* 1980 p. 131 in note 79; Mayrhofer *Lautlehre* 1986 p. 161 with note 267; A. Hardarson in *FS Rix* 1993 p. 164 with note 25. These three authors consider at least four different suffixes, namely, the verbal *-i̯o-, a nominal *-i̯o- with a vague meaning (according to its origins, presumably an -*i*-stem with a thematic vowel); a nominal *-ih_2-o- with a special indication of possession (by its origin, possibly an -*o*-derivation from an abstract noun featuring *-ih_2-: → G. Klingenschmitt in *Fachtagung Regensburg* 1973 [1975] p. 154 in note 10; or, what I consider more likely, an -*o*-derivation from -ih_2- constructions of the type of Ved. *vr̥kī́*: → Rubio Orecilla *Sufijo de derivación nominal* 1995 p. 316f.); a nominal locative *-i(i̯)-o- (by its origin an -*o*-derivation from the nominal locative singular forms in -*i*, cf. the type Ved. *dámiya-* 'domestic'). — The precise determination of the details is made more difficult by Proto-Indo-European variant forms resulting from the prior syllabic structure in the case of the forms of type I (for information on the change from *-i̯o- to *-ii̯o-, cf. L 218 § 1 on Sievers' Law), by PIE vanishing of *H*, which, when occuring in type III, leads to merger with type II, and finally by generalization in the IE languages of *-ii̯o- in type I, such that, after the vanishing of the laryngeal under *-ii̯o-, both true *-ii̯o- forms and those that were originally *-i̯o- and *-ih_2o- forms can be united. — The complexity of the situation is revealed by the example PIE *ph_2-tr-ii̯o- 'belonging to the *ph_2ter-, located at the *ph_2ter-, coming from the *ph_2ter-' = Lat. *patrius* = Gr. πάτριος = Ved. *pítriya-*, etc. If one assumes the presence of an original suffix -i̯o- (evidence in Italic suggests this basic form for the group of patronyms: → Rix *Gentilnamensystem* 1972 p 718f. with note 60), one should then expect to find *ph_2tr̥-i̯o-; the -*tr*- (and not -*tr̥*-) double consonance is only conceivable, if it was re-formed according to the model of the type gen. sg. *ph_2tr-és already in the Proto-Indo-European era; the variant *-ii̯o- (in place of *-i̯o-) would then simply be the phonetic consequence of the double-consonant -*tr*-. The form *-ii̯o-, suggested in IE languages, may just as well be traced back to *-ih_2-o-; further, it should not be excluded that both locative *-i(i̯)-o-, as well as *-i̯o- and *-ih_2-o- derivatives of *ph_2tr- first coexisted, and then merged. — See also the issue of Lat. *dīus* = Myc. Gr. *di-wi-jo* / *di-u-jo* i.e. *diu̯ii̯on* (secondarily also inner-Myc. *diu̯i̯on*) 'belonging to (in the realm of) *di̯eu̯- ,' 'shrine to Zeus' and *di-wi-ja* / *di-u-ja* i.e. *diu̯ii̯ā* (secondarily inner-Myc. *diu̯i̯ā*) female divinity 'belonging to *di̯eu̯-,' 'daughter of *di̯eu̯-' = Ved. *div(i)yá-* (RV+) 'heavenly, divine.' The substantive Hom. δῖα = Ved. *devī́* is separate from the adjective. Suggestions for further reading: → Risch *Kleine*

Schriften 1981 p. 580f.; Mayrhofer EWAia I p. 727 (which justly emphasizes that the Vedic form *devī́* cannot share a heritage with Gr. δῖα); Harđarson in *FS Rix* 1993 p. 164-166. Particularly concerning Mycenaean: → Aura Jorro *DMic* I 1985 p. 178ff.; A. Leukart in *Mykenaïka* 1992 p. 394 note 44. For information on the special group of patronyms, cf. W 302 § 3.

1b) I. Balles proposes a new view of the entire issue: → *Sprache* 39 1997 [2000] p. 141-167. The contribution is based upon a thesis paper from Vienna, which the author submitted in 1996 under the direction of J. Schindler. Following are the results in tabular form:

		I *-i̯o-*	II *-i(i̯)o-*
A) *-o*-abl. of *-i-* stem		λοῦσσον < **lóu̯ki̯-o-* τυρός (Myc. *tu-rjo*) < **tuHri̯-ó-* cf. Avest. *tuiri-* n. 'whey'	
B) *-o*-abl. of loc. *–i*	a) relational adjective	**med^{h}i̯-o-* > μέσ(σ)ος **ali̯-o-* > ἄλλος	*medius* *alius*
	b) compositional suffix		ἐφ-άλ-ιος
	c) denominative adjective	**sok^{w}h$_2$-i̯o-* > **soki̯o-* >	θαλάσσ-ιος *soc-ius* *tert-ius*
	d) verbal adjective	ἄπειρος < **n̥-per-i̯o-* Ved. *ajur-yá-* 12x (*-ia-* 1x)	ἄγ-ιος, *infer-ius*, *exim-ius* Ved. *mád-ia-* 12x (*-ya-* 1x)

Commentary: — The author postulates (*ibid.*, p.161f.) that the common starting point for the entire group are the *-o-* derivatives from *-i* locatives (B), which must be distinguished from the less numerous *-o-* derivatives of *-i-* stems (A), cf. λοῦσσον (Theophrastus) 'white core of pine' < **lou̯ki̯-o-* 'featuring whiteness [**lou̯ki-*]' (see also, *ibid.*, p. 162 note 44). — The example τυρός is my contribution. — Starting from B, constructions including the rare relational adjectives (Ba) as well as the productive possessive adjectives have developed, as well as various sub-groups (Bb-Bd). While in the group Ba, the derivative of *-i-o-* as *-i̯-o-* would be expected phonetically (just as in Bc and Gr. ἄπειρος in Bd) as a rule (see Bb-Bd), the syllabic form *-i-o-* would be conserved for morphological reasons, as well as for reasons of clarity (the hiatus filled by the glide *i̯* to the -*ii̯o*-form). The group Bd however represents a special case in which, in the case of Vedic verbal adjectives, the form -*ii̯o*- in longer word constructions, is shortened to -*i̯o*-.

2) A further possibility for marking possession through construction is attested by PIE **d-e-i̯u̯-ó*- 'belonging to the heavens' = OL (Duenos inscription) *deivo*- and Class.Lat. *deus* / *dīvus* (cf. L 217 § 3) = Ved. *devá*- (< **dai̯u̯á*-) 'divine; god' = OAv. *daēuua*- 'demon' = Lith. *diẽvas*, etc.: → Mayrhofer EWAia I p. 742f. The PIE **d-e-i̯u̯-ó*- is considered a Vr̥ddhi-derivative from PIE **di̯eu̯*- / **diu̯*- 'god of the day and/or sky' and has been described as an -*o*- derivative with additional insertion of -*e*-: → Darms *Vr̥ddhi* 1978 p. 376ff. — In just the same way, **n-é-u̯-o*- 'now; new, young' may be interpreted as a derivative of the temporal adverb PIE **nu* 'now.' — Further sources of information on this phenomenon which is common and has been systematized in Indo-Iranian include: → Wackernagel / Debrunner *Ai. Grammatik* II / 2 1954 § 34ff. W. Schulze wrote the classic work on this form of derivative: → Schulze *Kleine Schriften* 1966 p. 60ff. (in an essay from 1907). Schulze considers the example PIE **su̯ēḱuró*- (in which **su̯ēḱ*- < **su̯-e-eḱ*-) meaning 'who belongs to the father-in-law,' i.e. 'son of the father-in-law' with the Proto-Germanic descendant **su̯ēguró*- (cf. NHG *Schwager*) as a derivative from PIE **su̯éḱuro*- 'father-in-law' (for information on PIE **su̯éḱu̯r̥-h₂*- 'mother-in-law,' cf. L 217 § 4) with the Proto-Germanic descendant **su̯éχuro*- (cf. NHG *Schwäher*). For information on phonetics, cf. L 421 § 1, and further, cf. Kluge / Seebold 1995 p. 657 *s.v.* '*Schwager*' and '*Schwäher*.' — Cf. also L 331 §3 (which concerns Luw. *sii̯u̯al*).

3) Adjectives indicating material composition: — PIE *-*éi̯-o*-, cf. Lat. *aur-eus* 'golden,' Class. Gr. ἀργυρ-οῦς 'made of silver' (the contracted form may be traced to -*éo*- < -*éi̯o*- [Myc.]; the Homeric accentuation of the type nom. sg. ἀργύρεος vs. dat. sg. ἀργυρέῳ was secondarily formed according to the schema ἄνθρωπος vs. ἀνθρώπῳ; the older pattern *ἀργυρέος vs. ἀργυρέῳ is indirectly attested by the Classic/Attic Greek contracted forms), Ved. *hiraṇy-áya*-. — Suggestions for further reading: → I. Hajnal "*Die frühgriechische Flexion der Stoffadjektive und deren ererbte Grundlagen*" in *Fachtagung Zürich* 1992 [1994] p. 77-109 (Following the lead of A. Heubeck, the author postulates, using Mycenaean relations to the suffix forms -*e*-(*j*)*o* and -(*i*-)*jo*, the existence of a PIE feminine form *-*ih₂*- in addition to the masculine and neuter *-*éi̯-o*-). —

Concerning Latin: → Leumann LLFL 1977 p. 286f. (*-eus*) and p. 321 (*-inus*).

4) Adjectives indicating fullness, in the sense of 'rich in…': — For information on PIE **-u̯ent-*, cf. W 305.

5) Smaller groups: — Temporal adjectives: → O. Szemerényi "Latin hībernus and Greek χειμερινός, the formation of time-adjectives in the Classical languages" in Szemerényi *Scripta Minora* III 1987 (in an essay of 1959) p. 1141-1159.

W 203. Adjectives that are derived from verbs:

PIE **-tó-*, **-nó-* and **-ló-* are components of verbal adjectives which have been partially integrated into the various IE verbal systems as passive (or intransitive) perfect participles. The roles of these suffixes vary from one IE language to another, e.g. **-lo-*, which, in Slavic forms the perfect active participle, but which in Greek is very seldom: → Risch *Wortbildung* 1994 p. 107. In the case of the passive perfect participle, the languages alternate with **-to-* and **-no-*. Examples of the former are Latin, Greek, and Vedic; an example of the latter is Slavic: → Leumann LLFL 1977 p. 611. For further sources concerning **-to-* and **-no-*: → Szemerényi *Einführung* 1990 § 351f. Despite the limited use of **-no-*, there are also constructions that are common to IE languages that are attributable to Proto-Indo-European, cf. PIE **pl̥h$_1$-nó-* = Lat. *plēnus* (in place of **plānos*) = Ved. *pūrṇá-* 'full, filled' = Got. *fulls* and NHG *voll* (< Proto-Germ. **fulna-* < **fulHno-)* = Lith. *pìlnas*: → Mayrhofer EWAia II p. 156; cf. also L 332 § 4d.

W 204. Substantives that are derived from substantives or adjectives:

1) Terms that indicate feminine beings and that are derived from masculine forms: — The suffixes **-i-h$_2$-* and **-e-h$_2$* are examples of *-h$_2$-* constructions on *-i-* and *-o-* stems (cf. F 323 § 2 and F 312) and may with certainty be traced to Proto-Indo-European.

One example (among many) of **-e-h$_2$-* is the Proto-Indo-European construction **néu̯-eh$_2$-* '(the) new one (feminine, sc. woman)' = Lat. *nova* = Gr. νέα = Ved. *návā-* etc. Some constructions that appear to be of Proto-Indo-European origin, are in fact of later origin, cf. E 506 § 5.

The situation of **-i-h$_2$-* is more complex. Vedic features two different types of inflection: Type I = *devī́-*, Type II = *vr̥kī́-*. — The inflectional model Type I (according to MacDonell *Vedic Grammar* 1910 p. 274) features: nom. sg. *devī́*, acc. sg. *devī́m*; nom. pl. *devī́s*, acc. pl. *devī́n*, instr. pl. *devī́bhis*, etc. vs. gen. sg. *devyā́s*, dat. sg. *devyā́i*, and instr. sg. *devyā́*: → Mayrhofer EWAia I p. 744 *s.v. devī́*. — An example of the inflection model Type II (according to MacDonell *Vedic Grammar* 1910 p. 270ff, marked by B) is *rathī́-* (here masculine) 'wagon driver, charioteer': nom. sg. *rathī́s* (with *-s*!); dat. pl. *rathī́bhis*, acc. pl. *rathī́n* etc. vs. acc. sg. *rathíyam* (written *rathyàm*), gen. sg. *rathíyas* (*-yàs*), dat. sg. *rathíye* (*-yè*), instr. sg. *rathī́*; nom. acc. pl. *rathíyas* (*-yàs*). — Concerning the inflection of Type I, which is found almost purely apart from the *-a-* stems, and Type II, which indicates feminine gender in *-a-* stems and is common as a feminine form of possessive composites: → Wackernagel / Debrunner *Ai. Gramm.* III 1930 p. 163ff. and II / 2 1954 p. 368ff.; Mayrhofer EWAia II p. 570f. *s.v. vṛ́ka-*; by the same author, "*Zu iranischen Reflexen des vṛkī́-Typus*" in Mayrhofer *Kleine Schriften* II 1996 (in an essay of 1980) p. 353ff. — Type I is widely represented in the Indo-European branch of languages. Among the many examples, compare the feminine active present participles with *-nt-*, including PIE *$*h_1s$-n̥t-ih_2-* 'existing' = Proto-Gr. **-ehat-i̯a* > Myc. Gr. *-ehassa* = Ved. *sat-ī́-* (for information on the verb PIE *$*h_1es$-*, cf. E 502ff.; for more information on attestations of feminine participles in Greek: → Meier-Brügger *Gr. Sprachw.* II 1992 p. 63). — Type II is primarily present in Vedic; non-Indian examples are seldom: compare, on the one hand, Ved. *puruṣī́-* (RV+) 'woman,' from *púruṣa-* (RV+) 'person' and Ved. *naptī́-* 'granddaughter,' from *nápāt-* 'grandson'; and on the other hand, compare Ved. *ahī́-* 'mother cow' with corresponding forms in Old Avestan and Later Avestan *azī-* and Ved. *vṛkī́-* with the corresponding Old West Norse form *ylgr* 'she-wolf.' — The origins of Type I are unproblematic: nom. sg. *dev-ī́-* / gen. sg. *dev-yā́-s* < PIE **déi̯u-ih_2-* / **di̯u-i̯éh_2-s* (the accent of the nominative singular form is secondary, in place of **dévī-*). While the nominative singular accent in the Homeric Greek example δῖα is retained, its stem form originates from weak case forms. Suggestions for further reading: → H. Eichner in *Sprache* 20 1974 p. 28. — Additional information on **-ih_2-* and **-i̯éh_2-*: While zero grade **-ih_2-* yielded **-ī-* phonetically in IE languages (e.g. the Vedic and Latin suffix *-tr-ī-k-*, cf. F 101 § 2), a newly formed **-i̯h_2-* (with consonantal *i̯*) often resulted from *-i̯éh_2-*, as is the case in the Greek normal form *-i̯a*. Remnant *-ī-* forms are however attested, cf. nom. sg. *γλώχ-ῑ- 'tongue' (cf. Homeric γλωχῖς, 'yoke strap end'; a secondary *-īn-* stem was formed by sandhi via the acc. sg. *-īn V-*, in the sense of *-īn' V-*; the accented suffix is secondary as well) vs. Ion. gen. sg. γλασσᾶς (with the expected zero grade stem and *-ss-* [Att. *-tt-*] < **-k^h-i̯-*; on the other hand,

Class. Att. gen. sg. γλώττης with full grade root and accent placement according to the nominative singular form; while the normal nom. sg. form γλῶττα reveals the expected full grade and accent, the consonant-initial suffix form originates from the weak stem). — The Old West Norse example *ylgr* presumably offers clues about the origins of Type II: → Mayrhofer *Kleine Schriften* II 1996 p. 354 with note 12. While the information in Vedic suggests the Proto-Indo-European form **u̯l̥kʷī́s*, from which one would expect the form **ylfir* to derive phonetically, the transformation of the labiovelar k^w to the guttural *g*, which in fact takes place, is only attested when followed by consonantal *i̯*. This phonetic constellation is only possible when we assume, firstly, that the Type II group was originally based upon a hystero-dynamic type with a nom. sg. **u̯l̥kʷ-i̯éh₂-s* and a gen. sg. **u̯l̥k-ih₂-és*, and secondly, that the form and suffix of the weak stem, as well as the accent placement of the strong stem were generalized as a rule, as in Vedic: → Kuiper *Ved. Noun-Inflexion* 1942 p. 12f.; Mayrhofer *ibid.* in note 12; R. S. P. Beekes "*Le type gotique bandi*" in *Laryngales* 1990 p. 49-58. — For information on other assumptions about the suffix *-ih₂-*: → Mayrhofer *ibid.* p. 356; G. Klingenschmitt in *Fachtagung Regensburg* 1973 [1975] p. 154 note 10 (*-i-h₂-* lastly as a collective construction [from which a feminine construction developed] with *-h₂-* for adjectives featuring *-i-*, which indicate possession; and lastly also the possessive adjectives featuring **-ih₂-o-*, cf. W 202 § 1); Leumann LLFL 1977 p. 283 (for information on remnants of Type II in Latin); R. Lühr in *FS Schmid* 1999 p. 299-312 (for information on descendents of both types in Baltic).

2) Diminutives and hypocorisms: — PIE **-ko-* and **-lo-* (in the case of *-o-*stems, *-e-lo-*). Diminutives: → Meier-Brügger *Gr. Sprachw.* II W 408 § 2. Hypocorisms: → Meier-Brügger *Gr. Sprachw.* II W 408 § 3; further, Risch, *Wortbildung* 1974 p. 107 note 93.

3) Abstract nouns of the type **neu̯ó-teh₂t-* 'novelty' = Lat. *novitāt-* = Gr. νεότητ-: → Meier-Brügger *Gr. Sprachw.* II W 410 § 3 and Rix *ibid.* in W 205 § 2 p. 737.

4) Place names: — This is the appropriate rubric for the suffix PIE **-Hon-*, discovered by K. Hoffmann: → Hoffmann *Aufsätze* II 1976 (in contribution from 1955) p. 378ff. The suffix has possessive meaning and can (like PIE **-u̯ent-*, cf. W 305) indicate place names. However, the use is broader. E. P. Hamp proposes that **-Hon-* may be determined to be **-h₃on-*, cf. the critical comments in L 329 § 2: → N. Oettinger in *Arbeitstagung Erlangen* 1997 [2000] p. 393-400 (on the Old Indian name of a divinity, *Pūṣan-*); G.-J. Pinault in BSL 95 / 1 2000 p. 61-118 (concerning the Vedic *dámūnas-*).

W 205. Substantives that are derived from verbs:

1) Indicator of the agent (*nomina agentis*): — For information on PIE **dh₃-tér-* 'occasional giver' vs. **déh₃-tor-* 'habitual giver': → Tichy "*Die Nomina Agentis auf -tar- im Vedischen,*" 1995. Cf. F 101 § 2 for an example from Latin.

2) Verbal abstract nouns (*nomina actionis*): — H. Rix offers a list of Proto-Indo-European constructions in *FS Szemerényi* *65 II 1979 p. 737f.: Among the types featured on the list are those with suffixes such as **-ti-* (cf. F 317 § 7), **-tu-*; those with an *-o-* stem such as PIE **róu̯dʰ-o-* 'to whine'; feminine forms such as **bʰug-éh₂-* 'escape'; root nouns of the type **nék̑-* 'destruction' and *-t-* constructions of the type **stu-t-* 'high praise'; and also *-es-* neuter forms of the type **tép-es-* 'heat, warmth.'

3) Indicators of tools, means, and places: — For information on PIE **-tr-o-*, **-tl-o-*, **-dʰr-o-* and **-dʰl-o-* (which find their point of departure in the *-o-* derivations from *nomina agentis* with *-ter-* / *-tor-*, which, due to variations in root forms, are often misleadingly transformed to **-tl-o-* or **-dʰr-o-* or **-dʰl-o-*): → Risch *Wortbildung* 1974 p. 41; Olsen *Instrument Noun Suffix* 1988; M. V. Southern in MSS 60 2000 p. 89-133 (which concerns Lat. *tabula* and the suffix *-dʰlo-*). Further, cf. L 347 § 2.

W 206. Suffix systems, suffix associations: — Parts of the group described by W. Caland are demonstrably of Proto-Indo-European origin.

1) In his treatment of the Later Avestan word *xruu-i-drau-* 'who carries a terrible, bloody, wooden weapon,' W. Caland called attention to the fact that Avestan adjectives with *-ra-* and *-ma-* as the initial element in the case of compound adjectives replace the *-ra-* descriptively with *-i-*. See, for example the adjective *xrū-ra-* (corresponding to the compound example) 'bloody, terrible' or cf. Later Avestan *dərəz-ra-* 'tough, strong, capable' vs. Later Avestan *dərəz-i-raϑa-* 'who has a strong wagon': → KZ 31 1892 p. 267 and 32 1893 p. 592 ("It now [seems] probable to me that this characteristic lasts into the Indo-Êranic period"). In his piece "*ΑΡΓΙΚΕΡΑΥΝΟΣ und Genossen*" published in *Wackernagel Kleine Schriften* I 1969 (but which dates from 1897) p. 770, J. Wackernagel showed that the phenomena is of PIE origin: "The Caland Rule is thus common Indo-European." Wackernagel refers to Greek examples such as ἀργός 'white, bright, shiny, fast' (*argó-* developed either from **arg-ró-* and further by dissimulation from **-rgr-* > *-rg-* or directly from PIE **h₂r̥ǵ-ó-*, cf. L 333 § 1) vs. ἀργ-ι-κέραυνος 'who has bright shining flash.'

2) The synchronic description of the phenomenon is certain. Historically, however, it is quite improbable that the initial word elements of compound words represent adjectives, but rather abstract *-i-* nouns. Our modern English translation promotes the illusion that there is also an adjective in the word-initial element. It is indeed conspicuous that, in contrast with **-ro-* constructions, **-u-* adjectives also appear in compound forms, cf. Hom. Gr. ὠκύ-ποδ-ες (from horses) 'with fast feet' and Ved. *āśu-ratha-* 'having a fast wagon.'

3) Following the precedent of Caland and Wackernagel, an entire series of suffixes that originate with, and are more or less connected to, the core of **-ro-*/**-mo-*/**-i-*, which in some measure developed in a post-Proto-Indo-European period, are known under the name 'Caland,' along with adjective constructions with **-ro-*/**-mo-* and the **-i-* prefixes, including the stative *-eh₁-* verbs, the *-es-* neuters, including the **-i̯os-* comparatives and the **-is-to-* superlatives: → Risch *Wortbildung* 1974 p. 65ff. and p. 218f.; Meier-Brügger *Gr. Sprachw.* II 1992 p. 31f.; Jasanoff *Stative and Middle* 1978 p. 125 with note 13 (including references to work by C. Watkins, J. Schindler and the Harvard dissertation of A. Nussbaum); J. Schindler in *Fachtagung Wien* 1978 [1980] p. 390 and p. 392 with note 23; T. Meissner in *Fachtagung Innsbruck* 1996 [1998] p. 237-254 (concerning Greek).

4) As yet, there does not exist a monograph on these phenomena. A. J. Nussbaum is presently the leading expert on the subject. As he made clear in his block seminar in Berlin (March, 2001), when considering linguistic development from the Proto-Indo-European period on, one must depart from the idea of a living process of development, of internal and external derivations of substantives, from which possessive adjectives are derived, and from which in turn substantives are created. By external derivation, derivation by means of suffixes is meant. In the case of internal derivation, the word stem is not altered. A change in accent placement is characteristic, cf. the adjective, Gr. γλαυκός 'blue' vs. the name Γλαῦκος or the change of inflection type (cf. the acrostatic abstract noun PIE **pólh₁u-* 'fullness' with the strong stem **pólh₁u-* and weak stem **pélh₁u-* vs. the proterokinetic possessive adjectives **pélh₁u-* 'possessing **pólh₁u-*' with the strong stem **pélh₁u-* and weak stem **pl̥h₁éu̯-*: → Nussbaum *Two Studies* 1998 p. 147ff.).

5) An example in tabular form:

	A. root noun	B. adjective	C. abstract noun	D. adjective
IE	str. **króu̯h₂-*, wk. **kruh₂-′*	a. **kruh₂-ró-* b. **króu̯h₂-o-*	str. **króu̯h₂i-*, wk. **kréu̯h₂i-*	**kruh₂i-nó-*
later	Avestan *xrū-*	a. Avest. *xrūra-* b. German *roh*	Avestan prefix *xruui-*	Lith. *krùvinas*

Comment: Situated at the beginning of the chain of derivations is the root noun, **króu̯h₂-* (A) = LAv. *xrū-* 'bloody, raw meat,' from which the possessive adjectives **kruh₂-ró-* (Ba) = OAv. and LAv. *xrūra-* 'bloody, terrible' and **króu̯h₂o-* (Bb) = NHG *roh* were derived externally. Starting from the adj. **króu̯h₂o-* (Bb) the external derivation leads, via replacement of *-o-* by *-i-*, to **króu̯h₂i-* (C). It is incorporated as a prefix in the zero grade of compound forms, e.g. **kruh₂i-* = LAv. *xruui-drau-* 'who carries a bloody weapon.' The *-i-* abstract noun may be found indirectly in the possessive Ved. *-o-* derivation *kravyá-* 'bloody' (< **krou̯h₂i̯-ó-* 'possessing **króu̯h₂i-*'). The derivation then continues to the possessive **kruh₂i-nó-* (D) = Lith. *krùvinas* 'bloody,' etc. For more detailed information: → A. J. Nussbaum in *GS Schindler* 1999 p. 402.

6) A central insight for further understanding of compound formations is that there are no adjectives, only abstract nouns. The compound form *xruui-drau-* may first be understood in the sense of 'whose (wooden) weapon is characterized by blood.' However, the *-i-* abstract noun was quickly out of use, whereby the prefix was accorded adjectival value, and *xruui-drau-* was then interpreted as 'who has a bloody (wooden) weapon.' From the appearance of the commonly used adj. *xrūra-*, the impression arose that the adjective was also present in the prefix, with replacement of *-ra-* by *-i-*.

7) It may also be explained why, in contrast to the *-ro-* adjectives (e.g. *xrūra-*), the *-u-* adjectives (e.g. Gr. πολύς) appear as prefixes of compound forms. Even here appearances are misleading. The point of departure in this case is the internal derivation from the acrostatic abstract noun **pólh₁u-* 'fullness' and proterokinetic possessive adjective str. **pélh₁u-*, wk. **pl̥h₁éu̯-* 'having fullness, much,' cf. § 4. The abstract noun is present in the prefixes of compound forms, but since both the abstract noun and the adjective, owing to their internal deduction remain *-u*-stems, the impression thus arose much later, at a time when the abstract noun had disappeared, that the still-productive *-u-* adjective was reflected in the prefix. The *-u-* adjectives have generally established themselves with zero

stem roots, cf. here Ved. *purú-*. The *-o-* of Gr. πολύς was long misunderstood, but is now recognized as coming from an abstract noun.

3. Word Formation by Composition

W 207. The possibility of forming compound words dates from Proto-Indo-European and consists of the joining of two nominal stems, a first element, and a second element. —The first element is normally composed of a simple stem while the second element may be inflected: The stem is either used directly, or in combination with a suffix such as **-o-*, **-i-*, **-i̯o-*, etc. The new noun receives its own accent and a new meaning. —Two types of PIE models are the possessive compounds (called *bahuvrīhi* in Old Indian terminology, meaning 'having much rice') and the verbal government compounds. Proto-Indo-European itself features several established types of both models.

1) In the case of the possessive compound, nominal phrases such as Gr. ἵππος = μέλας 'the horse [is] black' becomes the noun μελάν-ιππο-. In this case, the compound form serves to characterize a person, namely one, 'who owns a black horse/rides on a black horse.' As a rule, prefixes find their origin in abstract nouns, cf. W 206 § 6. See further W 208 below.

2) In the case of the verbal government compound, a verbal sentence of the type Gr. κοῦρον τρέφει '(the wet nurse) feeds a male child' is nominalized to form κουρο-τρόφο-. In order to make the compound form possible, the finite verb is transformed into an abstract noun, here in the form of -τρόφο-. The newly formed word indicates a person 'who goes about the feeding of children.' See further W 209 below.

3) The genesis of compound forms that is described here, with the example of Greek, most likely took place in the pre-Proto-Indo-European period: → J. Wackernagel in Wackernagel / Debrunner *Ai. Gramm.* II / 1 1957 (first edition, 1905) p. 289 (dealing with possessive compound forms) and p. 186 (on verbal government compounds); Risch *Kleine Schriften* 1981 (in a contribution from 1945) p. 124, note 21.

4) Terminology concerning compound forms is not completely uniform. On the one hand, there is a relatively comprehensive Old Indian terminology which is fully adapted to the classical circumstances peculiar to Old Indian and built up purely in terms of content: → J. Wackernagel in Wackernagel / Debrunner *Ai. Gramm.* II / 1 1957 p. 140-142. On the other

hand, a separate terminology has evolved within IE linguistics, including terms already used by E. Risch in his early work such as: possessive compound, verbal government compound, determinative compound (cf. W 211), and prepositional government compound (cf. W 210): → Risch *Kleine Schriften* 1981 (in a contribution from 1944) p. 5 and p. 36 and (in a contribution of 1945) p. 112f.; Risch *Wortbildung* 1974 p. 182.

5) To date, there exists no comprehensive treatment of Proto-Indo-European compound forms. Sadly, his passing prevented J. Schindler from completing the planned volume on Indo-European grammar. However, the plan of his Madrid lecture is accessible: → "*Zur internen Syntax der indogermanischen Nominalkomposita*" in *Kolloquium Delbrück* Madrid 1994 [1997] p. 537-540.

6) More recent suggestions for further reading: → Mikkola *Kompositum* I 1971; Th. Linder *Lateinische Komposita* Innsbruck 1996; V. Sadovski in *Arbeitstagung Erlangen* 1997 [2000] p. 455-473 (concerning what are called entheos compounds and prepositional government compounds in the Rigveda); G. E. Dunkel *"On the origins of nominal composition in IE"* in *GS Schindler* 1999 p. 47-68.

W 208. Following is further information on IE possessive compound forms (see W 207 § 1): — The contents of ancient IE possessive compound forms often relate to appearance, property, fame, beauty, and power. The first element may be an adjective, substantive, number, or even a preposition, e.g. Lat. *con-cord-* 'having a heart that is together' meaning 'unanimous,' Gr. τρι-ποδ- 'having three feet' in the sense of 'a container with three feet' or Ved. *su-śrávas-* 'having powerful, positive fame' in the sense of 'glorious,' etc.

Suggestions for further reading: → Risch *Wortbildung* 1974 p. 182ff.; J. Schindler "*Zu den homerischen ῥοδοδάκτυλος-Komposita*' in *FS Risch* 1986 p.393-401; J. Uhlich '*Der Kompositionstyp 'Armstrong' in den indogermanischen Sprachen*' in HS 110 1997 p. 21-46.

W 209. The following section contains further information on verbal government compound forms (see W 207 § 2): → At least two different types of constructions are traceable to Proto-Indo-European:

1) Verbal government compound forms with verbal first element, e.g., Gr. ἐχέ-πωλο-ς 'he who keeps young horses' and Vedic *trasá-dasyu-* 'he who causes his enemies to tremble.' Suggestions for further reading: → Risch *Wortbildung* 1974 p. 190ff.

2) Verbal government compound forms with a verbal second element: — What are called root compound forms represent an archaic group, e.g., Lat. *prīn-ceps* < **prīmo-cap-* 'he who takes the first part' and *con-iug-* 'bound together,' Gr. χέρ-νιβ- (which was represented already in Mycenaean as *ke-ni-qa* i.e. *k^{h}err-nig^w-*) '(water) that washes hands' and Vedic *havir-ád-* 'eating the food of sacrifice.' The second element is not, as is generally supposed, a nominal root, but rather a verbal root: → Scarlata *Wurzelkomposita im R̥g-Veda* 1999 p. 765f. Suggestions for further reading: → In addition to Scarlata, see particularly Benedetti *Composti radicali* 1988. — The more common type in ancient IE languages is that exemplified by Gr. κουροτρόφος (cf. W 207) and Ved. *puṣṭim-bhará-* 'rendering plenty, nourishing.'

W 210. Further possibilities of Proto-Indo-European compound construction include what are called prepositional government compounds and derivation compounds, e.g. Lat. *suburbānus* 'near the city (sc. Rome),' in which case the expression *sub urbe* is nominalized with the help of the suffix *-ānus*: → Leumann LLFL 1977 p. 264f. — In the case of Greek, compare the Homeric form εἰν-άλ-ιος 'found in the sea' (applying to sea creatures) with the prepositional expression ἐν ἁλί 'inside of the sea': → Risch *Wortbildung* 1974 p. 187f. Suggestions for further reading: → E. Risch "*Griechische Komposita vom Typus μεσο-νύκτιος und ὁμο-γάστριος*" in Risch *Kleine Schriften* 1981 (dating from 1945) p. 112-124. — Concerning the Vedic *tri-vats-á-*, cf. L 217 § 1. — Also included in this group are what are called (numeral) complexive compound forms, e.g. Ved. *tri-div-á-* 'the complex of three heavens': → Sommer *Nominalkomposita* 1948 p. 46; Hoffmann *Aufsätze* II 1976 (in an essay of 1952/1956) p. 356f.

W 211. So-called determinative compound forms represent the majority of compound forms in NHG. Among the many examples are *Gießkanne*, *Teekanne* and *Kaffeekanne*. In the case of this group, the second element (usually a general expression) is presented (determined) by the first element: In contrast to the simplex *Kanne*, compound forms such as *Gießkanne* represent subgroups of a genre. Such determinative compound forms are conspicuously absent in ancient IE languages. In all probability, they were not yet common in Proto-Indo-European. — One must distinguish between true determinative compound forms and fusions such as **déms pot-* 'lord of the estate, of the family clan.' As a comparison of the Greek and Vedic forms reveals, (cf. Gr. δεσπότης and Ved. *pátir dán* along with *dámpati-*), although the expression **dems pot-* (*pot-* 'lord of' with genitive) dates to the Proto-Indo-European period, the fusion is post-Proto-Indo-European. For information on the archaic gen. sg. PIE **dém-s*, cf. F 320 § 1a.

Suggestions for further reading: → E. Risch "*Griechische Determinativkomposita*" in *Risch Kleine Schriften* 1981 (in the post-doctoral work published in IF 59 *Heft* 1 1944 and IF 59 *Heft* 3 1949) p. 1ff. Owing to the index in the *Kleinen Schriften*, a large part of the examples were explained for the first time.

W 212. For information on what are called *Āmreḍita*, e.g. Ved. *divédive* 'day for day,' se F 318 § 6a (at the end of the section).

C. The Lexicon of Names

1. General Information

W 300. In addition to the value of the word as an appellative, it also has its place as a name. "Each word of a language is a 'name' with regard to the act of designation": → B. Schlerath "Name and Word in Indo-European" in *FS Hamp* II 1997 p. 164-169.

The abstract noun **$h_1$néh$_3$-mn̥-* may be traced with certainty to Proto-Indo-European and means 'name, appellation, qualification' (= Lat. *nōmen*, Gr. ὄνομα, Ved. *nā́man-*, Hitt. *lāman-*, Got. *namo*, OCS *imę* etc.: → Mayrhofer EWAia II p. 35-37 and cf. F 317 § 10).

According to the evidence in individual IE languages, **$h_1$néh$_3$-men-* + **d^{h}eh$_1$-* 'to give a name to someone' was a feature of Proto-Indo-European. The naming of a newborn child, generally performed by the father, presumably took place on or after the ninth day after the baby's birth: → R. Schmitt in *Namenforschung* 1 1995 p. 616.

W 301. Proper nouns have a special role in the lexicon of a language. In contrast to appellatives, they indicate an individual and not a class, or genre.

The marking of the individual is not only important in designating individual people, but also in designating groups of people, geographical features, etc.

Due to space limitations, the following treatment is quite brief. For more information on the subject: → *Namenforschung* 1-2 1995-1996.

2. Names of Persons and Deities

W 302. The common manner of naming a person in our western world consists of a first name and a surname. The first name (German: *Vorname*; French: *prénom*) serves to identify a person. The surname, or family name (German: *Nachname*, French: *nom de famille*) generally reveals the genetic membership of a person in a family.

First names are determined by the parents (or rather, the father) and generally remain valid until the death of the named individual. The parents' choice of first names is dependent on a number of factors, which include (among many others): family tradition (that the son inherits the name of the grandfather), vision of the future, the parents' plans for the life of their child, e.g. that he should be successful, etc. While first names are freely chosen, family names are predetermined and may not be varied.

The current European naming practices including a first name and a family name took shape in a long evolutionary process starting in the 12th century A.D. The family name was originally an addition to the first name, and only later became inherited. One suggestion for further reading, among many others: → Bach *Deutsche Personennamen* 1943.

1) All evidence suggests that, in the ancient IE period, only the individual name was common, e.g. the Homeric Greek practice with examples such as Ἀχιλλεύς, Ἕκτωρ, Πατροκλῆς (with *-ēs* < **-éu̯ēs*; however, in place of the full name, the shortened form Πάτροκλος is common, which is formed from the vocative form Πάτροκλε, which itself is abbreviated from the full vocative form *Πάτροκλεες, cf. the less common full form Πατρόκλεις with *-ei̯s* < **-ees* in addition to the more common Πάτροκλε), etc., cf. the practice in OHG with *Hildebrand* and *Heribrand* in the *Hildebrandlied* (concerning the origins of these names: → Lühr *Hildebrandlied* I 1982 p. 356ff.), etc.

2) Ancient IE individual names are generally either composed of two stems (cf. Gr. Πατρο-κλῆς) or one stem (cf. Gr. Ἕκτωρ). Full names that are polysyllabic are often used in abbreviated forms. Individual names may further be modified through the use of suffixes to form hypocorisms. For details: → R. Schmitt "*Entwicklung der Namen in älteren indogermanischen Sprachen*" in *Namenforschung* 1 1995 p. 616-636; *ibid.*, "*Morphologie der Namen: Voll-*

namen und Kurznamen bzw. Kosenamen im Indogermanischen" *ibid.* p. 419ff.

3) Further, the syntactical indication of the father's name also dates from Proto-Indo-European, whether by adding the name of the father in the genitive, in the sense of 'son of X,' or by adding a possessive adjective that is derived from the name of the father. An example of the former is *Hadubrand Heribrandes suno*; an example of the latter is Myc. Gr. *a-re-ku-tu-ru-wo e-te-wo-ke-re-we-i-jo* i.e. *Alektruu̯ōn Eteu̯okleu̯ehii̯os* 'Alektruu̯ōn, son of Eteu̯okleu̯ēs' and Russ. *Nikolaj Sergejevič*. — Patronymics ending in *-ios* (later *-ius*) led to what is called the *nomine gentile* in Rome, compare *Gaius Iulius Caesar* with *Gaius* = *praenomen* < individual name, *Iulius* = *nomen gentile* < patronymic and *Caesar* = *cognomen*. The first step towards the system that is widespread in all of Middle Italy is the transferral to each person of the patronymic from the father. For more comprehensive information: → Rix *Gentilnamensystem* 1972 passim (For information on suffix functions in Proto-Indo-European, p. 71.). — For information on Greek patronymics: → Meier-Brügger *Gr. Sprachw.* II p. 21 (in section 3 below).

4) When considering the giving of names to individuals, one departs generally from the basis of the free male. Individual names of women have their own special issues and are directly related to the role of women in Indo-European society, as is shown in forms of address. Whereas the man is addressed using the individual name, a simple 'oh woman' suffices in the case of the woman. "The woman is treated more as a *typus*, the man as an individual": → J. Wackernagel "*Über einige antike Anredeformen*" in *Wackernagel Kleine Schriften* II 1969 (in an essay of 1912) p. 970ff. and particularly p. 993 (Wackernagel makes clear that the same forms of address were adopted for interactions with the gods. To say that the Indo-Europeans were not very different from the Romans and Greeks would not likely be too far from the mark). — In Rome, women generally carried only the *nomen gentile*, cf. *Cornelia*, *Iulia* etc.: → Rix *Gentilnamensystem* 1972 p. 704. — In the case of the Greeks, most names of women are simply feminine forms of masculine names of individuals, e.g. (already) Myc. *a-re-ka-sa-da-ra*, i.e. *Aleksandrā* (which corresponds to **Aleks-anōr*, meaning 'who fights off men'), Hom. Ἀνδρομάχη (which comes from Ἀνδρόμαχος, meaning 'who fights with men'), etc.: → G. Neumann (p. 132 a.O. in § 5); O. Masson "*Remarques sur les noms de femmes en grec*" in MH 47 1990 p. 129-138.

5) For further information: → Solmsen *Eigennamen* 1922; R. Schmitt "*Indogermanische (Personen-)Namen: nur Schall und Rauch?*" in *Fachtagung Innsbruck* 1996 [1998] p. 69-86; *Namenforschung* 1 1995 with chapter VIII,

"*Historische Entwicklung der Namen,*" containing contributions on various ancient IE languages: The authors include, among others, E. Seebold on word history and etymology, R. Schmitt on Old and Middle Indo-Aryan, O. v. Hinüber on Indian, O. Masson on Greek, H. Rix on the Etruscans and Romans, J. Untermann on the border zones of Italy, K. H. Schmidt on Celtic); *DNP s.v.* '*Personennamen.*' — Concerning the Greeks and Romans: → H. Rix in *Kl. Pauly 4 Sp.* 657-661; Meier-Brügger *Gr. Sprachw.* II 1992 p. 39-44; *Greek Personal Names* I-III *A* 1987-1997; G. Neumann "*Wertvorstellungen und Ideologie in den Personennamen der mykenischen Griechen*" in *Anzeiger der phil.-hist. Klasse der Österreich. Akademie der Wiss.* 131 1994 p. 127-166 (see also bibliographical information, p. 158-161); DNP 9 2000 *s.v.* '*Personennamen*' (J.-L. García-Ramón on Greece, H. Rix on Rome). — On Iranians: → *Iranisches Personennamenbuch*; Mayrhofer, *Altiranische Namen* 1979; S. Zimmer "*Zur sprachlichen Deutung sassanidischer Personennamen*" in *Altorientalische Forschungen* 18 1991 p. 109-150. — On Asia Minor: → Zgusta *Kleinasiatische Personennamen* 1964. — On the Germans: → R. Lühr "*Germanische Personennamen in ihrer zeitlichen Staffelung, Zwei Aspekte der althochdeutschen und voralthochdeutschen Namenüberlieferung*" in *Fachtagung Leiden* 1987 [1992] p. 271-282. — Concerning the Celts: Uhlich *Komponierte Personennamen des Altirischen,* 1993.

W 303. Names of gods may clearly be distinguished from individual names of people. While even the gods are generally thought of as individual agents, conceptions of them outlast the individual lifetime and lend them the appearance of immortality.

As a rule, IE names of gods are personifications of common nouns that are either concrete or abstract. There are also constructions which include the suffix PIE *-*Hno*- and thus indicate the realm of dominance of the divinity, e.g., Lat. *Neptūnus* and Proto-Germ. **Wōđanaz.* One may not separate concrete appellative meaning from personification. There is no essential difference. For more information on this: → B. Schlerath in *Fachtagung Innsbruck* 1996 [1998] p. 92ff.

The form PIE **d(i)i̯éu̯ ph₂ter* 'father heaven,' which includes **d(i)i̯éu̯*- 'daytime sky' and is often used in vocative form, may with certainty be dated to the Proto-Indo-European period, cf. E 512 § 3 and F 318 § 6a. A further general appellative that, in all probability, originates in Proto-Indo-European is PIE **$h_2$éu̯s-os*- (weak stem **$h_2$us-s*-: → Mayrhofer EWAia I p. 236 and cf. F 321 § 2) 'brightening of daylight, morning light' and 'goddess of the morning light' = Lat. *Aurōra*, Hom. Gr. ἠώς Ἠώς, Ved. *uṣás*-.

W 304. There are names of tribes, names of peoples, names of warrior groups, etc, that correspond to the diverse characters of groups of people that are determined socially and economically.

It is important to note whether the name of a tribe or group originates from within the group of from a neighboring group, e.g., the case of the Classical Greek word for 'Greek,' Ἕλληνες vs. Lat. *Graecī* (which originates from the Italian penninsula, from which perspective the name of the *Graecī* of Epirus [modern northwestern Greece and Albania] came to be the Latin term for all inhabitants of the region): → Biville *Emprunts* II 1995 p. 178 note 39 with suggestions for further reading.

The extent to which names of groups, tribes, and peoples may be traced to Proto-Indo-European is not clear. The Indo-Iranian self-descriptive term **ar*(*i*)*i̯á*- is old, for example. For more information on the associated issues: → Mayrhofer EWAia I p. 174f.; F. Bader "*Les noms des aryens: Ethniques et expansion*" in *Langues Indo-européennes* 1994 p. 65ff. — The Mycenaean Greeks apparently called themselves *Ak*^{h}*ai̯u̯ó*-: → Chantraine DELG I 1968 p. 149; Latacz *Troia und Homer* 2001 p. 150ff. (which includes information on the Homeric terms *Akhaiói*, *Danaói* and *Argéioi*).

3. Formation of Place Names

W 305. In addition to individuals and groups of individuals, the environments that surround the individuals and the places where they live are important points of orientation: mountains, rivers, bodies of water, settlements, cities, etc. These place names are stable and are transferred from generation to generation.

While individual IE languages are clearly linked to particular geographic regions, no such clarity exists for the Proto-Indo-European period, cf. E 512. It is thus practically impossible to determine whether particular place names are of Proto-Indo-European origin.

The comparison of IE habits in the formation of place names leads one to suppose, in the case of commonality among several languages, that these habits may be traced to speakers of Proto-Indo-European. Among these habits is surely the use of the IE suffix *-*u̯ent*- (sometimes with the ablaut *-*u̯ont*-, fem. *-*u̯n̥t-ih*$_2$) to characterize typical merits of a particular place, e.g. the Mycenaean place name dat. sg. *sa-ri-nu-wo-te* i.e. *Salin-u̯ont-ei̯* '(place) where celery flourishes' (in which case alphabetic Greek features Σελ- in place of *Sal*-. For more information: → Leukart

Frühgr. Nomina 1994 p. 116f. note 233); the Indo-Iranian name for a river and region **saras-u̯at-iH-* (= Ved. *sárasvatī-*, LAv. *harax^{v}aitī-*) meaning '(river or region) where there are many swamps'; the Lycian place name *Xada-wãti-* (hellenized as Καδύανδα), i.e. **ḫadá-u̯antī-* '(place) that is rich in grain' (→ Hajnal *Lyk. Vokalismus* 1995 p. 88). Suggestions for further reading: → R. Schmitt in *Namenforschung* 1995 p. 633f.

1) As a rule, place names originate from general appellatives, e.g., the Vedic river name *síndhu-* 'Indus,' which was originally an appellative that meant 'river': The Indus, like the Nile and the Rhine, is the unique prototypical river in its region.

2) Tribe names may be used to indicate places, e.g. Gr. Δελφοί as an accusative (of direction) plural tribe name 'to the Delphians' and dat. loc. pl. Δελφοῖς 'with/among the Delphians.' Since the Delphians inhabit a particular region and town, the accusative and dative/locative can be directly used to indicate them: Δελφοί, 'city in Phokis at the foot of mount Parnass.' Similar is the case of Old Indian loc. pl. *madréṣu* which means 'with/among the *madrá*-people,' which may be interpreted, 'in the area where the *madrá*-people dwell.' This characteristic of equating the tribe name with the name of the place where it lives is in all likelihood of Proto-Indo-European origin.

3) Place names and prehistory: Because place names are stable and remain linked to their objects, they are particularly instructive regarding the prehistory of a place. In addition to the place names that may be interpreted on the basis of the locally spoken language, there are as a rule names as well that may not be interpreted by any single language. When these names are very ancient, one may conclude that their appearance occurred at a time at which the locally spoken language was not yet known and another language was in use. However, when further documentation of such a language is missing, it is practically impossible to extrapolate information about the language based on place names. One difficulty among many are adaptations of the name to subsequent languages. — Greece presents an example: Place names that may not be understood on the basis of the Greek language, such as Κόρινθος and Ἀθῆναι (!) date, unlike comprehensible names such as Σελινοῦς (meaning 'rich in celery,' see above), from before the settlement of the land by the Greeks took place, and may thus be considered pre-Greek: → E. Risch "*Ein Gang durch die Geschichte der griechischen Ortsnamen*" in *Kleine Schriften* 1981 (in an essay from 1965) p. 145ff.. — Examples of European hydronymy: Names of rivers such as *Elbe* and *Rhine* are incomprehensible on the basis of Germanic and must therefore be of pre-Germanic origin. However, whether these names

are based upon Proto-Indo-European linguistic material and were thus created by speakers of Proto-Indo-European remains disputed, cf. E 513 § 3.

4) Helpful resources concerning place names: → J.-L. García-Ramón in DNP 4 1998 Sp. 930-934 *s.v.* "*Geographische Namen*"; *Namenforschung* 2 1996 with chapter X ('*Namengeographie*') and the chapters XV-XVII ('*Ortsnamen I: Siedlungsnamen*;' '*Ortsnamen II: Flurnamen*;' '*Gewässernamen*'); Tischler *Kleinasiatische Hydronymie* 1977; Zgusta *Kleinasiatische Ortsnamen* 1984; *Kleinasiatische Onomastik* in *Namenforschung* 1995 p. 636ff.; RGA *s.v.* '*Länder- und Landschaftsnamen.*'

VI. Bibliography and Key to Reference Citations

More than simply a list of works used in the preparation of this book and their shortened citations, the following bibliography aims at furnishing the reader with a representative overview of current Indo-European specialty literature as of mid-2001. Included are titles which will not be referred to elsewhere in the present work. Exhaustiveness is not pretended in any area. All publications are not equally good, but none of those listed is so poor that one cannot learn something from it, even if what is learned is simply how things are not.

Reviews and discussions of books constitute a separate genre of literature. Particular works are mentioned here and there in order to call attention to this type of information. It is heartily recommended to those who are penetrating a new field of study, or searching the newest positions on a certain problem, that they take into account the opinions, corrections, and completions of appropriate reviewers. However, it was never intended in this work that all the concerned reviews be named. I especially refer the reader to the publication for reviews and reports, *Kratylos*, published by the *Indogermanische Gesellschaft*, and of which the most recent volume available to me at the time of publication is 46 2001. Occasionally a note or comment from 'Idg. Chr.' will be referred to (see entry below).

The basis for the abbreviations of journals used in this text is the *Bibliographie Linguistique / Linguistic Bibliography*, the last volume of which that was consulted is that from 1994. In addition, a couple of particularly relevant titles appear in the list. For habitual lecture and consultation, the following (in alphabetical order) are recommended, among others: Diachronica, Glotta, HS (older abbreviations ZVS, and KZ), IF, JIES, MSS and Sprache.

The following bibliographical information is not always uniformly organized. In the case of newer works, indications are included at the end of the entry, when the work appeared in an particular series, such as a Supplementary volume to the ZVS / HS, an IBS volume, or the review of an academy. In the case of publications which have long been well-known, only the place of origin and year, and no additional bibliographical information, are given.

AAWL = *Abhandlungen der Akademie der Wissenschaften und der Literatur in Mainz.*

Adams *Dictionary* 1999 = D. Q. Adams, D.Q. 1999 *A Dictionary of Tocharian B.* Amsterdam and Atlanta, Ga (= Leiden Studies in Indo-European 10).

Adams *Tocharian* 1988 = Adams, D. Q. *Tocharian Historical Phonology and Morphology*. New Haven 1988 (= American Oriental Series 71).

Adiego *Studia Carica* 1993 = Adiego, I.-J. Lajara *Studia Carica, Investigaciones sobre la escritura y lengua carias*. Barcelona 1993.

Adrados *Manual*, see below, *Manual de lingüistica indoeuropea*

Aitzetmüller *Abulg. Gramm.* 1991 = R. Aitzetmüller 1991 Altbulgarische Grammatik als Einführung in die slavische Sprachwissenschaft. 2d ed, revised and expanded, Freiburg (= Monumenta Linguae Slavicae Nr. 30).

Akten 13. Österreich. Linguistentagung 1988 = Zinko, C., ed. 1988 *Akten der 13. Österreichischen Linguistentagung 1985 in Graz mit den Beiträgen der Tagung 1983 in Salzburg*. Graz.

Allen *Vox Graeca* 1987 = Allen, W. S. 1987 *Vox Graeca, A Guide to the Pronunciation of Classical Greek*. 3d ed. Cambridge.

Althochdeutsch I / II 1987 = Bergmann, R., H. Tiefenbach and L. Voetz eds. 1987 *Althochdeutsch*. Heidelberg: Volume I (*Grammatik. Glossen und Texte*); Volume II (*Wörter und Namen. Forschungsgeschichte*).

Ambrosini *Linguistica Indo-Europea* I / II 1996 = R. Ambrosini 1996 *Introduzione alla linguistica indo-europea*. I (*La ricostruzione dell' indoeuropeo*), II (*Le lingue indo-europee orientali e centrali*). Lucca.

Ammann *Untersuchungen* I 1922 = H. Ammann *Untersuchungen zur homerischen Wortfolge und Satzstruktur. 1. allgemeiner Teil.* Leipzig

1922; by the same author, vol 2: *Die Stellung des Verbums, im einzelnen untersucht* in IF 42 1924 p. 149-171 and 300-322.

Ancient IE Dialects 1963 [1966] = *Ancient Indo-European Dialects, Proceedings of the Conference on Indo-European Linguistics 1963* in Los Angeles, H. Birnbaum and J. Puhvel (eds). Berkeley / Los Angeles 1966.

Andersen (H.) *Prehistorical Dialects* 1996 = H. Andersen *Reconstructing Prehistorical Dialects, Initial Vowels in Slavic and Baltic*. Berlin 1996. Review: Chr. Koch in *Kratylos* 45 2000 p. 146-154.

Andersen (P. K.) *Word Order Typology* 1983 = P. K. Andersen *Word Order Typology and Comparative Constructions*. Amsterdam / Philadelphia 1983. Review: Ch. Lehmann in *Kratylos* 29 1984 [1985] p. 25-30.

Anttila PIE Schwebeablaut 1969 = R. Anttila Proto-Indo-European Schwebeablaut Berkeley / Los Angeles 1969. Review: J. Schindler in *Kratylos* 15 1970 [1972] p. 146-152.

AÖAW = *Anzeiger der Österreichischen Akademie der Wissenschaften, philosophisch-historische Klasse*.

Arbeitstagung Erlangen 1997 [2000] = *Indoarisch, Iranisch und die Indogermanistik, Arbeitstagung der Idg. Gesellschaft* 1997 in Erlangen, edited by B. Forssman and R. Plath (eds), Wiesbaden 2000. Review: B. Schlerath in OLZ 96 2000 p. 306-316.

Arbeitstagung Osk.-Umbr. Freiburg 1991 [1993] = *Oskisch-Umbrisch, Texte und Grammatik, Arbeitstagung der Idg. Gesellschaft und der Società Italiana di Glottologia* 1991 in Freiburg, edited by H. Rix, ed. Wiesbaden 1993.

Arbeitstagung (100 Jahre) Tocharologie Saarbrücken 1995 [1997] = *Arbeitstagung 100 Jahre Tocharologie, Kolloquium der Idg. Gesellschaft* 1995 in Saarbrücken, published as TIES 7 1997.

Arens *Sprachwissenschaft* I + II 1969 = H. Arens *Sprachwissenschaft, Der Gang ihrer Entwicklung von der Antike bis zur Gegenwart*. Frankfurt am Main 1969, I (*Von der Antike bis zum Ausgang des 19. Jahrhunderts*), II (*Das 20. Jahrhundert*).

Arlotto *Introduction* 1972 = A. Arlotto *Introduction to Historical Linguistics*. Boston 1972.

Arumaa *Urslav. Grammatik* I 1964 II 1976 III 1985 = P. Arumaa *Urslavische Grammatik*. Heidelberg: vol. I (*Einleitung, Lautlehre mit Vokalismus und Betonung*) 1964; vol. II (*Konsonantismus*) 1976; vol. III (*Formenlehre*) 1985.

ASNP = *Annali della Scuola Normale Superiore di Pisa: lettere, storia e filosofia*.

Aspects of Latin 1993 [1996] = *Aspects of Latin, Papers from the Seventh International Colloquium on Latin Linguistics* Jerusalem 1993, edited by H. Rosén, ed. Innsbruck 1996 (= IBS 86); see below, *s.v.* IKLL (ICLL / CILL) VII 1993 [1996].

Aspekte baltist. Forschung 2000 = *Aspekte Baltistischer Forschung*, edited by J- Range, ed. Essen 2000 (= *Schriften des Instituts für Baltistik der Ernst-Moritz-Arndt-Universität Greifswald 1*).

Assmann *Kulturelles Gedächtnis* 1997 = J. Assmann *Das kulturelle Gedächtnis. Schrift, Erinnerung und politische Identität in frühen Hochkulturen*. Munich 1997 (and re-editions).

Aufrecht *Hymnen des RV* 1877 = Th. Aufrecht *Die Hymnen des Rigveda*. 2 vols. 2d ed. 1877 (and reprints).

Aura Jorro *DMic.* I 1985 II 1993 = F. Aura Jorro *Diccionario micénico*. Madrid, vol. I (a-n) 1985, vol. II (o-z) 1993.

Autobiographische Berichte 1991 = *Wege in der Sprachwissenschaft, Vierundvierzig autobiographische Berichte, Festschrift für M. Wandruszka*, edited by H.-M. Gauger and W. Pöckl, eds. Tübingen 1991 (= *Tübinger Beiträge zur Linguistik*, vol. 362).

Bach *Deutsche Personennamen* 1943 = A. Bach *Die deutschen Personennamen*. Berlin 1943.

Baltische Sprachen 1994 = *Die baltischen Sprachen, Eine Einführung*, R. Eckert, Elvira-Julia Bukevičiūtė, F. Hinze. Leipzig / Berlin 1994. Review: F. Scholz in *Kratylos* 42 1997 p. 126-130.

Baltistik 1998 = *Baltistik, Aufgaben und Methoden*, edited by A. Bammesberger. Heidelberg 1998 (= *Indogermanische Bibliothek*, Reihe 3, vol. 19). Review: R. Matasović and W. P. Schmid in IF 105 2000 p. 342-351; F. Heidermanns in *Kratylos* 45 2000 p. 154-162.

Bammesberger *Abstraktbildungen* 1973 = A. Bammesberger *Abstraktbildungen in den baltischen Sprachen*. Göttingen 1973.

Bammesberger *Germ. Verbalsystem* 1986 = A. Bammesberger *Der Aufbau des germanischen Verbalsystems*. Heidelberg 1986 (= *Untersuchungen zur vergleichenden Grammatik der germanischen Sprachen*, vol. 1).

Bammesberger *Laryngaltheorie* 1984 = A. Bammesberger *Studien zur Laryngaltheorie*. Göttingen 1984 (= supplement to ZVS 33). Review: R. S. P. Beekes in *Kratylos* 31 1986 p. 70-75; F. O. Lindeman in IF 91 1986 p. 349-351. See also below *s.v. Laryngaltheorie* 1988.

Bammesberger *Pforzen und Bergakker* 1999 = *Pforzen und Bergakker, Neue Untersuchungen zu Runeninschriften*, edited by A. Bammesberger. Göttingen 1999 (= HS, *Ergänzungsheft* 41).

Bammesberger *Urgerm. Nomen* 1990 = A. Bammesberger *Die Morphologie des urgermanischen Nomens*. Heidelberg 1990 (= *Untersuchungen zur vergleichenden Grammatik der germ. Sprachen Nr. 2*).

Bartholomae *Air. Wörterbuch* 1904 = C. Bartholomae *Altiranisches Wörterbuch*. Strasbourg 1904. The second photomechanical reprint of 1979 contains supplements and improvements (vol. 1881-1900), as well as supplementary material and groundwork from 1906. Berlin 1979.

Bartschat *Methoden der Sprachwissenschaft* 1996 = B. Bartschat *Methoden der Sprachwissenschaft. Von Hermann Paul bis Noam Chomsky*. Berlin 1996.

BCH = *Bulletin de Correspondence Hellénique*.

Bechtel *Gr. Dialekte* 1921-1924 = F. Bechtel *Die griechischen Dialekte*, 3 vols. Berlin 1921-1924.

Bechtel *Hauptprobleme* 1892 = Fr. Bechtel *Die Hauptprobleme der indogermanischen Lautlehre seit Schleicher*. Göttingen 1892.

Beekes *Gatha-Avestan* 1988 = R. S. P. Beekes *A Grammar of Gatha-Avestan*. Leiden 1988. Review: J. E. Rasmussen in *Kratylos* 36 1991 p. 109-116. Cf. also, by the same author, "Historical Phonology of Iranian" in JIES 25 1997 p. 1-26.

Beekes *IE Nominal Inflection* 1985 = R.S.P. Beekes, *The Origins of the Indo-European Nominal Inflection*. Innsbruck 1985 (= IBS Nr. 46). Review: J. Schindler in *Idg. Chr.* 31a 1985 Nr.85.

Beekes *Introduction* 1995 = R. S. P. Beekes *Comparative Indo-European Linguistics, An Introduction*. Amsterdam 1995. Review: A. Bammesberger in HS 109 1996 p. 310-316; M. Kümmel in PFU 2-3 1996 / 1997 p. 113-125; Ch. de Lamberterie in BSL 92 / 2 1997 p. 143-149; St. Zimmer in PBB 119 / 2 1997 p. 276-282.

Beekes *Laryngeals* 1969 = R. S. P. Beekes *The Development of the Proto-Indo-European Laryngeals in Greek*. The Hague / Paris 1969. Review: C. J. Ruijgh in *Lingua* 26 1970 / 1971 p. 181-198 (= *Scripta Minora* I 1991 p. 330-347); H. Rix in *Kratylos* 14 1969 [1972] p. 176-187. Cf. also R. S. P. Beekes *Laryngeal Developments: A survey in Laryngeal Theory* 1988 p. 59-105.

Benedetti *Composti radicali* 1988 = M. Benedetti *I composti radicali latini: Esame storico e comparativo*. Pisa 1988.

Benfey *Geschichte der Sprachwissenschaft* 1869 = Th. Benfey *Geschichte der Sprachwissenschaft und orientalischen Philologie in Deutschland seit dem Anfange des 19. Jahrhunderts mit einem Rückblick auf die früheren Zeiten*. Munich 1869 (reprinted 1965).

Benveniste *Hittite et indo-européen* 1962 = E. Benveniste *Hittite et indo-européen, Études comparatives*. Paris 1962.

Benveniste *Institutions* I + II 1969 = E. Benveniste *Le vocabulaire des institutions indo-européennes*. 2 vols. Paris 1969. Translated into English with the title "*Indo-European Language and Society*," London 1973. Translated into German as "*Indoeuropäische Institutionen*." Translated by W. Bayer, D. Hornig, K. Menke, edited, and with an afterword by St. Zimmer. Frankfurt / New York 1993. Review: R. Schmitt in *Kratylos* 39 1994 p. 183f.

Benveniste *Noms d'agent* 1948 = E. Benveniste *Noms d'agent et noms d'action en indo-européen*. Paris 1948.

Benveniste *Origines* 1935 = E. Benveniste *Origines de la formation des noms en indo-européen*. Paris 1935.

Benveniste *Problèmes* I 1966 II 1974 = E. Benveniste *Problèmes de linguistique générale*. Paris vol. I 1966, vol. II 1974.

Benveniste, see also *s.v. Colloque E. Benveniste*.

Berlinische Lebensbilder - Geisteswissenschaftler 1989 = *Berlinische Lebensbilder*, edited by W. Ribbe: *vol. 4, Geisteswissenschaftler*, edited by M. Erbe. Berlin 1989.

Bibliographie d. Hethitologie 1-3 1996 (1998) = *Systematische Bibliographie der Hethitologie* 1915-1995, 3 vols., assembled by V. Souček and J. Siegelová. Prague 1996.

Bile *Crétois* 1988 = M. Bile *Le dialecte crétois ancien, Étude de la langue des inscriptions, Recueil des inscriptions postérieures aux IC* (= *Inscriptiones Creticae*). Paris 1988.

Binnig *Gotisches Elementarbuch* 1999 = W. Binnig *Gotisches Elementarbuch*. Berlin 1999 (This de Gruyter *Studienbuch* replaces H. Hempel *Gotisches Elementarbuch, Grammatik, Texte mit Übersetzungen und Erläuterungen*, Berlin 1966, *Sammlung Göschen* vol. 79/79a).

BiOr = *Bibliotheca Orientalis*.

Birkhan *Kelten* 1997 = H. Birkhan *Kelten*. Vienna 1997. Review: J. Uhlich in CMCS 39 2000 p. 65-73.

Bittel *Hattusha* 1970 = K. Bittel *Hattusha, The Capital of the Hittites*. Oxford 1970. See also, *s.v.* Neve *Ḫattuša* 1996.

Bittel *Hethiter* 1976 = K. Bittel *Die Hethiter: Die Kunst Anatoliens vom Ende des 3. bis zum Anfang des 1. Jahrtausends vor Christus*. Munich 1976.

Biville *Emprunts* I 1990 II 1995 = F. Biville *Les emprunts du latin au grec. Approche phonétique*. Louvain, Paris: vol. I (*Introduction et consonantisme*) 1990; vol. II (*Vocalisme et conclusion*) 1995.

BL = *Bibliographie linguistique / Linguistic Bibliography*. Boston / London.

Blažek *Numerals* 1999 = V. Blažek *Numerals: Comparative-Etymological Analysis of Numerals Systems and their Implications*. Brno 1999. Review: M. de Vaan in *Sprache* 39 / 2 1997 [2000] p. 239-245; V. Bubenik in JIES 28 2000 p. 450-454.

Bloch *Suppletive Verba* 1940 = A. Bloch *Zur Geschichte einiger suppletiver Verba im Griechischen*. Basel 1940.

Blümel *Aiol. Dialekte* 1982 = W. Blümel *Die aiolischen Dialekte, Phonologie und Morphologie der inschriftlichen Texte aus generativer Sicht*. Göttingen 1982 (= supplement ZVS Nr. 30).

Blümel *Untersuchungen* 1972 = W. Blümel *Untersuchungen zu Lautsystem und Morphologie des vorklassischen Lateins*. Munich 1972 (= MSS, *Beiheft*, *Neue Folge 8*).

BNF = *Beiträge zur Namenforschung*.

Bohl *Besitzverhältnis* 1980 = S. Bohl *Ausdrucksmittel für ein Besitzverhältnis im Vedischen und Griechischen*. Louvain-la-Neuve 1980.

Boisacq DELG 1950 = E. Boisacq *Dictionnaire étymologique de la langue grecque étudiée dans ses rapports avec les autres langues indoeuropéennes*. 4th edition, augmented with an index by Helmut Rix. Heidelberg 1950.

Boley *Hittite hark-construction* 1984 = J. Boley *The Hittite hark-construction*. Innsbruck 1984 (= IBS 44).

Boley *Sentence Particles* 1989 = J. Boley *The Sentence Particles and the Place words in Old and Middle Hittite*. Innsbruck 1989 (= IBS 60). Cf., by the same author, *The Hittite Particle -z / -za*. Innsbruck 1993 (= IBS 79).

Bopp *Albanesisch* 1855 = F. Bopp *Über das Albanesische in seinen verwandtschaftlichen Beziehungen*. Berlin 1855 (= Abhandlung der Preußischen Akadamie der Wissenschaften, Philosophisch-historische Klasse).

Bopp *Conjugationssystem* 1816 = F. Bopp *Über das Conjugationssystem der Sanskritsprache in Vergleichung mit jenem der griechischen, lateinischen, persischen und germanischen Sprache. Neben Episoden des Ramajan und Mahabharat in genauen metrischen Übersetzungen aus dem Originaltext und einigen Abschnitten aus den Veda's*. Frankfurt 1816.

Bopp-Symposion 1992 [1994] = *Bopp-Symposium* 1992, Humboldt-Universität zu Berlin, documents from the 1992 conference given to commemorate the 200th birthday of Franz Boppon 14 September 1991, edited by R. Sternemann. Heidelberg 1994.

Boretzky *Historische Linguistik* 1977 = N. Boretzky *Einführung in die historische Linguistik*. Reinbek, near Hamburg (Rowohlt) 1977.

Bornemann / Risch *Gr. Gr.* 1978 = E. Bornemann and E. Risch *Griechische Grammatik*. 2d ed. Frankfurt 1978. Additionally, compare W. Kastner *Sprachgeschichtliche Erläuterungen zur Griechischen Grammatik*. Frankfurt 1988.

Bräuer *Slav. Sprachw.* I 1961 II 1969 III 1969 = H. Bräuer *Slavische Sprachwissenschaft*. 3 vols. Berlin 1961-1969: I (*Einleitung, Lautlehre*) 1961, II (*Formenlehre, 1. Teil*) 1969, III (*Formenlehre, 2nd Teil*) 1969 (= *Sammlung Göschen* Nr. 1191, 1192 and 1236).

Brandenstein / Mayrhofer *Altpersisch* 1964 = W. Brandenstein and M. Mayrhofer *Handbuch des Altpersischen*. Wiesbaden 1964. See also, *s.v.* Mayrhofer *Supplement* 1978.

Braunmüller *Skandinav. Sprachen* 1991 = K. Braunmüller *Die skandinavischen Sprachen im Überblick*. Tübingen 1991 (= UTB 1635). Review: J. A. Harđarson in PFU 4 1998 p. 85-96.

Braune / Ebbinghaus *Got. Gr.* 1981= W. Braune *Gotische Grammatik*. 19th ed, revised by E. A. Ebbinghaus. Tübingen 1981.

Brixhe *Grec anatolien* 1987 = C. Brixhe *Essai sur le grec anatolien au début de notre ère*. new revised edition, Nancy 1987.

Brixhe *Koiné* I 1993 = *La Koiné grecque antique I: Une langue introuvable*, edited by C. Brixhe. Nancy 1993.

Brixhe *Pamphylie* 1976 = C. Brixhe *Le dialecte grec de Pamphylie, Documents et grammaire*. Paris 1976.

Brixhe *Phonétique et phonologie* 1996 = C. Brixhe *Phonétique et phonologie du grec ancien I, Quelques grandes questions*. Paris 1996 (= *Bibliothèque des Cahiers de l' Institut de Linguistique de Louvain Nr.* 82).

Brixhe / Lejeune *Paléo-phrygien* 1984 = C. Brixhe *Corpus des inscriptions paléo-phrygiennes*. 2 vols. Paris 1984.

Brugmann *Einfacher Satz* 1925 = K. Brugmann *Die Syntax des einfachen Satzes im Indogermanischen*. Berlin / Leipzig 1925.

Brugmann *Grundriß* I 1897 II-1 1906 II-2 1911 II-3 1916 = K. Brugmann [and B. Delbrück] *Grundriß der vergleichenden Grammatik der indogermanischen Sprachen*. 2d revised edition. Strasbourg: vol. I 1897 (*Einleitung, Lautlehre: die erste Hälfte* p. 1-622; *die zweite Hälfte* p.

623-1098; unchanged reprint of both parts 1930); vol. II containing three parts, namely II-1 1906 (*Allgemeines, Zusammensetzung* [compound forms], *Nominalstämme*: p. 1-688), II-2 1911 (*Zahlwörter, Genera, Kasus- und Numerusbildung, Pronomina, Adjektiv, Adverbia, Präpositionen*: p. 1-997) and II-3 1916 (*Verbum finitum* and *infinitum, Partikeln im einfachen Satz: die erste Hälfte* p. 1-496, *die zweite Hälfte* p. 497-1052). reprint Berlin / New York 1967. Regarding vols. III - V, see *s.v.* Delbrück *Vgl. Syntax*.

Brugmann *Kurze vgl. Gramm.* 1902-1904 = K. Brugmann *Kurze vergleichende Grammatik der indogermanischen Sprachen*. Strasbourg: 1. *Lieferung* (*Einleitung und Lautlehre*: p. 1-280) 1902, 2nd *Lieferung* (*Lehre von den Wortformen und ihrem Gebrauch*: p. 281-622) 1903, 3. *Lieferung* (*Lehre von den Satzgebilden und Sach- und Wörterverzeichnis*: p. 623-677) 1904. unchanged reprint Leipzig 1933, reprint 1970.

Brugmann / Thumb *Gr. Gr.* 1913 = K. Brugmann *Griechische Grammatik*. 4th ed. by A. Thumb. Munich 1913.

Brunner *Aengl. Gr.* 1965 = K. Brunner *Altenglische Grammatik nach der angelsächsischen Grammatik von Eduard Sievers*. 3rd ed. Tübingen 1965.

Bryce *Lycians* 1986 = T. R. Bryce *The Lycians in Literary and Epigraphic Sources*. Copenhagen 1986 (= volume I of the work by T. R. Bryce and J. Zahle: *The Lycians, A Study of Lycian History and Civilisation to the Conquest of Alexander the Great*).

Bryce *Kingdom* 1998 = T. Bryce *The Kingdom of the Hittites*. Oxford 1998.

BSL = *Bulletin de la société de linguistique*. Paris.

Buchholz / Fiedler *Alban. Gramm.* 1987 = O. Buchholz and W. Fiedler *Albanische Grammatik*. Leipzig 1987.

Buck *Comparative Grammar* 1963 = C. D. Buck *Comparative Grammar of Greek and Latin*. 9th ed. Chicago / London 1963.

Buck *Dict. of select. Syn.* 1949 = C. D. Buck *A Dictionary of Selected Synonyms in the principal Indo-European Languages*. Chicago 1949.

Buck *Greek Dialects* 1955 = C. D. Buck *The Greek Dialects, Grammar, Selected Inscriptions, Glossary*. 2nd ed. Chicago / London 1955 (and reprint).

Bühler *Sprachtheorie* 1934 = K. Bühler *Sprachtheorie. Die Darstellungsfunktion der Sprache*. Jena 1934.

Burkert *Griechische Religion* 1977 = W. Burkert *Griechische Religion der archaischen und klassischen Epoche*. Stuttgart 1977. Translated into English as: *Greek Religion*. Cambridge / Mass. 1985.

Burkert *Orientalisierende Epoche* 1984 = W. Burkert "*Die orientalisierende Epoche in der griechischen Religion und Literatur*," lecture given on 8 May 1982, Heidelberg 1984 (= SbHAW 1984 / 1). English translation: "The Orientalizing Revolution, Near Eastern Influence on Greek Culture in the Early Archaic Age." Cambridge / Mass. 1992.

Bussmann *Lexikon d. Sprachw.* 2nd ed. 1990 = H. Bussmann *Lexikon der Sprachwissenschaft*. 2nd, fully revised ed. Stuttgart 1990.

Bynon *Hist. Linguistics* 1977 (also: *Hist. Linguistik* 1981 = Th. Bynon *Historical Linguistics*. Cambridge 1977 [and reprints]) = *Historische Linguistik, Eine Einführung*. Munich 1981 (revised and expanded edition of the English original). Review of the German edition: J. Udolph in IF 96 1991 p. 258-262.

Campanile *Ricostruzione* 1990 = E. Campanile *La ricostruzione della cultura indoeuropea*. Pisa 1990.

Cas et prépositions en grec ancien 1994 = *Cas et prépositions en grec ancien*, Actes du colloque international de Saint-Étienne 1993, edited by B. Jacquinod. Saint-Étienne 1994.

Cardona *Them. Aorists* 1960 = G. Cardona *The Indo-European Thematic Aorists*. Ann Arbor 1960.

Cario 1993 [1994] = *La decifrazione del cario, Atti del 1° Simposio Internazionale* 1993 in Rome, edited by M. E. Giannotta, R. Gusmani, L. Innocente, D. Marcozzi, M. Salvini, M. Sinatra, P. Vannicelli. Rome 1994 (= *Consiglio Nazionale delle Ricerche, Monografie Scientifiche*).

Carling *Lokale Kasus im Toch.* 2000 = G. Carling *Die Funktionen der lokalen Kasus im Tocharischen*. Berlin / New York 2000.

Carruba *Palaisch* 1970 = O. Carruba *Das Palaische: Texte, Grammatik, Lexikon*. Wiesbaden 1970 (= StBoT 10).

Causatives and Transitivity 1993 = *Causatives and Transitivity*, edited by B. Comrie and M. Polinsky. Amsterdam / Philadelphia 1993 (= *Studies in Language Companion Series* 23).

CEG = *Chronique d'étymologie grecque*, see below, Chantraine DELG.

Celtic Languages 1992 = *The Celtic Languages*, edited by D. Macaulay. Cambridge 1992 (from the series *Cambridge Language Surveys*).

Celtic Languages 1993 = *The Celtic Languages*, edited by M. J. Ball together with J. Fife. London / New York 1993 (Routledge).

CFS = *Cahiers Ferdinand de Saussure*

Chadwick *Documents* 1973 = J. Chadwick *Documents in Mycenaean Greek*. 2nd ed. Cambridge 1973.

Chantraine DELG 1968-1980 = P. Chantraine *Dictionnaire étymologique de la langue grecque, Histoire des mots*. Paris I 1968, II 1970, III 1974, IV / 1 1977, IV / 2 1980. Since 1999, Chantraine DELG is available in a single-volume reprint of slightly reduced size, which includes a supplement (see below, CEG 1-3). Helpful addenda and corrigenda may be found in Ruijgh *Scripta Minora* I 1991 p. 571-632 and Szemerényi *Scripta Minora* III 1987 p. 1559-1607, among others. Cf. also the ongoing *Chronique d'étymologie grecque* (CEG), edited by A. Blanc, Ch. de Lamberterie and J. L. Perpillou: CEG 1 in RPh 70 1996 [1997] p. 103-138; CEG 2 in RPh 71 1997 [1998] p.147-179; CEG 3 1998 [1999] in RPh 72 1998 [1999] p. 119-148; CEG 4 1999 [2000] in RPh 73 1999 [2000] p. 79-108.

Chantraine *Formation des noms* 1933 = P. Chantraine *La formation des noms en grec ancien*. Paris 1933 (and reprints).

Chantraine *Gramm. hom.* I 1958 II 1953 = P. Chantraine *Grammaire homérique*. 2 vols. Paris: I (*Phonétique et Morphologie*) 3rd ed. 1958, II (*Syntaxe*) 1st ed. 1953.

Chantraine *Morphologie* 2nd ed. 1961 = P. Chantraine *Morphologie historique du grec*. 2nd ed. Paris 1961 (and reprints).

CHD = *The Hittite Dictionary of the Oriental Institute of the University of Chicago*, edited by H. G. Güterbock and H. A. Hoffner. Currently available are the volumes: L-N 1989; P-1 (pa - parā) 1994; P-2 (parā - (UZU)pattar A) 1995; P-3 ((UZU)pattar A - putkiya-) 1997.

CILL see below, IKLL.

Clackson *Armenian and Greek* 1994 = J. Clackson *The Linguistic Relationship between Armenian and Greek*. Oxford / Cambridge 1994. Review: Ch. de Lamberterie in *Kratylos* 42 1997 p. 71-78.

CMCS = *Cambrian Medieval Celtic Studies*.

Collinge *Laws* 1985 = N. E. Collinge *The laws of Indo-European*. Amsterdam / Philadelphia 1985. An update through the year 1998 by the same author may be found in JIES 27 1999 p. 355-377.

Coll. Myc. 1975 [1979] = *Colloquium Mycenaeum, Actes du sixième Colloque International* 1975 in Chaumont, edited by E. Risch and H. Mühlestein. Neuchâtel / Geneva 1979.

Colloque E. Benveniste I / II 1983 [1984] = E. Benveniste *aujourd'hui, Actes du colloque Tours* 1983, edited by G. Serbat. 2 vols. Paris 1984.

Colloque P. Chantraine 1989 [1992] = *La langue et les textes en grec ancien, Actes du colloque P. Chantraine* Grenoble 1989, edited by F. Létoublon. Amsterdam 1992.

Colloquium Caricum 1997 [1998] = *Colloquium Caricum, Akten der Internationalen Tagung über die karisch-griechische Bilingue von Kaunos* 1997 in Feusisberg near Zürich, published as *Kadmos* 37 1998.

Coll. Raur. 2 1991 = *Colloquium Rauricum*, vol. 2, *Zweihundert Jahre Homer-Forschung, Rückblick und Ausblick*, edited by J. Latacz. Stuttgart / Leipzig 1991. Review: R. Schmitt in *Kratylos* 38 1993 p. 73-79.

Compendium Ling. Iran. 1989 = *Compendium Linguarum Iranicarum*, edited by R. Schmitt. Wiesbaden 1989.

Complétives 1998 [1999] = "*Les complétives en grec ancien*," *Colloque Saint-Étienne* 1998, edited by B. Jacquinod. Saint-Étienne 1999.

Convegno Udine (Restsprachen) 1981 [1983] = "*Le lingue indoeuropee di frammentaria attestazione, Die indogermanischen Restsprachen*", *Atti del Convegno della Società Italiana di Glottologia e della Idg. Gesell.* 1981 in Udine, edited by E. Vineis. Pisa 1983.

Coseriu *Synchronie, Diachronie* 1974 = E. Coseriu *Synchronie, Diachronie und Geschichte, Das Problem des Sprachwandels*. Munich 1974.

Cotticelli-Kurras *Heth. 'sein'* 1991 = P. Cotticelli-Kurras *Das hethitische Verbum 'sein'*. Heidelberg 1991 (= *Texte der Hethiter* 18).

Cowgill *Einleitung* 1986 = W. Cowgill *Einleitung*, translated into German and with a bibliography by A. Bammesberger and M. Peters = 1. Halbband von vol. I of *Idg. Gr.* (see below). Heidelberg 1986.

CR = *Classical Review.*

CRAI = *Comptes rendus de l'Académie des Inscriptions et Belles-Lettres.*

Crystal *Enzyklopädie* 1995 = D. Crystal *Die Cambridge-Enzyklopädie der Sprache*. Frankfurt / New York 1995 (= German translation of the original in English, *The Cambridge Encyclopedia of Language*. Cambridge / New York / Melbourne 1987).

Darms *Vr̥ddhi* 1978 = G. Darms *Schwäher und Schwager, Hahn und Huhn. Die Vr̥ddhi-Ableitung im Germanischen*. Munich 1978 (= MSS *Beiheft* 9, *Neue Folge*).

De Boel *Goal accusative* 1988 = G. De Boel *Goal accusative and object accusative in Homer. A contribution to the theory of transitivity*. Brüssel 1988;

Debrunner *Gr. Wortbildung* 1917 = A. Debrunner *Griechische Wortbildungslehre*. Heidelberg 1917.

Debrunner, see below under Schwyzer / Debrunner and Wackernagel / Debrunner.

Degrassi *Inscriptiones* I-II 1965-1972 = A. Degrassi *Inscriptiones Latinae Liberae Rei Publicae*. 2nd ed. Florence: I (Nr. 1-503) 1965 (and reprints); II (Nr. 504-1277 and indexes) 1972. By the same author, *Imagines*. Berlin 1965.

Delaunois *Syntaxe* 1988 = M. Delaunois *Essai de syntaxe grecque classique, Réflexions et recherches*. Leuven / Brussels 1988.

Delbrück *Ablativ Localis Instrumentalis* 1867 = B. Delbrück *Ablativ Localis Instrumentalis*. Berlin 1867.

Delbrück *Ai. Syntax* 1888 = B. Delbrück *Altindische Syntax*. Halle 1888 (reprint Darmstadt 1968).

Delbrück Einleitung 1904 = B. Delbrück *Einleitung in das Studium der indogermanischen Sprachen*. 4th ed. Leipzig 1904.

Delbrück *Gr. Syntax* 1879 = B. Delbrück *Die Grundlagen der griechischen Syntax*. Halle 1879.

Delbrück *Synkretismus* 1907 = B. Delbrück *Synkretismus. Ein Beitrag zur germanischen Kasuslehre*. Strasbourg 1907.

Delbrück *Vgl. Syntax* I 1893 II 1897 III 1900 = B. Delbrück *Vergleichende Syntax der indogermanischen Sprachen*. 3 parts, Strasbourg: I 1893, II 1897, III 1900. The three parts are included in Brugmann's *Grundriß* as vols. III - V. Along with the *Grundriß*, they were reprinted in 1967.

DELG see above, Chantraine DELG.

DELL see below, Ernout / Meillet DELL.

Demiraj (B.) *Alban. Etymologien* 1997 = B. Demiraj *Albanische Etymologien, Untersuchungen zum albanischen Erbwortschatz*. Amsterdam / Atlanta 1997. Review: G. Bonnet in BSL 93 / 2 1998 p. 256-262.

Demiraj (S.) *Albanisch* 1993 = S. Demiraj *Historische Grammatik der albanischen Sprache*. Vienna 1993.

Denniston *Greek Particles* 1954 = J. D. Denniston *The Greek Particles*. 2nd ed., revised by K. J. Dover. Oxford 1954.

Der Neue Pauly = DNP = *Enzyklopädie der Antike*, edited by H. Cancik and H. Schneider. Stuttgart: vol. 1 (A - Ari) 1996; vol. 2 (Ark - Ci) 1997; vol. 3 (Cl - Epi) 1997; vol. 4 (Epo - Gro) 1998; vol. 5 (Gru - Iug) 1998; vol. 6 (Iul - Lee) 1999; vol. 7 (Lef - Men) 1999; vol. 8 (Mer - Op) 2000; vol. 9 (Or - Poi) 2000; 10 (Pol - Sal) 2001. Further, volumes of the *Rezeptions- und Wissenschafts-geschichte* that have already appeared include: vol. 13 (A-Fo) 1999 and vol. 14 (Fr - Ky) 2000.

Deutschsprachige Keltologen 1992 [1993] = *Akten des Ersten Symposiums deutschsprachiger Keltologen* 1992 Gosen near Berlin, edited by M. Rockel and St. Zimmer. Tübingen 1993. Further, see below, *Keltologen-Symposium* II 1997 [1999].

Devoto *Lingua di Roma* 1940 = G. Devoto *Storia della lingua di Roma*. Bologna 1940 (reprint 1944, further 1983 foreword by L. Prosdocimi; translated into German by I. Opelt as "*Geschichte der Sprache Roms*". Heidelberg 1968).

DGE = *Diccionario griego-espanol*. Madrid, under the direction of F. R. Adrados. vol. I (α -ἀλλά) 1980. The work is currently vol. IV 1997 and the word διώνυχος. Anejo I / II see above, Aura Jorro *DMic*; Anejo III = *Repertorio bibliográfico de la lexicografía griega* 1998.

Diachrony within Synchrony 1990 [1992] = *Diachrony within Synchrony: Language History and Cognition, Papers from the International Symposium 1990 in Duisburg*, edited by G. Kellermann and M. D. Morrissey. Frankfurt 1992 (= *Duisburger Arbeiten zur Sprach- und Kulturwissenschaft* 14).

Dialectes indo-aryennes 1986 [1989] = *Dialectes dans les littératures indo-aryennes*, edited by C. Caillat. Paris 1989.

Dialectologica Graeca 1991 [1993] = *Dialectologica Graeca, Actas del II Coloquio Internacional de Dialectología Griega* Madrid 1991, edited by E. Crespo, J. L. García Ramón, A. Striano. Madrid 1993. Concerning the third colloquium, cf. *Katà diálekton* 1996 [1999] below. The texts of the first colloquium (*Rencontre internationale*) in Nancy / Pont-à-Mousson were published in *Verbum* 10 1987.

Dialektologie 1 1982 2 1983 = *Ein Handbuch zur deutschen und allgemeinen Dialektforschung*, edited by W. Besch, U. Knoop, W. Putschke, H. E. Wiegand. Berlin / New York. 2 half-vols.: 1 1982; 2 1983 (= HSK 1.1 and 1.2).

Diehl Altlat. Inschriften 1965 = E. Diehl *Altlateinische Inschriften, mit Indizes*. 5th ed. Berlin 1964 (= *Kleine Texte*, commented by H. Lietzmann, Nr.38 / 40).

Di Giovine see below, Giovine.

Dionysios Thrax (2nd century B.C.) *Grammatik* = *La grammaire de Denys le Thrace, traduite et annotée par Jean Lallot*. 2nd ed. Paris 1998.

Disterheft *Infinitive* 1977 = D. Disterheft *The Syntax of the Infinitive in Indo-European: Evidence from Indo-Iranian, Celtic, and Hittite*. Ph.-D. dissertation. University of California, Los Angeles 1977 (microfilm Ann Arbor 1979).

DNP = see above, *Der Neue Pauly*.

Dobias-Lalou *Cyrène* 2000 = C. Dobias-Lalou *Le dialecte des inscriptions grecques de Cyrène*. Paris 2000.

Dressler *Verb. Pluralität* 1968 = W. Dressler *Studien zur verbalen Pluralität, Iterativum, Distributivum, Intensivum in der allgemeinen Grammatik, im Lateinischen und Hethitischen.* Vienna 1968.

dtv-Atlas Dt. Sprache 1998 = *dtv-Atlas Deutsche Sprache* 1998. Munich 1st ed. 1978, 12. ed. 1998.

Dubois *Arcadien* 1986 = L. Dubois *Recherches sur le dialecte arcadien.* Louvain-La-Neuve 1986: I (*Grammaire*), II (*Corpus dialectal*), III (*Notes, Index, Bibliographie*).

Duden *Grammatik* 1995 = *Der Duden in 12 Bänden*, vol. 4. *Grammatik der deutschen Gegenwartssprache*, 5th ed., fully revised and expanded, edited and revised by G. Drosdowski, together with P. Eisenberg, H. Gelhaus, H. Henne, H. Sitta and H. Wellmann. Mannheim / Leipzig / Vienna / Zürich 1995.

Egetmeyer *Wörterbuch* 1992 = M. Egetmeyer *Wörterbuch zu den Inschriften im kyprischen Syllabar.* Berlin 1992.

Egli *Gelenkheteroklisie* 1954 = J. Egli *Heteroklisie im Griechischen mit besonderer Berücksichtigung der Fälle von Gelenkheteroklisie.* Zürich 1954.

Eichner *Numeralia* 1982 = H. Eichner *Studien zu den indogermanischen Numeralia* (2-5). (unpublished) postdoctoral thesis. Regensburg 1982.

Einhauser *Junggrammatiker* 1989 = E. Einhauser *Die Junggrammatiker, Ein Problem für die Sprachwissenschaftsgeschichtsforschung.* Trier 1989.

Ernout *Recueil* 1947 = A. Ernout *Recueil de textes latins archaïques, Textes épigraphiques et littéraires.* 2nd ed. Paris 1947 (and reprints).

Ernout / Meillet DELL 1959 = A. Ernout and A. Meillet *Dictionnaire étymologique de la langue latine. Histoire des mots.* 4th ed., revised, corrected, and augmented with an index. Paris 1959.

Ethnogenese 1985 = *Studien zur Ethnogenese, Abhandlungen der Rheinisch-Westfälischen Akademie der Wissenschaften* vol. 72. Opladen 1985.

Etruschi e Roma 1979 [1981] = *Gli Etruschi e Roma, Atti dell' incontro di studio in onore di Massimo Pallottino* Rome 1979, edited by G. Colonna. Rome 1981. Review: D. Steinbauer in GGA 235 1983 p. 210-232.

Etrusker 1985 = *Die Etrusker*, edited by M. Christofani. Stuttgart / Zürich 1985.

Etter *Fragesätze* 1985 = A. Etter *Die Fragesätze im Ṛgveda.* Berlin / New York 1985. Review: J. S. Klein in *Kratylos* 33 1988 p. 79-83.

Etymologisches Wörterbuch 1983 = *Das etymologische Wörterbuch, Fragen der Konzeption und Gestaltung*, edited by A. Bammesberger. Regensburg 1983 (= *Eichstätter Beiträge* 8).

Euler *Gemeinsamkeiten* 1979 = W. Euler *Indoiranisch-griechische Gemeinsamkeiten der Nominalbildung und deren indogermanische Grundlagen*. Innsbruck 1979 (= IBS Nr. 30).

Evidence for Laryngeals 1965 = *Evidence for Laryngeals*, edited by W. Winter. London / The Hague / Paris 1965.

EWAhd = *Etymologisches Wörterbuch des Althochdeutschen*. Göttingen / Zürich. I (-a - bezzisto) 1988 by A. L. Lloyd and O. Springer; II (bî - ezzo) 1998 by A. L. Lloyd, R. Lühr and O. Springer. A separate booklet of word indexes belongs to vol. I.

EWAia see below, Mayrhofer EWAia.

Explanation in Historical Linguistics 1992 = *Explanation in Historical Linguistics*, edited by G. W. Davis and G. K. Iverson. Amsterdam / Philadelphia 1992 (= *Amsterdam Studies in the Theory and History of Linguistic Science*, IV *Current Issues in Linguistic Theory* 84).

Fachtagung Berlin 1983 [1985] = *Grammatische Kategorien, Funktion und Geschichte, Akten der VII. Fachtagung der Idg. Gesellschaft* 1983 in Berlin, edited by B. Schlerath. Wiesbaden 1985.

Fachtagung Bern 1969 [1973] = *Indogermanische und allgemeine Sprachwissenschaft, Akten der IV. Fachtagung der Idg. Gesellschaft* 1969 in Bern, edited by G. Redard. Wiesbaden 1973.

Fachtagung Innsbruck 1961 [1962] = Akten der II. Fachtagung der Idg. Gesellschaft 1961 in Innsbruck. Innsbruck 1962.

Fachtagung Innsbruck 1996 [1998] = *Sprache und Kultur der Indogermanen, Akten der X. Fachtagung der Idg. Gesellschaft 1996 in Innsbruck*. Innsbruck 1998 (= IBS Nr. 93).

Fachtagung Leiden 1987 [1992] = *Relative Chronologie, Akten der VIII. Fachtagung der Idg. Gesellschaft* 1987 in Leiden, edited by R. S. P. Beekes. Innsbruck 1992. Review: B. Forssman in *Kratylos* 39 1994 p. 48-55 (with a useful glossary [p. 53-55] in place of an index).

Fachtagung Regensburg 1973 [1975] = *Flexion und Wortbildung, Akten der V. Fachtagung der Idg. Gesellschaft* 1973 in Regensburg, edited by H. Rix. Wiesbaden 1975.

Fachtagung Tocharisch Berlin 1990 [1994] = *Tocharisch, Akten der Fachtagung der Idg. Gesellschaft* 1990 in Berlin, edited by B. Schlerath. Reikjavík 1994 (= *TIES, Suppl. Ser.* 4).

Fachtagung Wien 1978 [1980] = *Lautgeschichte und Etymologie, Akten der VI. Fachtagung der Idg. Gesellschaft* 1978 in Vienna, edited by M. Mayrhofer, M. Peters, O. E. Pfeiffer. Wiesbaden 1980.

Fachtagung Zürich 1992 [1994] = *Früh-, Mittel-, Spätindogermanisch, Akten der IX. Fachtagung der Idg. Gesellschaft* 1992 in Zürich, edited by G. E. Dunkel, G. Meyer, S. Scarlata, Chr. Seidl. Wiesbaden 1994. Review: J. S. Klein in *Kratylos* 42 1997 p. 24-32.

Feist *Got. Wörterbuch* 1939 = S. Feist *Vergleichendes Wörterbuch der gotischen Sprache.* 3rd revised ed. Leiden 1939. See also, Lehmann *Gothic Etymological Dictionary*1986.

Feist *Indogermanen* 1913 = S. Feist *Kultur, Ausbreitung und Herkunft der Indogermanen.* Berlin 1913.

Floreant *Studia Mycenaea* 1995 [1999] = Floreant *Studia Mycenaea, Akten des X. Internationalen Mykenologischen Colloquiums Salzburg 1995*, edited by S. Deger-Jalkotzy, S. Hiller and O. Panagl. 2 vols., Vienna 1999 (= *Denkschriften* 274, *Österr. Ak. der Wissenschaften*).

FoL = *Folia Linguistica.*

Formazione dell' Europa linguistica 1993 = *La formazione dell' Europa linguistica, Le lingue d'Europa tra la fine del I e del II millennio*, edited by E. Banfi. Florence 1993. Including, among others, "*Le lingue germaniche*" by M. Meli; "*Le lingue slave*" by A. Cantarini; "*Le lingue baltiche*" by P. U. Dini; "*Le lingue celtiche*" by P. Cuzzolin; *La lingua greca* by E. Banfi; "*La lingua albanese*" by S. Demiraj.

Forssman *Pindar* 1966 = B. Forssman *Untersuchungen zur Sprache Pindars.* Wiesbaden 1966.

Forssman, see also, Hoffmann / Forssman.

Fraenkel *Lit. etym. Wörterbuch* 1962-1965 = E. Fraenkel *Litauisches etymologisches Wörterbuch.* Heidelberg 1962-1965.

Fraenkel *Syntax der lit. Kasus* 1928 = E. Fraenkel *Syntax der litauischen Kasus.* Kaunas 1928.

Fraenkel *Syntax der lit. Postpositionen und Präpositionen* 1929 = E. Fraenkel *Syntax der litauischen Postpositionen und Präpositionen.* Heidelberg 1929.

Friedrich (J.) *Elementarbuch* I 1960 = J. Friedrich *Hethitisches Elementarbuch.* I (*Kurzgefaßte Grammatik*). 2nd ed. 1960.

Friedrich (J.) *Kleinas. Sprachdenkmäler* 1932 = J. Friedrich *Kleinasiatische Sprachdenkmäler.* Berlin 1932.

Friedrich (J.) / Kammenhuber HW = J. Friedrich *Hethitisches Wörterbuch.* 2nd ed. by A. Kammenhuber fully revised on the basis of edited Hittite texts. Heidelberg. installment 1 1974. Status at the end of 1998: installment 13 (Ḫ⟩ 1998.

Friedrich (P.) *Syntax* 1975 = P. Friedrich *Proto-Indo-European Syntax: The Order of Meaningful Elements*. Washington 1975 (= JIES, *Monograph* 1).

Frigi e Frigio 1995 [1997] = *Frigi e Frigio, Atti del 1° Simposio Internazionale* Rome 1995, edited by R. Gusmani, M. Salvini, P. Vannicelli. Rome 1997 (= *Consiglio Nazionale delle Ricerche, Monografie Scientifiche*).

Frisian Runes 1994 [1996] = *Frisian Runes and Neighbouring Traditions, Proceedings of the First International Symposium on Frisian Runes at the Fries Museum* 1994 in Leeuwarden, edited by T. Looijenga and A. Quak. Amsterdam 1996 (= *Amsterdamer Beiträge zur älteren Germanistik, Band* 45).

Frisk GEW 1960-1972 = H. Frisk *Griechisches etymologisches Wörterbuch*. Heidelberg 3 vols. 1960-1972: I (A - Kο) 1960, II (Kρ - Ω) 1972, III (*Nachträge, Wortregister, Corrigenda, Nachwort*) 1972. also reprints.

Fritz *Lokalpartikel* 1997 = M. Fritz *Die syntaktischen und semantischen Relationen der Lokalpartikeln mit drei Kasus bei Homer*. Berlin (dissertation at the Freie Universität) 1997.

FS = *Festschrift* (commemorative publications): For the sake of simplicity, only the name of the honored person shall be given, along with the date of publication. A longer list of *Festschriften* may be found in Mayrhofer EWAia I p. XXV - XXX and II p. XIII - XV. A few newer *Festschriften* are additionally listed here.

FS Beekes 1997 = *Sound Law and Analogy, Papers in Honor of R. S. P. Beekes*, edited by A. Lubotsky. Amsterdam / Atlanta 1997.

FS Belardi I 1994 = *Miscellanea di studi linguistici in onore di Walter Belardi*, edited by P. Cipriano, P. di Giovine, M. Mancini. Rome vol. I (*Linguistica indoeuropea e non indoeuropea*) 1994.

FS Dihle 1993 = *Philanthropia kai Eusebeia, Festschrift für Albrecht Dihle zum 70. Geburtstag*, edited by G. W. Most, H. Petersmann and A. M. Ritter. Göttingen 1993.

FS Forssman 1999 = *gering und doch von Herzen, 25 indogermanistische Beiträge B. Forssman zum 65. Geburtstag*, edited by J. Habisreitinger, R. Plath, S. Ziegler. Wiesbaden 1999.

FS Hamp 1990 = *Celtic Language, Celtic Culture: A Festschrift for Eric P. Hamp*, edited by A. T. E. Matonis and D. F. Melia. Van Nuys, California 1990.

FS Hamp I / II 1997 = *Festschrift for Eric P. Hamp*. Washington 1997 (= JIES Monographs 23 and 25).

FS Hoenigswald 1987 = *Festschrift for Henry M. Hoenigswald*, edited by G. Cardona and N. H. Zide. Tübingen 1987.

FS Knobloch 1985 = *Sprachwissenschaftliche Forschungen, Festschrift für J. Knobloch*, edited by H. M. Ölberg, G. Schmidt. Innsbruck 1985 (= IBS 23).

FS Kuiper 1968 = *Pratidānam, Indian, Iranian and Indo-European Studies Presented to Franciscus Bernardus Jacobus Kuiper on his sixtieth birthday*, edited by J. C. Heesterman, G. H. Schokker, V. I. Subramoniam. The Hague / Paris 1968.

FS Lejeune 1978 = *Etrennes de septantaine, Travaux de linguistique et de grammaire comparée offerts à Michel Lejeune*, edited by a group of his students. Paris 1978 (= *Études et Commentaires 91*).

FS Meid *60 1989 = *Indogermanica Europea, Festschrift für W. Meid zum 60. Geburtstag*, edited by K. Heller, O. Panagl, J. Tischler. Graz 1989.

FS Meid *70 1999 = *Studia Celtica et Indogermanica, Festschrift für W. Meid zum 70. Geburtstag*, edited by P. Anreiter, E. Jerem. Budapest 1999.

FS Narten 2000 = *Anusantatyai, Festschrift J. Narten*, edited by A. Hintze, E. Tichy. Dettelbach 2000 (= MSS, *Beiheft* 19. *N.F.*).

FS Neumann 1982 = *Serta Indogermanica, Festschrift für Günter Neumann zum 60. Geburtstag*, edited by J. Tischler. Innsbruck 1982.

FS Otten 1973 = *Festschrift Heinrich Otten*, edited by E. Neu and Chr. Rüster. Wiesbaden 1973.

FS Otten 1988 = *Documentum Asiae Minoris Antiquae. Festschrift für Heinrich Otten zum 75. Geburtstag*, edited by E. Neu and Chr. Rüster. Wiesbaden 1988.

FS Palmer 1976 = *Studies in Greek, Italic, and Indo-European Linguistics offered to Leonard R. Palmer*, edited by A. Morpurgo Davies and W. Meid. Innsbruck 1976.

FS Puhvel I 1997 = *Studies in Honor of J. Puhvel. I: Ancient Languages and Philology*, edited by D. Disterheft, M. Huld and J. Greppin. Washington 1997 (= JIES Monograph 20).

FS Ramat 1998 = *Ars Linguistica, Studi offerti a Paolo Ramat*, edited by G. Bernini, P. Cuzzolin, P. Molinelli. Rome 1998.

FS Risch 1986 = *o-o-pe-ro-si, Festschrift für Ernst Risch zum 75. Geburtstag*, edited by A. Etter. Berlin / New York 1986.

FS Rix 1993 = *Indogermanica et Italica, Festschrift für Helmut Rix zum 65. Geburtstag*, edited by G. Meiser. Innsbruck 1993.

FS Schlerath 1992 [1994] = *Die Indogermanen und das Pferd, Akten des Internationalen interdisziplinären Kolloquiums an der Freien Universität Berlin, 2nd-3. Juli 1992* [= *Festschrift für Bernfried Schlerath*], edited by B. Hänsel and St. Zimmer. Budapest 1994. Cf. report by St. Zimmer in *Ethnographisch-archäologische Zeitschrift* 33 1992 [1993] p. 297-301.

FS Schmeja 1998 = *Wort - Text - Sprache und Kultur, Festschrift für Hans Schmeja zum 65. Geburtstag*, edited by P. Anreiter and H. M. Ölberg. Innsbruck 1998 (= IBK 103).

FS Schmid 1999 = *Florilegium Linguisticum, Festschrift für Wolfgang P. Schmid*, edited by E. Eggers, J. Becker, J. Udolph, D. Weber. Bern, Frankfurt am Mainet al. 1999.

FS (K. H.) Schmidt 1994 = *Indogermanica et Caucasica, Festschrift für Karl Horst Schmidt zum 65. Geburtstag*, edited by R. Bielmeier and R. Stempel. Berlin / New York 1994.

FS Seebold 1999 = *Grippe, Kamm und Eulenspiegel, Festschrift für Elmar Seebold zum 65. Geburtstag*, edited by W. Schindler and J. Untermann. Berlin 1999.

FS Stimm 1982 = *Fakten und Theorien, Beiträge zur romanischen und allgemeinen Sprachwissenschaft, Festschrift für Helmut Stimm zum 65. Geburtstag*, edited by S. Heinz and U. Wandruszka. Tübingen 1982 (= TBL 191).

FS Strunk 1995 = *Verba et structurae, Festschrift für Klaus Strunk zum 65. Geburtstag*, edited by H. Hettrich, W. Hock, P.-A. Mumm and N. Oettinger. Innsbruck 1995. Review: R. S. P. Beekes in *Kratylos* 42 1997 p. 36-39.

FS Szemerényi *65 I / II 1979 = *Studies in Diachronic, Synchronic, and Typological Linguistics, Festschrift for Oswald Szemerényi*, edited by B. Brogyanyi. 2 vols. Amsterdam 1979.

FS Szemerényi *75 I / II 1992, III 1993 = *Prehistory, History and Historiography of Language, Speech and Linguistic Theory, Papers in Honor of Oswald Szemerényi* I, edited by B. Brogyanyi; *Historical Philology: Greek, Latin, and Romance, Papers in Honor of Oswald Szemerényi* II, edited by B. Brogyanyi and R. Lipp; *Comparative-Historical Linguistics: Indo-European and Finno-Ugric, Papers in Honor of Oswald Szemerényi* III, edited by B. Brogyanyi and R. Lipp. 3 vols. Amsterdam / Philadelphia 1992-1993 (= Current Issues in Linguistic Theory, Nr. 64, 87 and 97). Review: M. Egetmeyer in PFU (= PFU) 1 1994 [1995] p. 47-53 and p. 55-61; 4 1998 p. 69-76.

FS Thomas 1988 = *Studia Indogermanica et Slavica. Festgabe für Werner Thomas zum 65. Geburtstag*, edited by P. Kosta. Munich 1988.

FS Untermann 1993 = *Sprachen und Schriften des antiken Mittelmeer-raumes, Festschrift für Jürgen Untermann*, edited by F. Heidermanns, H. Rix and E. Seebold. Innsbruck 1993 (= IBS 78).

FS Watkins 1998 = *Mír Curad, Studies in Honor of Calvert Watkins*, edited by J. Jasanoff, H. Craig Melchert, L. Oliver. Innsbruck 1998 (= IBS 92).

FS Zaic 1989 = *Phonophilia, Untersuchungen zu Phonetik und Phonologie, F. Zaic zum 60. Geburtstag*, edited by W. Grosser et al. Salzburg 1989.

Fulk Quantitative Ablaut 1986 = R. D. Fulk *The Origins of Indo-European Quantitative Ablaut*. Innsbruck 1986 (= IBS 49). Review: G. Schmidt in *Kratylos* 32 1987 p. 37-46.

Gaedicke *Accusativ im Veda* 1880 = C. Gaedicke *Der Accusativ im Veda*. Breslau 1880.

Gamkrelidze / Ivanov *IE and IEs* 1995 = T. V. Gamkrelidze and V. V. Ivanov *Indo-European and the Indo-Europeans. A Reconstruction and Historical Analysis of a Proto-Language and a Proto-Culture*. 2 vols. Berlin / New York 1995. The work is the English translation of the original Russian *Indoevropejskij jazyk i indoevropejcy* that was published in 1984. The translation, dated 1995, reflects the status of research in 1984. Review: M. Mayrhofer in *Kratylos* 42 1997 p. 21-24; J. Gippert in BNF 33 1998 p. 39-54.

Gāters *Lettische Syntax* 1993 = A. Gāters *Lettische Syntax, Die Dainas*, posthum edited by H. Radtke. Frankfurt am Main et al. 1993.

Geiger *Pāli* 1916 = W. Geiger *Pāli, Literatur und Sprache*. Strasbourg 1916.

Geldner *RV Übersetzung* 1951-1957 = *Der Rig-Veda, Aus dem Sanskrit ins Deutsche übersetzt und mit einem laufenden Kommentar versehen von K. F. Geldner*. 4 vols. Leipzig 1951-1957. Although the translation was already complete in 1923, circumstances were such that the the work was first published only after the Second World War, cf. the foreword by J. Nobel (vol. IV p. V-VII).

Germanenprobleme in heutiger Sicht 1986 = *Germanenprobleme in heutiger Sicht*, edited by H. Beck. Berlin / New York 1986.

GGA = *Göttingische Gelehrte Anzeigen*.

Giacomelli *Lingua falisca* 1963 = G. Giacomelli *La lingua falisca*. Florence 1963.

Giacomelli *Lingua latina* 1993 = R. Giacomelli *Storia della lingua latina*. Rome 1993 (in the series *Guide allo studio della Civilità romana* IV. 1)

Giannakis *Reduplicated Presents* 1997 = G. K. Giannakis *Studies in the Syntax and Semantics of the Reduplicated Presents of Homeric Greek and Indo-European*. Innsbruck 1997 (= IBS 90). Review: E. F. Tucker in *Kratylos* 45 2000 p. 111-116.

Giovine *Perfetto* I 1990 II / III 1996 = P. Di Giovine *Studio sul Perfetto Indoeuropeo*. Rome: *Parte I* 1990 (*La funzione originaria del perfetto studiata nella documentazione delle lingue storiche*); *Parte II* 1996 (*La posizione del perfetto all' interno del sistema verbale indoeuropeo*); *Parte III* 1996 (*Indici*); also by the same author, *Le lingue anatoliche e il perfetto indoeuropeo: Una "petitio principii"?* in *FS W. Belardi* I. Rome 1994 p. 113-130. Review: J. A. Harđarson in *Kratylos* 46 2001 p. 36-44.

Gippert *Infinitive* 1978 = J. Gippert *Zur Syntax der infinitivischen Bildungen in den indogermanischen Sprachen*. Frankfurt / Bern / Las Vegas 1978.

Gippert *Iranica* 1993 = J. Gippert *Iranica Armeno-Iberica, Studien zu den iranischen Lehnwörtern im Armenischen und Georgischen*. 2 vols. Vienna 1993 (= SbÖAW Nr. 606).

Glotta = *Glotta. Zeitschrift für griechische und lateinische Sprache*. Göttingen.

Gmür *Mémoire* 1986 = R. Gmür *Das Schicksal von F. de Saussures "Mémoire". Eine Rezeptionsgeschichte*. Bern 1986. Review: M. Mayrhofer in *Kratylos* 33 1988 p.1-15 = *Kleine Schriften* II 1996 p. 271-285.

Godel *Classical Armenian* 1975 = R. Godel *An Introduction to the Study of Classical Armenian*. Wiesbaden 1975.

Gonda *Indo-European Moods* 1956 = J. Gonda *The Character of the Indo-European Moods*. Wiesbaden 1956. Review: E. Risch in Gnomon 33 1961 p. 174-178; J. Kuryłowicz and Hj. Seiler in *Kratylos* 1 1956 p. 123-135.

GORILA I - V 1976-1985 = L. Godart, J.-P. Olivier *Recueil des inscriptions en linéaire A*. Paris: I (*Tablettes éditées avant 1970*) 1976; II (*Nodules, Scellés et rondelles édités avant 1970*) 1979; III (*Tablettes, nodules et rondelles édités en 1975 et 1976*) 1976; IV (*Autres documents*) 1982; V (*Addenda, Corrigenda, Concordances, Index et planches des signes*) 1985 (= *École Française d'Athènes, Études Crétoises Nr. 21, 1-5*).

Gotō I. *Präsensklasse* 1987 = T. Gotō *Die "I. Präsensklasse" im Vedischen. Untersuchung der vollstufigen thematischen Wurzelpräsentia*. Vienna 1987. The 2nd ed. (1996) includes supplements and improvements. Review der 2nd ed.: St. W. Jamison in *Kratylos* 34 1989 p. 59-65.

Gotō *Materialien* Nr. 1-3 1990 Nr. 4-7 1991 Nr. 8-15 1993 Nr. 16-29 1997 = T. Gotō, *Materialien zu einer Liste altindischer Verbalformen. Bulletin of the National Museum of Ethnology, Osaka (Japan)*: Nr. 1-3 (1. *am*^{i}, 2. *ay/i*, 3. *as/s*) in Vol. 15 / 4 1990 p. 987-1012; Nr. 4-7 (4. *dogh/dugh/doh/duh*, 5. *sav/su*, 6. ^{1}*sav*^{i}*/sū*, 7. ^{2}(*sav*^{i}*/*)*sū* in Vol. 16 / 3 1991 p. 681-707; Nr. 8-15 (8. *ard/r̥d*, 9. *īṣ*, 10. *ukṣ*, 11. *eṣ/iṣ*, 12. *eṣ*^{i}*/iṣ*^{i}, 13. *ok/oc/uc*, 14. *kaṇ*, 15. *vakṣ/ukṣ*) in Vol.18 / 1 1993 p. 119-141; Nr. 16-29 (16. *chad*, 17. *chand/chad*, 18. *chard/chr̥d*, 19. *dagh/dhag*, 20. *dveṣ/dviṣ*, 21. *bandh/badh*, 22. ^{1}*man*, 23. ^{2}*man*, 24. *mnā*, 25. ^{1}*yav/yu*, 26. ^{2}*yav/yu*, 27. *san*^{i}, 28. *star/str̥*, 29. *star*^{i}*/str̥̄*) in Vol. 22 / 4 1997 [1998] p.1001-1059.

Grammatica ittita 1992 = *Per una grammatica ittita, Towards a Hittite Grammar*, edited by O. Carruba. Pavia 1992 (= *Studia Mediterranea* 7).

Grassmann *Wörterbuch* 1873 = H. Grassmann *Wörterbuch zum Rig-Veda*. Leipzig 1873 (and reprints). 6th revised, updated ed. by M. Kozianka 1996. Review of the 6th ed.: Th. Zehnder in PFU 4 1998 p. 77-84.

Graz (*125 Jahre Idg.*) 2000 = *125 Jahre Indogermanistik in Graz, Festband anläßlich des 125jährigen Bestehens der Forschungs-einrichtung „Indogermanistik" an der Karl-Franzens-Universität Graz*, edited by M. Ofitsch and Chr. Zinko, Graz 2000.

Greek Language in Cyprus 1988 = *The History of the Greek Language in Cyprus, Proceedings of an International Symposium Larnaca 1986*, edited by J. Karageorghis / O. Masson. Nicosia 1988.

Greek Particles 1996 [1997] = *New Approaches to Greek Particles, Proceedings of the Colloquium Amsterdam 1996*, edited by A. Rijksbaron. Amsterdam 1997.

Greek Personal Names I 1987 II 1994 III A 1997 = *A Lexicon of Greek Personal Names*, edited by P. M. Fraser, E. Matthews. Oxford. vol. I (*The Aegean Islands, Cyprus, Cyrenaica*) 1987; vol. II (*Attica*, edited by M. J. Osborne, S. G. Byrne) 1994; vol. III A (*The Peloponnese, Western Greece and Magna Graecia*) 1997.

Größere altkelt. Sprachdenkmäler 1993 [1996] = *Die größeren altkeltischen Sprachdenkmäler, Akten des Kolloquiums 1993 in Innsbruck*, edited by W. Meid and P. Anreiter. Innsbruck 1996 (= IBK, Sonderheft 95). Review: J. Uhlich in *Kratylos* 44 1999 p. 144-154.

Gr. Philologie 1997 = *Einleitung in die griechische Philologie*, edited by H.-G. Nesselrath. Stuttgart / Leipzig 1997.

GS = *Gedenkschrift* (memorial publication); a listing may be found in Mayrhofer EWAia I p. XXXII f., II p. XVII.

GS Brandenstein 1968 = *Studien zur Sprachwissenschaft und Kulturkunde, Gedenkschrift für W. Brandenstein*, edited by M. Mayrhofer. Innsbruck 1968 (= IBK Nr. 14).

GS Cowgill 1987 = *Studies in Memory of Warren Cowgill (1929-1985), Papers from the Fourth East Coast Indo-European Conference 1985*, edited by C. Watkins. Berlin / New York 1987 (= *Untersuchungen zur Indogermanischen Sprach- und Kulturwissenschaft*, N.F. 3).

GS Katz 2001 = *Fremd und Eigen, Untersuchungen zu Grammatik und Wortschatz des Uralischen und Indogermanischen, in memoriam Hartmut Katz*, edited by H. Eichner, P.-A. Mumm, O. Panagl, E. Winkler. Vienna 2001.

GS Kronasser 1982 = *Investigationes Philologicae et Comparativae. Gedenkschrift für Heinz Kronasser*. Wiesbaden 1982.

GS Kuryłowicz I / II 1995 = Kuryłowicz *Memorial Volume*, vol. I, edited by W. Smoczynski. Cracow 1995. vol. II was published as vol. 4 1995 of *Linguistica Baltica*. Review by I: A. Christol in BSL 92 / 2 1997 p. 131-135.

GS Schindler 1999 = *Compositiones indogermanicae in memoriam Jochem Schindler*, edited by H. Eichner and H. Chr. Luschützky. Prague 1999.

GS van Windekens 1991 = *Studia etymologica indoeuropea, Memoriae A. J. van Windekens (1915-1989) dicata*, edited by L. Isebaert. Leuven 1991.

Guiraud *Phrase nominale* 1962 = Ch. Guiraud *La phrase nominale en grec*. Paris 1962.

Gusmani *Lyd. Wörterbuch* 1964 = R. Gusmani *Lydisches Wörterbuch*. Heidelberg 1964.

Gusmani *Lyd. Wb. Erg.* 1986 = R. Gusmani *Lydisches Wörterbuch. Ergänzungsband*. Heidelberg 1986.

Haas *Heth. Religion* 1994 = V. Haas *Geschichte der hethitischen Religion*. Leiden / New York / Köln 1994.

Hackstein *Sigmat. Präsensstammbildungen* 1995 = O. Hackstein *Untersuchungen zu den sigmatischen Präsensstammbildungen des Tocharischen*. Göttingen 1995 (= HS, *Ergänzungsheft Nr. 38*). Review: J. H. W. Penney in *Kratylos* 43 1998 p. 92-96; H. Craig Melchert in TIES 9 2000 p. 145f.; G.-J. Pinault in BSL 95 / 2 2000 p. 157-163.

Hahn *Naming-Constructions* 1969 = E. A. Hahn *Naming-Constructions in some Indo-European Languages*. Ann Arbor 1969.

Hahn *Subjunctive and Optative* 1953 = E. A. Hahn *Subjunctive and Optative, Their origin as futures*. New York 1953.

Hajnal *Lyk. Vokalismus* 1995 = I. Hajnal *Der lykische Vokalismus: Methode und Erkenntnisse der vergleichenden anatolischen Sprachwissenschaft, angewandt auf das Vokalsystem einer Kleincorpussprache*. Graz 1995. Review: G. Neumann in HS 111 1998 p.372-376.

Hajnal *Myk. Kasussystem* 1995 = I. Hajnal *Studien zum mykenischen Kasussystem*. Berlin / New York 1995. Review: N. Guilleux (-Maurice) in BSL 92 / 2 1997 p. 200-216.

Hajnal *Myk. u. hom. Lexikon* 1998 = I. Hajnal *Mykenisches und homerisches Lexikon, Übereinstimmungen, Divergenzen und der Versuch einer Typologie*. Innsbruck 1998 (= IBS, *Vorträge und kl. Schriften 69*).

Hajnal *Sprachschichten* 1997 = I. Hajnal *Sprachschichten des Mykenischen Griechisch*. Salamanca 1997 (= *Minos Supl. 14*).

Hamm *Sappho und Alkaios* 1957 = E.-M. Hamm *Grammatik zu Sappho und Alkaios*. Berlin 1957.

Handbuch der Onomastik 1 1995 = *Namenforschung, Name Studies, Les noms propres, Ein internationales Handbuch zur Onomastik*, edited by E. Eichler, G. Hilty, H. Löffler, H. Steger, L. Zgusta. part 1. Berlin / New York 1995.

Happ *Grundfragen* 1976 = H. Happ *Grundfragen einer Dependenzgrammatik des Lateinischen*. Göttingen 1976.

Harđarson *Wurzelaorist* 1993 = J. A. Harđarson *Studien zum indogermanischen Wurzelaorist und dessen Vertretung im Indoiranischen und Griechischen*. Innsbruck 1993. Review: K. Strunk in *Kratylos* 39 1994 p. 55-68; M. Peters in *Idg. Chr. 35* Nr. A 789.

Haudry *Cas en védique* 1977 = J. Haudry *L'emploi des cas en védique. Introduction à l'étude des cas en indo-européen*. Lyon 1977. Review: G. Cardona in *Kratylos* 23 1978 [1979] p. 71-82.

Haudry *Les indo-européens* 1985 = J. Haudry *Les indo-européens*. Paris 1st ed. 1981, 2nd ed. 1985 (= *Collection Que sais-je ?* Nr. 1965).

Haudry *L'indo-européen* 1979 = J. Haudry *L'indo-européen*. Paris 1979 (= *Collection Que sais-je ?* Nr. 1798).

Hauri *-ena* 1963 = Ch. Hauri *Zur Vorgeschichte des Ausgangs -ena des Instr. Sing. der a-Stämme des Altindischen*. Göttingen 1963 (= ZVS, *Ergänzungsheft* Nr. 17).

Hauri *Futur* 1975 = H. W. Hauri *Kontrahiertes und sigmatisches Futur. Einflüsse von Lautstruktur und Aktionsart auf die Bildung des griechischen Futurs*. Göttingen 1975 (= ZVS, *Ergänzungsheft* Nr. 24). Review: C. J. Ruijgh in *Kratylos* 20 1975 [1977] p. 82-91 (= *Scripta Minora* I 1991 p. 368-377); F. M. J. Waanders in *Mnemosyne 33* 1980 p. 369-374.

Hauschild, see below, Thumb / Hauschild.

Haverling *sco-Verbs* 2000 = G. Haverling *On sco-Verbs, Prefixes and Semantic Functions*. Göteborg 2000.

Havers *Erklärende Syntax* 1931 = W. Havers *Handbuch der erklärenden Syntax, Ein Versuch zur Erforschung der Bedingungen und Triebkräfte in Syntax und Stilistik*. Heidelberg 1931.

Havers *Kasussyntax* 1911 = W. Havers *Untersuchungen zur Kasussyntax der indogermanischen Sprachen*. Strasbourg 1911.

Havers *Sprachtabu* 1946 = W. Havers *Neuere Literatur zum Sprachtabu*. Vienna 1946.

Hawkins *Corpus* 1 2000 / 2 1999 = D. Hawkins *Corpus of Hieroglyphic Luwian inscriptions*. Berlin / New York. vol. 1 (in 3 parts: *Inscriptions from the Iron Age*) by D. Hawkins 2000; vol. 2 (*Karatepe-Aslantas: the inscriptions; facsimile edition*) by H. Çambel 1999.

HED, see below, Puhvel HED.

HEG, see below, Tischler HEG.

Hehn *Cultivated Plants and Domesticated Animals* (1885) 1976 = V. Hehn *Cultivated Plants and Domesticated Animals in their Migration from Asia to Europe, Historico-linguistic studies, new edition prepared with a bio-bibliographical account of Hehn and a survey of the research in Indo-European prehistory*, edited by J. P. Mallory. Amsterdam 1976.

Heidermanns *Germ. Primäradjektive* 1993 = F. Heidermanns *Etymologisches Wörterbuch der germanischen Primäradjektive*. Berlin / New York 1993.

Hethitisch und Indogermanisch 1979 = *Hethitisch und Indogermanisch, Vergleichende Studien zur historischen Grammatik und zur dialektgeographischen Stellung der indogermanischen Sprachgruppe Altkleinasiens*, edited by E. Neu and W. Meid. Innsbruck 1979 (= IBS Nr. 25).

Hettrich *Agens* 1990 = H. Hettrich *Der Agens in passivischen Sätzen altindogermanischer Sprachen*. Göttingen 1990 (= NAWG 1990 / 2).

Hettrich *Hypotaxe* 1988 = H. Hettrich *Untersuchungen zur Hypotaxe im Vedischen*. Berlin / New York 1988. Review: S. W. Jamison in JAOS 110 1990 p. 535f.

Hettrich *Kontext und Aspekt* 1976 = H. Hettrich *Kontext und Aspekt in der altgriechischen Prosa Herodots*. Göttingen 1976. Review: C. J. Ruijgh in Gnomon 51 1979 p. 217-227 (= *Scripta Minora I* 1991 p. 764-774).

Heubeck *Kleine Schriften* 1984 = A. Heubeck *Kleine Schriften zur griechischen Sprache und Literatur*. Erlangen 1984. For supplemental information, cf. B. Forssman and R. Plath in HS 103 1990 p. 249-260.

Heubeck *Schrift* 1979 = A. Heubeck *Schrift*. Göttingen 1979 (= *Archaeologia Homerica* vol. III, chapter X).

Hiersche *Grundzüge* 1970 = R. Hiersche *Grundzüge der griechischen Sprachgeschichte bis zur klassischen Zeit*. Wiesbaden 1970.

Hiersche *Tenues aspiratae* 1964 = R. Hiersche *Untersuchungen zur Frage der Tenues aspiratae im Indogermanischen*. Wiesbaden 1964. Review: Mayrhofer *Kleine Schriften* II 1996 p. 298 note 17.

Hiller / Panagl *Frühgr. Texte aus myk. Zeit* 1976 = S. Hiller and O. Panagl *Die frühgriechischen Texte aus mykenischer Zeit*. Darmstadt 1976. 2nd, revised ed. 1986. Review of the 2nd ed.: C. J. Ruijgh in *Mnemosyne* 31 1978 p. 294-298.

Hilmarsson *Nasal Prefixes in Tocharian* 1991 = J. Hilmarsson *The Nasal Prefixes in Tocharian, A Study in Word Formation*. Reykjavík 1991 (= TIES, *Suppl. Ser. 3*).

Hilmarsson *Tocharian Dictionary* 1996 = J. Hilmarsson *Materials for a Tocharian Historical and Etymological Dictionary*. Reykjavík 1996 (= TIES, *Suppl. Ser. 5*).

Hintze *Zamyād Yašt* 1994 = A. Hintze *Zamyād Yašt, Avestan Text*, English translation, with glossary. Wiesbaden 1994 (= *Beiträge zur Iranistik 7*). Concerning the same text, see also H. Humbach and Pallan R. Ichaporia *Zamyād Yasht, Yasht 19 of the Younger Avesta, Text, Translation, Commentary*. Wiesbaden 1998.

Hinüber *Älteres Mittelindisch* 1986 = O. von Hinüber *Das ältere Mittelindisch im Überblick*. Vienna 1986 (= SbÖAW, 467. vol.).

Hirt *Gr. Laut- und Formenlehre* 1912 = H. Hirt *Handbuch der griechischen Laut- und Formenlehre*. 2nd, revised ed. Heidelberg 1912.

Hirt *Hauptprobleme* 1939 = H. Hirt *Die Hauptprobleme der indogermanischen Sprachwissenschaft*, edited by H. Arntz. Halle 1939.

Hirt *Idg. Gramm.* I - VII 1927-1937 = H. Hirt *Indogermanische Grammatik.* 7 parts Heidelberg: I (*Einleitung, Etymologie, Konsonantismus*) 1927; II (*Vokalismus*) 1921; III (*Nomen*) 1927; IV (*Doppelung, Zusammensetzung, Verbum*) 1928; V (*Akzent*) 1929; VI (*Syntax I, Syntaktische Verwendung der Kasus und der Verbalformen*) 1934; VII (*Syntax II, Die Lehre vom einfachen und zusammengesetzten Satz*) 1937, posthumous.

Hirt *Indogermanen* I 1905 II 1907 = H. Hirt *Die Indogermanen, Ihre Verbreitung, ihre Urheimat und ihre Kultur.* 2 vols. Strasbourg 1905-1907.

Hirt *Urgerm.* I-III 1931-1934 = H. Hirt *Handbuch des Urgermanischen.* Heidelberg 1931-1934.

Historical Linguistics Papers 1985 [1987] = *Historical Linguistics, Papers from the 7th International Conference on Historical Linguistics Pavia* 1985, edited by A. G. Ramat, O. Carruba and G. Bernini. Amsterdam / Philadelphia 1987 (= *Current Issues in Linguistic Theory 48*).

Historical Linguistics Papers 1989 [1993] = *Historical Linguistics, Papers from the 9th International Conference on Historical Linguistics Rutgers University 1989*, edited by H. Aertsen and R. J. Jeffers. Amsterdam / Philadelphia 1993 (= *Current Issues in Linguistic Theory* 106).

Historical Linguistics Problems 1993 = *Historical Linguistics: Problems and Perspectives*, edited by Ch. Jones. London / New York 1993 (= *Longman Linguistics Library*).

Historical Morphology 1980 = *Historical Morphology*, edited by J. Fisiak. The Hague / Paris / New York 1980 (= *Trends in Linguistics, Studies and Monographs 17*).

Historical Syntax 1984 = *Historical Syntax*, edited by J. Fisiak. Berlin et al. 1984 (= *Trends in Linguistics, Studies and Monographs 23*).

HL = *Historiographia linguistica.*

Hock *Historical Linguistics* 1986 = H. H. Hock *Principles of Historical Linguistics*. Berlin 1986.

Hock *Language History* 1996 = H. H. Hock *Language History, Language Change and Language Relationship: An Introduction to Historical and Comparative Linguistics*. Berlin / New York 1996. Review: Th. Krisch in *Kratylos* 44 1999 p. 174-176.

Hodot *Éolien* 1990 = R. Hodot *Le dialecte éolien d'Asie. La langue des inscriptions, VIIe s. a. C. - IVe s. p. C.* Paris 1990.

Hoenigswald *Historical linguistics* 1973 = H. M. Hoenigswald *Studies in Formal Historical Linguistics*. Dordrecht / Boston 1973.

Hoenigswald *Language Change* 1960 = H. M. Hoenigswald *Language Change and Linguistic Reconstruction*. Chicago 1960.

Hoffmann *Aufsätze* I 1975 II 1976 III 1992 = K. Hoffmann *Aufsätze zur Indoiranistik*. Wiesbaden 1975-1992.

Hoffmann *Gedenkfeier* 1996 [1997] = *Akademische Gedenkfeier für Professor Dr. Karl Hoffmann am 11. Juli 1996*. Erlangen 1997 (= *Akademische Reden und Kolloquien, Friedrich-Alexander-Universität Erlangen-Nürnberg, Bd. 12*).

Hoffmann *Injunktiv* 1967 = K. Hoffmann *Der Injunktiv im Veda. Eine synchronische Funktionsuntersuchung*. Heidelberg 1967.

Hoffmann / Forssman *Av. Laut- und Flexionslehre* 1996 = K. Hoffmann and B. Forssman *Avestische Laut- und Flexionslehre*. Innsbruck 1992 (= IBS Nr. 84). Review: X. Tremblay in BSL 92 / 2 1997 p. 180-184; R. S. P. Beekes in *Kratylos* 44 1999 p. 62-71.

Hoffmann / Narten *Sasanid. Archetypus* 1989 = K. Hoffmann and J. Narten *Der Sasanidische Archetypus, Untersuchungen zu Schreibung und Lautgestalt des Avestischen*. Wiesbaden 1989.

Hofmann *Lat. Umgangssprache* 1936 = J. B. Hofmann *Lateinische Umgangssprache*. Heidelberg 2nd ed. 1936, 4. ed. with index 1978.

Hofmann see *s.v.* Hofmann / Szantyr *Syntax*, and Leumann / Hofmann / Szantyr *Lat. Gr.*, and Walde / Hofmann LEW.

Hofmann / Szantyr *Syntax* 1965 = J. B. Hofmann *Lateinische Syntax und Stilistik*, revised by A. Szantyr. Munich 1965 (= 2nd vol. by Leumann / Hofmann / Szantyr *Lat. Gr.* in the *Handbuch der Altertumswissenschaft*).

Homeric Questions 1995 = *Homeric Questions, Essays in Philology, Ancient History and Archaeology*, edited by J. P. Crielaard. Amsterdam 1995.

Homers Ilias Gesamtkommentar 2000ff., see *Homers Ilias Prolegomena*.

Homers Ilias Prolegomena 2000 = *Homers Ilias, Gesamtkommentar*, edited by J. Latacz. *Prolegomena* as an independent volume by F. Graf, I. de Jong, J. Latacz, R. Nünlist, M. Stoevesandt, R. Wachter, M. L. West. Munich / Leipzig 2000. *Gesamtkommmentar*: vol. I, 1. *Gesang* (*Faszikel 1 Text und Übersetzung*; *Faszikel 2 Kommentar*) 2000.

Hooker *Linear B* 1980 = J. T. Hooker *Linear B, An Introduction*. Bristol 1980.

Hooker *Scripta Minora* 1996 = J. T. Hooker *Scripta Minora, Selected essays on Minoan, Mycenaean, Homeric and Classical Greek subjects*, edited by F. Amory, P. Considine, S. Hooker. Amsterdam 1996.

Horrocks *Greek* 1997 = G. Horrocks *Greek, A History of the Language and its Speakers*. London 1997.

Horrocks *Space and Time* 1981 = G. C. Horrocks *Space and Time in Homer. Prepositional and Adverbial Particles in the Greek Epic*. New York 1981.

Houwink ten Cate *Luwian Population Groups* 1965 = Ph. H. J. Houwink ten Cate *The Luwian Population Groups of Lycia and Cilicia Aspera during the Hellenistic Period*. Leiden 1965.

HS = *Historische Sprachforschung*, Göttingen. Prior to vol. 100 the abbreviation was ZVS (*Zeitschrift für Vergleichende Sprachforschung*), although it was commonly referred to as KZ (Kuhns Zeitschrift). For the vols. 1-100, there now exists an index (*Sachindex*), edited by A. Bammesberger, revised by I. Hajnal, Chr. Schaefer, G. Schaufelberger and S. Ziegler. Göttingen 1997. On the current internet site of the department for *Englische und Vergleichende Sprachwissenschaft* of the *Katholische Universität Eichstätt*, A. Bammesberger offers an additional index to the first hundred volumes.

HSK = *Handbücher zur Sprach- und Kommunikationswissenschaft*: Berlin / New York. vol. 1.1 and 1.2 see above, *Dialektologie* 1-2 1982-1983; vols. 2.1 and 2.2 see below, *Sprachgeschichte* 1-2 1998-1985; vols. 5.1 and 5.2 see below, *Wörterbücher* 1-3 1989-1991; vols. 9.1 and 9.2 see below, *Syntax* 1-2 1993-1995; vol. 10.1 and 10.2 see below, *Schrift und Schriftlichkeit* 1-2 1994-1996; vol. 11.1 and 11.2 see below, *Namenforschung* 1-2 1995-1996.

Hübschmann *Casuslehre* 1875 = H. Hübschmann *Zur Casuslehre*. Munich 1875.

Hübschmann *Kleine Schriften* 1976 = H. Hübschmann *Kleine Schriften zum Armenischen*, edited by R. Schmitt. Hildesheim / New York 1976. Further, cf. R. Schmitt "*Schriftenverzeichnis Heinrich Hübschmann*" in HS 111 1998 p. 185-190.

IBK = *Innsbrucker Beiträge zur Kulturwissenschaft*.

IBS = *Innsbrucker Beiträge zur Sprachwissenschaft*.

ICLL, see below, IKLL.

Idg. Chr. = *Indogermanische Chronik* in *Sprache*, since vol. 13 1967 including 13a. Last available: *Idg. Chr.* 35 / II in *Sprache* 37 / 3 1995.

Idg. Gr. I / 1 1986 I / 2 1986 II 1968 III / 1 1969 = *Indogermanische Grammatik*, founded by J. Kuryłowicz, edited by M. Mayrhofer. Heidelberg: I / 1 (*Einleitung*) 1986 see above, Cowgill *Einleitung* 1986; I / 2 (*Lautlehre*) 1986 see below, Mayrhofer *Lautlehre* 1986; II (*Akzent* .

Ablaut) 1968 see below, Kuryłowicz *Akzent . Ablaut* 1968; III (*Formenlehre*) / 1 (*Geschichte der indogermanischen Verbalflexion*) 1969 see below, Watkins *Verbalflexion* 1969.

IE and IEs 1970 = *Indo-European and Indo-Europeans*, edited by G. Cardona, H. M. Hoenigswald, A. Senn. Philadelphia 1970.

IE Subgrouping 1999 = *Special Session on Indo-European Subgrouping and Internal Relations*, edited by B. K. Bergen, M. C. Plauché, A. C. Bailey. Berkely 1998 (= *Berkely Linguistic Society, Proceedings of the Twenty-Fourth Annual Meeting*).

IEW, see below, Pokorny IEW.

IF = *Indogermanische Forschungen.*

IIJ = *Indo-Iranian Journal.*

IKLL (ICLL / CILL) I 1981 (1983); IV 1987 [1991]; V 1989; VII 1993 [1996]; VIII 1995 [1996]= *Internationales Kolloquium zur lateinischen Linguistik* [IKLL] (*International Colloquium on Latin Linguistics* [ICLL]/ *Colloque international de linguistique latine* [CILL]): — I 1981 [1983] *Latin Linguistics and Linguistic Theory, Proceedings of the 1st ICLL Amsterdam 1981*, edited by H. Pinkster. Amsterdam / Philadelphia 1983. — IV 1987 [1991]: *New Studies in Latin Linguistics, Selected papers from the 4th ICLL Cambridge 1987*, edited by R. Coleman. Amsterdam / Philadelphia 1991. — V 1989: *Actes du Ve CILL Louvain-la-Neuve / Borzée 1989*, edited by M. Lavency and D. Longré. Louvain-la-Neuve 1989. — VII 1993 [1996] see above, *Aspects of Latin* 1996. — VIII 1995 [1996]: *Akten des VIII. IKLL Eichstätt* 1995, edited by A. Bammesberger and F. Heberlein. Heidelberg 1996.

Iliad I-VI 1985-1993 = *The Iliad, A Commentary*, edited by G. S. Kirk. Cambridge: I (Books 1-4) and II (Books 5-8) by G. S. Kirk; III (Books 9-12) by B. Hainsworth; IV (Books 13-16) by R. Janko; V (Books 17-20) by M. W. Edwards; VI (Books 21-24) by N. Richardson.

Illič-Svityč *Nominal Accentuation* 1979 = V. M. Illič-Svityč *Nominal Accentuation in Baltic and Slavic*, translated from Russian by R. L. Leed and R. F. Feldstein. Cambridge / Mass. 1979.

Indo-European Languages 1998 = *The Indo-European Languages*, edited by A. G. Ramat and P. Ramat. London 1998. See also the Italian original, *s.v. Lingue indoeuropee* 1994.

Indo-Europeanization of Northern Europe 1996 = *The Indo-Europeanization of Northern Europe, Papers Presented at the International Conference in Vilnius 1994*, edited by K. Jones-Bley and M. E. Huld.

Washington 1996 (= JIES, Monograph 17). Review: B. Hänsel and B. Schlerath in *Kratylos* 46 2001 p. 55-62.

Indogermanische Dichtersprache 1968 = *Indogermanische Dichtersprache*, edited by R. Schmitt. Darmstadt 1968 (= *Wege der Forschung* CLXV).

Indologie 1979 = *Einführung in die Indologie, Stand, Methoden, Aufgaben*, edited by H. Bechert and G. von Simson. 1st ed. 1979, 2nd ed. 1993.

InL = *Incontri Linguistici*.

Insler *Gāthās* 1975 = S. Insler *The Gāthās of Zarathustra*. Teheran / Liège / Leiden 1975 (= *Acta Iranica* 8). Review: H.-P. Schmidt in IIJ 21 1979 p. 83-115.

Iranisches Personennamenbuch = *Iranisches Personennamenbuch*, edited by M. Mayrhofer and R. Schmitt. Vienna. vol. I 1979: M. Mayrhofer *Die altiranischen Namen* (which includes Avestan and Old Persian names: Cf., by the same author, *Zum Namengut des Avesta*. Vienna 1977 [= SbÖAW vol. 308, *Abhandlung* 5]). The *Iranische Personennamenbuch* an ambitious project which comprises altogether 10 vols. Along with vol. I, other fascicles and volumes have already been published, cf. vol. II *Faszikel* 2 1986 Ph. Gignoux *Noms propres sassanides en moyen-perse épigraphique*, vol. V *Faszikel* 4 1982 R. Schmitt *Iranische Namen in den indogermanischen Sprachen Kleinasiens (Lykisch, Lydisch, Phrygisch)*, vol. V *Faszikel* 6a 1990 Ph. Huyse *Iranische Namen in den griechischen Dokumenten Ägyptens*.

Italia alumna 1990 = *Italia omnium terrarum alumna, La civiltà dei Veneti, Reti, Liguri, Celti, Piceni, Umbri, Latini, Campani e Iapigi*. Milan: 1st ed. 1988, 2nd ed. 1990 (= *Credito Italiano, Antica Madre, Collana di studi sull' Italia antica* vol. 11, under the direction of G. P. Carratelli).

Italia parens 1991 = *Italia omnium terrarum parens, La civiltà degli Enotri, Choni, Ausoni, Sanniti, Lucani, Brettii, Sicani, Siculi, Elimi*. Milan: 1st ed. 1989, 2nd ed. 1991 (= *Credito Italiano, Antica Madre, Collana di studi sull' Italia antica* vol. 12, under the direction of G. P. Carratelli).

Jackson *Early Britain* 1953 = K. Jackson *Language and History in Early Britain, A Chronological Survey of the Brittonic Languages First to Twelfth Century A.D.* Edinburgh 1953.

Jacquinod *Double accusatif en grec* 1989 = B. Jacquinod *Le double accusatif en grec d'Homère à la fin du Ve siècle avant J.-C.* Louvain-La-Neuve 1989

Jamison *-áya-* 1983 = S. W. Jamison *Function and Form in the -áya-Formations of the Rig Veda and Atharva Veda.* Göttingen 1983 (= ZVS, *Ergänzungsheft* Nr. 31). Review: G. Pinault in *Kratylos* 29 1984 [1985] p. 47-51; M. Peters in *Idg. Chr.* 30a Nr. 242.

Janda *Stock und Stein* 1997 = M. Janda *Über „Stock und Stein", Die indogermanischen Variationen eines universalen Phraseologismus.* (dissertation) Vienna 1995 = MSS, *Beiheft* 18, N.F. 1997.

Janda *Eleusis* 1999 = M. Janda *Eleusis, Das indogermanische Erbe der Mysterien.* Innsbruck 1999 (= IBS 96).

Jankuhn *Passive Bedeutung* 1969 = H. Jankuhn *Die passive Bedeutung medialer Formen untersucht an der Sprache Homers.* Göttingen 1969 (= supplement to ZVS 21).

Jasanoff *Stative and Middle* 1978 = J. H. Jasanoff *Stative and Middle in Indo-European.* Innsbruck 1978.

JAOS = *Journal of the American Oriental Society.*

Jensen *Altarm. Gr.* 1959 = H. Jensen *Altarmenische Grammatik.* Heidelberg 1959.

JIES = *Journal of Indo-European Studies.* Washington D. C.

Joachim *Mehrfachpräsentien* 1978 = U. Joachim *Mehrfachpräsentien im Ṛgveda.* Frankfurt am Main / Bern / Las Vegas 1978 (= *Europäische Hochschulschriften Reihe* XXI vol. 4).

Joki *Uralier und Indogermanen* 1973 = A. J. Joki *Uralier und Indogermanen. Die älteren Berührungen zwischen den uralischen und indogermanischen Sprachen.* Helsinki 1973.

Jokl *Albanisch* = N. Jokl *Linguistisch-kulturhistorische Untersuchungen aus dem Bereiche des Albanischen.* Berlin / Leipzig 1923.

Kadmos = *Kadmos. Zeitschrift für vor- und frühgriechische Epigraphik.* Berlin.

Kammenhuber *Arier* 1968 = A. Kammenhuber *Die Arier im Vorderen Orient.* Heidelberg 1968.

Kammenhuber *Kleine Schriften* 1993 = A. Kammenhuber *Kleine Schriften zum Altanatolischen und Indogermanischen* (*1. Teilband* 1955-1968, *2. Teilband* 1969-1990) Heidelberg 1993. Review including much complementary information and many references: J. Catsanicos in BSL 92 / 2 1997 p. 156-179.

Kastner *Adjektive* 1967 = W. Kastner *Die griechischen Adjektive zweier Endungen auf -ΟΣ.* Heidelberg 1967. Review: E. Neu in IF 74 1969 p. 235-242.

Katà diálekton 1996 [1999] = *Katà diálekton, Atti del III Colloquio Internationale di Dialectologia Greca Napoli / Fiaiano d'Ischia* 1996, edited by A. C. Cassio, Naples 1999 (= *Annali dell' Istituto Universitario Orientale di Napoli, Sezione Filologico-Letteraria,* 19 [1997]). See above, *Dialectologica Graeca* 1991 [1993].

Katičić *Languages of the Balkans* 1976 = R. Katičić *Ancient Languages of the Balkans I.* The Hague / Paris 1976. Review: C. de Simone in *Kratylos* 22 1977 [1978] p. 113-119.

Katz (H.) *Lehnwörter* 1985 = H. Katz *Studien zu den älteren indoiranischen Lehnwörtern in den uralischen Sprachen.* postdoctoral paper Munich 1985. A posthumous publication is presently being prepared by R.-P. Ritter for *Verlag Winter.*

Katz (J.) *Personal Pronouns* 1998 = J. T. Katz *Topics in Indo-European Personal Pronouns.* dissertation. Harvard 1998. Cf. also, by the same author, the review of Schrijver *Celtic Pronouns and Particles* 1997 in *Kratylos* 46 2001 p. 1-23.

Kellens *Noms racines* 1974 = J. Kellens *Les noms-racines de l'Avesta.* Wiesbaden 1974 (= *Beiträge zur Iranistik vol.* 7). Review: R. Schmitt in *Kratylos* 19 1974 [1975] p. 56-60; J. Schindler in *Sprache* 25 1979 p. 57-60.

Kellens *Verbe avestique* 1984 + 1995 = J. Kellens *Le verbe avestique.* Wiesbaden 1984; by the same author, *Liste du verbe avestique.* Wiesbaden 1995.

Kellens / Pirart *Textes vieil-avestiques* I 1988 II 1990 III 1991 = J. Kellens, E. Pirart *Les textes vieil-avestiques.* Wiesbaden: vol. I (*Introduction, texte et traduction*) 1988; vol. II (*Répertoires grammaticaux et lexique*) 1990; vol. III (*Commentaire*) 1991. Reviews of vol. I 1988: P. O. Skjærvø in JAOS 111 1991 p. 659-662; S. W. Jamison in IIJ 36 1993 p. 244-251. Review of vols. I-III: N. Oettinger in *Kratylos* 38 1993 p. 43-49.

Keller (M.) *Verbes latins à infectum en -sc-* 1992 = M. Keller *Les verbes latins à infectum en -sc-, Étude morphologique à partir des informations attestées dès l'époque préclassique.* Brussels 1992 (= *Collection Latomus* 216).

Keller (R.) *Sprachwandel* 1994 = R. Keller *Sprachwandel, Von der unsichtbaren Hand in der Sprache.* 2nd ed. Tübingen and Basel 1994 (= UTB Nr. 1567).

Keltologen-Symposium II 1997 [1999] = *Akten des Zweiten Deutschen Keltologen-Symposiums in Bonn 1997*, edited by St. Zimmer, R. Ködderitzsch, A. Wigger. Tübingen 1999. See above, *Deutschsprachige Keltologen* 1992 [1993].

KEWA, see below, Mayrhofer KEWA.

Keydana *Absol. Konstr.* 1997 = G. Keydana *Absolute Konstruktionen in altindogermanischen Sprachen*. Göttingen 1997 (= *Ergänzungsheft* HS Nr. 40).

Kieckers *Gr. Gr.* III-IV 1926 = E. Kieckers *Historische Grammatik des Griechischen*. 4 parts. Berlin / Leipzig (*Sammlung Göschen*: vols. 117, 118, 924, 925) 1925-1926: I (*Lautlehre*) 1925; II (*Formenlehre*) 1926; III (*Syntax, erster Teil*) 1926; IV (*Syntax, zweiter Teil*) 1926.

Kieckers *Stellung des Verbs* 1911 = E. Kieckers *Die Stellung des Verbs im Griechischen und in den verwandten Sprachen, Erster Teil: Die Stellung des Verbs im einfachen Hauptsatze und im Nachsatze nach den griechischen Inschriften und der älteren griechischen Prosa, verglichen mit den verwandten Sprachen*. Strasbourg 1911.

Kienle *Histor. LFL d. Dt.* 1965 = R. von Kienle *Historische Laut- und Formenlehre des Deutschen*. 2nd ed. Tübingen 1965.

Kilian *Indogermanen* 1983 = L. Kilian *Zum Ursprung der Indogermanen, Forschungen aus Linguistik, Prähistorie und Anthropologie*. Bonn 1983. Review: F. Lochner von Hüttenbach in *Kratylos* 29 1984 [1985] p. 160-163.

Kimball *Hittite Historical Phonology* 1999 = S. E. Kimball *Hittite Historical Phonology*. Innsbruck 1999 (= IBS 95).

Klaproth *Asia polyglotta* 1823 = J. Klaproth *Asia polyglotta*. Paris 1823. The importance of this pioneering work should not be underestimated. Cf. G. Bolognesi in *FS Belardi* I 1994 p. 334ff.

Klein Discourse Grammar 1985 = J. S. Klein *Toward a Discourse Grammar of the Rigveda*. 2 parts. Heidelberg 1985. Review: H. Hettrich in *Kratylos* 33 1988 p. 72-79.

Klein *Particle u* 1978 = J. S. Klein *The Particle u in the Rigveda, A Synchronic and Diachronic Study*. Göttingen 1978 (= ZVS, *Ergänzungsheft* 27).

Klein Personal Deixis 1996 = J. S. Klein *On Personal Deixis in Classical Armenian, A Study of the Syntax and Semantics of the n-, s- and d-Demonstratives in Manuscripts E and M of the Old Armenian Gospels*. MSS, *Beiheft* 17, N.F. 1996.

Klein Verbal Accentuation 1992 = J. S. Klein *On Verbal Accentuation in the Rigveda*. New Haven 1992. Review: S. Migron in *Kratylos* 40 1995 p. 190-192.

Klingenschmitt *Altarm. Verbum* 1982 = G. Klingenschmitt *Das Altarmenische Verbum*. Wiesbaden 1982. Review: G. R. Solta in *Kratylos* 29 1984 [1985] p. 59-74.

Kl. Pauly = *Der Kleine Pauly, Lexikon der Antike*. 5 vols. Stuttgart / Munich 1964-1975 (= dtv 1979 Nr. 5963). See above, *s.v.* DNP.

Kluge *Stammbildungslehre* 1926 = F. Kluge *Nominale Stammbildungslehre der altgermanischen Dialekte*. 3rd ed. Halle 1926.

Kluge *Urgermanisch* 1913 = F. Kluge *Urgermanisch, Vorgeschichte der altgermanischen Dialekte*. Strasbourg 1913.

Kluge / Seebold 1995 = F. Kluge *Etymologisches Wörterbuch der Deutschen Sprache*. revised by E. Seebold. 23rd expanded ed., Berlin / New York 1995.

Koch *Aksl. Verbum* I / II 1990 = Ch. Koch *Das morphologische System des altkirchenslavischen Verbums*. Munich 1990: vol. I (*Text*); vol. II (*Anmerkungen*).

Kölver *Sekundäre Kasus* 1965 = B. Kölver *Der Gebrauch der sekundären Kasus im Tocharischen*. dissertation. Frankfurt 1965.

Koerner *Practicing Linguistic Historiography* 1989 = K. Koerner *Practicing Linguistic Historiography, Selected Essays*. Amsterdam / Philadelphia 1989 (= *Amsterdam Studies in the Theory and History of Linguistic* Science 50).

Kohrt *Problemgeschichte* 1985 = M. Kohrt *Problemgeschichte des Graphembegriffs und des frühen Phonembegriffs*. Tübingen 1985 (= *Reihe germanistische Linguistik Nr.* 61).

Koiné I 1993 II 1996 III 1998 = *La koiné grecque antique, sous la direction de Cl. Brixhe*. Nancy (= *Études anciennes* 10, 14, 17). vol. I 1993 (*une langue introuvable ?*); II 1996 (*La concurrence*); III 1998 (*Les contacts*).

Koivulehto *Uralische Evidenz für die Laryngaltheorie* 1991 = J. Koivulehto *Uralische Evidenz für die Laryngaltheorie*. Vienna 1991 (= SbÖAW, 566. vol.). Review: T. Hofstra and O. Nikkilä in *Kratylos* 38 1993 p. 36-39; R. P. Ritter in PFU 1 1994 / 1995 p. 3-8.

Kolb *Rom* 1995 = F. Kolb *Rom, Die Geschichte der Stadt in der Antike*. Munich 1995.

Kolloquium Delbrück Madrid 1994 [1997] = *Berthold Delbrück y la sintaxis indoeuropea hoy, Actas del Coloquio de la Idg. Gesellschaft*

1994 in Madrid, edited by E. Crespo and J.-L. García-Ramón. Wiesbaden 1997.

Kolloquium Germanisch Freiburg 1981 [1984] = *Das Germanische und die Rekonstruktion der indogermanischen Grundsprache, Akten des Freiburger Kolloquiums der Idg. Gesellschaft 1981 in Freiburg*, edited by J. Untermann and B. Brogyanyi. Amsterdam / Philadelphia 1984.

Kolloquium Idg., Slaw. u. Balt. Jena 1989 [1992] = *Indogermanisch, Slawisch und Baltisch, Materialien des Kolloquiums Jena 1989*, edited by B. Barschel, M. Kozianka, K. Weber. Munich 1992.

Kolloquium Keltisch Bonn 1976 [1977] = *Indogermanisch und Keltisch, Kolloquium der Idg. Gesellschaft 1976 in Bonn*, edited by K. H. Schmidt. Wiesbaden 1977.

Kolloquium Kühner Amsterdam 1986 [1988] = *In the Footsteps of R. Kühner, Proceedings of the International Coll. in Commemoration of the 150th Anniversary of the Publication of R. Kühner's Ausführliche Grammatik II: Syntaxe 1986 in Amsterdam*, edited by A. Rijksbaron, H. A. Mulder, G. C. Wakker. Amsterdam 1988.

Kolloquium Lat. u. Idg. Salzburg 1986 [1992] = *Latein und Indogermanisch, Akten des Kolloquiums der Idg. Gesellschaft 1986 in Salzburg*, edited by O. Panagl and Th. Krisch. Innsbruck 1992.

Kolloquium Pedersen Kopenhagen 1993 [1994] = *In honorem Holger Pedersen, Kolloquium der Idg. Gesellschaft 1993 in Copenhagen*, edited by J. E. Rasmussen. Wiesbaden 1994.

Kolloquium Syntax Pavia 1979 [1980] = *Linguistic Reconstruction and Indo-European Syntax, Proceedings of the Colloquium of the „Indogermanische Gesellschaft" 1979 in Pavia*, edited by P. Ramat. Amsterdam 1980.

Kolloquium Wackernagel Basel 1988 [1990] = *Sprachwissenschaft und Philologie, Jacob Wackernagel und die Indogermanistik heute, Kolloquium der Idg. Gesellschaft 1988 in Basel*, edited by H. Eichner and H. Rix. Wiesbaden 1990.

Kortlandt Slavic Accentuation 1975 = F. H. H. Kortlandt *Slavic Accentuation, A Study in Relative Chronology*. Lisse / Holland 1975.

Krahe *Idg. Sprachw.* I 1966 II 1969 = H. Krahe *Indogermanische Sprachwissenschaft*. Berlin: vol. I (*Einleitung und Lautlehre*) 5th ed. 1969 (= *Sammlung Göschen Nr. 59*); vol. II (*Formenlehre*) 5th ed. 1969 (= *Sammlung Göschen Nr. 64*). 6th ed. (unchanged) in one vol. 1985 (= *Sammlung Göschen Nr. 2227*). Concerning older editions, as well as previous work by R. Meringer, see p. IX above.

Krahe *Illyrier* I 1955 II 1964 = H. Krahe *Die Sprache der Illyrier*. Wiesbaden: vol. I (*Die Quellen*) 1955; vol. II 1964 (contains *Die messapischen Inschriften* by C. de Simone and *Die messapischen Personennamen* by J. Untermann).

Krahe *Vergl. Syntax* 1972 = H. Krahe *Grundzüge der vergleichenden Syntax der indogermanischen Sprachen*, edited by W. Meid and H. Schmeja. Innsbruck 1972 (= IBS 8).

Krahe / Meid *Germ. Sprachw.* I 1969 II 1969 III 1967 = H. Krahe and W. Meid *Germanische Sprachwissenschaft*. 3 vols. Berlin: I (*Einleitung und Lautlehre*) 4th ed. 1969; II (*Formenlehre*) 4th ed. 1969; III (*Wortbildungslehre*) 1st ed. 1967 (= *Sammlung Göschen Nr. 238, 780, 1218*).

Kratylos = *Kratylos. Kritisches Berichts- und Rezensionsorgan für indogermanische und allgemeine Sprachwissenschaft*. Wiesbaden.

Krause *Handb. d. Got.* 1968 = W. Krause *Handbuch des Gotischen*. 3. ed. Munich 1968.

Krause / Thomas *Toch. Elementarbuch* I 1960 II 1964 = W. Krause and W. Thomas *Tocharisches Elementarbuch*. Heidelberg: vol. I 1960; vol. II (W. Thomas) 1964.

Kretschmer *Einleitung* 1896 = P. Kretschmer *Einleitung in die Geschichte der griechischen Sprache*. Göttingen 1896.

Krisch *Konditionalsätze* 1986 = Th. Krisch *Überlegungen zur Herkunft und Entwicklung der irrealen Konditionalsätze des Altgriechischen*. Innsbruck 1986 (= IBS, *Vorträge und Kleinere Schriften 38*).

Krisch *Konstruktionsmuster* 1984 = Th. Krisch *Konstruktionsmuster und Bedeutungswandel indogermanischer Verben. Anwendungsversuche von Valenztheorie und Kasusgrammatik auf Diachronie und Rekonstruktion*. Frankfurt am Main, et al. 1984. Review: Chr. Koch in *Anzeiger für Slavische Philologie* 17 1986 p. 187-198.

Krisch *Perfekta mit langem Reduplikationsvokal* 1996 = Th. Krisch *Zur Genese und Funktion der altindischen Perfekta mit langem Reduplikationsvokal, Mit kommentierter Materialsammlung*. Innsbruck 1996 (= IBS 87). Review: G.-J. Pinault in BSL 93 / 2 1998 p. 139-143; St. W. Jamison in *Kratylos* 44 1999 p. 59-62.

Krogh *Stellung des Altsächsischen* 1996 = S. Krogh *Die Stellung des Altsächsischen im Rahmen der germanischen Sprachen*. Göttingen 1996 (= *Studien zum Althochdeutschen 29*).

KS = *Kleine Schriften*.

Kühner / Blass *Ausführliche Gramm. d. gr. Sprache* I / 1 1890 I / 2 1892 = R. Kühner *Ausführliche Grammatik der griechischen Sprache*. Hannover: *Erster Teil* (*Elementar- und Formenlehre*) revised by F. Blass, 3rd ed. in 2 vols. 1890 and 1892.

Kühner / Gerth *Ausführliche Gramm. d. gr. Sprache* II / 1 1898 II / 2 1904 = R. Kühner *Ausführliche Grammatik der griechischen Sprache.* Hannover / Leipzig: *Zweiter Teil* (*Satzlehre*) revised by B. Gerth, 3rd ed. in 2 vols. 1898 and 1904.

Kühner / Holzweissig *Ausführliche Gramm. d. lat. Sprache* I 1912 = R. Kühner *Ausführliche Grammatik der lateinischen Sprache. Erster Band.* (*Elementar-, Formen- und Lautlehre*) revised by F. Holzweissig.

Kühner / Stegmann *Ausführliche Gramm. d. lat. Sprache* II / 1 and II / 2 1955 = R. Kühner *Ausführliche Grammatik der lateinischen Sprache, Satzlehre*, revised by C. Stegmann, 2 parts. 3rd ed. revised A. Thierfelder. Leverkusen 1955.

Kümmel *Perfekt* 2000 = M. Kümmel *Das Perfekt im Indoiranischen, Eine Untersuchung der Form und Funktion einer erebten Kategorie des Verbums und ihrer Weiterbildung in den altindoeuropäischen Sprachen.* Wiesbaden 2000.

Kümmel *Stativ und Passivaorist* 1996 = M. Kümmel *Stativ und Passivaorist im Indoiranischen.* Göttingen 1996 (= HS *Ergänzungsheft* 39). Review: I. Hajnal in *Kratylos* 44 1999 p. 50-54.

Kuhn *Letztes Indogermanisch* 1978 = H. Kuhn *Das letzte Indogermanisch.* Mainz 1978 (= AAWL 1978 Nr. 4). Critical review: B. Schlerath in *Kratylos* 23 1978 [1979] p. 44-57.

Kuiper *Nasalpräsentia* 1937 = F. B. J. Kuiper *Die indogermanischen Nasalpräsentia. Ein Versuch zu einer morphologischen Analyse.* Amsterdam 1937 (first appeared as a dissertation in a shorter version in 1934).

Kuiper *Selected Writings* 1997 = F. B. J. Kuiper *Selected Writings on Indian Linguistics and Philology*, edited by A. Lubotsky, M. S. Oort, M. Witzel. Amsterdam 1997.

Kuiper *Ved. Noun-Inflexion* 1942 = F. B. J. Kuiper *Notes on Vedic Noun-Inflexion.* Amsterdam 1942 (reprinted in *Selected Writings* 1997 p. 437-530); see below, F 314 § 5.

Kuryłowicz *Accentuation* 1952 = J. Kuryłowicz *L'accentuation des langues indo-européennes.* Cracow 1952, 2nd ed. 1956.

Kuryłowicz *Akzent . Ablaut* 1968 = J. Kuryłowicz *Akzent . Ablaut* = vol. II der *Idg. Gr.* (see above,). Heidelberg 1968.

Kuryłowicz *Apophonie* 1956 = J. Kuryłowicz *L'apophonie en indo-européen.* Wrocław 1956.

Kuryłowicz *Esquisses* I 1973 II 1975 = J. Kuryłowicz *Esquisses linguistiques.* 2 vols. Munich: I 1st ed. 1960, 2nd ed. 1973; II 1975.

Kuryłowicz *Études* I 1935 = J. Kuryłowicz *Études indo-européennes* I. Cracow 1935.

Kuryłowicz *Inflectional Categories* 1964 = J. Kuryłowicz *The Inflectional Categories of Indo-European.* Heidelberg 1964.

Kuryłowicz, see also GS Kuryłowicz 1995 above.

KZ = *Zeitschrift für Vergleichende Sprachforschung.* founded by A. Kuhn. Presently published in Göttingen, see above, HS.

LALIES = LALIES. *Actes des sessions de linguistique et de littérature.* Paris.

Lambert *Langue gauloise* 1994 = P.-Y. Lambert *La langue gauloise.* Paris 1994.

Lamberterie *Adj. en -υς* 1990 = Ch. de Lamberterie *Les adjectifs grecs en -υς.* 2 vols. Louvain-la-Neuve 1990. Review: J. L. Perpillou in RPh 64 1990 [1992] p. 197-200; F. Bader and L. Dubois in BSL 86 / 2 1991 p. 145-149; M. Peters in *Idg. Chr.* 34 Nr. G 601; F. Mawet in REArm 24 1993 p. 301-305.

Lamberterie *Arménien classique* 1992 = Ch. de Lamberterie *Introduction à l'arménien classique* in LALIES 10 1992 p. 234-289.

langues indo-européennes 1994 = *langues indo-européennes*, edited by F. Bader. Paris 1994. reprint, with addenda 1997. Review: A. Blanc in BSL 92 / 2 1997 p. 141-143.

Language Typology 1988 [1991] = *Language Typology* 1988, *Typological Models in the Service of Reconstruction*, edited by W. P. Lehmann and H. J. Hewitt. Amsterdam / Philadelphia 1991 (= *Amsterdam Studies in the Theory and History of Linguistic Science*, Series IV: *Current Issues in Linguistic Theory* 81).

Lanszweert *Balt. Grundwortschatz* 1984 = R. Lanszweert *Die Rekonstruktion des baltischen Grundwortschatzes.* Frankfurt am Main 1984.

La Roche *Accusativ* 1861 = J. La Roche *Homerische Studien, Der Accusativ im Homer.* Vienna 1861

Laroche *Hiéroglyphes hittites* I 1960 = E. Laroche *Les hiéroglyphes hittites I (L'écriture).* Paris 1960.

Laroche *Hourrite* 1980 = E. Laroche *Glossaire de la langue hourrite.* Paris 1980.

Laroche *Louvite* 1959 = E. Laroche *Dictionnaire de la langue louvite.* Paris 1959.

Laryngales 1990 = *La reconstruction des laryngales*, edited by J. Kellens. Liège 1990. Review: G.-J. Pinault in BSL 86 / 2 1991 [1992] p. 116-118; F. O. Lindeman in *Kratylos* 37 1992 p. 58-62.

Laryngaltheorie 1988 = *Die Laryngaltheorie und die Rekonstruktion des indogermanischen Laut- und Formensystems*, edited by A. Bammesberger. Heidelberg 1988. Index by S. Ziegler 1990. Review: M. Peters in *Idg. Chr.* 33 Nr. G 231; F. O. Lindeman in HS 102 1989 p. 268-297; R. S. P. Beekes in *Amsterdamer Beiträge zur Älteren Germanistik* 33 1991 p. 237-245.

Latacz *Homer* 1989 = J. Latacz *Homer, Der erste Dichter des Abendlandes*. 2nd ed. Munich / Zürich 1989.

Latacz *Troia und Homer* 2001 = J. Latacz *Troia und Homer, Der Weg zur Lösung eines alten Rätsels*. Munich / Berlin 2001.

Lat. Philologie 1996 = *Einleitung in die lateinische Philologie*, edited by F. Graf. Stuttgart / Leipzig 1996. Review: W. Pfaffel in *Kratylos* 44 1999 p. 94-98.

LAW 1965 = *Lexikon der Alten Welt*. Zürich / Stuttgart 1965.

LDIA 1978 = *Lingue e dialetti dell' Italia antica*, edited by A. L. Prosdocimi. Rome 1978. revised and with indexes by A. Marinetti 1982.

Lehmann (Chr.) *Relativsatz* 1984 = Chr. Lehmann *Der Relativsatz, Typologie seiner Strukturen, Theorie seiner Funktionen, Kompendium seiner Grammatik*. Tübingen 1984 (= *Language Universals Series* 3).

Lehmann (W. P.) *Gothic Etymological Dictionary* 1986 = W. P. Lehmann, *A Gothic Etymological Dictionary, based on the third edition of Feist Gothisches Wörterbuch*. Leiden 1986.

Lehmann (W. P.) *Idg. Forschung* 1992 = W. P. Lehmann *Die gegenwärtige Richtung der indogermanischen Forschung*. Budapest 1992. Review: M. Kümmel in PFU 4 1998 p. 51-59.

Lehmann (W. P.) *PIE Syntax* 1974 = W. P. Lehmann *Proto-Indo-European Syntax*. Austin 1974.

Leisi *Sprach-Knigge* 1992 = I. and E. Leisi *Sprach-Knigge oder Wie und was soll ich reden ?* 1st ed. Tübingen 1992 (3rd ed. 1993).

Leisi *Streiflichter* 1995 = E. Leisi *Streiflichter: unzeitgemäße Essays zu Kultur, Sprache und Literatur*. Tübingen 1995.

Leisi *Wortinhalt* 1974 = E. Leisi *Der Wortinhalt*. 4th ed. Heidelberg 1974.

Lejeune *Lepontica* 1971 = M. Lejeune *Lepontica*. Paris 1971 (= *Monographies Linguistiques* 1).

Lejeune *Mémoires* I 1958 II 1971 III 1972 IV 1997 = M. Lejeune *Mémoires de philologie mycénienne*. 4 series. Paris: I (1955-1957) 1958; Rome: II (1958-1963) 1971; III (1964-1968) 1972; IV (1969-1996) 1997.

Lejeune *Notice* 1993 = M. Lejeune *Notice biographique et bibliographique, suivie de l'exposé "D'Alcoy à Espanca: Réflexions sur les écritures paléo-hispaniques"*. Leuven 1993.

Lejeune *Phonétique* 1972 = M. Lejeune *Phonétique historique du mycénien et du grec ancien*. 2nd ed. Paris 1972.

Lejeune Vénète 1974 = M. Lejeune *Manuel de la langue vénète*. Heidelberg 1974.

Leskien *Handb. d. abulg. (aksl.) Sprache* 1962 = A. Leskien *Handbuch der altbulgarischen Sprache*. Heidelberg 1962.

Lesky *Gr. Lit.* 1957-1958 = A. Lesky *Geschichte der griechischen Literatur*. 1st ed. Bern 1957-1958, 3rd ed. Bern and Munich 1971.

Leukart *Frühgr. Nomina* 1994 = A. Leukart *Die frühgriechischen Nomina auf -tās und -ās, Untersuchungen zu ihrer Herkunft und Ausbreitung (unter Vergleich mit den Nomina auf -eús)*. Vienna 1994 (= SbÖAW 558). Review: J.-L. Perpillou in *Kratylos* 42 1997 p. 81-86.

Leumann *Homerische Wörter* 1950 = M. Leumann *Homerische Wörter*. Basel 1950 (and reprint).

Leumann *Kleine Schriften* 1959 = M. Leumann *Kleine Schriften*, edited by H. Haffter, E. Risch and W. Rüegg. Zürich 1959.

Leumann *LLFL* 1977 = M. Leumann *Lateinische Laut- und Formenlehre*. new ed. Munich 1977 (= vol. 1 of Leumann / Hofmann / Szantyr *Lat. Gr.*). The new edition replaces an earlier version (1926-1928) from the hand of M. Leumann. The 1926-1928 version was included as the 5th edition of *Lateinischen Laut- und Formenlehre*, part of the greater work, *Handbuch der Altertumswissenschaft* and was written as a thorough revision of the 4th edition by F. Stolz. It is unsurpassed in brevity and conciseness.

Leumann *Neuerungen* 1952 = M. Leumann *Morphologische Neuerungen im altindischen Verbalsystem*. Amsterdam 1952.

Leumann / Hofmann / Szantyr *Allg. Teil* 1965 = M. Leumann, J. B. Hofmann and A. Szantyr *Allgemeiner Teil*. This work presents general reflections on Leumann / Hofmann / Szantyr *Lat. Gr.* and constitutes an appendix in Hofmann / Szantyr *Lat. Syntax* 1965.

Leumann / Hofmann / Szantyr *Lat. Gr.* = M. Leumann, J. B. Hofmann and A. Szantyr *Lateinische Grammatik*. Munich 1977 and 1965 (as part of the *Handbuch der Altertumswissenschaft*). The first volume is included in the present bibliography as Leumann LLFL 1977; the second volume, as Hofmann / Szantyr *Lat. Syntax* 1965. The general section (*Allgemeiner Teil*) is included as Leumann / Hofmann / Szantyr *Allg. Teil* 1965.

LEW = A. Walde *Lateinisches etymologisches Wörterbuch*. 3rd revised ed. by J. B. Hofmann. 3 vols. Heidelberg 1938-1956.

Lewandowski *Linguist. Wörterbuch* 1-3 1994 = Th. Lewandowski *Linguistisches Wörterbuch*. 6th ed. Heidelberg / Wiesbaden 1994 (= UTB 1518): 1 (A-H), 2 (I-R), 3 (S-Z).

Lex(icon) Gramm(aticorum) 1996 = *Lexicon Grammaticorum, Who's Who in the History of World Linguistics*, General Editor H. Stammerjohann. Tübingen 1996.

LfgrE = *Lexikon des frühgriechischen Epos*, edited by *Thesaurus Linguae Graecae* in Hamburg. Founded by B. Snell. Göttingen: Fascicle 1 (ἀ - ἀεικής) 1955. The fascicles 1-9 were published as vol. I (A) 1979; 10-14 as vol. II (B-Λ) 1991. The newest fascicles are 17 (ὁδός - ὁράω) 1999 and 18 (ὀργή - πᾶς) 2000.

Lindeman *Laryngeal Theory* 1997 = F. O. Lindeman *Introduction to the "Laryngeal Theory"*. revised and augmented edition of the Oslo 1987 edition. Innsbruck 1997 (= IBS Nr. 91). Review: B. Forssman in *Kratylos* 45 2000 p. 68-75. Review of the 1987 edition: H. Rix in IF 96 1991 p. 269-274; M. Mayrhofer in *Kratylos* 36 1991 p. 92-95. Cf. also F. O. Lindeman in HS 102 1989 p. 268-297 (review of *Laryngaltheorie*, 1988).

Lingue e dialetti 1978 = *Lingue e dialetti dell' Italia antica*, edited by A. L. Prosdocimi. *Aggiornamento e indici a cura di A. Marinetti*. Padua 1982.

Lingue indoeuropee 1994 = *Le lingue indoeuropee*, edited by A. Giacalone Ramat and P. Ramat. Bologna 1994. Review: B. Schirmer in *Kratylos* 42 1997 p. 39-43. Cf. the English translation, *s.v. Indo-European Languages* 1998.

Linguistic Change and Reconstruction Methodology 1990 = *Linguistic Change and Reconstruction Methodology*, edited by Ph. Baldi. Berlin / New York 1990 (= *Trends in Linguistics, Studies and Monographs* 45).

Lipp *Palatale* 1994 = R. Lipp *Die indogermanischen Palatale im Indoiranischen*. (dissertation). Freiburg 1994. Publication is imminent.

LIV 1998 = *Lexikon der indogermanischen Verben, Die Wurzeln und ihre Primärstammbildungen*, under the direction of H. Rix, revised by M. Kümmel, Th. Zehnder, R. Lipp, B. Schirmer. Wiesbaden 1998; see below, F 203. New edition, see below, LIV 2001. At the time of publication, it was no longer possible to integrate information in LIV 2001. Thus, all references to LIV refer to LIV 1998. Reviews of LIV 1998:

E. Seebold in IF 104 1999 p. 287-299; Ch. de Lamberterie in BSL 95 / 2 2000 p. 139-145. On the new revised edition see LIV 2001.

LIV 2001 = *Lexikon der indogermanischen Verben*. New revised edition by H. Rix and M. Kümmel. Wiesbaden 2001.

Lockwood *Idg. Sprachw.* 1982 = W. B. Lockwood *Indogermanische Sprachwissenschaft*. Tübingen 1982. English original: *Indo-European Philology*. London 1969.

Lockwood *Überblick* 1979 = W. B. Lockwood *Überblick über die indogermanischen Sprachen*. Tübingen 1979. English original: *A Panorama of Indo-European languages*. London 1972.

Lohmann *Genus und Sexus* 1932 = J. Lohmann *Genus und Sexus, Eine morphologische Studie zum Ursprung der indogermanischen nominalen Genus-Unterscheidung*. Göttingen 1932.

Lommel *Kleine Schriften* 1978 = H. Lommel *Kleine Schriften*. Wiesbaden 1978.

Lubotsky *Nominal Accentuation* 1988 = A. M. Lubotsky *The System of Nominal Accentuation in Sanskrit and Proto-Indo-European*. Leiden 1988. Review: S. W. Jamison in JAOS 111 1991 p. 419-422.

Lubotsky *RV Word Concordance* 1997 = A. Lubotsky *A R̥gvedic Word Concordance*. 2 Parts. New Haven 1997 (= *American Oriental Series* 82-83).

Lühr *Egill* 2000 = R. Lühr *Die Gedichte des Skalden Egill*. Dettelbach 2000 (= *Jenaer Indogermanistische Textbearbeitung* 1).

Lühr *Expressivität* 1988 = R. Lühr *Expressivität und Lautgesetz im Germanischen*. Heidelberg 1988.

Lühr *Hildebrandlied* I / II 1982 = R. Lühr *Studien zur Sprache des Hildebrandliedes*. Frankfurt am Main 1982: Part I (*Herkunft und Sprache*); Part II (*Kommentar*).

Lühr *Neuhochdeutsch* 1986 = R. Lühr *Neuhochdeutsch, Eine Einführung in die Sprachwissenschaft*. 4th ed. Munich 1986.

Luraghi *Casi e preposizioni* 1996 = S. Luraghi *Studi su casi e preposizioni nel greco antico*. Pavia 1996.

Luraghi *Hittite* 1997 = S. Luraghi *Hittite*. Munich / New Castle 1997 (= *Languages of the World, Materials* 114).

Luraghi *Old Hittite Sentence Structure* 1990 = S. Luraghi *Old Hittite Sentence Structure*. London / New York 1990.

MacDonell *Vedic Grammar* 1910 = A. A. MacDonell *A Vedic Grammar*. Strasbourg 1910 (Indian reprints).

Macqueen *Hittites* 1986 = J. G. Macqueen *The Hittites and their Contemporaries in Asia Minor*. 2nd ed. London 1986. paperback, 1996.

Mallory *In Search of the Indo-Europeans* 1989 = J. P. Mallory *In Search of the Indo-Europeans, Language, Archaeology and Myth*. London 1989. Critical review: B. Schlerath in *Praehistorische Zeitschrift* 67 1992 p. 132-137.

Mallory / Adams *Encyclopedia* 1997 = J. P. Mallory and D. Q. Adams *Encyclopedia of Indo-European Culture*. London and Chicago 1997. Review: St. Zimmer in JIES 27 1999 p. 105-163 and in *Kratylos* 45 2000 p. 46-52; A. Häusler in IF 105 2000 p. 314-318.

Mann *IE Comparative Dictionary* 1984 / 1987 = S. E. Mann *An Indo-European Comparative Dictionary*. Hamburg 1984 / 1987. Critical review: M. Mayrhofer in *Kratylos* 34 1989 p. 41-45 (p. 45: "*ein so schlechtes Buch*").

Manual de lingüistica indoeuropea I-III 1995-1998 = F. R. Adrados, A. Bernabé, J. Mendoza *Manual de lingüistica indoeuropea*. Madrid: I (*Prólogo, introducción fonética*) 1995; II (*Morfología nominal y verbal*) 1996; III (*Morfología: pronombres, adverbios, particulas y numerales; Syntaxis; Differenciación dialectal*) 1998.

Marazzi *Geroglifico* 1990 = M. Marazzi *Il geroglifico anatolico: Problemi di analisi e prospettive di ricerca*. Rome 1990.

Marinetti *Iscriz. sudpicene* 1985 = A. Marinetti *Le iscrizioni sudpicene*, I: *Testi*. Florence 1985 (= *Lingue e Iscrizioni dell' Italia Antica* 5). Review: G. Meiser in *Kratylos* 32 1987 p. 110-118.

Marouzeau *Latin littéraire* 1949 = J. Marouzeau *Quelques aspects de la formation du latin littéraire*. Paris 1949.

Martínez García *Nombres en -υ* = F. J. Martínez García *Los nombres en -υ del griego*. Frankfurt am Main 1994 (= *Europäische Hochschulschriften*, series XXI, vol. 166).

Masson (E.) *Immortalité* 1991 = E. Masson *Le combat pour l'immortalité, Héritage indo-européen dans la mythologie anatolienne*. Paris 1991.

Masson (O.) *Anatolian Languages* 1994 = O. Masson *Anatolian Languages in Cambridge Ancient History*, vol. III / 2nd ed. Cambridge 1991. Phrygian, p. 666-669; Lydian, p. 669-671; Lycian p. 671-674; Carian p. 674-676.

Masson (O.) ICS 1961 + Add. 1983 = O. Masson *Les inscriptions chypriotes syllabiques, Recueil critique et commenté*. Paris 1961. reprint with addenda nova 1983. Review of the 1st ed. 1961: E. Risch in *Kratylos* 10 1965 p. 88-94.

Matthews *Syntax* 1981 = P. H. Matthews *Syntax*. Cambridge et al. 1981.

Maurach *Lat. Dichtersprache* 1983 = G. Maurach *Enchiridion Poeticum, Hilfsbuch zur lateinischen Dichtersprache*. Darmstadt 1983. 2nd ed. 1989.

Mayrhofer *Altiranische Namen* 1979 = M. Mayrhofer *Die altiranischen Namen*. Vienna 1979. The work is part of the *Iranischen Personennamenbuches*, see above.

Mayrhofer EWAia = M. Mayrhofer *Etymologisches Wörterbuch des Altindoarischen*. Heidelberg 1986ff. Vols. I (*A-DH*) 1991 and II (*N-H*) 1996 are of great value.

Mayrhofer *Indo-Arier* 1966 = M. Mayrhofer *Die Indo-Arier im Alten Vorderasien. Mit einer analytischen Bibliographie*. Wiesbaden 1966. Cf. also, by the same author, *Die Arier im vorderen Orient - ein Mythos ?* Vienna 1974 (= SbÖAW, 294. vol., 3. *Abhandlung*).

Mayrhofer KEWA = M. Mayrhofer *Kurzgefaßtes etymologisches Wörterbuch des Altindischen*. 4 vols. Heidelberg 1956-1980.

Mayrhofer *Kleine Schriften* I 1979 II 1996 = M. Mayrhofer *Ausgewählte Kleine Schriften*. Wiesbaden: I 1979 edited by S. Deger-Jalkotzy and R. Schmitt; II 1996 edited by R. Schmitt.

Mayrhofer *Lautlehre* 1986 = M. Mayrhofer *Indogermanische Grammatik*, vol. I, 2nd half-volume, *Lautlehre*. Heidelberg 1986. Review: B. Forssman in *Kratylos* 33 1988 p. 56-63.

Mayrhofer *Pāli* 1951 = M. Mayrhofer *Handbuch des Pāli*. Part I: *Grammatik*; Part II: *Texte und Glossar*. Heidelberg 1951.

Mayrhofer *Sanskrit-Gramm.* 1978 = M. Mayrhofer *Sanskrit Grammatik mit sprachvergleichenden Erläuterungen*. 3rd ed. Berlin / New York 1978 (= *Sammlung Göschen Nr.* 2207).

Mayrhofer *Sanskrit und die Sprachen Alteuropas* 1983 = M. Mayrhofer *Sanskrit und die Sprachen Alteuropas, Zwei Jahrhunderte des Widerspiels von Entdeckungen und Irrtümern*. Göttingen 1983 (= NAWG, 1983, Nr. 5).

Mayrhofer *Supplement* 1978 = M. Mayrhofer *Supplement zur Sammlung der altpersischen Inschriften*. Vienna 1978 (= SbÖAW, 338. vol.).

Mayrhofer see also, Brandenstein / Mayrhofer above.

McCone *Old Irish Nasal Presents* 1991 = K. McCone *The Indo-European Origins of the Old Irish Nasal Presents, Subjunctives and Futures*. Innsbruck 1992.

McCone *Relative Chronology* 1996 = K. McCone *Towards a Relative Chronology of Ancient and Medieval Celtic Sound Change*. Maynooth 1996 (= *Maynooth Studies in Celtic Linguistics* I).

McCone / Simms *Progress in Medieval Irish Studies* 1996 = K. McCone and K. Simms *Progress in Medieval Irish Studies*. Maynooth 1996.

Meid *Archäologie und Sprachwissenschaft* 1989 = W. Meid *Archäologie und Sprachwissenschaft, Kritisches zu neueren Hypothesen der Ausbreitung der Indogermanen*. Innsbruck 1989 (= IBS, *Vorträge und Kleinere Schriften* 43). Critical review: B. Schlerath in *Praehistorische Zeitschrift* 67 1992 p. 137-139.

Meid */b/* 1989 = W. Meid *Das Problem von indogermanisch /b/*. Innsbruck 1989 (= *Vorträge und Kleinere Schriften* 44).

Meid *Botorrita* 1993 = W. Meid *Die erste Botorrita-Inschrift: Interpretation eines keltiberischen Sprachdenkmals*. Innsbruck 1993 (= IBS Nr. 76). Cf. by the same author, *Celtiberian Inscriptions*. Budapest 1994 and *Kleinere keltiberische Sprachdenkmäler*. Innsbruck 1996 (= IBS, *Vorträge und kleinere Schriften* 64).

Meid *Gaulish inscriptions* 1992 = W. Meid *Gaulish Inscriptions: Their Interpretation in the Light of Archaeological Evidence and their Value as a Source of Linguistic and Sociological Information*. Budapest 1992 (2nd Rev. Ed. 1994).

Meid, see also,Krahe / Meid.

Meier-Brügger *Gr. Sprachw.* I / II 1992 = M. Meier-Brügger *Griechische Sprachwissenschaft*. 2 vols. Berlin / New York 1992 (= *Sammlung Göschen* Nr. 2241 and Nr. 2242): I (*Bibliographie, Einleitung, Syntax*); II (*Wortschatz, Formenlehre, Lautlehre, Indizes*).

Meillet *Aperçu* 1975 = A. Meillet *Aperçu d'une histoire de la langue grecque*. Paris 1913. Reprints. 8th ed. 1975 with a bibliography by O. Masson. Regarding the reception of this epoch-making work: → A. Morpurgo Davies in *Meillet et la linguistique de son temps* 1988 p. 235-252.

Meillet *Arménien classique* 1936 = A. Meillet *Esquisse d'une grammaire comparée de l'arménien classique*. 2nd edition, completely revised. Vienna 1936.

Meillet *Esquisse* 1928 = A. Meillet *Esquisse d'une histoire de la langue latine*. Paris 1928.

Meillet et la linguistique de son temps 1988 = *Antoine Meillet et la linguistique de son temps*, edited by S. Auroux. Lille 1988 (= HEL [*Histoire, Épistémologie, Langage*] 10 / II).

Meillet *Introduction* 1949 = A. Meillet *Introduction à l'étude comparative des langues indo-européennes*. Paris 1949 (reprint of the 8th ed. Alabama 1964).

Meillet *Linguistique historique et linguistique générale* I 1921 II 1936 = A. Meillet *Linguistique historique et linguistique générale*. Paris I 1921, II 1936 (and various reprints).

Meillet *Méthode comparative* 1925 = A. Meillet *La méthode comparative en linguistique historique*. Oslo / Paris 1925 (and reprints).

Meillet / Vendryes *Grammaire comparée* 1924 = A. Meillet and J. Vendryes *Traité de grammaire comparée des langues classiques*. Paris 1924. A comparable work is Sihler *New Comparative Grammar* 1995 (*q.v.*).

Meiser *(Hist.) Laut- u. Formenlehre (d. lat. Sprache)* 1998 = G. Meiser *Historische Laut- und Formenlehre der lateinischen Sprache*. Darmstadt 1998. Review: B. Vine in *Kratylos* 46 2001 p. 118-126.

Meiser *Perfekt* 1991 = G. Meiser *Vorgeschichte und Ausbildung des lateinischen Perfektsystems*. postdoctoral work Freiburg im Breisgau 1991.

Meiser *Umbrisch* 1986 = G. Meiser *Lautgeschichte der umbrischen Sprache*. Innsbruck 1986 (= IBS Nr. 51).

Meister *Homer. Kunstsprache* 1921 = K. Meister *Die homerische Kunstsprache*. Leipzig 1921.

Meisterhans / Schwyzer *Att. Inschr.* 1900 = K. Meisterhans *Grammatik der attischen Inschriften*. 3rd ed., revised and expanded by E. Schwyzer. Berlin 1900.

Melchert *Abl. and Instr.* 1977 = H. C. Melchert *Ablative and Instrumental in Hittite*. (dissertation). Harvard 1977.

Melchert *Anatolian Historical Phonology* 1994 = H. C. Melchert *Anatolian Historical Phonology*. Amsterdam / Atlanta 1994. Review: E. Rieken in BiOr 55 1998 Sp. 473-475; N. Oettinger in *Kratylos* 43 1998 p. 96-108.

Melchert *Cuneiform Luvian* 1993 = H. C. Melchert *Cuneiform Luvian Lexicon*. Chapel Hill 1993.

Melchert *Hittite Historical Phonology* 1984 = H. C. Melchert *Studies in Hittite Historical Phonology*. Göttingen 1984 (= ZVS, *Ergänzungsheft* 32).

Melchert *Lycian* 1993 = H. C. Melchert *Lycian Lexicon*. 2nd fully revised ed. Chapel Hill 1993.

Méndez Dosuna *Noroeste* 1985 = J. Méndez Dosuna *Noroeste (Dialectos dorios del noroeste)*. Salamanca 1985.

Metzler Lexikon Sprache 1993 and 2000 = *Metzler Lexikon Sprache*, edited by H. Glück. 1st ed. Stuttgart / Weimar 1993. 2nd revised and expanded ed. 2000.

Meyer *Lat. Epigraphik* 1973 = E. Meyer *Einführung in die lateinische Epigraphik*. Darmstadt 1973.

MH = *Museum Helveticum*.

Mikkola *Abstraktion* 1964 = E. Mikkola *Die Abstraktion, Begriff und Struktur, Eine logisch-semantische Untersuchung auf nominalistischer Grundlage unter besonderer Berücksichtigung des Lateinischen*. Helsinki 1964.

Mikkola *Kompositum* I 1971 = E. Mikkola *Das Kompositum*, vol. I (see particularly the first chapter, '*Die Zusammensetzung, Begriff und Struktur*' p. 5ff. and the bibliography p. 56ff.). 2nd ed. 1971.

Miklosich *Vergl. Syntax* 1868-1874 = Fr. Miklosich *Vergleichende Syntax der slavischen Sprachen*. Vienna 1868-1874.

Minos = *Minos. Revista de filología egea*. Salamanca.

Monro *Homer. Dialect* 1891 = D. B. Monro *A Grammar of the Homeric Dialect*. 2nd ed. Oxford 1892.

Morpurgo *Davies Ottocento* 1996 = A. Morpurgo Davies *La linguistica dell' Ottocento*. Bologna 1996.

MSS = *Münchener Studien zur Sprachwissenschaft*.

Müller Nominativ und Akkusativ 1908 = C. F. W. Müller Syntax des Nominativs und Akkusativs im Lateinischen. Leipzig / Berlin 1908.

Mutzbauer *Gr. Tempuslehre* 1 1893 2 1909 = C. Mutzbauer *Die Grundlagen der griechischen Tempuslehre und der homerische Tempusgebrauch, Ein Beitrag zur historischen Syntax der griechischen Sprache*. 2 vols. Strasbourg 1893-1909.

Mutzbauer *Konj. und Opt.* 1908 = C. Mutzbauer *Die Grundbedeutung des Konjunktivs und Optativs und ihre Entwicklung im Griechischen*. Leipzig / Berlin 1908.

Mykenaïka 1990 [1992] = *Mykenaïka. Actes du IXe Colloque international sur les textes mycéniens et égéens* 1990 in Athens. Paris 1992 (= BCH, Suppl. 25).

Nagy = *Greek Dialects* 1970 = G. Nagy *Greek Dialects and the Transformation of an Indo-European Process*. Cambridge / Mass. 1970. Review: A. Morpurgo Davies in CR 22 1972 p. 371-374; C. J. Ruijgh in *Scripta Minora* I 1991 p. 635-650.

Namenforschung 1 1995 / 2 1996 = *Namenforschung / Name Studies / Les noms propres, Ein internationales Handbuch zur Onomastik*, edited by E. Eichler, G. Hilty, H. Löffler, H. Steger, L. Zgusta. Berlin / New York. 2 vols.: 1 1995; 2 1996 (= HSK 11.1 and 11.2). Review: R. Bergmann in BNF N.F. 32 / 4 1997 p. 457-471.

Narten *Kleine Schriften* I 1995 = J. Narten *Kleine Schriften*, edited by M. Albino and M. Fritz. vol. I Wiesbaden 1995.

Narten *Sigmatische Aoriste* 1964 = J. Narten *Die sigmatischen Aoriste im Veda*. Wiesbaden 1964.

Narten *Yasna Haptaŋhāiti* 1986 = J. Narten *Der Yasna Haptaŋhāiti*. Wiesbaden 1986.

Narten, see also Hoffmann / Narten.

NAWG = *Nachrichten der Akademie der Wissenschaften in Göttingen.*

Neu *Aheth. Glossar* 1983 = E. Neu *Glossar zu den althethitischen Ritualtexten*. Wiesbaden 1983 (= StBoT 26).

Neu *Aheth. Ritualtexte* 1980 = E. Neu *Althethitische Ritualtexte in Umschrift*. Wiesbaden 1980 (= StBoT 25).

Neu *Anitta* 1974 = E. Neu *Der Anitta-Text*. Wiesbaden 1974 (= StBoT 18). See also: → G. Steiner *Struktur und Bedeutung des sog. Anitta-Textes* in OA 23 1984 p. 53-73.

Neu *Hurritisch* 1988 = E. Neu *Das Hurritische: Eine altorientalische Sprache in neuem Licht*. Mainz 1988 (= AAWL 1988 Nr. 3).

Neu *Interpret. Mediopassiv* 1968 = E. Neu *Interpretation der hethitischen mediopassiven Verbalformen*. Wiesbaden 1968 (= StBoT 5).

Neu *Lokativ* 1980 = E. Neu *Studien zum endungslosen "Lokativ" des Hethitischen*. Innsbruck 1980 (= IBS, Vorträge und kleinere Schriften 23).

Neu *Mediopassiv* 1968 = E. Neu *Das hethitische Mediopassiv und seine indogermanischen Grundlagen*. Wiesbaden 1968 (= StBoT 6).

Neu, see also Rüster / Neu.

Neumann *Indogermanistik* 1967 = G. Neumann *Indogermanische Sprachwissenschaft* 1816 and 1966. Innsbruck 1967.

Neumann *Kleine Schriften* 1994 = G. Neumann *Ausgewählte kleine Schriften*. edited by E. Badali, H. Nowicki and S. Zeilfelder. Innsbruck 1994 (= IBS 77).

Neumann *Phrygisch und Griechisch* 1988 = G. Neumann *Phrygisch und Griechisch*. Vienna 1988 (= SbÖAW 499).

Neumann *Weiterleben* 1961 = G. Neumann *Untersuchungen zum Weiterleben hethitischen und luwischen Sprachgutes in hellenistischer und römischer Zeit*. Wiesbaden 1962.

Neve *Ḫattuša* 1996 = P. Neve *Ḫattuša - Stadt der Götter und Tempel, Neue Ausgrabungen in der Hauptstadt der Hethiter*. 2nd ed. Mainz 1996 (= *Sonderheft der Antiken Welt*).

New Sound of Indo-European 1989 = *The New Sound of Indo-European, Essays in Phonological Reconstruction*, edited by Th. Vennemann.

Berlin 1989 (= *Trends in Linguistics* 41). Review: O. Szemerényi in *Diachronica* 6 1989 p. 237-269.

Noreen *Altisländisch und Altnorwegisch* 1923 = A. Noreen *Altisländische und altnorwegische Grammatik unter Berücksichtigung des Urnordischen*. Halle 1923.

Noreen *Altschwedisch* 1904 = A. Noreen *Altschwedische Grammatik, Mit Einschluß des Altgutnischen*. Halle 1904.

Nowicki *s-Stämme* 1976 = H. Nowicki *Die neutralen s-Stämme im indoiranischen Zweig des Indogermanischen*. (dissertation in philology). Würzburg 1976.

NTS = *Norsk Tidskrift for Sprogvidenskap*.

Numerals 1992 = *Indo-European Numerals*, edited by J. Gvozdanović. Berlin / New York 1992 (= *Trends in Linguistics, Studies and Monographs* 57). Concerning the work, see below F 500 § 3b.

Nussbaum *Head and Horn* 1986 = A. J. Nussbaum *Head and Horn in Indo-European*. Berlin / New York 1986. Review: R. S. P. Beekes in *Kratylos* 34 1989 p. 55-59.

Nussbaum *Two Studies* 1998 = A. J. Nussbaum *Two Studies in Greek and Homeric Linguistics*. Göttingen 1998 (= *Hypomnemata* 120). Review: B. Forssman in *Kratylos* 46 2001 p. 113-117.

OA = *Oriens Antiquus*.

Odyssey I (Books i-viii) 1988 II (Books ix-xvi) 1989 III (Books xvii-xxiv) 1992 = *A Commentary on Homer's Odyssey*. Oxford: I by A. Heubeck (with *General Introduction*), S. West (with *The Transmission of the Text* and Books i-iv) and J. B. Hainsworth (with *The Epic Dialect* and Books v-viii); II by A. Heubeck (with Books ix-xii) and A. Hoekstra (with Books xiii-xvi) 1989; III by J. Russo (with Books xvii-xx), M. Fernández-Galiano (with Books xxi-xxii) and A. Heubeck (with Books xxiii-xxiv) 1992. The Oxford edition is a "Revised version, without text and translation, of the six-volume edition commissioned by the *Fondazione Lorenzo Valla* and published by *Mondadori Milano* 1981-1986".

Oertel *Dativi finales* 1941 = H. Oertel *Die Dativi finales abstrakter Nomina und andere Beispiele nominaler Satzfügung in der vedischen Prosa*. Munich 1942.

Oettinger *Verbum* 1979 = N. Oettinger *Die Stammbildung des hethitischen Verbums*. Nürnberg 1979. The same author offers the supplementary *Die hethitischen Verbalstämme in Grammatica Ittita* 1992 p. 214-252.

Ohlstadt 1994 [1996] = *Tagungsband „Hellenische Mythologie / Vorgeschichte"* (title also in Modern Greek) 1994 in Ohlstadt / Oberbayern, edited by N. Dimoudis and A. Kyriatsoulis. Altenburg 1996 (organizers: *Verein zur Förderung der Aufarbeitung der hellenischen Geschichte Weilheim* (Upper Bavaria) and the *Club Griechischer Akademiker München*).

Ohlstadt 1996 [1998] = *Tagung „Die Geschichte der hellenischen Sprache und Schrift"* (title also in Modern Greek and English) 1996 in Ohlstadt / Oberbayern, edited by N. Dimoudis and A. Kyriatsoulis. Altenburg 1998 (organizers: *Verein zur Förderung der Aufarbeitung der hellenischen Geschichte Weilheim* [Upper Bavaria]).

OLD = *Oxford Latin Dictionary*. Oxford 1968-1982.

Oldenberg *Kleine Schriften* 1967 = H. Oldenberg *Kleine Schriften*, edited by K. L. Janert. 2 parts. Wiesbaden 1967.

Oldenberg *Noten* 1909-1912 = H. Oldenberg *Ṛgveda, Textkritische und exegetische Noten*. I - VI Berlin 1909, VII - X Berlin 1912.

Old English Runes 1991 = *Old English Runes and their Continental Background*, edited by A. Bammesberger. Heidelberg 1991.

Olsen *Instrument Noun Suffix* 1988 = B. A. Olsen *The Proto-Indo-European Instrument Noun Suffix *-tlom and its variants*. Copenhagen 1988.

Olsen *Noun* 1999 = B. A. Olsen *The Noun in Biblical Armenian, Origin and Word-Formation - with special emphasis on the Indo-European heritage*. Berlin 1999 (= *Trends in Linguistics, Studies and Monographs* 119). Review: S. Zeilfelder in *Sprache* 40 1998 p. 105-109; R. Schmitt in *Kratylos* 46 2001 p. 80-88.

OLZ = *Orientalistische Literaturzeitung*

Palmer *Descriptive and Comparative Linguistics* 1972 = L. R. Palmer *Descriptive and Comparative Linguistics, A Critical Introduction*. London 1972.

Palmer *Greek Language* 1980 = L. R. Palmer *The Greek Language* London / Boston 1980. German translation by W. Meid. Innsbruck 1986 (= IBS Nr. 50).

Panzer *Slav. Sprachen* 1991 = B. Panzer *Die slavischen Sprachen in Gegenwart und Geschichte. Sprachstrukturen und Verwandtschaft*. Frankfurt am Main 1991 (= *Heidelberger Publikationen zur Slavistik, A. Linguistische Reihe* 3).

Partherreich [1996] 1998 = *Das Partherreich und seine Zeugnisse / The Arsacid Empire: Sources and Documentation, Beiträge des interna-*

tionalen Colloquiums 1996 in Eutin, edited by J. Wiesenhöfer. Stuttgart 1998.

PBB = *Beiträge zur Geschichte der deutschen Sprache und Literatur*. (Halle and) Tübingen (The abbreviation comes from H. Paul, W. Braune, *Beiträge ...*).

Pedersen *Cinquième déclinaison* 1926 = H. Pedersen *La cinquième déclinaison latine*. Copenhagen 1926.

Pedersen *Hittitisch* 1938 = H. Pedersen *Hittitisch und die anderen indoeuropäischen Sprachen*. Copenhagen 1938.

Pedersen *Kl. Schr. zum Arm.* 1982 = H. Pedersen *Kleine Schriften zum Armenischen*, edited by R. Schmitt. Hildesheim / New York 1982.

Pedersen *Tocharisch* 1941 = H. Pedersen *Tocharisch vom Gesichtspunkt der indoeuropäischen Sprachvergleichung*. Copenhagen 1942.

Pedersen *Vgl. Gramm. d. kelt. Spr.* I 1909 II 1913 = H. Pedersen *Vergleichende Grammatik der keltischen Sprachen*. 2 vols. Göttingen: I (*Einleitung und Lautlehre*) 1909; II (*Bedeutungslehre*) 1913.

Pellegrini / Prosdocimi *Lingua Venetica* I / II 1967 = G. B. Pellegrini and A. L. Prosdocimi *La lingua Venetica*. Padua 1967. I: *Le iscrizioni* by G. B. Pellegrini and A. L. Prosdocimi; II: *Studi* by A. L. Prosdocimi.

Peters *Laryngale* 1980 = M. Peters *Untersuchungen zur Vertretung der indogermanischen Laryngale im Griechischen*. Vienna 1980. Review: R. S. P. Beekes in *Kratylos* 26 1981 [1982] p. 106-115; J. Catsanicos in BSL 77 / 2 1982 p. 89-95; B. Forssman in ZVS 96 1982 [1983] p. 290-292; C. J. Ruijgh in *Mnemosyne* 36 1983 p. 373-380.

Petit **su̯e-* 1999 = D. Petit **Su̯e- en grec ancien: La famille du pronom réfléchi, Linguistique grecque et comparaison indo-européenne*. Louvan 1999 (= *Collection Linguistique, publiée par la Société de Linguistique de Paris*, 79).

Petit *Lituanien* 1999 = D. Petit *Lituanien*. Paris 1999 (in LALIES 19, Aussois 1998).

Pfeiffer *Klass. Philologie* I 1970 = R. Pfeiffer *Geschichte der klassischen Philologie, Von den Anfängen bis zum Ende des Hellenismus*. Reinbek near Hamburg 1970. *Klass. Philologie* is a translation (by M. Arnold) of the English original: "History of Classical Scholarship". Oxford 1968.

PFU = *Philologia Fenno-Ugrica*.

Pinault *Tokharien* 1989 = G.-J. Pinault *Introduction au tokharien*. Paris 1989 (in LALIES, *Actes des sessions de linguistique et de littérature* Nr.7, Aussois 1985).

Pinkster *Lateinische Syntax* 1988, i.e. *Latin Syntax* 1990 = H. Pinkster *Lateinische Syntax und Semantik.* Tübingen 1988 (= UTB Nr. 1462 published by the *Francke Verlag*). The text is a translation of the original, published in Dutch in 1984. An English version appeared in 1990 in London / New York with the title: *Latin Syntax and Semantics.*

Place de l' Arménien 1986 = *La place de l'arménien dans les langues indo-européennes*, edited by M. Leroy and F. Mawet. Louvain 1986.

Plath *Streitwagen* 1994 = R. Plath *Der Streitwagen und seine Teile im frühen Griechischen. Sprachliche Untersuchungen zu den mykenischen Texten und zum homerischen Epos.* Nürnberg 1994 (= *Erlanger Beiträge zur Sprache, Literatur und Kunst* 76). Review: I. Hajnal in *Kratylos* 42 1997 p. 78-81.

Poccetti *Nuovi Documenti Italici* see below, *s.v.* Vetter.

Pokorny IEW 1959-1969 = J. Pokorny *Indogermanisches etymologisches Wörterbuch.* I / II Bern / Munich 1959-1969.

Portraits I / II 1966 = *Portraits of Linguists, A Biographical Source Book for the History of Western Linguistics, 1764-1963*, edited by Th. A. Sebeok. Bloomington / London 1966: I (*From Sir William Jones to Karl Brugmann*); II (*From Eduard Sievers to Benjamin Lee Whorf*).

Porzig *Gliederung* 1954 = W. Porzig *Die Gliederung des indogermanischen Sprachgebiets.* Heidelberg 1954.

Porzig *Satzinhalte* 1942 = W. Porzig *Die Namen für Satzinhalte im Griechischen und im Indogermanischen.* Berlin 1942 (= *Untersuchungen zur indogermanischen Sprach- und Kulturwissenschaft* 10).

Porzig *Wunder der Sprache* 1971 = W. Porzig *Das Wunder der Sprache, Probleme, Methoden und Ergebnisse der Sprachwissenschaft.* 5th ed. revised by A. Jecklin and H. Rupp. Munich 1971 (= UTB 32). 8. ed. 1986. The first edition of this outstanding work was published in 1950.

Prins *Hittite neuter* 1997 = A. Prins *Hittite neuter singular - neuter plural, Some Evidence for a Connection.* Leiden 1997.

Probleme der lat. Gramm. 1973 = *Probleme der lat. Grammatik*, edited by K. Strunk. Darmstadt 1973 (= *Wege der Forschung* 93).

Probleme der Namenbildung 1986 [1988] = *Probleme der Namenbildung, Rekonstruktion von Eigennamen und der ihnen zugrundeliegenden Appellative, Akten eines internationalen Symposiums 1986 in Uppsala*, edited by Th. Andersson. Uppsala 1988.

Puhvel *Analecta Indoeuropea* 1981 = J. Puhvel *Analecta Indoeuropea, Delectus operum minorum ... annos 1952-1977 complectens.* Innsbruck 1981 (= IBS 35).

Puhvel HED 1 / 2 1984, 3 1991, 4 1997, 5 2001 = J. Puhvel *Hittite Etymological Dictionary*. Berlin / New York / Amsterdam: vol. 1 (*Words beginning with A*) and 2 (*Words beginning with E and I*) 1984; vol. 3 (*Words beginning with H*) 1991; vol. 4 (*Words beginning with K*) 1997; vol. 5 (*Words beginning with L*) 2001. Concerning vol. 4, cf. I. Hajnal in HS 112 1999 p. 305-315

Puhvel *Laryngeals and the IE Verb* 1960 = J. Puhvel *Laryngeals and the Indo-European Verb*. Berkeley 1960. Review: W. Cowgill in *Language* 39 1963 p. 248-270.

Radke *Archaisches Latein* 1981 = G. Radke *Archaisches Latein*. Darmstadt 1981 (= *Erträge der Forschung* 150).

Ramat see above, *Lingue indoeuropee* 1994.

Rasmussen *Morphophonematik* 1989 = J. E. Rasmussen *Studien zur Morphophonematik der indogermanischen Grundsprache*. Innsbruck 1989 (= IBS Nr. 55).

Rasmussen *Selected Papers* 1999 = J. E. Rasmussen *Selected Papers on Indo-European Linguistics*, 2 vols. Copenhagen 1999.

Raulwing *Horses* 2000 = P. Raulwing *Horses, Chariots and Indo-Europeans, Foundations and Methods of Chariotry Research from the Viewpoint of Indo-European Linguistics*. Budapest 2000. Review: K. Jones-Bley in JIES 28 2000 p. 440-449.

REArm = *Revue des Etudes Arméniennes*.

Rédei *Idg.-ural. Sprachkontakte* 1986 = K. Rédei *Zu den indogermanisch-uralischen Sprachkontakten*. Vienna 1986 (= SbÖAW 468).

Rehder *Slav. Sprachw.* 1998 = P. Rehder *Einführung in die slavische Sprachwissenschaft*. Darmstadt 3rd ed. 1998.

Reichler-Béguelin *Type mēns* 1986 = M.-J. Reichler-Béguelin *Les noms latins du type mēns*. Brussels 1986 (= *Collection Latomus* vol. 195). Review: F. Mawet in *Kratylos* 34 1989 p. 96-102.

REL = *Revue des études latines*.

Renfrew *Archaeology and Language* 1987 = C. Renfrew *Archaeology and Language: The Puzzle of Indo-European Origins*. London 1987. Review: E. Campanile in *Kratylos* 33 1988 p. 53-56.

Renou *Bibliographie* 1997 = *Bibliographie des travaux de Louis Renou*, by G. Pinault. Paris 1997 (= a supplement to the *Bulletin d'études indiennes* 13-14 1995-1996 [1997]).

Res Mycenaeae 1981 [1983] = *Res Mycenaeae, Akten des VII. Internationalen Mykenologischen Colloquiums 1981 in Nürnberg*, edited by A. Heubeck and G. Neumann. Göttingen 1983. Review: M. Peters in

Idg. Chr. 30a Nr. 581; W. Blümel in GGA 236 1984 p. 121-136; F. Bader in *Kratylos* 30 1985 p. 105-112.

RGA = *Reallexikon der Germanischen Altertumskunde*, founded by J. Hoops. 2nd ed., fully revised and considerably expanded by numerous experts under the editorship of R. Müller edited by H. Beck, H. Steuer and D. Tiempe. Status of publication: vol. 1 1973 - vol. 18 2001.

Riecke *jan-Verben* 1996 = J. Riecke *Die schwachen jan-Verben des Althochdeutschen, Ein Gliederungsversuch*. Göttingen 1996 (= *Studien zum Althochdeutschen* 32). Review: O. W. Robinson in *Kratylos* 44 1999 p. 127-130.

Rieken *Nom. Stammbildung* 1999 = E. Rieken *Untersuchungen zur nominalen Stammbildung des Hethitischen*. Wiesbaden 1999 (StBoT 44).

RIG = *Recueil des Inscriptions Gauloises*. Paris. vol. I 1985: M. Lejeune *Textes gallo-grecs*; vol. II 1 1988: M. Lejeune *Textes Gallo-Étrusques*, Textes *Gallo-Latins sur pierre*; vol. III 1986: P.-M. Duval *Les Calendriers*.

Rijksbaron *Verb in Class. Greek* 1994 = A. Rijksbaron *The Syntax and Semantics of the Verb in Classical Greek*. 2nd ed. Amsterdam 1994.

Ringe *Sound Changes in Tocharian* I 1996 = D. A. Ringe *On the Chronology of Sound Changes in Tocharian*. I (*From Proto-IE to Proto-Tocharian*). New Haven 1996 (= *American Oriental Series* 80).

Risch *Gerund.* 1984 = E. Risch *Gerundivum und Gerundium. Gebrauch im klassischen und älteren Latein. Entstehung und Vorgeschichte*. Berlin / New York 1984.

Risch *Kleine Schriften* 1981 = E. Risch *Kleine Schriften*. edited by A. Etter and M. Looser. Berlin / New York 1982.

Risch *Wortbildung* 1974 = E. Risch *Wortbildung der homerischen Sprache*. 2nd ed. Berlin 1974.

Ritter *Armeno antiguo* 1996 = R.-P. Ritter *Introducción al armeno antiguo*. Madrid 1996.

Rix *Etr. Texte* I / II 1991 = H. Rix *Etruskische Texte. Editio minor*, edited by H. Rix together with G. Meiser. Tübingen 1991: vol. I (*Einleitung, Konkordanz, Indizes*); vol. II (*Texte*).

Rix *Gentilnamensystem* 1972 = H. Rix *Zum Ursprung des römisch-mittelitalischen Gentilnamensystems*. Publishe as part of *Aufstieg und Niedergang der römischen Welt, Geschichte und Kultur Roms im Spiegel der neueren Forschung*, edited by H. Temporini. vol. I / 2. Berlin / New York 1972 p. 700-758.

Rix *Hist. Gramm. d. Gr.* 1976 = H. Rix *Historische Grammatik des Griechischen*. Darmstadt 1976. 2nd revised ed. 1992. Review of the 2nd ed.: G. Dunkel in AJPh 97 1976 p. 416-420; M. Peters in *Sprache* 23 1977 p. 65-67; F. Bader in BSL 72 / 2 1977 p. 134-140; C. J. Ruijgh in *Mnemosyne* 31 1978 p. 298-307.

Rix *Kleine Schriften* 2001 = H. Rix *Kleine Schriften, Festgabe für Helmut Rix zum 75. Geburtstag*. Bremen 2001.

Rix *Modussystem* 1986 = H. Rix *Zur Entstehung des urindogermanischen Modussystems*. Innsbruck 1986 (= IBS, *Vorträge und Kleinere Schriften Nr.* 36). Review: E. Risch in *Kratylos* 32 1987 p. 46-50.

Rix *Rätisch und Etruskisch* 1998 = H. Rix *Rätisch und Etruskisch*. Innsbruck 1998 (= IBS, *Vorträge und Kleinere Schriften* 68).

Rix *Termini der Unfreiheit* 1994 = H. Rix *Die Termini der Unfreiheit in den Sprachen Alt-Italiens*. Stuttgart 1994 (= *Forschungen zur Antiken Sklaverei* 25).

Rosén *Periphrase* 1992 = H. B. Rosén *Die Periphrase, Wesen und Entstehung*. Innsbruck 1992 (= IBS, *Vorträge und kleinere Schriften* 57).

RPh = *Revue de Philologie*.

Rubio Orecilla *Sufijo de derivación nominal* 1995 = F. J. Rubio Orecilla *El sufijo de derivación nominal *-i̯i̯o-/ *-i̯o- en los gerundios y gerundivos del Rg-Veda y el Avesta, Un estudio histórico-comparativo*. Zaragoza 1995. Review: M. Kümmel in *Kratylos* 43 1998 p. 81-83; J. Haudry in BSL 93 / 2 1995 p. 134-139; see below, W 202 § 1.

Rüster / Neu *Heth. Zeichenlexikon* 1989 = Chr. Rüster and E. Neu *Hethitisches Zeichenlexikon, Inventar und Interpretation der Keilschriftzeichen aus den Boğazköy-Texten*. Wiesbaden 1989.

Ruijgh *Études* 1967 = C. J. Ruijgh *Études sur la grammaire et le vocabulaire du grec mycénien*. Amsterdam 1967.

Ruijgh *Scripta Minora* I 1991 II 1996 = C. J. Ruijgh *Scripta Minora ad linguam Graecam pertinentia* I, edited by J. M. Bremer, A. Rijksbaron, F. M. J. Waanders. Amsterdam 1991; *Scripta Minora ad linguam Graecam pertinentia* II, edited by A. Rijksbaron, F. M. J. Waanders. Amsterdam 1996.

Ruijgh *„te épique“* 1971 = C. J. Ruijgh *Autour de „te épique“, Études sur la syntaxe grecque*. Amsterdam 1972.

Ruipérez *Ilias und Odyssee* 1999 = M. S. Ruipérez *Anthologie Ilias und Odyssee*. Wiesbaden 1999. Translation of the Spanish original that was published in 1963.

Ruipérez *Opuscula* 1989 = M. S. Ruipérez *Opuscula selecta, Ausgewählte Arbeiten zur griechischen und indogermanischen Sprachwissenschaft*, edited by J. L. García-Ramón. Innsbruck 1989 (= IBS Nr. 58).

Sandhi Phenomena 1986 = *Sandhi Phenomena in the Languages of Europe*, edited by H. Andersen. Berlin / New York / Amsterdam 1986.

Saussure *Cours* 1916 = F. Saussure *Cours de linguistique générale*, edited by Ch. Bally / A. Sechehaye / A. Riedlinger. Paris 1916 (and reprints). Concerning the diachronic aspect of this work: → P. Wunderli *Principes de diachronie, Contribution à l'exégèse du „Cours"*. Frankfurt 1990 (an announcement of the publication by M. Mayrhofer appeared in *Idg. Chr.* 34 Nr. A 89).

Saussure *Mémoire* 1879 = F. Saussure *Mémoire sur le système primitif des voyelles dans les langues indo-européennes*. Leipzig 1879 (*Wiederabdruck in Saussure Recueil* 1922 p. 1ff.; separate reprint Hildesheim 1987). Concerning the work and its reverberations: → M. Mayrhofer *Nach hundert Jahren, Ferdinand de Saussures Frühwerk und seine Rezeption durch die heutige Indogermanistik*, Heidelberg 1981 (= SbHAW 1981 / 8). Further, see above Gmür *Mémoire* 1986, as well asSaussure *Saggio* below.

Saussure *Recueil* 1922 = F. Saussure *Recueil des publications scientifiques de F. de Saussure*. Geneva 1922 (and reprints).

Saussure *Saggio* 1987 = F. Saussure *Saggio sul vocalismo indoeuropeo*, Italian edition of the *Mémoire* with an introduction and comments by G. C. Vincenzi. Bologna 1987.

SbBAW = *Sitzungsberichte der Bayerischen Akademie der Wissenschaften, phil.-hist. Klasse*, Munich.

SbHAW = *Sitzungsberichte der Heidelberger Akademie der Wissenschaften, phil.-hist. Klasse*, Heidelberg.

SbÖAW = *Sitzungsberichte der Österreichischen Akademie der Wissenschaften, phil.-hist. Klasse*, Vienna.

Scardigli *Goten* 1973 = P. Scardigli *Die Goten, Sprache und Kultur*. Munich 1973.

Scardigli *Weg zur deutschen Sprache* 1994 = P. Scardigli *Der Weg zur deutschen Sprache, Von der indogermanischen bis zur Merowingerzeit*. Bern et al. 1994 (= *German. Lehrbuchsammlung* 2).

Scarlata *Wurzelkomposita im R̥g-Veda* 1999 = S. Scarlata *Wurzelkomposita im R̥g-Veda*. Wiesbaden 1999.

Schaefer *Intensivum* 1994 = Ch. Schaefer *Das Intensivum im Vedischen* (= ZVS *Ergänzungsheft* 37). Review: E. Seebold in IF 101 1996 p. 299-302; St. W. Jamison in *Kratylos* 42 1997 p. 50-55; A. Lubotsky in JAOS 117 1997 p. 558-564.

Scherer *Lat. Syntax* 1975 = A. Scherer *Handbuch der lateinischen Syntax*. Heidelberg 1975.

Schindler *Wurzelnomen* 1972 = J. Schindler *Das Wurzelnomen im Arischen und Griechischen.* (dissertation) Würzburg 1972.

Schirmer *Wortschatz* 1998 = B. Schirmer *Studien zum Wortschatz der Iguvinischen Tafeln.* Frankfurt am Main et al. 1998 (= *Europäische Hochschulschriften, Reihe XXI Linguistik*, vol. 205). Review: M. Weiss in *Kratylos* 46 2001 p. 131-134.

Schleicher *Compendium* 1866 = A. Schleicher *Compendium der vergleichenden Grammatik der indogermanischen Sprachen, Kurzer Abriß einer Laut- und Formenlehre der indogermanischen Ursprache, des Altindischen, Alteranischen, Altgriechischen, Altitalischen, Altkeltischen, Altslawischen, Litauischen und Altdeutschen.* 2nd ed. Weimar / London / Paris 1866 (1st ed. 1861-1862).

Schlerath *Indogermanen* 1973 = B. Schlerath *Die Indogermanen. Das Problem der Expansion eines Volkes im Lichte seiner Sozialstruktur.* Innsbruck 1973 (= IBS, *Vorträge* 8). Review: K. Strunk in BNF N.F. 9 1974 p. 388-390.

Schlerath *Kleine Schriften* 2000 = B. Schlerath *Kleine Schriften.* 2 vols. Dettelbach 2000.

Schmid *Schriften* 1994 = W. P. Schmid *Linguisticae scientiae collectanea, Ausgewählte Schriften*, edited by J. Becker. Berlin / New York 1994.

Schmid *Studien* 1963 = W. P. Schmid *Studien zum baltischen und indogermanischen Verbum.* Wiesbaden 1963.

Schmidt (G.) *Personalpronomina* 1978 = G. Schmidt *Stammbildung und Flexion der indogermanischen Personalpronomina.* Wiesbaden 1978.

Schmidt (J.) *Neutra* 1889 = J. Schmidt *Die Pluralbildungen der indogermanischen Neutra.* Weimar 1889.

Schmidt (J.) *Verwantschaftsverhältnisse* 1872 = J. Schmidt *Die Verwantschaftsverhältnisse* (sic !) *der indogermanischen Sprachen.* Weimar 1872.

Schmidt (J.) *Vocalismus* I 1871 II 1875 = J. Schmidt *Zur Geschichte des indogermanischen Vocalismus.* Weimar: I 1871, II 1875.

Schmidt (K. H.) *Celtic* 1996 = K. H. Schmidt *Celtic: A Western Indo-European Language?* Innsbruck 1996 (= IBS, *Vorträge und Kleinere Schriften* 66).

Schmidt (K. T.) *Medium im Toch.* = K. T. Schmidt *Die Gebrauchsweisen des Mediums im Tocharischen.* Göttingen 1974 (dissertation, philology) Göttingen 1969.

Schmitt *Ap. Inschriften* 1999 = R. Schmitt *Beiträge zu altpersischen Inschriften.* Wiesbaden 1999.

Schmitt *Bisitun Inscriptions* 1991 = *The Bisitun Inscriptions of Darius the Great, Old Persian Text*, edited by R. Schmitt. London 1991 (= *School of Oriental and African Studies, Corpus Inscriptionum Iranicarum*, Pt. I (*Inscriptions of Ancient Iran*), Vol. I (*The Old Persian Inscriptions, Texts I*). Review: Ch. H. Werba in *Sprache* 35 (1991-1993) p. 140-145; S. W. Jamison in IIJ 37 (1994) p. 168-171. Also by R. Schmitt, *Epigraphisch-exegetische Noten zu Dareios' Bīsitūn-Inschriften*. Vienna 1990 (= SbÖAW, 561. vol.); and also *Ap. Inschriften* 1999.

Schmitt *Dichtersprache* 1967 = R. Schmitt *Dichtung und Dichtersprache in indogermanischer Zeit*. Wiesbaden 1967.

Schmitt *Gr. Dialekte* 1977 = R. Schmitt *Einführung in die griechischen Dialekte*. Darmstadt 1977.

Schmitt *Ir. Sprachen* 2000 = R. Schmitt *Die iranischen Sprachen in Geschichte und Gegenwart*. Wiesbaden 2000.

Schmitt *Klass. Arm.* 1981 = R. Schmitt *Grammatik des Klassisch-Armenischen mit sprachvergleichenden Erläuterungen*. Innsbruck 1982 (= IBS Nr. 32).

Schmitt-Brandt *Einführung* 1998 = R. Schmitt-Brandt *Einführung in die Indogermanistik*. Tübingen / Basel 1998 (= UTB Nr. 1506). Review: G. Keydana in IF 104 1999 p. 281-286; K. Stelter in *Kratylos* 46 2001 p. 200-202; see above, p. VIII.

Schneider *Lautgesetz* 1973 = G. Schneider *Zum Begriff des Lautgesetzes in der Sprachwissenschaft seit den Junggrammatikern*. Tübingen 1993 (= TBL 46).

Schön *Neutrum und Kollektivum* 1971 = I. Schön *Neutrum und Kollektivum, Das Morphem -a im Lateinischen und Romanischen*. Innsbruck 1971 (= IBS Nr. 6). Review: A. Morpurgo Davies in CR 25 1975 p. 248f.

Schrift und Schriftlichkeit 1 1994 2 1996 = *Schrift und Schriftlichkeit / Writing and its Use, Ein interdisziplinäres Handbuch internationaler Forschung*, edited by H. Günther, O. Ludwig. Berlin / New York. 2 parts: 1 1994; 2 1996 (= HSK 10.1 and 10.2).

Schrijver *British Celtic Phonology* 1995 = P. Schrijver *Studies in British Celtic Historical Phonology*. Amsterdam / Atlanta 1995.

Schrijver *Celtic Pronouns and Particles* 1997 = P. Schrijver *Studies in the History of Celtic Pronouns and Particles*. Maynooth 1997. Review: J. T. Katz in *Kratylos* 46 2001 p. 1-23.

Schrijver *Laryngeals in Latin* 1991 = P. Schrijver *The Reflexes of the Proto-Indo-European Laryngeals in Latin*. Amsterdam / Atlanta 1991. Review: H. Rix in *Kratylos* 41 1996 p. 153-163.

Schulze *Kleine Schriften* + *Nachtr.* 2nd ed. 1966 = W. Schulze *Kleine Schriften*, published by the *Idg. Seminar der Universität Berlin*. 2nd ed. with supplement (*Nachträge*), edited by W. Wissmann. Göttingen 1966.

Schulze-Thulin *o-stufige Kausativa / Iterativa und Nasalpräsentien* 2001 = B. Schulze-Thulin *Studien zu den urindogermanischen o-stufigen Kausativa / Iterativa und Nasalpräsentien im Kymrischen*. Innsbruck 2001 (= IBS 99).

Schwerdt *2. LV* 2000 = J. Schwerdt *Die 2. Lautverschiebung*. Heidelberg 2000.

Schwyzer *Kleine Schriften* 1983 = E. Schwyzer *Kleine Schriften*, edited by R. Schmitt. Innsbruck 1983 (= IBS 45).

Schwyzer *Gr. Gr.* I 1939 = E. Schwyzer *Griechische Grammatik*, vol. I (*Allgemeiner Teil, Lautlehre, Wortbildung, Flexion*). Munich 1939.

Schwyzer / Debrunner *Gr. Gr. II* 1950 = E. Schwyzer and A. Debrunner *Griechische Grammatik*, vol. II (*Syntax und syntaktische Stilistik*), completed and edited by A. Debrunner. Munich 1950.

Seebold *Etymologie* 1981= E. Seebold *Etymologie. Eine Einführung am Beispiel der deutschen Sprache*. Munich 1981.

Seebold *Germ. starke Verben* 1970 = E. Seebold *Vergleichendes und etymologisches Wörterbuch der germanischen starken Verben*. The Hague / Paris 1970.

Seebold *Halbvokale* 1972 = E. Seebold *Das System der indogermanischen Halbvokale. Untersuchungen zum sog. "Sieversschen Gesetz" und zu den halbvokalhaltigen Suffixen in den indogermanischen Sprachen, bes. im Vedischen*. Heidelberg 1972. Review: J. Schindler in *Sprache* 23 1977 p. 56-65.

Seebold *Personalpronomina* 1984 = E. Seebold *Das System der Personalpronomina in den frühgermanischen Sprachen*. Göttingen 1984 (= ZVS, *Ergänzungsheft* 34).

Seebold, see also Kluge / Seebold above.

SEG = *Supplementum Epigraphicum Graecum*.

Seiler *Relativsatz* 1960 = Hj. Seiler *Relativsatz, Attribut und Apposition*. Wiesbaden 1960.

Seiler *Sprache und Sprachen* 1977 = Hj. Seiler *Sprache und Sprachen, Gesammelte Aufsätze*. Munich 1977 (= *Structura* 11).

Seiler *Steigerungsformen* 1950 = Hj. Seiler *Die primären griechischen Steigerungsformen*. Hamburg 1950.

Senn *Handb. d. lit. Sprache* 1966 = A. Senn *Handbuch der litauischen Sprache*. 2 vols. Heidelberg: I (*Grammatik*) 1966; II (*Lesebuch und Glossar*) 1957.

Serbat *Cas et fonctions* 1981 = G. Serbat *Cas et fonctions, Etude des principales doctrines casuelles du Moyen Age à nos jours*. Paris 1981. Review: R. Amacker in *Kratylos* 27 1982 p. 5-8.

Sergent *Indo-Européens* 1995 = B. Sergent *Les indo-européens, Histoire, langues, mythes*. Paris 1995.

Sihler *New Comparative Grammar* 1995 = A. L. Sihler *New Comparative Grammar of Greek and Latin*. New York / London 1995.

SMEA = *Studi Micenei ed Egeo-Anatolici*.

SMID I 1968 II 1986 1979 1980-1981= *Studies in Mycenaean Inscriptions and Dialect*. The work offers a comprehensive bibliography with indexes. — SMID I (1953-1964) assembled by L. Baumbach from the SMID-vols. I-X (originally published by: The Institute of Classical Studies of the University of London). Rome 1968. — SMID II (1965-1978), assembled by L. Baumbach from the SMID-vols. XI-XXIII (originally published by: as part I, but the final fascicles were published by the British Association of Mycenaean Studies, Cambridge). Rome 1986. — SMID 1979, edited by E. Sikkenga. University of Texas at Austin, Department of Classics, Program in Aegean Scripts and Prehistory. 1995. — SMID 1980-1981, dito, 1997.

Smyth *Greek Grammar* 1956 = H. W. Smyth *A Greek Grammar (for Colleges)*, revised by G. M. Messing. Cambridge MA 1956 (and reprints).

Solmsen *Eigennamen* 1922 = F. Solmsen *Indogermanische Eigennamen als Spiegel der Kulturgeschichte*, edited by E. Fraenkel. Heidelberg 1922.

Solmsen *Untersuchungen* 1901 = F. Solmsen *Untersuchungen zur griechischen Laut- und Verslehre*. Strasbourg 1901.

Solta *Balkanlinguistik* 1980 = G. R. Solta *Einführung in die Balkanlinguistik mit besonderer Berücksichtigung des Substrats und des Balkanlateinischen*. Darmstadt 1980.

Solta *Stellung der lat. Sprache* 1974 = G. R. Solta *Zur Stellung der lateinischen Sprache*. Vienna 1974 (= SbÖAW 291. vol., 4. *Abhandlung*).

Solta *Stellung des Arm.* 1960 = G. R. Solta *Die Stellung des Armenischen im Kreise der indogermanischen Sprachen. Eine Untersuchung der indogermanischen Bestandteile des armenischen Wortschatzes.* Vienna 1960.

Sommer *Handbuch* 1948 = F. Sommer *Handbuch der lateinischen Laut- und Formenlehre. Eine Einführung in das sprachwissenschaftliche*

Studium des Lateins. Heidelberg 1948. See also Sommer / Pfister below.

Sommer *Heth.* 1947 = F. Sommer *Hethiter und Hethitisch.* Stuttgart 1947.

Sommer *Nachlaß* 1977 = F. Sommer *Schriften aus dem Nachlaß*. Munich 1977 (= MSS Beiheft 1, *Neue Folge*).

Sommer *Nominalkomposita* 1948 = F. Sommer *Zur Geschichte der griechischen Nominalkomposita*. Munich 1948.

Sommer *Vergl. Syntax* 1931 = F. Sommer *Vergleichende Syntax der Schulsprachen*. 3rd ed. Stuttgart 1931 (= 4th, unchanged reprint Darmstadt 1959).

Sommer / Pfister *Lautlehre* 1977 = F. Sommer *Handbuch der lateinischen Laut- und Formenlehre*. Heidelberg 1948. 4th revised ed.: vol. I (*Einleitung und Lautlehre*) by R. Pfister. Heidelberg 1977. The planned second volume was not published. Sonderegger *Althochdeutsch* 1987 = S. Sonderegger *Althochdeutsche Sprache und Literatur. Eine Einführung in das älteste Deutsch. Darstellung und Grammatik.* 2nd revised and expanded ed., Berlin / New York 1987.

Sonderegger *Deutsche Sprachgeschichte* I 1979 = S. Sonderegger *Grundzüge deutscher Sprachgeschichte. Diachronie des Sprachsystems*. vol. I (*Einführung, Genealogie, Konstanten*). Berlin / New York 1979.

Speyer *Syntax* 1896 = J. S. Speyer *Vedische u. Sanskrit-Syntax*. Strasbourg 1896.

Sprache = *Die Sprache. Zeitschrift für Sprachwissenschaft*. Wiesbaden / Vienna. Contains the important *Idg. Chr.*, see above, *s.v.*

Sprache Fünf Vorträge 1991 = *Sprache, Fünf Vorträge* by H. Kößler, I. Richter, B. Forssman, M. v. Engelhardt and R. Slenczka. Erlangen 1991 (= *Erlanger Forschungen, Reihe A Geisteswissenschaften* 54).

Sprachen im röm. Reich 1980 = *Die Sprachen im römischen Reich der Kaiserzeit, Kolloquium 1974*, edited by G. Neumann and J. Untermann. Köln / Bonn 1980.

Sprachgeschichte 1 1998 2 1985 = *Sprachgeschichte, Ein Handbuch zur Geschichte der deutschen Sprache und ihrer Erforschung*, edited by W. Besch, A. Betten, O. Reichmann, S. Sonderegger. Berlin / New York. 2 parts: 1 (2nd edition, fully revised) 1998; 2 1985 (= HSK 2.1 and 2.2).

Stair na Gaeilge 1994 = *Stair na Gaeilge in ómós do Pádraig Ó Fiannachta*, edited by K. McCone et al. Maigh Nuad 1994. Which includes a review of current research in Old Irish phonology and morphology by K. McCone p. 61-219.

Stang *Opuscula* 1970 = Ch. S. Stang *Opuscula linguistica, Ausgewählte Aufsätze und Abhandlungen*. Oslo / Bergen / Tromsø 1970.

Stang *Vgl. Gramm.* 1966 *Ergänzungsband* 1975 = Ch. S. Stang *Vergleichende Grammatik der baltischen Sprachen*. Oslo / Bergen / Tromsø: *Vgl. Gramm.* 1966; *Ergänzungsband, Register, Addenda und Corrigenda zur Vgl. Gramm.* 1975.

Starke *Kasus und Adv. im Aheth.* 1977 = F. Starke *Die Funktionen der dimensionalen Kasus und Adverbien im Althethitischen*. Wiesbaden 1977 (= StBoT 23).

Starke *Keilschr.-luw. Nomen* 1990 = F. Starke *Untersuchungen zur Stammbildung des keilschrift-luwischen Nomens*. Wiesbaden 1990 (= StBoT 31).

Starke *Keilschrift-luw. Texte* 1985 = F. Starke *Die keilschrift-luwischen Texte in Umschrift*. Wiesbaden 1985 (= StBoT 30).

Starke *Kikkuli* 1995 = F. Starke *Ausbildung und Training von Streitwagenpferden: Eine hippologisch orientierte Interpretation des Kikkuli-Textes*. Wiesbaden 1995 (= StBoT 41).

StBoT = *Studien zu den Boğazköy-Texten*.

Steinbauer *Denominativa* 1989 = D. H. Steinbauer *Etymologische Untersuchungen zu den bei Plautus belegten Verben der lateinischen ersten Konjugation. Unter besonderer Berücksichtigung der Denominative*. Altendorf near Bamberg 1989.

Stempel *Diathese* 1996 = R. Stempel *Die Diathese im Indogermanischen, Formen und Funktionen des Mediums und ihre sprachhistorischen Grundlagen*. Innsbruck 1996 (= IBS, *Vorträge und Kleinere Schriften* 67).

Storia d'Europa II 1994 = *Storia d'Europa*, vol. II (*Preistoria e antichità*), edited by J. Guilaine and S. Settis. Turin 1994.

Streitberg *Got. Bibel* 1971 = *Die gotische Bibel*, edited by W. Streitberg. 2nd ed. Part I (*Der gotische Text und seine griechische Vorlage*) Heidelberg 1919; 2nd ed. Part II (*Gotisch-griechisch-deutsches Wörterbuch*) Heidelberg 1928. 6th ed. Heidelberg 1971. 7th ed. (Part I with an afterword by P. Scardigli).

Streitberg *Urgerm. Gr.* 1896 = W. Streitberg *Urgermanische Grammatik, Einführung in das vergleichende Studium der altgermanischen Dialekte*. Heidelberg 1896 (reprint 1943).

Strunk *Lachmanns Regel* 1976 = K. Strunk *Lachmanns Regel für das Lateinische*. Göttingen 1976 (= ZVS *Ergänzungsheft* Nr.26). Review: A. Morpurgo Davies in CR 29 1979 p. 259f.

Strunk *Nasalpräsentien und Aoriste* 1967 = K. Strunk *Nasalpräsentien und Aoriste*. Heidelberg 1967.

Strunk *'Vorhersagbarer' Sprachwandel* 1991 = K. Strunk *Zum Postulat 'vorhersagbaren' Sprachwandels bei unregelmäßigen oder komplexen Flexionsparadigmen*. Munich 1991 (= SbBAW 1991, *Heft* 6).

Studi di linguistica greca 1993 [1995] = *Studi di linguistica greca, Materiali linguistici*, dossier from a conference in Pavia 1993, edited by P. Cuzzolin. Milan 1995. Review: R. Hodot in BSL 93 / 2 1998 p. 165-168.

Stud. z. idg. Wortschatz 1987 = *Studien zum indogermanischen Wortschatz*, edited by W. Meid. Innsbruck 1987. Review: J. Untermann in *Kratylos* 34 1989 p. 45-54.

Stumpf *Westtocharisch* 1990 = P. Stumpf *Die Erscheinungsformen des Westtocharischen*. Reykjavík 1990 (= TIES, *Suppl. Ser.* 2).

Svennung *Anredeformen* 1958 = J. Svennung *Anredeformen, Vergleichende Forschungen zur indirekten Anrede in der dritten Person und zum Nominativ für den Vokativ*. Uppsala / Wiesbaden 1958.

Syntax 1 1993 2 1995 = *Syntax, Ein internationales Handbuch zeitgenössischer Forschung*, edited by J. Jacobs, A. v. Stechow, W. Sternefeld, Th. Vennemann. Berlin / New York. 2 parts: 1 1993; 2 1995 (= HSK 9.1 and 9.2).

Syntaxe des langues indo-iraniennes anciennes 1993 [1997] = *Syntaxe des langues indo-iraniennes anciennes, Colloque international Sitges 1993*, edited by E. Pirart. Barcelona 1997.

Szantyr see above, Hofmann / Szantyr and Leumann / Hofmann / Szantyr.

Szemerényi *Einführung* 4. ed. 1990 = O. Szemerényi *Einführung in die vergleichende Sprachwissenschaft*. 4th revised ed. Darmstadt 1990. The *Einführung* first appeared in 1970, the 2nd ed. in 1980, 3rd ed. in 1989. — Italian translation: *Introduzione alla linguistica indoeuropea*, edited by G. Boccali, V. Brugnatelli and M. Negri. Milan 1985. — English translation: *Introduction to Indo-European Linguistics*. Oxford 1996. — Many reviews have been written. Reviews of the 1st ed. 1970 include: W. Meid in *Kratylos* 16 1971 [1973] p. 41-49; B. Forssman in *Anglia* 94 1976 p. 441-450. Reviews of the 3rd ed. 1989: R. Schmitt in *Gnomon* 62 1990 p. 365-367; W. Meid in *Kratylos* 36 1991 p. 87-91; E. Eggers in IF 96 1991 p. 261-266 (including in note 1 the reviews from BL (*q.v.*) of the first and second editions up to 1986). Reviews of the 4th ed. 1990 include: I. Hajnal in PFU 1 1994-1995 p. 39-46.

Szemerényi *Lat. Wortschatz* 1989 = O. Szemerényi *An den Quellen des lateinischen Wortschatzes*. Innsbruck 1989. Review: M. Peters in *Idg. Chr.* 34 Nr. H 659.

Szemerényi *Numerals* 1960 = O. Szemerényi *Studies in the Indo-European System of Numerals*. Heidelberg 1960.

Szemerényi *Richtungen d. mod. Sprachw.* I 1971 II 1982 = O. Szemerényi *Richtungen der modernen Sprachwissenschaft*. Heidelberg: I (*Von Saussure bis Bloomfield*, 1916-1950) 1971; II (*Die fünfziger Jahre, 1950-1960*) 1982. Review: M. Mayrhofer in *Sprache* 29 1983 p. 182-186.

Szemerényi *Scripta Minora* I 1987 II 1987 III 1987 IV 1991 Suppl. 1992 = O. Szemerényi *Scripta Minora. Selected Essays in Indo-European, Greek, and Latin*, edited by P. Considine and J. T. Hooker. Parts I-III Innsbruck 1987 (= IBS 53 with 3 parts): I (Indo-European) p. 1-588; II (Latin) p. 589-1076; III (Greek) p. 1077-1643; Part IV (Indo-European Languages other than Latin and Greek) Innsbruck 1991 (= IBS 63). As a supplement, *Word Index* 1992. By the same author *Summing up a Life, Autobiographie und Schriftenverzeichnis*. edited by B. Brogyanyi. Freiburg 1991. Concerning Szemerényi, see also *FS O. Szemerényi* *65 1979 and *75 1992 above. Also cf. HS 110 1997 p. 1-3 which includes comments on O. Szemerényi's publications. Lastly, cf. B. Brogyanyi *Schriftenverzeichnis: O. Szemerényi (1913-1996)* in PFU 2-3 1996-1997 p. 53-80.

Szemerényi *Syncope* 1964 = O. Szemerényi *Syncope in Greek and Indo-European and the Nature of Indo-European Accent*. Naples 1964. Review: G. Cardona in *Language* 43 1967 p. 757-773.

Tavola di Agnone 1994 [1996] = *La Tavola di Agnone nel contesto italico, Convegno di Studio 1994 in Agnone*, edited by L. del Tutto Palma. Florence 1996 (= *Lingue e Iscrizioni dell' Italia Antica* 7). Review: E. Nieto Ballester in *Kratylos* 44 1999 p. 98-106.

TBL = *Tübinger Beiträge zur Linguistik*.

Tense and Aspect in IE 1997 = *Tense and Aspect in Indo-European: Theory, Typology, Diachrony*, edited by J. Hewson and V. Bubenik. Amsterdam / Philadelphia 1997. Review: E. C. Polomé in JIES 25 1997 p. 482.

Ternes *Phonologie* 1987 and 1999 = E. Ternes *Einführung in die Phonologie*. 1st ed. Darmstadt 1987; 2nd revised and expanded ed. 1999.

Tesnière *Syntaxe structurale* 1959 = L. Tesnière *Eléments de syntaxe structurale*. Paris 1959.

Textdatierung 1979 = S. Heinhold-Krahmer, I. Hoffmann, A. Kammenhuber, G. Mauer *Probleme der Textdatierung in der Hethitologie*. Heidelberg 1979 (= *Texte der Hethiter* 9).

Thieme *Heimat* 1954 = P. Thieme *Die Heimat der indogermanischen Gemeinsprache*. Wiesbaden 1954.

Thieme *Kleine Schriften* I 1971 II 1995 = P. Thieme *Kleine Schriften*. Wiesbaden: I. vol. 1972; II. vol. 1995.

Thieme *Studien* 1952 = P. Thieme *Studien zur indogermanischen Wortkunde und Religionsgeschichte*. Berlin 1952.

Thomas *Der tocharische Obliquus* 1983 = W. Thomas *Der tocharische Obliquus im Sinne eines Akkusativs der Richtung*. Wiesbaden 1983.

Thomas *Erforschung des Toch.* 1985 = W. Thomas *Die Erforschung des Tocharischen (1960-1984)*. Stuttgart 1985.

Thomas *Vergangenheitstempora* 1957 = W. Thomas *Der Gebrauch der Vergangenheitstempora im Tocharischen*. Wiesbaden 1957.

Thomas, see also Krause / Thomas above.

Threatte *Attic* I 1980 II 1996 = L. Threatte *The Grammar of Attic Inscriptions*. Berlin: I (*Phonology*) 1980; II (*Morphology*) 1996.

Thumb see above, *s.v.* Brugmann / Thumb.

Thumb / Hauschild *Handb. d. Skr.* I / 1 1958 I / 2 (+3) 1959 = A. Thumb *Handbuch des Sanskrit. Eine Einführung in das sprachwissenschaftliche Studium des Altindischen*. 3rd ed. by R. Hauschild. Heidelberg: I / 1 (*Einleitung und Lautlehre*) 1958; I / 2 (+3) (*Formenlehre, Compositum und Satzbau*) 1959.

Thumb / Kieckers *Gr. Dial.* I 1932 = A. Thumb *Handbuch der griechischen Dialekte*. Heidelberg. 2nd ed.: vol. I 1932 by E. Kieckers.

Thumb / Scherer *Gr. Dial.* II 1959 = A. Thumb *Handbuch der griechischen Dialekte*. Heidelberg. 2nd ed.: vol. II 1959 by A. Scherer.

Thurneysen *Old Irish* 1946 = R. Thurneysen *A Grammar of Old Irish*. Dublin 1946.

Tichy *Grundwissen* 2001 = E. Tichy *Indogermanistisches Grundwissen für Studierende sprachwissenschaftlicher Disziplinen*. Bremen 2001.

Tichy *Nom. ag. auf -tar-* 1995 = E. Tichy *Die Nomina agentis auf -tar- im Vedischen*. Heidelberg 1995. Review: H. Hettrich in *Kratylos* 43 1998 p. 84-91.

Tichy *Onomatop. Verbalbildungen* 1983 = E. Tichy *Onomatopoetische Verbalbildungen des Griechischen*. Vienna 1983 (= SbÖAW, vol. 409).

TIES = *Tocharian and Indo-European Studies*. vol. 1 1987 - vol. 6 1993 Reykjavík; vol. 7 1997 Copenhagen. (vol. 7 1997 included the dossier *Arbeitstagung 100 Jahre Tocharologie Saarbrücken 1995* [1997]).

The *Supplementary Series* includes Stumpf *Westtocharisch* 1990 as vol. 2, *Hilmarsson Nasal Prefixes in Tocharian* 1991 as vol. 3, *Fachtagung Tocharisch Berlin 1990* [1994] as vol. 4, Hilmarsson *Tocharian Dictionary* 1996 as vol. 5.

Tischler HEG = J. Tischler *Hethitisches etymologisches Glossar*. Innsbruck (= IBS Nr. 20): Part I (A-K) 1983; Part II with fascicles 5-6 (L-M) 1990 and fascicle 7 (N) 1991; Part III with fascicle 8 (T, D / 1) 1991, fascicle 9 (T, D / 2) 1993 fascicle 10 (T, D / 3) 1994.

Tischler *Kleinasiatische Hydronymie* 1977 = J. Tischler *Kleinasiatische Hydronymie, Semantische und morphologische Analyse der griechischen Gewässernamen*. Wiesbaden 1977.

TPhS = *Transactions of the Philological Society*. Oxford.

Tract. Myc. 1985 [1987] = *Tractata Mycenaea, Proceedings of the Eighth International Colloquium on Mycenaean Studies Ohrid 1985*, edited by P. H. Ilievski and L. Crepajac. Skopje 1987.

Tucker *Early Greek Verbs* 1990 = E. F. Tucker *The Creation of Morphological Regularity: Early Greek Verbs in -éō, -áō, -óō, -úō and -íō*. Göttingen 1990 (= HS, *Ergänzungsheft* 35). Review: R. Schmitt in HS 103 1990 p. 301-304; M. Peters in *Idg. Chr.* 34 Nr. G 615.

UCLA *IE Conference 1999* [2000] = *Proceedings of the Eleventh Annual UCLA IE Conference 1999*, edited by K. Jones-Bley, M. E. Huld, A. Della Volpe. Washington 2000.

UCLA *IE Studies* = *University of California Los Angeles Program in IE Studies*, edited by V. V. Ivanov and B. Vine. Vol. 1 1999.

Uhlich *Komponierte Personennamen des Air.* 1993 = J. Uhlich *Die Morphologie der komponierten Personennamen des Altirischen*. Witterschlick / Bonn 1993.

Untermann *Monumenta (Linguarum Hispanicarum)* = J. Untermann *Monumenta Linguarum Hispanicarum*. Wiesbaden. vol. I (*Die Münzlegenden:* 1 *Text,* 2 *Tafeln*) 1975; vol. II (*Die Inschriften in iberischer Schrift aus Südfrankreich*) 1980; vol. III (*Die iberischen Inschriften aus Spanien:* 1 *Literaturverzeichnis, Einleitung, Indices,* 2 *Die Inschriften*) 1990; vol. IV (*Die tartessischen, keltiberischen und lusitanischen Inschriften*) 1997. Review of Monumenta IV: F. Villar and C. Jordan in *Kratylos* 46 2001 p. 166-181.

Untermann Wb. *Osk.-Umbr.* 2000 = J. Untermann *Wörterbuch des Oskisch-Umbrischen*. Heidelberg 2000.

Urheimat 1968 = *Die Urheimat der Indogermanen*, edited by A. Scherer. Darmstadt 1968 (= *Wege der Forschung* 116).

UTB = *UTB für Wissenschaft, Uni-Taschenbücher.*

Väänänen *Latin vulgaire* 1981 = V. Väänänen *Introduction au latin vulgaire*. 2nd ed. Paris 1967; 3rd ed. Paris 1981.

Vaillant *Vieux slave* 1948 = A. Vaillant *Manuel du vieux slave*. Paris 1948.

Vasmer REW 1953-1958 = M. Vasmer *Russisches etymologisches Wörterbuch*. 3 vols. Heidelberg 1953-1958.

Večerka *Aksl. Syntax* I 1989 II 1993 III 1996 = R. Večerka *Altkirchenslavische (altbulgarische) Syntax*, prepared by F. Keller and E.Weiher. Freiburg (*Monumenta Linguae Slavicae Dialecti Veteris*): I (*Die lineare Satzorganisation*) 1989 (= MLS 17); II (*Die innere Satzstruktur*) 1993 (= MLS 34); III (*Die Satztypen*) 1996 (= MLS 36).

Vetter Handb. d. ital. Dialekte I 1953 = E. Vetter Handbuch der italischen Dialekte. I (Texte mit Erklärung, Glossen, Wörterverzeichnis). Heidelberg 1953. A useful supplement is P. Poccetti Nuovi Documenti Italici, a complemento del Manuale di E. Vetter. Pisa 1979. H. Rix has been preparing a new edition of Vetter's Handbuch for some time; further see above, Untermann Wb. Osk.-Umbr. 2000.

Villar *Celtiberian Grammar* 1995 = F. Villar *A New Interpretation of Celtiberian Grammar*. Innsbruck 1995 (= IBS, *Vorträge und Kleinere Schriften* 62).

Vine *Archaic Latin* 1993 = B. Vine *Studies in Archaic Inscriptions*. Innsbruck 1993 (= IBS Nr. 75). Review: R. Gerschner in *Sprache* 38 / 2 1996 [1999] p. 231-237.

Vine *Deverbative* *-etó- 1998 = B. Vine *Aeolic ὄρπετον and Deverbative *-etó- in Greek and Indo-European*. Innsbruck 1998 (= IBS, *Vorträge und Kleinere Schriften* 71).

Volkart *Brugmanns Gesetz* 1994 = M. Volkart *Zu Brugmanns Gesetz im Altindischen*. Bern 1994 (= *Universität Bern, Institut für Sprachwissenschaft, Arbeitspapiere* 33). Review: Th. Zehnder in CFS 48 1994 [1995] p. 177-184; R. Lubotsky in *Kratylos* 42 1997 p. 55-59.

von Hinüber see above, Hinüber.

Vottéro *Béotien* I 1998 = G. Vottéro *Le dialecte béotien (7ᵉ s. - 2ᵉ s. av. J.-C.)*. Nancy. vol. I (*L'écologie du dialecte*) 1998. At least three further volumes have been announced.

Vries AnordEW 1962 = J. de Vries *Altnordisches etymologisches Wörterbuch*. 2nd, revised ed. Leiden 1962 (= 3rd ed. 1977).

Waanders *Local Case Relations* 1997 = F. M. J. Waanders *Studies in Local Case Relations in Mycenaean Greek*. Amsterdam 1997.

Wachter *Altlat. Inschriften* 1987 = R. Wachter *Altlateinische Inschriften. Sprachliche und epigraphische Untersuchungen zu den Dokumenten bis etwa 150 v. Chr.* Bern 1987. Review: M. Peters in *Idg. Chr.* 32b Nr. 1045; M. Lejeune in REL 65 1987 [1989] p. 285-287.

Wackernagel *Kleine Schriften* I / II 1969 III 1979 = J. Wackernagel *Kleine Schriften*, 3 vols., edited by the *Akademie der Wissenschaften zu Göttingen*. I - II (p. 1-1426, edited by K. Latte) 1st ed. Göttingen 1953, 2nd ed. 1969; III (p. 1427-1905, edited by B. Forssman) Göttingen 1979.

Wackernagel *Untersuchungen* 1916 = J. Wackernagel *Sprachliche Untersuchungen zu Homer*. Göttingen 1916.

Wackernagel *Vorlesungen* I 1926 II 1928 = J. Wackernagel *Vorlesungen über Syntax, 2 Reihen*. 2nd ed. Basel 1926-1928 (1st ed. 1920-1924).

Wackernagel, see also *Kolloquium Wackernagel* above.

Wackernagel, see also Wackernagel / Debrunner below.

Wackernagel / Debrunner *Ai. Grammatik* I + II / 1 1957 II / 2 1954 III 1930 = J. Wackernagel *Altindische Grammatik*. Göttingen: vol. I (*Lautlehre*), reprint of the 2nd ed. 1896 with an introduction by L. Renou and additional contributions by A. Debrunner 1957; vol. II / 1 (*Einleitung zur Wortlehre. Nominalkomposition*), reprint of the 1905 text with addition contributions by A. Debrunner 1957; vol. II / 2 (*Die Nominalsuffixe*) von A. Debrunner 1954; vol. III (*Nominalflexion, Zahlwort, Pronomen*) by A. Debrunner and J. Wackernagel 1930 (The sections on number words and pronouns are by J. Wackernagel, as well as §§ 83-101 and §159). R. Hauschild published the index to vols. I - III in 1964; vol. IV (*Verbum und Adverbium*) remains missing.

Walde *Vgl. Wb.* 1927-1932 = A. Walde *Vergleichendes Wörterbuch der indogermanischen Sprachen*, edited by J. Pokorny. Berlin 1927-1932 = reprint 1973.

Walde / Hofmann LEW = A. Walde *Lateinisches etymologisches Wörterbuch*, revised, starting with the 3rd ed., by J. B. Hofmann. 4th ed. Heidelberg 1965 (and reprints).

Warmington *Remains of Old Latin* I-IV 1935-1940 = E. H. Warmington *Remains of Old Latin*, newly edited and translated. 4 vols. Cambridge / Mass.: I (*Ennius and Caecilius*) 1935 (reprint 1956); II (*Livius Andronicus, Naevius, Pacuvius and Accius*) 1936 (reprint 1957); III (*Lucilius, The Twelve Tables*) 1938 (reprint 1957); IV (*Archaic Inscriptions*) 1940 (reprints since 1953)

Wathelet *Traits éoliens* 1970 = P. Wathelet *Les traits éoliens dans la langue de l'épopée grecque*. Rome 1970.

Watkins *How to kill a dragon* 1995 = C. Watkins *How to kill a dragon, Aspects of IE Poetics*. New York / Oxford 1995. Review: G. E. Dunkel in *The Classical Journal* 92 1997 p. 417-422; F. Bader in BSL 93 / 2 1998 p. 116-130; B. Schlerath in *Kratylos* 45 2000 p. 36-46.

Watkins *Selected Writings* 1994 = C. Watkins *Selected Writings*, edited by L. Oliver. 2 vols. Innsbruck 1994 (= IBS 80).

Watkins *Verbalflexion* 1969 = C. Watkins *Geschichte der indogermanischen Verbalflexion* = vol. III 1 of the *Idg. Gr.* (see above). Heidelberg 1969. Concerning Watkins, see also *FS Watkins* above.

Wegner *Hurritisch* 2000 = I. Wegner *Einführung in die hurritische Sprache*. Wiesbaden 2000.

Weinrich *Linguistik der Lüge* 1974 = H. Weinrich *Linguistik der Lüge, Kann Sprache die Gedanken verbergen ?* 5. ed. Heidelberg 1974.

Weinrich *Textgrammatik* 1993 = H. Weinrich *Textgrammatik der deutschen Sprache*. Mannheim / Leipzig / Vienna / Zürich 1993.

Weiss *Italic Nominal Morphology* 1993 = M. Weiss *Studies in Italic Nominal Morphology*. (dissertation). Cornell University 1993.

Weitenberg *Heth. u-Stämme* 1984 = J. J. S. Weitenberg *Die hethitischen u-Stämme*. Amsterdam 1984. Review: H. C. Melchert in *Kratylos* 29 1984 [1985] p. 79-82.

Werba *Verba IndoArica* (VIA) I 1997 = C. Werba *Verba IndoArica: Die primären und sekundären Wurzeln der Sanskrit-Sprache*. Part I (*Radices primariae*). Vienna 1997. Review: B. Schlerath in HS 111 1998 p. 369-371.

West *Ilias* I 1998 = M. L. West *Homerus, Ilias*, Part I: *Rhapsodiae* I-XII. Stuttgart / Leipzig 1998.

West *Theogony* 1966 = M. L. West *Hesiod, Theogony*, edited with *Prolegomena and Commentary*. Oxford 1966.

West *Works & Days* 1978 = M. L. West *Hesiod, Works & Days*, edited with *Prolegomena and Commentary*. Oxford 1978.

Wheeler *Nominalaccent* 1885 = B. I. Wheeler *Der griechische Nominalaccent*. Strasbourg 1885.

Windisch *Sanskritphilologie* I 1917 II 1920 = E. Windisch *Geschichte der Sanskritphilologie*. 2 parts: I Strasbourg 1917; II Berlin / Leipzig 1920.

Winkler *Germanische Casussyntax* I 1896 = H. Winkler *Germanische Casussyntax*, I. *Der Dativ, Instrumental, örtliche und halbörtliche Verhältnisse*. Berlin 1896.

Wissenschaft vom Altertum am Ende des 2nd Jt. n. Chr. 1995 = *Die Wissenschaft vom Altertum am Ende des 2nd Jahrtausends n. Chr.*, edited by E.-R. Schwinge. Stuttgart and Leipzig 1995.

Wörterbücher 1 1989 2 1990 3 1991 = *Wörterbücher / Dictionaries / Dictionnaires, Ein internationales Handbuch zur Lexikographie*, edited by F. J. Hausmann, O. Reichmann, H. E. Wiegand, L. Zgusta. Berlin / New York. 3 parts: 1 1989; 2 1990; 3 1991 (= HSK 5.1, 5.2, 5.3).

Yoshida (D.) *Aheth. Gen.* 1987 = D. Yoshida *Die Syntax des althethitischen substantivischen Genitivs*. Heidelberg 1987 (= *Texte der Hethiter* 13).

Yoshida (K.) *Endings in -ri* 1990 = K. Yoshida *The Hittite Mediopassive Endings in -ri*. Berlin / New York 1990 (= *Untersuchungen zur idg. Sprach- und Kulturwissenschaft*, N.F. 5). Review: G. Pinault in BSL 86 / 2 1991 p. 134-141.

ZCP = *Zeitschrift für celtische Philologie*.

ZDL = *Zeitschrift für Dialektologie und Linguistik*.

ZDMG = Zeitschrift der Deutschen Morgenländischen Gesellschaft.

Zehnder *AVP 2* 1999 = Th. Zehnder, *Atharvaveda-Paippalāda, Buch 2, Text, Übersetzung, Kommentar, Eine Sammlung altindischer Zaubersprüche vom Beginn des 1. Jahrtausends v. Chr.* Idstein 1999.

Zgusta *Kleinasiatische Ortsnamen* 1984 = L. Zgusta *Kleinasiatische Ortsnamen*. Heidelberg 1984 (= BNF N.F. Beiheft 21).

Zgusta *Kleinasiatische Personennamen* 1964 = L. Zgusta *Kleinasiatische Personennamen*. Prague 1964.

Ziegler *Ogam-Inschriften* 1994 = S. Ziegler *Die Sprache der altirischen Ogam-Inschriften*. Göttingen 1994 (= HS *Ergänzungsheft* Nr. 36).

Zimmer *Satzstellung* 1976 = St. Zimmer *Die Satzstellung des finiten Verbs im Tocharischen*. The Hague / Paris 1976.

Zimmer *Ursprache* 1990 = St. Zimmer *Ursprache, Urvolk und Indogermanisierung. Zur Methode der Indogermanischen Altertumskunde*. Innsbruck 1990 (= IBS, *Vorträge u. kleinere Schriften* Nr. 46). Review: J. Untermann in *Kratylos* 39 1994 p. 68-70.

Zinsmeister *Gr. Gr.* I 1954 = H. Zinsmeister *Griechische Grammatik* I, *Laut- und Formenlehre*. Munich 1954. revised edition. Heidelberg 1990.

ZVS see above, HS.

Zweihundert Jahre Homer-Forschung 1991 = *Zweihundert Jahre Homer-Forschung. Rückblick und Ausblick*, edited by J. Latacz. Stuttgart / Leipzig 1991.

Zwolanek *Anrufungsformen* 1970 = R. Zwolanek *„vā́yav índraśca“, Studien zu Anrufungsformen im Vedischen, Avestischen und Griechischen*. Munich 1970 (= MSS, *Beiheft* 5, N. F.).

VII. Index

The following index has two goals: In addition to serving as a traditional index, it directs the reader not only from an entry to its corresponding paragraphs, but also occasionally informs the reader on subjects that are not explicitly discussed in the text and offers additional bibliographical information. There are also entries for individual Indo-European linguists and historical linguists, particularly those from the first generations following 1816.

In addition to *Metzler Lexikon Sprache* 2000, general assistance may be found in the *Sachindex* of *HS* 1-100 (1997), see bibliography, *s.v. HS*. See also Mallory/Adams *Encyclopedia* 1997. What I could not yet accomplish in the eighth edition is the addition of a complete index of vocabulary.

miscellaneous languages (IE): → Convegno *Udine* 1981 [1983]
Mitanni-Indic E 404 (1)
mobilia F 303 (2), W 204 (1)
mode S 303ff.
monophthongs (Lat.) E 503 (9), L 220 (1)
morpheme E 502 (2), F 100 (1)
morphology F 100 (2)
morphonology L 418
murmel vowel L 202, L 318
muta cum liquida L 406
mutation (Germ.) L 208, L 307 (1)
Mycenaean E 418
names of gods W 303
names W 300ff.
Narten present F 203 (1b)
nasalis sonans L 305
nasals L 300ff.
National Socialism: Abuse of linguistics in support of then-current views. As a frightening example, see W. Wüst "*Indogermanisches Bekenntnis*" in *Die Weltliteratur*, *Folge* 7, 17 1942 p. 134-142.
negation: → Meier-Brügger *Gr. Sprachw.* I 1992 p. 108ff.
neo-grammarians E 306
neuter p. XVIII, F 303, F 313
noem: The smallest unity of that which one wishes to express: → Hoffmann *Aufsätze* II 1976 p. 524ff.
nomen actionis W 205 (2)
nomen agentis W 205 (1)
nomen gentile W 302 (3)
nomen loci W 205 (3)
nominal compounds W 207
nominal root F 101 (3)
nominal sentences S 206, W 207
nominal stems F 100 (1)
nominal suffixes W 202ff.
nominal types F 304
nominative S 405
Northwest Indo-Germ. E 435 (4)
Nostratic E 437
notations p. XVIIff.
number F 304, S 302, S 415
numbers F 500
numerals F 500
numerical adverbs F 504
Nuristani: → Buddruss in MSS 36 1977 p. 19ff.
occlusive L 335ff.
Ogam inscriptions E 431 (2)
Old Bulgarian, cf. Old Church Slavic
Old Church Slavic E 433
Old Indian E 404 (2)
Old Iranian E 405
Old Irish E 431 (2)
Old Persian E 407
Old Phrygian E 423
Old Prussian E 434
Old Saxon E 432 (3)
onomatopoeia: → Tichy *Onomatop. Verbalbildungen* 1983
optative F 207 (2), S 313
orality E 400
ordinal numbers F 503
orthoepic diaskeuasis: (RV authoritative text): → Hoffmann *Aufs.* II 1976 p. 546
orthotone F 400 (2), F 401 (1), F 403
Oscian E 429
Osthoff, Hermann (1847-1909): → *Portraits* I 1966 p. 555-562; *Lex. Gramm.*, 1996 p. 683; Os-

proterodynamic F 315 (4), F 317
proterokinetic F 315 (4), F 317
Proto-Germanic culture E 512 (3)
Proto-Indo-European E 410
psilosis (Gr.) L 309 (2)
Punic E 426 (3B)
qualitative ablaut L 409
quantitative ablaut L 409
quantitative metathesis F 317 (7), F 318 (6c)
-r-/-n- heteroclitics F 314 (6)
Rask, Rasmus Kristian (1787-1832): → *Portraits* I 1966 p. 179ff.; Lex. Gr. 1996 p. 774ff.
reconstruction methods E 507
reduction grade L 203
referent S 403 (2), S 410, S 413
reflexive pronouns F 401 (2)
relative chronology L 107
relative clause S 205
relative pronouns F 404
Renou, Louis (1896-1966): → G. Pinault in *Lex. Gramm.*, 1996 p. 785f.
rhotacism E 503 (4), L 309 (1), F 325 (1b)
Rigveda (RV) E 404 (2)
Rix's Law L 333
Romance languages E 427 (6)
root F 101 (3)
root aorist F 203 (Typ 2a)
root compound W 209
root noun → Schindler *Wurzelnomen* 1972; L 211 (6), W 206 (5)
root present E 502 (4), F 203 (1a), F 206
root structure L 321
ruki rule E 502 (6), L 309 (3)
runes E 432
Sabellian E 426 (1), E 429
sa-figé F 405
sandhi L 404f.
Sanskrit E 404
satem languages L 339 (3), L 341
Saussure, Ferdinand de (1857-1913): E 307, L 315; → *Portraits* II 1966 p. 87-110; Saussure's Law L 330
Scandinavian languages E 432 (2)
Schindler, Jochem L 103, L 304 (3), L 313 (4), F 315 (1), W 207
Schleicher, August (1821-1868): E 305; → *Portraits* I 1966 p. 374-395; K. Koerner in *Lex. Gramm.*, 1996 p. 835f.
Schmidt, Johannes (1843-1901): E 304f.; → Lex. Gr. 1996 p. 837f.
school grammar F 102
Schulze, Wilhelm (1863-1935): → B. Schlerath in *Lex. Gramm.*, 1996 p. 843f.
schwa primum (Indogerm.) L 202, L 318, L 324 (2)
schwa secundum L 203, L 304 (3), L 313 (3), see also s.v. weak vowels
Schwebeablaut L 417 (3)
Schwyzer, Eduard (1874-1943): → *Lex. Gramm.*, 1996 p. 845f.
secondary ending E 502 (9) (11), F 202 (4), F 209
secondary stem F 202 (1), F 209
secondary suffix F 202 (1)
semivowels L 212ff.
sentence S 102
sentence accent S 209
Serbian E 433
Serbo-Croatian E 433
seṭ roots E 502 (14), L 315 (1)

transformation (through laryngeals) L 211 (8), L 323 (2)
transitivity S 300 (2)
tree models E 513
types of actions F 202 (2), F 206, S 305
typology S 100 (3)
Umbrian E 429
Umlaut (Germ.) L 208, L 418
Universalien E 501 (1)
Uralic languages E 436
Vr̥ddhi derivation L 331 (3), W 202 (2)
Vr̥ddhi L 413 (1)
vr̥kī́-inflection W 204 (1)
Vasmer, Max (1886-1962) → *Lex. Gramm.*, 1996 p. 959f.
Vedic E 404 (2)
Vendryes, Joseph (1875-1960) → *Portraits* II 1966 p. 385-393, *Lex. Gramm.*, 1996 p. 962-964
Venetian E 430
Vennemann, Th. E 437
verbal accents F 214
verbal adjectives W 203
verbal government compounds L 215 (2), L 420 (3), W 207, W 209
verbal inflection F 102, F 200ff.
verbal root E 502 (2)
verbal stem F 100 (1), F 202 (1)
Verner, Karl (1846-1896) → *Portraits* I 1966 p. 538-548; *Lex. Gramm.*, 1996 p. 965; Verner's Law L 421
visarga p. XX, L 309 (3)
vocative S 406
voice S 314
vowel weakening (Lat.) L 108, L 204, L 217 (3), L 325, L 411
vowels L 200ff.
Vulgar Latin E 427 (6)
Wackernagel, Jacob (1853-1938): → *Portraits* II 1966 p. 52-55; R. Schmitt in *Lex. Gramm.* 1996 p. 986f.; Wackernagel's Law S 209
wave theory: → J. Schmidt *Verwantschaftsverhältnisse* 1872; J. Goebl in *Zeitschr. f. Sprachwiss.* 2 1983 p. 3-44; E 305
weak cases F 314 (1)
weak vowels E 503 (5), E 504 (9), L 103, L 202f., L 304 (3), L 324 (1)
Whitney, William Dwight (1827-1894): → *Portraits* I 1966 p. 399-439; *Lex. Gramm.*, 1996 p. 1007-1009
word L 400
word accent L 403, L 419
word formation W 200ff.
word groups W 101
word limits L 403
writing E 400
zero grade L 409
Zeuss, Johann Kaspar (1806-1856): → S. Ziegler in *Lex. Gramm.* 1996 p. 1041f.
Zipf, George Kingsley (1902-1950):→Lex. Gr. 1996 p. 1043f.
Zirkumstanten S 210